POST-WAR CINEMA AND MODERNITY

A FILM READER

Edited by
John Orr and Olga Taxidou

EDINBURGH UNIVERSITY PRESS

© Introductions, selection and
editorial material, John Orr and
Olga Taxidou, 2000

Transferred to digital print 2007

Edinburgh University Press Ltd
22 George Square, Edinburgh

Typeset in Sabon and Gill Sans
by Bibliocraft Ltd, Dundee, and
printed and bound in Great Britain
by CPI Antony Rowe, Eastbourne

A CIP record for this book is available
from the British Library

ISBN 0 7486 1282 3 (hardback)
ISBN 0 7486 1281 5 (paperback)

CONTENTS

LIST OF ILLUSTRATIONS

ACKNOWLEDGEMENTS

Grateful acknowledgement is made to the following sources for permission to reproduce material previously published elsewhere. Every effort has been made to trace the copyright holders, but if any have been inadvertently overlooked, the publisher will be pleased to make the necessary arrangements at the first opportunity.

André Bazin, 'Neorealism: An Aesthetic of Reality', from *What is Cinema?* vol. 2, translated/edited by Hugh Gray. Copyright © 1967, The Regents of the University of California; Les Editions du Cerf.

J. P. Telotte, '*Noir* Narration', from *Voices in the Dark: The Narrative Patterns of* Film Noir. Copyright © 1989 by the Board of Trustees of the University of Illinois. Used with the permission of the University of Illinois Press.

Pier Paolo Pasolini, 'The Cinema of Poetry', from *Heretical Empiricism*, pp. 167–186, translated by Louise Barnett and Ben Lawton, Indiana University Press, 1988. Used with the permission of Indiana University Press.

Christian Metz, 'The Modern Cinema and Narrativity', from *Film Language* by Christian Metz, translated by Michael Taylor. Translation copyright © 1974 by Oxford University Press. Used by permission of Oxford University Press, Inc.

Noël Burch, 'Spatial and Temporal Articulations', from *Film Theory and Practice*. Copyright © Princeton University Press, 1981. Reprinted by permission of Princeton University Press.

Bruce F. Kawin, 'The Mind's Eye', from *Mindscreen: Bergman, Godard and First-Person Film*, Princeton University Press, 1978. Copyright © 1978 by Bruce F. Kawin. All rights reserved.

Gilles Deleuze, 'Beyond the Movement-Image', from *Cinema 2: The Time-Image*, translated by Hugh Tomlinson and Robert Galeta. Copyright © The Athlone Press, 1989; University of Minnesota Press, 1989.

Teresa de Lauretis, 'Imaging', from *Alice Doesn't: Feminism, Semiotics, Cinema*. Copyright © Indiana University Press, 1984; Macmillan, 1984.

Fredric Jameson, 'Totality as Conspiracy', *The Geopolitical Aesthetic: Cinema and Space in the World System*. Copyright © BFI, 1991.

Paul Virilio, 'The Travelling Shot over Eighty Years', from *War and Cinema*, Verso, London, 1991.

Peter Wollen, 'Cinema and Technology: A Historical Overview', from *Readings and Writings: Semiotic Counter-strategies*, Verso, London 1978.

Jacques Aumont, 'The Role of the Apparatus', from *The Image*. Copyright © BFI, 1997.

Andrew Tarkovsky, 'Time, Rhythm, Editing', from *Sculpting in Time* © Bodley Head, 1987.

Bill Nichols, 'The Fact of Realism and the Fiction of Objectivity', from *Representing Reality*, pp. 165–198, Indiana University Press, 1991. Used with the permission of Indiana University Press.

Scott Bukatman, 'The Artificial Infinite: On Special Effects and the Sublime', from *Visual Display: Culture Beyond Appearances*, edited by Lynne Cooke and Peter Wollen. Copyright © The New Press, 1995.

Nestor Almendros, 'Days of Heaven', from *A Man with a Camera*, translated by Rachel Phillips Belash. Copyright © 1984 by Farrar, Straus and Giroux, LLC. Reprinted by permission of Farrar, Strauss and Giroux, LLC; Copyright © Faber and Faber.

Michael Chapman, 'Michael Chapman', from *Masters of Light: Conversations with Contemporary Cinematographers* edited by Dennis Schaefer and Larry Salvato. Copyright © 1984 The Regents of the University of California.

Donald Richie, 'Introduction to Ozu', from *Ozu: His Life and Films*. Copyright © 1974 The Regents of the University of California.

Tania Modleski, 'Femininity by Design: *Vertigo*', from *The Woman Who Knew Too Much: Hitchcock and Feminist Film Theory*. Copyright © 1998. Reproduced by permission of Routledge, Inc.

Terry Comito, 'Introduction to *Orson Welles, Director*', from *Touch of Evil* edited by Terry Comito. Copyright © 1985 by Rutgers, The State University. Reprinted by permission of Rutgers University Press.

Paul Schrader, 'Bresson', from *Transcendental Style in Film: Ozu, Bresson, Dreyer*. Copyright © Paul Schrader, 1972.

Susan Sontag, excerpts from 'Godard', an essay that first appeared in *Styles of Radical Will*, Bodley Head, 1970. Copyright © Susan Sontag. Reprinted with the permission of Susan Sontag.

Angela Dalle Vacche, 'Michelangelo Antonioni's *Red Desert*', from *Cinema and Painting: How Art is Used in Film*. Copyright © 1996. Reprinted with permission of The Athlone Press and the University of Texas Press.

Timothy Corrigan, 'Transformation in Fassbinder's *Bitter Tears of Petra von Kant*', from *New German Film: The Displaced Image*, Indiana University Press, 1994. Used with the permission of Indiana University Press.

Ismail Xavier, '*Black God, White Devil*: The Representation of History', from *Brazilian Cinema* edited by R. John and R. Stam. Copyright © 1995 by Columbia University Press. Reprinted with the permission of the publisher.

Colin MacCabe, 'The Shoot', from *Performance*. Copyright © 1998, Colin MacCabe, BFI, 1998. Reprinted by permission of Colin MacCabe.

Laura Mulvey, 'The Carapace that Failed: Ousmane Sembene's *Xala*', from *Fetishism and Curiosity*, BFI, 1996. Copyright © 1996, Laura Mulvey. Reprinted by permission of Laura Mulvey.

David Pascoe, 'The Book Depository', first published in *Peter Greenaway: Museums and Moving Images* by David Pascoe (London, Reaktion Books, 1997), © David Pascoe, 1997.

Rey Chow, 'The Force of Surfaces: Defiance in Zhang Yimou's Films', from *Primitive Passions* by Rey Chow. Copyright © 1995 by Columbia University Press. Reprinted with the permission of the publisher.

Peter Harcourt, 'Imaginary Images: An Examination of Atom Egoyan's Films', from *Film Quarterly*, vol. 48, no. 3, Spring 1995, pp. 2–13. Copyright © 1995 by The Regents of the University of California.

Denise Youngblood, '*Repentance*: Stalinist Terror and the Realism of Surrealism', from *Revisioning History: Film and the Construction of a New Past* edited by Robert Rosenstone. Copyright © 1995, Princeton University Press. Reprinted by permission of Princeton University Press.

SECTION I
FILM THEORY AND FILM FORM

Theory and Culture

INTRODUCTION

John Orr

Just as film has its own chronology so criticism has followed in its footsteps. The changing critical forms we find in film writing are themselves responses to a changing cinema. Transformations of style, genre, technology and narrative are the foundation of changes in criticism. Though Part 1 of the Reader is divided into two sections, this summary will show how they dovetail by discussing them in unison. The following selection tries to incorporate two things; first the immediacy of critical response to films in this period and second, the studied, retrospective look upon film of an earlier period. The essays by Telotte, Wollen and Virilio are in that sense retrospective while the essays by Bazin, Pasolini and Metz are more immediate. Other critics, by contrast, adopt a range that looks to both past and present and, in some cases, to the future. Whatever their differences, all the writers here are passionately engaged with their subject matter and still astute, original and often path-breaking in their analysis. Film criticism is a meeting point of so many different strands of writing – aesthetics, ontology, history, sociology and many more – that at best it is no half-hearted hybrid but a genuine synthetic skill, which tells as much about the world of modernity as the world of the big screen.

1

In the immediate post-war period we have chosen key variants of dominant movements in world cinema – Italian neo-realism, British and American neo-expressionism and Japanese formalism. While Donald Richie looks at formalism through the films of Ozu, André Bazin's essay on the post-war Italian cinema is a key source of his continuous engagement with film and representation. Bazin's strength, later inherited by the younger critics of *Cahiers du Cinéma* lay in his immediate response to new movements, which he saw as an empowering method for understanding the nature of cinema itself. The films of Italian neo-realism are celebrated as an advance in the filmic verve for registering great changes in twentieth-century life. The moving image captures a society in upheaval through an 'aesthetic of reality' using location shooting, explorations of city and landscape, non-professional actors, episodic tales, forms that are all fragments in a wider mosaic. The star system, the studio set and the neat finished melodramas of Hollywood genre are discarded. In films like Rossellini's *Paisà*, the changing nature of filmic reality is brought to light through the detail of *mise-en-scène*, in the nature of 'the image-fact' which Bazin casts enigmatically as the aesthetic anchor of cinematic realism. While many semiologists have dismissed Bazin by refusing to read him closely, this key term in his ontology has outlived their contempt and is with us still, open, ambiguous, elusive.

Bazin's template provides a springboard for Bill Nichols's extended reflections on feature-film and documentary representation. Nichols looks with a fresh eye at the early greats, Grierson, Jennings and Flaherty before considering more recent developments in documentary film. Intrigued by the 'enormous ellipses – or rather great holes' which Bazin saw in the narrative of *Paisà* he sees the new realism which inflects documentary as being a contingent form of observing that is neither purely subjective, allowing for identification with the onscreen figure or purely objective, the demonstration of an absolute truth. Yet he recognises documentary form as gravitating to a narrative of 'subjects-as-victims' and often given, by the power of the engaged voice-over, the illusion of omniscience. In a telling comparison between the opening sequences of *Touch of Evil* and *Louisiana Story* he locates the main difference between fiction and documentary in the facticity of place. Both Welles and Flaherty use similar narrative constructions in editing to tell their respective 'stories' but while Venice, California, serves as a fictional Mexican border town, Flaherty's bayou is a given landscape his film then explores. In fiction, the location is subordinate to the story, while in documentary the story is subordinate to actualities of time and place.

An alternative development in post-war film lies in the expressionist legacy. Two key forms of neo-expressionism are explored here in different ways. J. P. Telotte looks at film noir as a Hollywood genre that adapts expressionist style to its distinctive set of urban themes, while Duncan Petrie looks at the contribution of neo-expressionist cinematography to British cinema in the same decade. Telotte's essay points out the many ambiguities of the *noir* label. It can be seen as a hard-boiled extension of the fictions of Hammett, Chandler and Jim Thomson in its witnessing of city criminality, but also a style-incorporation of the dark and distorting features of German expressionism. While some critics stress darkness of setting, others stress darkness of motive and the form itself straddles many other genres. Telotte identifies four very different narrative strategies present in noir; the third-person narrative, the voice-over/flashback, the documentary mode and the subjective camera. The ambiguities of definition here are comparable, Telotte suggests, to those Foucault had discovered in the historical discourse of madness. In contrast to the stress on genre, Petrie looks at the defining role of the camera in post-war British cinema through the work of Rober Krasker in black and white film and Jack Cardiff in the new three-strip Technicolor. In Reed's *Odd Man Out* and *The Third Man* Krasker gives a defining look to the post-war European city that subtly incorporates the subjective camera, its hallucinations and distortions. In Powell's *Black Narcissus* and *The Red Shoes*, Cardiff uses colour as a remarkably diffuse emotional force in Powell's narratives of exotic unreality. Through their innovating techniques, both cinematographers expand and develop quite significantly the auteurist vision of their respective directors.

The role of cinematography is reprised in the modernist period of the American cinema where Nestor Almendros analyses his work for Malick's epic narrative of American rural life, *Days of Heaven*, and Michael Chapman discusses his collaboration with Scorsese on *Taxi Driver* and *Raging Bull*. Both pieces link back to the post-war period. Almendros shows how the technical innovations of the 1970s, such as the greater mobility of the Panaflex and Panaglide cameras, could be used to enhance cinematic reality in a way that affirms Bazin's vision but also shows up the technical limitations of the post-war period the French critic had discussed. Similarly technical advances vindicated Malick's insistence on twilight or 'magic hour' shooting, and on extensive night scenes, with Almendros using to great effect the sensitivity of film stock whose negatives could be successfully pushed in the laboratory. While Malick's film was an abstract transformation of Bazinian ontology, Scorsese's films often fused the neo-realist and neo-expressionist legacies of the post-war era for similar effect. Echoing Krasker's work for Reed, Chapman mentions the vital role of the subjective camera in *Taxi Driver* to create the paranoid feel of New York City in the 1970s. Echoing Cardiff's work on *The Red Shoes* ballet, he also dissects the choreography of the fight scenes in *Raging Bull*, noting that elsewhere in the film the enhancing of reality by wide-angle panning shots is made possible by Scorsese's flair for abstraction in the *mise-en-scène*. Though it shares much with neo-realism in setting, technique and period, the style and tone of the film are crucially altered by Scorsese's vision.

II

The decade of the 1960s was vital for the modernist, or neo-modern turn in the cinema and provoked in turn a response to the changes in film form taking place in that turbulent decade. One of the most powerful and polemical responses came from filmmaker Pier Paolo Pasolini. In his essay on the 'cinema of poetry' he argued that a new film had emerged which enhanced our understanding of film itself. Pasolini's argument is a complex mixture of the essentialist and the historicist. On the one hand he sees cinematic images as a form of pre-linguistic communication, an irrational speech without language, which emerges from the human capacity for dream and memory. On the other he sees a specific form of narrative technique – free indirect subjectivity – as an essential element of the new modernist filmmaking of the 1960s, in particular the work of Godard, Antonioni and Bertolucci. Here invisible narration is punctured by the visible presence of the camera as an intruding force and by a new form of subjectivity which substitutes for representation the deranged vision of the neurotic subject, a vision which is itself converted by the cineaste into a new aesthetic of film form. This is a vision of poetic narrative clinically immersed in a delirium of images, and made possible, in Pasolini's Marxist perspective, by the deep crisis of bourgeois society during the Cold War.

The response of Christian Metz to the filmic innovations of the 1960s and especially the French New Wave, was somewhat different. He rejects a whole raft of critical approaches viewing the modern, as opposed to the classical cinema, in terms of an erosion of narrativity. Narrative forms may change but narrativity remains an essential feature of all film. He thus looks at various conceptual pairings given by critics as models of the difference between classical and modern film and sees in all a chimerical belief that narrative has been superseded, particularly since many instances of the modern are a repetition of techniques used in silent cinema prior to the Hollywood genres of the sound period. Instead he demonstrates that the non-diegetic features of the French New Wave, such as in the escape sequence in *Pierrot le fou*, do not signal the end of narrativity but form a counterpoint with the narrative syntax of the film, thus reinventing narrativity rather than liquidating it. Yet this reinvention leads him in his later work to search for a fundamental cinematographic syntax, which he imagined would explain all narrative variations. While he criticises Pasolini for moving to a historicist position based on faulty essentialist principles, Metz himself moved to an essentialist position on the basis of a reductive reading of film history, namely that specific narratives could only be understood though a knowledge of fundamental semiological laws, that he was never able in his later work to uncover.

Teresa de Lauretis provides a vital in-depth summary of this critical debate on semiology and the cinema of poetry, not only analysing Eco's complex attempt to find a *via media* between the polarised positions of Metz and Pasolini, but also showing the relevance of the whole controversy to the feminist theorising of the image and filmic spectacle in the 1980s. Analysing the films of Bergman and Godard, Bruce Kawin expands on the modernist ambiguities in the relationship of filmmaker and film hero by elaborating a paradigm for cinematic thinking, for filming thought, he calls 'mindscreen'. This is a form that goes beyond the use of simple voice-over or point-of-view techniques to fuse the vision of the *auteur* and the subjectivity of the onscreen character in increasingly sophisticated ways. John Orr glosses the same paradigm by analysing the growing use of Pasolini's 'free indirect subjectivity' in film narrative after 1965 in a variety of thematic and stylistic forms, including the relationship between colour and perception, the liminality of the neurotic or psychotic subject and the synthetic reworking of surreal and expressionist techniques. All three critics see the vexed question of subjectivity as central to the theory and practice of contemporary film. Moreover the critical discourse of the poetic image is an enduring one that carries over into another key polarity between philosopher and filmmaker. After the clash of Metz and Pasolini, we might say, come the significant variations of Deleuze and Tarkovsky.

As a fellow cineaste, Tarkovsky was as fixated as Pasolini on the relationship between poetry and film. Yet he theorised it in a very different manner. For him, the world of dream and memory the film image recreates is inextricable from our experience of time. The film sequence according to his aesthetic should not only capture images of dream and memory but also capture our experience of their duration in time. Tarkovsky sees the sequence-shot as the vital technical means of capturing the rhythms of time on film and of unfolding or revealing the essential truths of human experience. He places it, aesthetically and polemically, against Eisenstein's theory of montage with its stress upon the primacy of editing and the cut. He endows film time with a positive moral value so that it resurrects not just the personal world of time past but also the wider, public world of previous generations. The politics of this position can be read as an implicit stance against the selective amnesia that characterised Soviet politics during Tarkovsky's lifetime.

Profoundly influenced by the philosophy of Nietzsche and Bergson, Gilles Deleuze gives us a very different reading of cinematic time to that of Tarkovsky. He contrasts the 'movement-image' of classical cinema with the 'time-image' of modern cinema, translating Bergson's distinction between matter and memory into filmic terms. In the extract here from the second volume of his landmark work, he takes up the challenge to continue where Bazin left off, looking at the movement out of neo-realism in Italy and France. Here, he contends, there is a breakdown in the sensory-motor effects of cinematic perception in classical cinema where narrative firmly integrates situation and action. Instead there emerges a cinema of pure optical and sonic signs, a narrative form that is lyrical in its meandering distractions combining both elements of the song and the circular route which he calls a 'ba(l)lade' and a Nietzschean concern with the recurrence of the past within the present, most pronounced in Welles and Resnais, that questions the ontology of the image and invokes 'the powers of the false'.

In the case of time as memory, Deleuze stressed the falsity of cinematic time against Tarkovsky's vision of its inner moral strength but in considering time as duration in work of Antonioni and Fellini, or Godard and Rivette, he also poses the time-image as a form that upends Bazinian ontology. Instead of a modernist movement towards perceptual subjectivity, as implied in Pasolini, Delueuze suggests the more complex paradox of a double movement. The most objective of filmmaking in Antonioni or Godard can possess a fierce hallucinatory quality while the subjective cinemas of Fellini or Rivette delineate a detailed and tactile world of the senses. The classic division between Lumière and Méliès, between reality and fantasy, as two generic kinds of cinema, thus breaks down under the narrative weight of the time-image. The uncertainties of the past in the films of Resnais and Welles and are matched by the uncertainties of the present in the films of Rivette and Godard. No final separation of subjective from objective cinema becomes possible.

III

These narrative transformations are aided of course by changing styles, technologies and techniques of cinematography, which all lead on in turn to broader questions of perception. Noël Burch and Jacques Aumont deal with specific aspects of spatial and temporal framing in the modernist period, while Peter Wollen and Scott Bukatman focus on specific dimensions of the relationship between technology and perception. Paul Virilio, by contrast, proposes a grand theory of cinematic 'derealisation' based on the affinity between war and cinema in the logistics of perception. In analysing American political film in the 1970s and 1980s, Fredric Jameson suggests that key changes in narrative and perception demand the abandonment of the modernist paradigm in favour of a theory of postmodernity where film complements other cultural forms.

The essays by Burch and Aumont both engage, in editing and composition, the question that Metz had posed at the level of narrative. The breaking of narrative convention depends upon their currency and intelligibility for audiences. Writing soon after Metz, Burch looks at the conventions of filmic articulation in much the same way. How shots and sequences are matched to one another in space and time depends not upon fixed rules but established conventions. In the post-war period there is, he detects, an increasing rejection of the conventions of classical cinema and much greater innovation in spatial and temporal framing. In a similar vein but in a more contemporary piece, Aumont explores the wider conventions of framing in the plastic arts, the important relationship of film to painting and consequently, the different forms of the 'de-framing' which innovating filmmakers use, either in signalling the absent presence of offscreen space or by using the close-up as an intrusive shot that disrupts the conventions of *mise-en-scène*. In subverting conventions, therefore, filmmakers make them more transparent, exposing the myth of their invisibility.

Modernist departures from filmic conventions are many and various but Paul Virilio suggests that the source of this cinematic 'derealisation' lies elsewhere, in the logistics of perception imposed by military technologies. Thus the changing forms of the electronic simulation of the real, from radar to laser-guided bombs, can generate forms of disorientation that invade whole domains of our culture. The technologies of film are inseparable from the technologies of war and, consequently, the forms of representation that Bazin saw in post-war film would, in Virilio's eyes, be made redundant by the technologies of that very war. While also acknowledging the crossover between military and film technologies, Wollen guards against technological determinism and sees film as an autonomous form where decisions to use new technologies come from a wide variety of motives. Some visual technologies developed by science and medicine are not used in the cinema at all while advances in film stock and new lightweight cameras have made possible the advance of avant-garde and experimental filmmaking on low budgets. Wollen's stress on growing diversity in the 1970s is echoed in the low-budget opportunities now afforded by digital technology at the end of the century.

While Virilio's supreme example of the crossover between war and cinema in the realm of derealisation would be *Apocalypse Now*, Scott Bukatman suggests the most apt departure from cinematic realism in this period lies in the American genre of science fiction. It is in future and non-terrestrial worlds that special effects technologies come into their own through their remaking of the 'sublime', a structure of feeling that excites both fear and fascination in the viewer. This, he suggests, from comes from the American experience, which transforms the source of the sublime from nature and landscape in nineteenth-century painting to technologies of war and space exploration in late twentieth-century film. This is not an auteur cinema so much as an 'effects' cinema in which designers like Douglas Trumbull are as important as directors like Ridley Scott. Bukatman sees in this technical making-over a vital source of the cinematic post-modern, a different but related approach from that of Jameson, who locates the post-modern in a wide number of protean forms, both technical and cultural.

In the specific argument there, delivered in the rambling baroque that is Jameson's trademark, the link with Bukatman lies most of all in the pervasiveness of paranoia. In science fiction this is part of the fateful encounter with the sublime whereas in the political thriller it is taken as an iconic sign of conspiracy. Jameson dissects recent political thrillers in North-America cinema, from *The Day of the Condor to Videodrome* that map out conspiracy as the key form of paranoid vision. Paranoia, for Jameson, can be produced as a junk cultural commodity in late-capitalism, and is thus post-modern, bereft of the ideas and world-views that motivated the modernist text in fiction and film. The illusion of closure is thus produced by what he has called 'a poor man's cognitive mapping', and the interaction of ideal and society that characterises the art of the modern is replaced by a culture anxiously immersed in the detritus of information and consumerism. By implication, the fragmentations of modernist film from Godard onwards are displaced by a new illusion of totality in post-modern cinema that is pathological in the extreme and will define cinema at the end of the twentieth century.

I

AN AESTHETIC OF REALITY: NEOREALISM (CINEMATIC REALISM AND THE ITALIAN SCHOOL OF THE LIBERATION)

André Bazin

The historical importance of of Rossellini's film *Paisà* has been rightly compared with that of a number of classical screen masterpieces. Georges Sadoul has not hesitated to mention it alongside *Nosferatu*, *Die Nibelungen*, or *Greed*. I subscribe wholeheartedly to this high praise as long as the allusion to German expressionism is understood to refer to the level of greatness of the film but not to the profound nature of the aesthetics involved. A better comparison might be with the appearance in 1925 of *Potemkin*. For the rest, the realism of the current Italian films has been frequently contrasted with the aestheticism of American and, in part, of French productions. Was it not from the outset their search for realism that characterized the Russian films of Eisenstein, Pudovkin, and Dovjenko as revolutionary both in art and politics, in contrast to the expressionist aestheticism of the German films and Hollywood's mawkish star worship? *Paisà*, *Sciuscà*, and *Roma Città Aperta*, like *Potemkin*, mark a new stage in the long-standing opposition between realism and aestheticism on the screen. But history does not repeat itself; we have to get clear the particular form this aesthetic quarrel assumes today, the new solutions to which Italian neorealism owed its triumph in 1947.

Confronted with the originality of the Italian output, and in the enthusiasm engendered by the surprise that this has caused, we have perhaps neglected to go deeply into the origins of this renaissance, preferring to see it rather as something spontaneously generated, issuing like a swarm of bees from the decaying

From: Andre Bazin, 'Neorealism: An Aesthetic of Reality', in Hugh Gray (trans./ed.), *What is Cinema?* Vol. 2 (The Regents of the University of California; Les Éditions du Cerf, 1967).

corpses of fascism and the war. There is no question that the Liberation and the social, moral, and economic forms that it assumed in Italy have played a decisive role in film production. We shall return to this later. It was simply a lack of information about the Italian cinema that trapped us into believing in a sudden miracle.

It could well be that, today, Italy is the country where the understanding of film is at its highest, to judge by the importance and the quality of the film output. The Centro Sperimentale at Rome came into existence before our own Institut des Hautes Etudes Cinématographiques; above all, intellectual speculation in Italy is not, as it is in France, without its impact on film-making. Radical separation between criticism and direction no more exists in the Italian cinema than it does in France in the world of literature.

Furthermore, fascism, which, unlike Nazism, allowed for the existence of artistic pluralism, was particularly concerned with cinema. One may have reservations about the connection between the Venice film festival and the political interests of the Duce but one cannot deny that the idea of an international festival has subsequently made good, and one can measure its prestige today by the fact that five or six European countries are vying for the spoils. The capitalists and the Fascist authorities at least provided Italy with modern studios. If they turned out films which were ridiculously melodramatic and overly spectacular, that did not prevent a handful of bright men, smart enough to shoot films on current themes without making any concessions to the regime, from making high-quality films that foreshadowed their current work. If during the war we had not been, albeit justifiably, so prejudiced, films like *SOS 103* or *La Nave Bianca* of Rossellini might have caught our attention more. In addition, even when capitalist or political stupidity controlled commercial production completely, intelligence, culture, and experimental research took refuge in publications, in film archive congresses, and in making short films. In 1941, Lattuada, director of *Il Bandito* and, at the time, the head of the Milan archive, barely escaped jail for showing the complete version of *La Grande Illusion.*

Beyond that, the history of the Italian cinema is little known. We stop short at *Cabiria* and *Quo Vadis*, finding in the recent and memorable *La Corona di ferro* all the proof we need that the supposed characteristics of films made beyond the Alps remain unchanged: a taste, and a poor taste at that, for sets, idealization of the principal actors, childish emphasis on acting, atrophy of *mise en scène*, the dragging in of the traditional paraphernalia of *bel canto* and opera, conventional scripts influenced by the theater, the romantic melodrama and the *chanson de geste* reduced to an adventure story. Undoubtedly too many Italian films do their best to justify such a caricature and too many directors, including some of the best, sacrificed themselves, sometimes with self-irony, to commercial necessity. The great spectacles like *Scipio Africanus* were, of course, the primary export. There was another artistic vein, however, almost exclusively reserved for the home market. Today, when the thunder of the charging elephants of Scipio is only a distant rumble, we can the better lend an ear to the discreet but delightful sounds made by *Quattro passi fra le nuvole*.

The reader, at least one who has seen this latter film, will undoubtedly be as surprised as we were to learn that this comedy with its unfettered sensibility, brimming over with poetry, the lightly handled socialist realism of which is directly related to the recent Italian cinema, was shot in 1942, two years after the famous *La Corona di ferro* and by the same director: Blasetti, to whom, about the same time, we owe *Un'avventura di Salvator Rosa* and most recently *Un Giorno nella vita*. Directors like Vittorio De Sica who made the admirable *Sciuscià* were always concerned to turn out human and sensitive comedies full of realism, among them, in 1942, *I Bambini ci guardano*. Since 1932, Camerini has made *Gli uomini che mascalzoni*, the action of which, like *Roma Città Aperta*, is laid in the streets of the capital and *Piccolo Mondo Antico*, no less typically Italian.

As a matter of fact, there are not so many new names among the directors in Italy today. The youngest, like Rossellini, started to make films at the beginning of the war. Older directors, like Blasetti and Mario Soldati, were already known in the early days of the talkies.

But let us not go from one extreme to the other and conclude that there is no such thing as a new Italian school. The realist trend, the domestic, satirical, and social descriptions of everyday life, the sensitive and poetic verism, were, before the war, minor qualities, modest violets flowering at the feet of the giant sequoias of production. It appears that from the beginning of the war, a light began to be shed on the papier-maché forests. In *La Corona di ferro* the style seems to parody itself. Rossellini, Lattuada, Blasetti were striving toward a realism of international importance. Nevertheless it is the Liberation that set these aesthetic trends so completely free as to allow them to develop under new conditions that were destined to have their share in inducing a noticeable change in direction and meaning.

THE LIBERATION: RUPTURE AND RENAISSANCE

Some components of the new Italian school existed before the Liberation: personnel, techniques, aesthetic trends. But it was their historical, social, and economic combination that suddenly created a synthesis in which new elements also made themselves manifest.

Over the past two years, Resistance and Liberation have furnished the principal themes, but unlike the French, and indeed one might say unlike the European cinema as a whole, Italian films have not been limited to themes of the Resistance. In France, the Resistance immediately became legendary. Recent as it was, on the day of the actual Liberation it already belonged to the realm of history. The Germans having departed, life began again. By contrast, in Italy the Liberation did not signify a return to the old and recent freedom; it meant political revolution, Allied occupation, economic and social upheaval. The Liberation came slowly through endless months. It had a profound effect on the economic, social, and moral life of the country. Thus, in Italy, Resistance and Liberation, unlike the Paris uprising, are in no sense just words with a historical connotation. When Rossellini made *Paisà*, his script was concerned with things actually happening at the time. *Il Bandito* showed how prostitution and the black market developed on the heels of the advancing army, how disillusion and lack of employment turned a liberated prisoner into a gangster. Except for unmistakable Resistance films like *Vivere in Pace* or *Il Sole Sorge Ancora*, the Italian cinema was noted for its concern with actual day-to-day events. The French critics had not failed to emphasize (whether in praise or blame but always with solemn surprise) the few specific allusions to the postwar period that Carné deliberately introduced into his last film. If the director and his writer took so much trouble to make us understand this, it is because nineteen out of twenty French films cannot be dated within a decade. On the other hand, even when the central scene of the script is not concerned with an actual occurrence, Italian films are first and foremost reconstituted reportage. The action could not unfold in just any social context, historically neutral, partly abstract like the setting of a tragedy, as so frequently happens to varying degrees with the American, French, or English cinema.

As a result, the Italian films have an exceptionally documentary quality that could not be removed from the script without thereby eliminating the whole social setting into which its roots are so deeply sunk.

This perfect and natural adherence to actuality is explained and justified from within by a spiritual attachment to the period. Undoubtedly, the tide of recent Italian history cannot be reversed. Thus, the war is felt to be not an interlude but the end of an era. In one sense Italy is only three years old. But other effects could have resulted from the same cause. What is a ceaseless source of wonder, ensuring the Italian cinema a wide moral audience among the Western nations, is the significance it gives to the portrayal of actuality. In a world already once again obsessed by terror and hate, in which reality is scarely any longer favored for its own sake but rather is rejected or excluded as a political symbol, the Italian cinema is certainly the only one which preserves, in the midst of the period it depicts, a revolutionary humanism.

LOVE AND REJECTION OF REALITY

The recent Italian films are at least prerevolutionary. They all reject implicitly or explicitly, with humor, satire or poetry, the reality they are using, but they know better, no matter how clear the stand taken, than to treat this reality as a medium or a means to an end. To condemn it does not of necessity mean to be in bad faith. They never forget that the world *is*, quite simply, before it is something to be condemned. It is silly and perhaps as naïve as Beaumarchais' praise of the tears induced by melodrama. But does one not, when coming out of an Italian film, feel better, an urge to change the order of things, preferably by persuading people, at least those who can be persuaded, whom only blindness, prejudice, or ill-fortune had led to harm their fellow men?

That is why, when one reads resumés of them, the scenarios of many Italian films are open to ridicule. Reduced to their plots, they are often just moralizing melodramas, but on the screen everybody in the film is overwhelmingly real. Nobody is reduced to the condition of an object or a symbol that would allow one to hate them in comfort without having first to leap the hurdle of their humanity.

I am prepared to see the fundamental humanism of the current Italian films as their chief merit. They offer an opportunity to savor, before the time finally runs out on us, a revolutionary flavor in which terror has yet no part.

AN AMALGAM OF PLAYERS

What naturally first struck the public was the high quality of the acting. *Roma Città Aperta* enriched the world's screen with a performer of the first order, Anna Magnani, the unforgettable pregnant young woman, Fabrizzi the priest, Pagliero, a member of the Resistance, and others whose performances rival in retrospect the most stirring of film characterizations in the past. Reports and news items in the public press naturally made a point of letting us know that *Sciuscà* was filled with genuine street urchins, that Rossellini shot crowds taken at random at the scene of the action, that the heroine of the first story of *Paisà* was an illiterate girl discovered on the dockside. As for Anna Magnani, admittedly she was a professional but from the world of the *café-concert*. Maria Michi, well, she was just a little girl who worked in a movie house.

Although this type of casting is unusual in films, it is not new. On the contrary, its continual use, by various realistic schools ever since the days of Lumière, shows it to be a true law of the cinema, which the Italian school simply confirms and allows us to formulate with conviction. In the old days of the Russian cinema too, we admired its preference for nonprofessional actors who played on the screen the roles of their daily lives. Actually, a legend has grown up around the Russian films. The theater had a strong influence on certain Soviet schools and although the early films of Eisenstein had no actors, as realist a film as *The Road to Life* was in fact played by professionals from the theater and ever since then the actors in Soviet films have continued to be professionals, just as they have in other countries.

No major cinematographic school between 1925 and the present Italian cinema can boast of the absence of actors, but from time to time a film outside the ordinary run will remind us of the advantage of not using them. Such a film will always be specifically only slightly removed from a social document. Take two examples: *L'Espoir* and *La Dernière Chance*. Around them, too, a legend has grown up. The heroes in the Malraux film are not all part-time actors called on for the moment to play their day-to-day selves. It is true that some of them are, but not the principal characters. The peasant, for example, was a well-known Madrid comic actor. As regards *La Dernière Chance*, the Allied soldiers were actually airmen shot down over Switzerland, but the Jewish woman was a stage actress. Only productions like *Tabu* are entirely without professional actors, but here, as in children's films, we are dealing with a special genre in which a professional actor would be almost unthinkable. More recently, Rouquier in *Farrebique* set out to play the game to the hilt. While noting his success, let us also note that it is practically unique and that the problems presented by a peasant film, so far as the acting is concerned, are no different from those of an exotic film. So far from being an example to be followed, *Farrebique* is a special case in no way invalidating the law that I propose to call the law of the amalgam. It is not the absence of professional actors that is, historically, the hallmark of social realism nor of the Italian film. Rather, it is specifically the rejection of the star concept and the casual mixing of professionals and of those who just act occasionally. It is important to avoid casting the professional in the role for which he is known. The public should not be burdened with any preconceptions. It is significant that the peasant in *Espoir* was a theater comedian, Anna Magnani a singer of popular songs, and Fabrizzi a music-hall clown. That someone is an actor does not mean he must not be used. Quite the opposite. But his professionalism should be called into service only insofar as it allows him to be more flexible in his response to the requirements of the *mise en scène*, and to have a better grasp of the character. The nonprofessionals are naturally chosen for their suitability for the part, either because they fit it physically or because there is some parallel between the role and their lives. When the amalgamation comes off – but experience shows that it will not unless some "moral" requirements are met in the script – the result is precisely that extraordinary feeling of truth that one gets from the current Italian films. Their faithfulness to a script which stirs them deeply and which calls for the minimum of theatrical pretense sets up a kind of osmosis among the cast. The technical inexperience of the amateur is helped out by the experience of the professionals while the professionals themselves benefit from the general atmosphere of authenticity.

However, if a method so beneficent to the art of the cinema has only been employed here and there, it is because unfortunately it contains within itself the seeds of its own destruction. The chemical balance of the amalgam is of necessity unstable, and nothing can prevent it evolving to the point at which it reintroduces the aesthetic dilemma it originally solved – that between the enslavement of the star and the documentary without actors. This disintegration can be observed most clearly and quickly in children's films or films using native peoples. Little Rari of *Tabu*, they say, ended up as a prostitute in Poland, and we all know what happens to children raised to stardom by their first film. At best they turn out to be infant actor prodigies, but that is something else again. Indispensable as are the factors of inexperience and naïveté, obviously they cannot survive repetition. One cannot envisage the Farrebique family appearing in half a dozen films and finally being signed up by Hollywood. As for the professionals who are not stars, the process of disintegration operates a little differently. The public is to blame. While an accepted star is received everywhere as himself, the success of a film is apt to identify the ordinary actor with the role he plays in it. Producers are only too glad to repeat a success by catering to the well-known public fondness for seeing their favorite actors in their established roles. And even if an actor has sense enough to avoid being confined to a single role, it is still a fact that his face and some recurring mannerisms in his acting having become familiar will prevent the amalgam with nonprofessionals from taking place.

Aestheticism, Realism and Reality

Faithfulness to everyday life in the scenario, truth to his part in an actor, however, are simply the basic materials of the aesthetic of the Italian film.

One must beware of contrasting aesthetic refinement and a certain crudeness, a certain instant effectiveness of a realism which is satisfied just to present reality. In my view, one merit of the Italian film will be that it has demonstrated that every realism in art was first profoundly aesthetic. One always felt it was so, but in the reverberations of the accusations of witchcraft that some people today are making against actors suspected of a pact with the demon of art for art's sake, one has tended to forget it. The real like the imaginary in art is the concern of the artist alone. The flesh and blood of reality are no easier to capture in the net of literature or cinema than are gratuitous flights of the imagination. Or to put it another way, even when inventions and complexity of forms are no longer being applied to the actual content of the work, they do not cease thereby to have an influence on the effectiveness of the means. Because the Soviet cinema was too forgetful of this, it slipped in twenty years from first to last place among the great film-producing nations. *Potemkin* turned the cinema world upside down not just because of its political message, not even because it replaced the studio plaster sets with real settings and the star with an anonymous crowd, but because Eisenstein was the greatest montage theoretician of his day, because he worked with Tissé, the finest cameraman of his day, and because Russia was the focal point of cinematographic thought – short, because the "realist" films Russia turned out secreted more aesthetic knowhow than all the sets and performances and lighting and artistic interpretation of the artiest works of German expressionism.

It is the same today with the Italian cinema. There is nothing aesthetically retrogressive about its neorealism, on the contrary, there is progress in expression, a triumphant evolution of the language of cinema, an extension of its stylistics.

Let us first take a good look at the cinema to see where it stands today. Since the expressionist heresy came to an end, particularly after the arrival of sound, one may take it that the general trend of cinema has been toward realism. Let us agree, by and large, that film sought to give the spectator as perfect an illusion of reality as possible within the limits of the logical demands of cinematographic narrative and of the current limits of technique. Thus the cinema stands in contrast to poetry, painting, and theater, and comes ever closer to the novel. It is not my intention here to justify this basic aesthetic trend of modern cinema, be it on technical, psychological, or economic grounds. I simply state it for this once without thereby prejudging either the intrinsic validity of such an evolution or the extent to which it is final.

But realism in art can only be achieved in one way – through artifice.

Every form of aesthetic must necessarily choose between what is worth preserving and what should be discarded, and what should not even be considered. But when this aesthetic aims in essence at creating the illusion of reality, as does the cinema, this choice sets up a fundamental contradiction which is at once unacceptable and necessary: necessary because art can only exist when such a choice is made. Without it, supposing total cinema was here and now technically-possible, we would go back purely to reality. Unacceptable because it would be done definitely at the expense of that reality which the cinema proposes to restore integrally. That is why it would be absurd to resist every new technical development aiming to add to the realism of cinema, namely sound, color, and stereoscopy. Actually the "art" of cinema lives off this contradiction. It gets the most out of the potential for abstraction and symbolism provided by the present limits of the screen, but this utilization of the residue of conventions abandoned by technique can work either to the advantage or to the detriment of realism. It can magnify or neutralize the effectiveness of the elements of reality that the camera captures. One might group, if not classify in order of importance, the various styles of cinematography in terms of the added measure of reality. We would define as "realist," then, all narrative means tending to bring an added measure of reality to the screen. Reality is not to be taken quantitatively. The same event, the same object, can be represented in various ways. Each representation discards or retains various of the qualities that permit us to recognize the object on the screen. Each introduces, for didactic or aesthetic reasons, abstractions that operate more or less corrosively and thus do not permit the original to subsist in its entirety. At the conclusion of this inevitable and necessary "chemical" action, for the initial reality there has been substituted an illusion of reality composed of a complex of abstraction (black and white, plane surface), of conventions (the rules of montage, for example), and of authentic reality. It is a necessary illusion but it quickly induces a loss of awareness of the reality itself, which becomes identified in the mind of the spectator with its cinematographic representation. As for the film maker, the moment he has secured this unwitting complicity of the public, he is increasingly tempted to ignore reality. From habit and laziness he reaches the point when he himself is no longer able to tell where lies begin or end. There could never be any question of calling him a liar because his art consists in lying. He is just no longer in control of his art. He is its dupe, and hence he is held back from any further conquest of reality.

[...]

As we have thus far attempted to describe it, the style of Italian films would appear to belong with a greater or less degree of skill and mastery of technique or feeling to the same family as quasi-literary journalism, to an ingenious art, pleasing, lively, and even moving, but basically a minor art. This is sometimes true even though one may actually rank the genre fairly high in the aesthetic hierarchy. It would be unjust and untrue to see such an assessment as the final measure of this particular technique. Just as, in literature, reportage with its ethic of objectivity (perhaps it would be more correct to say with its ethic of seeming objectivity) has simply provided a basis for a new aesthetic of the novel, so the technique of the Italian film makers results in the best films especially in *Paisà*, with its aesthetic of narrative that is both complex and original.

Paisà is unquestionably the first film to resemble closely a collection of short stories. Up to now we had only known the film composed of sketches – a bastard and phony type of film if ever there was one. Rossellini tells us, in succession, six stories of the Italian Liberation. This historical element is the only thing they have in common. Three of them, the first, the fourth, and the last, are taken from the Resistance. The others are droll or pathetic or tragic episodes occurring on the fringes of the Allied advance. Prostitution, the black market, and a Franciscan convent alike provide the story material. There is no progression other than a chronological ordering of the story beginning with the landing of an Allied force in Sicily. But their social, historical, and human foundation gives them a unity enough to constitute a collection perfectly homogeneous in its diversity. Above all, the length of each story, its form, contents, and aesthetic duration gives us for the first time precisely the impression of a short story. The Naples episode of the urchin – a black-market expert, selling the clothes of a drunk Negro soldier – is an excellent Saroyan story. Another makes us think of Hemingway, yet another (the first) of Faulkner. I am not merely referring to the tone or the subject, but in a profound way to the style. Unfortunately one cannot put a film sequence in quotation marks like a paragraph, and hence any literary description of one must of necessity be incomplete. However, here is an episode from the final story which reminds me now of Hemingway, now of Faulkner:

> 1. A small group of Italian partisans and Allied soldiers have been given a supply of food by a family of fisher folk living in an isolated farmhouse in the heart of the marshlands of the Po delta. Having been handed a basket of eels, they take off. Some while later, a German patrol discovers this, and executes the inhabitants of the farm. 2. An American officer and a partisan are wandering at twilight in the marshes. There is a burst of gunfire in the distance. From a highly elliptical conversation we gather that the Germans have shot the fishermen. 3. The dead bodies of the men and women lie stretched out in front of the little farmhouse. In the twilight, a half-naked baby cries endlessly.

Even with such a succinct description, this fragment of the story reveals enormous ellipses – or rather, great holes. A complex train of action is reduced to three or four brief fragments, in themselves already elliptical enough in comparison with the reality they are unfolding. Let us pass over the first purely descriptive fragment. The second event is conveyed to us by something only the partisans can know – distant gunfire. The third is presented to us independently of the presence of the partisans. It is not even certain that there were any witnesses to the scene. A baby cries besides its dead parents. There is a fact. How did the Germans discover that the parents were guilty? How is it that the child is still alive? That is not the film's concern, and yet a whole train of connected events led to this particular outcome. In any case, the film maker does not ordinarily show us everything. That is impossible – but the things he selects and the things he leaves out tend to form a logical pattern by way of which the mind passes easily from cause to effect. The technique of Rossellini undoubtedly maintains an intelligible succession of events, but these do not mesh like a chain with the sprockets of a wheel. The mind has to leap from one event to the other as one leaps from stone to stone in crossing a river. It may happen that one's foot hesitates between two rocks, or that one misses one's footing and slips. The mind does likewise. Actually it is not of the essence of a stone to allow people to cross rivers without wetting their feet any more than the divisions of a melon exist to allow the head of the family to divide it equally. Facts are facts, our imagination makes use of them, but they do not exist inherently for this purpose. In the usual shooting script (according to a process resembling the classical novel form) the fact comes under the scrutiny of the camera, is divided up, analyzed, and put together again, undoubtedly without entirely losing its factual nature; but the latter, presumably, is enveloped in abstraction, as the clay of a brick is enveloped by the wall which is not as yet present but which will multiply its parallelipeds. For Rossellini, facts take on a meaning, but not like a tool whose function has predetermined its form. The facts follow one another, and the mind is forced to observe their resemblance; and thus, by recalling one another, they end by meaning something which was inherent in each and which is, so to speak, the moral of the story – a moral the mind cannot fail to grasp since it was drawn from reality itself. In the Florentine episode, a woman crosses the city while it is still occupied by a number of Germans and groups of Italian Fascists; she is on her way to meet her fiancé, a leader of the Italian underground, accompanied by a man who likewise is looking for his wife and child. The attention of the camera following them, step by step, though it will share all the difficulties they encounter, all their dangers, will however be impartially divided between the heroes of the adventure and the conditions they must encounter. Actually, everything that is happening in a Florence in the throes of the Liberation is of a like importance. The personal adventures of the two individuals blend into the mass of other aq. ventures, just as one attempts to elbow one's way into a crowd to recover something one has lost. In the course of making one's way one sees in the eyes of those who stand aside the reflections of other concerns, other passions, other dangers alongside which one's own may well be merely laughable. Ultimately and by chance, the woman learns, from a wounded partisan, that the man she is looking for is dead. But the statement from which she learned the news was not aimed straight at her – but hit her like a stray bullet. The impeccable line followed by this recital owes nothing to classical forms that are standard for a story of this kind Attention is never artificially focused on the heroine. The camera makes no pretense at being psychologically subjective. We share all the more fully in the feelings of the protagonists because it is easy for us to sense what they are feeling; and also because the pathetic aspect of the episode does not derive from the fact that a woman has lost the man she loves but from the special place this drama holds among a thousand others, apart from and yet also part of the complete drama of the Liberation of Florence. The camera, as if making an impartial report, confines itself to following a woman searching for a man, leaving to us the task of being alone with her, of understanding her, and of sharing her suffering.

In the admirable final episode of the partisans surrounded in the marshlands, the muddy waters of the Po Delta, the reeds stretching away to the horizon, just sufficiently tall to hide the man crouching down in the little flat-bottomed boat, the lapping of the waves against the wood, all occupy a place of equal importance with the men. This dramatic role played by the marsh is due in great measure to deliberately intended qualities in the photography. This is why the horizon is always at the same height. Maintaining the same proportions between water and sky in every shot brings out one of the basic characteristics of this landscape. It is the exact equivalent, under conditions imposed by the screen, of the inner feeling men experience who are living between the sky and the water and whose lives are at the mercy of an infinitesimal shift of angle in relation to the horizon. This shows how much subtlety of expression can be got on exteriors from a camera in the hands of the man who photographed *Paisà*.

The unit of cinematic narrative in *Paisà* is not the "shot," an abstract view of a reality which is being analyzed, but the "fact." A fragment of concrete reality in itself multiple and full of ambiguity, whose meaning emerges only after the fact, thanks to other imposed facts between which the mind establishes certain relationships. Unquestionably, the director chose these "facts" carefully while at the same time respecting their factual integrity. The closeup of the door knob referred to earlier was less a fact than a sign brought into arbitrary relief by the camera, and no more independent semantically than a preposition in a sentence. The opposite is true of the marsh or the death of the peasants.

But the nature of the "image facts" is not only to maintain with the other image facts the relationships invented by the mind. These are in a sense the centrifugal properties of the image – those which make the narrative possible. Each image being on its own just a fragment of reality existing before any meanings, the entire surface of the scene should manifest an equally concrete density. Once again we have here the opposite of the "door-knob" type of scene, in which the color of the enamel, the dirt marks at the level of the hand, the shine of the metal, the worn-away look are just so many useless facts, concrete parasites of an abstraction fittingly dispensed with.

In *Paisà* (and I repeat that I imply by this, in varying degrees, all Italian films) the closeup of the door knob would be replaced, without any loss of that peculiar quality of which it is part, by the "image fact" of a door whose concrete characteristics would be equally visible. For the same reason the actors will take care never to dissociate their performance from the decor or from the performance of their fellow actors. Man himself is just one fact among others, to whom no pride of place should be given *a priori*. That is why the Italian film makers alone know how to shoot successful scenes in buses, trucks, or trains, namely because these scenes combine to create a special density within the framework of which they know how to portray an action without separating it from its material context and without loss of that uniquely human quality of which it is an integral part. The subtlety and suppleness of movement within these cluttered spaces, the naturalness of the behavior of everyone in the shooting area, make of these scenes supreme bravura moments of the Italian cinema.

2

NOIR NARRATION

J. P. Telotte

The deep of night is crept upon our talk,
And nature must obey necessity.
– Shakespeare

In the darkened movie theater, it is understood, we are supposed to be silent. Sometimes reminders appear on the screen to prompt us, and there are always the irritated looks of fellow filmgoers to reinforce the custom. If for some reason we have to speak, we know not to raise our voices above a whisper, for here it is the *movie's* role to talk and ours to listen. Most popular American films seem to take this injunction a bit further; that is, they seldom appear to speak above a whisper about the problems that weigh most heavily upon us. Instead, they usually talk in what we might term a *conventional* way: encoding our concerns within patterns of generic conventions, reducing them to a kind of sign language, and thereby resolving them for us in an imaginary, almost silent way. Such quiet "speech," however, has generally proved quite useful for a culture like ours, propelled as it is by such varied and contradictory dreams that their unmuffled or shrill expression might well create problems rather than resolve them.

Violations, of course, always occur; in the theater someone invariably talks and spoils our concentration. The same thing happens in our film. For from time to time, despite a possibility of disturbing viewers, our films will speak directly and even forcefully about our cultural and human problems. They do so not

From: J. P. Telotte, '*Noir* Narration', in *Voices in the Dark: The Narrative Patterns of* Film Noir, The Board of Trustees of the University of Illinois (University of Illinois Press, 1989).

only because, as Walker Percy warns, "silence prolonged can induce terror," but also because talk, even when it addresses those "unspeakable feelings" that "nobody wants to hear about," can serve a therapeutic function of sorts. "Through its re-presenting," Percy explains, our alienation, fear, or cultural anxiety can undergo "an aesthetic reversal," producing a measure of comfort in the very "speakability" of our problems. Seen in this context, the violation of a customary silence, or the raising of popular film's narrative voice, seems a natural response to a kind of need. It is a need whose satisfaction points up the basic contradictions that, in the modern world, seem to structure both our speech and our silences.

When we look at the group of films we call *film noir*, we find both a notable instance of such violation and a revealing articulation of the sort of tensions that shape our film narratives. This large body of films, flourishing in America in the period 1941–58, generally focuses on urban crime and corruption, and on sudden upwellings of violence in a culture whose fabric seems to be unraveling. Because of these typical concerns, the *film noir* seems fundamentally *about* violations: vice, corruption, unrestrained desire, and, most fundamental of all, abrogation of the American dream's most basic promises – of hope, prosperity, and safety from persecution. Taken as a whole, the *noir* films are noteworthy neither for their subtlety of expression nor their muting of our cultural problems; to the contrary, they deploy the darkest imagery to sketch starkly disconcerting assessments of the human and social condition. In their vision, crime and corruption seem almost a matter of decor, dark trappings of a world suddenly shown in a new and most revealing light.

Admittedly, American films have periodically focused on such violations. D. W. Griffith's *Musketeers of Pig Alley* (1912), for example, with its naturalistic detailing of urban crime, already looks toward the gangster cycle of the 1930s, as well as to such typical *films noir* as *Kiss of Death* (1947), *Cry of the City* (1948), and *The Asphalt Jungle* (1950). But what makes the *noir* voice so distinctive is that the patterns of violation it speaks of also appear to be the patterns of our cultural and human order. That identity, of course, forestalls any easy or conventional imaginary resolution. Moreover, it adds a special inflection to the narrative voice that drives these films, which talks not simply about crime and corruption but about how we understand and give formulation to self and society; it asks how we see ourselves, individually and culturally. If that voice at times seems a bit loud, even coarse, directly addressing us in ways we are not accustomed to in the cinema, it is also generally a therapeutic voice. For by speaking forthrightly, it helps us to recognize, understand, and perhaps better cope with the problems it so starkly describes.

To continue in what might seem an uncinematic analogy, I would suggest that what makes *noir*'s social commentary both possible and distinctive is this different manner of speech, the form's narrative voice. One aspect of that difference is the form's ambiguous posture on the borders of genre. As critics have often noted, at times the films seem to adopt what we might term a generic voice, following the conventions and stylistic characteristics that usually mark our popular narrative formulas; yet at other times they defy formula and even capitalize on the disrupting of our narrative expectations. Is *noir*, then, simply a cycle of films that flourished in the backwash of World War II and the early cold war days, borrowing its markings from a variety of established genres; or is it a genre in its own right, simply appearing, disappearing, and then reappearing, in keeping with the usual principles of audience popularity and *need*? Those who see it as a unique and time-bound phenomenon argue the former, while those who find the *noir* spirit repeatedly resurfacing, notably in such more recent films as *Chinatown* (1974), *Body Heat* (1981), *Blood Simple* (1985), and *D.O.A.* (1988), hold to the latter. It is an argument that finally has as much to do with criticism itself, especially with the varying ways that we define film genres, as it does with the *film noir*, and thus one that we probably cannot fully resolve here.

What we can quickly note, though, is that a similar ambiguity marks the *film noir*'s relationship to the dominant style of its period, what we term classical film narrative. This conventional voice is characterized by a seemingly objective point of view, adherence to a cause-effect logic, use of goal-oriented characters to direct our attention and elicit our sympathies, and a progression toward narrative closure. In the *noir* family we find many films that seem by turns to contravene and to support these classical conventions. In fact, this form may be most remarkable not just for the subjects it addresses but for its efforts at finding an adequate voice for those subjects, as if the normal manner of film narrative had come to be perceived as unsuitable, inadequate, or, like the various structures of daily life it examines, even suspect. It is, after all, the *film noir* that, energized by some singular literary models of the pre- and postwar era, popularized the voice-over and flashback devices which implicitly challenge conventionally linear narratives, while it also developed the extended subjective camera sequence and brought into vogue a variety of documentary techniques that influenced our whole sense of film realism.

Ultimately, I want to argue, these are not just isolated violations of conventional styles but telling indicators of a curious phenomenon: when viewed as a group, these films demonstrate a remarkable pattern of narrative experimentation, certainly one that is unique for a particular cycle or, if you will, genre of films. In fact, not since the days of film pioneers like Griffith, Thomas Ince, and William DeMille had the American cinema experienced such a fascination with the mechanics and the *possibilities* of storytelling. In this consistent pattern of narrative experimentation, violation, and development, then, we can see both one of the form's most distinctive characteristics (one that could argue for its generic status), and the extent of its departure from a tradition of American films depicting cultural violation.

The *film noir*'s historical context, that is, its appearance in the closing years of World War II and its flourishing in the immediate postwar era, obviously has much to do with this curious mixture of violations. For example, one of the war's immediate effects was to radically curtail the export market for American films, even as home attendance saw a steady rise. Reacting to this shift in audience, Hollywood apparently intensified its focus on the specific concerns of American moviegoers. Of course, this focus was partly prompted by government calls to support the war effort and avoid any potentially divisive subject matter. But as Colin Shindler notes, it was also generally true that "What Hollywood feared above all else was deep division in the country that would cloud the image of America that the majority of film-makers tried to reflect." As the war began to wind down and those governmental and ideological pressures eased, however, the culture gradually came into a more critical focus. American life was viewed not simply as the subject of some outrageous violation by an outside force – Japanese or Germans – but as the very locus of various long disguised, almost invisible violations of our individual and cultural dreams. And in the unsatisfying return to normalcy that the war's conclusion brought to America – a return punctuated by rampant inflation, unemployment, labor strife, shifting social patterns, and the rapidly growing anxieties of the cold war – this pattern of self-examination and self-critique seemed increasingly justified.

As if inspiring a voice of violation, then, the calamitous troubles that had convulsed the world became internalized by postwar American culture and, as we might expect, were reflected in its films. Fittingly, it is the German critic Siegfried Kracauer who, recalling his experience of Nazi Germany, noted this trend, observing an almost obsessive concern with crime and the criminal mind in our postwar films. In them he saw an image of "the weird, veiled insecurity of life under the Nazis," now "transferred to the American scene. Sinister conspiracies incubate next door, within the world considered normal – any trusted neighbor may turn into a demon." But why this transference and the almost ritualistic mirroring of the world's violations it implies? Kracauer believes these films reflect both a cultural and human failing that the American cinema had, intentionally or not, previously overlooked. On the one hand, he felt, they show the "uncertainties" Americans had begun to feel about their own system and its ability to cope with problems the war had uncovered; on the other, they evoke a larger sense of fear and anxiety that increasingly seemed to be "accepted as inevitable and almost inscrutable."

While he is mainly trying to describe Fascism's destructive lure of order and simplicity, laying bare its potential attraction for a disillusioned America, Kracauer also points to a deeper, almost semantic significance in these films. Drawing on his interpretation, we might see them as signs of a disturbing lack of adequate models or terms for dealing with a broken, seemingly deranged world: as emblems of a failure not just in our culture but in its conventional genres, in its narrative techniques – by which we try to make imaginary sense of our world – in effect, in the very voice with which it spoke. Seen in this context, the *film noir* seems most remarkable for the various ways in which it copes with and casts into relief these different failings. What I want to suggest is that these films served a significant liberating function for the American cinema that merits more careful examination. For not only did they manage to voice violation, to articulate what the classical cinema might normally have muted or stifled, but they also called attention – and at times fell prey – to the very power of our cultural discourse to permit speech and to impose silence.

That same function had already been taken up by our literature – or at least by a significant subset of the literary canon, the hard-boiled and mystery fiction of the 1930s. And that example not only helped clear the narrative ground for the *film noir*, through the work of writers like Dashiell Hammett, Raymond Chandler, Cornell Woolrich, and James M. Cain, but it also continued in the vein of the cinema, developing into a kind of *noir* literary genre in the works of such novelists as Jim Thompson, David Goodis, and Dorothy B. Hughes, among others. In fact, the strongest argument for *noir* as a genre might ultimately be based on this point, that it is a narrative form with specific conventions and concerns which bulk beyond the cinema's limited confines, in much the way that, say, the melodrama does.

In their pioneering overview of *noir*, the French critics Raymond Borde and Etienne Chaumeton made much of this literary influence. The *film noir*'s "immediate source," they asserted, "is clearly the American or English detective thriller novel," exemplified by the work of Hammett, Chandler, Cain, W. R. Burnett, and Graham Greene, and they noted that early *noirs* seem marked by "a total submission by the cinema to literature" as a source. Alain Silver and Elizabeth Ward's "encyclopedic reference" book on the *film noir* largely bears out that assessment. For of thirty-six *noirs* listed from the early period of 1940–45, twenty-seven are based on previously published works – novels, short stories, or plays – while seven derive from unpublished stories, and only two are original film scripts.

Hammett and Chandler are the two figures who most often surface in discussions of these literary origins, in part because of the kind of characters and world they depicted, but also because of their approach to those depictions. Hammett's protagonists, such as the anonymous Continental Op of what may be the prototype *noir* story, *Red Harvest*, and the more well known Sam Spade of *The Maltese Falcon*, move through a dark and corrupt world (Poisonville, the nickname for the city in *Red Harvest*, would fit any of Hammett's locales). Whether his protagonist narrates the tale or is only its focal point, though, he provides a kind of measure of that world through his ability to remain apart from its corruption; as Terry Curtis Fox notes, "The Op's voice is never neutral ... every descriptive sentence carries an emotional and moral judgment on the matter at hand." What results is a constant tension between the lure of that corrupt world and his characters' stance – one that at times seems nearly pointless, given the pervasive criminality, and at other times self-destructive, because of the dangers it involves. But that stance is finally crucial to the attraction of these tales, for the moral center it fashions reassures us that, individually, man can cling to some human values, even as he is faced by corruption on all sides.

Raymond Chandler's oft-quoted prescription for the detective, "down these mean streets a man must go," clearly suggests his link to Hammett. His characters, especially the detective Philip Marlowe, move through a world with which they are at odds. They are like knights in a realm where, as Marlowe notes in *The Big Sleep*, "knights had no meaning." But that figure with no "meaning" controls both our perspective and our sympathies for, thanks to Chandler's first-person narration, all that we see in the Marlowe novels is what the detective himself sees; his experiences – and his thoughts – are ours. This outer-directedness ultimately proves just as important as Marlowe's moral stance (style an equivalent of theme), since it equally defines our relationship to the world he inhabits. Through Marlowe we become different from, and in many ways stronger than, that world. We perceive its truth, understand its ways, and avoid its pitfalls as no one else in the novels can. What this singular experience produces, in effect, is a new vantage on the relation of psyche and surface, as *how* we perceive becomes our one sure proof against *what* awaits on those "mean streets."

For James Cain, author of such *noir* source novels as *Double Indemnity, Mildred Pierce,* and *The Postman Always Rings Twice*, the question of narrative technique was a fundamental issue, and his solution was akin to Chandler's. He has confessed that he initially found the novel form "hopeless," because "I didn't seem to have the least idea where I was going with it, or even which paragraph should follow which. But my short stories, which were put into the mouth of some character, marched right along, for if I in the third person faltered and stumbled, my characters in the first person knew perfectly well what they had to say ... I began to wonder if *that* wouldn't be the medium I could use to write novels." Of course, the first-person, pointedly retrospective format became the key to Cain's best work, providing him with both a narrative pattern and a way of organizing all that occurs in the narrative. Cain's characters look back at a series of events that have led up to their present situation, like the impending execution of Frank Chambers in *The Postman Always Rings Twice*, and what they recollect is just what they could have seen, experienced, or heard about. It is, moreover, constantly being weighed, often for ironic effect, against all that they know *now*.

More than simply a narrative formula, then, that retrospective approach, which was retained for the screen versions of the novels mentioned above, contributed to a complex vision of the individual in modern society. Like Chandler's, Cain's approach clearly foregrounds the consciousness, gives center stage to reason as it attempts to sort out a welter of past events. But Cain's protagonists hardly rival Marlowe in the ability to puzzle out their world; as one critic puts it, "reason doesn't stand a chance" in his novels. Whether his characters are trying to manipulate others or simply hoping to figure out how their plans went wrong, they invariably find that things do not make sense, or that, as Frank Chambers bluntly puts it, "When I start to figure, it all goes blooey." What Cain has done is to fashion a disturbing dialectic between the passions that led his characters to their current pass and a mind that, in the present, must sort out and make sense of all that has transpired. While his first-person narrators thus give order and reason to their narratives, much as Chandler's do, the very things of which they speak – the passions and pathological acts that defy all reason – give us pause, call into question their ability ever to sort out or explain their lives.

That paradox becomes the driving force behind the fiction of Jim Thompson, whose work appears at the height of the *film noir*'s popularity and continues beyond its day, and who contributed to the script of Stanley Kubrick's *noir* film. *The Killing* (1956). Besides a reporter's eye for detail – at various times he wrote for the *New York Daily News* and *Los Angeles Times Mirror* – that ranks his work alongside Chandler's and Hammett's for effective and telling description, Thompson also brought to the hard-boiled/crime novel a fascination with exploring various narrative approaches that gives his work a distinctly modernist stamp. In addition to straightforward first-person narratives much in the Chandler and Cain mold, we find in his works multiple-narrator novels like *The Criminal*; narratives that break into alternate versions, like *A Hell of a Woman*'s final chapter, which tells two stories in alternate lines of type, one the story the narrator consciously wishes to relate and the other the truth which he simply cannot escape or ignore any longer; and narrators who seem to be dying or, in the pattern of one of the most famous *noir* films, *Sunset Boulevard* (1950), already dead as they speak (*Savage Night*'s narrator describes his reactions as his girl hacks him to death with an axe). In such a character, who is being physically reduced even as he recounts events, Thompson seems to be playing at the very margins of narration, exploring, in much the way that the *film noir* as a form did, the limits of conventional storytelling practice.

In describing *Savage Night*'s conclusion, Geoffrey O'Brien notes how "being itself erodes, right in front of us." It is, though, not just being but Thompson's narrative that typically "erodes" or, perhaps, deconstructs itself, reminding us that we have simply been attending to a voice in a void that has sought to construct its own version of reality, and thereby to stay a tendency for erosion, for the gradual eating away of whatever we fashion. What Thompson does, in the best *film noir* fashion, is lure us into a seemingly unified narrative, only to violate our expectations, revealing finally how illusory that unity is. Having drawn us into a human consciousness – or several consciousnesses – he then springs a narrative trap of sorts that leaves us in a hallucinatory realm – the realm of the human psyche deprived of all the customary supports that normal experience leads us to expect.

In this pattern, I believe, Thompson models or reflects the narrative developments found in the *films noir* more than he influences them. While several of his novels have been successfully adapted to the screen – and we might particularly note *The Getaway* (1972) and the later *Coupe de Torchon* (1981), based on Thompson's *Pop. 1280* – most of those adaptations appeared long after the period of *film noir*'s greatest appeal. His importance for this study, though, lies in the way his fiction mirrors the patterns we find repeatedly worked out in the *noir* mainstream, as his narrators set about providing us privileged access to a world, only to find that the path they have staked out is full of obstacles and pitfalls, in fact that, like truth itself, it seems virtually to disappear before us. Thus even as he narrates his fast-eroding situation, *Savage Night's* Charlie Bigger notes how language itself has become almost empty and meaningless: "after a while everything was said that we could say and it would have been like talking to yourself. So we talked less and less, and pretty soon we were hardly talking at all. And then we *weren't* talking at all. Just grunting and gesturing and pointing at things. It was like we'd never known how to talk." Not only is the fragile order of his life rapidly disappearing, but even the means of describing that situation, of accounting for the mystery, seems to have vanished. Still, he goes on speaking, the narrative itself a kind of straw at which he clutches, as a last desperate hope or human gesture against a world marked by an inhuman violence and cruelty.

Most other studies of the *film noir* examine this literary background in far more depth than the brief sketch offered here. And in doing so they follow the lead of the French critic Nino Frank, who in 1946 drew the very term *film noir* from the similarity of these works to the novels then being published in Gallimard's *Serie Noire*. But that linkage never answers the real question, never tells us what the *film noir* is, only what it is *like*. It resembles, in both themes and narrative patterns, a variety of popular literature that appears prior to the *film noir* and that continues beyond its heyday. This material helps cast into relief several of *noir's* most distinctive narrative developments, but that literary perspective alone does not let us see the form's larger scheme. To do so, we have to turn to the film themselves.

The primary difficulty facing most inquiries into the *film noir* is its very amorphous nature. It simply does not sit still for an accurate or conventional portrait. While many historians describe it as a discrete genre with its own conventions, others see it as nothing more than a limited cycle, a strange outgrowth of various social factors at a special time in our history. Certainly, *noir* seems to push at the normal bounds of genre designation, its varied settings, subjects, and actions confounding the sort of easy classification that samples of the Western, musical, or science fiction genres allow. More often, a *noir* film seems related to other, established genres, for example, to the gangster or detective formulas, or to straddle generic lines, drawing simultaneously on a variety of conventions and expectations. The historical limits often cited for the form, the period from 1941 to 1958, further block thinking of *noir* as we do of other, seemingly longer-lived genres with their implicitly mythic appeal. For such reasons, Paul Schrader flatly asserts that "*film noir* is not a genre": "It is not defined, as are the western and gangster genres, by conventions of setting and conflict, but rather by the most subtle qualities of tone and mood." And following this lead, J. A. Place and L. S. Peterson argue that "visual style" alone proves the "consistent thread that unites the very diverse films that together comprise this phenomenon," as they then attempt to describe precisely what constitutes this peculiar "*film noir* style."

The question of style, however, only broadens the debate about what the *film noir* is. After all, a number of distinct "looks," as well as various combinations of them, mark the *noir* canon. Thus we might take *style* to mean the baroque play of light and dark, of line and volume that *noir* drew from its roots in German expressionist films of the 1920s. But it could also refer to the stark realism and urban locations that Schrader and others link to the influence of Italian neorealist films in the postwar period. Then too the documentary look of films like *Boomerang* (1947), *The Naked City* (1948), and *Panic in the Streets* (1950) owes much to the impact of war documentaries and newsreels on American audiences, as well as to various technical advances that made location shooting commonplace. Seldom, though, do we find the documentary style combined with the surrealistic imagery and distorted perspectives of yet another, more fantastic offshoot of the *noir* style, glimpsed in the Dali-designed dream sequences of *Spellbound* (1945), as well as those of *Murder, My Sweet* (1944) or *The Dark Past* (1949). The *noir* "style," I would suggest, ultimately seems as curiously diverse as its subject matter, and equally as inadequate for accurately defining the form.

The very disagreement underlying practically every discussion of *film noir* is significant, though. For despite a lack of consensus, critics generally agree on which films merit a *noir* classification. The *noir* filmographies published by John S. Whitney, Foster Hirsch, and Alain Silver and Elizabeth Ward, for example, differ mainly in two respects. First, they disagree about which *modern* films to put in their groupings as inheritors of the *noir* tradition. And we might read into this a hint of their common bias toward seeing the form not as a singular, time-bound cycle but as a true genre, recurring through time as cultural conditions dictate. Second, they differ in terms of the minor or "B" films which, because of their elusiveness and limited distribution, may have been seen by one compiler and not by another. As James Damico suggests, therefore, it might seem "self-evident that the foremost task of any inquiry into the category ought to be the identification of exactly what it is that causes films intuitively classed as FN [*film noir*] to appear to share affinities." In effect, we must consider how to account for the general agreement in classifying these films when the definitions that might justify such classification seem so elusive.

In exploring Western culture's changing perceptions of "madness," Michel Foucault faced a similar difficulty. Judging from the "multiplicity of objects" that supposedly constituted madness and the variety of commentaries that made up "a discourse, concerning madness," he found coming to any universally acceptable definition of the condition almost impossible. As a result, he adopted a broadly inclusive strategy, concluding that "mental illness" has been "constituted by all that was said in all the statements that named it, divided it up, described it, explained it, traced its developments, indicated its various correlations, judged it, and possibly gave it speech by articulating, in its name, discourses that were to be taken as its own." One approach he initially entertained recalls that of Schrader, Place, and Peterson, namely an effort to examine his subject from a vantage determined "not so much by its objects or concepts as by a certain *style*, a certain constant manner of statement." However, aware that such "descriptions could not, in any case, be abstracted from the hypotheses" about his subject, in effect that "style" depended upon a prior select group, he rejected such a stance. In its place, he tried to isolate certain "discursive formations" or regularities that marked our identification of the objects and events of madness, as well as the various ways in which we speak of them. With this approach, he began to isolate and analyze "small islands of coherence," and then examine the various strategies that embrace the disparate objects, shifting styles of description, and changing contexts of his study.

This approach might well serve our thinking about the *film noir*, since it lets us account for both the play of difference noted by most commentaries on the form and the "intuitive" perception of unifying factors Damico describes. By trying to describe *noir*'s primary discursive formations, we might obviate – or at least postpone – the question of its generic status, while also avoiding the simplistic notion of "style" as the determining factor – especially since it only hides an unexplained predetermination of what films are truly *noir*. This study thus takes a broadly inclusive focus, accepting for the purposes of a discursive description all that is usually grouped within the time-bound or traditional *noir* canon. Thereafter, regardless of whether we think of *noir* as a discrete genre (with an unnaturally restricted life span or irregular cycle of recurrence), or as a congealing of forces and attitudes operating in various genres in a specific era, our vantage on those formations can remain stable, our analysis securely anchored in the works themselves.

When viewed from this perspective, the *film noir* seems to mirror both the large cultural forces and the immediate human impulses that shape our lives and that seem to generate their own discourse. On the one hand, then, we shall see *noir* in a *reactive* context, as a response or resistance to the dominations of power in society, and thus as a generic effort at revealing, examining, and, as far as possible, gaining some freedom from the forces that both structure and violate our daily lives. In this sense it is a social myth, one evoked by the particular conditions of postwar America. On the other hand, we shall see it as a symptom, a distortion that cuts across generic lines and that is caused by the same desires and powers that propel our culture and our lives. But whether viewed as a response to distortion or as itself a stylistic and thematic distortion that infects our prevailing cultural myths – thereby producing, for example, *noir* Westerns like *Rancho Notorious* (1952) and *Johnny Guitar* (1954) – the *film noir* can designate a field of deviation that mirrors the problems of modern America in particular and modern man in general. And this field is characterized by a remarkable variety of discursive formations, as Foucault would term them, through which the form manages to articulate a rising awareness of the limitations and paradoxes that shape our culture, our lives, and the stories we tell of them both.

A survey of the large body of films usually classed as *noir* suggests that one of its most distinctive yet often overlooked features is its singular concern with or awareness of the nature of narration. For more than any other body of popular films, and certainly more so than its near relative, the gangster genre, *film noir* pushes at the very boundaries of classical narrative, particularly with its frequent use of voice-over narrators, flashbacks (even flashbacks within flashbacks, as in *Sorry, Wrong Number* [1948] and *The Enforcer* [1951]), convoluted time schemes, and subjective camera techniques. Schrader and others basically pass these varied approaches off as further examples of *noir* stylistics, seeing them as evidence of "a love of romantic narration" that mainly serves to establish "a mood of *temps perdu*: an irretrievable past, a predetermined fate and an all-enveloping hopelessness." Foster Hirsch, however, distinguishes between two complementary elements of the typical *noir* narrative, noting that "*noir* tells its stories in a particular way, and in a particular visual style." While he neither explores nor identifies this range of *noir* narrative patterns, he does point us in a valuable direction by recognizing that the form's curious rhetoric is as remarkable as its look and tone. This observation is, I believe, crucial to understanding the *film noir*.

My survey of the *noir* form, based on a sampling of more than 130 films, isolates four dominant narrative strategies or discursive for mations: 1 the classical, third-person narrative. 2, the voice-overy/flashback style-3, the subjective camera technique, 4 the documentary mode. Because they emerge from an industry dominated by the classical pattern, we should expect that a majority of *noir* films largely follow this first approach, with its linear unfolding of events from a third-person or "objective" vantage. Certainly some of the best-known *noirs*, such as *The Maltese Falcon* (1941), *In a Lonely Place* (1950), and *Kiss Me Deadly* (1955), work in this way, using a traditional narrative approach to counterbalance the disturbing or unconventional events they depict. Most *noir* critics, though, find the combination of voice-over and flashback, with its implicit suggestion that the viewer has privileged access to a mind meditating on the past, to be more symptomatic of the form. In describing the typical *noir* film, Robert Porfirio, for instance, takes this view, noting that "instead of writing his story, the hero tells it to us directly, and the combined techniques of first person narration and flashback enhance the aura of doom. It is almost as if the narrator takes a perverse pleasure in relating the events leading up to his current crisis." While not quite the "typical" style critics would have it, this basically subjective approach surfaces often, and it occurs in one of the earlier and most influential of *films noir*, *Double Indemnity* (1944). Following its successful application in this film, more than forty other *noirs* would use the same narrative approach.

It remained for a third strategy to explore more fully the possibility of subjective narration. A subjective camera, used either with a voice-over or as a separate narrative device, promised viewers a far more radical sense of shared consciousness, by literally giving them a character's vantage on events for large portions of the narrative. Robert Montgomery's experiment with almost completely subjective narration, *The Lady in the Lake* (1947), is the most famous instance of this briefly popular style. A fourth discursive formation, that of the documentary-style *noir* worked a compromise between the first two strategies we have described. Films like *Boomerang* and *The Naked City* use the camera as an objective recorder of events, but they also yoke it to a voice-over commentary that guides our point of view and testifies to the truth of what we see. Transported into the streets, among the people and locales where the factually based events occurred, we were supposed to gain in these films a new view of reality, of our world stripped of its veneer of custom and habit. Of course, we were also supposed to overlook the irony implicit in this approach: the notion that through the natural, by evoking film's mimetic capacity, these documentary-style works sought much the same sort of revisioning of the commonplace that other *films noir* pursued in more fantastic ways, through expressionistic imagery, distorted camera angles, and chiaroscuro lighting.

What this variety of discursive formations quickly points up is the extent to which the *film noir* reflects a new openness toward narrative experimentation and development. That this exploration occurs in a period still dominated by the practices of classical film narrative and, for the most part, in an industry that was historically reluctant to alter or challenge any proven profitable procedure, seems equally significant. Certainly it suggests the sort of tensions and contradictions that we typically find in *noir* narratives – tensions that, Foucault would offer, ultimately mark all forms of discourse. Even more significantly, though, this exploration points to a deeper identifying characteristic of the form: a compelling urge to understand, formulate, and articulate the human situation at a time when our old formulations, as well as the means of expression underlying them, no longer seemed adequate. That urge, I feel, drives the *film noir*, and gives reason to the basic commitment to expression it evidences even in the face of the obvious limitations and conventions that condition all cinematic speech.

3

THE 'CINEMA OF POETRY'

Pier Paolo Pasolini

I believe that it is no longer possible to begin to discuss cinema as an expressive language without at least taking into consideration the terminology of semiotics. Quite simply, the problem is this: while literary languages base their poetry on the institutionalized premise of usable instrumentalized languages, the common possession of all speakers, cinematographic languages seem to be founded on nothing at all: they do not have as a real premise any communicative language. Literary languages thus have an immediate legitimacy as instruments (pure and simple instruments), which do, in fact, serve to communicate. Cinematographic communication would instead seem to be arbitrary and aberrant, without the concrete instrumental precedents which are normally used by all. In other words, people communicate with words, not images; therefore, a specific language of images would seem to be a pure and artificial abstraction.

If this reasoning were correct, as it would appear to be, cinema would simply not exist; or, if it did, it would be a monstrosity, a series of meaningless signs. Instead, cinema does communicate. This means that it, too, is based on a patrimony of common signs.

Semiotics confronts sign systems without differentiating among them: it speaks of "systems of *linguistic* signs," for example, because they exist, but this does not exclude at all the theoretical possibility that there may be other systems of signs – for example, systems of gestural signs. As a matter of fact, in

From: Pier Paolo Pasolini, 'The Cinema of Poetry', in Louise Barnett and Ben Lawton (trans.), *Heretical Empiricism* (Indiana University Press, 1988).

the real world it is actually necessary to invoke a system of gestural signs to complement the spoken language.

In fact, a word (lin-sign or language sign) spoken with a certain facial expression has one meaning; spoken with another expression it has another meaning, possibly actually its opposite. Let's assume that it is a Neapolitan who is speaking: a word followed by one gesture has one meaning; followed by another gesture, it has another meaning, etc.

This "system of gestural signs" that in actual oral communication is interwoven with and completes the system of linguistic signs can be isolated under laboratory conditions and studied autonomously. One can actually imagine, as an abstract hypothesis, the existence of a single system of gestural signs as the single instrument of human communication (all deaf-mute Neapolitans, in other words). It is on such a hypothetical system of visual signs that the language of the cinema founds its practical ability to exist, its right to be conceivable as the result of a series of natural communicative archetypes.

This would be very little, certainly. But then it is necessary to add immediately that the intended audience of the cinematographic product is also accustomed to "read" reality visually, that is, to have an instrumental conversation with the surrounding reality in asmuch as it is the environment of a collectivity, which also expresses itself with the pure and simple optical presence of its actions and habits. A solitary walk in the street, even with stopped up ears, is a continual conversation between us and an environment which expresses itself through the images that compose it: the faces of people who pass by, their gestures, their signs, their actions, their silences, their expressions, their arguments, their collective reactions (groups of people waiting at traffic lights, crowding around a traffic accident or around the fish-woman at Porta Capuana); and more – billboards, signposts, traffic circles, and, in short, objects and things that appear charged with multiple meanings and thus "speak" brutally with their very presence.

But there is more, a theoretician would say: that is, there is an entire world in man which expresses itself primarily through signifying images (shall we invent, by analogy, the term im-signs?): *this is the world of memory and of dreams.*

Every effort to reconstruct a memory is a "sequence of im-signs," that is, in a primordial sense, a film sequence. (Where did I see that person? Wait ... I think it was at Zagorà – image of Zagorà with its pale green palm trees set off against the pink earth – in the company of Abd el-Kader ... image of Abd el-Kader and of the "person" as they walk, with the small barracks of the former French outpost in the background, etc.) In this sense every dream is a sequence of im-signs, which have all the characteristics of film sequences: close-ups, long shots, extreme close-ups, etc. In short, there is a complex world of meaningful images – both gestural and environmental – that accompany the lin-signs, and those proper to memories and dreams, which prefigure and offer themselves as the "instrumental" premise of cinematographic communication.

And so it will be immediately necessary to make a parenthetical observation: while the instrumental communication which lies at the basis of poetic or philosophical communication is already extremely elaborate – it is, in other words, a real, historically complex and mature system – the visual communication which is the basis of film language is, on the contrary, extremely crude, almost animal-like. As with gestures and brute reality, so dreams and the processes of our memory are almost prehuman events, or on the border of what is human. In any case, they are pregrammatical and even premorphological (dreams take place on the level of the unconscious, as do the mnemonic processes; gestures are an indication of an extremely elementary stage of civilization, etc.). *The linguistic instrument on which film is predicated is, therefore, of an irrational type:* and this explains the deeply oneiric quality of the cinema, and also its concreteness as, let us say, object, which is both absolute and impossible to overlook.

More specifically, I am saying that every system of lin-signs is collected and enclosed in a dictionary. Beyond that dictionary there is nothing – with the exception, perhaps, of the gestures which accompany the signs in spoken usage. Each of us thus has in his head a lexically incomplete but practically perfect dictionary of the linguistic signs of his circle and of his country. The work of the writer consists of taking words from this dictionary, where they are kept as if in a shrine, in order to use them in a specific manner: specific in respect to the historical moment of the word and of the writer. The result of this process is to increase the historical value of the word, that is, to increase the meaning of the word.

If that writer should amount to something, in future dictionaries his "specific use of the word" will be cited as an additional meaning of the institutionalized word. The writer's expressive process, that is, his invention, therefore adds to the historicity, that is, to the reality of the language; therefore, he works on the language both as an instrumental linguistic system and as a cultural tradition. His act, if one were to describe it toponymically, is one alone: the reworking of the meaning of the sign. The sign was there, in the dictionary, pigeonholed, ready to be used.

For the filmmaker, however, the action, although fundamentally similar, is much more complicated. There is no dictionary of images. There is no pigeonholed image, ready to be used. If by any chance we wanted to imagine a dictionary of images, we would have to imagine an *infinite dictionary*, as infinite as the dictionary of *possible words*.

The filmmaker does not have a dictionary; he has infinite possibilities. He does not take his signs (im-signs) from a shrine, a protective sheath, or from some baggage, but from chaos, where they are nothing more than possibilities or shadows of a mechanical, oneiric communication. The activity of the cinematographic author, thus toponymically described, is not *single*, but *double*. As a matter of fact, he must take the im-sign from the meaningless jumble of possible expressions (chaos), make its individual existence possible, and conceive of it as placed in a dictionary of meaningful im-signs (gestures, environment, dream, memory); [and he must] fulfill the writer's function, that is, add to such a purely morphological sign its individual expressive quality.

In other words, while the activity of the writer is an aesthetic invention, that of the filmmaker is first linguistic and then aesthetic.

It is true that a kind of dictionary of film, that is, a convention has established itself during the past fifty years of film. This convention is odd for the following reason: it is stylistic before it is grammatical.

Let us take the image of the wheels of a train which turn among puffs of steam: it is not a syntagma, it is a stylema. This leads us to suppose that – because cinema obviously will never be able to achieve a real set of grammatical rules, if not, so to speak, those of a stylistic grammar – each time a filmmaker makes a film he is compelled to repeat the *twofold process* mentioned above. And he must be satisfied, insofar as rules are concerned, with a certain number of expressive devices which lack in articulation, and which, born as stylemas, have become syntagmas.

On the positive side of the ledger, the filmmaker, instead of having to refine a centuries-old stylistic tradition, works with one whose history is counted in decades. In practical terms this means that there is no convention to upset by excessive outrage. His "historical addition" to the im-sign is attached to a very short-lived im-sign. Hence, perhaps, a certain sense that film is transitory proceeds from this. Its grammatical signs are the objects of a world which is chronologically exhausted each time it is depicted: the clothes of the thirties, the automobiles of the fifties – these are all "things" without an etymology, or with an etymology that finds its expression in the corresponding word systems.

The evolution that presides over the fashion which creates clothing or which invents the shapes of cars is followed by the meaning of the words – the latter, in other words, adapt themselves to the former. Objects, instead, are impenetrable. They do not move, nor do they say about themselves what they are in a particular moment. The dictionary in which the filmmaker places them in his activity is not sufficient to give them a historical background meaningful for everyone, immediately and at a later date.

Thus it should be observed that the object which becomes a film image is characterized by a degree of unity and determinism. And it is natural that it be so, because the lin-sign used by the writer has already been refined by an entire grammatical, popular, and cultural history, while the im-sign employed by the filmmaker ideally has been extracted – by the filmmaker himself, and no one else – from the insensitive chaos of objects in a process analogous to the borrowing of images from a dictionary intended for a community able to communicate only through images.

But I must insist: while the images or im-signs are not organized in a dictionary and do not possess a grammar, they nonetheless belong to a common patrimony. All of us, with our eyes, have seen the famous steam engine with its wheels and its pistons. It belongs to our visual memory and to our dreams. If we see it in the real world, "it says something to us." Its apparition in a barren wasteland, for example, *tells us* how touching mankind's industriousness is, and how enormous is the capacity of industrialized society and, therefore, of capitalists to annex the territories of new consumers. At the same time, it *tells* some of us that the train engineer is an exploited man who nevertheless performs his job with dignity for a society which is what it is, even if it is his exploiters who are identified with it. As object the steam engine can tell us all these things as a possible cinematographic symbol in direct communication with us; and indirectly, with others, as a part of the common visual patrimony.

"Brute objects" therefore do not exist in reality. All are sufficiently meaningful in nature to become symbolic signs. It is for this reason that the activity of the filmmaker is legitimate. He chooses a series of objects, or things, or landscapes, or persons as syntagmas (signs of a symbolic language) which, *while they have a grammatical history invented in that moment* – as in a sort of happening dominated by the idea of selection and montage – *do, however, have an already lengthy and intense pregrammatical history.*

In short, much as the pregrammatical qualities of the spoken signs have the right to citizenship in the style of a poet, so the pregrammatical qualities of objects will have the right to citizenship in the style of a filmmaker. This is simply another way of saying what I had already said above: film is fundamentally oneiric because of the elementary nature of its archetypes (which I will list once again: habitual and thus unconscious observation of the environment, gestures, memory, dreams), and because of the fundamental prevalence of the pregrammatical qualities of objects as symbols of the visual language.

One more observation: in his search for a dictionary as fundamental and preliminary activity, the filmmaker can never collect abstract terms. This is probably the principal difference between literary and cinematographic works (if such a comparison matters). The linguistic or grammatical world of the filmmaker is composed of images, and images are always concrete, never abstract (only if one looks thousands of years into the future can one foresee image-symbols which undergo a process similar to that of words, or at least roots which, originally concrete, through the effects of repeated use have become abstract). For now, therefore, cinema is an artistic and not a philosophic language. It may be a parable, but never a directly conceptual expression. This, then, is a third way of restating the dominant artistic nature of cinema, its expressive violence, its oneiric physical quality.

All this should, in conclusion, make one think that the language of cinema is fundamentally a "language of poetry." Instead, historically, in practice, after a few attempts which were immediately cut short, the cinematographic tradition which has developed seems to be that of a "language of prose," or at least that of a "language of prose narrative."

This is true, but as we shall see, it's a question of a specific and surreptitious prose, because the fundamentally irrational nature of cinema cannot be eliminated. The truth is that cinema, in the very moment in which it established itself as a new "technique" or "genre" of expression, also established itself as a new technique or genre of escapist performance, with a number of consumers unimaginable for all other forms of expression. This means that it immediately underwent a rather foreseeable and unavoidable rape. In other words, all its irrational, oneiric, elementary, and barbaric elements were forced below the level of consciousness; that is, they were exploited as subconscious instruments of shock and persuasion. That narrative convention which has furnished the material for useless and pseudocritical comparisons with the theater and the novel was built on this hypnotic "monstrum" that a film always is. This narrative convention belongs without question, by analogy, to the language of prose communication, but it has in common with such a language only the external manifestation – the logical and illustrative processes – while it lacks one fundamental element of the "language of prose": rationality. Its foundation is that mythical and infantile subtext which, because of the very nature of cinema, runs underneath every commercial film which is not unworthy, that is, [which is] fairly adult aesthetically and socially.

Nevertheless, as we shall see later, *art films have also adopted as their specific language this "language of prose,"* this narrative convention deprived of expressive, impressionistic, and expressionistic highlights, etc.)

It can be stated, however, that the tradition of film language, as it has developed during these first decades, is primarily naturalistic and objective. This is such an intriguing contradiction that its causes and its deepest technical connotations deserve to be observed carefully.

In fact, to recapitulate synoptically what I have said so far, we see that the linguistic archetypes of the im-signs are the images of our memories and our dreams, that is, images of "communication with ourselves" (and of only indirect communication with others in that the image that the other person has of a thing of which I speak to him is a reference we have in common). Those archetypes thus lay a direct base of "subjectivity" for the im-signs, which consequently belong in the highest degree to the world of poetry. Thus the tendency of film language should be expressively subjective and lyrical.

But the im-signs, as we have seen, also have other archetypes: the amplification of the spoken by gestures and by visually observed reality, with its thousands of signs which function only as signals. Such archetypes are profoundly different from those of memory and dreams. They are, in other words, brutally objective; they belong to a kind of "communication with others" which is as common as possible to everyone and is strictly functional. Thus the tendency that they impress upon the language of the im-signs is rather flatly objective and informative.

Third: the first action which must be performed by the director – that is, the choice of his vocabulary of im-signs as possible usable linguistic entity – certainly does not have the objectivity of an actual, common, established vocabulary such as the one of words. There is thus already a first subjective moment in such a process, too, in that the first choice of images cannot avoid being determined by the filmmaker's ideological and poetic vision of reality at that moment. And so the language of the im-signs is compelled to undergo yet another tendentially subjective coercion.

But this fact, too, is contradicted. The brief stylistic history of cinema, in fact, because of the expressive limitation imposed by the enormous size of the audience of film, has caused the stylemas – which immediately became syntagmas in cinema, and thus were reincorporated into the institution of language – to be very few and, in the final analysis, crude (remember the eternal example of the wheels of the locomotive; the infinite series of always identical close-ups, etc., etc.). All the above stands as a conventional moment in the language of im-signs and guarantees it once again an elementary conventional objectivity.

In short, cinema, or the language of im-signs, has a double nature: it is both extremely subjective and extremely objective (to such an extent that it reaches an unsurpassable and awkward naturalistic fate). The two moments of the above-mentioned nature are closely intertwined and are not separable even in the laboratory.

Literary language is also, naturally, predicated upon a double nature, but its two natures are separable; there is a language of poetry and a language of prose, so completely differentiated from each other that they are, in fact, diachronic – they follow two different histories.

Through words, by performing two different operations, I can create a "poem" or a "tale." Through images, at least until now, I can only make a film (only through its shadings will it tend to be more or less poetic or more or less prosaic – this, in any case, in theory; in practice, as we have seen, a tradition of the "language of narrative film prose" was quickly established).

There are, to be sure, borderline cases in which the poetic quality of the language is foregrounded beyond all reason. For example, Buñuel's *Le chien andalou* is avowedly produced according to canons of pure expressivity. But, for this reason, it must be labeled surrealistic. And it must be said that, as a surrealistic product, it is outstanding. Very few other works can compete with it, be they literary or pictorial, because their poetic quality is corrupted and rendered unreal by their content – that is, by the poetics of surrealism, a sort of rather harsh representationalism (through which the words or the colors lose their expressive purity and are enslaved by a monstrous impurity of content). On the other hand, the purity of film images is exalted rather than obfuscated by a surrealistic content – because it is the real oneiric nature of dreams and of the unconscious memory which surrealism reactivates in film.

I have already stated that cinema, lacking a conceptual, abstract vocabulary, is powerfully metaphoric; as a matter of fact, *a fortiori* it operates immediately on the metaphoric level. Particular, deliberately generated metaphors, however, always have some quality that is inevitably crude and conventional. Think of the frenzied or joyous flights of doves which are meant to express metaphorically the state of anxiety or joy in the mind of the character. In short, the nuanced, barely perceptible metaphor, the poetic halo one millimeter thick – the one which separates by a whisper and by an abyss the language of "To Sylvia" from the institutional Petrarchan/arcadian language – would not seem possible in cinema. Whatever part of the poetically metaphoric which is sensationalistically possible in film, it is always in close osmosis with its other nature, the strictly communicative one of prose. The latter, in the end, is the one which has prevailed in the brief tradition of the history of cinema, embracing in a single linguistic convention art films and escapist films, the masterpieces and the serials.

However, the entirety of the most recent film production, from Rossellini, elevated to the position of a latter-day Socrates, to the "*nouvelle vague*," to the production of these recent years, of these months (including, I would imagine, the majority of the films of the first Festival of Pesaro), tends toward a "cinema of poetry."

The following question arises: how is the "language of poetry" theoretically explicable and practically possible in cinema?

I would like to answer this question outside a strictly cinematographic context, that is, by breaking this logjam and acting with the freedom which is guaranteed by a special and concrete relationship between cinema and literature. Thus I will temporarily transform the question "is a language of poetry possible in cinema?', into the question "is the technique of free indirect discourse possible in cinema?"

We will see later the reasons for this sudden change in direction. We will see how the birth of a technical tradition of the "language of poetry" in cinema is tied to a particular form of free indirect cinematographic discourse. However, a couple of words are necessary first in order to establish what I mean by "free indirect discourse." It is, simply, the immersion of the filmmaker in the mind of his character and then the adoption on the part of the filmmaker not only of the psychology of his character but also of his language.

Cases of free indirect discourse have always existed in literature. There is a potential and emblematic free indirect discourse even in Dante, when, for mimetic reasons, he uses words which it is unimaginable that he used himself and which belong to the social circle of his characters: expressions of polite language from the illustrated romantic tales of his time for Paolo and Francesca; swear words for the common *Lazaronitum*, etc.

Naturally the use of the "free indirect" exploded first in naturalism (consider the archaizing and poetic naturalism of Verga), and then in crepuscular intimist literature; in other words, the nineteenth century expresses itself very fully through reanimated speech.

The constant characteristic of all reanimated speech is the author's inability to avoid a certain sociological awareness of the environment that he evokes. It is, in fact, the social condition of a character that determines his language (specialized language, slang, dialect, or however dialect-like language has become).

It will also be necessary to make a distinction between interior monologue and free indirect discourse: the interior monologue is speech reanimated by the author for a character who may, at least ideally, be of his generation and share his economic and social class. The language [of the author and of the character] may therefore well be identical. The psychological and objective individuation of the character is not a question of language but of style. "Free indirect" discourse is more naturalistic in that it is an actual direct discourse without quotation marks and thus implies the use of the language of the character.

In middle-class literature, which is lacking in class consciousness (that is, it identifies itself with the whole of humanity), "free indirect" discourse is often-times a pretext: the author constructs a character, who may speak an invented language, in order to express a particular interpretation of the world. It is in this "indirect" discourse, whose function is a pretext – at times for good reasons, at others for bad – that one can find a narrative in which large amounts of the text are taken from the "language of poetry."

In cinema direct discourse corresponds to the point-of-view shot. In direct discourse the author stands aside and cedes speech to his character, putting what he says in quotation marks: "And now the poet was climbing before me and saying: 'Come on now: the meridian is touched by the sun, and on the shore night now sets its foot on Morocco.'" Through direct discourse Dante reports the words of the gentle teacher, exactly as they were spoken. When a screen-writer uses the expressions "*As seen* by Accattone, Stella walks through a small, filthy field," or "Close-up of Cabiria who looks and sees . . . down there, among the acacias, some boys advance toward her playing instruments and dancing," he is sketching the outline of those shots which, as the film is shot, and to a greater extent edited, will become *points-view shots*. There is no lack of famous point-of-view shots, perhaps because of their extravagance. Think back to the shot seen from the point of view of the cadaver who sees all the world as it might be seen by someone who is lying inside a coffin, that is, from the bottom up and in motion.

Much as writers do not always have a precise technical awareness of a process such as free indirect discourse, so directors, too, have until now established the stylistic premises for such a process either with the most absolute lack of awareness or with a very relative awareness. That nevertheless a free indirect discourse may also be possible for cinema is certain. Let us call this process a "free indirect point-of-view shot" (which, when compared to the analogous process in literature, can be infinitely less articulated and complex). And, seeing that we have established a difference between "free indirect" and "interior monologue," it will be necessary to see to which of the two processes the "free indirect point of view" is closer.

In the first place, it cannot be an actual "interior monologue," since cinema does not have the possibilities of interiorization and abstraction that the word has. It is an "interior monologue" of images, that's all. In other words, it lacks the entire abstract and theoretical dimension which is explicitly involved in the evocative and cognitive act of the character's monologue. Thus the absence of one element – the one which in literature is constituted by thoughts expressed by abstract or conceptual words – means that a "free indirect point-of-view shot" will never correspond perfectly to the interior monologue in literature.

Moreover, in the history of cinema, I would not be able to cite any cases of the total disappearance of the filmmaker into a character – at least until the early sixties. In other words, I don't think a film exists which is entirely a "free indirect point-of-view shot" in that the entire story is told through the character, through an absolute internalization of his inner system of allusions.

While the "free indirect point-of-view shot" does not correspond entirely to the "interior monologue," it corresponds still less to actual "free indirect discourse."

When a writer recreates the speech of one of his characters, he immerses himself in his psychology, but also in his *language*. Free indirect discourse is therefore always linguistically differentiated when compared to the language of the writer. The writer has the possibility of reproducing the various languages of the different types of social conditions by reanimating them because they exist. Every linguistic reality is a totality of socially differentiated and differentiating languages, and the writer who uses "free indirect discourse" must be aware of this above all – an awareness which in the final analysis is a form of class consciousness.

But the reality of the possible "institutional film language," as we have seen, does not exist, or is infinite, and the author must cut out his vocabulary from this infinity every time. But also, in such a vocabulary, the language is of necessity interdialectal and international, because our eyes are the same the world over. They cannot take into consideration, because they don't exist, special languages, sublanguages, slang – in short, social differences. Or if they do exist, as in fact they do, they are totally beyond any possibility of classification and use.

Because, in fact, the "gaze" of a peasant, perhaps even of an entire town or region in prehistoric conditions of underdevelopment, embraces another type of reality than the gaze given to that same reality by an educated bourgeois. Not only do the two actually see different sets of things, but even a single thing in itself appears different through the two different "gazes." However, all this cannot be institutionalized; it is purely inductive. In practice, therefore, on a possible common linguistic level predicated on "gazes" at things, the difference that a director can perceive between himself and a character is only psychological and social. *But not linguistic.* He therefore finds himself in the complete impossibility of effecting any naturalistic *mimesis* of this language, of this hypothetical "gaze" at reality by others.

Thus, if he immerses himself in his character and tells the story or depicts the world through him, he cannot make use of that formidable natural instrument of differentiation that is language. *His activity cannot be linguistic; it must, instead, be stylistic.*

Moreover, a writer, too, if he were hypothetically to reanimate the speech of a character socially *identical to himself*, can differentiate his psychology from that of his character not by means of a language which is his own language, but by means of a style – that is, in practical terms, through certain characteristic traits of the "language of poetry." Thus the fundamental characteristic of the "free indirect point-of-view shot" is not linguistic but stylistic. And it can therefore be defined as an interior monologue lacking both the explicit conceptual element and the explict abstract philosophical element. This, at least in theory, causes the "free indirect point-of-view shot" in cinema to imply the possibility of an extreme stylistic articulation. In fact, it causes it to free the expressive possibilities compressed by the traditional narrative convention through a sort of return to the origins until the original oneiric, barbaric, irregular, aggressive, visionary quality of cinema is found through its technical devices. In short, it is the "free indirect point-of-view shot" which establishes a possible tradition of the "technical language of poetry" in cinema.

As concrete examples of all this, I will drag into my laboratory Antonioni, Bertolucci, and Godard – but I could also add Rocha from Brazil, or Forman from Czechoslovakia, and naturally many others (presumably, almost all the filmmakers of the Festival of Pesaro).

As for Antonioni (*The Red Desert*), I don't want to linger on those aspects of the film which are universally recognized as "poetic', which are certainly numerous in his film. For example, those two or three out-of-focus violet flowers in the foreground in the shot in which the two protagonists enter the house of the neurotic worker; and those same two or three violet flowers which reappear in the background, no longer out of focus, but aggressively in focus, in the shot of the exit. Or, consider the sequence of the dream, which, after so much delicacy of color, is suddenly conceived in an almost blatant technicolor (in order to imitate, or better, to reanimate through a "free indirect point-of-view shot" the comic-book idea that a child has of tropical beaches). Or, consider also the sequence of the preparation for the trip to Patagonia, the workers who listen, etc. – that stupendous close-up of a distressingly "real" Emilian worker, followed by an insane pan from the bottom up along an electric blue stripe on the whitewashed wall of the warehouse. All this testifies to a deep, mysterious, and – at times – great intensity in the formal idea that excites the fantasy of Antonioni.

But, to demonstrate that it is this formalism which is, in essence, the premise of the film, I would like to examine two aspects of an extremely meaningful stylistic operation (the same one which I will also examine in Bertolucci and Godard). The two parts of the process are the following: 1. the sequential juxtaposition of two insignificantly different points of view of the same image; that is, the sequence of two shots which frame the same piece of reality, first from nearby, then from *a bit* further; or, first frontally and then *a bit* more obliquely; or, finally, actually on the same axis but with two different lenses. This leads to an insistence that becomes obsessive, as it becomes the myth of the actual, distressing, autonomous beauty of things. 2. The technique of making the characters enter and leave the frame, as a result of which, in an occasionally obsessive manner, the editing comes to consist of a series of "pictures" – which we can call informal – where the characters enter, say or do something, and then go out, leaving the picture once again to its pure, absolute significance as picture. This picture is followed by another analogous picture, where the characters enter, etc. So that the world is presented as if regulated by a myth of pure pictorial beauty that the personages invade, it is true, but adapting themselves to the rules of that beauty instead of profaning them with their presence.

Film's internal law of "obsessive framing" thus clearly demonstrates the prevalence of formalism as a finally liberated and therefore poetic myth. (My use of the word formalism does not imply a value judgment. I know very well that there is an authentic, sincere formalistic inspiration: the poetry of language.)

But how has this liberation been possible for Antonioni? Very simply, it has become possible by creating the "stylistic condition" for a "free indirect point-of-view shot" that coincides with the entire film.

In *Red Desert* Antonioni no longer superimposes his own formalistic vision of the world on a generally committed content (the problem of neuroses caused by alienation), as he had done in his earlier films in a somewhat clumsy blending. Instead, he looks at the world by immersing himself in his neurotic protagonist, reanimating the facts through her eyes (she, not by accident, clearly needs professional care, having already tried to commit suicide). By means of this stylistic device, Antonioni has freed his most deeply felt moment: he has finally been able to represent the world seen through his eyes, *because he has substituted in toto for the world view of a neurotic his own delirious view of aesthetics*, a wholesale substitution which is justified by the possible analogy of the two views. And if there were something arbitrary in such a substitution, there could be no objections. It is clear that the "free indirect point-of-view shot" is a pretext, and Antonioni took advantage of it, possibly arbitrarily, to allow himself the greatest poetic freedom, a freedom which approaches – and for this it is intoxicating – the arbitrary.

The obsessive immobility of the frame is also typical of Bertolucci's film *Before the Revolution*. However, it has a different meaning than it does for Antonioni. It is not a fragment of the world, enclosed in a frame and transformed by the frame into a piece of self-sufficient figurative beauty, that interests

Bertolucci as instead it interests Antonioni. The formalism of Bertolucci is infinitely less pictorial, and his framing does not act metaphorically on reality subdividing it into so many pieces which are as mysteriously autonomous as paintings. Bertolucci's frame adheres to reality according to a standard that is somewhat realistic (according to a technique of poetic language followed, as we shall see, by the classics, from Charlot to Bergman). The immobility of the frame of a piece of reality (the river Parma, the streets of Parma, etc.) testifies to the elegance of a deep and uncertain love, precisely for that piece of reality.

In practical terms, the entire stylistic system of *Before the Revolution* is a long "free indirect point-of-view shot," predicated on the dominant state of mind of the protagonist of the film, the young neurotic aunt. But while in Antonioni we find the wholesale substitution of the filmmaker's vision of feverish formalism for the view of the neurotic woman, in Bertolucci such a wholesale substitution has not taken place. Rather, we have a mutual contamination of the worldviews of the neurotic woman and of the author. These views, being inevitably similar, are not readily distinguishable – they shade into each other; they require the same style.

The only expressively sharp moments of the film are, precisely, the "insistent pauses" of the framing and of the rhythms of the editing. The programmatic realism of these devices (the Rossellinian neorealistic heritage, and the mythic realism of some younger masters) is charged during the abnormal duration of a shot or of an editing rhythm until it explodes in a sort of technical scandal. This insistence on particulars, especially on certain details of the digressions, is a deviation in relation to the method of the film: *it is the temptation to make another film*. It is, in short, the presence of the author, who transcends his film in an abnormal freedom and who constantly threatens to abandon it, detoured by a sudden inspiration which is, finally, the latent inspiration of the love for the poetic world of his own vital experiences. A moment of barefaced subjectivity, natural in a film in which the subjectivity is completely mystified through that process of false objectivism that is the result of a pretextual "free indirect point-of-view shot." In short, beneath the technique produced by the protagonist's state of mind – which is disoriented, incapable of coordination, obsessed by details, attracted by compulsory kindness – the world as it is seen by the no less neurotic filmmaker continually surfaces, dominated by an elegant, elegiac spirit, which never becomes classicist.

There is, instead, a somewhat brutal and even slightly vulgar quality in Godard's cultural formation. The elegy is inconceivable to him because, being a Parisian, he cannot be touched by such a provincial, rustic sentiment. Nor can he conceive of Antonioni's formal classicism, for the same reason. He is completely post-Impressionistic. He retains nothing of the old sensuality which stagnates in the conservative, marginal area between the Po and Rome, even when it has become very Europeanized, as it has in Antonioni. Godard has not accepted any moral imperative. He feels neither the obligations of Marxist commitment (old stuff), nor the bad faith of academia (provincial stuff). His vitality is without restraints, modesty, or scruples. It reconstitutes the world within itself. It is also cynical toward itself. The poetics of Godard is ontological – it is called cinema. His formalism is thus a technicality which is intrinsically poetic: everything that is captured in movement by a camera is beautiful. It is the technical, and therefore poetic, restoration of reality.

Naturally, Godard also plays the usual game; he too needs a "dominant condition" of the protagonist to guarantee his technical freedom, a neurotic and scandalous dominant condition in the relationship with reality. Thus, Godard's protagonists are also sick; they are exquisite flowers of the bourgeoisie, but they are not under medical treatment. They are extremely ill, but vital; they have not yet passed over the threshold into a pathological condition. They simply represent the average of a new anthropological type. Obsession also characterizes their relationship with the world: the obsessive attachment to a detail or a gesture (and here cinematographic technique, which can intensify situations even better than literary technique, comes into play). But in Godard we are not confronted by an insistence on a given individual object which exceeds all bearable limits. In him there is neither the cult of the object as form (as in Antonioni), nor the cult of the object as symbol of a lost world (as in Bertolucci). Godard has no cult, and he puts everything on the same level, head on. His pretextual "free indirect discourse" is a confrontational arrangement which does not differentiate between the thousand details of the world, without a break in continuity edited with the cold and almost self-satisfied obsession (typical of his amoral protagonist) of a disintegration reconstituted into unity through that inarticulate language. Godard is completely devoid of classicism; otherwise, one could speak of neocubism in reference to him. But we would speak of an atonal neocubism. Beneath the events of his film, under the long "free indirect point-of-view shots" which imitate the state of mind of his protagonists, there is always a film made for the pure pleasure of restoring a reality fragmented by technique and reconstituted by a brutal, mechanical, and discordant Braque.

The "cinema of poetry" – as it appears a few years after its birth – thus has the common characteristic of producing films with a double nature. The film that is seen and ordinarily perceived is a "free indirect point-of-view shot." It may be irregular and approximate – very free, in short, given that the filmmaker makes use of the "dominant psychological state of mind in the film," which is that of a sick, abnormal protagonist, in order to make it a continual *mimesis* which allows him great, anomalous, and provocative stylistic freedom.

Beneath this film runs another film, the one that the filmmaker would have made even without the pretext of the *visual mimesis* of his protagonist – a film whose character is completely and freely expressive/expressionistic.

Proofs of the presence of such an unrealized, subterranean film are, precisely, as we have seen in the specific analyses, the obsessive shots and editing rhythms. This obsessiveness contradicts not only the norm of the common film language, but the very internal organization of the film as a "free indirect point-of-view shot." It is, in other words, the moment in which language, following a different and possibly more authentic inspiration, frees itself of function and presents itself as "language as such" – style.

The "cinema of poetry" is in reality, therefore, profoundly based, for the most part, on the practice of style as sincerely poetic inspiration, to such an extent as to remove all suspicion of mystification from the pretextual use of the "free indirect point-of-view shot."

What does all this mean? It means that a common technical/stylistic tradition is taking form; a language, that is, of the cinema of poetry. This language by now tends to be placed diachronically in relation to the language of film narrative, a diachronism that would appear destined to be always more pronounced, as happens in literary systems. This emerging technical/stylistic tradition is based on the totality of those film stylemas that developed almost naturally as a function of the anomalous psychological excesses of the pretextually chosen protagonists; or better, as a function of a substantially formalistic vision of the world (informal in Antonioni elegiae in Bertolucci, technical in Godard, etc.). To express this internal vision necessarily requires a special language with its own stylemas and its own techniques equally present alongside the inspiration. This inspiration, precisely because it is formalistic, finds both its instrument and its object in its stylemas and techniques.

The series of "film stylemas" thus born and catalogued in a scarcely established tradition (still without norms other than those which are intuitive and, I would say, pragmatic) all coincide with the typical processes of specifically cinematographic expression. They are pure linguistic facts, and therefore they require specific linguistic expressions. To list them implies tracing a possible and not yet codified "prosody," whose normativity, however, is already potential (from Paris to Rome, from Prague to Brasilia).

The first characteristic of these signs which constitute a tradition of the cinema of poetry consists of that phenomenon that is normally and banally defined by persons in the business as "allowing the camera to be felt." In short, the great principle of wise filmmakers, in force up to the first years of the sixties ("Do not allow the camera to be felt!"), has been replaced by the opposite principle. These two canons, gnoseological and gnomic opposites, are there to define unequivocally the presence of two different ways of making films, of two different film languages.

But then it must be said, in the great film poems – from Charlot to Mizoguchi to Bergman – the general and common characteristic was that "the camera was not felt." They were not, in other words, shot according to the canons of the "language of poetry." Their poetry was elsewhere than in language as technique of language. The fact that the camera wasn't felt meant that the language adhered to the meanings, putting itself at their service. It was transparent to perfection; it did not superimpose itself on facts, violating them through the insane semantic deformations that are attributable to its presence as continuous technical/stylistic awareness.

Let us recall the boxing sequence in *City Lights* [1931] between Chaplin and a champion who, characteristically, is much stronger than he. The stupendous comical nature of Chaplin's ballet, those symmetrical, useless steps taken first here and then there, is heart-rending and irresistibly ridiculous. Well, the camera was there, motionless, filming whatever "totality" was in front of it. It wasn't felt. Or, let us recall one of the latest products of the classical "cinema of poetry." In Bergman's *The Devil's Eye* [1960], when Don Giovanni and Pablo leave after three hundred years, and see the world once again, the apparition of the world – something so extraordinary – is presented by Bergman as a "long shot" of the two protagonists in a somewhat wild stretch of springtime country landscape, one or two extremely ordinary "close-ups," and a great "establishing shot" of a Swedish panorama of disturbing beauty in its transparent and humble insignificance. The camera was still; it framed those images in an absolutely normal manner. It was not felt.

The poetic nature of classical films was thus not obtained using a specifically poetic language. This means that they were not poems, but stories. Classical cinema was and is narrative. Its language is that of prose. Poetry is internal to it, as, for example, in the tales of Chekhov or Melville. Conversely, the creation of a "language of film poetry" thus implies the possibility of making pseudostories written with the language of poetry. The possibility, in short, of an art prose, of a series of lyrical pages whose subjectivity is ensured by the pretextual use of the "free indirect point-of-view shot," and whose real protagonist is style.

The camera is therefore felt for good reasons. The alternation of different lenses, a 25mm and a 200mm on the same face; the proliferation of wasted zoom shots, with their lenses of very high numbers which are on top of things, expanding them like excessively leavened bread; the continuous, deceptively casual shots against the light, which dazzle the camera; the hand-held camera movements; the more sharply focused tracking shots; the wrong editing for expressive reasons; the irritating opening shots; the interminable pauses on the same image, etc – this entire technical code came into being almost out of impatience with the rules, out of a need for an irregular and provocative freedom, out of an otherwise authentic or delicious enjoyment of anarchy. But then it quickly became the canon, the linguistic and prosodic patrimony that interests contemporary filmmaking the world over.

Of what use is it to have singled out and, in some way, to have baptized this recent technical/stylistic tradition of a "cinema of poetry'? Obviously, it simply offers a useful terminology which is meaningless unless one proceeds subsequently to a comparative examination of this phenomenon in a vaster cultural, social, and political context.

Film, probably since 1936, the year *Modern Times* appeared, has always anticipated literature, or at least has catalyzed, with a timeliness that made it be first chronologically, the deep sociopolitical themes that would characterize literature soon thereafter. For this reason cinematographic neorealism (*Rome, Open City* [1945]) prefigured all the Italian literary neorealism of the postwar years and of part of the fifties; the neodecadent and neoformalist films of Fellini or Antonioni prefigured the Italian neo-avant-garde revival or the fading of neorealism; the "new wave" anticipated the "*école du regard*," making its first symptoms sensationally public; the new cinema of some of the socialist republics is the first and most interest in the formalism of Western origin, as manifestation of the resumption of an interrupted twentieth-century theme, etc.

In short, in general terms, the formation of a tradition of a "language of poetry of film" may be posited as revealing a strong general renewal of formalism as the average, typical production of the cultural development of neocapitalism. (Naturally, there is my reservation, due to my Marxist morality, that there is a possible alternative: that is, of a renewal of the writer's mandate, which at this time appears to have expired.)

And so, in conclusion: 1 The technical/stylistic tradition of a cinema of poetry is born within the bounds of neoformalistic research, which corresponds to the tangible and prevalently linguistic/stylistic inspiration that is once again current in literary production. 2 The use of the "free indirect point-of-view shot" in the cinema of poetry, as I have repeated several times, is pretextual. It serves to speak indirectly – through any narrative alibi – in the first person singular. Therefore, the language used for the interior monologues of pretextual characters is the language of a "first person" who sees the world according to an inspiration which is essentially irrational. Therefore, to express themselves they must make recourse to the most sensational expressive devices of the "language of poetry." 3 The pretextual characters cannot be chosen from outside the cultural limits of the filmmaker; that is, they are analogous to him in culture, language, and psychology – they are exquisite "flowers of the bourgeoisie." If they should belong to another social world, they are mythicized and assimilated by being categorized as abnormal, neurotic, or hypersensitive, etc. In short, the bourgeoisie, also in film, identifies itself with all of humanity, in an irrational interclassicism.

All of this is part of that general attempt on the part of bourgeois culture to recover the ground lost in the battle with Marxism and its possible revolution. And it insinuates itself into that in some ways grandiose movement of what we might call the anthropological evolution of capitalism; that is, the neocapitalism that discusses and modifies its own structures and that, in the case in point, once again, ascribes to poets a late humanistic function: the myth and the technical consciousness of form.

4

THE MODERN CINEMA AND NARRATIVITY

Christian Metz

I

A deep, permanent ambiguity underlies the definition of the "modern" cinema. It is often suggested, and sometimes even affirmed, that the "young cinema," or the "new cinema," has developed beyond the stage of the *narrative*, that the modern film is an absolute object, a work to be read in any direction, and that it had thrown off narrativity, the earmark of the classical film. This is the great argument of the "breakdown of narrativity."

In recent years this argument has appeared under a variety of forms in the writings of many film critics. Here are some examples taken from a debate which attempted to produce a synthesis of positions: For René Gilson, it was "nondramatization" ("*dédramatisation*"), which defined a sort of "Antonioni tendency," which Marcel Martin, in turn, associated with Mizoguchi; for Michel Mardore and Pierre Billard, it was the idea of a more direct approach to reality, a certain type of fundamental realism which would more or less displace the old narrative habits. For others, it was the concept of a cinema of improvisation, suggested by "*cinéma verité*," "*cinéma direct*," and similar approaches (Michel Mardore); for Marcel Martin, it was a "film-maker's cinema," which has taken the place of the "scriptwriter's cinema." Or it was a cinema of the "shot," replacing the old, directly narrative cinema, where one galloped from shot to shot (Michel Mardore). Or, finally, it was a cinema of freedom, open to multiple readings, a cinema of "contemplation" and

From: Christian Metz, 'The Modern Cinema and Narrativity', in Christian Metz (Michael Taylor, trans.), *Film Language* (Oxford University Press, 1974).

"objectivity," which rejected the rigid, authoritarian concatenations of the classical film, and rejected the theater, substituting *"mise en présence"* for *"mise en scène"* (Marcel Martin).

[...]

Finally, for all of these critics, the recent period has witnessed the birth of a free cinema, a cinema permanently liberated from the supposedly syntactic rules of "cinematographic language."

In this account of partially overlapping positions – admittedly a very incomplete account, of which I have given only samples – one recognizes the updated echo of the famous analyses of André Bazin, Roger Leenhardt, Francois Truffaut, and Alexandre Astruc: rejection of the movie spectacle in favor of a "language cinema" (*cinéma langage* – Truffaut), rejection of the too impeccable "quality" production (Truffaut again), rejection of the too evident "signs" that do violence to the ambiguity of reality (Bazin), rejection of the pseudo-syntactic arsenal dear to the old theoreticians (Leenhardt), rejection of the cinema of pure plot, as well as the movie spectacle, in favor of a cinema of "writing" (*cinéma d'écriture*), a docile and flexible means of expression (Astruc).

My purpose in this text is not to take up arms against any one of these analyses – especially since each one of them contains, to my mind, a great deal of truth – but rather to confront, by means of a successive (and never total) questioning of these different positions, a *great libertarian myth*, which is not fully expressed in any one of the analyses, but which underlies them all and actuates them all.

[...]

There remains, finally, the notion, recently suggested by Pier Paolo Pasolini, of a distinction between the "cinema of prose" and the "cinema of poetry." As attractive as it may seem, the idea is nevertheless basically fragile. For the concepts of "prose" and "poetry" are too linked to the use of the verbal language to be easily carried over to the cinema. Or else, if one takes "poetry" in its broadest sense – as the immediate presence of the world, the sense of things, the inner quickness beneath the surface of externality – one will have to recognize that the cinematographic enterprise, whether successful or not, is *always* initially poetic. But if one considers poetry in its technical sense – the use of verbal idiom according to some orderly procedure, with supplementary restrictions added to those of the language, a second code capping the first – one encounters a difficulty which hardly seems surmountable: The absence of a first unitary and complete code in the cinema, that is, the absence of a specifically cinematographic idiom. Pasolini is aware of this problem; indeed he outlines it with great precision. But he believes that, all things considered, it can be circumvented. I believe, on the contrary, that this is impossible, and later I will show why. Further more, to these obstacles one must add still another: the concept of "prose," in whatever sense it is given, has no plausible equivalent in the cinema; and if a prose does exist in the lexical domain, it is only in distinction to poetry and because a long rhetorical tradition has divided into two a domain that is *initially literary* (for prose, properly speaking, is literary prose, that of a Chateaubriand or of a Stendhal, and not that which Monsieur Jourdain discovered; prose is already the artistic use of language and is already distinct from utilitarian language; it creates objects that have their own value, and at which the thrust of language ceases). As for the cinema, it is *never* used for daily communication; it always creates works. The distinction between poetry and prose has meaning only within a broader distinction, one that separates *literature* from the simple use of idiom as a tool. And it is this primary distinction that is lacking in the cinema, so that no film can pertain to prose in the strict sense, nor, strictly, to poetry.

So much for the linguistic implications of Pasolini's theory – at least for the time being, for I will return to them later; let us examine his thesis in the light of the history of the cinema. If there is any single trend running through all of this history, it is indeed the one that leads from the poem-cinema to the novel-cinema – that is to say, in a certain way from the "cinema of poetry" to the "cinema of prose," and not the other way around. Pasolini tends to confuse poetic *accents* – which are not rare in the modern cinema – with poetic *structures*; he tends also to compare the most beautiful contemporary films to the dullest traditional movies, and he does not consider the very early films. Obviously there is more poetry in À *Double tour, Lola, Shoot the Piano Player, The Knack, Pour la Suite du monde,* or *8½,* than in *Le Président, Un Grand patron, Volpone,* or *Dernier atout*. But is it not simply that the substance and form of each one of the first-mentioned films are more poetic and less radically vulgar than the form and substance of each of the older films; and is one quite sure that the language of the first differs fundamentally from that of the second group? Can one be sufficiently certain that the "free indirect subjectivity" of which Pasolini speaks represents a procedure *precise* enough for one to see in it the beginnings of a *technical language of poetry* for the cinema? And is it not in the final analysis, confused with that inevitable subjective coloration of the filmic object by its filming perception – which is a characteristic of all cinema – so that the only real difference would finally be that of poetic and prose perceptions, which can only be clarified by the analysis of each film and does not, in the cinema, necessarily coincide with the existence of general restrictions peculiar to any "poetry" distinguished from "prose"? Furthermore, if one extends the matter further back, is it not, among the films that seem the most outmoded today – but not always rightly – that one encounters the most coherent and systematic attempts to construct a film as one structures a poem? What about Pudovkin's "lyrical montage," which Jean Mitry has so well analyzed? What about the coronation scene in *Ivan the Terrible,* or the procession before Vakulintchuk and the scenes of mist in *Potemkin*? What about Abel Gance in *Napoleon and La Roue*? And the attempts of the "pure cinema" to substitute a cinema of *themes* for the story-cinema? And Jean Epstein's enthusiastic analyses of the poetic value of the close-up shot? And the use of slow motion in the dormitory scene in *Zero for Conduct*? And all the systems of montage mentioned earlier, whose aim was to formalize the various filmic counterpoints, to solidify the thematic "depth" in the normative prescriptions of a formal syntagmatic system? And the accelerated filming in the scene with the black coach in *Nosferatu*? And the incredible aerial traveling shot in the beginning of Murnau's *Faustus*? They are all, indeed, instances of those "grammatical elements as poetic functions" that Pasolini tends to identify with the new cinema. In truth, though today's cinema is at times rich in poetic resonances, though the bad films of every period by definition exclude the so-called poetry "of things" and the poetry of their organization, the fact remains that the only attempts that have been undertaken toward not only a poetic cinema but also a cinema as organized poetic *idiom* – since this is what Pasolini is talking about – were, precisely, in the old cinema. And the fact is that, since its birth, the cinema has practically never ceased to evolve in the direction of an ideal (*technically* prosaic) flexibility and a freedom that are entirely novelesque, as is shown, in different ways, by the analyses of François-Régis Bastide (the cinema as a modern sociological substitute for the traditional novel), André Bazin and the filmologist critics (the cinema pertains to the novel rather than to the theater), Jean Mitry (progressive victory of narrative montage over the "lyrical," "intellectual," and "constructive" types of montage), and Edgar Morin (withdrawal of the archetypal, naïve imagination peculiar to many of the first films to the advantage of a more sophisticated use of the powers of the fabulous within the framework of the relatively late "realistic" film's verisimilitude). More generally, one will observe that the so-called fantastic cinema, which in certain early periods came very close to merging with one of the mainstreams of the cinema as a whole (German-Swedish expressionism from 1910 to 1930, the fantastic films of the period 1930–35, such as *Frankenstein, The Invisible Man*, and *King Kong*), eventually became a *genre*, and a rather special genre at that, which even in part overlaps what the French call the *cinéma-bis*: horror films, grade-B Italian movies, sadistic Japanese films, Soviet fantasy films, British terror films, etc. As a corollary, the so-called realistic film, which has long been contrasted to the fantastic film or to the film of the marvelous as if they were the two great poles of the cinema (and this is simply the famous theme: "Lumière *vs* Méliès"), has taken over almost the whole of modern film.

Pasolini also defines the new cinema as the *noticeable presence of the camera*; whereas, in traditional films, on the contrary, the camera tried to make its presence unfelt, to make itself invisible before the spectacle it was presenting. But, while it is true that this analysis may apply to certain films of the not-so-distant past – the classical American comedy, for example, and in general all the films related to what Bazin called "classical editing" ("*découpage classique*"), which was made to appear invisible – it cannot describe the various tendencies of the very early cinema whose aesthetics, on the contrary, were based on the aggressive presence of the camera: montage in Eisenstein, Pudovkin, or Abel Gance, camera movements in the expressionist or *Kammerspiel* films, the optical distortions and unusual angles in the films of the French "avant-garde," Dreyer's close-ups in *The Passion of Joan of Arc* – in a word, the aesthetics that theoreticians like Epstein, Eisenstein, Balàzs, Arnheim, or Spotiswoode had in mind when they insisted constantly on the specific enriching that the filmed object derives from the filming. And conversely, within the modern cinema there is a tendency one might call "objectivist" – Rohmer, some aspects of Antonioni, of De Seta, and of the *cinéma direct*, etc. – and that carefully "erases" any camera effects; thus, on this point I am in agreement with Eric Rohmer.

II

Spectacle and nonspectacle, theater and nontheater, improvised and controlled cinema, dramatization and nondramatization, basic realism and contrivance, film-maker's cinema and script-writer's cinema, shot cinema and sequence cinema, prose cinema and poetic cinema, the camera-in-presence and the invisible camera: none of these distinctions seems to me to account for the specific character of the modern cinema. In each one of these conceptual pairs, the feature claimed as "modern" is too often found in the films of yesterday and too often is lacking in the films of today. Each one of these antitheses was proposed with implicit reference to certain films of the past and to certain modern films – and to that extent therefore remains partially true – but with no effort sufficient to account for the greatest possible number of historically known circumstances. Of course such an attempt is no simple one and is hardly likely to be fully satisfied in the few pages that follow. But it is not forbidden to try; one accepts in advance the inevitable incompleteness of the results ...

I note, first, that if all of the conceptual pairs examined above are insufficient, they are so perhaps all for the same reason. They are so many partial expressions of a same underlying idea: that in the past the cinema was entirely narrative and no longer is so today, or is so at least to a much lesser extent. I believe on the contrary that the modern film is more narrative, and more satisfyingly so, and that the main contribution of the new cinema is to have enriched the filmic narrative.

More or less associated with this idea of a presumed "breakdown" or weakening of narrativity is, among many critics, the notion of a breakdown of the "grammar" or "syntax" of the cinema. I would say, on the contrary, that the cinema has *never* had either a grammar or a syntax in the precise linguistic sense of these terms (some theoreticians believed that it did, but that is another matter), rather it has always obeyed, and today still obeys, a certain number of fundamental semiological laws that pertain to the most profound necessities of the transmission of any information – semiological laws that are extremely difficult to isolate, but whose models are to be sought in general linguistics, or general semiotics, and not in the grammar or normative rhetorics of specific languages. The whole muddle of the latter approach derives from the fact that one looks for "language" among the various highly derived and specific (and consequently very removed from cinematographic reality) idiomatic manifestations, without reflecting that the filmic laws are most probably located far beyond the place one usually expects to find them – that is to say, on a much deeper level, a level in some ways prior to the differentiation of verbal language (with all its idioms) from other human semiotic systems.

We are told that "cinematographic syntax" no longer exists, that it was suited to the silent film, but that the living film wants nothing to do with such a burden. But the *syntagmatic* articulations – rather than being actually syntactic articulations, for, as Ferdinand de Saussure observed, syntax is only one part of the syntagmatic category – are like Monsieur Jourdain's prose. Every discourse must be governed by them, willingly or not, or else it becomes unintelligible. The occasionally excessive reactions of some of the devotees of the young cinema can be explained and excused by the corresponding excesses of a "syntax" that, during the period of "*ciné langue*" and even later, was considered to be as strict as the grammar of a verbal language. But the new, more flexible, forms of the cinema are governed just as much by the great fundamental figures without which no information would be possible; a discourse of some length is always, in one way or another, divisible. The study of "cinematographic language" became a burden only when it tried to be normative. Today it no longer pretends to govern films; its aim is only to study them; it no longer pretends to precede them, but it admits to following them. Similarly, in the domain of verbal language, the most elaborate linguistic theory cannot influence the future evolution of our languages. And we know the extent of the gap between the linguist and the normative "grammarian," which was illustrated in 1963 by the exchange, published in *Arts*, between Etiemble and Martinet. Even the most "advanced" films still pertain to a semiological approach, though in order to apprehend new objects, the latter may have to become more flexible, as I will show in several examples further on.

In short two very different things are meant by "rules" of the cinema: on one hand, there is a corpus of prescriptions derived from a *normative aesthetics* that can reasonably be considered outdated or uselessly restrictive; on the other hand, there are a certain number of structural configurations that are in actual fact laws and whose details are constantly evolving. When one says that the films of the "new wave," for example, have completely "dismantled the narrative," or that they have "entirely displaced syntax," one is really taking a very limited view of the problems involved; one is considering "narrative" and "syntax" in a very narrow way, and thus one is unwittingly giving credit to the devotees of the aesthetics one is fighting against (for it is the latter who restrict the meaning of "narrative" and "syntax" to the order of a purely ideological or commercial codification, with no relation to the codified structures peculiar to the filmic vehicle as a whole). It is precisely to the extent that they react against such prejudices that the innovations of the young cinema are interesting; but, in doing so, far from demonstrating the nonexistence of "syntax," they are really discovering new syntactic regions while remaining (at least as long as they are intelligible, as is the case almost always) entirely submissive to the functional requirements of filmic discourse. *Alphaville* and *Last Year at Marienbad* are still, from one end to the other, diegetic films, and they were still conceived in relation to the requirements of narrative fiction, despite their undoubted originality, their editing, and their montage. *Impossible constructions do exist in the cinema.* Thus, any progression of a hero along a precise itinerary excludes the descriptive syntagma; an autonomous shot cannot begin in Moscow and end in Paris (at least in the present state of cinematographic techniques); a non-diegetic image must in one way or another be linked to a diegetic image, or it will not appear to be nondiegetic, etc. But such orderings have never been seriously tried by film-makers, unless perhaps – and even then one would have to examine the matter more closely – by some extreme avant-gardist who had deliberately abandoned the effort to make himself understood (and, then, usually in cinematographic "genres" initially foreign to the narrative fiction film). And the reason that the other film-makers never attempt to construct such combinations, or even to imagine that they might exist, is precisely because the main figures of cinematographic intelligibility inhabit their minds to a much greater extent than they are aware of. Similarly, the most original writer does not attempt to fashion an entirely new language.

III

That is why we must now stop looking at the history of the cinema and take a more semiological and technical approach, and from this vantage point return to the critique of the Pasolinian theories, which, more than any other attempt at defining filmic modernity, try to define their subject precisely and go beyond the stage of general impressions.

The 'im-segni' or iconic analogy?

At fist glance, our author says, there is nothing in the cinema corresponding to what *idiom* is for the writer. That is to say, there is no codified instance prior to the actual aesthetic undertaking. Fine. Nevertheless, Pasolini continues, one must assume that there is something in the cinema that, in one way or another, assumes the same role as language in literature, since the constant fact is that the cinema is not an "abortion," that it is able to communicate. It is at this point, I believe, that the more questionable statements begin: an artistic semiotic system, such as the cinema, can function perfectly well without the assistance of an initial codified *language*. The cinema is in the same position as figurative painting in Claude Lévi-Strauss's analysis in *The Raw and the Cooked*: the first level of articulation is replaced by the "natural" – that is, the cultural signification that perception invests in the objects represented in the picture (or on the screen).

Literature requires language, because the *sound* produced by the vocal organs possesses no intrinsic meaning. Therefore it has to be *articulated* to acquire meaning, which is withheld from "inarticulate shouts," and the two articulations that constitute language – that of the phonemes and that of the monemes, in André Martinet's terminology – are nothing other than the inevitable creative instances of literal signification (i.e., denoted signification), lacking which the poet would have nothing on which to project the interplay of connotations. But the film-maker does not work with vocal sound initially deprived of meaning. His raw material is the image – that is to say, the photographic duplication of a real spectacle, which always and already has a meaning. Consequently, this codified, or at least codifiable, language, which Pasolini postulates and which he defines as an indefinite, labile, but virtually organizable body of "im-segni" (image signs) existing prior to the cinema, is to my mind a dubious, burdensome artifact. Simple iconic analogy, photographic resemblance, replaces it quite advantageously. Indeed, film "communicates," but that is not a mystery whose elucidation justifies the introduction into theory of an additional instance openly presented by Pasolini as being hypothetical and adventurous – it is, much more simply, because the dullest and least connoted photograph of an automobile will have "automobile" for its meaning and thus will yield to the film-maker a significate, which a verbal language could attain only by means of its two articulations (that of its phonemes (/o/, /t/ ,/m/ , /b/ , etc.) and that of its monemes (distinguished within the language "automobile" from "train," "wagon," "airplane," etc.) The cinema arrives at the same results *with no code other than that of perception with its psychosociological and cultural conditionings*, in short with no *language-like* code.

These "im-segni," which, incidentally, Pasolini analyzes very skillfully, do, I am persuaded, exist, and they play the major role in our comprehension of the particular images of particular films – but not within the deepest mechanism of filmic intellection. How is one to understand films, Pasolini asks, without somehow possessing a knowledge of the symbolic values of these visual images: dream images, images of the memory, of emotional experience, images of daily life with their whole load of implicit extensions for each society and each period? Certainly, the total understanding of a given film would be impossible if we did not carry within us that obscure but quite real dictionary of "im-segni" Pasolini talks about; if, to take a single example, we did not know that Jean-Claude Brialy's car in *Les Cousins* was a sports car, with all that this implies in twentieth-century France, the diegetic period of the film. But all the same we would know, because we would *see* it, that it is a car, and that would be enough for us to grasp the *denoted* meaning of the passage. Let no one object that an Eskimo with no experience of industrial civilization might not even be able to recognize the car! For what the Eskimo would be lacking in would not be the ability to translate, but a specific acculturation; it would not be his language of "im-segni" that would be deficient but his *perception* as an aggregate of psychosocial integrations. A manufactured object – a car – as soon as it exists in the world, becomes an object of perception like all other objects of perception, and a child in our society has no more trouble identifying a truck than he does a cat.

From the presumed existence of a primary language of "im-segni" (which is codifiable, but never really codified), Pasolini deduces the idea that the film-maker is obliged to invent a language *first* (i.e., the attempt to isolate clearly the "im-segni"), and then an art – whereas the writer, who already possesses the language, can allow himself to invent only on the aesthetic plane. It is in that *first* that all the misunderstanding lies. If it is true that *cinematic invention* is inevitably a mixture of artistic inspiration and language-like fashioning, the fact remains that the film-maker is always foremost an artist and that it is through his endeavors to order the things of reality differently, through his aesthetic intentions and his strivings for connotation, that he is occasionally able to bequeath some eventually conventional form liable to become a "fact of language." If filmic denotation today is rich and diverse, as indeed it is, that is only as a result of the strivings for connotation in the past.

The renewal of 'cinematographic syntax'

We know that image structures, such as the parallel syntagma, the alternate syntagma, the bracket syntagma, inserts, episodic sequences, etc., which I have analyzed elsewhere – and still other image structures, such as the *flashback* (i.e., succession as the signifier for precession) for example, or the *flash forward* (immediate succession as the signifier for distant succession), etc – are among those figures of connotation that have, in time, also become intelligible patterns of denotation. Now, what is important to note is that most of these semiological figures have not fallen out of use at all but are, on the contrary, in current use in the modern cinema. Not, of course, that the stock of figures has remained unchanged from Griffith to our times. In the cinema, too, there is a diachrony. It would be easier to pick out procedures that have aged: the nondiegetic metaphor (except as renewed by Godard, as we will see in an example further on), slow-motion, accelerated motion, the use of the iris diaphragm (except for nostalgic and humorous "quotation": *Shoot the Piano Player*), the excessive reliance on "punctuation" (except in the instance of a deliberate renewal of this technique: the first sequence in *Une Femme mariée*), the use of shot/reverse-shot in its mechanical form imitated from ping-pong (but the scene in the Paris apartment with the white walls, in *Pierrot le fou*, with Anna Karina's love song, is handled in a more flexible form of shot/reverse-shot), etc. Despite these normal evolutions, one should think twice before asserting that cinematographic syntax lias been "completely thrown overboard." The license of poetic inspiration must not be confused with some impossible license on the level of the deeper articulations, which, even if they are partially arbitrary and are furthermore in a constant state of evolution, nevertheless guarantee, within given synchronic conditions, the correct transmission of information. Only the isolated and unexpressed thought – if such a thing exists – can (perhaps) be removed from such a law. From the moment that *saying* occurs (i.e., the desire to communicate, concern for the public, etc.), a certain number of semiological restrictions appear, which characterize the expression of thought rather than thought itself, that is, if the two things are not identical. Thus, as linguists have observed, the sentence is *first* of all a unit of speech, not of thought, reality, or perception.

Rather than some cataclysmic "breakdown" of filmic syntax, we are witnessing with the new cinema a vast and complex trend of renewal and enrichment, which is expressed by three parallel developments: 1. Certain figures are for the time being more or less abandoned (example: slow motion or accelerated motion filming); 2. others are maintained, but as more flexible variations, which must not prevent one from recognizing the permanence of a deeper semiological mechanism (examples: the shot/reverse-shot, the scene, the sequence, alternate montage, etc.); 3. finally, new figures evolve, increasing the cinema's possibilities of expression. Let us consider the last point.

So far, I have identified, from the origins of the cinema to the present, only a limited number (eight) of large *basic* syntagmatic types. Now, there is a passage in Godard's *Pierrot le fou* that cannot be reduced to any of these models, or to any variation of these models. It is the moment when the two protagonists hurriedly leave the white-walled Paris apartment by sliding down a drain pipe, and flee in a red 404 Peugeot along the banks of the Seine. This "sequence," which is in fact not a sequence, freely alternates shots taken from the sidewalk in front of the building (the last few feet of the descent along the drainpipe, the race into the 404 parked in front of the building, the car taking off, and the brief appearance of the dwarf with his transistor radio, etc.) with other images that, from the diegetic point of view, occur several minutes later in another location, since we now see the 404 driving rapidly along the banks of the river. The passage thus yields several unusual repetitions: from the banks of the river we go back to the drainpipe; the entrance of the car at the foot of the building is itself shown two or three times with slight variations in the position and in the movements of the characters (variations that remind us rather of a construction dear to Robbe-Grillet: *Le Voyeur, La Maison de rendez-vous*).

Therefore, in this syntagma, time does not function according to a vectorial scheme – a scheme that corresponds to the simplest and most common narrative procedure; it cannot be a linear narrative syntagma (i.e., scene, ordinary sequence, or episodic sequence). Nor is it an alternate syntagma, for the alternating images do not refer to simultaneous events but to clearly succeeding events (the shots of the roadway along the river obviously come later); nor does the alternating of the images indicate an alternating of events (i.e., "alternative" variation of the alternate syntagma), since the protagonists have not made several trips back and forth between the building and the river bank; still less does it correspond to a counterpoint of pure connotation, with a momentary absence of the significate of temporal denotation (i.e., parallel syntagma), for the events shown follow a precise chronological order, and only one order, on the level of the significate (diegesis): first entering the car and second driving along the river. And the passage is not a descriptive syntagma either, since it presents us with the evidence of temporal consecution, and not just that of spatial coexistence. Any "frequentative" modality is likewise excluded, since the passage in no way indicates a customary or repetitive action, but quite clearly a single succession of unique occurrences. Nor is it an example of the bracket syntagma, for in this instance the film obviously shows a singular event in its own terms and not in terms of some other event (that is, there is not the slightest attempt at categorization). Last, it is not an autonomous shot, since it contains several images corresponding to a single unit of the diegesis. It is in fact a kind of dislocated sequence, highly expressive of the mad rush, the fever, and the randomness of existence (clearly identifiable significates of denotation). In the midst of the frenzy of the hasty departure (significate of the denotation), it presents as equal possibilities – which implies a sort of self-confession of narrativity, an awareness of its own fablic nature – several *slightly* different variations of a frantic escape, sufficiently similar to each other nevertheless for the event that really did occur (and which we will never know) to take its place among a class of quite clearly outlined occurrences. One is reminded of certain of Marcel Proust's observations, for, faced with the different circumstances of life, Proust had an acute and accurate sense of other psychologically possible or likely occurrences but claimed he was incapable of predicting in advance which one would actually be realized. (We might remark that this Proustian distinction corresponds fairly well to a typology that anyone can observe in his own experience: there are indeed, from this point of view, two types of mind or two forms of intelligence, and the one able to predict the possible outcome to "emerge" often lacks penetration and psychological acuteness in the imaginative description of the different variants that, in the given context, are just as probable as the possibility that is realized.) In the passage we are considering, Jean-Luc Godard would seem to belong to the second type, since he is able to suggest with a great deal of truth, but without determining the outcome, several possibilities at the same time. So he gives us a sort of *potential sequence* – an undetermined sequence – that represents a new type of syntagma, a novel form of the "logic of montage," *but that remains entirely a figure of narrativity* (i.e., two protagonists, different events, places, times, one diegesis, etc – in the same way that in the same film the shots of the Renoir paintings constitute a revitalization of the old nondiegetic metaphor, considerably aged, by the way, since the days of Eisenstein and the symbolically moving statues of *October*.

There would be many other examples to examine: the still photograph, which had been little used up to now and to which Rudolf Arnheim gave only a very modest place in his montage chart, is now, with the modern cinema, experiencing its first real flowering: the examples of Jeanne Moreau's face in *Jules and Jim*, the sequence "I bet you can't do everything I can do" in *A Woman is a Woman*, and, finally *La Jetée* or *Salut les Cubains* (entirely composed of still photographs). The use of the off-screen voice in various modern films is especially rich: occasionally it is the voice of an anonymous commentator – much less the incarnation of the author than of narrativity itself, as Albert Laffay observed in another context – occasionally it is that of the film's protagonist addressing himself directly to the audience – a new form of aside: Belmondo's voice in *Pierrot le fou*, the first sequence in *Marienbad*. To these two examples one must add the on-screen voice in dialogued scenes and the frequent use of written titles (in Godard, Agnès Varda, and others), and also the on-screen voice itself when it assumes the recitative mode and acquires a sovereign density that pulls it away from the image and transforms it from within into a kind of off-screen voice, thus to some extent subtracting it from the diegesis (*Hiroshima mon amour*, *La Pointe courte*, etc.). Thus the film is able to play on five levels of speaking: five possible ranges, five "personae." One could write a whole study of the voice in a Godard or Resnais film on the problem of "Who is speaking?" And one could write another study on the revitalization of what used to be called "subjective images" in Fellini (*8½*, *Juliet of the Spirits*), Resnais (*Marienbad*) or Robbe-Grillet (*L'Immortelle*).

5

SPATIAL AND TEMPORAL ARTICULATIONS

Noël Burch

The terminology a film-maker or film theoretician chooses to employ is a significant reflection of what he takes a film to be. The French term *découpage technique* or simply *découpage* with its several related meanings is a case in point. In everyday practice, *découpage* refers to the final form of a script, incorporating whatever technical information the director feels it necessary to set down on paper to enable a production crew to understand his intention and find the technical means with which to fulfill it, to help them plan their work in terms of his. By extension, but still on the same practical workaday level, *découpage* also refers to the more or less precise breakdown of a narrative action into separate shots and sequences *before filming*. French film-makers, of course, are not the only ones to have a term for this procedure. Both English- and Italian-speaking film-makers have a similar term for this final version of the script – called a "shooting script" in English and a *copione* in Italian – though they always speak of "writing" it or "establishing" it, thereby indicating that the operation the word describes is no more important in their minds than any other in the making of a film. A third French meaning of *découpage*, however, has no English equivalent. Although obviously derived from the second meaning of a shot breakdown, it is quite distinct from it, no longer referring to a process taking place before filming or to a particular technical operation but, rather, to the underlying structure of the *finished* film. Formally, a film consists of a succession of fragments excerpted from a spatial and temporal continuum.

From: Noël Burch, 'Spatial and Temporal Articulations', in *Film Theory and Practice* (Princeton University Press, 1981).

Découpage in its third French meaning refers to what results when the spatial fragments, or, more accurately, the succession of spatial fragments excerpted in the shooting process, converge with the temporal fragments whose duration may be roughly determined during the shooting, but whose final duration is established only on the editing table. The dialectical notion inherent in the term *découpage* enables us to determine, and therefore to analyze, the specific form of a film, its essential unfolding in time and space. *Découpage* as a structural concept involving a synthesis is strictly a French notion. An American film-maker (or film critic, in so far as American film critics are interested in film technique at all) conceives of a film as involving two successive and separate operations, the selection of a camera setup and then the cutting of the filmed images. It may never occur to English-speaking film-makers or English-speaking critics that these two operations stem from a single underlying concept, simply because they have at their disposal no single word for this concept. If many of the most important formal break-throughs in film in the last fifteen years have occurred in France, it may be in part a matter of vocabulary.

An examination of the actual manner in which the two partial *découpages*, one temporal and the other spatial, join together to create a single articulated formal texture enables us to classify the possible ways of joining together the spaces depicted by two succeeding camera setups and the different ways of joining together two temporal situations. Such classification of the possible forms of temporal and spatial articulations between two shots might seem to be a rather academic endeavor, but to my knowledge no one has previously attempted such a classification, and I believe that it may well open up some important new perspectives.

Setting aside such "punctuation marks" as dissolves and wipes, which may be regarded as mere variations on the straight cut, five distinct types of temporal articulation between any two shots are possible.

The two shots, first of all, may be absolutely continuous. In a certain sense, the clearest example of this sort of temporal continuity is a cut from a shot of someone speaking to a shot of someone listening, with the dialogue continuing without a break in voice-over. This is, of course, precisely what happens whenever a shot is followed by a reverse-angle shot. Although the term "straight match-cut," as is made clear later on in this chapter, refers more specifically to spatial continuity, it is also another example of absolute temporal continuity. If shot A shows someone coming up to a door, putting his hand on the doorknob, turning it, then starting to open the door shot B, perhaps taken from the other side of the door, can pick up the action at the precise point where the previous shot left off and show the rest of the action as it would have "actually" occurred with the person coming through the door and so on. This action could even conceivably be filmed by two cameras simultaneously resulting in two shots that, taken together, preserve an absolute continuity of action seen from two different angles. To obtain as complete a continuity in the edited film, all we would have to do is cut the tail of shot A into the head of shot B on the editing table.

A second possible type of temporal relationship between two shots involves the presence of a gap between them, constituting what might be called a *temporal ellipsis* or *time abridgement*. Referring again to the example of someone opening a door filmed by two cameras (or by the same camera from two different angles), a part of the action might be omitted when these two shots are joined together (in shot A someone puts his hand on the doorknob and turns it; in shot B he closes the door behind him). Even the most conventional films frequently use this technique as a means of tightening the action, of eliminating the superfluous. In shot A someone might perhaps start up a flight of stairs, and in shot B he might already be on the second or even the fifth floor. Particularly when a simple action such as opening a door and walking through it is involved, it might be emphasized that the ellipsis or abridgement can occur in any one of a large number of possible variations; the "real" action might span some five or six seconds, and the time ellipsis might involve the omission of anything from a twenty-fourth of a second to several seconds, and might occur at any point in the action. This is equally true in the case of absolute temporal continuity; the transition between shots may occur anywhere. A film editor might maintain that in both cases there is only one "right" point at which to make a straight match-cut or abridge the action, but what he really means is that there is only one place where the shot transition will not be consciously noticed by the viewer. This may well be. But if we are seeking a film style that is less "smooth," that actually stresses the structures that it is based upon, a whole range of possibilities remains open.

This first type of temporal ellipsis involves, then, an omission of a time-span that is not only perceptible but *measurable* as well. The occurrence and the extent of the omission are necessarily always indicated by a more or less noticeable break in either a visual or an auditory action that is potentially capable of being completely continuous. (A continuous temporal-auditory action, verbal or otherwise, occurring in conjunction with a discontinuous temporal-visual action, as in Jean-Luc Godard's *Breathless* and Louis Malle's *Zazie dans le Métro*, is, of course, not at all precluded.) In the previous examples of going through a door or going up a flight of stairs we become aware of the existence of a temporal discontinuity or gap as a result of the spatial continuity having been forcefully enough maintained to allow the viewer to determine mentally that some portion of a continuous action has been omitted and even enable him to "measure" the actual extent of the omission. (Temporal *continuity* can likewise only be measured relative to some other *uninterrupted* visual or auditory continuity.) Thus, if a shot transition takes us from one location to another, more distant one without there being any way of relating the two distinct spaces (such as a telephone or some other means of communication), the temporal continuity between them will remain indefinite unless it is preserved through the use of such clumsy devices as successive close-ups of a clock-dial or some convention such as cross-cutting, an emphatic alternation between two actions occurring in two distinct spaces.

A third type of temporal articulation and a second type of abridgement are possible, the *"indefinite ellipsis."* It may cover an hour or a year, the exact extent of the temporal omission being measurable only through the aid of something "external" – a line of dialogue, a title, a clock, a calendar, a change in dress style, or the like. It is closely related to the scenario, to the actual narrative and visual content, but it nonetheless performs a genuine temporal function, for, even though the time of the narrative obviously is not the same as the time of the film, the two time spans can nevertheless be related in a rigorously dialectical manner. The reader may object that the boundary between the "measurable" ellipsis and the "indefinite" ellipsis is not clear. Admittedly a segment of time abridged in the process of splicing together two shots showing someone walking through a door can be measured rather accurately – namely, as that part of the action that we know must be gone through but do not see, whereas we are less capable of measuring "the time it takes to climb five flights of stairs." However, "the time it takes to climb five flights of stairs" still constitutes a unit of measurement, much as "one candle power" is the amount of light furnished by one candle; this is not at all the case, on the other hand, when we realize that something is occurring "a few days later," as in an indefinite ellipsis.

A *time reversal* constitutes another type of possible temporal articulation. In the example of someone walking through a door, shot A might have included the entire action up to the moment of going through the door, with shot B going back to the moment when the door was opened, repeating part of the action in a deliberately artificial manner. This procedure constitutes what might be called a *short time reversal*, or an overlapping cut, such as Sergei Eisenstein used so often and to such striking advantage – as in the bridge sequence in *October (Ten Days That Shook the World)* – and such as certain avant-garde film-makers have used (see also Fraçois Truffaut's *La Peau douce* and Luis Buñuel's *The Exterminating Angel*. At this point, however, it is worth noting that time reversals, like time ellipses, are commonly used on a very small scale, involving the omission or repetition of only a few frames, as a means of preserving *apparent* continuity. The preservation of an appearance of continuity is, of course, what is always involved in any conventional use of time abridgement. What we are referring to now, however, no longer involves simple mental deception – that is to say, making an action that is not visually continuous convey a "spirit" of continuity – but the actual physical deception of the eye. When it comes to "match-cutting" two shots showing someone walking through a door, for perceptual reasons which are quite beyond the scope of this book), a few frames of the action may be omitted or repeated in order that the filmed action may seem more smoothly continuous than would have been the case had the shot been picked up *precisely* where the previous one left off.

The flashback is a more usual form of time reversal. Just as a time ellipsis can span either just a few seconds or several years, so too can a time reversal. The fifth and last type of temporal articulation thus is the *indefinite time reversal*, which is analogous to the *indefinite time ellipsis* (the exact extent of a flashback is as difficult to measure without outside clues as is the extent of a flashforward) and the opposite of a *measurable time reversal*. The reason why the flashback so often seems such a dated and essentially uncinematic technique today is that, aside from its use by Alain Resnais and in a few isolated films such as Marcel Carné's *Le Jour se lève* and Marcel Hanoun's *Une Simple histoire*, the formal function of the flashback and its precise relationship to other forms of temporal articulation have never been understood. Like the voice-over, the flashback has remained little more than a convenient narrative device borrowed from the novel, although both have recently begun to assume other functions.

But might not this inability to measure the exact temporal duration spanned by either flashback or flashforward point to some basic and previously over-looked truth? Are not jumps forward and backward in time really identical on the formal organic level of a film? Are there not ultimately, then, only four kinds of temporal relationships, the fourth consisting of a great jump in time, either forward or backward? Alain Robbe-Grillet obviously believes this is so, and in that sense, his and Resnais's *Last Year at Marienbad* perhaps comes closer to the organic essence of film than it is currently fashionable to believe.

Three types of articulation between the spaces depicted in two successive shots are possible – apart from, and independent of, temporal articulations, even though they have obvious analogies to them.

A first kind of possible spatial relationship between two shots involves the preservation of spatial continuity in a manner similar to that in which temporal continuity is preserved, *although this spatial continuity may or may not be accompanied by temporal continuity*. The door example in all three variations is an instance of spatial continuity; in each case, the same fragment of space fully or partially seen in shot A is also visible in shot B. Any change in angle or scale (matching shots, that is, taken from the same angle but closer or farther away) with relation to the same camera subject or within the same location or the same circumscribed space generally establishes a spatial continuity between two shots. That much is obvious. It seems to follow that there is only one other form of possible spatial articulation between two shots: spatial *discontinuity* – in other words, anything not falling into the first category. This discontinuity, however, can be divided into two distinct subtypes bearing a rather curious resemblance to the two distinct subtypes of time ellipses and reversals. While showing a space different in every way from the space visible in shot A, shot B can show a space that is obviously in close *proximity* to the spatial fragment previously seen (it may, for instance, be within the same room or other closed or circumscribed space). This type of spatial discontinuity has given rise to a whole vocabulary dealing with spatial orientation, and the fact that such a vocabulary should be necessary serves to emphasize how essentially different this type is from an obvious third possibility, complete and radical spatial discontinuity.

This vocabulary dealing with spatial orientation brings us to a key term, one of some concern to us here: the "match" or "match-cut." "Match" refers to any element having to do with the preservation of continuity between two or more shots. Props, for instance, can be "match" or "not match." On a sound stage one can often hear remarks such as "these glasses are not match," meaning that the actor was not wearing the same glasses or was not wearing glasses at all in a shot that has already been filmed and is supposed to "match" with the shot at hand. "Match" can also refer to space, as in eye-line matches, matches in screen direction, and matches in the position of people or objects on screen. There are also spatiotemporal matches, as in the door example, where the speed of movement in the two shots must "match," that is, must *appear* to be the same. To clarify this notion of "match" or "match-cutting," a brief history of how it developed is in order.

When, between 1905 and 1920, film-makers started bringing their cameras up close to the actors and *fragmenting* the "proscenium space" that early cinema had left intact, they noticed that, if they wanted to maintain the illusion of theatrical space, a "real" space in which the viewer has an immediate and constant sense of orientation (and this was, and still remains, the essential aim for many directors), certain rules had to be respected if the viewer was not to lose his footing, to lose that instinctive sense of direction he always has in traditional theater and believes he has in life. This was the source of the concepts of eye-line match, matching screen direction, and matching screen position.

Eye-line match and matching screen direction concern two shots that are spatially discontinuous but in close proximity. When two shots show two different persons supposedly looking at each other, person A must look screen right and person B screen left, or vice versa, for if both look in the same direction in two successive shots, the viewer will inevitably have the impression that they are not looking at each other and will suddenly feel that he has completely lost his orientation in screen space. This observation on the part of the second generation of film-makers contains a basic truth that goes far beyond the original goal of matching. Only the Russian directors, however (before Stalinism brought film experimentation to an abrupt halt), were beginning to glimpse what this really implied: that only what happens in frame is important, that the only film space is screen space, that screen space can be manipulated through the use of an infinite variety of *possible* real spaces, and that disorienting the viewer is one of a film-maker's most valuable tools. We will come back to this idea later.

As a corollary to eye-line match, film-makers also discovered the principle of matching screen direction: someone or something exciting frame left must always enter a new frame showing a space that is supposedly close by or contiguous from the right; if this does not occur it will seem that there has been a change in the direction the person or object is moving in.

It was also noticed, finally, that in any situation involving two shots preserving spatial continuity and showing two people seen from relatively close up, their respective screen positions as established in the first shot, with one of them perhaps to the right and the other to the left, must not be changed in succeeding shots. To do so risks confusing the viewer's eye, for he invariably will read any shift in screen position as necessarily corresponding to a shift in "real" space.

As the techniques for breaking down an action into shots and sequences were developed and refined, these continuity rules became more and more firmly fixed, methods ensuring that they would be respected were perfected, and their underlying aim, to make any transition between two shots that were spatially continuous or in close proximity *imperceptible*, became increasingly apparent. The introduction of sound brought an increased emphasis on film as an essentially "realistic" medium, an erroneous conception that soon resulted in what we might call the "zero point of cinematic style," at least in so far as shot transitions were concerned. The Russian experiments exploring an entirely different idea of *découpage* were soon considered outdated or at best only marginally important. "Jump cuts" and "bad" or "unclear" matches were to be avoided because they made the essentially *discontinuous* nature of a shot transition or the *ambiguous* nature of cinematic space too apparent (the over-lapping cuts in *October* were viewed as "bad" matches, and the *découpage* of Alexander Dovzhenko's *Earth* was thought to be "obscure"). Attempting thus to deny the many-sided nature of the cut, film-makers eventually had no well-defined aesthetic reason whatsoever for cutting from one shot to the next, often doing so for reasons of pure convenience, until by the end of the 1940's some of the most rigorous directors (Luchino Visconti in *La Terra trema*. Alfred Hitchcock in *Rope*, Michelangelo Antonioni in *Cronaca di un amore*) began wondering whether cuts were necessary at all, whether they should not be purely and simply eliminated or used very sparingly and endowed with a very special function.

The time has now come to change our attitude toward the function and nature of cinematic articulation, both between individual shots and in the film over all, as well as its relation to narrative structure. We are just beginning to realize that the formal organization of shot transitions and "matches" in the strict sense of the word is the essential cinematic task. Each articulation, as we have seen, is defined by two parameters, the first temporal, the second spatial. There are, therefore, fifteen basic ways of articulating two shots, that being the number of possible combinations of the five temporal types and the three spatial types of transitions. Each of these possibilities, moreover, can give rise to an almost infinite number of permutations, determined not only by the extent of the time ellipsis or reversal but also, and more importantly, by another para-meter that is capable of undergoing an almost infinite number of variations too: the changes in camera angle and camera-subject distance (not to mention deliberate discrepancies in eye-line angles or matching trajectories, which are less easy to control but almost as important). I am not saying that these are the only elements that play a role in a transition between shots. But other elements such as camera and subject movement, frame content and composition, and the like can define only the particular nature of a given match and not the function of articulations in general. As regards the content of the film image, it may be interesting to know that a close-up of a man's expressionless face followed by a shot of a bowl of soup creates the impression that the man is hungry; but this relationship between the content of two shots is a *syntactical* one that merely helps us determine the *semantic* relationship between them. Although film remains largely an imperfect means of communication, it is nonetheless possible to foresee a time when it will become a totally immanent object whose semantic function will be intimately joined with its plastic function to create a *poetic function*. Although camera movements, entrances into and exits from frame, composition, and so on can all function as devices aiding in the organization of the film object, I feel that the shot transition will remain the basic element in the infinitely more complex structures of the future.

One of the possible forms that this over-all organization of film articulations might take can already be foreseen, for the fifteen types of shot transitions can give rise to patterns of *mutual interference*, resulting in yet another controllable set of permutations. At the moment of transition, the articulation between two shots might seem to fit into any one of the five temporal categories and any one of the three spatial categories, but then something in shot B or some other subsequent shot might *retrospectively* reveal that the transition actually belongs in an altogether different temporal or spatial category, or perhaps even both. Examples of this procedure exist even in relatively conventional film-making. In a scene in Hitchcock's *The Birds*, Tippi Hedren, who has lingered too long at the home of the local schoolteacher, telephones her fiancé. The first shot shows her in a medium close-up. The next shot shows the teacher starting to sit down in an armchair, blocking part of the frame at the beginning of the shot. Because of the alternation between shots to which we have become accustomed in similar scenes, and more importantly because of the absence of any other clue to the spatial orientation, we have the impression the camera is aimed at some other part of the set; hence there appears to be preservation of temporal continuity (Tippi Hedren continuing her conversation off screen) along with spatial discontinuity. When the teacher is finally seated, however, she reveals the part of the set in the background that she has previously blocked from view, and we see Tippi Hedren in a medium-long shot at the telephone. Spatial continuity had in fact been preserved as well (it is a matching shot from the same angle). Our first impression of the situation was an erroneous one, and we are belatedly forced to correct our initial misconception. This is a much more complex process of awareness, to say the least, than that implied in the "invisible" match. The exact nature of the relationship between the two shots remains vague for several seconds and becomes obvious only sometime after the transition has occurred. The variable duration of this interval may furnish another parameter.

Another frequently employed technique involves having a distant shot of someone followed by a closer one, with this second shot subsequently turning out to be occurring at some other time and perhaps even in some other place. Although this procedure is commonly used in flashbacks and time ellipses, it has hidden potentialities that allow more complex formal structures to be created (as in *Une Simple histoire*).

It is, however, important to note that this sort of disorientation presupposes a "coherent" spatial and temporal continuity, a previously created context built around immediately comprehensible relationships between shots. A more systematic, more structural use of the disorientation created by these "retro-active matches" would depend on establishing some sort of dialectical relation-ship between such matches and others that are immediately comprehensible, a dialectic in which the "deferred" match might perhaps still be an exceptional device but would no longer remain a gratuitous or merely stylistic "gimmick."

Still other possibilities can result from the nonresolution of these "open" matches, films that would have this very ambiguity as their basis, films in which the viewer's sense of "real" space would be constantly subverted, films in which he could never orient himself. Resnais's *Last Year at Marienbad* and Jean-Marie Straub's *Nicht Versöhnt*, especially in their use of indefinite time ellipses and reversals, already provide examples.

I have just briefly outlined a set of formal "objects" – the fifteen different types of shot transitions and the parameters that define then – capable of rigorous development through such devices as rhythmic alternation, recapitu-lation, retrogression, gradual elimination, cyclical repetition, and serial varia-tion, thus creating structures similar to those of twelve-tone music. None of this is as abstractly theoretical as might be imagined.

As early as 1931, Fritz Lang's masterpiece *M* was entirely structured around a rigorous organization of the film's formal articulations, starting with sequences in which each shot is temporally and spatially autonomous, with time ellipses and changes in location playing the obviously predominant role, then gradually and systematically evolving toward the increasing use of the continuity cut, finally culminating in the famous trial sequence in which temporal and spatial continuity are strictly preserved for some ten minutes. In the course of this progression a certain number of "retroactive matches" also occur, the most striking of which takes place when the gangsters leave the building in which they have captured the sadistic child-murderer. Lang repeats a shot, already used several times, of a housebreaker seen through the hole in the floor he has made to get into a locked bank. The thief asks for a ladder so he can climb out. A ladder is thrown down and he clambers out, only to discover that it is the police and not his gangster friends who are there waiting for him. We then realize that the time between the mob's departure and the arrival of the police has been completely skipped over in a time ellipsis, that instead of occurring immediately after the departure of the thief's pals this shot in fact happens a good deal later than we initially thought.

A more recent film, Marcel Hanoun's little-known masterpiece *Une Simple histoire*, is entirely structured around principles similar to the one I have been describing. Although these principles are arrived at in Hanoun's case in a purely empirical manner, they are nevertheless applied with utmost rigor.

The contemporary film narrative is gradually liberating itself from the constraints of the literary or pseudo-literary forms that played a large part in bringing about the "zero point of cinematic style" that reigned supreme during the 1930's and 1940's and still remains in a position of some strength today. It is only through systematic and thorough exploration of the *structural* possibilities inherent in the cinematic parameters I have been describing that film will be liberated from the old narrative forms and develop new "open" forms that will have more in common with the formal strategies of post-Debussyian music than with those of the pre-Joycean novel. Film will attain its formal autonomy only when these new "open" forms begin to be used organically. What this principally involves is the creation of a truly consistent relationship between a film's spatial and temporal articulations and its narrative content, formal structure determining narrative structure as much as vice versa. It also implies giving as important a place to the viewer's disorientation as to his orientation. And these are but two of the possible multiple dialectics that will form the very *substance* of the cinema of the future, a cinema in which *découpage* in the limited sense of breaking a narrative down into scenes will no longer be meaningful to the real film-maker and *découpage* as defined here will cease to be experimental and purely theoretical and come into its own in actual film practice. It is this cinema of the future that the following pages will hopefully help to bring forth.

6

THE MIND'S EYE

Bruce F. Kawin

Film is a dream – but whose? One rests in the dark, and sees; one is silent, and hears. One submits to the dream-field, yet actively scans it – for play, for release, for community, solitude, truth. The viewer's interplay between passivity and creation is analogous to the sleeper's, since both forget, almost continuously, that the dream-world is "made"; only while picking the fantasy over in the daylight or breaking contact with the narrative field is one moved to congratulate oneself, or the artist, for thinking up so many wonders. In the dark one participates, thinks, and guides the eye. Whether the film is nonrepresentational or documentary, whether it tells a story or simply weaves the light, it presents itself to the audience as privileged vision: an image the mind can search, a revelation to deny or accept.

The filmmaker dreams in the daylight – stages, blocks, budgets, points, shoots, edits, writes, acts – solo or as a member of a collective: but always with reference to the image he creates for the dark. The film lives under his eyelids, till the means of reproduction make it public. Between the dreaming artist and the dreaming audience, the artifact mediates.

Most analyses of film consciousness have swung on these two gates and left out the garden. Might not the artifact, too, have or imitate mindedness? The dialectic between the world before the camera and the image before the projector; the relationships between the artist's intentions, the emotive capacity of the image, and the audience's response; the mutual influence of guided

From: Bruce F. Kawin, 'The Mind's Eye', in *Mindscreen: Bergman, Godard and First-Person Film* (Princeton University Press, 1978).

fantasy and willed behavior – all these have been opened to question. Auteur criticism, in particular, has paid so much attention to the ways an artist (director or not) manifests himself in his work that the questions of who *narrates* the work and of how, as a pseudo-autonomous text, the film might construct or comment upon itself, have come to sound almost foolish. Marxist semiotics, on the other hand, has reacted against the bourgeois emphasis of much auteur criticism and has called attention to the ways an image itself can be encoded and thence to the ways an audience deals with this culturally predetermined iconography.

I do not mean to oversimplify or disparage the achievements of film theory and criticism here, but there does appear to be a need for a more complex rhetoric of film than has yet been attempted. The issues of narrative conscious-ness and reflexivity have hardly been defined for film. The "impersonal" nature of photography, for instance, appears to have dominated many of our rhetorical assumptions, so that a wide range of film theorists generally accept that a film must be narrated in the third person, whether it tells a story or not. The image, however encoded or manipulated, is presumed to consist of *he*s and *she*s and *it*s. While it seems reasonable to agree with one of the implications of this approach – that the organizer of the image must be offscreen – it does not seem necessary to deny the possibility that the organizer, as a persona of the artist or even just as a character, can be fictitious, and that he can include an image of himself (or an indicator of his offscreen presence) in the filmed field without compromising his status as narrator. I do not mean to negate the importance of such nonfictional organizers of the image as the filmmakers, the interpretive audience, or the culture itself; clearly, they exist, and contribute to what can be structured, presented, and seen. Clearly, the selective intelligence of the filmmaker is always at work, whether he keeps a large field in deep focus, or interrelates its fragments through montage, or fires the camera "at random." The frame itself is selective; two-dimensionality itself is artificial; the world itself is politicized and emotive. There is much to analyze, much that is seen to be *meant*, in even the most third-person photographs.

Still, any art would be impoverished if it could speak only in the third person. The reader of *Moby-Dick*, for example, recognizes his own creative inter-pretation of the novel's world, and Melville's structural intentions, and whal-ing as a capitalist process that exists in reality – but he is also aware of the narrator, Ishmael, who is neither Melville nor the reader nor whaling. As an essential condition of one's response to the novel, one forgets at some point that Ishmael is Melville's puppet, just as one forgets that the camera is not independent.

The audience at a film is presented with a world; the question remains, what is "a fictitious presenter"? How can it be recognized, how responded to? If a film, which is already both the dream of its maker and the dream of its audience, can present itself as the dream of one of its characters, can it, finally, appear to dream itself? Implicit in my ordering of these questions is the assumption that there are several narrative modes and voices in film; I shall try to clarify these before going further.

A narrator is someone who does not simply speak, but tells. As a medium of presentation and communication occurring in time, film is no less a "language" (or system of signification) than literature. Although it is "spoken" by some combination of filmmaker and movie theater, it can *appear* to be spoken by a character within the fiction, or by the filmmaker who intrudes in his own voice.

The simplest kind of narration to recognize is, of course, the purely verbal or voice-over. Buñuel's *Land without Bread (Las Hurdes*, 1932), for instance, includes a mock-travelogue voice-over commentary by Pierre Unik. The audience feels, with some justification, that it is not simply eavesdropping on the people of Las Hurdes but is being *told* about them. Both here and in Resnais's *Night and Fog* (1956; commentary by Jean Cayrol), the voice-over narration counterpoints rather than simply explains what one is seeing, so that both word and image function as narrative units. The camera, as an active presence, probes and relates, but does not assign its viewpoint to any character. In the later work of Resnais and Buñuel, however, the subjectivity of both camera and commentary is often fictionally assigned, as when the soldier narrates his death-dream in *The Discrete Charm of the Bourgeoisie* (1972), or the actress her visit to the museum in *Hiroshima, mon amour* (1959).

Voice-over narration is a literary device – one that is, in fact, often used to anchor an adaptation in its literary source. *Finnegans Wake* (1965), for instance, like *The Reivers* (1969) or *A Clockwork Orange* (1971), is haunted by the eloquence of the novel, and continually returns to the voice of the story teller as if to an oasis – not because the imagery is unable to sustain interest or clarity, but because the film aspires, among other things, to some kinship with literature.

When the voice-over narration is assigned to a fictitious speaker, it expresses not the filmmaker's judgments on his material (as in *Night and Fog*) but the character's interpretive response to his own experience. Whether the narrator talks directly to the audience, as Alex in *A Clockwork Orange*, or to himself, as Charlie in *Mean Streets* (1973), one understands that the film is limited to this character's point of view, that one is seeing the world as Alex or Charlie presents it. I say "presents" rather than "experiences" so as not to exclude the possibility of a narrator who lies, and to maintain the emphasis on narrativity rather than subjectivity. It is necessary, however, to clarify the nature of subjective presentation before returning to the issue of narration.

Subjectivity is essential to any first-person construct, but many uses of subjective imagery function without specifically first-person narrative intent. When a fight scene is heightened by a shot of a fist's heading straight for the camera, one understands that the victim's angle of vision is being shared for a moment, but one does not necessarily go chasing through the film in search of a consistently subjective point of view. In this case the subjective angle is merely one of many available camera positions.

In the opening sequence of *Rebecca* (1940), however, both the tracking camera and the moody voice-over explicitly belong to a first-person narrator. Her opening line, "Last night I dreamed I went to Manderley again," makes it clear that the image takes place in her dreaming mind (or that her narrating mind is re-creating the image of her dream). Even when the heroine appears before the camera, one understands that this is still *her* story; it is not necessary, in other words, for the audience to share her angle of vision in order to feel itself confined to her point of view. (In order not to lose sight of this distinction, I have avoided the term "point of view shot," or POV, to describe subjective camera.)

In another Hitchcock film. *Spellbound* (1945), several varieties of first-person narration occur. At the end of the film, one shares the villain's angle of vision as he looks from behind his revolver at his accuser, then turns the revolver to fire point-blank at himself; no voice-over is necessary to make the audience understand that this is a first-person image. In the more complicated sequence of the hero-doctor's dream, however, voice-over combines with subjective imagery (designed by Salvador Dali) to give the impression not only that one is sharing the dreamer's experience (as one shares the sight of the gun), but also that the hero is deliberately telling his dream as he relives it. As a whole, *Spellbound* is narrated anonymously, in the third person, but includes first-person sequences.

There are, then, two ways of using what is generally called "subjective camera": to show what the character sees, or to show what he thinks. The first mode is that of the physical eye, the second is that of the mind's eye. The modes overlap in many Surrealist and Expressionist sequences, but it will clarify matters to examine them separately.

The first mode, as has been suggested above, is commonly used only to achieve momentary identification between character and audience, or for shock effects (the revolver in *Spellbound*). For technical reasons, it is rarely used at length; the most noteworthy exceptions are Robert Montgomery's *Lady in the Lake* (1946) – where the hero appears only in mirrors – and the first half of Delmer Daves's *Dark Passage* (1947). (It is also worth mentioning Orson Welles's unproduced *Heart of Darkness* [1940], in which both subjective camera and a Welles voice-over were to embody Marlow with Welles appearing before the camera as Kurtz – an intriguing way to dramatize Conrad's "secret sharer" theme.) One of this mode's recent vehicles, the wide-angle close-up, appears strikingly unrealistic when the near object (or the camera) moves. The huddling faces in John Frankenhemier's *Seconds* (1966), for example, are much harder to accept than the hovering face of the scientist in Chris Marker's *La Jetée* (1962), a film made up almost entirely of stills. Such distortion paradoxically contributes to the realism of a film like *2001* (1968), however, in which the eye of the character (HAL) is *supposed* to be a wide-angle lens. Such effects become ludicrous when they are not perfectly executed in terms of the human facial anatomy – as when a glass of wine is raised to lens height and poured out just below camera range to give the illusion of drinking, or where the filmed subject attempts a passionate kiss of the tripod. Most such shots leave out those portions of the face and body one's own eye normally sees. Furthermore, most camera movements are slower than eye movements (so the image can remain clear) and of a completely different nature: more akin to movements of the head, complicated by a neckbrace. And a cut, short of blinking, is virtually out of the question.

Resnais gets around these problems by deliberately ignoring the conventions of animal movement. His fluid trackings through the corridors at Marienbad or the hospital and museum at Hiroshima are movements of the mind more than of the physical eye. As the characters fantasize, remember, or concentrate on certain places and events, the camera acts out the movements of their attention. At times Resnais achieves great realism by juxtaposing both modes of subjective camera, as when the actress in *Hiroshima* sees the twitching hand of her Japanese lover in one shot, and remembers the twitching hand of her German lover in the next-but-one (a shot of her own face intervenes).

The earliest use of this second mode occurs in Edwin S. Porter's *Life of an American Fireman* (1903). As described in the Edison Catalogue:

> The fire chief is dreaming and the vision of his dream appears in a circular portrait on the wall. It is a mother putting her baby to bed, and the impression is that he dreams of his own wife and child. He suddenly awakens and paces the floor in a nervous state of mind, doubtless thinking of the various people who may be in danger from fire at the moment.

Here a first-person shot is vignetted within a third-person shot as a sort of thought balloon. In 1908, D. W. Griffith arrived at a more flexible and sophisticated device for showing what a character might be thinking: the subjective cutaway. In his first version of Tennyson's *Enoch Arden* (*After Many Years*), Griffith cut from a shot of Enoch's wife (disconsolate over his long absence) to a shot of Enoch himself, stranded on a remote island. Since Annie has in fact no idea where Enoch is, it is perhaps necessary to describe this as a primitive instance of parallel cutting, but the impression is nevertheless given that Annie is thinking of Enoch, whether or not the inserted shot precisely incarnates her fantasy. By the time he made *Judith of Bethulia* (1914) Griffith had learned how to make it explicit that a character is imagining what is shown in this kind of cutaway. The heroine of that film, wavering in her resolve to kill Holofernes, "sees" images of her people starving in the streets of Bethulia, then cuts off the head of her lover/enemy. If this were a third-person insert shot of her people's troubles instead of a direct presentation of Judith's thought process, the reason for her change of heart would not be clear; as it is, the subjective insert and its aftermath (the murder) stand in an evident cause-and-effect relationship.

In his masterpiece, *Mother* (1926), Pudovkin experimented with more complex uses of subjective camera and subjective montage. Early in the film, the mother watches her son, Pavel, hide a parcel of guns and leaflets under a floorboard. She is half-asleep, and the image comes only gradually into focus. The camera's position is hers, in bed; an iris indicates the concentration of her attention on Pavel; and the shifting focus unmistakably identifies the image as her visual field. Later on, just before the police question Pavel in this same room, the mother remembers (via a cutaway) what she saw; a series of dissolves goes on to make her *thinking* manifest. She looks at the loose floorboard; a dissolve appears to penetrate the floor and reveal the parcel; a further dissolve to the "opened" parcel reveals the guns. In the "Tomorrow!" sequence near the end of this film, a montage of images of exuberance expresses Pavel's emotion on discovering a plan to release him from prison. Clearly, he is not looking at a happy child or rushing water; he is probably not even thinking of them. But the images express, metaphorically, what his thinking feels like, and belong therefore to the second subjective mode.

There are, then, three familiar ways of signifying subjectivity within the first-person narrative field: to present what a character says (voice-over), sees (subjective focus, imitative angle of vision), or thinks. The term I propose for this final category is *mindscreen*, by which I mean simply the field of the mind's eye. From here on I shall use the term *subjective camera* to denote only the field of the character's physical eye.

All three modes can include distortion. A voice-over narrator can lie, contradicting either what appears in the visual field ("You saw nothing at Hiroshima") or what the audience surmises "really happened" (*Rashomon*, 1950). Subjective camera can imitate anything from nearsightedness to X-ray vision, as in Roger Corman's *X – The Man with the X-Ray Eyes* (1963). And the mindscreen can present the whole range of visual imagination – not just Dorothy's dream of Oz (1939), or the unverifiable memories of Marienbad (1961), but also the interpretive bias of private experience (*Citizen Kane*, 1941).

The opening of *Rebecca*, then, though it includes both voice-over and what appears to be subjective camera, is primarily an instance of mindscreen, since it presents what the character imagined in her sleep. There are numerous examples of such overlap, some of which do not admit of resolution. In Abel Gance's Surrealist short, *La Folie du Docteur Tube* (1914), the world is presented as a mad doctor sees it after experimenting on himself. There is no way to determine whether these stretched, spread, and otherwise grotesquely distorted images belong to the doctor's physical or mind's eye. (In *X*, it is obviously the physical eye that is affected, as in Emile Cohl's *Hasher's Delirium* or Porter's *Dream of a Rarebit Fiend* – both 1906 – it is the mind's.) There are instances, too, where the modes occur not in confusion but in combination. Like that of *Rebecca*, the opening of *Hiroshima* employs both voice-over and mindscreen. The shot in *8½* that presents Guido's being handed a glass of mineral water by his fantasy-angel instead of by the mundane attendant employs subjective camera to identify itself as *his* fantasy. It is entirely possible, of course, for the "dreamer" to occur as a "he," or object, in his own mindscreen, as is the case in *The Wizard of Oz* or *An Occurrence at Owl Creek Bridge* (1961).

It is, then, comfortable to include in one's response to an image the possibility of its fictitious origin. Indeed, once one admits the notion of the *authorial* persona (or fictionalized author), it becomes much easier to deal with apparently unmotivated subjective imagery. *Persona* (1966), for instance, continually appeals outside itself to a dreaming mind that it would be simplistic to identify as either Bergman's or the boy's in the morgue. The sets of *The Scarlet Empress* (1934), and the image of Dietrich herself, on the other hand, appear to have proceeded, without the intervention of a persona, directly from the mind of Von Sternberg. (To the extent that *The Scarlet Empress* successfully integrates this imagery into its own "world," however, its subjectivity comes to seem internally motivated, and therefore autonomous.)

In this latter sense, many films as wholes – those of Stan Brakhage, for instance – literally represent the mindscreens of their makers. Lest the term get out of hand, however, let me suggest that in such cases the authors are acting as narrators, and that not only certain first-person sequences, but also sustained narrations can be identified as the visualized mentations of their "speakers." Even with this qualification, mindscreen begins to suggest itself as an encyclopedic term for "visual narration." It must be emphasized, then, that mindscreens belong to, or manifest the workings of, *specific* minds. A mindscreen sequence is narrated in the *first person*. There will be times the filmmaker casts himself as a narrator, whether in the flesh ("This is what *we* saw at Las Hurdes …") or as a persona. The filmmaker may posit a fictitious persona ("Last night I dreamed I went to Manderley again"), a credible one (the budgeteers at the opening of Godard's *Tout va bien* [1972]), or a version of himself. When the filmmaker keeps himself out of it and presents his images in the third person (as Lumière does, for instance), his therapist can call the film a mindscreen, but we do not have to.

All three modes of first-person discourse, then – voice-over, subjective camera, and mindscreen can be presented as if they were fictitious in origin. (8½ is Fellini's mindscreen, but presents itself intermittently as Guido's.) All three present their origins as outside the image field; the audience is led to imagine an offscreen speaker, seer, or image-maker who is not necessarily the auteur. When the image-maker appears within the field, the audience understands that this is his imagined self-portrait (Dorothy is offscreen, in bed). The intimacy of these modes contrasts markedly with those of the stage, where a narrator must appear in the flesh and talk about his experience. (*Strange Interlude* is a relevant exception, in which one hears the characters" unspoken thoughts.) When the narrative techniques of *Our Town* are used in film, as in *Amarcord* (1974), one tends to reject them and seek out a more cinematic "first person" – in the case of *Amarcord*, the boy whose experience is the center of attention, in preference to the "citizen" who addresses the camera. Film is closer to literature, then, in its ability to allow the audience to participate in – rather than hear about – a character's life-space. It is insufficient, however, to identify modes of first-person narration; it remains to establish just what narrativity is.

As Christian Metz has observed – taking his cue from Albert Laffay – the very existence of an image indicates that it has been selected and arranged by some narrating intelligence, whether that be the intelligence of the filmmaker, of "the film itself as a linguistic object," or of "a sort of 'potential linguistic focus' situated somewhere behind the film." The viewer "is leafing through an album of predetermined pictures, and it is not he who is turning the pages but some 'master of ceremonies,' some 'grand image-maker.' ..." (Such a discussion applies to third- as well as first-person narration, of course, with the distinction arising from the manner in which this "linguistic focus" is characterized – or, more precisely, ascribed.) The image does not simply *appear*, but gives the impression of having been *chosen*. It is in this sense that the distinction I asserted earlier between speech and narration – that the narrator *tells* – becomes applicable to cinema. An image is the result, and the indicator, of directed attention. The filmmaker (or his surrogate) points the audience's eye *at* something, whether the film documents a period in history (*The Sorrow and the Pity* [1970]), tells a story (*Psycho* [1960]), or is the product of a wild night with salt and pepper and thumbtacks (*Return to Reason* [1923]). Although this last example reminds one that a film can be made without the use of a camera, it will simplify matters to identify the camera as the narrator's vehicle, his principal means of guiding the audience's attention. (This is not to ignore the eye-attractance of *mise en scène*, movement within the frame, composition, etc.) To point a camera at something, then, may indicate discursive intent. In the cinema, to show deliberately is to tell. Just as "discourse is not language," a perceptibly random series of images fails to generate the sense of narrativity. It is "filmic manipulation," as Metz observes, that "transforms what might have been a mere visual transfer of reality into discourse."

It is unnecessary, then, to present a character in a conventional "story-telling" pose in order to identify him to the audience as a narrator (as Wilder and Chandler do in *Double Indemnity* [1944], whose hero relates his story into a dictaphone – and, subsequently, voice-over). One is alerted by camera position, montage, etc., to narrative intent, and by what emerges as the logic of their changes to narrative bias. A short look at Bergman's *Cries and Whispers* (1972) should help to clarify the ways in which bias and intent can be ascribed, so that they become not just properties inherent in the image field as a "linguistic" object, but recognizable elements of the fiction.

Cries and Whispers is the story of four women: Agnes, who is dying of cancer; her two sisters, Karin and Maria; and Anna, her maid. The film is carefully, almost geometrically structured to explore two contrasts: that between community and isolation, and that between spiritual and physical pain. Agnes, who thrives on loving companionship, suffers intense physical pain; she is nurtured by Anna, who freely and physically comforts her. The fact that both Anna and Agnes are devout is something of a red herring (as the minister's speech and the final sequence from Agnes's diary make explicit): their principal comfort, and their means of banishing the "whispers and cries" that beset them, is their commitment to love and friendship. (This theme, which is general in Bergman's work, is here most convincingly divorced from the issue of religion, although it finds related expression in *Wild Strawberries* [1957], *Through a Glass Darkly* [1961], and to some extent *Persona.*) Karin, who is terrified of – and starving for – intimacy, is in spiritual (or psychological) pain, but has for her nurturer only the selfish and insincere Maria. When Agnes dies, halfway through the film, the emphasis shifts from her pain to Karin's.

Each of the women is presented in her aloneness and in relationship with the others. Each woman has an extended first-person sequence, and among these sequences there is a structure of ascending intimacy. (The burden of the film, then, appears to be on the side of loving, of community, and of self-knowledge.) In response to the vastly differing capacities for openness and loving touch each woman possesses, their subjective sequences achieve different degrees of intimacy. The audience is encouraged to enter deeply the mind of Anna, for instance, but is largely kept outside of Maria and Karin. Appropriately, Bergman exploits the differences in intimacy of the various narrative modes to control the intimacy of the respective sequences.

The film as a whole is third person: there is no character to whom the film's overall narrativity is ascribed. The opening montage of dawn and clocks is an objective introduction to the house in which the action takes place. (Compare the opening of Resnais's *Providence* [1977].) Agnes wakes up in pain and goes to her diary, where she writes (and we hear), "It is early Monday morning and I am in *pain.*" This is the most literary first-person mode. She looks into the next room, where Maria is sleeping; the mode is subjective camera. Soon afterward, Agnes begins to think about her mother. While she addresses herself (and the eavesdropping audience) in the first person, voice-over, her mindscreen presents images both of the mother and of herself as a young girl. The voice-over makes plain that Agnes is attempting to organize and understand this experience – that the sequence is not a directorial flashback but a deliberate and presented memory: a first-person narrative in both word and image, rather literary in feel, but – for the audience – more interior than either the diary entry or the shot of Maria asleep.

The next private sequence, Maria's, is introduced voice-over by a male. He informs the audience that the forthcoming scenes took place "some years ago." One watches Maria's attempt to seduce the family doctor, and her husband's aborted suicide attempt, with the understanding that although Maria is the central figure in these scenes, she is not their narrator. The mode is third person, but might be more precisely designated "point of view," in that the story is confined to Maria's experience; the narrator avoids the appearance of omniscience and limits himself to presenting the world as Maria sees it. (This is the method of *The 400 Blows* [1959] and *The Maltese Falcon* [1941], as it is of most of Henry James's major fiction.)

Karin's sequence, too, is presented by the male narrator. Like Maria's, it presents a dinner scene, a bedroom scene, and an act of bloody self-mutilation (although here the woman, not her husband, performs the act). Again the mode is point of view, but the impression of self-knowledge is more intense. Whereas Maria's sequence is tied into the plot by a simple act of association (another attempt to seduce the doctor), Karin's appears not simply to explain but to influence her behavior during the second half of the film, as if she had been *considering* her fear of intimacy.

Anna's sequence, however, is pure mindscreen. No voice-over is necessary; one understands almost immediately that Anna is having a dream in which Agnes demands to be comforted after death. (This is not to deny the possibility that Agnes does need such loving, and is, as a ghost, appearing to Anna in a dream.) One sees the world as Anna imagines it; one shares her mental experience. Point of view is not operative here, since Anna, the dreamer, is creating, or deliberately manipulating, the image. (It is not necessary that she be aware of presenting the image to an audience, as a narrator often is in first-person literature; if she were, however, I would propose that the mode be identified as self-consciousness. As with Agnes, the audience here is eavesdropping on a first-person sequence, rather than being addressed and acknowledged.)

Each sequence is bracketed by dissolves between a close-up of the character's face and a field of intense red. Although there are numerous ways to interpret Bergman's use of red (and its counterpart, white) in this film, the one that seems most interesting in this context is the possibility that the image field is retinal: that of all the blood in this film, the most inescapable is that which circulates through the retina and which, analogously, gives color to the eyelids closed against intense light. Such an interpretation is consistent with the device's intent here – which is to introduce a sequence of private "vision'– as well as useful in suggesting that the screen is itself retinal. (Bergman has defended his color scheme and, by implication, the use of this red field, on the ground that it somehow signifies the "moist membrane" of the soul.)

The final sequence, which fades to red only at its conclusion, emphasizes the theme of community in a manner that the foregoing discussion can help to clarify. Anna reads Agnes's diary entry of a day in which she was thoroughly happy and at peace. As in Agnes's "Mother" sequence, the words of the diary are heard voice-over, and the image includes Agnes along with Karin, Maria, and Anna. But the image must in some manner be taken as Anna's, since it is she who is reading. The narrator of the diary is Agnes; the narrator of the mindscreen is Anna. Their private experiences have, as a fact of the image, conjoined. It is at this point possible to argue that the red field has become communal, that it indicates a "mind's eye of the film." Although this last statement may reflect an overdose of *Persona*, it is clear in any case that there is a structure of ascending privacy from Agnes's literary first person, through Maria's and Karin's more cinematic, although less deliberately "presentational," points of view, to Anna's mindscreen; and it is in keeping with the film's apparent intent to suggest that increased intimacy (in which Bergman has led the audience to participate) results not in isolation but in community.

Another reading of Karin's and Maria's sequences is possible: they may be mindscreens, identified by the male narrator as having their basis in the factual past. The "red membrane" and bracketing close-ups may be taken to indicate that Maria and Karin are deliberately remembering these experiences. It is further possible that Karin's self-mutilation is entirely fantastic – an extension, originating in the present, of her memory of the tense dinner. If these sequences are not flashbacks but mindscreens, they are still more closely tied to the shared, "real" world than the sequence of Anna's dream (the structure is still one of ascending intimacy), but Maria's is a memory, Karin's a memory that may or may not shift to fantasy, and Anna's an entirely *created* mental event. There is no need for a mindscreen to present itself as fact-based; the point is that Karen's self-mutilation is a mental event in the film's present (and in her mental present, if this interpretation is followed) whether or not it is also a physical event in the past.

To recapitulate: subjectivity can be indicated through voice-over, subjective camera, and mindscreen. The narrative voices possible in cinema are, broadly: third person – in which there is no apparent narrator except the anonymous "grand image-maker"; point of view – a variety of third-person cinema in which the "grand image-maker" presents the experience of a single character, subjectivizing the world but not the narrative; first person – where a character appears to present his own view of himself and his world; and self-consciousness – which can exist in combination with (or as an aspect of) any of these voices, and in which the film itself, or the fictious narrator, is aware of the act of presentation. It bears mention at this point that self-consciousness most often expresses itself through mindscreen, characterizing the aural and visual fields as those of *its own* mentation.

So far I have confined my discussion of sound to the pseudo-literary technique of voice-over narration; I should now like to make a few points about subjective sound. Although some aspect of each of these narrative modes and categories was explored, and is demonstrable, in silent film, any series of demonstrations that aspires to thoroughness must acknowledge that sound has become integral to the presentational field. Sound is not, as was first feared, a "third leg," but a highly expressive aspect of the filmed world. It is as indicative of subjectivity to present what a character hears as to present what he sees. Owing to the prevalence of the literary first person in our culture, and the dearth of analyses of visual narration, one tends to identify auditory with verbal narration, to consider that only by speaking can one narrate in sound. (The assumption holds even in music, where the sounds" presentation is identified with the point of origin.) But it should be clear that a narrator "speaks" simply by presenting what is meant or encountered, and that it is a simple matter, in the sound film, to present what is heard, just as in subjective camera one presents what is seen. The narrator does not have to "tell" sounds orally, but can allow the audience to share his ears, just as he does not have to construct the landscape in front of him. The issue is still that of narrativity as deliberate manipulation or selection (which can include both creation and re-creation), of telling as presenting.

The "finger-twitch" sequence from *Hiroshima, mon amour* provides a straightforward example of the uses of subjective sound. From fade-in to fade-out, the sequence runs less than two minutes and includes thirteen shots, ten of which average four seconds in length; indeed, the cutting is so dynamic and revelatory that one hardly has time to pay attention to the sound. An outline of the visual track, then, may prove helpful in understanding the visual/aural relationships (shot durations are approximate):

1. Full shot, 24 seconds: Fade in. Bicyclists pass the actress's hotel. The camera pans from them to the actress on her balcony, holding a cup of coffee. She turns and walks back toward her room.
2. Mid-shot (reverse angle), 8 seconds: She completes her swing over a low divider, then leans against the door-frame and looks down toward the bed.
3. Mid-shot, 7 seconds: The Japanese lover, asleep in bed. His hand twitches slightly.
4. Close-up, 3 seconds: Her face in the doorway.
5. Close-up, 4 seconds: The twitching hand of her German lover; then a rapid pan up to his bloody face, which she is kissing.
6. Mid-shot, 3 seconds: The Japanese lover in bed.
7. Close-up, 2 seconds: Her face in the doorway.
8. Mid-shot, 8 seconds: The Japanese lover in bed. Waking, he moves his arm and starts to turn.
9. Close-up, 3 seconds: Her face in the doorway. She snaps herself back to the present.
10. Mid-shot, 4 seconds: He completes his turn, sits up, and ruffles his hair.
11. Mid-shot, 7 seconds: She comes over to him, smiling, and offers coffee.
12. Mid-shot, 18 seconds: He smiles and rests on his elbow, accepts the offer. She enters the frame, kneeling, and pours coffee. He drinks it.
13. Mid-shot (closer in), 21 seconds: She rests against the bed; he looks at his hands; they talk. She settles her head on her forearm. Fade out.

Three sound tracks are used here: dialogue, music, and natural. The natural sounds shortly precede the fade-in: bicycle bells, a train whistle. As the actress starts to walk, light Japanese-sounding music begins, but one still hears her footsteps on the balcony. During shots 2 to 5, one hears only music. At the start of shot 2, the actress enters a shadow; at shot 3, the music deepens in pitch and mood; the flutes are replaced by bass woodwinds and (if I heard correctly) some brass. At the first twitch, the music becomes louder; as the note is held, it continues to increase in volume and intensity. The bass continues through shot 4, with flutes laid in. The music peaks at the beginning of shot 5, then ceases altogether. During the pan, one has the impression of silence; as she kisses the face, one becomes aware of the return of natural sound, which in this case is primarily room tone, but which is recognized during shot 6 as the "silence" before the train whistle. Natural sound is continuous from shot 6 to the end of the sequence; no music returns. In shot 7, the street sounds are noticeable. In shot 8, a second train whistle continues to motivate the man's waking up and the woman's return to the present. In shot 9, room tone increases, and the sound of his arm on the sheet is quite loud. The train whistle repeats in shot 10, and shots 11 through 13 use room tone and dialogue.

Natural sound and music combine, in the first shot, to define the actress's mood and environment. The disappearance of natural sound during her "flash" indicates that she has become disoriented, has ceased to listen to the street, etc. The music indicates her change of mood, from peace to apprehension to crisis; it also controls the audience's expectations. The return of natural sound *during* shot 5 brings both her and the audience back to "the present." My point is that the music here functions both impersonally and in the service of point of view – registering the levels of tension in the story (and controlling those of the audience) on the one hand, and indicating how the woman feels on the other. (An example of music as purely subjective sound can be found in Hitchcock's *Strangers on a Train* [1951], where Bruno hears/remembers "The Band Played On" when he is struck by the resemblance between Barbara and his victim.) The presence or absence of natural sound, however, here forms a first-person structure. Where the visuals tend to alternate between the modes of point of view (shots 1, 2, 4, 7, 9, 11, 12, 13) and subjective camera (shots 3, 6, 8, 10), with shot 5 a mindscreen – the natural sound track is consistently limited to what the actress hears. In this sense, subjective sound is analogous, as a first-person mode, to subjective camera. It remains arguable that the music track functions, in this sequence, as a nonliteral, aural element of her mindscreen.

The first step in mindscreen analysis, then, is the recognition and attribution of selectivity. Once one has recognized that the opening duet of *Hiroshima*, for instance, is not spoken "aloud," and may in fact be the film's autonomous expression of the implications of the lovers" encounter (despite the fact that much of that sequence imitates the woman's point of view), one can go on to interpret not simply the film's narrative structure, but the effect of that structure. The question of voice becomes, finally, the question of mind, and both are inseparable from the question of meaning.

7

BEYOND THE MOVEMENT-IMAGE

Gilles Deleuze

1

Against those who defined Italian neo-realism by its social content, Bazin put forward the fundamental requirement of formal aesthetic criteria. According to him, it was a matter of a new form of reality, said to be dispersive, elliptical, errant or wavering, working in blocs, with deliberately weak connections and floating events. The real was no longer represented or reproduced but 'aimed at'. Instead of representing an already deciphered real, neo-realism aimed at an always ambiguous, to be deciphered, real; this is why the sequence shot tended to replace the montage of representations. Neo-realism therefore invented a new type of image, which Bazin suggested calling 'fact-image'. This thesis of Bazin's was infinitely richer than the one that he was challenging, and showed that neo-realism did not limit itself to the content of its earliest examples. But what the two theses had in common was the posing of the problem at the level of reality: neo-realism produced a formal or material 'additional reality'. However, we are not sure that the problem arises at the level of the real, whether in relation to form or content. Is it not rather at the level of the 'mental', in terms of thought? If all the movement-images, perceptions, actions and affects underwent such an upheaval, was this not first of all because a new element burst on to the scene which was to prevent perception being extended into action in order to put it in contact with thought, and, gradually, was to subordinate the image to the demands of new signs which would take it beyond movement?

From: Gilles Deleuze, 'Beyond the Movement Image', in Hugh Tomlinson and Robert Galeta (trans.), *Cinema 2: The Time-Image* (University of Minnesota Press, 1989).

When Zavattini defines neo-realism as an art of encounter – fragmentary, ephemeral, piecemeal, missed encounters – what does he mean? It is true of encounters in Rossellini's *Paisa*, or De Sica's *Bicycle Thief*. And in *Umberto D*, De Sica constructs the famous sequence quoted as an example by Bazin: the young maid going into the kitchen in the morning, making a series of mechanical, weary gestures, cleaning a bit, driving the ants away from a water fountain, picking up the coffee grinder, stretching out her foot to close the door with her toe. And her eyes meet her pregnant woman's belly, and it is as though all the misery in the world were going to be born. This is how, in an ordinary or everyday situation, in the course of a series of gestures, which are insignificant but all the more obedient to simple sensory-motor schemata, what has suddenly been brought about is a *pure optical situation* to which the little maid has no response or reaction. The eyes, the belly, that is what an encounter is … Of course, encounters can take very different forms, even achieving the exceptional, but they follow the same formula. Take, for example, Rossellini's great quartet, which, far from marking an abandonment of neo-realism, on the contrary, perfects it. *Germany Year 0* presents a child who visits a foreign country (this is why the film was criticized for not maintaining the social mooring which was held to be a condition of neo-realism), and who dies from what he sees. *Stromboli* presents a foreign woman whose revelation of the island will be all the more profound because she cannot react in a way that softens or compensates for the violence of what she sees, the intensity and the enormity of the tunny-fishing ('It was awful …'), the panic-inducing power of the eruption ('I am finished, I am afraid, what mystery, what beauty, my God …'). *Europe 51* shows a bourgeoise woman who, following the death of her child, crosses various spaces and experiences the tenement, the slum and the factory ('I thought I was seeing convicts'). Her glances relinquish the practical function of a mistress of a house who arranges things and beings, and pass through every state of an internal vision, affliction, compassion, love, happiness, acceptance, extending to the psychiatric hospital where she is locked up at the end of a new trial of Joan of Arc: she sees, she has learnt to see. *The Lonely Woman* [*Viaggio in Italia*] follows a female tourist struck to the core by the simple unfolding of images or visual clichés in which she discovers something unbearable, beyond the limit of what she can personally bear. This is a cinema of the seer and no longer of the agent [*de voyant, non plus d'actant*].

What defines neo-realism is this build-up of purely optical situations (and sound ones, although there was no synchronized sound at the start of neo-realism), which are fundamentally distinct from the sensory-motor situations of the action-image in the old realism. It is perhaps as important as the conquering of a purely optical space in painting, with impressionism. It may be objected that the viewer has always found himself in front of 'descriptions', in front of optical and sound-images, and nothing more. But this is not the point. For the characters themselves reacted to situations; even when one of them found himself reduced to helplessness, bound and gagged, as a result of the ups and downs of the action. What the viewer perceived therefore was a sensory-motor image in which he took a greater or lesser part by identification with the characters. Hitchcock had begun the inversion of this point of view by including the viewer in the film. But it is now that the identification is actually inverted: the character has become a kind of viewer. He shifts, runs and becomes animated in vain, the situation he is in outstrips his motor capacities on all sides, and makes him see and hear what is no longer subject to the rules of a response or an action. He records rather than reacts. He is prey to a vision, pursued by it or pursuing it, rather than engaged in an action. Visconti's *Obsession* rightly stands as the forerunner of neo-realism; and what first strikes the viewer is the way in which the black-clad heroine is possessed by an almost hallucinatory sensuality. She is closer to a visionary, a sleepwalker, than to a seductress or a lover (similarly, later, the Countess in *Senso*).

In Volume 1 the crisis of the action-image was defined by a number of characteristics: the form of the trip/ballad, the multiplication of clichés, the events that hardly concern those they happen to, in short the slackening of the sensory-motor connections. All these characteristics were important but only in the sense of preliminary conditions. They made possible, but did not yet constitute, the new image. What constitutes this is the purely optical and sound situation which takes the place of the faltering sensory-motor situations. The role of the child in neo-realism has been pointed out, notably in De Sica (and later in France with Truffaut); this is because, in the adult world, the child is affected by a certain motor helplessness, but one which makes him all the more capable of seeing and hearing. Similarly, if everyday banality is so important, it is because, being subject to sensory-motor schemata which are automatic and preestablished, it is all the more liable, on the least disturbance of equilibrium between stimulus and response (as in the scene with the little maid in *Umberto D*), suddenly to free itself from the laws of this schema and reveal itself in a visual and sound nakedness, crudeness and brutality which make it unbearable, giving it the pace of a dream or a nightmare. There is, therefore, a necessary passage from the crisis of image-action to the pure optical-sound image. Sometimes it is an evolution from one aspect to the other: beginning with trip/ballad films [*films de bal(l)ade*] with the sensory-motor connections slackened, and then reaching purely optical and sound situations. Sometimes the two coexist in the same film like two levels, the first of which serves merely as a melodic line for the second.

It is in this sense that Visconti, Antonioni and Fellini are definitely part of neo-realism, in spite of all their differences, *Obsession*, the forerunner, is not merely one of the versions of a famous American thriller, or the transposition of this novel to the plain of the Po. In Visconti's film, we witness a very subtle change, the beginnings of a mutation of the general notion of situation. In the old realism or on the model of the action-image, objects and settings already had a reality of their own, but it was a functional reality, strictly determined by the demands of the situation, even if these demands were as much poetic as dramatic (for instance, the emotional value of objects in Kazan). The situation was, then, directly extended into action and passion. After *Obsession*, however, something appears that continues to develop in Visconti: objects and settings [*milieux*] take on an autonomous, material reality which gives them an importance in themselves. It is therefore essential that not only the viewer but the protagonists invest the settings and the objects with their gaze, that they see and hear the things and the people, in order for action or passion to be born, erupting in a pre-existing daily life. Hence the arrival of the hero of *Obsession*, who takes a kind of visual possession of the inn, or, in *Rocco and his Brothers*, the arrival of the family who, with all their eyes and ears, try to take in the huge station and the unknown city: this will be a constant theme in Visconti's work, this 'inventory' of a setting – its objects, furniture, tools, etc. So the situation is not extended directly into action: it is no longer sensory-motor, as in realism, but primarily optical and of sound, invested by the senses, before action takes shape in it, and uses or confronts its elements. Everything remains real in this neo-realism (whether it is film set or exteriors) but, between the reality of the setting and that of the action, it is no longer a motor extension which is established, but rather a dreamlike connection through the intermediary of the liberated sense organs. It is as if the action floats in the situation, rather than bringing it to a conclusion or strengthening it. This is the source of Visconti's visionary aestheticism. And *The Earth Trembles* confirms these new parameters in a singular way. Of course the fishermen's situation, the struggle they are engaged in, and the birth of a class consciousness are revealed in this first episode, the only one that Visconti completed. But this embryonic 'communist consciousness' here depends less on a struggle with nature and between men than on a grand vision of man and nature, of their perceptible and sensual unity, from which the 'rich' are excluded and which constitutes the hope of the revolution, beyond the setbacks of the floating action: a Marxist romanticism.

In Antonioni, from his first great work, *Story of a Love Affair*, the police investigation, instead of proceeding by flashback, transforms the actions into optical and sound descriptions, whilst the tale itself is transformed into actions which are dislocated in time (the episode where the maid talks while repeating her tired gestures, or the famous scene with the lifts). And Antonioni's art will continue to evolve in two directions: an astonishing development of the idle periods of everyday banality; then, starting with *The Eclipse*, a treatment of limit-situations which pushes them to the point of dehumanized landscapes, of emptied spaces that might be seen as having absorbed characters and actions, retaining only a geophysical description, an abstract inventory of them. As for Fellini, from his earliest films, it is not simply the spectacle which tends to overflow the real, it is the everyday which continually organizes itself into a travelling spectacle, and the sensory-motor linkages which give way to a succession of *varieties* subject to their own laws of passage. Barthélemy Amengual produces a formula which is true for the first half of this work: 'The real becomes spectacle or spectacular, and fascinates for being the real thing ... The everyday is identified with the spectacular ... Fellini achieves the deliberate confusion of the real and the spectacle' by denying the heterogeneity of the two worlds, by effacing not only distance, but the distinction between the spectator and the spectacle.

The optical and sound situations of neo-realism contrast with the strong sensory-motor situations of traditional realism. The space of a sensory-motor situation is a setting which is already specified and presupposes an action which discloses it, or prompts a reaction which adapts to or modifies it. But a purely optical or sound situation becomes established in what we might call 'any-space-whatever', whether disconnected, or emptied (we find the passage from one to the other in *The Eclipse*, where the disconnected bits of space lived by the heroine – stock exchange, Africa, air terminal – are reunited at the end in an empty space which blends into the white surface). In neo-realism, the sensory-motor connections are now valid only by virtue of the upsets that affect, loosen, unbalance, or uncouple them: the crisis of the action-image. No longer being induced by an action, any more than it is extended into one, the optical and sound situation is, therefore, neither an index nor a synsign. There is a new breed of signs, *opsigns* and *sonsigns*. And clearly these new signs refer to very varied images – sometimes everyday banality, sometimes exceptional or limit-circumstances – but, above all, subjective images, memories of childhood, sound and visual dreams or fantasies, where the character does not act without seeing himself acting, complicit viewer of the role he himself is playing, in the style of Fellini. Sometimes, as in Antonioni, they are objective images, in the manner of a *report*, even if this is a report of an accident, defined by a geometrical frame which now allows only the existence of relations of mea-surement and distance between its elements, persons and objects, this time transforming the action into displacement of figures in space (for instance, the search for the vanished woman in *The Adventure*). It is in this sense that the critical objectivism of Antonioni may be contrasted with the knowing sub-jectivism of Fellini. There would be, then, two kinds of opsigns, reports [*constats*] and 'instats', the former giving a vision with depth, at a distance, tending towards abstraction, the other a close, flat-on vision inducing involve-ment. This opposition corresponds in some respects to the alternative as defined by Worringer: abstraction or *Einfühlung*. Antonioni's aesthetic visions are inseparable from an objective critique (we are sick with Eros, because Eros is himself objectively sick: what has love become that a man or a woman should emerge from it so disabled, pitiful and suffering, and act and react as badly at the beginning as at the end, in a corrupt society?), whilst Fellini's visions are inseparable from an 'empathy', a subjective sympathy (embrace even that decadence which means that one loves only in dreams or in recollec-tion, sympathize with those kinds of love, be an accomplice of decadence, and even provoke it, in order to save something, perhaps, as far as is possible ...). On both sides these are higher, more important, problems than commonplaces about solitude and incommunicability.

The distinctions, on one hand between the banal and the extreme, and on the other between the subjective and the objective, have some value, but only relatively. They are valid for an image or a sequence, but not for the whole. They are still valid in relation to the action-image, which they bring into question, but already they are no longer wholly valid in relation to the new image that is coming into being. They mark poles between which there is continual passage. In fact, the most banal or everyday situations release accumulated 'dead forces' equal to the life force of a limit-situation (thus, in De Sica's *Umberto D*, the sequence where the old man examines himself and thinks he has fever). In addition, the idle periods in Antonioni do not merely show the banalities of daily life, they reap the consequences or the effect of a remarkable event which is reported only through itself without being explained (the break-up of a couple, the sudden disappearance of a woman ...). The method of report in Antonioni always has this function of bringing idle periods and empty spaces together: drawing all the consequences from a decisive past experience, once it is done and everything has been said. 'When everything has been said, when the main scene seems over, there is what comes afterwards ...'

As for the distinction between subjective and objective, it also tends to lose its importance, to the extent that the optical situation or visual description replaces the motor action. We run in fact into a principle of indeterminability, of indiscernibility: we no longer know what is imaginary or real, physical or mental, in the situation, not because they are confused, but because we do not have to know and there is no longer even a place from which to ask. It is as if the real and the imaginary were running after each other, as if each was being reflected in the other, around a point of indiscernibility. We will return to this point, but, already, when Robbe-Grillet provides his great theory of descriptions, he begins by defining a traditional 'realist' description: it is that which presupposes the independence of its object, and hence proposes a discernibility of the real and the imaginary (they can become confused, but none the less by right they remain distinct). Neo-realist description in the *nouveau roman* is completely different: since it *replaces* its own object, on the one hand it erases or *destroys* its reality which passes into the imaginary, but on the other hand it powerfully brings out all the reality which the imaginary or the mental *create* through speech and vision. The imaginary and the real became indiscernible. Robbe-Grillet will become more and more conscious of this in his reflection on the *nouveau roman* and the cinema: the most objectivist determinants do not prevent their realizing a 'total subjectivity'. This is what was embryonic from the start of Italian neo-realism, and what makes Labarthe remark that *Last Year in Marienbad* is the last of the great neo-realist films.

We can already see in Fellini that a particular image is clearly subjective, mental, a recollection or fantasy – but it is not organized into a spectacle without becoming objective, without going behind the scenes, into 'the reality of the spectacle, of those who make it, who live from it, who are absorbed in it': the mental world of a character is so filled up by other proliferating characters that it becomes inter-mental, and through flattening of perspectives ends 'in a neutral, impersonal vision ... all our world' (hence the importance of the telepath in 8½). Conversely, in Antonioni, it is as if the most objective images are not formed without becoming mental, and going into a strange, invisible subjectivity. It is not merely that the method of report has to be applied to feelings as they exist in a society, and to draw from them such consequences as are internally developed in characters: Eros sick is a story of feelings which go from the objective to the subjective, and are internalized in everyone. In this respect, Antonioni is much closer to Nietzsche than to Marx; he is the only contemporary author to have taken up the Nietzschean project of a real critique of morality, and this thanks to a 'symptomatologist' method. But, from yet another point of view, it is noticeable that Antonioni's objective images, which impersonally follow a becoming, that is, a development of consequences in a story [récit], none the less are subject to rapid breaks, interpolations and 'infinitesimal injections of a temporality': for example, the lift scene in *Story of a Love Affair*. We are returned once more to the first form of the any-space-whatever: disconnected space. The connection of the parts of space is not given, because it can come about only from the subjective point of view of a character who is, nevertheless, absent, or has even disappeared, not simply out of frame, but passed into the void. In *The Outcry*, Irma is not only the obsessive, subjective thought of the hero who runs away to forget, but the imaginary gaze under which this flight takes place and connects its own segments: a gaze which becomes real again at the moment of death. And above all in *The Adventure*, the vanished woman causes an indeterminable gaze to weigh on the couple – which gives them the continual feeling of being spied on, and which explains the lack of co-ordination of their objective movements, when they flee whilst pretending to look for her. Again in *Identification of a Woman*, the whole quest or investigation takes place under the presumed gaze of the departed woman, concerning whom we will not know, in the marvellous images at the end, whether or not she has seen the hero curled up in the lift cage. The imaginary gaze makes the real something imaginary, at the same time as it in turn becomes real and gives us back some reality. It is like a circuit which exchanges, corrects, selects and sends us off again. From *The Eclipse* onwards, the any-space-whatever had achieved a second form: empty or deserted space. What happened is that, from one result to the next, the characters were objectively emptied: they are suffering less from the absence of another than from their absence from themselves (for example, *The Passenger*). Hence, this space refers back again to the lost gaze of the being who is absent from the world as much as from himself, and, as Ollier says in a phrase which is true for the whole of Antonioni's work, replaces 'traditional drama with a kind of *optical drama* lived by the character'.

In short, pure optical and sound situations can have two poles – objective and subjective, real and imaginary, physical and mental. But they give rise to opsigns and sonsigns, which bring the poles into continual contact, and which, in one direction or the other, guarantee passages and conversions, tending towards a point of indiscernibility (and not of confusion). Such a system of exchange between the imaginary and the real appears fully in Visconti's *White Nights*.

The French new wave cannot be defined unless we try to see how it has retraced the path of Italian neo-realism for its own purposes – even if it meant going in other directions as well. In fact, the new wave, on a first approxima-tion, takes up the previous route again: from a loosening of the sensory-motor link (the stroll or wandering, the ballad, the events which concern no one, etc.), to the rise of optical and sound situations. Here again, a cinema of seeing replaces action. If Tati belongs to the new wave, it is because, after two ballad-films, he fully isolates what was taking shape in these – a burlesque whose impetus comes from purely optical and, in particular, sound, situations. Godard begins with some extraordinary ballads, from *Breathless* to *Pierrot le fou*, and tends to draw out of them a whole world of opsigns and sonsigns which already constitute the new image (in *Pierrot le fou*, the passage from the sensory-motor loosening, 'I dunno what to do', to the pure poem sung and danced, 'the line of your hips'). And these images, touching or terrible, take on an ever greater autonomy after *Made in USA*; which may be summed up as follows: 'A witness providing us with a series of reports with neither conclusion nor logical connection . . . without really effective reactions.' Claude Ollier says that, with *Made in USA*, the violently hallucinatory character of Godard's work is affirmed for itself, in an art of description which is always being renewed and always replacing its object. This descriptive objectivism is just as critical and even didactic, sustaining a series of films, from *Two or Three Things I Know about Her*, to *Slow Motion*, where reflection is not simply focused on the content of the image but on its form, its means and functions, its falsifica-tions and creativities, on the relations within it between the sound dimension and the optical. Godard has little patience with or sympathy for fantasies: *Slow Motion* will show us the decomposition of a sexual fantasy into its separate, objective elements, visual, and then of sound. But this objectivism never loses its aesthetic force. Initially serving a politics of the image, the aesthetic force is powerfully brought out for its own sake in *Passion*: the free build-up of pictorial and musical images as *tableaux vivants*, whilst at the other end the sensory-motor linkages are beset by inhibitions (the stuttering of the female worker and the boss's cough). *Passion*, in this sense, brings to its greatest intensity what was already taking shape in *Le Mépris*, when we witnessed the sensory-motor fail-ure of the couple in the traditional drama, at the same time as the optical representation of the drama of Ulysses and the gaze of the gods, with Fritz Lang as the intercessor, was soaring upwards. Throughout all these films, there is a creative evolution which is that of a visionary Godard.

For Rivette, *Le pont du Nord* has exactly the same perfection of provisional summary as *Passion* for Godard. It is the ballad of two strange women strollers to whom a grand vision of the stone lions of Paris will present pure optical and sound situations, in a kind of malicious snakes and ladders where they replay the hallucinatory drama of Don Quixote. But, from the same starting-point, Rivette and Godard seem to mark out the two contrasting sides. This is because, with Rivette, the break in the sensory-motor situations – to the benefit of optical and sound situations – is connected to a knowing subjectivism, an empathy, which most frequently works through fantasies, memories, or pseudo-memories, and finds in them a unique gaiety and lightness (*Celine and Julie Go Boating* is certainly one of the greatest French comic films, along with the work of Tati). Whilst Godard drew inspiration from the strip cartoon at its most cruel and cutting, Rivette clothes his unchanging theme of an international conspiracy in an atmosphere of fable and children's games. Already in *Paris Belongs to Us*, the stroll culminates in a twilight fantasy where the cityscape has no reality or connections other than those given by our dream. And *Celine and Julie Go Boating*, after the stroll-pursuit of the girl with a double, has us witness the pure spectacle of her fantasy, a young girl whose life is threatened in a family novel. The double, or rather the woman double [*la double*], is herself present with the aid of magic sweets; then, thanks to the alchemical potion, she introduces herself into the spectacle which no longer has viewers, but only behind the scenes, and finally saves the child from her appointed fate as a little boat takes her off into the distance: there is no more cheerful a fairy-tale. *Twilight* does not even have to get us into the spectacle; the heroines of the spectacle, the solar woman and the lunar woman, who have already passed into the real, under the sign of the magic stone track down, make disappear or kill the surviving characters who would still be capable of being witnesses.

Rivette could be said to be the most French of the new wave authors. But 'French' here has nothing to do with what has been called the French quality. It is rather in the sense of the pre-war French school, when it discovers, following the painter Delaunay, that there is no struggle between light and darkness (expressionism), but an alternation and duel of the sun and the moon, which are both light, one constituting a circular, continuous movement of complementary colours, the other a faster and uneven movement of jarring, iridescent colours, the two together making up and projecting an eternal mirage on to the earth. This is the case with *Twilight*. This is the case with *Merry-go-round*, where the description made of light and colours constantly begins again in order to obliterate its objects. Rivette takes this to the highest level in his art of light. All his heroines are daughters of fire, all his work is under this sign. In the end, if he is the most French of film-makers, it is in the sense that Gérard de Nerval could be called the supreme French poet, could even be called the 'Good Gerard', singer of the Ile de France, just like Rivette, singer of Paris and its rustic streets. When Proust asks himself what there is behind all these names that were applied to Nerval, he replies that in fact it is some of the greatest poetry that there has been in the world, and madness itself or the mirage to which Nerval succumbed. For, if Nerval needs to see, and to walk in the Valois, he needs this like some reality which has to 'verify' his hallucinatory vision, to the point where we no longer have any idea what is present or past, mental or physical. He needs the Ile de France as the real that his speech and his vision create, as the objective in his pure subjectivity: a 'dream lightning', a 'bluish and purple atmosphere', solar and lunar. The same goes for Rivette and his need of Paris. Here again, we have to conclude that the difference between the objective and the subjective has only a provisional, relative value, from the point of view of the optical-sound image. The most subjective, the knowing subjectivism of Rivette, is utterly objective, because it creates the real through the force of visual description. And conversely what is most objective, Godard's critical objectivism, was already completely subjective, because in place of the real object it put visual description, and made it go 'inside' the person or object (*Two or Three Things I know about Her*). On both sides, description tends towards a point of indiscernibility of the real and the imaginary.

A final question: why does the collapse of traditional sensory-motor situations, in the form these had in the old realism or in the action-image, allow only pure optical and sound situations, opsigns and sonsigns, to emerge? It will be noted that Robbe-Grillet, at least at the beginning of his reflections, was even harsher: he renounced not merely the tactile, but even sounds and colours as inept for the report, too tied to emotions and reactions, and he kept only visual descriptions which operated through lines, surfaces and sizes. The cinema was one of the causes of his evolution, because it made him discover the descriptive power of colour and sounds, as these replace, obliterate and re-create the object itself. But, even more, it is the tactile which can constitute a pure sensory image, on condition that the hand relinquishes its prehensile and motor functions to content itself with a pure touching. In Herzog, we witness an extraordinary effort to present to the view specifically tactile images which characterize the situation of 'defenceless' beings, and unite with the grand visions of those suffering from hallucinations. But it is Bresson, in a quite different way, who makes touch an object of view in itself. Bresson's visual space is fragmented and disconnected, but its parts have, step by step, a manual continuity. The hand, then, takes on a role in the image which goes infinitely beyond the sensory-motor demands of the action, which takes the place of the face itself for the purpose of affects, and which, in the area of perception, becomes the mode of construction of a space which is adequate to the decisions of the spirit. Thus, in *Pickpocket*, it is the hands of the three accomplices which connect the parts of space in the Gare de Lyon, not exactly through their seizing an object, but through brushing it, arresting it in its movement, giving it another direction, passing it on and making it circulate in this space. The hand doubles its prehensile function (of object) by a connective function (of space); but, from that moment, it is the whole eye which doubles its optical function by a specifically 'grabbing' [*haptique*] one, if we follow Riegl's formula for indicating a touching which is specific to the gaze. In Bresson, opsigns and sonsigns cannot be separated from genuine tactisigns which perhaps regulate their relations (this is the originality of Bresson's any-space-whatevers).

2

Although he was subject, from the outset, to the influence of certain American authors, Ozu built up in a Japanese context a body of work which was the first to develop pure optical and sound situations (even so he came quite late to the talkie, in 1936). The Europeans did not imitate him, but came back to him later via their own methods. He none the less remains the inventor of opsigns and sonsigns. The work borrows a trip/ballad [bal(l)ade] form, train journey, taxi ride, bus trip, a journey by bicycle or on foot: the grandparents' return journey from the provinces to Tokyo, the girl's last holiday with her mother, an old man's jaunt ... But the object is everyday banality taken as family life in the Japanese house. Camera movements take place less and less frequently: tracking shots are slow, low 'blocs of movement'; the always low camera is usually fixed, frontal or at an unchanging angle: dissolves are abandoned in favour of the simple *cut*. What might appear to be a return to 'primitive cinema' is just as much the elaboration of an astonishingly temperate modern style: the montage-cut, which will dominate modern cinema, is a purely optical passage or punctuation between images, working directly, sacrificing all synthetic effects. The sound is also affected, since the montage-cut may culminate in the 'one shot, one line' procedure borrowed from American cinema. But there, for instance, in Lubitsch, it was a matter of an action-image functioning as an index, whereas Ozu modifies the meaning of the procedure, which now shows the absence of plot: the action-image disappears in favour of the purely visual image of what a character *is*, and the sound image of what he *says*, completely banal nature and conservation constituting the essentials of the script (this is why the only things that count are the choice of actors according to their physical and moral appearance, and the establishment of any dialogue whatever, apparently without a precise subject-matter.

It is clear that this method immediately presents idle periods, and leads to their increase in the course of the film. Of course, as the film proceeds, it might be thought that the idle periods are no longer important simply for themselves but recoup the effect of something important: the shot or the line would, on this view, be extended by a quite long silence or emptiness. But it is definitely not the case, with Ozu, that we get the remarkable *and* the ordinary, limit-situations *and* banal ones, the former having an effect on, or purposely insinuating themselves into, the latter. We cannot follow Paul Schrader when he contrasts, like two phases, 'the everyday' on one hand and, on the other, 'the moment of decision', 'the disparity', which introduce an inexplicable break or emotion into daily banality. This distinction would seem strictly more valid for neo-realism. In Ozu, everything is ordinary or banal, even death and the dead who are the object of a natural forgetting. The famous scenes of sudden tears (that of the father in *An Autumn Afternoon* who starts to weep silently after his daughter's wedding, that of the daughter in *Late Spring* who half smiles as she looks at her sleeping father, then finds herself on the verge of tears, that of the daughter in *Dernier caprice* who makes a sharp comment about her dead father, then bursts into tears) do not mark out a strong period which might be contrasted with the weak periods in the flow of life, and there is no reason to suggest the emergence of a repressed emotion as 'decisive action'.

The philosopher Leibniz (who was not unaware of the existence of the Chinese philosophers) showed that the world is made up of series which are composed and which converge in a very regular way, according to ordinary laws. However, the series and sequences are apparent to us only in small sections, and in a disrupted or mixed-up order, so that we believe in breaks, disparities and discrepancies as in things that are out of the ordinary. Maurice Leblanc wrote a very good serial which comes close to a Zen kind of wisdom: the hero, Balthazar, 'professor of everyday philosophy', teaches that there is nothing remarkable or exceptional in life, that the oddest adventures are easily explained, and that everything is made up of ordinary things. It is just that we have to admit that, because the linkages of the terms in the series are naturally weak, they are constantly upset and do not appear in order. An ordinary term goes out of sequence, and emerges in the middle of another sequence of ordinary things in relation to which it takes on the appearance of a strong moment, a remarkable or complex point. It is men who upset the regularity of series, the continuity of the universe. There is a time for life, a time for death, a time for the mother, a time for the daughter, but men mix them up, make them appear in disorder, set them up in conflicts. This is Ozu's thinking: life is simple, and man never stops complicating it by 'disturbing still water' (as in the three companions in *Late Autumn*). And if, after the war, Ozu's work does not at all fall into the decline that has sometimes been suggested, it is because the post-war period helps confirm this thinking, but by renewing it, by reinforcing and going beyond the theme of conflicting generations: American ordinariness helps break down what is ordinary about Japan, a clash of two everyday realities which is even expressed in colour, when Coca-Cola red or plastic yellow violently interrupt the series of washed-out, unemphatic tones of Japanese life. And, as the character says in *The Flavour of Green Tea over Rice*: what if the opposite had occurred, if saki, samisen and geisha wigs had suddenly been introduced into the everyday banality of Americans ... ? On this point it seems to us that nature does not, as Schrader believes, intervene in a decisive moment or in a clear break with everyday man. The splendour of nature, of a snow-covered mountain, tells us one thing only: everything is ordinary and regular, everything is everyday! Nature is happy to renew what man has broken, she restores what man sees shattered. And, when a character emerges for a moment from a family conflict or a wake to contemplate the snow-covered mountain, it is as if he were seeking to restore to order the series upset in his house but reinstated by an unchanging, regular nature, as in an equation that provides us with the reason for apparent breaks, 'for the turns and returns, the highs and the lows', as Leibniz puts it.

Daily life allows only weak sensory-motor connections to survive, and replaces the action-image by pure optical and sound images, opsigns and sonsigns. In Ozu, there is no universal line which connects moments of decision, and links the dead to the living, as in Mizoguchi; nor is there any breathing space or encompasser to contain a profound question, as in Kurosawa. Ozu's spaces are raised to the state of any-space-whatevers, whether by disconnection, or vacuity (here again Ozu may be considered one of the first inventors). The false continuity of gaze, of direction and even of the position of objects are constant and systematic. One case of camera movement gives a good example of disconnection: in *Early Summer*, the heroine goes forward on tiptoe to surprise someone in a restaurant, the camera drawing back in order to keep her in the centre of the frame; then the camera goes forward to a corridor, but this corridor is no longer in the restaurant, it is in the house of the heroine who has already returned home. As for the empty spaces, without characters or movement, they are interiors emptied of their occupants, deserted exteriors or landscapes in nature. In Ozu they take on an autonomy which they do not immediately possess even in neo-realism, which accords them an apparent value which is relative (in relation to a story) or consequential (once the action is done with). They reach the absolute, as instances of pure contemplation, and immediately bring about the identity of the mental and the physical, the real and the imaginary, the subject and the object, the world and the I. They correspond in part to what Schrader calls 'cases of stasis', Noël Burch 'pillow-shots', Richie 'still lifes'. The question is to know whether there is not all the same a distinction to be made at the centre of this category itself.

Between an empty space or landscape and a still life properly so called there are certainly many similarities, shared functions and imperceptible transitions. But it is not the same thing; a still life cannot be confused with a landscape. An empty space owes its importance above all to the absence of a possible content, whilst the still life is defined by the presence and composition of objects which are wrapped up in themselves or become their own container: as in the long shot of the vase almost at the end of *Late Spring*. Such objects are not necessarily surrounded by a void, but may allow characters to live and speak in a certain soft focus, like the still life with vase and fruit in *The Woman of Tokyo*, or the one with fruit and golf-clubs in *What Did the Lady Forget?* It is like Cézanne, the landscapes – empty or with gaps – do not have the same principles of composition as the full still lifes. There comes a point when one hesitates between the two, so completely can their functions overlap each other and so subtle are the transitions that can be made: for instance, in Ozu, the marvellous composition with the bottle and the lighthouse, at the beginning of *A Story of Floating Weeds*. The distinction is none the less that of the empty and the full, which brings into play all the nuances or relations in Chinese and Japanese thought, as two aspects of contemplation. If empty spaces, interiors or exteriors, constitute purely optical (and sound) situations, still lifes are the reverse, the correlate.

The vase in *Late Spring* is interposed between the daughter's half smile and the beginning of her tears. There is becoming, change, passage. But the form of what changes does not itself change, does not pass on. This is time, time itself, 'a little time in its pure state': a direct time-image, which gives what changes the unchanging form in which the change is produced. The night that changes into day, or the reverse, recalls a still life on which light falls, either fading or getting stronger (*That Night's Wife, Passing Fancy*). The still life is time, for everything that changes is in time, but time does not itself change, it could itself change only in another time, indefinitely. At the point where the cinematographic image most directly confronts the photo, it also becomes most radically distinct from it. Ozu's still lifes endure, have a duration, over ten seconds of the vase: this duration of the vase is precisely the representation of that which endures, through the succession of changing states. A bicycle may also endure; that is, represent the unchanging form of that which moves, so long as it is at rest, motionless, stood against the wall (*A Story of Floating Weeds*). The bicycle, the vase and the still lifes are the pure and direct images of time. Each is time, on each occasion, under various conditions of that which changes in time. Time is the full, that is, the unalterable form filled by change. Time is 'the visual reserve of events in their appropriateness'. Antonioni spoke of 'the horizon of events', but noted that in the West the word has a double meaning, man's banal horizon and an inaccessible and always receding cosmological horizon. Hence the division of western cinema into European humanism and American science fiction. He suggested that it is not the same for the Japanese, who are hardly interested in science fiction: one and the same horizon links the cosmic to the everyday, the durable to the changing, one single and identical time as the unchanging form of that which changes. It is in this way that nature or stasis was defined, according to Schrader, as the form that links the everyday in 'something unified and permanent'. There is no need at all to call on a transcendence. In everyday banality, the action-image and even the move-ment-image tend to disappear in favour of pure optical situations, but these reveal connections of a new type, which are no longer sensory-motor and which bring the emancipated senses into direct relation with time and thought. This is the very special extension of the opsign: to make time and thought perceptible, to make them visible and of sound.

8

IMAGING

Teresa de Lauretis

Cinema has been studied as an apparatus of representation, an image machine developed to construct images or visions of social reality and the spectators' place in it. But, insofar as cinema is directly implicated in the production and reproduction of meanings, values, and ideology in *both* sociality and subjectivity, it should be better understood as a signifying practice, a work of semiosis: a work that produces effects of meaning and perception, self-images and subject positions for all those involved, makers and viewers; and thus a semiotic process in which the subject is continually engaged, represented, and inscribed in ideology. The latter emphasis is quite consonant with the present concerns of theoretical feminism in its effort to articulate the relations of the female subject to ideology, representation, practice, and its need to reconceptualize women's position in the symbolic. But the current theories of the subject – Kristeva's as well as Lacan's – pose very serious difficulties for feminist theory. Part of the problem, as I have suggested, lies in their derivation from, and overwhelming dependence on, linguistics. It may well be, then, that part of the solution is to start elsewhere, which is not to say that we should ignore or discard a useful concept like signifying practice, but rather to propose that we rejoin it from another critical path.

If feminists have been so insistently engaged in practices of cinema, as film makers, critics, and theorists, it is because there the stakes are especially high. The representation of woman as image (spectacle, object to be looked at,

From: Teresa de Laurentis, 'Imaging', in *Alice Doesn't: Feminism, Semiotics, Cinema* (Macmillan, 1984).

vision of beauty – and the concurrent representation of the female body as the *locus* of sexuality, site of visual pleasure, or lure of the gaze) is so pervasive in our culture, well before and beyond the institution of cinema, that it necessarily constitutes a starting point for any understanding of sexual difference and its ideological effects in the construction of social subjects, its presence in all forms of subjectivity. Moreover, in our "civilization of the image," as Barthes has called it, cinema works most effectively as an *imaging* machine, which by producing images (of women or not of women) also tends to reproduce woman as image. The stakes for women in cinema, therefore, are very high, and our intervention most important at the theoretical level, if we are to obtain a conceptually rigorous and politically useful grasp of the processes of imaging. In the context of the discussion of iconic signification, the feminist critique of representation has raised many questions that require critical attention and further elaboration. In very general terms, what are the conditions of presence of the image in cinema and film? And vice versa, what are the conditions of presence of cinema and film in imaging, in the production of a social imaginary?

More specifically, what is at stake, for film theory and for feminism, in the notion of "images of women," "negative" images (literally, *clichés*), or the alternative, "positive" images? The notion circulates widely and has acquired currency in private conversations as well as institutional discourses from film criticism to media shop talk, from academic courses in women's studies to scholarly conferences and special journal issues. Such discussions of images of women rely on an often crude opposition of positive and negative, which is not only uncomfortably close to popular stereotypes such as the good guys versus the bad guys, or the nice girl versus the bad woman, but also contains a less obvious and more risky implication. For it assumes that images are directly absorbed by the viewers, that each image is immediately readable and meaningful in and of itself, regardless of its context or of the circumstances of its production, circulation, and reception. Viewers, in turn, are presumed to be at once historically innocent and purely receptive, as if they too existed in the world immune from other social practices and discourses, yet immediately susceptible to images, to a certain power of iconism, its truth or reality effect. But this is not the case. And it is precisely the feminist critique of representation that has conclusively demonstrated how any image in our culture – let alone any image of woman – is placed within, and read from, the encompassing context of patriarchal ideologies, whose values and effects are social and subjective, aesthetic and affective, and obviously permeate the entire social fabric and hence all social subjects, women as well as men. Thus, since the historical innocence of women is no longer a tenable critical category for feminism, we should rather think of images as (potentially) productive of contradictions in both subjective and social processes. This proposition leads to a second set of questions: by what processes do images on the screen produce imaging on and off screen, articulate meaning and desire, for the spectators? How are images perceived? How do we *see?* How do we attribute meaning to what we see? And do those meanings remain linked to images? What about language? Or sound? What relations do language and sound bear to images? Do we image as well as imagine, or are they the same thing? And then again we must ask: what historical factors intervene in imaging? (Historical factors might include social discourses, genre codification, audience expectations, but also unconscious production, memory, and fantasy.) Finally, what are the "productive relations" of imaging in filmmaking and filmviewing, or spectatorship – productive of what? productive how?

These questions are by no means exhaustive of the intricate problematic of imaging. Moreover, they demand consideration of several areas of theoretical discourse that are indispensable in the study of cinematic signification and representation: semiotics, psychoanalysis, ideology, reception and perception theories. In the following pages I will discuss some points at issue in the theoretical accounts of the image given by semiotics and by recent studies of perception; and in so doing I will attempt to outline the notion of imaging more precisely as the process of the articulation of meaning to images, the engagement of subjectivity in that process, and thus the mapping of a social vision into subjectivity.

PROEMIUM

It is customary to begin such epic tales with a classical verse as propitiatory invocation. Therefore: in the beginning was the word. In its earlier stages semiology was developed in the wake of Saussurian linguistics as a conceptual, analytical framework to study sign systems – or better, to study a certain functioning of certain elements, called signs, in the social production of meaning. In the Saussurian account, the system of language is defined by a double articulation of its elementary units, its signs, the smallest meaningful units of language (morphemes, roughly corresponding to words). The first articulation is the combination, linking, or sequential ordering of morphemes into sentences according to the rules of morphology and syntax; the second articulation is the combination of certain distinctive units, sounds in themselves meaningless (the phonemes), into significant units, into signs, according to the rules established by phonology. Each sign, said Saussure, is constituted by an arbitrary or conventional (socially established) bond between a *sound-image* and a *concept*, a signifier and a signified. Note that from the very beginning in semiology the idea of image, of representation, is associated with the signifier, not with the signified, which is defined as "concept." This may be partly responsible for the disregard in which the signified (hence meaning) was held. If we were to call the signified "a mental image," thereby associating meaning with representation rather than with the purely conceptual, we would have, I think, a better sense of the complexity of the sign. For representation (verbal, visual, aural) is in both components of the sign; better still, representation *is* the sign-function, the social work of the sign.

The Saussurian account prompted the assumption that analogous operations were at work in nonverbal sign systems – systems composed of images, gestures, sounds, objects – and the representational apparati utilizing them, such as painting, advertising, the cinema, the theatre, dance, music, architecture. If the first thorough semiological investigations of cinema yielded the result that no exact parallelism, no homology with verbal language could be drawn, nonetheless semiotics has continued to be concerned with the modes and conditions of iconic coding, the rules of visual communication. So it may be useful to retrace something of the history of semiotics from the debate around cinematic articulation, which took place during the mid-sixties around the *Mostra del nuovo cinema* in Pesaro, Italy (also known as the Pesaro Film Festival), and practically set off the semiological analysis of cinema.

CINEMATIC ARTICULATION AND ICONICITY

The debate on articulation in the early years of semiology seemed to crystallize around an opposition between linguistic signs and iconic signs, between verbal language and visual images. Their difference was thought to be inherent in two irreducible modes of perception, signification, and communication: verbal language appeared to be mediated, coded, symbolic, whereas iconism was assumed to be immediate, natural, directly linked to reality. Cinema was at the very center of this theoretical storm, for its status as a semiotic system (a language, as it was then assumed any semiotic system would be) depended on the possibility of determining an articulation, preferably a double articulation, for the cinematic signs. Although a narrow linguistic notion of articulation has proved to be something of a theoretical liability and is no longer adequate to the concerns of film theory, the questions "what is cinematic articulation, how is cinema articulated, what does it articulate?" are still very much at issue. Hence it is important to review the terms of the argument and to follow its development over the years.

According to Metz's first paper on the topic, "Le cinéma: langue ou language?" (1964), taking a position which he later revised, cinema can only be described as a language without a code or language-system ("un langage sans langue"), for it lacks altogether the second articulation (at the phonemic level). Though meaningful, cinematic images cannot be defined as signs in the Saussurian sense, because they are motivated and analogical rather than arbitrary or conventional, and because each image is not generated by a code with a series of fixed rules and (largely unconscious) operations, as a word or a sentence is. The cinematic image is instead a unique, a one-time-only, combination of elements that cannot be catalogued, as words can be, in lexicons or dictionaries. Saussure had said that language is a storehouse of signs, from which all speakers equally draw. But no such thing could be claimed for cinema; for the images it puts together, there is no paradigm, no storehouse. In the cinematic image, concluded Metz, meaning is released naturally from the total signifier without recourse to a code.

Pasolini, on the other hand, maintained that cinema was a language with a double articulation, though different from verbal language and in fact more like written language, whose minimal units were the various objects in the frame or shot (*inquadratura*); these he called *cinémi*, "cinemes," by analogy with *fonemi*, *phonemes*. The cinemes combine into larger units, the shots, which are the basic significant units of cinema, corresponding to the morphemes of verbal language. In this way, for Pasolini, cinema articulates reality precisely by means of its second articulation: the selection and combination of real, profilmic objects or events (faces, landscapes, gestures, etc.) in each shot. It is these profilmic and pre-filmic events or objects in reality (*"oggetti, forme o atti della realtà"* – and hence already *cultural* objects) that constitute the paradigm of cinema, its storehouse of significant images, of image-signs (*im-segni*).

Yet, contended Eco, another participant in the debate, the objects in the frame do not have the same status as the phonemes of verbal language. Even leaving aside the problem of the qualitative difference between objects and their photographic image (a difference central to semiotics, for the real object, the referent, is neither the signified nor the signifier but "the material precondition of any coding process"), the objects in a frame are already meaningful units, thus more like morphemes. In fact, within the idea of cinema as a system of signs, the cinematic code could be better described as having not two (as for Pasolini), nor one (as for Metz), but three articulations, which Eco designates as follows. He calls *seme* (semantic nucleus, meaningful unit) each recognizable shape (Pasolini's "object"); each seme is made up of smaller *iconic signs* such as /nose/ or /eye/; each iconic sign can be further analyzed in *figurae* (e.g., angles, curves, light-dark effects, etc.) whose value is not semantic but positional and oppositional, like the phonemes'. The iconic signs (nose, eye, street) would thus be formed from a paradigm of possible iconic *figurae* (angles, curves, light); and this would be the third articulation. In turn the iconic signs would combine into a seme (human figure, landscape), the second articulation. Finally, the combination of semes into a frame would constitute the first articulation. But the process does not stop there. Not only do semes combine to form a frame, but, given that cinema is pictures in motion, a further combination takes place in the projected film, in the passage from frame (or photogram) to shot. Here each iconic sign and each iconic seme generates what kinesics calls *cinemorphs*, i.e., significant units of movement, gestural units. If, continues Eco, kinesics finds difficulty in identifying the non-meaningful units, the *figurae*, of a gesture (the equivalent of phonemes), cinema does not: it is the specific property of the camera that allows cinema to break down the unity of perceived movement, the gestural continuum, into discrete units which in themselves are not significant. It is precisely the motion picture camera that provides a way to analyze kinesic signs in their non-meaningful, differential units, something of which human natural perception is incapable.

Eco's line of reasoning is correct enough, but then a further distinction must be made. The breakdown of movement into photograms is still mechanically imposed, no less than it was in, say, futurist paintings. The "units of movement" are established by the speed of the camera, they are not discrete units in the gesture itself, whereas phonemes are distinguishable and in finite number in language. Then, since cinema depends on the objects whose imprint the light rays inscribe on the film stock, one would also need to distinguish between the articulation of *real* movement (the movement of the objects, studied by kinesics), cinematic movement (the movement of the frames effected by the pull-down mechanism in the camera or the blades of the projector shutter), and apparent movement or motion (perceived by the viewer). And here semiotics must rejoin the study of visual and motion perception.

But let us assume with Eco that cinema, considered as a sign system (independently, that is, of a viewing situation and actually considered merely as image-track), does have a triple articulation. This assumption would explain, for instance, the greater perceptual richness we experience – the so-called impression of reality – and our conviction that cinema is better equipped than verbal language to transmit, capture, or express that reality; it would also account for, as he notes, the various metaphysics of cinema. The question then is: even assuming that we may correctly speak of a triple articulation of the cinematic signs, is it worthwhile to do so? The notion of articulation is an analytical notion, whose usefulness rests on its ability to account for the phenomenon (language, cinema) economically, to account for a maximum of events with a minimum of combinable units. Now the "phenomenon," the events of cinema are not the photogram, the still image, but at the very least the shot (cf. Pasolini's emphasis on *inquadratura*), images in motion which construct not only linear movement but also a depth, an accumulation of time and space that is essential to the meaning, the reading of the image(s). At the conclusion of this phase of the debate Eco admitted that, if cinema as a language can be said to possess a triple articulation, film as discourse is constructed on, and puts into play, many other codes – verbal, iconographic, stylistic, perceptual, narrative. Therefore, he himself remarked, "honesty requires that we ask ourselves whether the notion of triple articulation itself is not possibly complicit with a *semiotic* metaphysics."

With the shift from the notion of language to the notion of discourse began to appear the limitations, theoretical and ideological, of the early semiological analyses. First, the determination of an articulated code (be it a single, double, or triple articulation), even if possible, would offer neither an ontological nor an epistemological guarantee of the event, of what cinema is – to cite the title of Bazin's famous book. For indeed, as Stephen Heath observes, one never encounters "cinema" or "language," but only practices of language, or practices of cinema. And this, I will suggest, is what Pasolini was attempting, unsuccessfully, to formulate: the idea of cinema as a signifying practice, not cinema as system. Second, that notion of articulation, concerned as it was with minimal units and the homogeneity of the theoretical object, and "vitiated [in Pasolini's phrase] by the linguistic mould," was predicated on an imaginary, if not metaphysical, unity of cinema as system, independent, that is, of a viewing situation. Thus it tended to hide or make non-pertinent the other components of the signifying process; for example, to hide the fact that cinematic signification and signification in general are not systemic but rather discursive processes, that they not only engage and overlay multiple codes, but also involve distinct communicative situations, particular conditions of reception, enunciation, and address, and thus, crucially, the notion of spectatorship – the positioning of spectators in and by the film, in and by cinema.

In short, spectators are not, as it were, either in the film text *or* simply outside the film text; rather, we might say, they intersect the film as they are intersected by cinema. Therefore, it is the usefulness of that notion of iconic and cinematic articulation, and its pretension to provide the proper semiotic definition of the phenomenon cinema, that must be challenged.

This said, however, iconicity – the articulation of meanings to images – does remain an issue for semiotics and for film theory. It should not be too quickly cast aside as irrelevant, false, or superseded, for at least two reasons. On one front, it is important to pursue the question of iconic representation and its productive terms in the relations of meaning as a sort of theoretical resistance: one should not meekly yield to the current trend in semiotics toward an increasing grammatization of discursive and textual operations, toward, that is, logico-mathematical formalization. On another front, it continues to be necessary to reclaim iconicity, the visual component of meaning (including above all visual pleasure and the attendant questions of identification and subjectivity), not so much *from* the domain of the natural or *from* an immediacy of referential reality, as *for* the ideological; to wrench the visual from its vision, as it were, or, as Metz might say, to reclaim the imaginary of the image for the symbolic of cinema.

This is no simple task. For even as most forms of visual communication have become accepted as conventional (coded), our idea of what constitutes "reality" has changed. The paradox of live TV, our "window to the world," is that reality is only accessible as televised, as what is captured by an action camera. The paradox of current Hollywood cinema is that reality must surpass in visual fascination the horrors of, say, Carpenter's *Halloween* or Romero's *Dawn of the Dead*, must be fantasm-agoria, revel-ation, apocalypse here and now. The problem is, the very terms of the reality-illusion dichotomy have been displaced. Thus it is not by chance that all the nature-culture thresholds are being thematized and transgressed in recent movies: incest, life/death (vampires, zombies, and other living dead), human/non-human (aliens, clones, demon seeds, pods, fogs, etc.), and sexual difference (androgyns, transsexuals, transvestites, or transylvanians). Boundaries are very much in question, and the old rites of passage no longer avail. Cinema itself can no longer be the mirror of a reality unmediated, pristine, originary, since industrial technology has forfeited our claim in the earth, now lost to us through ecological disaster. Yet technology alone can simulate the Edenic plenitude of nature and remember it for us.

Think of the pastoral landscape unfolding in full color, bathed in the stereophonic sound of Beethoven's Sixth, on the wide screen of the death chamber in *Soylent Green*, the ambiguous title barely hiding a most gruesome irony. The film commemorates at once that loss of Eden and its own loss of innocence, the earlier innocent belief in cinema's perfect capacity to reproduce Eden's perfection, to render reality in its fullness and beauty. But elegy itself is simulated in today's cinema, where reality is hyperreality, not only coded but *absolutely* coded, not merely artificial, artful, made-up, masqueraded, tranvested or perverted, but permanently so, like the vision of its viewers, irreversibly transformed. The eyes of Tommy/David Bowie in *The Man Who Fell to Earth* are an apt metacinematic metaphor for both this elegy of cinema and the glorification of its artfulness, its immense power of vision.

Cinema's hyperreality, its total simulation – as Baudrillard would say – as precisely, conspicuously *image*, visually and aurally constructed, and represented as such (think of Truffaut playing the xylophone in *Close Encounter of the Third Kind*, or the canned Muzak and soft pastels of *American Gigolo*). And language becomes more and more incidental, as music used to be in silent cinema, often simply redundant or vaguely evocative, allusive, mythical. The hollow men of Eliot hyper-recited by Kurz/Brando in *Apocalypse Now*, the operatic arias in Bertolucci's *Luna*, serve solely to allude, refer to – not engage – a symbolic order, an abstract code; not to engage the code of opera in all its cultural, historical weight as Visconti does in *Senso*, or in its narrative, thematic, and rhythmic closure as Potter does in *Thriller*, as Rainer does in *Film About a Woman Who* .... The opera in *Luna* and myth in Coppola's *Golden Bough* are codes no longer intelligible. But it doesn't matter. What matters is once again the spectacle, as in the earliest days of cinema. Contradiction, paradox, ambiguity in the image as well as in the textualized overlay of sound, language, and image no longer produce distancing effects by baring the device of cinema and thus inducing rationality and consciousness. *They are the spectacle*, the no longer simple but excessive, "perverse" pleasure of current cinema.

In short, cinema's imaging, its complex iconicity, its textual overlay of visual, aural, linguistic, and other coding processes continues to be a crucial problem. And since the old polarity natural-conventional has been displaced, not only in film or semiotic theory, but in the social imaginary through the reality effect produced by the social technology that is cinema, I propose that the question of imaging – the articulation of meaning to image, language, and sound, and the viewer's subjective engagement in that process – must be reformulated in terms that are themselves to be elaborated, recast, or posed anew. Where shall we look for clues or ideas? My present inclination is to go back and read again, think through some of the notions we have taken for granted or perhaps disposed of prematurely. Indeed semiotics, too, has moved along these lines, to some extent, toward the analysis of reading processes and text pragmatics. Eco's own critique of iconism, by displacing the notion of articulation as well as the classical notion of sign to a much less central position in his theory of semiotics, provides a starting point.

Eco's critique of the so-called iconic signs, which he only outlined at the time of the Pesaro debate, has been more fully developed in *A Theory of Semiotics*. There he argues that iconism in fact covers many semiotic procedures, "is a collection of phenomena bundled together under an all-purpose label (just as in the Dark Ages the word 'plague' probably covered a lot of different diseases)" (p. 216). Thus the difference between the image of a dog and the word /dog/ is not the "trivial" difference between iconic (motivated by similarity) and arbitrary (or "symbolic") signs. "It is rather a matter of a complex and continuously gradated array of different modes of producing signs and texts, every sign-function (sign-unit or text) being in turn the result of many of these modes of production" (p. 190), every sign-function being in fact a text. Even if in a given iconic continuum, an image, one can isolate pertinent discrete units or *figurae*, as soon as they are detected, they seem to dissolve again. In other words, these "pseudo-features" cannot be organized into a system of rigid differences, and their positional as well as semantic values vary according to the coding rules instituted each time by the context. In studying iconic signification one sees "the classical notion of sign dissolve into a highly complex network of changing relationships" (p. 49). The very notion of sign, he emphasizes, becomes "untenable" when equated with the notion of significant elementary *units* and *fixed* correlations. Finally, Eco concludes, there is no such thing as an iconic sign; there are only visual texts, whose pertinent units are established, *if at all*, by the context. And it is the code, a purposefully established correlation between expressive and semantic units, that "decides on what level of complexity it will single out its own pertinent features" (p. 235).

The key concepts here are context, pertinence, and purposefulness (of the codes). The context establishes the pertinence of the units, of what counts or functions as a sign in an iconic text for a certain communicational act, a particular "reading." And the purposefulness of the codes, which is embedded in any practice of signification as a condition of communication, determines the level of complexity of the particular communicational act, that is to say, of what and how much one sees or "reads" in an image. Obviously, the definition of context is crucial. While the purpose of the code is not intended by Eco as idiosyncratic motive or individual intentionality (codes are socially and culturally established and usually work, not unlike linguistic structures, below the conscious awareness of the viewers), nevertheless it is possible to link purposefulness to subjectivity. Eco himself speaks of particular communicational acts which establish new codes, and calls them inventions or aesthetic texts, thus admitting the possibility of a subjective purposefulness, such as an artist's creativity, for at least some instances of code-making. The notion of context, however, is more restrictively defined as co-text, as everything that is included within the frame of the picture, so to speak. And although he does take into account the work of intertextuality in the reading of the image, intertextuality too is understood literally, as the relay to other images or other texts; it does not stretch to encompass nontextualized discourses, discursive formations, or other heterogeneous social practices, which however must be assumed to inform the viewer's subjective processes.

The importance, but also the insufficiency of this notion of context for my present concern, imaging, is apparent. Insofar as the notion is applicable to film spectators, it does not admit the possibility of a different reading of the filmic images by, say, women and men; it does not account, that is, for gender or other social factors that overdetermine the engagement of subjectivity in the semiotic process of spectatorship. In light of the developments within semiotics and especially of Eco's critique of iconism, it is interesting to reread Pasolini's essays on cinema, written in the mid-sixties and at the time quickly dismissed as un-semiotic, theoretically unsophisticated, or even reactionary. Ironically, from where we now stand, his views on the relation of cinema to reality appear to have addressed perhaps the central issues of cinematic theory. In particular, his observation that cinematic images inscribe reality as representation and his insistence on the "audio-visuality" of cinema (what I call the articulation of meaning to images, language, and sound) bear directly on the role that cinema's imaging has in the production of social reality.

Pasolini's often quoted slogan, "cinema is the language of reality," was in part provocatively outrageous, in part very earnestly asserted. To be exact, the words he used (it is the title of his best known essay on cinema) were "cinema is the *written language of reality*." This he explained as follows: the invention of the alphabet and the technology of writing revolutionized society by "revealing" language to men (men, this is also the word he used), making them conscious of spoken language as representation; previously, thought and speech must have appeared as natural, whereas written language *instituted a cultural consciousness of thought as representation*. In the same way cinema is a kind of "writing" (*scrittura, écriture*) of reality, in that it permits the conscious representation of human action; hence cinema is "the written language of action," or "the written language of reality". For Pasolini, human action, human intervention in the real, is the first and foremost expression of men, their primary "language"; primary not (or not just) in the sense of originary or prehistoric, but primary to the extent that it encompasses all other "languages" – verbal, gestural, iconic, musical, etc. In this sense he says, what Lenin has left us – the transformation of social structures and their cultural consequences – is "a great poem of action."

Another statement: cinema, like poetry (poetic writing, as a practice of language), is "translinguistic." It encodes human action in a grammar, a set of conventions, a vehicle; but as soon as it is perceived, heard, received by a reader/spectator, the convention is discarded and action (reality) is "recreated as a dynamics of feelings, affects, passions, ideas" in that reader/spectator. Thus in living, in practical existence, in our actions, "we represent ourselves, we perform ourselves. Human reality is this double representation in which we are at once actors and spectators: a gigantic happening, if you will." Cinema, then, is the recorded, stored, "written" moment of a "natural and total language, which is our action in the real."

It is easy to see why Pasolini's arguments could have been so easily dismissed. He himself, only half-jokingly, asked: "What horrible sins are crouching in my philosophy?" and named the "monstrous" juxtaposition of irrationalism and pragmatism, religion and action, and other "fascist" aspects of our civilization (p. 240). Let me suggest, however, that an unconventional, less literal or narrow reading of Pasolini's pronouncements (for such they undoubtedly were), one that would accept his provocations and work on the contradictions of his "heretical empiricism," could be very helpful in resisting, if not countering, the more subtle seduction of a logico-semiotic humanism.

This is not the place for an extensive reading of essays, articles, screenplay notations, interventions and interviews spanning nearly a decade; or for a reassessment of the originality of his insights with regard to, for example, the function of montage as "negative duration" in the construction of a "physio-psychological" continuity for the spectator or the qualities of "physicality" (*fisicalità*) and *oniricità*, the dreamlike state film induces in the spectator – insights which he tried to couch in the terms of the theoretical discourse of semiology (and they did not fit) but which, several years later, recast in psycho-analytic terms, were to become central to film theory's concern with visual pleasure, spectatorship, and the complex nexus of imaging and meaning that Metz was to locate in the "imaginary signifier." That relation of image and language in cinema, wrote Pasolini in 1965, is *in* the film and *before* the film; it is to be sought in "a complex nexus of *significant images* [imaginary signifiers?] which *pre-figures* cinematic communication and acts *as its instrumental foundation*." What Pasolini touches upon here is possibly one of the most important and most difficult problems confronting cinematic theory and iconic, as well as verbal, signification: the question of inner speech – of forms of "imageist, sensual, pre-logical thinking" already suggested by Eikhenbaum and Eisemstein in the twenties about the relation of language to sensory perception, of what Freud called word-presentation and thing presentation in the interplay of primary and secondary processes. A question that, clearly, could not be answered by semiology – but through no fault, no limitation, of Pasolini's – and has been more recently and fruitfully addressed by Paul Willemen.

I will take up just a few other points with regard to Pasolini. First, he imagines cinema as the conscious representation of social practice (he calls it action, reality – reality as human practice). This is exactly, and explicitly, what many independent filmmakers are in fact doing or trying to do today. Pasolini, of course, speaks as a film maker – *en poète*, as he said. He is concerned with film as expression, with the practice of cinema as the occasion of a direct encounter with reality, not merely personal, and yet subjective. He is not specifically taking on, as others are, cinema as institution, as a social technology which produces or reproduces meanings, values, and images *for* the spectators. But he is keenly aware, nevertheless, in the passages I quoted and elsewhere, that cinema's writing, its representation of human action, institutes "a cultural consciousness" of that encounter with reality. That is why he says – and this is my second point – that cinema, like poetry, is *trans*linguistic: it exceeds the moment of the inscription, the technical apparatus, to become "a dynamics of feelings, affects, passions, ideas" in the moment of reception. Cinema and poetry, that is, are not languages (grammars, articulatory mechanisms), but discourses and practices of language, modes of representing – signifying practices, we would say; he said "the written language of pragma." The emphasis on the subjective in three of the four terms, "feelings, affects, passions, ideas," cannot be construed as an emphasis on the merely "personal," that is to say, an individual's existential or idiosyncratic response to the film. On the contrary, it points to the current notion of spectatorship as a site of productive relations, of the engagement of subjectivity in meaning, values, and imaging. It therefore suggests that the subjective processes which cinema instigates are "culturally conscious," that cinema's binding of fantasy to images institutes, *for* the spectator, forms of subjectivity which are themselves, unequivocally, social.

One could go on recontextualizing, intertextualizing, overtextualizing Pasolini's "extravagant" statements. But I must go back to semiotics, where it all started – not only my reading of Pasolini's text but also the theoretical discourse on cinema through which I have been reading it. Pasolini's use of semiology, aberrant as it might have seemed, was in fact prophetic. The notion of *im-segno* proposed in the 1965 essays "*Il cinema di poesia*" and "*La sceneggiatura come 'struttura chevuol essere altra struttura'*" is much closer to Eco's notion of sign-function than anyone would have suspected, way back then. And so is Pasolini's attempt to define the "reader's collaboration" in the *sceno-testo*, the screenplay as text-in-movement, as diachronic structure or structure-in-process – another of his scandalous contradictions, yet no longer so if we compare it with Eco's recent reformulation of the notion of open text. As for the question of cinematic articulation and iconism, the *context* of cinema, as Pasolini outlines it, the context which makes certain "features" pertinent and thus produces meaning and subjectivity, is not only a discursive context or a textual co-text (linguistic or iconic), as Eco defines it; it is the context of social practice, that human action which cinematic representation articulates and inscribes from both sides of the screen, so to speak, for both filmmakers and spectators as subjects in history.

[...]

MAPPING

According to physiologist Colin Blakemore, our apparently unified view of the outside world is in fact produced by the interconnected operations of diverse neural processes. Not only are there different kinds of neuron or nerve cells in the brain and in the retina (the retina, the photosensitive layer at the back of the eye, is actually part of the cortex, composed of the same tissue and nerve cells); and not only do those nerve cells have different functions (for example, "the main function of the nucleus is not to process visual information by transform-ing the messages from the eyes, but to filter the signals, depending on the activity of the other sense organs"); but each neuron responds to a specific responsive field, and its action is inhibited or excited by the action of other, adjacent cortical cells. Different parts of the retina project through the optic nerves to different parts of the visual cortex and of the brain stem (the superior colliculus, in the lower part of the brain), producing two maps of the visual world or rather a discontinuous map in which are represented certain features of objects (edges and shapes, position, orientation). In other words, these interacting processes do not merely *record* a unified or preconstituted visual space, but actually constitute a discontinuous *map* of the external world. "Map" is the term used by Blakemore: the activity of the optical and cortical cells constitutes, he says, "a mapping of visual space on to the substance of the brain" (p. 14).

The perceptual apparatus, then, does not copy reality but symbolizes it. This is supported by the fact that "unnatural" stimulations of the retina or cortex (surgical, electrical, or manual) produce visual sensations; hence the familiar comic book truth that a blow on the head makes one see stars. This happens because "the brain always assumes that a message from a particular sense organ is the result of the *expected* form of stimulation" (p. 17). The term "expected" here implies that perception works by a set of learned responses, a cognitive pattern, a code; and further, that the principle of organization or combination of sensory input is a kind of inference (it has been called "unconscious infer-ence"). The perceptual apparatus, moreover, is subject to adaptation or cali-bration, for expectations are readjusted on the basis of new stimuli or occurrences. Finally, perception is not merely patterned response but active anticipation. In the words of R. L. Gregory, perception is "predictive": "the study of perception shows that nothing is seen as 'directly' as supposed in common sense." To perceive is to make a continuous series of educated guesses, on the basis of prior knowledges and expectations, however unconscious.

The term "mapping," interestingly enough, is also used by Eco to define the process of semiosis, sign-making, the production of signs and meanings (with-out, to the best of my knowledge, any intended reference to Blakemore or psychophysiology). Mapping, for Eco, is the transformation of percepts into semantic units into expressions, a transformation that occurs by transferring – mapping – certain pertinent elements (features that have been recognized as pertinent) from one material continuum to another. The particular rules of articulation, the conditions of reproducibility or of invention, and the physical labor involved are the other parameters to be taken into account in Eco's classification of what he calls the modes of sign production. Eco's view of sign production, especially of the mode he calls invention, associating it with art and creativity, is from the perspective of the *maker* – the speaker, the artist, the producer of signs; it stems from his background in classical aesthetics as well as marxism.

Inventions are radically different because, by establishing new codes, they are capable of transforming both the representation and the perception of reality, and thus eventually can change social reality. The perceptual model, on the contrary, is focused on the spectator, so to speak, rather than the film maker. While Eco's model requires that, in order to change the world, one must produce new signs, which in turn will produce new codes and different meanings or social values, the other model says nothing about purposeful activity and rather stresses adaptation to external events. But that adaptation is nonetheless a kind of production – of sensation, cognition, memory, an ordering and distribution of energy, a constant activity for survival, pleasure, self-maintenance.

The notion of mapping common to these two models implies that perception and signification are neither direct or simple reproduction (copy, mimesis, reflection) nor inevitably predetermined by biology, anatomy, or destiny; though they are socially determined and overdetermined. Put another way, what is called reproduction – as women well know – is never simply natural or simply technical, never spontaneous, automatic, without labor, without pain, without desire, without the engagement of subjectivity. This is the case even for those signs that Eco calls replicas, strictly coded signs for which the code is ready-made and neither requires nor allows invention. Since replicas, like all other signs, are always produced in a communicational context, their (re)pro-duction is still embedded in a speech act; it always occurs within a process of enunciation and address that requires the mapping of other elements or the making pertinent of other features, and that also involves memory, expecta-tions, decisions, pain, desire – in short, the whole discontinuous history of the subject. If, then, subjectivity is engaged in semiosis at all levels, not just in visual pleasure but in all cognitive processes, in turn semiosis (coded expectations, patterns of response, assumptions, inferences, predictions, and, I would add, fantasy) is at work in sensory perception, inscribed in the body – the human body and the film body. Finally, the notion of mapping suggests an ongoing but discontinuous process of perceiving-representing-meaning (I like to call it "imaging") that is neither linguistic (discrete, linear, syntagmatic, or arbitrary) nor iconic (analogical, paradigmatic, or motivated), but both, or perhaps neither. And in this imaging process are involved different codes and modalities of semiotic production, as well as the semiotic production of difference.

Difference. Inevitably that question comes back, we come back to the question of imaging difference, the question of feminism. Which is not, can no longer be, a matter of simple oppositions between negative and positive images, iconic and verbal signification, imaginary and symbolic processes, intuitive perception and intellectual cognition, and so forth. Nor can it be simply a matter of reversing the hierarchy of value which underlies each set, assigning dominance to one term over the other (as in the feminine-masculine or female-male dichotomies). The fundamental proposition of feminism, that the personal is political, urges the displacement of all such oppositional terms, the crossing and recharting of the space between them. No other course seems open if we are to reconceptualize the relations that bind the social to the subjective. If we take up the notion of mapping, for instance, and allow it to act as a foot-bridge across the two distinct theoretical fields of psychophysiology and semiotics, we can envision a connection, a pathway between spheres of material existence, perception, and semiosis, which are usually thought of as self-contained and incommensurable.

Much the same way as classical semiology opposed iconic and verbal signs, perception and signification are usually considered distinct processes, often indeed opposed to one another as pertaining respectively to the sphere of subjectivity (feeling, affectivity, fantasy, prelogical, pre-discursive, or primary processes) and to the sphere of sociality (rationality, communication, symbol-ization, or secondary processes). Very few manifestations of culture, notably Art, are thought to partake of both. And even when a cultural form, such as cinema, clearly traverses both spheres, their presumed incommensurability dictates that questions of perception, identification, pleasure, or displeasure be accounted for in terms of individual idiosyncratic response or personal taste, and hence not publicly discussed: while a film's social import, its ultimate meaning, or its aesthetic qualities may be grasped, shared, taught, or debated "objectively" in a generalized discourse. Thus, for example, even as the feminist critique of representation began with, and was developed from, the sheer displeasure of female spectators in the great majority of films, no other public discourse existed prior to it in which the question of displeasure in the "image" of woman (and the attendant difficulties of identification) could be addressed. Thus, whenever displeasure was expressed, it would be inevitably dismissed as an exaggerated, oversensitive, or hysterical reaction on the part of the indivi-dual woman. Such reactions appeared to violate the classic rule of aesthetic distance, and with it the artistic-social character of cinema, by an impingement of the subjective, the personal, the irrational. That the focus on "positive" images of woman is now another formula in both film criticism and filmmaking is a measure of the social legitimation of a certain feminist discourse, and the consequent viability of its commercial and ideological exploitation (witness the recent crop of films like *The French Lieutenant's Woman, Tess, Gloria, Nine to Five, Rich and Famous, Personal Best, Tootsie,* (etc.).

Feminist film theory, meanwhile, has gone well beyond the simple opposition of positive and negative images, and has indeed displaced the very terms of that opposition through a sustained critical attention to the hidden work of the apparatus. It has shown, for instance, how narrativity works to anchor images to non-contradictory points of identification, so that the "sexual difference" is ultimately reconfirmed and any ambiguity reconciled by narrative closure. The symptomatic reading of films as filmic texts has worked against such closure, seeking out the invisible subtext made of the gaps and excess in the narrative or visual texture of a film, and finding there, concurrent with the repression of the female's look, the signs of her elision from the text. Thus, it has been argued, it is the elision of woman that is represented in the film, rather than a positive or a negative image; and what the representation of woman *as* image, positive *or* negative, achieves is to deny women the status of subjects both on the screen and in the cinema. But even so an opposition is produced: the image and what the image hides (the elided woman), one visible and the other invisible, sound very much like a binary set. In short, we continue to face the difficulty of elaborating a new conceptual framework not founded on the dialectic logic of opposition, as all hegemonic discourses seem to be in Western culture. The notion of mapping and the theoretical bridge it sets up between perception and signification suggest a complex interaction and mutual implication, rather than opposition, between the spheres of subjectivity and sociality. It may be useful as a model, or at least a guiding concept in understanding the relations of imaging, the articulation of images to meanings in the cinema, as well as cinema's own role in mediating, binding, or indeed mapping the social into the subjective.

In what is now considered one of the most important texts of feminist film criticism, Laura Mulvey stated that an alternative, politically and aesthetically avant-garde cinema could only exist in counterpoint to mainstream film as analysis, subversion, and total negation of Hollywood's pleasurable obsessions and its ideological manipulation of visual pleasure. "Unchallenged, mainstream film coded the erotic into the language of the dominant patriarchal order"; woman, inscribed in films as once the representation/image, is at once the support of male desire and of the filmic code, the look, that defines cinema itself.

The challenge to classical narrative cinema, the effort to invent "a new language of desire" for an "alternative" cinema, entails nothing short of the destruction of visual pleasure as we now know it. But if "intellectual unpleasure" is not the answer, as Mulvey well knows (and her films strive against that problem, too), it nevertheless seems the unavoidable consequent in a binary set whose first term is visual pleasure, when that set is part of a series of oppositional terms subsumed under categories of the type A and non-A: "mainstream" (Hollywood and derivatives) and "non-mainstream" (political-aesthetic avant-garde). The importance of Mulvey's essay, marking and summing up an intensely productive phase of feminist work with film, is not to be diminished by the limitations of its theoretical scope. Indeed the fact that it has not yet been superseded is a major argument for our continued engagement with its problematic and the questions it raises – or one, the impasse reached by a certain notion of political avant-garde, a notion which, like Godard's cinema, today retains its critical force only to the extent that we are willing to historicize it and to give it up as the paragon or absolute model of any radical cinema.

9

TOTALITY AS CONSPIRACY

Fredric Jameson

If everything means something else, then so does technology. It would be a mistake to reduce the menacing object-world of allegorical conspiracies to that first, fresh fear of spy systems and informants in the 1960s, when right-wingers discovered a whole new generation of just the right gadgets and someone was listening to you, but only to you personally. J. Edgar Hoover would make a most anachronistic mascot for late capitalism; while the anxieties about privacy seem to have diminished, in a situation in which its tendential erosion or even abolition has come to stand for nothing less than the end of civil society itself. It is as though we were training ourselves, in advance, for the stereotypical dystopian rigors of overpopulation in a world in which no one has a room of her own any more, or secrets anybody else cares about in the first place. But the variable that gears the rest, as always, is the more fundamental abstract category of property: here disclosing a fundamental transition from the private to the corporate, the latter unmasking the former and thereby problematizing the very juridical system on which it is itself constructed. How there could be private things, let alone privacy, in a situation in which almost everything around us is functionally inserted into larger institutional schemes and frameworks of all kinds, which nonetheless belong to *somebody* – this is now the nagging question that haunts the camera dollying around our various life-worlds, looking for a lost object the memory of which it cannot quite retain. Older aesthetics guide its fumbling attempts – old-fashioned interiors, and

From: Fredric Jameson, 'Totality as Conspiracy', in *The Geopolitical Aesthetic: Cinema and Space in the World System* (BFI, 1991).

equally old-fashioned nightmare spaces, ancient collectibles, nostalgia for handicrafts – in a situation in which the appropriate new habits have been unable to form and the antique stores (Balzac, *La Peau de chagrin*) have all disappeared. What has happened to the objects of our object-world is neither youth nor age, but their wholesale transformation into instruments of communication; and this now takes the place of the older surrealist metamorphoses, the oneiric city, the domestic space of the incredible shrinking man, or the horror of the organic of so much science fiction, where brushing against an inanimate object suddenly feels like being touched by someone's hand.

Yet in hindsight, and with the appropriate rewriting, all of that might have been an anticipation of this, whose fundamental precondition is the disappearance of nature as such. Once its eclipse is secured, oppositions like those between animate and inanimate are themselves relegated to a historical lumber room that looks less like a museum or a junk-shop than the place information goes when a word-processor is accidentally erased. Once plants have become machines – and even though not a breath of wind has ruffled the selfsame landscape equal to itself – every object changes and becomes a human sign (not unexpectedly drawing all the theories of language and sign systems after it). Now not the magical speaking beasts or the 'flowers that look back at you,' but the marching automata of *Blade Runner*'s last cavernous private apartment (Ridley Scott, 1982): these are anachronisms that overspring the present into the far future of android technology; and now all of our things, of whatever fabric and purpose, are inhabited by the possibility of becoming nasty dolls with needle teeth that bite (*Barbarella* [Roger Vadim, 1968]).

This is the intuition embodied by the new magic realism of Derek Jarman and Raoul Ruiz: that surrealism was both impossible and unnecessary, since in some other sense it was already real (such had been Alejo Carpentier's original formulation of the style in the preface to his *Kingdom of This World*, which he attributed to the uneven development of Latin America, but which now seems to belong to all of us). Even late Buñuel (*The Discreet Charm* [1972], *The Obscure Object* [1977]) is closer to this than to the heroic period of surrealist desire and Wagnerian longing: *L'Age d'or* (1930) remains a breathtaking relic from the age of gods and heroes, but it is no longer for us, since it would be comical to wish the social burden of bourgeois respectability and elaborate moral taboo back into existence merely to re-endow the sex drive with the value of a political act.

Nonsynchronicity was also the condition, in the surrealist Europe of the 20s, for the eruption of archaic moments of Spanish feudality, French medieval romance, or even Rousseau's state of nature itself, into an incompletely modernized present staffed by the grande and the petite bourgeoisie. All that seems to remain of such effects are the simulations of occult film, which accompany the so-called religious revival like its wish-fulfillment. In Jarman and Ruiz, however, the most 'surrealist' moments are those in which modern technological artifacts – a pocket computer, say, or a once mint roadster covered in dust and housed beneath the grand staircase – are inconspicuously planted among the Renaissance splendor of Roman prelates, their costumes and palaces (*Caravaggio*, 1986); but Buñuel's mumbling bishops turned to bones, leaving only their robes behind them on the rocky promontory where the city was to be founded. That flight into deep geological time takes a different direction from this particular future shock: indeed, insisting that his work has nothing in common with surrealism, Ruiz has cherished incongruities of the type exemplified by the shot in *Cleopatra* in which an airliner can be glimpsed in the distant sky above the togaed actors. This is no longer Breton's 'objective chance,' I think, but rather a Nietzschean affirmation that there is no past, and thus, finally, no time at all – something one often feels in Ruiz's films when this or that chance marker abruptly 'situates' their magical events in modern chronology once more.

Communicational and information technologies – the scientific machineries of reproduction rather than of production (which, however, then trail the latter in their wake and turn it inside out, as their misunderstood predecessor) – foreground and dramatize this transformation of the object-world like its material idea. But they themselves become magical only when grasped as the allegories of something else, of the whole unimaginable decentered global network itself. The new ingredients are already registered in the opening credits of *Three Days of the Condor* (Pollack, 1975), elegantly telexed in stylish computer graphics. Indeed, in postmodern film, the credits have become an inconspicuous yet crucial space in which the desired perceptual habits of a viewer are, as in the old musical modes, generically cued towards either techno- or deco-graphics, respectively.

The relationship between this technology and death itself is then inscribed in *Condor*'s opening sequence – the apparently mistaken liquidation of a whole bureau of minor espionage researchers and specialists – by the clacking of the word-processors among the silence of the sprawling corpses as the machines continue to affirm their mechanical existence and to go on producing 'text' in a haunting sonorous surcharge (which it is instructive to juxtapose with the organic menace of vaguely flapping wings and chicken scratches in the attic during the opening scenes of *The Exorcist* [Friedkin, 1973]).

But who says 'media' traditionally includes and encompasses transportation as well. Not the least beautiful and pertinent feature of the Pollack film is its incorporation of the great traffic networks: not merely the outsized bridges and highways of Manhattan, but also the New York – Washington shuttle in flight, and the dialectical extremes of the helicopter and the little truck, along with the residual insertion of the railway system that infers the other end of this spatial map somewhere in the snows of Vermont.

This X-ray of functional mediations in space was completed, as a kind of program, by John Schlesinger's *Marathon Man* (1976), a virtual anthology of types of space and climate, which suggests the totalizing vocation of such a geographical collection, often required as a kind of backing or after-image for

those narratives that set out to map the social totality in some more fundamental structural fashion.

It may, however, be convenient to take a masterwork of the older aesthetic,
Hitchcock's *North by Northwest*, as a genealogical precursor in this development. As its title suggests, the narrative grid of this film, which propels us from
one empty hotel room to another across continental North America, re-enacts
that empty outline of the forty-eight states that all good American citizens carry
like a logo etched into their mind's eye. From Mies' newly built Seagram
Building in Manhattan to a famous cornfield in Illinois, from the CIA headquarters in Washington, DC, to the balding stone crown of the figures of Mount
Rushmore and a cantilevered modern house on the Canadian border – indeed
on the very edge of the world itself (its planes taking off for the darkest Iron
Curtain) – this sequence makes moves in which the various landscapes emit
specific but complementary narrative messages, as though in a return at the very
end of modernity to the semiotic landscapes of those tribal or oral narratives
Lévi-Strauss de-crypted for us in such studies as *The Epic of Asdiwal*.

The frenzy of the pursuit, however – notoriously, in Hitchcock, motivated
only in the most perfunctory way by the espionage intrigue, but more basically
by the love triangle – lends this displacement something of the passion and the
value of the epistemological itself: wanting to grasp the beast itself, as Mailer
has said of that desire called The Great American Novel; covering all the ground
and all the bases in the distracted feeling that this gigantic *objet petit a* somehow
contains the very secrets of Being itself: comparable in that only to the desperate
ride, in Philip K. Dick's novel *Ubik* (1969), from a formerly La Guardia Airport
in New York City to a Des Moines, Iowa, funeral home, in which historical time
is relentlessly disintegrating around the hapless protagonist, jet planes of the
future downgraded to small bi-planes, high technology fading away as in a
dream, space enlarging ominously as the means of transport become ever more
primitive – the most brilliant of all Dick's nightmares, in which each incre-
mental progress back into time enlarges just ever so more slightly your distance
from your heart's desire.

Condor, however, deploys such geographical motifs as a mere signal of the
'intent to totalize'. As for its plot in some literary sense, the neatly tied themes
(Redford is a 'reader,' the CIA wargames are structurally connected and
opposed to the deciphering of codes in printed stories and novels) are trendily
inappropriate for its thriller context, and are thereby trivialized. Alongside this
ideational window-dressing, the concrete and more genuinely filmic and spatial
working through of these themes can be found in the descent into the interior of
the telephone central. Redford as informational mechanic and industrial worker is more interesting than as English major and intellectual, and the great
banks of switches and synapses recall again the ghostly proletarian content of
other contemporary films such as *Alien* (Scott, 1979), if not indeed of the heist
genre itself – always in one way or another an inscription of collective non-
alienated work that passes the censor by way of its rewriting in terms of crime

and sub-generic entertainment. Archetypal journeys back beyond the surface appearance of things are also here dimly reawakened, from antiquity and Dante all the way to Goffman's storefront/backroom, with its canonical form in Marx's great invitation to 'leave this noisy sphere, where everything takes place on the surface and in full view of everyone, and follow [the owner of money and the owner of labor-power] into the hidden abode of production, on whose threshold there hangs the notice 'No admittance except on business'. This promise of a deeper inside view is the hermeneutic content of the conspiracy thriller in general, although its spatialization in *Condor* seems somehow more alarming than the imaginary networks of the usual suspects: the representational confirmation that telephone cables and lines and their interchanges follow us everywhere, doubtling the streets and buildings of the visible social world with a secondary secret underground world, is a vivid, if paranoid, cognitive map, redeemed for once only by the possibility of turning the tables, when the hero is able to tap into the circuits and bug the buggers, abolishing space with his own kind of simultaneity by scrambling all the symptoms and producing his messages from all corners of the map at the same time.

But no matter how systematically reorganized and postmodernized, telephone technology is still marked as relatively old-fashioned or archaic within the new post-industrial landscape (we will find that representation seems to have demanded a similar regression in the technologies of *All the President's Men*). Whether representation can draw directly, in some new way, on the distinctive technology of capitalism's third stage, whose video- and computer-based furniture and object-world are markedly less photogenic than the media and transportation technology of the second (not excluding telephones), remains one of the great open questions of postmodern culture generally. Surely the newer spy novels, with their bewildering multiplication of secret or private espionage operations within public ones, their dizzying paper structures (more philosophically dematerialized and ideal than the stock market) turning on the facile but effective device of the double agent, so that whole teams of villains can be transformed into heroes at the flip of a switch – surely these go a certain way towards declaring at least the intent to construct a narrative which is in some way an *analogon* of and a stand-in for the unimaginable overdetermination of the computer itself. But in representations like these, the operative effect is confusion rather than articulation. It is at the point where we give up and are no longer able to remember which side the characters are on, and how they have been revealed to be hooked up with the other ones, that we have presumably grasped the deeper truth of the world system (certainly no one will have been astonished or enlightened to discover that the head of the CIA, the Vice President, the Secretary of State, or even the President himself, was secretly behind everything in the first place). Such confusions – which evidently have something to do with structural limits of memory – seem to mark a point of no return beyond which the human organism can no longer match the velocities or the demographies of the new world system. That the symptom betrays some deeper incapacity of the postmodern subject to process history itself can be argued from a variety of other, related, but less officially political, phenomena. One noted long ago, for example, in Ross MacDonald's oedipal detective stories, that it was growing harder and harder to keep the parental generation separate from that of the grandparents: the feeling is now endemic in a whole new generation of detective stories that betray the need to incorporate history.

In high literature, Pynchon comes to mind unavoidably as a body of writing which does not avoid the weaknesses in plot construction of the spy novel (although it negotiates them at a greater level of quality and intensity), but which is marked out for our purposes as a matter of a somewhat different kind of interest, as a space in which new cybernetic figures are forged and elaborated: static op-art afterimages spun off the bewildering rotation of just such cyber-plots. Kenneth Burke's narratological categories, in which *scene* is pressed into service as a form of *agency*, seem extraordinarily apt for those now distant but still hallucinatory 60s California moments in *The Crying of Lot 49* (1966), when the conspiracy of property development suddenly resonates with some well-nigh runic message.

[...]

But in this, far and away the most politically radical of Pynchon's texts, and a belatedly 60s anti-authoritarian attack on the Reagan decade, one wonders sometimes whether the stereotypical wiring that is the classic Pynchon inner form has not been reversed, so that the moments of fear are derived from what we already know about the Nixon/Reagan years and their internal conspiracies, rather than the other way round, projecting a fresh breath of hitherto unexperienced anxiety onto plots that seem as comically inept as they may be prophetic.

The structural alternative, then, to a situation in which technological objects are endowed with symbolic power by their narrative contexts, can be expected to lie in objects whose very function itself generates the narrative and produces the conspiracy in their own right, and in such a way that attention is diverted from their visual inadequacy. Those Japanese apartment buildings constructed like stacks of audio-cassettes can now no longer be inserted into the tape player of the macrocosm; but the media in *Blow Out* (de Palma, 1981) do not merely write their own check, they rewrite the world itself – or at least its soundtrack – and release as many alternate histories. The telltale sound of the assassin's rifle shot can be excised or replaced, while the 'true' or documentary soundtrack of a real murder can be spliced into a fictional horror film, so as not to let anything go to waste.

As its overt organizing allusion to Antonioni's *Blow-up* (1966) suggests, films like *Blow out*, or *The Conversation* (Coppola, 1974), are best grasped as moments in the historical process of postmodernization, in which the decisive modulation from the visual image to the auditory one is as fundamental as it is paradoxical, given the universal affinity of postmodern culture with visibility and spatiality. Perhaps, indeed, the very omnipresence of the visual commodity requires estrangement and the passage through a different sensory register, endowed with a discontinuous temporal logic more apt to frame its events and components. Meanwhile, the deeper tendency of the postmodern towards a separation and a co-existence of levels and sub-systems has everywhere – in film theory fully as much as in film practice – made for a keener sense of the semi-autonomy of sound and the requirement that it counterpoint sight rather than simply underscore it.

At any rate, although both *Blow Out* and *The Conversation* retain the referent around which Antonioni's film turned far more problematically (was there really a murder in the first place?), the shift from the visual to the auditory has the (very postmodern) effect of annulling Antonioni's Heideggerian and metaphysical dimension, since it can no longer offer some bewildering Bazinian field of Being for desperate inspection. Not unsurprisingly, this occultation of the 'question of Being' now leaves the text fungible and open to all the manipulations the corporate world can muster. The artist-photographer of the Antonioni film, who still secured the philosopher's art function although he earned a living by shooting fashion models, here gives way to technicians for sale to the highest bidder.

Significantly, both these newer films (*Blow Out*, *The Conversation*), share a key episode, which must now be considered autoreferential: namely, the destruction of the apparatus of reproduction itself – the return to the ransacked laboratory in which great spools of tape festoon the work-place in derision, like eviscerated entrails. This destruction, which fills or implodes space, is of a peculiar type, quite unlike some mute savagery visited on a single object or instrument (as at the end of Faulkner's *The Bear*). Here, not the value of the physical object – which it is a pity to see broken to pieces – but rather its literal and essential worthlessness, is foregrounded: the unreproducible work of art, denied its capacity for reproduction, and reduced to blank high-tech waste. It is clearly an obligatory *scène à faire* which emblematically underscores the lack of iconic force in the newer reproductive technology, in that sense quite unlike the great streamlined 'media objects' of high modernist production, such as the ocean liner or the airplane. In *Blow-up* it was the images themselves, the photographic icons, which were silently and tactfully removed; the physical mayhem here aims at the non-visual inessentiality of the vehicles of reproduction – TV console, cassettes, computer print-outs and the like – which sung the dirge for the human dead in *Three Days of the Condor* and which Pynchon tried to tease into some final plastic exceptionality in *The Crying of Lot 49*. Trashing the apparatus thus underscores the gap between form and content in such postmodern representations of totality, where neither the plot nor its unique new technological object-world can bear the freight and import of the conspiratorial ideologeme that was to have revealed, not merely this specific political secret, but the very secret of the world system itself.

It is a gap which rebukes the traditional claim of the works of high culture to take their content up into form in a seamless web, thereby showing up on their surface as the flaw in the crystal or the fly in the ointment. By the same token, it blocks out the representational privileges of low culture or trash in this respect, since it is very precisely that gap between form and content that must be the fundamental content – and also the form – of the conspiratorial allegory of late capitalist totality. The value-paradoxes of allegory – indeed of post-modernism itself – are then here endlessly replayed, where structural failure is a new kind of success in its own right, and what is worst about such art-works may also often be better than what is best about them.

These are also the paradoxes that account for the unique status of David Cronenberg's *Videodrome* (1983) within our paradigm, a film which owes its canonical, well-nigh classical position to its triumphant evasion of virtually all high cultural qualities, from technical perfection to the discriminations of taste and the organon of beauty. In it, the owner of a porno television channel in Toronto (James Woods), while exploring the possibility of acquiring genuine snuff films, discovers that the product in question (produced by an outfit called Videodrome) contains a subliminal signal that causes hallucinations and eventually fatal brain damage. This turns out to be a right-wing conspiracy against the degeneration of moral values for which pornography and television alike are held responsible. Woods' discovery then brings into view a counter-conspiracy of a more protelevision, religious type, in which the cathode ray is used as therapy and an instrument of regeneration. But by that time, the Philip K. Dick-like reality-loops and hallucinatory after-effects are so complex as to relieve the viewer of any further narrative responsibility, who can only passively witness the manipulation of the hapless James Woods by both sides, as he becomes assassin-avenger, duped suicidal victim and sacrifice all at once.

Here, a Western, commercial version of the Third-World political aesthetic of Cuban 'imperfect cinema' is deployed, and not only in the function of B-film generic signals (the shoestring horror film, and so on). In another place, I argued something pre-eminently relevant here, namely, that the ideologeme of elegance and glossiness, expensive form, in postmodernism, was also dialectically at one with its opposite number in sleaze, punk, trash and garbage art of all kinds. Meanwhile, in the spirit of the return to origins of much contemporary cinema (Godard's hand-held cameras, the quintessential plebeian archetype of the home movie), this production also re-enacts those more humble predecessors, which are, in *Videodrome*, pornography as such and snuff film 'in reality'. Here too, then, authenticity in the grain and in the camera work means a gradual approximation to the palpable grubbiness of the archetypal model, not exclud-ing a wonderfully garish and cheap color, and this deeper formal affinity is distinct from any passionate, ideological or religious, adherence to B-film status. Finally, the positioning of this film and its production in the world system is no mere external accident either; as we shall see, it marks the content and is thematized in its own right. But even in terms of a signal system, the

Canadian provenance of *Videodrome* (and of Cronenberg himself) marginalizes the work internally and assigns it a semi-peripheral resonance, particularly since it is not designed to exemplify some national (or at least English-Canadian) cultural production, even though its deeper ideological values (a horror of US pornography, for example) are very Canadian, or at least Torontonian, indeed.

Yet there is another reason why the new conspiratorial film in general cannot aspire to high aesthetic status. This has to do with the breakdown of the opposition between high art and mass culture generally in the postmodern, but more specifically with the waning of the prestige of the literary and of its older structures. We have already seen how in Pynchon the official ideas or intellectual themes were somehow drawn back inside the representation, so that a slogan like 'paranoia' is no longer of the same order as the 'ideas' debated by the characters of Dostoyevsky or Thomas Mann, or the hyperintellectual speculations of Proust or Musil. Rather such words themselves become a media object and a piece of commercial cultural junk which is embedded in the montage and assimilated to the content of the work rather than to its authorial intentions or its ideological messages. This discrediting of the 'literary,' and the assimilation to it of themes and ideas of the older type, is omnipresent in contemporary (Western) film production, which has triumphantly liquidated its high modernist moment – that of the great *auteurs* and their stylistic 'worlds' – and along with them the genuine 'philosophies' to which film-makers like Bergman and Welles, Hitchcock and Kurosawa, could palpably be seen to aspire.

Yet the outer shell of the older form is here preserved; and *Videodrome* carefully explains its 'themes' to us – the social perniciousness of television and mass culture generally, McLuhanite reflections on the physical changes and perceptual mutations involved in prolonged exposure to the new medium, even the old philosophical questions about the Good and whether the masses' cultural appetites automatically lead them to it. These are all serious issues, with long and distinguished traditions of philosophical speculation and debate behind them; but who would wish to argue that *Videodrome* represents a serious contribution to their development? Equally clearly, however, the film does not misrepresent them in any trendy or lowbrow way, although the viewer may sometimes be tempted to think of it as a tribute to one of Canada's greatest thinkers. My sense is that in the new dimensionality of postmodern cultural space, ideas of the thing like by-products and after-images flung up on the screen of the mind and of social production by the culturalization of daily life. The dissolution of philosophy today then reflects this modification in the status of ideas (and ideology), which itself retroactively unmasks any number of traditional philosophical 'concepts' as having been just such consciousness-symptoms all the while, that could not be identified as such in the culturally impoverished, pre-media, and residually 'natural' human societies (or modes of production) of the past. What is today called Theory is of course another sign of this momentous historical development, which, by rendering Culture absolute, has deeply problematized the vocation of any of its individual products, texts or works (if they can no longer 'mean' something or convey ideas or messages, even in the form of the 'theme' or the 'problem,' what new function can they claim?).

It is worth adding that the 'concepts' I have identified above in the text of *Videodrome* are all in one way or another 'media' concepts: perhaps then, it is only the unique family of concepts of that kind that can no longer achieve respectable philosophical abstraction? Or are we to draw the more somber conclusion that all abstract philosophical concepts were always 'media concepts' in some deeper way without our being aware of it? At any rate, the notion of cognitive mapping that underpins the present investigation hints at some new vocation for the postmodern cultural work, at the same time as it specifies the fundamental function of the 'media idea' in any successful act of social triangulation or cognitive mapping, an act which always seems (as in some new postmodern version of high modernist autoreferentiality) to include the representation of its own media system within itself.

But the crisis of an older literary thematics also brings distinct new formal advantages to a henceforth themeless film of this kind, which has of course covered its tracks by way of simple generic affiliation and its identification as a horror film. (*Videodrome* faithfully reproduces the pornographic rhythms of ever greater and more horrifying physical violence that reach their climax with the exploding – now android, *Alien*-type – body, and their characteristic melancholy after satiation in the final suicide.) What happens on the level of meanings, however, is that immense dedifferentiation of the traditional levels which has seemed to characterize so much else in contemporary society and culture and its theories. With the expansion of the former cultural sphere to encompass and include within itself everything else in social life (something that could also be thought of as an immense commodification and commercialization, the virtual completion of the process of the colonization by the commodity form begun in classical capitalism), it becomes impossible to say whether we are here dealing any longer with the specifically political, or with the cultural, or with the social, or with the economic – not to forget the sexual, the historical, the moral, and so on. But this conflation, which surely presents some signal disadvantages in the realm of thought and action, uniquely intensifies the signifying power of this work that, rotated on its axis, can be said to comment on any of the above, virtually inexhaustibly.

Is *Videodrome* not, for example, the story of the classical struggle between a small businessman and entrepreneur and a great faceless corporation? The owner of the small independent television Channel 83 (James Woods) is indeed eventually suborned by the gigantic optical corporation behind Videodrome, which seizes on its competitor and incorporates it into itself. The post-contemporary spin given to this traditional heroic narrative then clearly involves the tendential international monopolization of the media and the various local culture industries (not excluding the publishing houses). So we have here a fairly explicit economic reading of the text as a narrative about business and competition; and it is worth measuring the distance between this overt and explicit commercial content (which most viewers will however take as a secondary pretext for the rest) and that deepest allegorical impulse of all, which insists on grasping this feature as an articulated nightmare vision of how we as individuals feel within the new multinational world system. It is as though the narrowly economic had to be thematized and thereby marginalized, in order for the deeper socio-economic allegory to pass the censorship.

Meanwhile, a host of political readings also compete for the surface of the text, flickering in and out: the assassination sequence is clearly a topical one, with its manipulation of the hero as a fall guy (shades of Pakula's 1974 *Parallax View*). A residual atmosphere of global 60s and 70s politics also shrouds the narrative, with its Third World reaches, its terrorists and infiltrators, its revolutionary puritanism; indeed, the confusion of torture with sex makes it initially unclear whether we have to do with political executions or with S & M pornography in the first emissions of Videodrome, which seem to be coming from somewhere in Malaysia. The unchanging 'set' of the telecast features a clay wall of a most un-Western type, presumably electrified; while, reversing the issue for a moment, the characters observe that pornography as such – if that is what the Videodrome broadcasts are really supposed to be – is a political matter in many Third World countries and punishable by death.

When the correct source of the transmission is identified (it turns out to be Pittsburgh, even then becoming a movie capital), the implications of the revised reading are no less political, but clearly shift their ground. The Canadian undertheme of economic and cultural marginalization is still present in this selection of a non-central, semi-peripheral, formerly industrial US urban area (something like a sister city to Toronto in marginality). Indeed in Pittsburgh, as with the economically stagnant parts of Toronto shown here, the run-down downtown is associated with cultural trash, no doubt by way of peep-shows and X-rated book stores. (It is also worth recalling that Pittsburgh was the setting for George Romero's vampire film, *Martin* [1978], one of the most extraordinary achievements of the recent B- or horror-film revival.)

But the spatial margins also connote a different set of political interests, that might euphemistically be styled 'grass-roots'. These are the vigilante and paramilitary networks that flourish outside the urban centers, powered by narrow-minded moralisms of generally racist and gender varieties. So it is that Videodrome is at length revealed, as has already been said, as a moral-majority conspiracy which, revolted by the permissive immorality everywhere encouraged by the media in our societies, has set forth on an unusual campaign of extermination: a subliminal signal beamed through the pornographic emissions causes an incurable tumor, accompanied by hallucinations and reality-warps worthy of Philip K. Dick, and will eventually be used on the degenerate viewing public of the advanced countries. The political movement here, therefore, cuts across class lines, uniting right-thinking businessmen with mechanics and technicians of a suitably post-Vietnam paramilitary variety. It could conceivably be everywhere, and bide its time, camouflaged comfortably within the familiar social fabric: 'it has something you don't have, Max; it has a philosophy, and that's what makes it dangerous.' In this particular hermeneutic, the appearance of an end of ideology and a universal instauration of cynical reason (when not the profit motive and the almighty dollar) are stripped away to show the ominous survival of true belief.

Not surprisingly, therefore, this Klan-type-fantasy reading gives way to a somewhat different kind of politics, the religious revival proper: only a new religion – Video New Flesh – can compete with the corporate paramilitary movement. Organized around the doctrines of the dead McLuhanite professor, it offers video therapy to desocialized vagrants and urban delinquents, promising something of an evolutionary leap or mutation to the species by way of its new perceptual prosthesis in the cathode ray. Optimistically, Video New Flesh considers that the Videodrome tumor is merely the way-station towards the development of a new perceptual organ, with functions as yet undreamed of. Here, then, anticipations and premonitions of transfiguration are coded along the recto and verso of a transformation of (technological) culture and a reappearance of religion (Catholicism also played a fundamental role in McLuhan's thinking).

What is finally most interesting about this titanic political struggle between two vast and faceless conspiracies (in which the hapless Max is little more than a pawn) is that they are finally the same, the twin faces of our unconscious meditation on the inevitable mutations a now repressed history has in store for us: fear and hope alike, the loathing for the new beings we ourselves are bound to become in the shedding of the skins of all our current values, intimately intertwined, as in some DNA of the collective fantasy, with our quasi-religious longing for social transubstantiation into another flesh and another reality. But they are also the same in the more humdrum changing of the valences on which the conventional narrative mechanism depends. Just as the moral fervor of the conspiratorial enemy (which we cannot altogether share) comes as something of a shock – fanatics or not, these high-tech media wreckers stand for Goodness and Righteousness in all its traditional senses – so also the seemingly benign or 'white' conspiracy of the New Flesh does not scruple ruthlessly to send James Woods to his death. Certainly this dualism of the flip-a-switch off/on conspiracy is narratively preferable to that proliferation of private surveillance networks and sub-CIAs that has taken place cancerously within the old genre of the spy novel; but it presents its own formal problems, which will be touched on in conclusion.

Yet if *Videodrome* owes its remarkable political polysemousness to the space freed by the end of traditional ideas, concepts and themes, it is thereby also enabled to participate in that reduction to the body everywhere present in the postmodern, here adroitly manipulated by way of those deeper unconscious physical fears and sexual revulsions that persist autonomously and independently in the social body but can occasionally, as in this case, be tapped for the deeper libidinal energy of the work as in a cultural and psychoanalytic ion-exchange. Primary here is no doubt the fear of the subliminal itself; the television screen as part of the eye; that sense of incorporating unclean or harmful substances that runs all the way from yesterday's phobias about fluorinated water and what it can do to our 'precious bodily fluids' back into the deep witchcraft and envy of village and triba societies. The discrepancy between the video monitor and the movie screen, to be sure, wedges a monkey-wrench into any absolute autoreferentiality. Still, the putative subliminal signals of the Videodrome image can be seen to be intensifications of Buñuel's inaugural assault on the viewer's eyeball (with a straight razor), while the deeper fantasy about the lethal properties of commodity consumption runs at least from the legendary coke in Coca-Cola all the way to the first new anxieties of the age of hucksters, dramatized in Pohl and Kornbluth's SF novel *Space Merchants* (1953), with its addictive brand of coffee. The originality of Philip K. Dick was then to have reunited the twin fears of addiction and of schizophrenia (with its reality-loops and hallucinatory alternate worlds) in a lethal combina-tion which Cronenberg's media nightmare transcends, replaces, and intensifies all at once, translating it into the society of the spectacle or image capitalism.

Physiological anxieties are also tapped by the grotesquely sexual nightmare images, in which males are feminized by the insertion of organic cassettes (if not revolvers) into a newly opened dripping slot below the breast bone. Corporeal revulsion of this kind probably has the primary function of expressing fears about activity and passivity in the complexities of late capitalism, and is only secondarily invested with the level of gender itself, which however knows a separate or semi-autonomous figuration elsewhere in the plot. For the three women – the older Greek or Slavic woman, distantly aristocratic, who makes her living as a go-between in semi-pornographic and bohemian spectacles; the intensely sexual radio therapist (Debbie Harry), whose experiments with S & M lead her directly into Videodrome and presumably to her death; the professor's daughter and spiritual heir, who administers the Cathode Ray Chapel and also the white conspiracy of the New Flesh – form a triad that clearly spells out for Max the ancient male fantasy structure of the triple goddess: mother, wife, and daughter. It is a structure which strengthens the film in two distinct ways: first of all by endowing *Videodrome* with an independent kind of closure that overdetermines it and also functions as a kind of secondary generic block in its own right, forestalling embarrassing questions about the contingencies of the plot and its cast of characters. But it also offers up a new register for just those effects of soiling and degradation on which the film depends: the bad mother, whose already illicit sexuality is incestuously directed towards young boys; the insatiable wife, whose drives reinvent, beyond the current permissibility of 'normal' sex relations, the taboo of torture and death; and the chill vestal, who represents the law of another, absent father, and, after deliberately exposing Max to the ray, sends him on into his own manipulated suicide.

Closure is, to be sure, one of the fundamental formal questions one wishes to ask of conspiratorial representations of this type, where its effect is clearly fundamentally related to the problem of totality itself. For the sense of closure here is the sign that somehow all the bases have been touched, and that the galactic dimensions and co-ordinates of the now global social totality have at least been sketched in. It should be obvious that, just as such totalities can never be perceived with the naked eye (where they would remain, in any case, purely contemplative and epistemological images), so also closure in the postmodern, after the end of the (modernist) organic work, has itself become a questionable value, if not a meaningless concept. It will be desirable therefore to speak of a closure-effect, just as we speak of mapping out triangulating, rather than perceiving or representing, a totality.

10

A CINEMA OF POETRY

John Orr

By 1965 controversy over film form had spread into the realm of colour as it became standard for features throughout Western cinema. We can note the bold experiments of Jean-Luc Godard in *Le Mépris* and *Pierrot le fou*, but two other films also stand out as markers for the cinema of the next thirty years: Hitchcock's much-pilloried *Marnie* with Tippi Hedren, and Michelangelo Antonioni's *The Red Desert* with Monica Vitti. Like Godard, both directors experiment with expressive uses of colour to explore the world of the senses, a world embodied in the texture of the screen image. Both show a social order seen through the eyes of a young woman who is marginal to it, who is neither pure heroine nor pure victim, but was to the audiences of the time disarmingly neurotic. That vision is unstable and for that reason a new challenge to film form, a challenge taken up immediately by Luis Buñuel in his remarkable study of female subjectivity with Catherine Deneuve, *Belle de Jour* (1967). All three films make an important juncture in the continuous experimenting which characterises the 1960s, and *The Red Desert* is a key text in Pier Paolo Pasolini's enduring case for a 'Cinema of Poetry', first delivered to the Pesaro film conference in 1965.

Pasolini's endorsement of a new 'poetic' cinema first pays homage to *Un Chien Andalou*, Buñuel's silent surrealist short of 1929 but equally it prophesies the coming age of what he called 'free indirect subjectivity'. What did he mean by this? Technically speaking, it entails immersion of the filmmaker in the experience of the subject who possesses some clear affinity with the auteur. This cannot

From: John Orr, 'A Cinema of Poetry', in *Contemporary Cinema*, (Edinburgh University Press, 1998).

operate, like fiction, through written narrative and spoken dialogue. It must be expressed primarily through visual style. Unlike novelists who immerse themselves in both the language and psychology of their central characters – elsewhere Pasolini mentions Italian writers as diverse as Ariosto and Moravia – filmmakers have no abstract language. They must work with concrete images possessing a pre-grammatical and irrational history. The film images is irrational. This does not move the image away from the Real but towards it. Gilles Deleuze has pointed out that Pasolini's critique signalled a shift from the arid formalism of semiology towards a new kind of language system, a language system of reality. Deleuze judges this 'reality-system' vital to a new understanding of film, where movement and image are inseparable, for the naive critical isolation of images as 'objects' presupposes an immobility of objects which is not only misleading but goes against the grain of the film medium itself. Thus the false semiological distinction between the object as mere referent and the image as a component of the signified, breaks down. In film, image and object are inseparable. Film is not a succession of represented objects but a series of moving images. A film language exists through its response to non-linguistic material which it then transforms, and narration is grounded in the image itself. The filmmaker cannot 'use' the character's language in the same way as the novelist. 'His activity cannot be linguistic,' Pasolini asserts, 'it must instead be stylistic'.

This is the basis of what he calls a 'free indirect point-of-view shot' which works, he insists, through analogy in two distinctive ways. In the first instance there is a juxtaposition of multiple POVs of the same image, with only a minor shift in angle, in distance, in lens length, or in some combination of any of these to signify a decentring of the point-of-view, a technique used recurrently in *The Red Desert*. Second, there is the further device of making characters enter and leave the frame in such a way that the picture in the frame gains significance both from their presence *and* their absence. This, it can be added, was an extension of the out-of-field techniques Antonioni and Godard had developed in their black-and-white cinema. For Pasolini this obsessive framing means 'the world is presented as if regulated by a myth of pure pictorial beauty that the personages invade, it is true, but adapting themselves to the rules of that beauty instead of profaning them with their presence'.

In *The Red Desert* Antonioni moves back and forth from his central subject Vitti, to the autonomous beauty of things. Moreover he looks at the world by immersing himself in the neurotic subject (Vitti) and then re-animating the facts of the world through her eyes. The narrative technique works not through identification or sympathy with the heroine as it would in melodrama, but by analogy: 'Antonioni has freed his most deeply felt moment: he has finally been able to represent the world through his eyes, *because he has substituted in toto for the world-view of a neurotic his own delirious view of aesthetics*, a wholesale substitution which is justified by the possible analogies of the two views.' This homology is the key to the double-register of the cinema of poetry, the subject's disturbed vision of the world and, by substitution, the director's artistic representation of it. Neither is possible without the other. Pasolini contrasts this substitution with the different technique of Bertolucci's *Before the Revolution* (1964). Here his assistant director on *Accatone* is seen as portraying a neurotic heroine (Adriana Asti) too close to his own sensibility, a harsh, misleading judgement by Pasolini since Asti is very much the object of the male gaze, in particular that of her nephew-lover, Fabrizio, in this the most dazzling and lyrical of Bertolucci's films. For Pasolini *The Red Desert* suggests in contrast a double reading through homology – the world as subjectively disturbed, the world as deliriously aesthetic. To this we can add our own coda. The historic transformation of the cinema of poetry lies in the world viewed. We see industrial Ravenna of 1965, not a studio facsimile. Through the figure of its disturbed subject Antonioni's camera seeks out the toxic eco-spaces of the 'red desert'.

The camera here is both objective and subjective, a feature of the modern cinema discussed at length by Deleuze and Jean Mitry, whose dissection of the ambiguities in tracking and shot/reverse shot sequences lead him towards the concept of a generalised semi-subjective image. That is to say, the camera is always moving among its characters but is not identical with any one of them. For Deleuze this camera-consciousness is the 'truly cinematographic *Mitsein*' of an unidentified other who bears witness to the events filmed. Yet it is also a filmic artifice which has no status in natural perception. Assessing the films of Godard, Antonioni and Bertolucci, Pasolini had provided a crucial link between the Heideggerian *Mitsein*, the filmic being-with-others, and free indirect subjectivity. The *Mitsein* or witnessing camera enacts homology, the double-register of style and psychic disturbance. Yet as Deleuze points out, Pasolini allows himself the slippage to a technically incorrect term, mimesis, which he uses for a very different reason, but one no less significant. Mimesis connotes the *sacred* nature of filming itself. In making *Accatone* a few years earlier he had already discovered the 'technical sacredness' of the long lens shot, a form of unmediated reality made possible by the movie camera alone. The lens records reality in the raw, without embellishment, and that, for the director of *The Gospel According to St Matthew*, is sacred.

There is a sense here in which Pasolini directly challenges Plato's devaluation of mimesis to the third order of truth in the tenth section of the *Republic*. Plato, we may recall, had seen the craftsman's form as an attempt to replicate the pure form of the object ordained by the Divine and seen art in turn as a third-order praxis, a copy of the craftsman's copy, an imitation of the craftsman's imitation of Divine form. Film technology affords a unique chance in Pasolini's view to short-circuit this triad. The world captured on film in its raw purity is not mere imitation like painting or mythic narrative. The style of the camera is nourished by sacred immediacy, in which advanced technologies have recovered the possibility of the sacred in a secular world. The power of the Human is made possible by imitating reality in the raw but subjecting it at the same time to the double-register of the cinema of poetry. The auteur attains pure Form by virtue of film's raw content. Pasolini uses a number of adjectives to delineate this ideal cinema 'oneiric, barbaric, irregular, aggressive, visionary' and cruci-ally,' expressive/expressionistic'. For him, the irrational works through form more than through content. As visual style pursues its free expression, rules of narrative continuity and editing no longer apply.

Although poetry for Pasolini means narrative poetry, and works against Sartre's distinction between prose as writing referring to a world outside itself and poetry as writing referring only to itself, there are still ambiguities over form. Key history films of the 1970s, for example, such as Herzog's *Aguirre*, Malick's *Days of Heaven* and Peter Weir's *Picnic at Hanging Rock*, can be seen as 'poetic' by virtue of their lyric style and sparse dialogue. Equally their narratives convey stories of the past with a precise naturalistic detail, a lucid concern with time, place and culture. For that reason we might place them closer to fiction than poetry, especially in its modernist forms, where in the English language Imagism has had such a powerful impact. The closer analogy in twentieth-century writing lies not with poetry but with the poetic prose of modernist fiction. Here Pasolini argues that interior mono-logue is the closest literary form to the free, indirect POV shot, and the immediacy of the shot would seem at times to correspond to the present tense of the interior 'I' in prose. Yet in English language fiction, the poetic prose which prefigures poetic cinema is a 'third person stream-of-consciousness', described by Banfield as a discourse of represented thought and speech. It makes use less of present tense than of past tense to conjure up the imme-diacy of the reader's mind. It is less the 'I' of Joyce's Molly in 'Penelope' and more the Stephen of 'Wandering Rocks', more the 'she' of Woolf's Clarissa Dalloway or Grassic Gibbon's Chris Guthrie in *Sunset Song*, more 'The Consul' (Geoffrey Firmin) hallucinating with delirium tremens in Lowry's *Under the Volcano*. In each case narration moves fluidly in and out of consciousness so that Stephen in 'Wandering Rocks' is seen both from the inside and the outside, seeing as he is being seen, an interior protean sensi-bility but also a figure on a coastal landscape. Yet a crucial difference remains. Film is a medium of the present. It happens on screen. It also has no set discourse for representing thought.

Contemporary film seems closer to this style of writing than it is to the self-conscious fabulating of Pynchon, Barth, Fowles or Calvino. There is no self-conscious author present to play with our response. Or is there? The other pole of Pasolini's double-register is Godard where the camera continually makes its presence felt in its poetic epiphanies. Here free indirect subjectivity is that of the libertarian technicist who makes unpredictable forays in the space of his own narrative. The presence of the camera charges the force-field of the narrative, not least through its recurrent dissonance. In *Le Mépris* Fritz Lang plays himself as a director of a Hollywood movie in Capri based on *The Odyssey* while the journey of return moves on a parallel plane in the modern triangle of screenwriter Michel Piccoli who sees himself as Odysseus to the Penelope of his contemptuous spouse Brigitte Bardot, and her would-be lover,

Hollywood producer Jack Palance. The reflexive motif gives us two films for the price of one and for Deleuze Godard becomes the prime exemplar of free indirect vision. In *Pierrot le fou* (1965) he moves more openly into the double-register. Jean-Paul Belmondo is both aesthete and criminal, Godard and not-Godard, aficionado of the quotation and the handgun. His flight south with Anna Karina, shot by Raoul Coutard in brilliant summer colours, is complete with multi-coloured captions, chapter headings, chance digressions and end-less quotations to prove Godard is at his best when he combines visual freedom with emotional doom. As the love affair of Ferdinand and Marianne falls apart, the technical virtuosity intensifies, but the presence of the camera does not dilute expressive power. Baudelaire had claimed that the clinical detachment of the artist strolling through Parisian crowds sharpened the visceral power of the artwork. A hundred years later, this is what happens in the cinema of poetry. But it happens because pure form is transcended in the act of filming. Form is born out of the intensity of theme and the irrational, not the aesthetic, remains the raw datum on which the filmmaker works.

Pasolini's Marxist critique is sadly too narrow in its view of bourgeois neurosis as a symptom of class decadence under advanced capitalism. The cinema of the poetry has featured strongly in Polish and Russian films of the late Soviet period, especially those of Andrei Tarkovsky and Krzysztof Kie-ślowski, and the films of the Chinese 'fifth generation' directors such as Chen Kaige and Zhang Yimou. Pasolini assumes an incestuous kinship between the neurotic bourgeois and the bourgeois auteur. But the parameters of resem-blance and difference stretch, historically speaking, much wider. Indeed we can say poetic form is at its best when the auteur *plays more upon difference than upon resemblance*. While gender transference works, as we have seen, through neurosis, class transference (male-to-male) often works through psychosis, thus echoing ironically the sexual difference noted by critics in Freud's casework. While for Freud the neurotic female tries to ignore existing reality but does not disavow it, the psychotic male disavows it and replaces it with a purely imaginary world. Yet female ignoring is also a complex form of resisting the wrongs of a specific male domination. We have already seen this in Vitti and Hedren but we may single out other cases. The most striking which come to mind over the last two decades are Krystyna Janda in the dark reveries of recent Polish history, *Man of Marble* (1977) and *The Interrogation* (1981), Sandrine Bonnaire in Agnès Varda's *Vagabond* (1987), Juliette Binoche in *Three Colours: Blue* (1992), and Gong Li in Zhang Yimou's *Shanghai Triad* (1996). Contrast this with the male-centred subjectivities of the same period. Overwhelming psychosis defines De Niro in *Taxi Driver* (1975) and *Raging Bull* (1980), Martin Sheen in *Badlands* (1974) and *Apocalypse Now* (1979), Jack Nicholson in *The Shining* (1980), David Thewlis in Mike Leigh's *Naked* (1993), Bruce Willis in *12 Monkeys* (1996). Resistance to the psychosis of imaginary worlds, resistance to the lure of the paranoid gaze defines David

Hemmings in *Blow-Up* (1966), Jack Nicholson in *Chinatown* (1974) and *The Passenger* (1975), Gene Hackman in *The Conversation* (1974), Griffin Dunne in *After Hours* (1985), Harrison Ford in *Blade Runner* (1982). While paranoia is the resistible temptation of the bemused modern investigator, the psychopathic violence of the socially excluded to which paranoia is integral, becomes a key motif in the nightmare vision of the present and future city.

In *Taxi Driver* Scorsese, Schrader and De Niro constructed through the deranged figure of Travis Bickle a working-class mirror of their complex urban paranoia, the shared paranoia of the streets of Manhattan expressed through the free indirect subjectivity of a Vietnam Vet trapped in the nightmare of his Yellow Cab. In Kieślowski's powerful and savage *Short Film About Killing* (1988), filmed in Warsaw through slime-green filters, Jacek is the country boy adrift and alone in a hostile city which finally makes him homicidal. In *Cyclo* (1996), echoing *Taxi Driver*, the young French-Vietnamese auteur Tran Anh Hung charts the Hadean descent of a Saigon cyclo cabby into an inferno of sexual commerce and multiple murder where East and West, communism and capitalism, insanely collide. The endlessly circulating traffic of the streets with its myriad bicycles, is shot in high-angle from dilapidated balconies to affirm metonymically the eternal recurrence of the hero's bad dream, his Vietnamese *fleur du mal*. In 1993, two American independents forged disturbing poetries of psychosis in a minor key, reminding us further of the sociopathic underside of contemporary capitalism while resisting Hollywood's great mythic temptation, the pseudo-documentary of the serial killer. In Lodge Kerrigan's 16mm feature, *Clean, Shaven*, Peter Greene plays a released schizophrenic in search of his young daughter in a fishing community on the Canadian Atlantic seaboard. Through a mosaic of visual fragments and weirdly strident sounds which comprise his perceptual world, Kerrigan recreates the disintegration of his schizoid subject whose mind is haunted by an unbearable self-hatred, a self-loathing clinched in the image of the razor in the mirror by which he constantly bloodies his own face. In Bryan Singer's *Public Access*, Ron Marquette is the psychotic but well-dressed drifter who starts up his own Cable talk show in the small Western town of Brewster and then murders those he tempts into challenging the official rhetoric of 'our town' which he generates over the airwaves. Looking the spitting image of Clark Kent, the crossover here which comes to mind is somewhat different. Mr Deeds changes into Norman Bates. The contrast between these films and *Three Colours: Blue* is quite fundamental, highlighting the sexual difference in the poetics of psychic disturbance. Here redemption is female. Binoche, amnesiac, traumatised by the crash which has badly injured her and killed spouse and child, is sado-dispassionate, turning cruelly and clinically against grief and compassion. Yet her Parisian journey takes her to the other side of trauma, through the art of music, to a dream of Christian redemption but also a reunion with the daily world of her past life. In the filmic liturgies of male psychosis redemption is impossible.

The essence of the double-register would seem to exclude from Pasolini's poetics the autobiographical cinema so prevalent in Fellini where Marcello Mastroianni proved to be such a brilliant and enduring version of his director's persona. In general, autobiography does not generate sufficient tension between style and theme, the vital springboard for free indirect vision. One extraordinary exception to this rule is the short episode which Rainer Werner Fassbinder made for the landmark composite of New German Cinema *Germany in Autumn* (1978). Like other episodes in the film Fassbinder lends a distinctive gloss to Germany's terrorist crisis of the time, to the polarised reaction to the killing of Hans Martin-Schleyer by the Baader-Meinhof group. He brings politics back into the home and charts the effect of the crisis on his relationships with his gay lover and his uncomprehending mother. The effect of separation here, between Fassbinder as creator and Fassbinder as subject, is alarmingly schizophrenic but dramatically effective. He turns himself inside out and shows us not only the collapse of the mother-son relationship through the generational impasse in German politics, but also the collapse of the gay intimacy which has no shield to protect itself against the eruption of political crisis. Meanwhile the narcissism of Fassbinder the subject is mercilessly scrutinised by the Brechtian camera of Fassbinder the filmmaker as he rolls naked on the floor with his lover in a fit of paranoia, and then finally kicks out of his flat the degraded object of his self-regarding desire.

This play of identity and difference also operates on the plane of memory, memory as reverie of a lived past not as objective remembering. Pasolini points out that in film the present is transformed into the past by the very feature of editing, yet the past still appears as present in filmic projection for the audience by virtue of the immediacy of the image. This immediacy is a poetic affirmation of the presentness of the past unique to the medium. It gives us also a new insight into the 'history' film. For this phenomenology of film form translates reflexively into thematic treatments of history as reverie or history as lived immediacy, into the poetic cinema of Bergman's *Cries and Whispers* or Bertolucci's *The Conformist*. History becomes a dream or a nightmare of difference, in which time itself is an integral part of the double-register. For Bergman in this case the historic other is female and dying. For Bertolucci, the historic other is fascist and repressed. Between the two films another key difference emerges. The singular nature of Marcello Clerici's persona gives us a single poetic subject. By contrast, Bergman's quest to reduce film to pure-dream state, 'a dark, flowing stream' as he puts it, creates a collective subject of three sisters whose emotions merge at times into one another, like the characters of *Persona* and *The Silence*, as aspects of a single soul before they finally hive apart. The legacy of *Cries and Whispers* can be seen most strongly in Terence Davies's *Distant Voices/Still Lives* (1987). Its title split because it had been filmed for cash reasons in two instalments, it emerged as one of the great films of the 1980s. Like Bergman, Davies used the family as collective subject who face a hideous death within their midst, the father-husband dying of cancer. But

Davies went further. Family memories are shared by mother and siblings but there is no chronological order to the flashbacks and no ascription of a single point-of-view. The past is a collage of interwoven memories, some individual, some shared, and these spring to life out of still photographs which capture the family rituals of birth, marriage and mourning. These still tableaux, filmed in washed-out sepia and developed in post-production through a 'bleach-bypass' technique eliminating primary colour, then spring into the moving images of shared experiences. The double-register of the collective subject, mother, brother and sisters, from which Davies absents his biographical self is more powerful than his sequel *The Long Day Closes* where he reinstates himself as a young boy at the centre of the narrative. This is because Davies creates a double-register in which the subjectivities of the family weave in and out of one another as phantasmic memories.

Yet there is still a key concept missing. We need to conceive the camera's *Mitsein* or active witnessing more precisely to stress its diffuse and fluid nature, to avoid the trap presented by the lure of that simplistic phrase, point-of-view. We also have to add a key dimension seen by Tarkovsky as linking cinema and poetry – the world of dreams. A reductive discourse of self is no use here since film is first and foremost a visual language. Since 'POV shot' is often an ambiguous term we can adopt Bruce Kawin's more fertile concept 'mindscreen' which interrogates subjectivity from a different angle. Kawin opposes the filmed thought of mindscreen to its verbal expression in the voice-over and its purely subjective point-of-view shot. Here I would disagree that such hard-and-fast distinctions can be made. It seems to me that mindscreen is by its nature fluid and can only work if it incorporates all three, the verbal, the physical and the mental, something which is implicit in Kawin's excellent discussion of subjective sound. Mindscreen, then, has to be a fusion of 'sightscreen' and 'soundscreen'. It would thus incorporate the verbal *Mitsein* or witnessing of such voice-overs as *Badlands* (Sissy Spacek) and *Days of Heaven* (Linda Ganz), whose teenage girls are part of the action they witness but mostly do not make it happen and where, unlike the fall-guy narrators of film noir, they are not ultimate victims but survivors, part of the tragic action but also apart from it. This naive narration is an aural 'following' to match the visual following of the camera which goes beyond, indeed deconstructs the POV shot. The travelling shot, so typical of Kieslowski's work, follows the movement of his central characters yet is never identical with them. In *Blue* for example, the camera tracks Binoche through space and time and films her POV sporadically through the still shot. In Polanski's *Chinatown* there is a similar effect. John Alonzo's camera is right behind the ear of Jack Nicholson (Jake Gittes) as he tracks Mulwray, the city's water commissioner to a dried-out riverbed, then to the Pacific at dusk and onto a rowing-boat on the lake in Echo Park. The *Mitsein* of the camera is thus a form of mindscreen which fuses body, voice and psyche by creating a montage of different shot-sequences of a singular vision. The resulting composite image resembles different aspects of the subject's world, both real and imaginary.

Tarkovsky's poetic logic of dream is a world where landscape, dream, memory and fantasy all have the same ontological status. His own films, *Mirror* (1974) and *Stalker* (1978), show just how much poetic cinema can free dream from the signifiers which, conventionally, would top and tail it, from the dissolve over eyes closing to the sudden start of the frightened subject waking from nightmare. In mindscreen, by contrast, the exterior world is contiguous with the interior world. In this context filmmakers have constantly challenged the POV shot. In Atom Egoyan's *Exotica* (1993) his distressed tax inspector (Bruce Greenwood) obsessively recalls the pastoral setting of a search party in which he himself is not present. Present in the scene however are the current object of his desire, Mia Kirshner, dancer at the Exotica club who also recalls the scene quite separately, and her slimeball MC, Elias Kotias who is with her in a search party in the meadow (searching, we later learn, for the body of Greenwood's murdered daughter). Both wear the casual hippy clothes of a previous decade. After the recurrent 'flashback' the film usually flashes forward to either Kirshner or Kotias at the Exotica as fashionable black Goths, but never to Greenwood, the tax inspector. The objects of Greenwood's original gaze – is it daydream or memory? – then become the screen's subjects while the original subject (Greenwood himself) is now completely absent. The puzzle about the origin of the shot increases – whose point of view? In different variations on free indirect subjectivity the point-of-view itself is often rendered problematic, and is no longer a fixed point through which the viewer can read the film.

Form and Process

11

A TRAVELLING SHOT OVER
EIGHTY YEARS

Paul Virilio

This story could have begun in 1854, at the siege of Sebastopol during the Crimean War, or seven years later with the American Civil War, since in both conflicts abundant use was made of modern techniques: repeating weapons, photographic records, armoured trains, aerial observation . . . But I have chosen to start in 1904, the first year of the 'war of light'. For it was then, a year after the Wright brothers flew in the *Kitty Hawk*, that a searchlight was used for the first time in history, in the Russo-Japanese war.

Trained on the heights of Port Arthur, the focused incandescence of war's first *projector* seemed to concentrate all the torches and all the fires of all the wars before it. Its beam pierced more than the darkness of the Russo-Japanese war; it illuminated a future where observation and destruction would develop at the same pace. Later the two would merge completely in the target-acquisition techniques of the *Blitzkrieg*, the cine-machineguns of fighter aircraft, and above all the blinding Hiroshima flash which literally photographed the shadow cast by beings and things, so that every surface immediately became war's *recording* surface, its *film*. And from this would come directed-light weapons, the coherent light-beam of the laser.

[. . .]

If we remember that it was an optics professor, Henri Chrétien, whose work during the First World War perfecting naval artillery telemetry laid the

From: Paul Virilio, 'A Travelling Shot over Eighty Years', *War and Cinema* (Verso, London, 1991).

foundations for what would become Cinemascope thirty-six years later, we can better grasp the deadly harmony that always establishes itself between the functions of eye and weapon. And, indeed, while the advance of panoramic telemetry resulted in wide-screen cinema, so the progress of radio-telemetry led to an improved picture: the *radar picture*, whose electronic image prefigured the electronic vision of video. From the commanding heights of the earliest natural fortifications, through the architectonic innovation of the watch-tower, and the development of anchored observation balloons, or the aerial reconnaissance of World War I and its 'photographic reconstruction' of the battlefield, right up to President Reagan's latest early warning satellites, there has been no end to the enlargement of the military field of perception. Eyesight and direct vision have gradually given way to optical or opto-electronic processes, to the most sophisticated forms of 'telescopic sight'. The strategic importance of optics was already clear in World War I, one indication being the dramatic rise during the war in French production of optical glass (for rangefinders, periscopes and camera lenses; for telemetry and goniometry) – from 40 tonnes to 140 tonnes a year, half the total Allied output.

[...]

Just as weapons and armour developed in unison throughout history, so visibility and invisibility now began to evolve together, eventually producing *invisible weapons that make things visible* – radar, sonar, and the high-definition camera of spy satellites. The Duke of Wellington once said he had spent his life guessing what was on the other side of the hill. Today's military decision-makers don't have to guess: their task is to avoid confusing the forms of a representation which, while covering the broadest regions of the front, must take in the minute details always liable to influence the outcome of a conflict. The problem, then, is no longer so much one of masks and screens, of camouflage designed to hinder long-range targeting; rather, it is a problem of ubiquitousness, of handling simultaneous data in a global but unstable environment where the image (photographic or cinematic) is the most concentrated, but also the most stable, form of information.

The camera-recording of the First World War already prefigured the statistical memory of computers, both in the management of aerial observation data and in the ever more rigorous management of the simultaneity of action and reaction.

[...]

It was in 1912 that the German Alfred Maul launched a powder-fuelled rocket with a small photographic device in its nose cone. When it reached its highest point, the rocket took a single photograph and came back to earth at a slower speed (a military experiment which built upon Nadar first aerostatic pictures). Twenty years later at RCA's laboratories Vladimir Zworykin invented the

'Iconoscope', the first name for the electronic television. He presented it not as a mass medium but as a way of expanding the range of human vision – indeed, anticipating the Pioneer and Voyager space probes by many years, he even wanted to place a camera on a rocket to observe inaccessible regions.

This urge to expand the range of vision and detection eventually found a scientific answer in the electro-magnetic radar beam, which at the time of the Battle of Britain gave the air the transparency of ether. Watson-Watt spread out a mysterious, invisible screen in the atmosphere, reaching to such a height that no air vessel could pass through without being detected somewhere on the ground, in the form of a blob of light in a darkened room. What had once taken place in the darkroom of Niepce and Daguerre was now happening in the skies of England. The war room in London filled up with senior officers and female assistants – hostesses, one might say, of a strategic office imitating real war – who organized the flow of 'Chain Home' radar information and coordinated the RAF combat formations. Brief exchanges between crews and their 'war hostesses' passed through the ether, as if the couples were together in the same room. Duly warned, guided and consoled, the fighter-pilots were ceaselessly followed by these offstage voices. It was not only the war film that had become a talkie. For the pilots could visualize the audience in the operations room and punctuated their brilliant feats of arms with exclamations and commentaries. The female assistants contributed to their leader's success, as well as to the derealization of a battle in which ghosts played an ever greater role – screen ghosts of enemy pilots served to confirm that they had been shot down, and ghostly radar images, voices and echoes came through on the screens, radios and sonars. The projection of light and waves had replaced the old projection of arrows and javelins.

Although military force depends on its relationship to outward appearance, this power has over the years lost its verisimilitude in a profusion of camouflage, decoys, jamming, smoke-screens, electronic countermeasures, and so on. The offensive arsenal has equipped itself with new devices for a conflict in which optical and motor illusion have fused in the cinematic delirium of lightning-war. Here what counts is the speed at which objects, images and sounds travel through space, until the moment of the nuclear flash.

In the spring of 1940, unlike 1914–18, reconnaissance aircraft had a constant short-wave radio link with the ground, over a range that would increase from a few dozen kilometres to five hundred by the end of the war. In the autumn of the same year, RAF night-fighters became the first to have onboard radar which enabled pilots to see on cockpit screens a Dornier or Messerschmitt-110 flying through the dark over five kilometres away. The pilot's gift of double sight thus introduced a new doubling of the warrior's personality: with his head up, atmospheric transparency and ocular targeting; head down, the transparency of the ether, long-distance vision. Two military spaces, one close and one faraway, corresponded to a single battle, a single war. Later these technologies led to the development of over-the-horizon weapons systems.

As for the night-bombers, which had to face the blinding light of 200 million candlepower searchlights, they gradually acquired new resources and procedures to help them accomplish their mission. Whereas in 1940 the Luftwaffe dropped incendiaries to mark the bombing area in London and Coventry, in 1941 the Allies' 'Operation Millennium' used impact flare-bombs to sketch out in the darkness a rectangle of red lights for the Halifaxes and Lancasters to release their destructive load over Cologne. 'Subsequently the Allies developed the magnesium flare and the electronic flash, which allowed USAF bombers not only to light up the ground but, more importantly, to dazzle enemy defences for a few moments. (Such innovations were taken further by Sam Cohen in the Vietnam War, when it became possible to blind the enemy for more than an hour: the latest development in this line is the stun grenade used against terrorists in Mogadishu and London.)

By 1942 ground-based electronic devices were able to direct Flying Fortress squadrons over a very long distance, helping them to drop their bomb-loads by day or night and under any weather conditions. The two ground stations involved were known as 'The Cat' and 'Mickey Mouse'. Aircraft fitted with a special receiver picked up the cat's beam and let themselves be passively guided to the vicinity of the target. The mouse, which had so far followed the operation in silence from a distance of some four hundred kilometres, then took over and, having calculated the moment when the bomber should release its load, transmitted the instruction by radar – all with a margin of error of a mere hundred metres.

This sophisticated electronic network covering Western Europe was first known as GEE. But as it continually improved, its name changed to the call-sign OBOE and finally, in 1943, to H2S, by which time it could give pilots not just a radar signal but a 'radar image', a luminous silhouette of the target over which they were flying. The bombing apparatus was equipped with a transmitter that beamed centimetric waves in a perpendicular line to ground level, the echoes then returning and forming on a cathode screen an electronic image of fifteen square kilometres. The system was used for the first time in Operation Gomorrah, which devastated Hamburg.

The visible weapons systems of artillery, machine-guns, and so forth thus became entangled with the invisible weapons systems of a continent-wide electronic war. No longer were objects on the ground invisible to pilots, who in the past had related to natural conditions both as a source of protective concealment from enemy fire and as a hindrance that masked their own target. Anti-aircraft defences benefited in turn from the ubiquitousness of war: the Kammhuber Line, for example, whose operational centre was at Arnhem in Holland, organized the German fighter response with an air-raid warning system that covered key areas from the North Sea to the Mediterranean. A network of 'panoramic radar' installations, each tracking a circle of three hundred kilometres, could cable an electronic image of the sky to the anti-aircraft batteries of *Festung Europa*. This total visibility, cutting through darkness, distance and natural obstacles, made the space of war translucent and its military commanders clairvoyant, since response time was continually being cut by the technological processes of foresight and anticipation.

The air-raid alert system also played a major psychological role on the Continent. Advance warning could be given to civilian populations as soon as enemy squadrons crossed the coast, and this was translated into a full-scale alert once they veered towards their target city. With the compression of space–time, danger was lived simultaneously by millions of attentive listeners. For want of space to move back into, their only protection was time given to them by the radio.

The Allied air assault on the great European conurbations suddenly became a *son-et-lumière*, a series of special effects, an atmospheric projection designed to confuse a frightened, blacked-out population. In dark rooms that fully accorded with the scale of the drama, victims-to-be witnessed the most terrifying night-time fairy theatre, hellish displays of an invading cinema that reproduced the Nuremberg architecture of light. Albert Speer, organizer of the Nazi festivities at Zeppelinfeld, wrote as follows of the bombing of Berlin on 22 November 1943:

> The raid offered a spectacle whose memory cannot be erased. You constantly had to remember the appalling face of reality if you were not to let yourself be entranced by this vision. Parachute-rockets – 'Christmas trees', as Berliners called them – suddenly lit up the sky; then came the explosion whose glare was engulfed by the smoke of incendiaries. On every side, countless searchlights scoured the night and a gripping duel began when an aeroplane, caught in the pencil of light, tried to make its escape. Sometimes it was hit and for a few moments became a blazing torch. It was an imposing vision of apocalypse.

Hitler's architect was well placed to measure the small distance from the hell of images to the image of hell:

> For the Nuremberg Party Congress in 1935, I used 150 anti-aircraft searchlights whose perpendicular, skyward beams formed a luminous rectangle in the night. Within these walls of light, the first of their kind, the congress unfolded in all its ritual. It was a fairy-like decor, reminding one of the glass castles imagined by poets in the Middle Ages. I now have a strange feeling when I think that my most successful architectural creation was a phantasmagoria, an unreal mirage.

Not a mirage, but rather a dress rehearsal for the war, a holographic harbinger which used material available to the army for more than thirty years.

Transparency, ubiquitousness, instant information – it was the time of the great 'command operas' where, in London as in Berlin, stage-directors moved the naval and air fleets around. 'The headquarters transmission centre was a model of its kind,' writes Speer.

> From his table in the conference room, Hitler was able to command all the
> divisions on the fields of battle. The worse the situation became, the more
> this instrument of modern warfare served to underline the divorce
> between reality on the ground and the fantasy which presided over the
> conduct of operations at that table.

Commanders were now able to exercise their authority with a minimum of
go-betweens. Hitler acted the warlord by radio-telephoning orders to his
generals and depriving them of initiative, but in the end the whole system of
communications, in both camps, worked to strengthen the supreme commander's control over his subordinates. *Power was now in a direct link-up*. If, as the
strategist Se-Ma put it, an army is always strong when it can come and go, move
out and back, as it pleases, we have to say that in this period of war the comings
and goings were less those of troops than of the output from detection and
transmission equipment. Visual or audiovisual technology now began to
reproduce not only the forced march or distant incursion – as it did in the
1914–18 war – but the actual movement of armies, with automatic feed-back
and retransmission in real time. How else can we understand the introduction of
PK units in the Wehrmacht, or the Allied armies' use not just of war corre-
spondents but of their own cine-commando units – how else but by the need for
ever more advanced mediation of military action, so that the pilot's 'gift of
double sight' could be extended to a high command at once absent and
omnipresent?

In making attack unreal, industrial warfare ceased to be that huge funeral
apparatus denounced by moralists and eventually became the greatest mystification of all: an apparatus of deception, the lure of deterrence strategy.
Already in the Great War, as we have seen, the industrialization of the repeating
image illustrated this cinematic dimension of regional-scale destruction, in
which landscapes were continually upturned and had to be reconstituted with
the help of successive frames and shots, in a cinematographic pursuit of reality,
the decomposition and recomposition of an uncertain territory in which film
replaced military maps.

Cinematic derealization now affected the very nature of power, which
established itself in a technological Beyond with the space–time not of ordinary
mortals but of a single war machine. In this realm sequential perception, like
optical phenomena resulting from retinal persistence, is both origin and end of
the apprehension of reality, since the seeing of movement is but a statistical
process connected with the nature of the segmentation of images and the speed
of observation characteristic of humans. The macro-cinematography of aerial
reconnaissance, the cable television of panoramic radar, the use of slow or
accelerated motion in analysing the phases of an operation – all this converts the
commander's plan into an animated cartoon or flow-chart. In the Bayeux
Tapestry, itself a model of a pre-cinematic march-past, the logistics of the
Norman landing already prefigured *The Longest Day* of 6 June 1944.

Now, it should not be forgotten that inductive statistics developed from the calculations that Marshal Vauban used to make during his long and repetitive journeys to the same place at different times. On each of these trips, Louis XIV's commissioner-general of fortifications became a kind of 'commissioner for displays'. The kingdom paraded before his eyes, offering itself up for general inspection. This was not just a troop muster for the logistical benefit of the officer in charge of army comportment; it was a full-scale review of the country, a medical examination of its territorial corpus. Instead of the ordinary situation in which serried ranks used to pass back and forth before the watchful gaze of the king's administrator, it was the country's provinces, drawn up as on parade, which were passed in review by his inspector-general. However, these repeated trips, which caused the regional film to unwind, were no more than an artifice or cinematic trick for the sole benefit of the itinerant observer. Alone as he watched the situations and sequences dissolve, he gradually lost sight of local realities and ended up demanding a reform of fiscal law in favour of administrative norms.

Statistics brings us to the dawn of political economy, which rested on the persistence of the sign and of dominant trends, not on the merely chronological succession of facts. It is the same movement of ideas which led from the Enlightenment to photographic recording, Muybridge's multiple chambers, Marey's chronophotography and the Lumière brothers' film-camera, not forgetting Méliès, the inventor of the mystification of montage.

Winston Churchill, it is well known, believed that whereas episodic events used to have greater importance than tendencies, in modern wars the tendency had gained the upper hand over episodes. Mass phenomena do indeed elude immediate apprehension and can only be perceived by means of the computer and interception and recording equipment which did not exist in earlier times (hence the relative character of Churchill's judgement). We should therefore conclude that total war has made an essential contribution to the rise of projection equipment which can reveal and finally make possible the totalitarian tendencies of the moment.

The development of 'secret' weapons, such as the 'flying bomb' and stratospheric rockets, laid the basis for Cruise and intercontinental missiles, as well as for those invisible weapons which, by using various rays, made visible not only what lay over the horizon, or was hidden by night, but what did not or did not yet exist. Here we can see the strategic fiction of the need for armaments relying on atomic radiation – a fiction which, at the end of the war, led to the 'ultimate weapon'.

As we saw in the first chapter, many epilogues have been written about the nuclear explosions of 6 and 9 August 1945, but few have pointed out that the bombs dropped on Hiroshima and Nagasaki were *light-weapons* that prefigured the enhanced-radiation neutron bomb, the directed-beam laser weapons, and the charged-particle guns currently under development. Moreover, a number of Hiroshima survivors have reported that, shortly after it was detonated, they thought it was a *magnesium bomb* of unimagined power.

The first bomb, set to go off at a height of some five hundred metres, produced a nuclear flash which lasted one fifteen-millionth of a second, and whose brightness penetrated every building down to the cellars. It left its imprint on stone walls, changing their apparent colour through the fusion of certain minerals, although protected surfaces remained curiously unaltered. The same was the case with clothing and bodies, where kimono patterns were tattooed on the victims' flesh. If photography, according to its inventor Nicéphore Niepce, was simply a method of engraving with light, where bodies inscribed their traces by virtue of their own luminosity, nuclear weapons inherited both the darkroom of Niepce and Daguerre and the military search-light. What appears in the heart of darkrooms is no longer a luminous outline but a shadow, one which sometimes, as in Hiroshima, is carried to the depths of cellars and vaults. The Japanese shadows are inscribed not, as in former times, on the screens of a shadow puppet theatre but on a new screen, the walls of the city.

A-bomb, 1945; H-bomb, 1951. Korean War ... After the war everything speeded up: firepower referred not just to firearms but to the jet-pipes of fighter aircraft. The sound barrier was crossed in 1952, the 'heat barrier' in 1956. As to the light barrier, that was for later. In the skies, Strategic Air Command bombers were in constant readiness, and Air Defense Command interceptors spread their protective umbrella for the eventuality of a Soviet long-range attack. The danger was all the greater in that the USSR exploded its first hydrogen bomb on 12 May 1953.

For the United States, it was becoming an urgent matter to have new information-gathering methods at its disposal. And so it was that Eastman Kodak came up with its Mylar-based film and Dr Edwin Land of Hycon Corporation with the high-resolution camera – both of which laid the basis for regular aerial reconnaissance over the Soviet Union. The sequel is well known. October 1961 saw the beginning of the Cuban crisis, with the threat of a third world war. On 29 August 1962, a U-2 aeroplane came back from a mission over Fidel Castro's island with film evidence of Soviet missile instal-lations. This sparked off the confrontation between Khrushchev and Kennedy which, after several months, led to a hot-line link-up between the two heads of state, an instant interface between their operations rooms.

We should remember that the U-2, still in service over Iran and the Persian Gulf, is fitted not only with photographic and electronic surveillance systems but also with a telescopic collimator or 'cine-drift indicator' which allows the spy pilot to follow ground contours at a height of more than twenty-five thousand metres.

Also in 1962, at a time when there were already ten thousand American advisers in Vietnam, the first electronic war in history was devised at Harvard and MIT. It began with the parachute-drops of sensors all along the Ho Chi-Minh Trail, and continued in 1966 with the development of the electronic 'MacNamara Line', consisting of fields of acoustic (Acouboy, Spikeboy) and seismic (Adsid, Acousid) detectors spread along the Laos access routes, around US army bases and especially the Khe Sanh stronghold.

At that time Harvard Professor Roger Fisher developed the strategic concept of a 'land-air dam', relying on up-to-the-minute technology to keep an effective watch on enemy movements. It would use infra-red devices and low-lighting television, combined with the most advanced means of aerial destruction such as the F-105 Thunderchief fighter, the Phantom jet, and the Huey-Cobra helicopter gunship. Transport aircraft (the Douglas AC-47 and, above all, the Hercules C-130) were converted into flying batteries with the latest electronic equipment: laser targeters capable of guiding bombs with absolute precision; a night-vision and image-enhancer system; and computer-controlled, multi-barrelled Minigums, descendants of the old Gatling gun which could fire six thousand rounds a minute.

With this sophisticated alert-system, made necessary by the fact that enemy movement usually took place by night, the black-out was a thing of the past, and darkness the fighter's best ally, while the daylight theatre also became a darkened cinema for the shadowy combatants. Hence the Americans' frenzied efforts to overcome this blindness by having recourse to pyrotechnic, electrical and electronic devices, most of which employed light intensification, photo-grammetry, thermography, infra-red scanning, and even specially invented infra-red film. All these weapons systems resulted in a new staging of war, massive use of synthetic images, and automatic feed-back of data. They also gave rise to chemical defoliation, whereby it finally became possible to empty the screen of parasitic vegetation.

In October 1967, the Nakhon Phanom electronic surveillance centre in Thailand was picking up, interpreting and displaying on screen data sent from ground-interceptors and relayed by Lockheed Bat-Cat aeroplanes. In these offices, the new nodal point of the war, an IBM 360.35 computer automatically sorted the data, producing a 'snapshot' which showed the time and place when the interceptors had been activated. On the basis of this information, analysts drew up a schedule of enemy movement and passed on to fighter-bomber crews the 'Skyspot' combat data that enabled them to go into action with the greatest dispatch and precision. Most interesting from our point of view, however, was the pilotless Drone, an aircraft with a wing-span of approximately three metres whose camera could take two thousand pictures and whose onboard television could broadcast live to a receptor station 240 kilometres away.

'*Il pleut mon âme, il pleut mais il pleut des yeux morts*', wrote Apollinaire in 1915, refering to enemy fire. With the advent of electronic warfare, this figure has become out of date. Projectiles have awakened and opened their many eyes: heat-seeking missiles, infra-red or laser guidance systems, warheads fitted with video-cameras that can relay what they see to pilots and to ground-controllers sitting at their consoles. The fusion is complete, the confusion perfect: nothing now distinguishes the functions of the weapon and the eye; the projectile's image and the image's projectile form a single composite. In its tasks of detection and acquisition, pursuit and destruction, the projectile is an image or 'signature' on a screen, and the television picture is an ultrasonic projectile propagated at the speed of light. The old ballistic projection has been succeeded by the projection of light, of the electronic eye of the guided or 'video' missile. It is the life-size projection of a film which would have overjoyed Eugène Promio, the inventor of the travelling platform, and even more Abel Gance, who wanted to launch his cameras like snowballs into the Battle of Brienne.

Ever since sights were superimposed on gun-barrels, people have never stopped associating the uses of projectiles and light, that light which is the soul of gun-barrels. Recent inventions have included the photon accelerator and the light intensifier, and now there are the laser weapons, directed beams, charged-particle guns, and so on. Not content with barrel-mounting, the experts have inserted a sighting device into the inner tube of artillery in order to improve performance. At ballistic and aerodynamic research laboratories in both France and the United States, 'hyperballistic firing tunnels' nearly a hundred metres long can launch scale-models of 're-entry bodies' (the projectiles being tested) at a speed of 5,000 metres a second. 'Cineradiographic' flash equipment, with a capacity for 40 million images a second, is then used to visualize their path in the bore of the gun. This takes us back to the origins of cinema, to Marey's first chronophotographic rifle which had a lens in the barrel and a cylinder for moving round the light-sensitive plate.

Since Vietnam and throughout the seventies, the mediation of battle has grown ever more pronounced. At the time of the Korean War a USAF Sabre already required more than forty kilometres to turn a Mig-15, but in Vietnam (as in the Six Days War) a Phantom needed an instrument-backed firing system if it was to have any hope of bringing down a Mig-21. The Phantom's targeting system subsequently led to the 'Fire and Forget' concept and to the Over-the-Horizon weapons systems which allow an attack to be conducted off the field.

The disintegration of the warrior's personality is at a very advanced stage. Looking up, he sees the digital display (opto-electronic or holographic) of the windscreen collimator; looking down, the radar screen, the onboard computer, the radio and the video screen, which enables him to follow the terrain with its four or five simultaneous targets, and to monitor his self-navigating Sidewinder missiles fitted with a camera or infra-red guidance system. However, this war of the waves had some major drawbacks, as Colonel Broughton, an F-105 Thunderchief pilot in Vietnam, has explained:

> The radio chatter was really picking up about this time – in fact, it was so dense with all the Mig and Sam warnings and everyone shouting direc-tions and commands that it was almost impossible to interpret what was going on. This is a real problem and once it starts, it just keeps getting worse and worse and is almost impossible to stop ... you see something

that you know you have to tell other people about in a desperate hurry to protect them and to protect yourself, and the temptation is to blurt it out as quickly as possible without using the proper call sign. The result is that everyone in the air immediately gets a shot of confusion and wonders who is talking about whom.

Such confusion was often exacerbated by poor weather conditions in North Vietnam:

> The weather over there is the thickest I have ever seen and when you get inside one of those big thunder-bumpers you are in for a good ride. Most clouds you fly through have their share of bumps but the visibility inside is usually good enough so that you can sit on the wing of another aircraft and fly formation off him. You just maintain the position you want and when he turns or rolls his aircraft, you roll right along with him. You have no idea where you are if you are on the wing, but that is up to the leader. The only time you get into trouble on the wing is when you try to fly position and also try to outguess the leader. This usually winds up in a case of spatial disorientation called vertigo. If this happens you can be sitting straight and level and swear that you are cocked up in a 60-degree bank going sideways. It is a most distressing sensation and sometimes almost impossible to get rid of. You can shake your head and holler at yourself and sometimes it won't go away, and it can be fatal. . . . For a real thrill, I recommend you try this type of flying on a black night.

The weightlessness that Ernst Jünger felt during artillery barrages in the First World War is reproduced in this account. However, the confusion of sensations involves not a panic-stricken terror but a technological vertigo or purely cinematic derealization, which affects the sense of spatial dimension. Tied to his machine, imprisoned in the closed circuits of electronics, the war pilot is no more than a motor-handicapped person temporarily suffering from a kind of possession analogous to the hallucinatory states of primitive warfare. We should not forget that the first stimulants were developed in response to the needs of Luftwaffe pilots.

Narcotics were to become the plague of the US expeditionary corps in Vietnam. From the beginning, they suffered from the hallucination of techno-logical combat-delirium, which blurred the distinction between the real and the imaginary. In this war of images, Broughton writes:

> Unfortunately, the groups known as photo interpreters are not always of the highest level of skill or experience, and their evaluation quite often does not agree with that of the men doing the work. I have bombed, and seen my troops bomb, on specific targets where I have watched the bombs pour in and seen the target blow up, with walls or structures flying across the area, only to be fragged right back into the same place because the film didn't look like that to the lieutenant who read it way back up the line. I

have gone back on these targets and lost good people and machines while doing so, and found them just as I expected, smashed. But who listens to a stupid fighter pilot?

People used to die for a coat of arms, an image on a pennant or flag; now they died to improve the sharpness of a film. War has finally become the third dimension of cinema.

It is a curious fact that much of the new matériel – helicopter gunships, missiles, telecommunications, detection systems – was being produced by the Hughes Aircraft Company, whose celebrated founder, Howard Hughes, had directed a film in 1930 about a First World War bomber crew (*Hell's Angels*). This schizophrenic magnate, who died in 1976, built an industrial empire by associating cinema and aviation, and Hughes Aircraft remains today one of the largest companies in the United States. In 1983, for example, it was working on improvements to the TOW anti-tank missile's guidance system, introducing an optical tracking device that allowed missiles to be precisely aimed despite the pitching and vibrating of the helicopter from which they were fired. But it was also developing equipment for in-flight entertainment, making it possible for infra-red rays to carry music and films to the passengers of regular airlines and business jets.

After the Vietnam defeat, Pentagon scientists and industrialists did not give up their drive to perfect electronic warfare. The MacNamara Line was transferred to the south of the United States – or, more precisely, the border with Mexico – with the supposed aim of detecting illegal immigrant workers. As for the anti-personnel interceptors, they gave birth in 1971 to a wild plan sponsored by the National Security Agency for the development of a personalized tracking device that could be used by the police. This electronic 'transponder', as it was known, was designed to record the distance, speed and path of an offender's movements and to transmit the information several times a minute, via relay-receivers, to a central screen-computer. Having checked these data against the permitted itineraries, the computer could immediately alert the police if the person wearing the 'tracking bug' went elsewhere or tried to remove it. Although the original idea was to use it for prisoners on parole, this system of *electronic incarceration* finally enabled a kind of prison reform. The cell would be replaced by a tiny black box, by confinement to the shadows through the stage direction of everyday life.

In 1974, spurred on by the oil crisis, this process of derealization acquired fantastic proportions with the boom in military flight and combat simulators, which effectively took the place of the old 'home trainer'. The production of synthetic 'daylight' images had meant that at last pilots could be trained without interruption in all aspects of a combat mission, covering the customary phases of navigation, penetration and attack. An instructor could teach them not just to pilot an aircraft with instruments but to pilot a series of startlingly realistic images. This *mise-en-scène* of war led a few years later to an event that went unnoticed: namely, the recognition of an equivalence between simulator time and real flight time. If we bear in mind the strictness of certification procedures for aeroplane pilots, we shall better understand the importance of such a decision.

Today, techniques have improved still further and a 'dogfight simulator', consisting of two spherical cabins, can simulate an attack by two enemy aircraft. It should be noted at this point that simulation has long since spread to the other two branches of the military. The Sperry Corporation – one of the main manufacturers, together with Thomson, of this type of equipment – produces for armoured units as well as for the navy and the air force. Moreover, within the East – West framework of direct non-aggression that has resulted from the strategy of nuclear deterrence, military manoeuvres have also gradually taken on the aspect of large-scale electronic games, a *Kriegspiel* requiring whole territories over which the various procedures and materials of modern war are reconstituted.

In the Nevada Desert, a special practice range known as 'Red Flag' has been created to simulate exposure to a Soviet defence system. Authentic Soviet surface-to-air missiles and accompanying radar equipment – whether Israeli war booty or old supplies to Egypt – help to re-create a perfectly realistic electronic environment of radar beams, firing procedures, radio transmissions, and so forth, which the American crews are trained to recognize and then neutralize. The aerial force participating in such exercises includes an AWACS flying control-tower and an Aggressor Squadron made up of aircraft whose features are similar to those of the Mig-21 and Mig-23. Similarly, in the Mojave Desert in California, the Army's National Training Center simulates war in the most life-like way. Thanks to 'Miles' (the Multiple Integrated Laser Engagement System), the soldiers' weapons on both sides project laser or infra-red rays with a range and trajectory roughly comparable to those of real ammunition. The various targets, fitted with silicon plates, are linked up to 'black boxes'. Both the troops and their weaponry also carry sensitive plates on their most vulnerable surfaces, so that when one is hit by a laser beam, the micro-processor in the black box calculates the impact and communicates it to Headquarters, which then adds up the score. A host of other simulation devices and special film effects complete the picture.

In the same order of ideas we should mention the Tactical Mapping System, a video-disc produced by the Advanced Research Project Army. By speeding up or slowing down the procession of fifty-four thousand images, and changing the direction or season as one might switch television channels, the viewer is able to build up a continuous picture of the small Colorado town of Aspen. The town is thus transferred to a sort of ballistic tunnel for tank-pilots, who use this method to train in street combat. Let us not forget that the Dykstraflex camera made by John Dykstra for the film *Star Wars* – a camera in the service of a computer which records its own movements – was actually descended from a pilot training system.

The same kind of technological spin-off lies behind the SPAACE camera, an automatic tracking system that two Frenchmen developed for the cinema on the basis of an anti-aircraft radar platform. This new-style camera, with its powerful telephoto lens, can follow the actors' spontaneous movements without any difficulty, even locking on to the face of a jet pilot executing a low-altitude figure. The fact is that once the energy crisis had made the simulation industry profitable, the pace of technological innovation grew more frantic towards the end of the seventies and culminated in the automation of the war machine.

The complexity of manoeuvres, the ever greater air speeds, the assistance of satellites, and the necessity for ground-attack aircraft to fly supersonically at very low altitudes eventually led the engineers to automate piloting itself. On the F-16 'AFT1,' for example, developed by Robert Swortzel, the pilot never touches the controls but navigates by voice. In return, an on-screen display keeps him informed of his flight plan and 'firing plan' and throws up on the windscreen the anticipated acceleration and countdown time, as well as the kind of manoeuvres that the pilot will have to execute. For the firing operation, the pilot has a special sighting helmet linked to a laser and infra-red targeting system; all he has to do is fix the target and give a verbal instruction for the weapons to be released. This revolutionary apparatus, designed in 1982 for the United States Air Force, the Navy and NASA, combines a number of advanced technologies, particularly in the field of laser-targeting. The Eye-Tracked synchronization system fixes the pilot's gaze, however sudden the movement of his eyes, so that firing can proceed as soon as binocular accomodation is achieved.

Finally, there is the 'homing image', which joins together an infra-red ray and an explosive projectile fitted with a special device. This device acts in the manner of an eye, picking up the image of the infra-red-lit target. The projectile then makes its way towards the image – and thus towards the target for destruction – with all the ease of someone going home. This system, which is attached to the latest missiles, once again illustrates the fateful confusion of eye and weapon.

We can now understand better the concern on both sides to perfect weapons that are as undetectable as a submerged submarine – Stealth bombers, 'smart' missiles, invisible not just to the human eye but above all to the piercing, unerring gaze of technology. In the 1980s there was a significant shift or 'conversion' in global strategy, as East – West conflict passed into North – South confrontation. Notwithstanding the tensions in the Middle East and the Euromissiles controversy, military space is being shifted and organized around the oceans, in the Pacific, the Indian Ocean and the South Atlantic. Indeed, the Malvinas War can be seen as a rehearsal for a nuclear conflict, in the use of American and Soviet satellites, British nuclear submarines, and French missiles capable of destroying highly exposed surface-ships. But it was also a war of electronic counter-measures – naval decoys whose main feature was to super-impose upon the incoming missile's optical or infra-red radar image an entirely manufactured image that would appear both more important and more attractive than the real ship, as well as being equally credible to the enemy missile. Once this was achieved, the missile's automatic navigator locked on to the centre of gravity of the 'decoy-image-cum-ship-image', and all that remained was to exploit the spectre of the decoy to draw the missile far over the ship. The whole operation lasted barely a few seconds.

One could go on for ever listing the technological weapons, the panoply of light-war, the aesthetic of the electronic battlefield, the military use of space whose conquest was ultimately the conquest of the image – the electronic image of remote detection; the artificial image produced by satellites as they endlessly sweep over the surface of continents drawing automatic maps; life-size cinema in which the day and the light of film-speed succeed the day and the light of astronomical time. It is subliminal light of incomparable transparency, where technology finally exposes the whole world.

In the summer of 1982, the Israeli preventive war in Lebanon, baptized 'Peace in Galilee', drew on all the resources of the scientific arsenal: Grumman 'Hawkeye' aircraft-radar capable of simultaneously locating two hundred and fifty targets for F-15 and F-16 fighter-bombers; and, above all, the remote-piloted 'Scout' automata, with a wing-span of less than two metres, which were massively and systematically deployed for the first time in the history of battle. This toy craft, worthy of Ernst Jünger's *Glass Bees*, was a veritable Tsahal's eye fitted with TV cameras and thermal-image systems. As it skimmed the rooftops of the besieged city of Beirut, flying over the most exposed Palestinian districts, it provided images of population movement and thermal graphics of Palestinian vehicles for Israeli analysts sitting at their video consoles more than a hundred kilometres away.

In the autumn of 1982, the United States established a military high command for space and announced the impending launch of an early-warning satellite. In the spring of 1983, on 23 March to be precise, President Reagan painted a picture of an anti-ballistic-missile system employing nuclear energy, enhanced rays, directed beams and charged particles.

Last summer, on 5 July 1983, an American KC-135 aircraft fitted with a laser system shot down a Sidewinder missile travelling at 3,000 kilometres an hour.

Scan. Freeze frame.

12

CINEMA AND TECHNOLOGY: A HISTORICAL OVERVIEW

Peter Wollen

I would like to give an overview, necessarily schematic, of the history of technological change and innovation in the cinema, together with a few theoretical comments, bringing out the implications of my reduced empirical material. The paper is intended as introductory and the main stress I want to make is on the heterogeneity of the economic and cultural determinants of change and the way in which innovations in one area may help to produce conservatism and even 'retreat' in another – history not simply with 'differential' times, but even with 'reverse' times. In dealing with the heterogeneity of film technology, I want to stress the presence of three distinct phases – recording, processing, and projecting or exhibiting – and the way in which developments in one may cause repercussions in the others. In general, I believe too much attention is usually paid to the recording stage at the expense of the laboratory and the theatre – a serious distortion because exhibition, rather than production, is economically dominant in the film industry, at least as far as the timing and impact of technological changes are concerned.

I am aware that, despite this, my own approach is probably too traditional in bias, if only because the available data has itself been determined by the bias of previous researchers. The history of the technique of editing, for instance, is rather neglected. I happened recently to see again Vertov's *Man With A Movie Camera* with its shots of Svilova editing with a pair of scissors and was reminded then of the changes that have taken place in editing equipment.

From: Peter Wollen, 'Cinema and Technology: A Historical Overview', in *Readings and Writings: Semiotic Counter-strategies* (Verso, London, 1978).

Even an apparently extraneous and trivial invention like Scotch tape has had an enormous impact on editing technique. It is difficult to escape entirely from those myths of film history that concentrate on only the recording phase and narrate this history in terms of four legendary moments. The first moment is that of Lumière and the first Lumière programme (often condensed into the train entering the station at La Ciotat). The second moment is the arrival of sound and its instance is *The Jazz Singer*. Then there is colour (strictly speaking, three-colour Technicolor) with the Disney cartoons and *Becky Sharp*. Fourthly, there is the moment of wide screen and 3-D (*The Robe, This is Cinerama*). This series, of course, suggests possible extensions in the future, in line with Bazin's celebrated myth of total duplication of reality.

In fact, I think, the crucial changes in the recording process have involved not the camera itself, as the Lumière example suggests, but changes in film stock. The camera itself is a very simple piece of mechanical equipment. As Hollis Frampton once pointed out, it represents the culmination of the Age of Machines and was superseded almost as soon as it was invented. Lumière's own inspiration was the sewing machine, itself a typical piece of nineteenth-century machinery. Lumière regarded the invention, of the film camera as a simple task in comparison with the invention of the Autochrome colour photography process that he also introduced. The camera is not an extremely elaborate piece of equipment even by nineteenth-century standards. Most of the devices necessary were the product of tinkering by skilled enthusiasts – the Maltese cross, the Latham loop, all the things that occupy chapters in books and really acquired significance through patents litigation. Most changes in camera efficiency are involved with the optical rather than the mechanical system (better light transmission through the lens; the post-war explosion of zoom; improvements in focusing systems), with miniaturization and portability and with by-products of other innovations (soundproofing, for instance). In one cinematographer's words, 'of course, the new camera is easier to use, with many labour-saving gadgets, but the final result looks the same.'

The real breakthroughs have been in the technology of film stock, in chemistry rather than mechanics. The precondition for the invention of cinema was the invention of celluloid (first used as a substitute for ivory in the manufacture of billiard balls and for primitive false teeth) which provided a strong but flexible base for the emulsion. Later the history of film stock is one of steadily improving speed/grain ratios, faster and more sensitive emulsions without adverse graininess. There is an important paradox here. Improved stocks have made film-making much more accessible, allowing films to be made in lower and lower levels of available light and creating the possibility of 8mm and 16mm film-making on a wide scale. Yet at the same time a good deal of the pressure for improved emulsions came because the development of sound and colour made filming much more difficult – colour demanded more light, and sound too made lighting much more cumbersome (hence, the well-known lag in deep-focus cinematography between the silent period and *Citizen Kane*). The innovations that restricted access to film-making, that demanded enormous capital investment and caused real set-backs, have attracted attention, while the steady development of stock – chemical rather than optical or electronic – has never been comprehensively chronicled.

I would like to dwell a little on the adverse effects of the introduction of sound. It was with sound that the truly modern technology of electronics first made a real impact on the cinema. In fact the breakthrough in sound technology is associated much more with the third of the phases that I described at the start than with the first, more with projection than with recording. The problems were twofold. First, image and sound had to be synchronized. Second, sound had to be amplified to fill a large theatre (Edison had shown sound films but only in a peepshow with a primitive listening-tube: in fact, it was his wish to incorporate sound, without any means of amplification, that led him towards the peepshow rather than theatrical projection). The two crucial discoveries were the audion tube which made possible advances in loudspeaker and public address technology that could eventually feed into the cinema and, of course, the photoelectric cell (leading in time to television as well) which made possible an optical sound-track that could be picked up, with absolutely precise synchronization, by a component within the projector, rather than demanding, as previous systems did, synchronization between the projector and a separate sound system.

The introduction of sound had a series of effects. A technical advance on one front brought retreats on others: one step forward, two steps backwards. In the first place, the economic effects must be mentioned. (The introduction of sound, also, of course, had economic determinants: principally, saving in labour costs through the elimination of orchestras and between-the-screenings entertainers.) The conversion costs were enormous and led to a vastly increased role for banks in the industry in alliance with the giant electronics firms that controlled the relevant patents. (Fox, who tried to challenge the patents, was driven to bankruptcy and gaol.) In comparison with the twenties, the thirties was a period in which very little independent or experimental film-making took place. In Hollywood, the power of the producer was enormously enhanced.

Technically, sound, while it introduced new possibilities (scarcely realized), also introduced new obstacles and a chain of bizarre secondary problems and solutions. The carbon lights hummed and the hum came through on the sound-track. The tungsten lights that replaced them were at the red end of the spectrum and so the old orthochromatic film, blind to red, had to go, to be replaced by panchromatic stock (like so much else, a spin-off from military technology – it had been originally developed for reconnaissance fog photography). This change brought changes in make-up; the fortunes of Max Factor date from this period. Studios replaced locations; multiple camera set-ups were introduced; the craft of script-writing was transformed. Most important of all, the laboratory was completely reorganized. The need for sound-image synchronization meant that every aspect of timing had to be standardized. On the set, the camera was no longer hand-cranked. New equipment was introduced: for example the sensitometer and densitometer. Every aspect of the laboratory was automated and there were standardized development and printing procedures. In this way, the laboratory became completely divorced from the work of the director and cinematographer; it became an automated, industrial process with its own standard operating procedures. Anyone who has made a film will be familiar with the opacity of the laboratory, something that dates from this period.

It was not until after World War II that new developments in sound technology were universalized, thus permitting immediate set-backs to be overcome. The crucial breakthrough was the advent of magnetic tape, invented in Germany and, like reflex focusing, the hand-held camera and monopack colour stock, part of the booty of victory. Tape made sound recording much easier, and cheaper; it transformed dubbing and mixing and, with the subsequent development of the Nagra and crystal-synchronization, led to much easier location filming and the whole *cinéma-vérité* movement, with subsequent new definitions of 'realism' in film. It is worth noting, perhaps, that the main limitations on sound currently come at the projection stage; poor speakers and poor acoustics make working to the full potentiality of modern recording and mixing technology pointless.

The history of the development of colour is similar to that of sound: a breakthrough that proved to be a set-back. There were attempts to introduce colour from the very beginning – with hand-tinting, toning and various experimental systems, including two-colour technicolor – out the successful invention was that of three-colour Technicolor in the early thirties by Herbert Kalmus. The success of Technicolor derived from Kalmus's realisation that he had to devise a system that not only recorded colour but would also be acceptable to exhibitors. Once again the projection stage proved to be the determining factor. At the production end Technicolor produced new obstacles. The beam-splitter camera was extremely bulky and could only be leased together with an approved Technicolor cinematographer. Colour consultants came on the set, led by Natalie Kalmus, and keyed colour to eye and lip tones; filters and unconventional effects were barred until Eastman Color arrived and Huston broke free with *Moulin Rouge* in the fifties. Technicolor required more light which meant a lower effective film speed. Film memoirs are full of complaints by cinematographers about the limitations Technicolor imposed.

As with sound, the next step came after the war with the appropriation by the victorious allies of Agfacolor, fruit of superior German dye technology, developed within the IG Farben group. Russian and American armies raced to get to the Agfa works and, though the Russians won (hence Sovcolor), the destruction of patents and diffusion of new technical information led to the appearance of Eastman Color with *The Robe* in 1953. (The new colour process was linked to Cinemascope: Technicolor beam-splitter cameras could not be fitted with scope lenses.) Eastman's problems were essentially matching Technicolor's speed, and then improving on it, without losing colour correction. Every new dye introduced as a corrective would tend to slow the film down. There was also a strong economic incentive, of course, in improving film speed, namely to reduce lighting costs. Again, the strength of Eastman Color lay in its greater accessibility, though there was a time-lag of twenty years or more.

Colour, like sound, also demanded standardization in the laboratory. Elaborate controls were developed and matching and grading colour became crucial parts of the laboratory's work. It is still extremely difficult and expensive to get really detailed control over complex colour effects. The opacity and autonomy of the laboratory was further accentuated. It might be added that one of the attractions of colour video, which uses electronic rather than chemical technology for colour, is that there is no laboratory involved. In video the three phases of articulation are much more closely connected and, of course, are not separated in time in the same way that they are in film. It is only a matter of time before electronic technology gains the ascendancy in image as well as sound.

Both sound and colour had to meet the requirements of the exhibitor. Projection has been the most conservative side of film technology. Exhibitors, for instance, defeated 3-D – an attempt by Polaroid to challenge Eastman's supremacy in the film stock market. Cinerama (derived from aerial gunnery simulation) never succeeded except in a few big city theatres. Cinemascope (another military spin-off – emanating from tank gun sighting periscopes) was able to make headway because it involved minimal adaptation of the projector, under the economic pressure of competition from TV (and also to eliminate 3-D). Exhibitors have consistently resisted conversion costs.

The economic strength of the exhibitors has always rested on the real estate value of the theatres. Production companies, in contrast, have been subject to recurrent crises, bankruptcies and take-overs throughout their history. They have simply not been able to afford research and development projects, except for a limited involvement in special effects, ironing out secondary technical problems and adapting technology developed elsewhere. Almost all the major technical innovations have been introduced by outsiders with the support of economic interests wishing to break into the industry. Dupont and 3M have tried to enter through magnetic tape and polyester film bases; Polaroid was fought off over stereoscopic film. New challengers will come from video and presumably laser technology. Moreover, the interests of the major technology-producing companies are not limited to Hollywood, which is only a small part of their market. The general industrial and also domestic markets are much more significant and here there are no entrenched exhibitors to contend with. It is here that, on the one hand, expensive laser and fibre optics 'cinema' and, on the other, cheap 8mm synch sound and video disc 'cinema' will first make headway.

At this point I would like to shift focus from Hollywood to experimental and avant-garde forms of film-making. This area, of course, has been crucially dependent on the improved quality and accessibility of 16mm and, to some extent, 8mm film-making: faster stock, portable equipment, miniaturization and so on. Up until the 1950s histories of avant-garde film list almost every experimental film made; there were so few. Clearly this was because of the difficulty and prohibitive cost of making films independently. Since then, however, there has been an enormous explosion in the number made following the introduction of the Eclair camera and the Nagra tape recorder (first used in 1960 in Rouch and Morin's *Chronique d'un Eté*), together with increased subsidies, either through state or para-state arts funding bodies or through the educational system. The entire new field of independent film has begun to appear between home movies and the industry.

Dependent for its expansion of these technical advances, avant-garde film has had other technological implications. First, of course, there has been the mis-use of existing technology, its use to transgress the norms implicit in it. On the whole, this has not involved very advanced technology: flicker films counteract the use of the shutter, and so on. A variety of mis-use is hyperbolic use – thus the hyperbolic use of the zoom lens (as in *Wavelength*), or the optical printer or the projector or the geared head (as in *Riddles of the Sphinx*). Then there is an area in which technological innovations have actually taken place – Chris Welsby's landscape films or Michael Snow's *La Région Centrale* for which ingenious contraptions were devised for the camera to permit realization of a project that would otherwise have been technically impossible. In all these areas, I think, there is an ambivalence between contravening legitimate codes and practices (a negative act) and exploring possibilities deliberately overlooked within the industry, or tightly contextualized (in contrast, a positive act).

Finally, a few theoretical, or pre-theoretical, remarks. I would like first to stress that the technology of cinema is not a unified whole, but is extremely heterogeneous. It covers developments in the fields of mechanics, optics, chemistry and electronics. It covers the Latham loop, Scotch tape, the densito-meter, the zoom lens, magnetic tape, and so on and on (the list is long). In the past theorists have tended to stress and even essentialize one or other area of technology at the expense of the others. Cinema is seen in terms of the camera and the recording process or reproduction and the printing process or projection and the physical place of the spectator (Bazin, Benjamin, Baudry). In this way the heterogeneity of the cinema is reduced to one subset of determinations in a reductionist manner. In effect a myth of the cinema (Bazin's own term) is thereby created, which serves to efface the reality of production.

Within the avant-garde too (or perhaps I should say within the theory of the avant-garde) there has been a parallel tendency to create an ontology, seeing means not as secreting a teleology, but as ends in themselves, as essences. This new ontology can easily be disguised as a materialism, since it seems to fore-ground means of production rather than 'images'. Yet implicit within it is an assumption that the equipment used for making films is an essential bedrock rather than itself the product of a variety of historical determinations, at the interface where the economies of capital and libido interlock. The forms of matter taken by the technical apparatus of film are determined by the forms taken by the material vicissitudes of labour and instinct, within history (or rather, as history).

At the same time, however, it is within the avant-garde that we find resistance to the perpetual anthropomorphization of technology in the cinema. It is instructive to re-read Vertov's rhapsodies on the camera-eye. Technological developments outside the cinema have already produced microphotography, X-ray photography, infra-red and thermal photography, magnetic photography and many varieties of photography which Vertov never saw. Yet these have had almost no impact on the cinema. The eye of the camera is still assimilated to the human eye, an eye whose imaginary is constructed around a range of differences within a basic unity, rather than a search for a fundamentally different form of vision. The problem is not one of representation as such, so much as the dominant and cohesive mode of representation. It is here that a specious unity exists, rather than within the technology itself, and it is here, by understanding the different and heterogeneous determinations at work and struggling to release them from the interlock in which they are bound, that we can conceive and construct a new cinema, not necessarily with a new technology, but certainly with a new place of and for technology.

13

THE ROLE OF THE APPARATUS

Jacques Aumont

THE SPATIAL DIMENSION OF THE APPARATUS

Plastic Space, the Spectator's Space

To look at an image is to make contact with a spatial reality, the reality of the image, which is quite different from the reality of our everyday world. The first function of the apparatus is to offer concrete solutions to the management of this unnatural contact between the spectator's space and the space of the image, which we will call plastic space.

The elements in the image which can be called 'plastic' (be it a figurative image or not) are those which characterise it as an ensemble of visual forms, and which allow these forms to be distinguished:

- the *surface* of the image, and its organisation, traditionally called its composition. In other words, the pattern of geometric relationships between the different parts of the surface;
- the range of *values*, linked to the degree of luminosity or brightness of each area of the image, and the contrasts that this range generates;
- the range of *colours*, and its range of contrasts;
- the *graphic* elements, especially important in all 'abstract' images;
- the *materiality* of the image itself in so far as this affects perception (for instance, the painterly brush strokes in certain kinds of art or the grain of a photographic image).

From: Jacques Aumont, 'The Role of the Apparatus', in *The Image* (BFI, 1997).

These are the basic plastic elements of the image, and they are the ones the spectator first encounters.

CONCRETE SPACE, ABSTRACT SPACE

The primary function of any apparatus of the image is to regulate the psychic space between the spectator and an image composed of the interaction between the plastic values outlined above, taking into account the fundamental fact that they do not share the same space and that there is, to use a term derived from André Michotte's remarks (1948) about film, a segregation of spaces, a distinction between plastic and spectatorial spaces.

One of the most important components of this relationship is the spectator's perception of a representational space, that is to say, a three-dimensional, imaginary and fictional space that nevertheless, through indices of analogy, can be referred to real space. However, there is a further link in this chain: the spectator not only perceives the representational, figurative space of the image, he or she also perceives the plastic space of the image in itself. Up to a point, that is what is implied by the notion of a 'double reality', but only up to a point, since this notion claims that, in the perception of represented space, the perception of surface is taken into account. Here we have to add that, regardless of whether a space is represented in the image or not, the spectator has to deal with plastic space. In order better to understand the spatial aspects of the apparatus (and especially the frame), we need to address the issue of the subject's capacity to enter into a direct relation with plastic space. This is what the art historian and sociologist Pierre Francastel has attempted to deal with in a number of books.

Francastel (1965) has analysed those aspects of our relationship to the image based on the active construction of imaginary space. There is no need to dwell on those aspects here. His originality, however, lies in the fact that he also emphasises another aspect of that relationship: that of the construction of a material, 'concrete' space which relates directly to the plastic values of the image. For Francastel, imaginary space rests on a particular, abstract conception of space: that of the average Western adult. However, there are other, less abstract ways of relating to space, prior even to any encounter with images, ways less rigidly constructed by perspectival geometry. Francastel sums up the range of these ways of relating to space under the term topology. In fact, in mathematics, topology is merely the study of spatial relations and includes, among other things, the study of perspective. However, Francastel uses the term in the specialist sense, developed in the 40s by psychologists such as Henri Wallon, to describe a child's conception of space. According to Wallon, a child learns about space gradually and before acquiring a point of view liable to be 'perspectivised', a child apprehends space in terms of close proximities, relying on relations such as 'next to', 'around' and 'inside', rather than through concepts of 'near', 'far', 'in front of' and 'behind'. For Francastel, these first relations to the actual space that surrounds us never entirely disappear and are never completely erased by the subsequent acquisition of a more total and abstract sense of space. In our relation to the image (artistic, pictorial, filmic), this original experience of space based on the body is reactivated, and to our perspectival organisation of social space is added, at times in contradictory manner, the genetic space of our 'topological' organisation.

WAYS OF SEEING

Francastel's thesis proposes that every spectator has two distinct and simultaneous, at times partly opposed, ways of perceiving space. In this respect, Francastel reprises, symptomatically, the German art historian Heinrich Wölfflin's famous thesis formulated in his *Fundamental Principles of the History of Art* (1915) that art (meaning Western art, of course) has developed in relation to two ways of seeing which range from the 'tactile' to the 'visual'. Wölfflin developed this thesis, which is reminiscent of Hildebrand's intuition into an explanatory principle of the history of art, and did so more rigorously than his colleagues Worringer or Riegl. For Wölfflin, the tactile form of vision is also a plastic form linked to the sensation of objects seen in close-up, organising the visual field according to a hierarchy which is close to Francastel's notion of topology. On the other hand, what he calls the visual form of seeing is the properly pictorial form linked to a distant and subjective vision of space, a unified vision of space and light which organises the totality of spatial relationships between the whole and the parts on geometric principles.

This idea seduced a number of art historians and critics because of its explanatory power and relatively elegant appearance. José Ortega y Gasset, the great Spanish critic, adhered strictly to Wölfflin's theory and set out to apply it to the history of figurative art from Giotto, who concentrated on the figuration of people, through Velasquez's ability to achieve a figurative representation of space by 'stepping back' from the canvas, through to the Impressionists, who 'stepped back' as far as it is possible to go in order to achieve the figuration of the sensation of light and, finally, to early-twentieth-century Expressionism and Cubism, in which an even greater distance leads the artist to represent ideas (and which, paradoxically, thus return to tactile values, closing the circle of the history of art).

Around the same time in the 40s, Eisenstein also took up this thesis, notably in his essay, 'Rodin and Rilke and the Problem of Space in Figurative Arts' (1945), in which he extended Wölfflin's thesis to suggest that not only the history of art, but the entire history of people's relation to space moves from the concave to the convex, from interior to exterior (that is to say, from the tactile to the visual), from a 'hollow' psychological situation to an understanding of 'plenitude'. Nevertheless, it is difficult to accept the *explanatory* dimension of this thesis, if only beacuse it places too much faith in its metaphor of the two different kinds of vision, near and far, which are ultimately reduced to functions of the seeing subject conceived as a completely ahistorical being. However, it remains an important intuition and, in combination with Francastel's work, it helpfully identifies the nature of the problem, reminding us that our relationship to the image is not due simply to our adaptation to the century-long dominance and ubiquity of photographic imagery. On the contrary, that relationship is based on an accumulation of prior experiences which go back to childhood, as well as to the 'childhood of art', and which emerge through photographic ways of seeing.

THE SIZE OF THE IMAGE

To repeat, the image is first and foremost an object in the world, with physical characteristics, just like any other object, that make it perceptible. Among these characteristics is one that is especially important for the apparatus: the size of the image.

Michelangelo's *Last Judgement*, the *Mona Lisa*, a daguerrotype, a film frame, all can these days be found side by side in the form of reproductions of identical size in an illustrated book, even though Michelangelo's fresco takes up an entire wall of the Sistine Chapel, Leonardo's painting is about one metre high and a daguerrotype is less than ten centimetres square. As for a film frame, it measures about 20×35mm on a celluloid reel, but can become huge when projected on to a screen. Our main sources of images, such as books, magazines and television screens, dramatically reduce the variety of an image's dimensions and habituate us to a spatial relationship with them based on average distances.

It is therefore very important to realise that every image has been made to occupy a specific place in the environment, which determines the way it is seen. The frescoes by Masaccio and Masolino in the Brancacci Chapel in Florence are not only much larger than their commonly available reproductions, but they are also painted one above the other on the walls of a fairly narrow chapel. *In situ*, they give an impression (to those who have only encountered them in art history books) of being heaped up and crammed in, which, among other things, greatly reduces their power of illusionism and emphasises their status as texts *to be read*. One of the great innovations of the Renaissance was the production of work that could be detached from the walls, *tableaux* (canvas paintings), and which were generally much smaller than the frescoes in the churches. The relationship of the spectator to the painting thus becomes not only more intimate, it also becomes more purely visual. It is remarkable that when frescoes were once again painted on walls and ceilings in the 17th and 18th centuries, they were influenced by the ideology of 'tableau' painting and tried to reproduce that kind of visual relationship rather than the kind of relationship characteristic of the pre-Renaissance fresco tradition. Examples are the vault ceiling of San Ignazio or the walls and ceilings of the Venetian palazzos decorated by Tiepolo.

The size of the image is thus one of the fundamental elements which determine the relationship that a spectator can establish between his or her own space and the plastic space of the image. In fact, the spectator's *spatial* relationship to the image is even more fundamental: in every era artists have been conscious of, for example, the power that a large image can exert when a specator is forced to be close to it, forcing him or her not only to see its surface, but also to be dominated, even crushed, by it. This spatial fact is used as a central component in a number of contemporary works, including installations. In the exhibition *Passages de l'image* (Centre Pompidou, 1990), a piece by Thierry Kuntzel juxtaposed a gigantic and a tiny image, one static, the other moving. Moreover, the smaller image presented an extreme close-up whereas the larger image presented a more inclusive perspective. The juxtaposition produced a perturbation of the spectator's spatial reference points. On the other hand, the small scale of certain images such as most photographic images enables the subject to enter into a relation of proximity, possession, even fetishisation with the image.

THE EXAMPLE OF THE CLOSE-UP

The success of the Lumière brothers' Cinématograph was largely due to the size of the projected image, which was significantly larger than the image size achieved by Edison's kinetoscope. However, the image size felt to be appropriate to represent expansive outdoor scenes became quite disturbing when film began to show human bodies in close-up. The first shots framing only a person's torso or head were rejected, not only because they were deemed unrealistic, but because these enlargements were experienced as monstrous. Critics referred to 'big heads' and 'dumb giants', and film-makers were accused of 'not knowing that a head cannot move by itself, without the help of a body and legs'. In short, the close-up seemed to be against nature. However, a few years later, in the 20s, Jean Epstein could say that the close-up was 'the soul of cinema'. What had originally been an eccentric characteristic of the cinematic apparatus had by then been transformed into a specific aesthetic element.

The close-up is a constantly repeated example of the power of the apparatus:

- It produces effects of 'Gulliverisation' or 'Lilliputisation', to quote Philippe Dubois, playing on the relative sizes of *the* image and the object represented in it (in early cinema, the close-up was often thought to represent an object seen through a magnifying glass or a telescope); however, the great directors of silent films knew how to use cinema's ability to make these strange enlargements, turning a telephone into a sort of monument (Epstein), a cockroach into a monster larger than an elephant (Eisenstein);
- It transforms the sense of distance, leading the spectator to extreme psychic proximity or intimacy (Epstein), as in the series of close-ups of Falconetti in Dreyer's *La Passion de Jeanne d'Arc* (1927). This intimacy can sometimes become excessive, as in Williamson's famous short film *The Big Swallow* (1901), in which the character filmed in close-up opens his mouth and, continuing to move towards the camera, ends up by swallowing it;

- It materialises, almost literally, the metaphor of visual touch, accentuating simultaneously, and contradictorily, the surface of the image (because its graininess becomes more perceptible) and the imaginary volume of the filmed object (detaching it from the surrounding space, the depth of which seems to have been abolished).

The close-up very soon became one of the most widely and consistently discussed aspects of film theory. Not only Epstein but also Eisenstein (who wrote a number of texts on it up to the 40s) and Béla Balázs were preoccupied with theorising the close-up at an early stage, recognising that it could become one of the major assets of cinema if the cinema was to become something more than a simple reproduction of reality. The theory of the close-up as a technique for heightening expressiveness has been extended more recently by Pascal Bonitzer (1982, 1985) and Philippe Dubois (1984–85). For Bonitzer, the close-up is a supplement of 'the drama, cutting into the primitive integrity of the cinematic scene', 're-marking the discontinuity of the cinematic space, and sweeping vision, the image, along in the substitutive movement of (cinematic) writing'. In such a notion of cinema, the close-up becomes an emblem of the heterogeneity of the film text, 'wrecking' the linear conception of montage and celebrating the fragmentary nature of the shot found in Eisensteinian concepts. Dubois emphasises the instinctual effects the close-up can produce, its ability to focus in its vertigo-effect ('a stone splits open and reveals a precipice'), its Medusa-effect which fascinates and repulses at the same time.

In all these cases, the close-up is seen as the image par excellence that produces a psychic distance specific to cinema, encompassing a sense of staggering proximity and irreducible remoteness.

The Frame

The image is a finite object with measurable dimensions: it has a size. The vast majority of images are objects that can be isolated perceptually, if not always materially, from their environment. The limited, often detachable, even portable nature of the image is also one of the essential characteristics that defines the image-apparatus. There is no concept that incarnates these characteristics better than the *frame*.

CONCRETE FRAME, ABSTRACT FRAME

All images have a material base. They are all objects. The frame is first and foremost the *edge* of this object, its material, tangible boundary. Very often, this edge is strengthened by the addition of another object to the object-image, which we will call an *object-frame*. For paintings exhibited in museums, an object-frame, whether sculpted, ornately decorated, gilded, and so on, is almost mandatory. Even snapshots displayed on the mantlepiece, posters on an adolescent's bedroom wall, the projected cinema image, and even the television image, all have their object-frame, even though its significance varies enormously, as does its materiality, its thickness, size and form. For instance, the object-frame of television was much more present in the early television sets. Their obtrusive oval-shaped window-frame almost overwhelmed the image within, whereas the current sets with square corners and flat screen aim to render the frame as invisible as possible.

The frame is also, and more fundamentally, that which demarcates the closure of the image, its finiteness. It is the edge of an image in another, intangible sense: it is its perceptible limit. In that sense, it is a *limit-frame*. The limit-frame is where the image ends, defining its field by separating it from what it is not; in this way, it constitutes an *out-of-frame*. Object-frame and limit-frame usually go together, but it is important to realise that this is not necessarily so. Many pictorial works, especially those of the 20th century, have never been framed. On a more mundane level, the amateur photos developed and printed by machine are produced, not only without a frame, but also without a border. In these cases, the image only has a limit-frame and no object-frame. Inversely, some images with an object-frame barely have a limit-frame. For instance, the many Chinese paintings on horizontal or vertical scrolls, which provides a kind of frame since the scrolls containing the images have edges, but the limits of the painted area are not marked in any way and so there is no particular signifier of a perceptible limit to the separate images themselves.

The frame, in both its phenomenal forms, is what gives form, or rather, a *format* to the image. A format can be defined by two parameters: the absolute size of the image, and the relative size of its main dimensions. Frames come in all shapes and sizes, even highly improbable ones, but with the notable exception of a widespread vogue for round frames in classic Italian painting, the immense majority of frames have been rectangular. In such cases, the format is defined by the relation of the vertical to the horizontal edges. There are no precise statistics on the predominant formats at different periods, but we can safely say that while cinema has familiarised us with horizontal images (from its use of the standard format of the 1:1.33 ratio, through to the widescreen format of the 1:2.5 ratio), all portrait photography of the 19th century, informed by a well-established tradition in painting, used a vertical format. As for the proportions of the image, they are most frequently similar to a slightly elongated rectangle (some old statistic confirms that a ratio of 1:1.6 between the two dimensions is not only the most common, but is 'preferred' by the majority of spectators.

THE FUNCTIONS OF THE FRAME

The gilded cornice frame seen frequently around paintings in our museums has been widely used since the 16th century. Previously, from ancient Greek painting onwards, other types of objects were used. Many mural paintings and mosaics of the Hellenistic era also had painted or sculpted frames. In other words, the frame, in both its aspects, has existed in our culture for a very long time. The durability of such a convention over a period of more than 2000 years can only be explained if it fulfils useful or important *functions*. The functions of the frame are potentially numerous:

- *Visual functions*. The frame is what separates the image from its perceptual environment. The effects of this perceptual function are multiple: the object-frame, by isolating a segment of the visual field, singles out and enhances its perception; it plays the part of a visual transition, an intermediary, between the interior and the exterior of the image, facilitating a smoother passage from inside to outside. (Classical painters were very sensitive to this transitional function, particularly to the way that the gilded frame enabled the canvas to be bathed in a soft, golden light, considered to be favourable to the vision of the painting.)

  Object-frame and limit-frame, together, ensure the perceptual isolation of the image. They contribute to its double perceptual reality by creating a special zone in the visual field, producing indices of analogy while organising the image into a visual 'force field', that is to say, it contributes to the organisation of the image's plastic aspects, traditionally called 'composition'.

- *Economic functions*. Framing, in the form that we know it, appeared at more or less the same time as the modern concept of a painting as a detachable, exchangeable object able to circulate as merchandise within economic circuits. The frame, therefore, soon turned into a visible signifier of the painting's market value. It is no accident, from this point of view, that the frame has for some time been a precious object in its own right, skilfully made and at times using precious materials such as gold, or embedded with precious stone.

- *Symbolic functions*. Simultaneously extending its visual function of separating and isolating the image, and its economic function of conferring value on the painting, the frame is also a kind of *index* which 'tells' the spectator that he or she is looking at an image which, because it is framed in a certain way, should be viewed in relation to certain conventions, and possibly has a certain value.

  Like all symbolic functions, this one is diverse, changing according to the reigning symbolic regime. For a long time, the framing of the image had a fairly straightforward value, signifying that it was art, and that it should be viewed accordingly. This idea has not altogether disappeared, and we find a faint echo of it in the proliferation of framed images in contemporary petit-bourgeois interiors or, until about 1960, in the way photographers (in France) 'framed' amateur photographs with a narrow white border, sometimes with patterns in relief. Other values have appeared with 'new' images: the television set which frames the televisual image (by locating it within the interior design of a room) gives this image a specific status, as far from art as possible, desanctifying it and giving it a status more like that of a 'conversation', an uninterrupted 'flow'. The televisual image seems to be addressed to me personally and, potentially, it goes on forever.

- *Representational and narrative functions.* As an index of vision designating a discrete world, the frame is intensified when the image is figurative or narrative, or when the image has a particularly *imaginary* value. The frame then becomes like an opening which gives access to the imaginary world, to the diegesis figured by the image. The famous metaphor of a frame as a 'window on the world', often repeated with variations, goes back at least as far as Leon Battista Alberti, the fifteenth-century Renaissance mathematician and painter who was one of the codifiers of perspective.

  In this instance, we are dealing primarily with a limit-frame, although some paintings have cleverly used their object-frames to extend the diegetic world of the painting through illusionism. Throughout the figurative tradition, from the Renaissance onwards and still today, the edges of an image are what limits the image, but also what builds a connection between the interior of an image, its 'field' with its imaginary extensions 'off-screen' (literally, in French, 'out-of-field' – *hors-champ*)

- *Rhetorical functions.* In many contexts the frame can be understood as 'making a statement' in a more or less autonomous way, although this may sometimes be difficult to distinguish from the symbolic values of the frame. In certain periods one can notice a veritable 'rhetoric of the frame', with recurrent and fixed motifs.

  This rhetoric is perhaps most evident where the painter has supplied his painting with a false frame painted in *trompe l'oeil*, deliberately playing with all the meanings of a frame. But it can also be seen at work in many other ways, especially when the frame is particularly expressive in relation to the representaional content of the image within it. For instance, in many Japanese cinemascope films of the 60s (for example the work of Shohei Imamura) the frame is sometimes animated by autonomous movements such as a rotation on its axis or a vigorous trembling, which cannot be justified by the diegetic content, but which 'express' in a directly visible form an emotion that the director wanted to associate with that diegetic content: trembling to signify a character's sense of profound disturbance; rotation to signify a disorienting, strange atmosphere, and so on.

CENTRING AND DECENTRING

Several of these functions of the frame (economic, symbolic, rhetorical) are relatively abstract and relate to the social conventions that regulate the production and consumption of images. On the other hand, the visual and representational functions are more directly aimed at the subject-spectator.

In his book *The Power of the Center* (1981), Rudolf Arnheim studied the relationship between the spectator conceived as an imaginary 'centre' of the world and images in which centring phenomena come to play a major part. Arnheim's thesis is interesting in its generality; there are several centres of various types in an image: a geometric centre, a visual centre of gravity, centres that are secondary to the composition, and diegetic and narrative centres. To view images (art images as it happens) means to order these different centres in relation to the 'absolute' centre of the subject-spectator.

Arnheim's thesis is important in spite of its psychologically dubious premises, because under the generic notion of centring it offers a unified theory of, on the one hand, phenomena otherwise left to the mercies of crude empiricism, such as the conventional understanding of 'composition' and, on the other, the relation between composition at the level of the image's plastic aspects and the organisation of the figurative image 'in depth'. The *dynamic* nature of Arnheim's theory adds to its seductiveness, conceiving the image as a force field and viewing as an active process creating often unstable relations. Arnheim's analyses are most convincing when he is considering *ex-centred* or *decentred* images in which there is a strong competition between centres, which increases the importance of the spectator's role. It could almost be said that more than a theory of centring, he develops an aesthetics of permanent decentring: an image is only interesting, and only functions well, if something in it is decentred and can therefore be imaginarily confronted with the absolute but unstable centre where we, the viewers, are.

Framing and Point of View

THE VISUAL PYRAMID

The figurative image, in the form most familiar to us, has often been conceived as representing a fragment of a larger, potentially unlimited space (see the notion of visual field mentioned earlier and the notion of 'representative field' discussed below). It has often been compared to 'natural' sight, in so far as the latter already consciously, or unconsciously, segments visual space. From the Renaissance onwards this analogy becomes more ubiquitous with the metaphor of the visual pyramid, which is itself derived from the notion of a ray of light. For Alberti, the eye's look is thought of as a kind of searchlight sweeping through space (even though light emanates from a searchlight whereas it enters the eye), making the eye the apex of a cone consisting of an infinite number of light rays. This cone extends sidewards very widely and is in fact relatively formless. The notion of a *visual pyramid* thus corresponds to an abstraction of one part of the solid angle formed by this cone, the part having an object of vision as its base and the observer's eye as its apex.

This notion is obviously not very scientific. It also echoes an ancient concept of vision, prevalent in the Middle Ages, which held that light rays emanated from the eye and were reflected back by objects. As the understanding of spatial geometry improved, this notion was superseded in the 16th and 17th centuries by a number of constructions which facilitated the perfection of the technique of perspective. Later, the notion of the visual pyramid continued to function implicitly in painting, then as an implicit or explicit fantasy informing concepts of photography.

FRAMING

Although it had been present in painting for centuries, the camera, especially when it became portable towards the middle of the 19th century, made visible the idea that the centring of an image is in some way the materialisation of a particular visual pyramid (it is, in a slightly different form, the same metaphor as that of 'the window on the world'; *see* §I.2.2 above). It is worth noting that, as Peter Galassi has shown (1981), this identification of the frame with the visual pyramid, and especially the imaginary mobility of this pyramid and its associated frame, had been around since well before the invention of photography. Obvious traces of it can be found in many paintings, especially landscapes, towards the end of the 18th century in work which deployed the 'visual pyramid' to produce a pictorial description of space thought to be in line with the freedom and arbitrariness of spontaneous, 'natural' vision.

Framing (*cadrage*) and 'centring' within the frame are terms often used interchangeably in film to designate the mental and material process which guides subject-spectators to a particular field of vision, seen from a certain angle within specific limits. Framing is therefore what the frame does, implying its potential mobility, the unending motion of the 'window' to which the frame is equated. Framing works like this in all figurative images which imply a reference to a look, even a 'generic', totally anonymous and disembodied look of which the image would then be the trace.

In the earliest films, the distance between the camera and the filmed object was almost always the same, and centring within the frame enabled characters to be represented full figure. However, the idea of moving the camera closer or further away caught on very soon, resulting in people becoming 'lost' in much larger settings or becoming much too large so that only a part of them can be seen. In order to come to terms with these possible variations in the relationship between camera-distance and the apparent size of the filmed object, a fairly empirical and crude typology of image-scales was developed. In English, this scale is measured in terms of distance, going from extreme long shot to extreme close-up.

By a natural slippage of meaning, framing rapidly came to signify certain specific positions of the frame vis-à-vis the scene represented. Here again, it is cinema that has most influenced the vocabulary for this relationship. Because the film image exists in time, its framing is eminently suited to be regarded as the visible embodiment of the virtual or actual mobility of the frame in general.

Framing, or centring, is thus the scanning (and sometimes the fixing) of the visual world by an imaginary visual pyramid. All framing establishes a relation between a fictional eye (of the painter, of the camera, and so on) and a group of objects organised into a scene. In Arnheim's terms, framing is thus part of a permanent process of centring and decentring, of creating visual centres, of balancing a variety of different centres in reference to an 'absolute centre', the apex of the pyramid, the Eye.

The question of framing also impinges onto the question of *composition*. This issue is particularly pronounced in photography which has tried for a long time to establish itself as an art, trying to establish a perfect balance between a notion of documentary framing and the achievement of a geometrically interesting composition. The relationship between framing and centring is just as evident in cinema. In the vast majority of so-called classical films, the image is constructed around one or two visual centres, often people, to such an extent that 'classic realism' is often synonymous with an essentially 'centred' style.

In this context, it is worth noting the frequent use in cinema of 'frames within frames' (or 'over-framing'), for instance through the inclusion of a mirror or a window. Equally important is the device of reframing, that small movement of the frame which is made in order to keep a chosen subject in the centre of the image. Of course, this kind of centring is a hangover from an academic concept of pictorial composition and is not ubiquitous in cinema. There are a number of styles, such as those of Antonioni, Dreyer or Straub, which are based on a rejection of centring, on a deliberate and active decentring, usually aiming to emphasise certain expressive values of the frame.

POINT OF VIEW

The notion of framing, by way of the fantasy of the visual pyramid, invites us to establish an equivalence between the eye of the image-maker and that of the spectator. It is this assimilation of one to the other that also informs the many forms of the concept of point of view. Contemporary language uses this term in three different senses. Point of view can designate:

- a real or imaginary place from which a scene is viewed;
- the different ways in which a question can be considered;
- an opinion or a feeling about a phenomenon or event.

The first of these meanings corresponds to the embodiment of the look within framing. The question then arises as to whose look is being represented: that of the image-maker, that of the apparatus or, in the narrative forms of the image (which may already be an imaginary construct), a character within the diegesis. The two other meanings of point of view entail different connotative values of framing. They suggest that, in a narrative context, the notion of point of view refers to all those aspects of the image which convey 'subjective', 'focused' vision and, more generally, to all those aspects which imply that framing implies a judgment about what is being represented, valuing or devaluing it, drawing attention to a detail in the foreground, and so on.

Framing is one of the main tools for the construction of this third sense of point of view, but it is not the only one. Other expressive means can also convey this, for example the contrast between values and colours, soft focus, and so on. The French cinema of the 20s known as the impressionist school extensively deployed such effects. In Marcel L'Herbier's *El Dorado* (1921), a shot of the heroine, lost in thought, shows her in soft focus surrounded by her friends who are seen in sharp focus. This image offers a synthesis of a visually centred point of view and a connotative, qualifying one.

THE DECENTRED FRAME (DÉCADRAGE)

So far, we have emphasised the tendency to equate framing with the materialisation of a point of view, more or less centred and capable of being altered or recentred. However, in the twentieth-century figurative tradition, this equation has often been experienced as mistaken and ideologically pernicious. A whole section of contemporary image history is characterised by the will to avoid centring, to displace or subvert it. The most spectacular example is what Pascal Bonitzer (1985) has called *décadrage* (literally, deframing), decentered or deviant framing, marked as such and aiming to disturb the automatic equation between framing and point of view.

'Deframing' and centring. The traditional concept of composition is based on what occupies the centre of an image. Deframing, in Bonitzer's definition, consists of removing signifying objects from the centre, which thus becomes a relatively insignificant aspect of the representation. Deframing is a decentring in Arnheim's sense, introducing a strong visual tension, since the spectator almost automatically tries to fill the vacant centre.

Deframing and the edges of the image. Compositional decentring operates simultaneously in relation to both the window-frame and the limit-frame. Deframing is a more abstract process, more concerned with the limit-frame: by removing the signifying zones from the image's centre (often occupied by characters), attention is drawn to the edges of the image. The deliberate, visibly arbitrary aspect of these edges emphasises the fact that they are what separates the image from its visual environment 'beyond the frame'. In other words, deframing operates in a theoretical manner, implicitly marking the discursive value of the frame. As Louis Marin (1972) has said, 'The frame tells us that the painting is a discourse.'

Deframing makes the edges of the frame appear to slice into the representation, emphasising their power to 'cut off'. In this respect, deframing is an echo of the fantasy of the visual pyramid in paintings of the late 18th century and early 19th. Deframing means that an imaginary movement of the visual pyramid has enabled a deliberate 'centring elsewhere'. When Dégas, a master of deframing, decided to depict the Paris stock exchange by means of a fragment of a column and a group of men in suits and top hats exiled right of centre and cut-through by the right edge of the canvas, he was making a clear statement about his desire to frame it in this way, that he wanted to place his attention a bit 'to one side' of the scene's real centre of interest. Deframing is always an explicit 'framing otherwise'.

Deframing and sequentiality. The 'normal' tendency of the viewer, who is used to centred images which mimic the 'usual' way of looking, is to want to cancel the deframing which is felt to be a potentially irritating anomaly. A fixed image such as a painting or photograph, of course, cannot be cancelled or altered. Deframing derives aesthetic value from this fact. It becomes accepted as a sign of a style and, after a while, the spectator stops wanting to reframe it, accepts and possibly even enjoys the composition. The same is not true of moving and time-based images such as film and video, nor of multiple images such as comic strips. In their case, the desire to 'normalise' may be satisfied by transformations internal to the image (such as a slight reframing action by the camera) or through the sequentiality of images (in a comic strip, a later image may reframe what an earlier image deframed). Consequently, decentring has an even stronger impact in those kinds of images because it must be deliberately maintained against a much greater possibility of recentring. This is one of the reasons why decentring in cinema is, still today, perceived as stranger and even more scandalous than in painting or in photography.

The viewer's question really comes down to: 'Why keep the character on the edge of the frame, cut in half, when it would be so simple to move the camera slightly?' It hardly needs to be pointed out that, in cinema, decentring is always a sign of a deliberate intention, stylistic or ideological, to escape the centring characteristic of 'classical' representational styles. In the films of Jean-Marie Straub and Danielle Huillet, where there is a lot of decentring, deframing aims to establish a strong relationship between the character and the place by breaking with the more conventional, expected relationship between this character and other characters, or even by removing a character from the frame altogether, thus making the relation to off-screen space more ambiguous.

By displaying the frame as the site and the material of the relation between the image and its spectator, decentring draws attention to the apparatus. This is why it was initially described as an ideological, denaturalising process. Although it has somewhat lost its power in this sense, deframing remains a factor that calls into question the spectator's relation to the image and its frame in an immediately perceptible manner.

14

TIME, RHYTHM, EDITING

Andrei Tarkovsky

Turning now to the film image as such, I immediately want to dispel the widely held idea that it is essentially 'composite'. This notion seems to me wrong because it implies that cinema is founded on the attributes of kindred art forms and has none specifically its own; and that is to deny that cinema is an art.

The dominant, all-powerful factor of the film image is *rhythm*, expressing the course of time within the frame. The actual passage of time is also made clear in the characters' behaviour, the visual treatment and the sound – but these are all accompanying features, the absence of which, theoretically, would in no way affect the existence of the film. One cannot conceive of a cinematic work with no sense of time passing through the shot, but one can easily imagine a film with no actors, music, décor or even editing. The Lumière brothers' *Arrivée d'un Train* was like that. So are one or two films of the American underground: there is one, for instance, which shows a man asleep; we then see him waking up, and, by its own wizardry, the cinema gives that moment an unexpected and stunning aesthetic impact.

Or Pascal Aubier's ten-minute film consisting of only one shot. First it shows the life of nature, majestic and unhurried, indifferent to human bustle and passions. Then the camera, controlled with virtuoso skill, moves to take in a tiny dot: a sleeping figure scarcely visible in the grass, on the slope of a hill. The dramatic dénouement follows immediately. The passing of time seems to be speeded up, driven on by our curiosity. It is as if we steal cautiously up to him

From: Andrei Tarkovsky, 'Time, Rhythm, Editing', in *Sculpting in Time* (Bodley Head, 1987).

along with the camera, and, as we draw near, we realise that the man is dead. The next moment we are given more information: not only is he dead, he was killed; he is an insurgent who has died from wounds, seen against the background of an indifferent nature. We are thrown powerfully back by our memories to events which shake today's world.

You will remember that the film has no editing, no acting and no décor. But the rhythm of the movement of time is there within the frame, as the sole organising force of the – quite complex – dramatic development.

No one component of a film can have any meaning in isolation: *it is the film that is the work of art*. And we can only talk about its components rather arbitrarily, dividing it up artificially for the sake of theoretical discussion.

Nor can I accept the notion that editing is the main formative element of a film, as the protagonists of 'montage cinema', following Kuleshov and Eisenstein, maintained in the 'twenties, as if a film was made on the editing table.

It has often been pointed out, quite rightly, that every art form involves editing, in the sense of selection and collation, adjusting parts and pieces. The cinema image comes into being during shooting, and exists *within* the frame. During shooting, therefore, I concentrate on the course of time in the frame, in order to reproduce it and record it. Editing brings together shots which are already filled with time, and organises the unified, living structure inherent in the film; and the time that pulsates through the blood vessels of the film, making it alive, is of varying rhythmic pressure.

The idea of 'montage cinema' – that editing brings together two concepts and thus engenders a new, third one – again seems to me to be incompatible with the nature of cinema. Art can never have the interplay of concepts as its ultimate goal. The image is tied to the concrete and the material, yet reaches out along mysterious paths to regions beyond the spirit – perhaps that is what Pushkin meant when he said that 'Poetry has to be a little bit stupid.'

The poetics of cinema, a mixture of the basest material substances such as we tread every day, is resistant to symbolism. A single frame is enough to show, from his choice and recording of matter, whether a director is talented, whether he is endowed with cinematic vision.

Editing is ultimately no more than the ideal variant of the assembly of the shots, necessarily contained within the material that has been put onto the roll of film. Editing a picture correctly, competently, means allowing the separate scenes and shots to come together spontaneously, for in a sense they edit themselves; they join up according to their own intrinsic pattern. It is simply a question of recognising and following this pattern while joining and cutting. It is not always easy to sense the pattern of relationships, the articulations between the shots, particularly if the scene has been shot inexactly, in which case you will have not merely to join the pieces logically and naturally at the editing table, but laboriously to seek out the basic principle of the articulations. Little by little, however, you will slowly find emerging and becoming clearer the essential unity contained within the material.

In a curious, retroactive process, a self-organising structure takes shape during editing because of the distinctive properties given the material during shooting. The essential nature of the filmed material comes out in the character of the editing.

To refer again to my own experience, I must say that a prodigious amount of work went into editing *Mirror*. There were some twenty or more variants. I don't just mean changes in the order of certain shots, but major alterations in the actual structure, in the sequence of the episodes. At moments it looked as if the film could not be edited, which would have meant that inadmissible lapses had occurred during shooting. The film didn't hold together, it wouldn't stand up, it fell apart as one watched, it had no unity, no necessary inner connection, no logic. And then, one fine day, when we somehow managed to devise one last, desperate rearrangement – there was the film. The material came to life; the parts started to function reciprocally, as if linked by a bloodstream; and as that last, despairing attempt was projected onto the screen, the film was born before our very eyes. For a long time I still couldn't believe the miracle – the film held together.

It was a serious test of how good our shooting had been. It was clear that the parts came together because of a propensity inherent in the material, which must have originated during filming; and if we were not deceiving ourselves about its being there despite all our difficulties, then the picture could not but come together, it was in the very nature of things. It had to happen, legitimately and spontaneously, once we recognised the meaning and the life principle of the shots. And when that happened, thank God! – what a relief it was for everyone.

Time itself, running through the shots, had met and linked together.

There are about two hundred shots in *Mirror*, very few when a film of that length usually has about five hundred; the small number is due to their length.

Although the assembly of the shots is responsible for the structure of a film, it does not, as is generally assumed, create its rhythm.

The distinctive time running through the shots makes the rhythm of the picture; and rhythm is determined not by the length of the edited pieces, but by the pressure of the time that runs through them. Editing cannot determine rhythm (in this respect it can only be a feature of style); indeed, time courses through the picture despite editing rather than because of it. The course of time, recorded in the frame, is what the director has to catch in the pieces laid out on the editing table.

Time, imprinted in the frame, dictates the particular editing principle; and the pieces that 'won't edit' – that can't be properly joined – are those which record a radically different kind of time. One cannot, for instance, put actual time together with conceptual time, any more than one can join water pipes of different diameter. The consistency of the time that runs through the shot, its intensity or 'sloppiness', could be called time-pressure: then editing can be seen as the assembly of the pieces on the basis of the time-pressure within them.

Maintaining the operative pressure, or thrust, will unify the impact of the different shots.

How does time make itself felt in a shot? It becomes tangible when you sense something significant, truthful, going on beyond the events on the screen; when you realise, quite consciously, that what you see in the frame is not limited to its visual depiction, but is a pointer to something stretching out beyond the frame and to infinity; a pointer to life. Like the infinity of the image which we talked of earlier, a film is bigger than it is – at least, if it is a real film. And it always turns out to have more thought, more ideas, than were consciously put there by its author. Just as life, constantly moving and changing, allows everyone to interpret and feel each separate moment in his own way, so too a real picture, faithfully recording on film the time which flows on beyond the edges of the frame, lives within time if time lives within it; this two-way process is a determining factor of cinema.

The film then becomes something beyond its ostensible existence as an exposed and edited roll of film, a story, a plot. Once in contact with the individual who sees it, it separates from its author, starts to live its own life, undergoes changes of form and meaning.

I reject the principles of 'montage cinema' because they do not allow the film to continue beyond the edges of the screen: they do not allow the audience to bring personal experience to bear on what is in front of them on film. 'Montage cinema' presents the audience with puzzles and riddles, makes them decipher symbols, take pleasure in allegories, appealing all the time to their intellectual experience. Each of these riddles, however, has its own exact, word for word solution; so I feel that Eisenstein prevents the audience from letting their feelings be influenced by their own reaction to what they see. When in *October* he juxtaposes a balalaika with Kerensky, his method has become his aim, in the way that Valéry meant. The construction of the image becomes an end in itself, and the author proceeds to make a total onslaught on the audience, imposing upon them his own attitude to what is happening.

If one compares cinema with such time-based arts as, say, ballet or music, cinema stands out as giving time visible, real form. Once recorded on film, the phenomenon is there, given and immutable, even when the time is intensely subjective.

Artists are divided into those who create their own inner world, and those who recreate reality. I undoubtedly belong to the first – but that actually alters nothing: my inner world may be of interest to some, others will be left cold or even irritated by it; the point is that the inner world created by cinematic means always has to be taken as reality, as it were objectively established in the immediacy of the recorded moment.

A piece of music can be played in different ways, can last for varying lengths of time. Here time is simply a condition of certain causes and effects set out in a given order; it has an abstract, philosophical character. Cinema on the other hand is able to record time in outward and visible signs, recognisable to the feelings. And so time becomes the very foundation of cinema: as sound is in music, colour in painting, character in drama.

Rhythm, then, is not the metrical sequence of pieces; what makes it is the time-thrust within the frames. And I am convinced that it is rhythm, and not editing, as people tend to think, that is the main formative element of cinema.

Obviously editing exists in every art form, since material always has to be selected and joined. What is different about cinema editing is that it brings together time, imprinted in the segments of film. Editing entails assembling smaller and larger pieces, each of which carries a different time. And their assembly creates a new awareness of the existence of that time, emerging as a result of the intervals, of what is cut out, carved off in the process; but the distinctive character of the assembly, as we said earlier, is already present in the segments. Editing does not engender, or recreate, a new quality; it brings out a quality already inherent in the frames that it joins. Editing is anticipated during shooting; it is presupposed in the character of what is filmed, programmed by it from the outset. Editing has to do with stretches of time, and the degree of intensity with which these exist, as recorded by the camera; not with abstract symbols, picturesque physical realia, carefully arranged compositions judiciously dotted about the scene; not with two similar concepts, which in conjunction produce – we are told – a 'third meaning'; but with the diversity of life perceived.

Eisenstein's own work vindicates my thesis. If his intuition let him down, and he failed to put into the edited pieces the time-pressure required by that particular assembly, then the rhythm, which he held to be directly dependent on editing, would show up the weakness of his theoretical premise. Take for example the battle on the ice in *Alexander Nevsky*. Ignoring the need to fill the frames with the appropriate time-pressure, he tries to achieve the inner dynamic of the battle with an edited sequence of short – sometimes excessively short – shots. However, despite the lightning speed with which the frames change, the audience (at any rate those among them who come with an open mind, who have not had it dinned into them that this is a 'classical' film, and a 'classical' example of editing as taught at S.I.C.) are dogged by the feeling that what is happening on the screen is sluggish and unnatural. This is because no time-truth exists in the separate frames. In themselves they are static and insipid. And so there is an inevitable contradiction between the frame itself, devoid of specific time-process, and the precipitate style of editing, which is arbitrary and superficial because it bears no relation to any time within the shots. The sensation the director was counting on never reaches the audience, because he didn't bother to fill the frame with the authentic time-sense of the legendary battle. The event is not recreated, but put together any old how.

Rhythm in cinema is conveyed by the life of the object visibly recorded in the frame. Just as from the quivering of a reed you can tell what sort of current, what pressure there is in a river, in the same way we know the movement of time from the flow of the life-process reproduced in the shot.

It is above all through sense of time, through rhythm, that the director reveals his individuality. Rhythm colours a work with stylistic marks. It is not thought up, not composed on an arbitrary, theoretical basis, but comes into being spontaneously in a film, in response to the director's innate awareness of life, his 'search for time'. It seems to me that time in a shot has to flow independently and with dignity, then ideas will find their place in it without fuss, bustle, haste. Feeling the rhythmicality of a shot is rather like feeling a truthful word in literature. An inexact word in writing, like an inexact rhythm in film, destroys the veracity of the work. (Of course the concept of rhythm can be applied to prose – though in quite another way.)

But here we have an inevitable problem. Let us say that I want to have time flowing through the frame with dignity, independently, so that no-one in the audience will feel that his perception is being coerced, so that he may, as it were, allow himself to be taken prisoner voluntarily by the artist, as he starts to recognise the material of the film as his own, assimilating it, drawing it in to himself as new, intimate experience. But there is still an apparent dichotomy: for the director's sense of time always amounts to a kind of coercion of the audience, as does his imposition of his inner world. The person watching either falls into your rhythm (your world), and becomes your ally, or else he does not, in which case no contact is made. And so some people become your 'own', and others remain strangers; and I think this is not only perfectly natural, but, alas, inevitable.

I see it as my professional task then, to create my own, distinctive flow of time, and convey in the shot a sense of its movement – from lazy and soporific to stormy and swift – and to one person it will seem one way, to another, another.

Assembly, editing, disturbs the passage of time, interrupts it and simultaneously gives it something new. The distortion of time can be a means of giving it rhythmical expression.

Sculpting in time!

But the deliberate joining of shots of uneven time-pressure must not be introduced casually; it has to come from inner necessity, from an organic process going on in the material as a whole. The minute the organic process of the transitions is disturbed, the emphasis of the editing (which the director wants to hide) starts to obtrude; it is laid bare, it leaps to the eye. If time is slowed down or speeded up artificially, and not in response to an endogenous development, if the change of rhythm is wrong, the result will be false and strident.

Joining segments of unequal time-value necessarily breaks the rhythm. However, if this break is promoted by forces at work within the assembled frames, then it may be an essential factor in the carving out of the right rhythmic design. To take the various time-pressures, which we could designate metaphorically as brook, spate, river, waterfall, ocean – joining them together engenders that unique rhythmic design which is the author's sense of time, called into being as a newly formed entity.

In so far as sense of time is germane to the director's innate perception of life, and editing is dictated by the rhythmic pressures in the segments of film, his handwriting is to be seen in his editing. It expresses his attitude to the conception of the film, and is the ultimate embodiment of his philosophy of life. I think that the film-maker who edits his films easily and in different ways is bound to be superficial. You will always recognise the editing of Bergman, Bresson, Kurosawa or Antonioni; none of them could ever be confused with anyone else, because each one's perception of time, as expressed in the rhythm of his films, is always the same.

Of course you have to know the rules of editing, just as you have to know all the other rules of your profession; but artistic creation begins at the point where these rules are bent or broken. Because Lev Tolstoy was not an impeccable stylist like Bunin, and his novels lack the elegance and perfection which mark any of Bunin's stories, Bunin cannot be declared greater than Tolstoy. You not only forgive Tolstoy his ponderous and often unnecessary moralising and his clumsy sentences, you even begin to be fond of them as a trait, a feature of the man. Faced with a really great figure, you accept him with all his 'weaknesses', which become the distinguishing marks of his aesthetic.

If you extract Dostoievsky's descriptions of his characters from the context of his work you cannot but find them disconcerting: 'beautiful', 'with bright lips', 'pale faces', and so on and so forth ... But that simply doesn't matter, because we're talking not of a professional and a craftsman, but of an artist and a philosopher. Bunin, who had an infinite regard for Tolstoy, thought *Anna Karenina* abominably written, and, as we know, tried to rewrite it – with no success. Works of art are, as it were, formed by organic process; whether good or bad they are living organisms with their own circulatory system which must not be disturbed.

The same applies to editing: it is not a question of mastering the technique like a virtuoso, but of a vital need for your own, distinct individual expression. Above all you have to know what brought you into cinema rather than into some other branch of art, and what you want to say by means of its poetics. Incidentally, in recent years one has met more and more young people coming into cinema schools already prepared to do 'what you have to' – in Russia, or what pays best – in the West. This is tragic. Problems of technique are child's play; you can learn any of it. But thinking independently, worthily, is not like learning to do something; nor is being an individual. Nobody can be forced to shoulder a weight that is not merely difficult, but at times impossible to bear; but there is no other way, it has to be all or nothing.

The man who has stolen in order never to thieve again remains a thief. Nobody who has ever betrayed his principles can have a pure relationship with life. Therefore when a film-maker says he will produce a pot-boiler in order to give himself the strength and the means to make the film of his dreams – that is so much deception, or worse, self-deception. He will never now make *his* film.

15

THE FACT OF REALISM AND THE FICTION OF OBJECTIVITY

Bill Nichols

REALISM IN DOCUMENTARY FILM

As a general style, documentary realism negotiates the compact we strike between text and historical referent, minimizing resistance or hesitation to the claims of transparency and authenticity. Along with the more specific matters of perspective and commentary, personal style and rhetoric, realism is the set of conventions and norms for visual representation which virtually every documentary text addresses, be it through adoption, modification, or contestation.

Yet, documentary realism is not the realism of fiction. It possesses antecedents and characteristics of its own; it answers to needs and suggests tensions that differ from those of narrative fiction. In fiction, realism serves to make a plausible world seem real; in documentary, realism serves to make an argument about the historical world persuasive. Realism in fiction is a self-effacing style, one that deemphasizes the process of its construction. The vision or style of a realist filmmaker emerges from the rhythms and textures of an imaginary world, from aspects of mise-en-scène, camera movement, sound, editing, and so on that seem at first natural, inevitable, or simply at the service of the story. The "vision" of the documentarist is more likely a question of voice: how a personal point of view about the historical world manifests itself. Leni Riefenstahl's paean to fascism, *Triumph of the Will*, or Grierson's tribute to

From: Bill Nichols, 'The Fact of Realism and the Fiction of Objectivity', in *Representing Reality* (Indiana University Press, 1991).

fishermen, *Drifters*, voice similar but contrasting points of view: the celebration of men in action, an enchantment with ritual, and for Riefenstahl, fascination with ceremony and its power to define a common cause; for Grierson, respect for the ordinary working man and willingness to contribute to the common good. Similar stylistic techniques come into play but the end result is a distinct mix of style and rhetoric, authorial personality and textual persuasion, that differs from that of fiction.

Realism builds upon a presentation of things as they appear to the eye and the ear in everyday life. The camera and sound recorder are well suited to such a task since – with proper lighting, distance, angle, lens, and placement – an image (or recorded sound) can be made to appear highly similar to the way in which a typical observer might have noted the same occurrence. Realism presents life, life as lived and observed. Realism is also a vantage point from which to view and engage with life. In classic Hollywood narrative, realism combines a view of an imaginary world with moments of authorial overtness (commonly at the beginning and end of tales, for example) to reinforce the sense of a moral and the singularity of its import. In modernist narrative (most European art cinema, for example), realism combines an imaginary world rendered through a blend of objective and subjective voices with patterns of authorial overtness (usually through a strong and distinctive personal style) to convey a sense of extensive moral ambiguity. In documentary, realism joins together objective representations of the historical world and rhetorical overtness to convey an argument about the world. Schematically, the differences look something like this:

Type of Cinema	Type of World	Authorial Address via	Viewer Works to Interpret
Classic Hollywood	Imaginary, Unitary	Style and Plot, Realism	A Singular Moral
European Art Cinema	Imaginary, Fragmentary	Style and Plot, Modernism	Pervasive Ambiguity
Documentary	Historical	Commentary and Perspective, Rhetoricy	An Argument

In each case a claim is made that "This is so, isn't it?" Such claims build on the indexical quality of the image and a realist style of representation. But realism in fiction relates primarily to sensibility and tone: it is a matter of an aesthetic. Realism in documentary, marshaled in support of an argument, relates primarily to an economy of logic. Realism underpins rationalism more than an aesthetic. It supports a commonsensical view of the world, one where a reasoned perspective appears to subordinate and mobilize passion for its own purposes rather than orchestrate feelings to address or resolve contradictions that remain intractable to reason or that follow from patterns of social organization (hierarchy, dominance, control, repression, rebellion, and so on). Ideological entailments follow in either case, but the starting point and emphasis differ. Documentary realism is not only a style but also a professional code, an ethic, and a ritual.

NEOREALISM AND DOCUMENTARY

Documentary realism as buttress for rationalism begins with the beginnings of cinema in the travelogues and news reports of the Lumière cameramen and others and becomes elaborated into something of an aesthetic and political agenda with Dziga Vertov, Flaherty, and the British school of documentary under John Grierson. The aesthetic dimension remained underdeveloped and even less openly discussed than in Hollywood. Documentary had a social mission to perform. It set itself apart from the spectacle and clamor of fiction, as we have already seen. But with the neorealist movement in postwar Italy, documentary realism gained a fictional ally in relation to its ethical calling as a responsible, if not committed form of historical representation. Neorealism, too, placed its faith in reality, but sought an aesthetic more than a logic that could serve that faith. Neorealism, as a fiction film movement, accepted the documentary challenge to organize its aesthetic around the representation of everyday life not simply in terms of topics and character types but in the very organization of the image, scene, and story. Its success and limitations help sharpen the difference between fiction and documentary.

The strong causal connections of the well-made Hollywood film that motivated every line of dialogue, every off-screen glance, every camera movement and cut fell away, leaving serendipity, contingency, and chance. The time and space of lived experience gained an imaginative representation in films like *Paisa, La Terra Trema, Shoeshine, Bicycle Thief*, and *Umberto D*. Such films melded the observational eye of documentary with the intersubjective, identificatory strategies of fiction.

These films worked less to subordinate characters to the great narrative machinery of dramatic rise, climax, and resolution than to suggest an autonomy to individual lives that happened to contain small dramas of their own. Conversations faltered; actors conveyed the awkwardness of first encounters and the clumsiness of actions not rehearsed to a smooth grace. Events occurred on location, outside the conjurings of a studio set; the harsh, high contrast lighting came from whatever was available at the scene, replacing the sculpted shades of key, fill, rim, and backlights all carefully balanced, positioned, and softened; the plots left many things unexplained or unstated; events took on a laconic quality.

Andre Bazin captured the feel of such a realism when he wrote of the last episode in *Paisa*: "This fragment of the story reveals enormous ellipses – or rather, great holes. A complex train of action is reduced to three or four brief fragments, in themselves already elliptical enough in comparison with the reality they are unfolding." The sense of a vaster, untold, and untellable realm of experience and insight, which resulted from a rhetorical ploy in classic fiction, results, here, from the narrative structure itself. In classic fiction, the sense of a greater plenitude within the bounds of the story, but beyond the reach of the narration, is what Roland Barthes dissected as a rhetorical ploy in *Sarrasine*: "And the Marquise remained pensive," uses pensiveness to signify the inexpressive, "as though, having filled the text but obsessively fearing that it is not *incontestably* filled, the discourse insisted on supplementing it with an *et cetera* of plenitudes." Neorealism reconstitutes the form of subjective experience and our own halting attempts to lend narrative shape to our lives.

Robert Kolker, in his excellent study of an international, modernist cinema, takes up the attack on Hollywood that we have already heard from Dziga Vertov and Paul Rotha, but now on behalf of a new alternative: Italian neorealism.

Neorealism, like documentary, but in the tradition of a socially conscious *trompe l'oeil* aesthetic, set out to establish as complete a congruence as possible between its representation of reality and the lived experience of postwar Italian reality. Within it, individual characters elude reification into objects or symbols controlled by the powers of narrative. We cannot love or hate them without first having to face the hurdle of their humanity. The image and, through temporal extension, the shot, puts its quality of being "sticky stuff" at the service of historical representation. Strange juxtapositions, expressionistic techniques, the smooth continuities of classic narrative and psychological realism drop away to leave unadorned moments, strung together with something of the catch-as-catch-can, see-for-yourself quality of documentaries at the mercy of events beyond direct control. There is in this the art of artlessness, of "the refusal to make more of the image than is there, and an attempt to allow the fewest and simplest faces, gestures, and surroundings to speak what they have to say and then to move on."

And yet, this refusal to make more of the image never forbade narrative structure itself and the fabrication of a fictional world. As Luigi Chiarini wrote, "Facts speak through the suggestive force of neo-realism; not as brutal documentary, because absolute objectivity is impossible and is never 'purified' out from the subjective element represented by the director." At the level of the individual scene, the subjectivity might be highly muted. As Bazin notes regarding the Florence episode of *Paisa*, in which a young Italian searches the city for her fiancé only to learn of his death, this discovery strikes her like a stray bullet, as a ricochet from the news of a wounded partisan: "The impeccable line followed by this recital owes nothing to the classical forms that are standard for a story of this kind. Attention is never artificially focused on the heroine. The camera makes no pretense at being psychologically subjective." But this oblique quality is precisely the aesthetic technique needed to convey the force of the accidental and tragic as they converge in this one incident. It serves to heighten a subjective, empathetic bond between viewer and character without resorting to the centripetal pull of continuity editing, subjective point-of-view shots, and a musical crescendo.

The contingent, coincidental tone of the plot replaces these centripetal alternatives for building empathy between audience and character. Fresh, raw, compellingly "real," the "ricochet" plot remains a technique aimed at audience engagement on an intersubjective plane. Such a structure, though aesthetically powerful, does not provide the "logic" documentary requires. In fact, it moves in the opposite direction, toward that asymptotic congruence with the real that documentary must avoid, ultimately, if it is to constitute a representation or argument about the real.

The controlling presence of narrative form is more directly felt in the overall structure of neorealist films. Neorealism not only provides a repertoire of techniques for giving the formal effect of representing a reality that evades the control of the filmmaker – a repertoire put to imaginative use in documentary by observational filmmakers where the argument is tacit or implied by the perspective – it also lapses back toward the very conventions at an overall level that it avoids at a local one. The documentary tradition of the victim described by Brian Winston gains powerful support from neorealism: "Flaherty's contribution to the notion of the documentary (the individual as subject, and the romantic style) when mixed with Grierson's (social concern and propaganda) leads directly to privileging 'victims' as subject matter." The very objectivity of the style, its tendency to catch at a glance the drama-laden moments of ordinary lives, simultaneously stresses the passivity and endurance of the poor and working class. Fate – and, for Bazin or Flaherty, faith – loom large. Wonder, and a child-like state of reverence, lead, when things go wrong, to disappointment and resignation, or vague intuitions of conspiracy. Emotional tugs of sympathy occur at the edges of almost every scene and add up to a pathos that is close to melodrama in its intensity.

The emphasis in neorealism remains with story more than argument, with a fictional representation more than a historical one, with imaginary characters more than social actors. It breaks with some of the conventions that seem to separate fiction from documentary most sharply: the compositional quality of the image; the remove of the world of the image from the domain of history; the reliance on continuity editing; the tendency to motivate, in the formal sense of providing a plausible justification for the presence of objects, characters, actions, and setting as much as possible.

Like the observational documentary, neorealism eschews overt commentary for perspective or vision but it also avoids many of the ethical issues that the taking of a perspective entails for the documentarist. Although the impression may be otherwise, the lives of the characters we follow, whether played by nonprofessionals or not, terminate at the borders of the frame and at the conclusion of the film. The filmmaker need not be accountable for what happens next to them, in history, even if the aesthetic force of the film is to suggest that we, the viewers, ought. Neorealism retains the fictional quality of metaphor: it presents a world *like* the historical world and asks that we view it, and experience the viewing of it, *like* the viewing, and experience, of history itself. Neorealism demonstrates the ways in which narrative can be placed at the service of a documentary impulse by imparting a sense of autonomy to the image and shot, by developing an elliptical style of editing, by constructing a weakly motivated, coincidental form of plot, and by placing all these devices at the service of a world rendered with objective accuracy and subjective intensity. Although qualities such as these have been taken up by documentary, neorealism remains just the other side of the boundary between fiction and fact, narrative and exposition, story and argument.

TYPES OF REALISM

Neorealism is one particular form of realism situated in history and identifiable as a movement. Realism can also be considered from a less historical perspective in terms of at least three levels or types of mimetic verisimilitude: empirical, psychological, and historical realism.

Empirical realism can be considered the underpinning for naturalism, but its potential uses extend beyond a style devoted to the accumulation of factual detail and the accurate placement of characters and objects within specific milieus. It also provides the foundation to what Michael Schudson, in his *Discovering the News*, refers to as the "naive empiricism" of journalists up until, roughly, the Treaty of Versailles and the acceptance of propaganda (or rhetorical suasion) as a convenient tool for governing. The naive empiricists did not segregate fact from value, objective from subjective; "they believed that facts are not human statements about the world but aspects of the world itself, given in the nature of things rather than a product of social construction."

Ien Ang uses empirical realism in her *Watching Dallas* to describe the factual, socially recognizable aspects of the Ewing family world that exhibit its distinctive place within 1980s America: particular styles of clothing and cars, the architecture and furnishings of the Ewing mansion, even certain colloquialisms and references to topical events. "Dallas" is not a show that could be considered naturalist by any stretch of the imagination, but this level of realism is clearly at work, placing melodramatic issues within a world built up from pieces of a recognizable social environment. Those historically accurate replicas and facsimiles of costumes and weapons, times and places that figure in historical narratives like *Ben-Hur*, *Spartacus*, *Revolution*, *Heaven's Gate*, and *American Graffiti* perform a similar function, anchoring the story to a ground of empirical realism at the level of fact and detail.

More generally, we might consider empirical realism to be the domain of the indexical quality of the photographic image and recorded sound. "Mere film" – isolated long takes, amateur footage, scientific recordings – these types of cinematographic record depend for their value on their indexical relationship to what occurred in front of the camera. Empirical verisimilitude provides no guarantee of historical accuracy at the higher level of significance or interpretation, as we have already noted, but it does secure an existential bond between image and referent whether it is a particular evening gown worn by Sue Ellen in "Dallas," the grimaces and hesitations of subjects in Stanley Milgram's experiments seen in *Obedience*, the 1960s cars driven by Terry the Toad, John, and Curt in *American Graffiti*, or a distinct set of gestures and spacings peculiar to the greeting rituals of Turkana women in *A Wife among Wives*. This quality of empirically accurate observation stands behind all forms of camera surveillance as well, although here, too, ambiguities immediately arise when it comes to interpretation, as the trials of Patty Hearst and John DeLorean and such fiction films as *Blow Up*, *Blow Out*, and *The Conversation* demonstrate.

Empirical realism, the indexical bond of image and referent, stylistic naturalism – this family of patterns of verisimilitude does not exhaust the most common understandings of realism. A broader sense that "life's like that" arises most profoundly at a psychological rather than empirical level. Psychological realism conveys the sense of a plausible, believable, and accurate representation of human perception and emotion. In stylistic terms, it may depart sharply from the empirical underpinning it relies on for part of its "reality effect." Extreme states may be realistically represented by extreme styles – as expressionism, which attempts to convey mood and tone accurately by means of form, demonstrates. It is also at this level that a Stan Brakhage or a Picasso can claim a realist motivation to their formal innovations as ways of addressing accurately how we might perceive the world outside the constraints of social convention and routinizing experience.

Most commonly, though, psychological realism involves a recognition that characters and situations are lifelike in a universalizing way. Both "Dallas" and *An American Family*, both *Platoon* and *Dear America*, both *No Lies* and *Not a Love Story* locate themselves within concrete situations set in a specific time and place, but they also invite their audiences to acknowledge the emotional chords struck as common ones, as the ties that bind us one to another, wherever we might be. Jealousy and love, trust and fear, humiliation and anger – these emotions take off from the plane of the concrete and move toward a more universal realm of shared experience. Fictional style and documentary rhetoric strive to emphasize that commonality, to draw us in, to make the experience of characters and social actors stand for the experience we (despite myriad distinctions among this "we") might also have and that we, the audience, can have empathetically.

A prime example of a psychological realism that departed radically from any literal empiricism of time and place was the Live-Aid concert of July 13,

1985. Broadcast to as many as two billion people across the world via thirteen satellites, Live-Aid had twin, empirical roots in the actual concert by famous performers and in the empirical fact of starvation in parts of Africa. What resulted, though, was a universalization of subjectivities that allowed concern to manifest itself in an AT&T advertising jingle done for the program as a rearrangement of the previous "Reach out and touch someone" campaign. This epitomized an ethic of good intentions that reduced the starving to the abstract, nameless category of victim. Commentary or perspective on the human, political, or economic reasons for hunger fell by the wayside. Instead, someone else's misery became an occasion to celebrate our own (white, Western) compassion, a compassion conveniently in harmony with musical pleasure, television entertainment, and effortless identification by means of familiar icons. The empirical fact of hunger and the empirically authentic images of the starving were subsumed into a narrative accounting that, as African critics of the event pointed out, denied individual dignity and overlooked African forms of aid to the stricken regions, in order to reinterpret events in a universalizing, psychologically realist, and therefore highly loaded manner.

Realism aids and abets empathy. The constructedness of the story or argument itself may be readily admitted. as it is in almost all musicals, cartoons, pornography, ethnography, and expository documentary, but the empathetic or identificatory bonds are very rarely treated as constructs: they transcend the fabrication, they triumph in spite of it, they rely on the complex dynamic of suspended disbelief or an acceptance of things we know to be other than what they seem. In *Singin' in the Rain*, Gene Kelly consciously arranges a sound stage to evoke a romantic setting in which to serenade Debbie Reynolds: his actions blatantly disclose what illusionism normally hides – the fabrication of scene and mood; his feelings for Cathy Seldon (Reynolds), though, are still meant to be understood as genuine. We are meant to identify with a feeling of romance, not its fabrication.

Fans of "Dallas" may say things like, "Do you know why I like watching it? I think it's because those problems and intrigues, the big and little pleasures and troubles, occur in our own lives too. You just don't recognize it and we are not so wealthy as they are." The exaggeration is noted but, rather than serving to expose the fabrications of the narrative, it only stresses a *fact* of social difference across which common problems readily travel. Similarly, an appreciative viewer of *Lonely Boy* may say that the documentary lets him or her feel what it is like to be a young man who makes a Mephistophelian pact to transform himself willingly into the image of a young, "lonely boy" that will make him a star even as we see and hear how this image is carefully constructed. The image may be contrived and the text may display its own contrivances as well as those of its subjects, but the sense of realism remains: it really is like this; this is Paul Anka, as he is; he is human, like me, even if he is only what he chooses to appear to be.

A similar, enigmatic realism pervades *Don't Look Back* where the "real" Bob Dylan remains an elusive figure. We emerge with the sense of a psychologically realistic portrait of elusiveness and of the ability of performers to confuse us about their level of performance both on and off stage. An identificatory bond takes shape in relation to this complex game of self-presentation. But a complex game of levels of knowingness and quests for a "real" self are not a necessary part of documentary realism. Documentaries like the Middletown series, Fred Wiseman's studies of institutions, majority of film biographies like *Antonia, The King of Colma, The Most, The Day after Trinity*, and social biographies like *Reds, Rosie the Riveter, With Babies and Banners* evince a more straight-forward realism that promises fairly direct access to the emotional states and psychological make-up of specific individuals. Whether enigmatic and self-conscious or clear and direct, psychological realism poses as a transparency between representation and emotional engagement, between what we see and what there is.

Although psychological realism may depart from the mimicry of normal perception to convey unusual states or feelings, it is most often associated with a "zero-degree" style that minimizes its own status as part of a socially con-structed reality in order to maximize the impression of direct, immediate access to the emotional reality it represents (in documentary) or fabricates (in fiction). This style derives most forcefully from the classic Hollywood film and the principles of continuity editing. Such editing relies heavily on the formal principle of motivation: each cut is justified not for its own sake but for how it serves to efface itself in order to maximize our identification with character, scene, action, and story. Maintaining consistent screen direction and eye-line matches across cuts; editing in relation to movements that draw attention away from the cut; building, in general, a sense of coherent physical orientation and spatial volume that centers on the intersubjective realm of character relations leads to the achievement of a realism that directs all of our curiosity, anticipa-tion, empathy, and suspicion to the realm of the story itself.

A similar style prevails in many documentaries where the measure of success might be that the film draws attention to the issue it addresses and not to itself. (A documentary filmmaker once remarked to me that she considered a film successful if the audience discussed the issue and not the film.) A documentary "zero-degree" style effaces itself sometimes in favor of the domain of individ-uated characters (as in many observational films), generally in favor of the historical world and the representations made about it (as in many expository films where evidentiary editing illustrates the point in ways harmonious with these patterns of psychological realism). Documentary editing, evidentiary or otherwise, tends to conform to guidelines similar to those for Hollywood continuity editing, but screen direction, eye-line matches, and cuts on move-ment may be less strongly linked to specific characters. A great deal of the editing in the Why We Fight series and in *Triumph of the Will* (the two works share some of the same footage) achieves continuity not in relation to any one character we come to know but through cuts on movement that retain screen direction, line, volume, or eye-line match with social actors who come and go. They function, at a formal level, primarily as a pivot or relay for the flow of images (crowd scenes where people look off-screen right or left followed by cuts to what they presumably see are a prime example). These scenes also exemplify the concept of a social subjectivity where our own identification is brought into play but less with any one individual than with the sense of collective participation itself.

In fiction the sound track often assists in the creation of continuity. Lines of dialogue, music, and sound effects can all carry across a cut, helping to minimize any jarring effect since our attention is given over, in part, to the continuing sound. Documentary relies on similar sound bridges with great frequency. The most significant contrast lies in the difference between dialogue, which is normally attached to specific characters and their spatial surround, and commentary, which has the license to roam disembodied, calling on images from diverse times and places to support its points. Because of this license, documentary continuity may be less coherent in terms of geographic consistency, spatial contiguity, or orientation from the standpoint of an individuated character. The continuity instead derives from the logic of the commentary which the images illustrate, counter-point, or metaphorically extend. Jumps in time and space that would be disruptive in the fiction film unless motivated through a character (through memories, fantasy, anticipation), can, in documentaries that rely on evidentiary editing, be easily and smoothly assimilated.

Raul Ruiz, in fact, addresses part of his self-reflexive *Of Great Events and Ordinary People* to this very property of "logical discontinuity" when we hear a voice-over commentary describe how the film will construct space with shot/reverse shots of two people in the street. We see two intercut series of images of a Parisian street with an unindividuated social actor in the foreground, the series performing no other function than to construct a spatial relationship. In another instance, Ruiz, speaking in voice-over, announces, "One of the film's themes is the peculiar dispersal of documentary across a series of heterogeneous objects," after he has presented a series of still-life images whose only continuity, in this case, is their evocation of the classic oil painting genre.

The commentary in Ruiz's film reflexively demonstrates the achievement of continuity at the same time it puts the construction of such continuity on display. Unlike the forms of self-confessed constructedness found in *Singin' in the Rain* or *Lonely Boy* that still allow for subjective engagement with an imaginary or historical world, this construction arrests attention. The "heterogeneous objects" illustrate no representation of the world as much as their own representationalism. No argument is made apart from the one directed at the strategies of documentary itself. They do not allow a process of identification to continue; blockage occurs. The logic of discontinuity, the logic of evidentiary editing, and the construction of a representation are put on display such that we must attend to the display rather than the referent.

REALISM IN POSTSTRUCTURAL PERSPECTIVE

Through most of the seventies and the beginning of the 1980s, poststructural criticism had realism under siege. The attempt to represent a world illusionistically had the quality of deceit about it. The critique of illusionism argued that not only were we encouraged to overlook the fabrication involved but also the apparatus that supported the fabrication: the cinema as institution and industry. "The cinematic apparatus," to use a phrase of some popularity, schooled viewers to occupy passive, masculinist positions in relation to stories involving active males and desirable females. Narrative policed the flow of sounds and images, holding them "on track," insuring that their temporal succession remained motivated by the requirements of the story. Realism contributed the lynchpin to this operation, drawing our attention past the apparatus and machination, past the enunciation and its ideology of containment, past the seeing to the scene and its imaginary, lifelike autonomy. Documentary, which often seemed to endorse realism and its effects uncritically, merited little discussion since, no matter what issue it addressed, it remained a prisoner to the ideology of the style and system it used to address that issue.

Other writers have contested this view, and, even more importantly, have begun to suggest viable alternatives that question whether entire aesthetic systems or specific "apparatuses" achieve this sort of unitary effect. The best poststructural critiques of realism never claimed it was monolithic in any simple way, but they also drew attention away from the specific text as a source of unique interpretive problems in order to stress its value as example or symptom of a larger mechanism. Countercritiques to this poststructural tendency have offered a better sense of what diversity in structure, strategy, and response might mean. This has come about through the introduction of different methodologies such as phenomenology and neoformalism, and through attention to previously neglected or too readily generalized aspects of realism such as the social dynamics of viewer-response, the cognitive process required to comprehend fiction films, and concepts like excess and masquerade.

A provisional and contingent, situated appraisal of realism can serve us well. The poststructural critiques of realism never offered a very satisfactory perch for the criticism of specific works: since the effects were generalizable, the individual work became a demonstration of how specific tactics achieved the same general results time after time. The possibility that specific tactics might yield significantly different results even though they continued to rely on realism for their effect did not receive systematic consideration, nor did the possibility that different viewers might have very different readings in ways that did more than demonstrate idiosyncrasy among viewers. Tania Modleski's *Loving with a Vengeance*, Ien Ang's *Watching Dallas*, and David Morley's *The "Nationwide" Audience* suggest how class, gender, nationality, and history all contribute to significant differences in how texts are understood even when the texts are fundamentally realist in their style.

The poststructuralist critique of realism may be best seen, and used, as a misplaced manifesto for the avant-garde. This critique almost always implicitly calls for what Laura Mulvey makes explicit: "The first blow against the monolithic accumulation of traditional film conventions (already undertaken by radical film-makers) is to free the look of the camera into its materiality in time and space and the look of the audience into dialectics, passionate detachment." Drawing most frequently on the theories of Bertolt Brecht but giving them a strongly formalist orientation by valuing the disruption of the classic form of illusionism and psychological identification with characters, such calls tend to write off mainstream cinema and realism as retrograde. In doing so, they move outside the arena of popular culture and its debate and enter the realm of experimental art and avant-garde politics. These critiques are richly suggestive in their denunciations and proposals, in their ability to locate ideologies of sexism, racism, and class at the levels of form and apparatus even more than content, and to provoke thought about alternative systems and forms. But if we wish to apply our theory and criticism to works that remain within the popular mainstream, as most documentaries do, without driving them all into the same ideological corner, a more open-ended conception of realism and its possible effects will have to be entertained.

The most compelling critique of realism involves the subordinated position of women, not simply in terms of roles but also in terms of narrative structure. Although they may be contested and qualified, arguments for the pervasiveness of fetishistic and voyeuristic relations between a masculine viewer and a female image as object of visual pleasure have great persuasive power. Such a dynamic exists in documentary as well, although since we encounter individuated characters less consistently and find both space and time less tightly organized around them, it is not so common for entire texts to be organized around such a dynamic (the films of von Sternberg and Hitchcock provide two immediate examples of fictional work that is).

In keeping with the tendency of documentary to bridge evidence and argument, the concretely historical and the conceptual generalization, the issue of gender may revolve more abstractly around the body. How shall it be represented? What subjectivity can be attached to it when it is not an imaginary construct to begin with (a fictitious character) but a participant in the historical world (a social actor)? What elements of sexism pervade not only the roles and subjectivities made available to women in the world but the representations of the body as image and Other (male or female)? And what responsibilities accrue to the filmmaker when people, made more widely known by their exposure on film, resume their lives after the film, possibly subject to insult or injury as a result of the film?

Such questions are the exception in fiction. Risk or injury to the actor, rather than the character, is required before they are posed. They arise in the aftermath of tragic incidents like the crash of the helicopter that took three lives during the filming of John Landis's portion of *The Twilight Zone*. They arose in the wake of 9½ *Weeks* when reports surfaced that playing her (masochistic) role had affected Kim Basinger personally. Such questions are central to documentary representations of the human body, however. In fact, the presence of such issues in pornography vividly demonstrates its status as documentary when it comes to matters of the body: what subjectivity operates in performers who engage in sexual encounters designed primarily to be documented; what self-image arises for performers whose bodies are rendered as appendages to sex organs, and what responsibilities arise when, as in most contemporary pornography, the act of intercourse takes place in defiance of almost every known precaution against the risk of AIDS? Sexism in documentary may revolve more around issues of power than pleasure, control than fascination, distance than identification.

Realism, then, has both empirical and psychological dimensions that repeat some of the objective, subjective polarities of our culture. Documentary realism also presents a pointedly historical dimension. It is a form of visual historiography. Its combination of representations *of* the world and representations *about* the world, of evidence and argument, give it the ambivalent status that the word "history" also enjoys: history is at once the living trajectory of social events as they occur and the written discourse that speaks about these events. We live in history but we also read histories. We see documentaries but we also see past them. We engage with their structures but we also recognize a realist representation of the world as it is.

Historical or documentary realism refers to those aspects of realism that are distinctive to documentary. Not only is there the empirical element of an indexical link between image and referent (usually presumed to be a historical referent), not only is there the psychological realism of subjectivity and empathetic engagement, there is also a historical realism that gives questions of style a distinctive ring in documentary.

EPISTEPHILIA

A realist style supports an illusionistic mode of reception. Even if the style of the text is blatant, the blatancy is motivated by the pathetic fallacy: stylistic vividness evokes or mimics qualities of the world represented. In fiction film, realism aligns itself with a scopophilia, a pleasure in looking, that often establishes a masculine position for the viewer where the pleasure of seeing male characters comes from recognizing and identifying with a potential ego-ideal and the pleasure of seeing female characters comes from activating sexual, voyeuristic, or fetishistic desire. Historical or documentary realism may well retain some of these characteristics but they are seldom quite so dominant as they are in fiction, where heightened attention to subjectivity brings ego-centered and libidinous relations to the fore. More likely, documentary realism supports – in addition to identification, voyeurism, and fetishism – an illusionistic mode of reception where style vivifies the physical texture and social complexity of the historical world itself.

Documentary realism aligns itself with an epistephilia, so to speak, a pleasure in knowing, that marks out a distinctive form of social engagement. The engagement stems from the rhetorical force of an argument about the very world we inhabit. We are moved to confront a topic, issue, situation, or event that bears the mark of the historically real. In igniting our interest, a documentary has a less incendiary effect on our erotic fantasies and sense of sexual identity but a stronger effect on our social imagination and sense of cultural identity. Documentary calls for the elaboration of an epistemology and axiology more than of an erotics.

The subjective dynamics of social engagement in documentary revolve around our confrontation with a representation of the historical world. What we see and hear ostensibly reaches beyond the frame into the world we, too, occupy. The subjectivity John Grierson exhorted the documentarist to support was one of informed citizenship – an active, well-informed engagement with pressing issues such that progressive, responsible change could be accomplished by governments. Other subjectivities are also possible – from curiosity and fascination to pity and charity, from poetic appreciation to anger or rage, from scientific scrutiny to inflamed hysteria – but all function as modes of engagement with representations of the historical world that can be readily extended beyond the moment of viewing into social praxis itself.

The credo that a good documentary is one that draws attention to an issue and not itself follows from the documentary's epistephilic foundations. Engagement is the aim more than pleasure. But both engagement and pleasure presuppose an exterior object, a target for cathexis or concern. And both stop short of erasing the gap between subject and object, viewer and representation, self and Other. Both, in fact, depend upon an aesthetics predicated on the preservation of distance (if not distanciation). (Were there no distance, the text itself would dissolve back into the world it represents and our engagement would be with this world directly.) The realist illusion of transparency complicates this aesthetic of distance by denying its omnipresent activity, but realism *is* a style, a form of textual construction, and a means of achieving specific effects one of which is the appearance of a nonproblematic relationship to representation itself. We seem to enter into a subjective relationship to the represented world aided, rather than impeded, by the work of rhetoric and style.

Humphrey Jennings's classic documentary, *Listen to Britain*, exemplifies the fusion of subjective and objective representation with an overall style that may seem surprisingly modern in its absence of voice-over commentary. Though apparently observational in this regard, it fractures the time and space of its scenes from the visible world of wartime Britain into a large number of dissociated impressions. The result is a poetic form of exposition rather than the observation of life unfolding before a subordinated camera. *Listen to Britain* presents situations and events in the spirit of evocation and remembrance: recognize this, remember that. In many instances the evocation is objective in the sense that the camera's gaze attaches to no specific human agency. We are not prompted to ask, "Whose gaze is this?" when we see shots of industrial Britain, of women at work bobbing and nodding in time to music coming from the factory loudspeakers, of men stoking the furnaces of a steel mill. But at other moments, we are invited to adopt the subjective perspective of specific social actors. This is most often true in the concert scenes when singers, pianists, and orchestras perform for representatives of a hard-working, culturally appreciative nation. Repeatedly the camera singles out members of the audience and then, using eye-line match editing, constructs a reverse-angle, point-of-view shot of the performance. Sometimes the pattern is the classic A/B/A where we return to the audience member to note his or her facial response to the music.

These classic forms of subjective editing depart from the unstated convention of fiction films that point-of-view shots develop around characters with whom we come to identify (by following their initiation of and response to a series of actions and events). Although point-of-view reaction shots tied to an undifferentiated audience are quite acceptable in fiction, they are not the lifeblood of narrative subjectivity, only a secondary variation. In documentary, though, such shots can become the foundation for a *social* subjectivity. This is subjectivity dissociated from any single individuated character. Our identification is with the audience as a collectivity, anchored by subjective shots that align us with specific audience members but without any prelude or follow-up that gives these particular members meaning or significance beyond their representative quality and position as emotional relays within the film.

By this means Jennings evokes the social subjectivity of viewing, or listening, itself. We share the spatial position of audience members at the wartime concerts. They become a mirror for our own act of viewing and listening to Britain. They represent pleasure that derives from shared, subjective experience. Jennings creates a form of affiliation through point-of-view editing while also emphasizing the social dimension to this affiliation rather than a strictly personal one. We engage with a historical realism that represents collective experience subjectively.

This relationship of subjective engagement retains, as a basic prerequisite, distance. The irony of this distance is that it supports the impression that we have achieved a direct form of engagement that has bypassed and even replaced the need for any other, more direct engagement with the world. What documentary may produce (like fiction) is less a disposition to engage directly with the world than to engage with more documentary (or fiction). The aesthetic of epistephilia, like that of scopophilia, nourishes itself, not its own alternative or replacement. We come to value and look forward to the pleasure of engaging the world at a distance, looking out through the windows of our theaters and living rooms onto a world that truly remains "out there," with all the assurance this provides about the importance of our engagement with a historical world that we have simultaneously postponed in order to attend to a representation of it.

AUTHENTICITY AND DOCUMENTARY REALISM

As we have seen, historical realism does not support the same aesthetic as fictional realism even though it uses many of the same techniques, nor does it necessarily support the same forms of subjectivity. By the same token, realist style in documentary plays a somewhat different function from the one it has in fiction. Fictional realism has most often been celebrated for its self-effacing quality. It allows unimpeded access to the world of the representation. And yet different directors have different styles that are noticeably distinct. These distinctions contribute to the sense of a personal vision, individual perspective, or unique point-of-view on an imaginary world. When we encounter a predominance of point-of-view shots within a fictional world heavily centered around the fascination and danger of heterosexual relationships, we enter the world of Alfred Hitchcock. When we encounter a tightly organized series of modulations in camera placement, movement, and character action along with a highly attenuated sense of emotional expressivity, we enter the world of Robert Bresson.

In documentary, style plays a somewhat different role. Individual filmmakers do display different styles in a manner similar to fiction film directors and these differences define different perspectives on the world, but realist style in documentary also grounds the text in the historical world. It is a mark of authenticity, testifying to the camera, and hence the filmmaker, having "been there" and thus providing the warrant for our own "being there," viewing the historical world through the transparent amber of indexical images and realist style.

Even if a fiction film is shot on location, as neorealist and many Hollywood films of the postwar period were, the centripetal force of the narrative draws such signs of authenticity into the woof and warp of the story; the location becomes one more signifying element, more or less well motivated in relation to the plot. In *Call Northside 777*, for example, the authentic urban locations enhance the indexical or empirical realism of the reporter/detective story while in *Niagara*, the location shots of a thunderous Niagara Falls serve to underscore the psychological realism of a story of infidelity and murder. In either case, the gravity of an imaginary world draws the location photography into its force field, holding it in place as one more element of plot and story.

In a documentary, location shooting is a virtual sine qua non. (Staged re-creations fail this basic requirement but usually adhere to strict claims of fidelity to actual events. This may also cause them to forfeit the peculiar fascination of engaging the historical world itself as Bazin noted in his comments on *Scott of the Antarctic*.) Location shots do not require motivation in relation to a plot line; instead their motivation lies in the documentary impulse itself: to represent the world in which we live. Compare, for example, two highly similar opening sequences, those of *Louisiana Story* and *Touch of Evil*.

Touch of Evil begins with a tour de force. The first shot is a long take that sets the entire film in motion. The camera travels near and across the Mexican-American border, picking up the crucial bits of evidence that will sustain the story. A man plants a bomb in a car; newlyweds Mike and Susan Vargas stroll from Mexico to the United States; Mike has broken up part of the Grandi gang; the car with the bomb contains another man and a woman, Linnekar and Zita; the two pairs of characters cross paths at the border but no one takes Zita seriously when she complains of a ticking noise in her head; a moment later the car explodes, disrupting Mike and Susan's kiss. They won't get another one until an hour and a half later, at the end of the film.

The opening draws us into an imaginary world with enormous rapidity. A highly unstable equilibrium prevails, full of darkness, uncertain borders, ambiguous and missed communications. A bomb explodes, precipitating yet further confusion and creating the experience of loss or lack that drives the remainder of the narrative forward (the loss of life and the lack of romantic solitude). The location has the air of authenticity of the sort we expect in fiction. Border towns are *like* this: danger and intrigue surround us at every step, the night is full of mystery, people live in jeopardy of wandering across lines they ought not cross, one's identity and self are put at risk. The metaphorical power of fiction operates at full force. Even though the scene was shot in Venice, California – hundreds of miles from the Mexican border – Welles has caught the likeness of a border town that we recognize as real (probably more on the basis of how such places figure in other fictions than of our own experience).

Flaherty, on the other hand, catches the thing itself: Petit Anse Bayou in Southern Louisiana (or at least a vividly indexical representation of it). Like Welles's *Touch of Evil*. Flaherty's film also features a fluid, poetic camera and a strong sense of rhythmic movement as we enter into the world of the bayou, first noting small, distinctive features such as lotus leaves and exotic birds before picking up the trail of the young boy, Alexander Napoleon Ulysses Latour (played by a nonprofessional actor from the bayou). Unlike the omniscient camera movements of *Touch of Evil* that choreograph the cold destiny of numerous characters. *Louisiana Story* brings us into alignment with the point of view of the boy. We see the bayou as he sees it and share his pleasure in the discovery of a young raccoon and his sense of excitement in a subsequent hunt.

There is more enchantment and mystery here than threat and danger. A long, graceful tracking shot passes through the swamp with its clusters of silvery Spanish moss, picking up the boy in the far background as he steers between the trees. The brightness of the grays (more silver than drab gray) contrasts with the deep black of Welles's night-for-night photography. The water may be everywhere and dark but it supports a world of brightness and wonder. Shots of an alligator prompt Virgil Thompson's score to sound deeper, more ominous notes, but when Napoleon beams an enormous broad smile at the young raccoon, the music shifts to a lighter, cheerful key: generic convention assures us this will be a happy story.

"Story" is, indeed, an apt word since Flaherty's film is barely distinguishable, structurally, from Welles's baroque fiction. Flaherty, too, relies on actors; he, too, constructs his opening to present the basic tonal values he wants to establish and to introduce a disruption, lack, threat, or disequilibrium. The explosion of the car in *Touch of Evil* is matched by the explosion of the bayou itself. The bursts of soil and vegetation abruptly interrupt Napoleon's hunt and dwarf the power of his little rifle. Just as the romantic interlude sought by Mike and Susan is massively disrupted, so too is Napoleon's relation to his beloved bayou, in this case by an oil derrick.

The largest difference is not in the fabrication of a fiction versus the found quality of Flaherty's world but in the method by which construction proceeds. Welles worked from a script, the equivalent of a composition or orchestral score. Flaherty worked without one, composing his scenes ex post facto in the editing process.

His editor, Helen van Dongen, describes the nature of this process well. She writes, "The choice of these scenes [for the opening] and their continuity was not decided upon *a priori*." The selection and arrangement depended on content, spatial movement, tonal value (the shades of black and white), and emotional content, a somewhat ill-defined quality analogous to what we have identified as the goal of psychological realism. This realism grows more powerful, for van Dongen, as shots are brought into association with one another.

[...]

The end result is no less constructed, no less a creature of Soviet montage theory in this case than *Touch of Evil* is of a long-take style. In fact, *Louisiana Story* is in most ways far more a companion piece to *Touch of Evil* than its opposite even though it presents itself as documentary. We may affiliate Flaherty with poetic realism rather than film noir, but the fictional elements of the film are never far from sight.

What restores the documentary balance – apart from the film's own claim to historical specificity as "an account of certain adventures of a Cajun boy who lives in the marshlands of Petit Anse Bayou in Louisiana" – is the representation of indexical fidelity. The images (much more than the sound with its musical score and lack of synchronous location recording) attest to the historical facticity of the bayou. The swamp has not been fabricated or recreated. Flaherty was there. He has brought back images – poetic, wonderful images – that celebrate that land and affirm the harmony people can enjoy with it even in the midst of technological change and commercial exploitation. The location photography escapes from the relatively weak force field of a "slight narrative'. We are invited to observe what we see not simply as an imaginary world of mystery and enchantment but as an argument about how enchantment and mystery can be discovered in the historical world itself.

As indexically forged evidence, the location photography testifies to the nature of *the* world and to the active presence of Robert Flaherty within it. He was there, in the realm of alligators and moss, pirogues and raccoons, and he now presents these images as testimony not only to a personal vision, not even simply to a perspective on the historical world, but as testimony to the very existence of such a world. What the Hollywood musical always insisted was a question of will – put on a happy face, smile and the world smiles with you – Flaherty argues is an aspect of reality itself: the world *is* a place of hope and optimism, of boyish wonder and childlike playfulness. We do not need will power so much as an ability to see. Documentary realism will help us see what we may not yet have seen, but which is there, in the world, awaiting our discovery.

Documentary realism, then, testifies to presence. The filmmaker was there, the evidence proves it. Rather than moving us into an unproblematic relationship to an imaginary world, it provides a foothold on the historical world itself. To see what we would have seen had we been there, to see what would have happened even if the camera had not recorded it – these impressions of reality anchor us to the world as it is. Rather than effortless transport into the nether regions of fantasy, documentary realism transports us into the historical world of today through the agency of the filmmaker's presence. (In television news, reporters serve as agents of presence who dutifully stand before capitols, angry crowds, blazing fires, battlefields, stock exchanges or fields of wheat; they serve as the sensory receptors of a larger news gathering organism whose head and heart remain at a remove.)

Realist style undergoes an inversion in documentary. Rather than bringing the sensibilities and vision of the filmmaker to the fore, it situates the filmmaker in the historical world. The helpless, accidental, humane, interventionist, and professional gazes testify less to a metaphorical vision of the world than to the real presence of the filmmaker in the face of historical events beyond his or her control. The shaky camera shots of *The Battle of San Pietro* seem less the artistic embellishment of a creative vision than evidence of risk and danger that required no invention. Those occasional moments in an observational film like *Soldier Girls* or the much more frequent moments in an interview-rich film like *In the Year of the Pig* when an individual looks directly into the camera and acknowledges its presence are not entirely or, often, even partially disruptive. Rather than shattering the realist illusion of an autonomous, imaginary world such moments authenticate the presence of characters (or social actors) and filmmakers on the same plane of historical coexistence.

But just as the indexical quality of the image is no guarantee of its historical authenticity (only of the bond between image and what was present before the camera), so realist style may be less a guarantee of historical reality – that which always exists *elsewhere* – than of the historically real recording of a situation or event, whatever its status. Signs of presence – recognizable people, places, and things, of familiar sounds and images; signs of incomplete control over what occurs or how it unfolds – imperfect framing, missing elements of action, loud background noises – such signs may be less evidence of the historical world than of the real recording of a world whose status as representation remains open to question and debate. These signs testify to presence, but not necessarily to the presence of historical reality. They more properly testify to the presence of the recording apparatus and the reality of the recording process, which we, often on faith, assume to have occurred in the face of pell-mell contingency.

Thus visible, audible clapper boards and the rough beginnings or ends of takes authenticate the act of recording itself – here we are, they announce; this is what was said or done – rather than the historical authenticity of what gets recorded. The empirical fact of such recording, represented as taking place in the historical world, underpins objectivity. Whatever challenge might be put to the veracity of what is said, the reality of the recording itself, the authenticity of the representation escapes debate. The filmmaker was really there. We have a heightened sense of the actual process of recording what was said and done. This sense may be imaginatively constructed – as it is in the hand-held combat camera style of the attack on Burpelson Air Force Base in *Dr. Strangelove* or the impromptu, morally loaded exchanges between filmmaker and civil defense personnel in Peter Watkins's *The War Game* – or it may be more securely rooted historically – as it is in *Harlan County, U.S.A.* or *The Sorrow and the Pity*. It is an *impression* of authenticity based on the reality of representation more than the representation of reality.

16

THE ARTIFICIAL INFINITE: ON SPECIAL EFFECTS AND THE SUBLIME

Scott Bukatman

All my modes of conveyance have been pictorial.
  – Charles Dickens, 'Some Account of an Extraordinary Traveler' (1885)

INTRODUCTION

In the eighteenth and nineteenth centuries, as new technologies and social formations displaced the haptic in favor of the visual as a source of knowledge about an increasingly complicated set of lived realities, popular culture offered a surfeit of spectacular forms, which compensated for the lack of touch with what might be termed a hyperbole of the visible. An apparently direct address toward the spectator depended upon techniques of perspectival composition, trompe l'oeil, a hiding or de-emphasis of the frame, an often overwhelming scale, and a mimesis of the natural. Historians tend to agree that underlying the fascination with such displays was an anxiety regarding urban growth, technological development, and social change. The spectacle was a simulacrum of reality, but spectators weren't fooled by these illusions – by paying admission, the customer indicated a comprehension of the terms of the exhibition. Some pleasure, however, clearly derived from responding to these entertainments *as if they were real*. Visual spectacle provided reassurance in the form of a panoptic power – the human subject was, after all, capable of perceiving and comprehending the new conditions of physical reality through the projection of an almost omnipotent gaze out into the represented world.

From: Scott Bukatman, 'The Artificial Infinite: On Special Effects and the Sublime', in Lynne Cooke and Peter Wollen (eds) *Visual Display: Culture Beyond Appearances* (The New Press, 1995).

The cosmic displays of science fiction cinema, produced by technologically advanced optical effects, surely derive from a similar drive for scopic mastery. The overwhelming perceptual power granted by these panoramic displays addressed the perceived loss of cognitive power experienced by the subject in an increasingly technologized world. In acknowledging anxiety while ultimately producing a sense of cognitive mastery, these entertainments frequently evoked the rhetorical figures of the sublime. The nature of popular, commercial entertainment suggests that this was actually tamed sublime and not truly awe-inspiring, transcendental visions; nevertheless, the sublime became an important mode for these mareoramas, landscape paintings, stereoscopic views, and science fiction films.

The stock scripts and relatively wooden performances of science fiction cinema shouldn't distract one from the articulations of meaning located in the mise-en-scène as well as the state-of-the-art technological spectacle on display. While there are relatively few director-auteurs in science fiction film, cinematic style (as well as authorial consistency) can be located in the fields of art- and effects-direction. The special-effects work of Douglas Trumbull is particularly distinctive and sustained in its evocation of the sublime, and this essay will concentrate on sequences from his films. Trumbull supervised the Stargate sequence of *2001:A Space Odyssey* (1968) and produced the luminous alien spacecraft for *Close Encounters of the Third Kind* (1977). He worked in conjunction with "visual futurist" Syd Mead on *Star Trek: The Motion Picture* (1979) and *Blade Runner* (1982). Beyond his work as an effects designer, Trumbull directed two features, *Silent Running* (1972) and *Brainstorm* (1983) – both interesting in themselves – while developing his 65 mm, 60 fps Showscan exhibition system. Finally turning away from Hollywood and a system that was, as he put it, "multiplexing itself to death," Trumbull turned to "special venue" productions, developing multimedia technologies for theme parks or World's Fair exhibitions. The popularity of simulation rides in a surprising range of settings has provided new opportunities for Trumbull to experiment with the kind of experiential cinema that has been his forte since the 1960s. The attention to spectacle and the simulative conditions of theme parks and fair exhibitions recall the early history of the cinema as well as the history of precinematic phantasmagoria.

In Trumbull's effects sequences, the sublime is elicited around a massive technological object or environment: the Stargate (*2001*), the mothership (*Close Encounters*), V'ger (*Star Trek*), and the city (*Blade Runner*). Inspiring the sensations characteristic of sublimity, technology alludes to the limits of human definition and comprehension. The special effect unfolds before the human gaze and becomes susceptible to the encompassing control that inheres in the very act of seeing. Trumbull's sequences, however, are different from other effects work in their ambivalence: they are neither unabashedly celebratory (*Star Wars* [1977]) nor darkly condemning (*Alien* [1979]). As with the panoramas and other displays of the last two hundred years, Trumbull's effects are rooted in an ambivalent relation to new technologies; like those other forms, Trumbull's effects too often depend upon new technologies to succeed.

[...]

CORPOREAL MAPPINGS

Now the sense of displacement or disorientation produced by the environment of the industrial city gave rise to new entertainments, which produced a cognitive and *corporeal* mapping of the subject into a previously overwhelming and intolerable space. Panoramic perception became a fundament of the Machine Age, a function of new architectures of steel and glass; it defined the arcades and department stores of consumerist abundance, as well as a set of spectacular forms that reinforced the new dominance of an epistemology of vision. Telescopes, microscopes, maps of continents, geological periods, and human anatomy further extended the reach of human perception, as Stafford notes:

> The extension of vision permitted a new form of travel. Opaque depths were opened up, becoming transparent without the infliction of violence. The veil of the invisible was gently and noninvasively lifted. The eye could easily voyage through and beyond the densities of a plane, or silently journey beneath the stratified level.

Travel provided the metaphor for a broad evocation of a spatiotemporal continuity wedded to a utopian dedication to "progress"; Susan Buck-Morss writes that "Railroads were the referent, and progress the sign, as spatial movement became so wedded to the concept of historical movement that these could no longer be distinguished." Journeys to new heights, new perspectives, and new worlds became the substance of such recreations as the packaged tour, the panorama, the scenic garden, and the World's Fair. In popular literature, Jules Verne took his readers aloft in a hot-air balloon to go *Around the World in Eighty Days* and fired them from a cannon to bring them *From the Earth to the Moon*. As Buck-Morss notes, new modes of conveyance became linked to new fields of knowledge and new possibilities for human advancement.

Here, then, was the start of at least one thread of what we have come to refer to as the Information Age, as an abundance of physical data was fitted to the epistemological desires and requirements of the public consciousness. Spectacular displays depended upon a new mode of spectatorial address – essentially, *you are there* (even though you're not) – linked to new technologies of visual representation. Of course, these presentations can, in their turn, be traced to the geometric specificities of perspectival composition, which situated the observer in relation to the scene observed: now the spectator was provided with panoptic views of the inside of the human body, astronomical phenomena, and newsworthy events. Panoramas of exotic ports evoked an illusory immersion in faraway places:

> The panorama struck a responsive chord in the nineteenth century. It satisfied, or at least helped to satisfy, an increasing appetite for visual information. A revolution in travel had made the world seem smaller. The growth of a literate middle class and the burgeoning newspaper industry meant that many more people were aware of a greater number of happenings over a larger area of the globe. It is not surprising that people should desire visual images of a world of which they were becoming increasingly aware through the printed word. The panorama supplied a substitute for travel and a supplement to the newspaper.

Bodily experience and cognitive understanding were thus supplemented, or replaced by a reliance on vision within a simulacrum of the real.

Most popular were panoramas of one's own city. One was positioned at the precise center of a 360-degree space that had, until now, been imperceptible and overwhelming in its entirety. If the visual was now released from the confirmation of haptic experience (a fundament of the Information Age), then the visual would become a hyperbolically self-sufficient source of knowledge and information for the general public, as well as for the scientist. The panorama and its successor, the diorama, would eventually incorporate simulated motion, lighting, and sound effects, platforms to rock or even move the audience, photography, and even, in the case of Hale's Tours, cinema. Such attractions have made an important return: Trumbull has developed the "Ridefilm Theater," a simulator-theater system, which features a fifteen-passenger motion base encompassed by a 180-degree spherically curved screen. High-resolution images are projected with synchronized movement to produce a remarkable sense of immersion in a complex technological space.

SPECIAL EFFECTS

A too-easy historicism has tended to divide cinematic representations into naturalist and anti-naturalist categories (Siegfried Kracauer's realist versus formalist debate). Within this dichotomous schema, special effects hark back to the imagistic manipulations of Georges Meliès, but it should be clear that even the supposedly naturalistic Lumière brothers were purveyors of spectacle and novelty. Cinema is, of course, a special effect, and that is how it was regarded by its initial audiences. The illusion of motion, with its consequent sensations of temporal flow and spatial volume, provided enough innovation for spectators already familiar with a range of spectacular visual novelties. If cinema's unique blend of spatiotemporal solidity and metamorphic fluidity was largely assigned to the representation of narrative, the effect(s) of the medium nevertheless remained central to the spectatorial experience.

Writings on early cinema by both Tom Gunning and Miriam Hansen describe a "cinema of attractions" – an "unabashed eclecticism" that was figured in a direct address to the viewer."[T]his is an exhibitionistic cinema," Gunning claims, while Hansen, following Jean Mitry, writes that "The frontality and uniformity of viewpoint is clearly the mark of a presentational mode as opposed to representational – conception of space and address." The presentational mode ultimately yielded to a more univocal narrational system that stabilized space and introduced "the segregation of the fictional space-time on the screen from the actual one of the theater or, rather, the subordination of the latter under the spell of the former."

Nevertheless, Gunning argues that the fascination of the attraction "does not disappear with the dominance of narrative, but rather goes underground, both into certain avant-garde practices and as a component of narrative films, more evident in some genres (e.g. the musical) than in others." The genre of science fiction often exhibits its spectatorial excess in the form of the special effect, which is especially effective at bringing the narrative to a spectacular halt. Science fiction participates in the presentational mode through the prevalence of optical effects that in fact reintegrate the virtual space of the spectacle with the physical space of the theater.

Special effects redirect the spectator to the visual (and auditory and even kinesthetic) conditions of the cinema, and thus bring the principles of perception to the foreground of consciousness. This idea is at the center of Annette Michelson's superb analysis of *2001:A Space Odyssey*. The expansion of the visible field to cineramic proportions, the removal of perceptual clues to verticality and other conditions of physical orientation, the sustained evocation of bodily weightlessness, the imposition of the rhythms of respiration and circulation on the soundtrack all contributed to the profound redefinition of haptic experience undergone by the voyagers in the audience. If *2001* is more radical in its affect than other works of narrative cinema, visual effects remain central to it and all science fiction. "If we think of what it is that science fiction 'does,'" writes Brooks Landon, "surely we must acknowledge that its frequently mentioned 'sense of wonder' derives from 'a new way of seeing.'"

The optical effects of the contemporary cinema are thus only a more recent manifestation of spectacular technologies of vision, which combine large-scale display with direct spectatorial address to create an immersive and apparently immediate sensory experience. Trumbull's work inherits from an entire history of visual displays, including "Renaissance" and aerial perspectives, panoramas, landscape paintings, dioramas, and the cinema (the cinema of attractions).

SUBLIME SPACE AND SCIENCE FICTION

The presentational mode described by Gunning and Hansen exceeds the logics of narrative and exaggerates the poetics of spectacle, and thus bears a relation to certain conceptions in poetry and painting of *the sublime* – especially the sublime as figured in American art of the nineteenth century. The classical conception of the sublime, as described by Longinus in relation to spoken rhetoric, emphasizes its power to enthrall and elevate the mind of man; in a famous passage, Longinus celebrated its unambiguous glory through his own little special-effects sequence, writing that "our soul is uplifted by the true sublime; it takes a proud flight, and is filled with joy and vaunting, as though it had itself produced what it has heard." Joseph Addison and Edmund Burke were largely responsible for transforming the sublime from Kantian doctrine to aesthetic strategy. The field of the sublime was comprised of the majestic, the awe-inspiring, and the literally overpowering: it spoke the languages of excess and hyperbole to suggest realms beyond human articulation and comprehension. The sublime was constituted through the combined sensations of astonishment, terror, and awe that occur through the revelation of a power greater, by far, than the human. Those commingled sensations result from the rhetorical construction of grandeur (either grandly large or small) and the infinite. The object of sublime rhetoric is often not all available to vision or description: uniformity (the similarity of all parts) and succession (a sense that the object extends on and on) characterize this "obscurity." The sublime initiates a crisis in the subject by disrupting the customary cognized relationship between subject and external reality. It threatens human thought, habitual signifying systems, and, finally, human prowess: the mind is hurried out of itself by a crowd of great and confused images, which affect because they are crowded and confused. The final effect is not a negative experience of anxious confusion, however, because it is almost immediately accompanied by a process of appropriation of, and identification with, the infinite powers on display. The phenomenal world is transcended as the mind moves to encompass what cannot be contained.

As telescopes provided tantalizing glimpses of worlds beyond our own, astronomy provided a new and exalted ground for the rhetoric of the sublime. In 1712 Addison wrote of the infinitude of the heavens in language typical of the mode:

> When we survey the whole earth at once, and the several planets that lie with in its neighbourhood we are filled with a pleasing astonishment, to see so many worlds, hanging one above another, and sliding round their axles in such an amazing pomp and solemnity. If, after this, we contemplate those wild fields of ether, that reach in height as far as from Saturn to the fixed stars, and run abroad almost to an infinitude, our imagination finds its capacity filled with so immense a prospect, and puts itself upon the stretch to comprehend it. But if we rise higher, and consider the fixed stars as so many vast oceans of flame, that are each of them attended with a different set of planets, and still discover new firmaments and new lights that are sunk further into those unfathomable depths of ether, so as not to be seen by the strongest of our telescopes, we are lost in such a labyrinth of suns and worlds, and confounded with the immensity and magnificence of nature.

Here, in a sense, the cosmic trajectories of *2001* are prefigured not only in the evocation of astronomical *scale*, but in the description of successive levels of macrocosmic order that signal the limits of our abilities to comprehend the vastness of the universe.

The universe is without end, it confounds us, but the rhetoric of the sublime paradoxically permits an understanding of these sensory and conceptual limits (the rhetorical threat posed by the sublime is finally, then, not really that much of a threat). In the twentieth century, the genre of science fiction has continued this representational tradition. The precise function of science fiction, in many ways, is to *create* the boundless and infinite stuff of sublime experience, and thus to produce a sense of transcendence beyond human finitudes (true to the form of the sublime, most works produce transcedence of, and acknowledgment of, human limits). Indeed, science fiction is characterized by a spatio-temporal grandeur revealed by its titles alone: *A Space Odyssey, When Worlds Collide* (1951), *The Star Maker* (1939); also consider the titles of early science fiction magazines: *Astounding, Amazing, Thrilling Wonder Stories, Weird Tales*. The conclusion of Richard Matheson's *The Incredible Shrinking Man* (1956) links the micro- and macro-cosmic in an infinite continuum of religious transcendence. Science fictional objects are sublimely obscure: the city of Trantor in Isaac Asimov's Foundation series covers an entire planet – one of the boundless cities of the genre – and there is the spaceship that begins *Star Wars*: too large for the screen – or our consciousness – to hold. Science fiction is immediately and deeply bound to the tropes of the sublime. Burke's "artificial infinite" is echoed in *2001*'s story "Jupiter and Beyond the Infinite": rhetorical allusions to the unrepresentable forms of infinity.

LANDSCAPE EFFECTS

The figures of sublime rhetoric were developed and understood primarily with reference to poetic language, and were first related to the register of the visual arts only with suspicion. With the unintentional influence of Burke, however, painting became a site for the instantiation of the sublime. The representation of natural phenomena – mountains, sky, flora – became the means of meditating upon the magnificence of their Creator (and the magnificent powers of reason that could ruminate upon that magnificence).

The landscape sublime is rooted in an activity of contemplation, in the attempt to grasp what, fundamentally, cannot be grasped. The breadth of Nature proves ideal for stimulating the dynamic cognitive processes that exalt the mind. The artworks most closely associated with the sublime, therefore, are often detailed, scrupulous revelations of nature's grandeur – but less from an impulse toward mimesis than from a wish to encourage specific spectatorial behaviors. For landscape painting to inspire dynamic contemplation, however, duplication of external form is not enough. Many artists, J. M. W. Turner and Frederick Church among them, provided a kind of viewing instruction in the depiction of a frequently tiny figure fixed in contemplation of the very wonders that the painter chose to embellish.

Spectacular and monumental elements, all encompassed by a dynamic spectatorial gaze, are easily found among the plethora of special-effects sequences in the history of the cinema, especially in the films with effects by

Douglas Trumbull. A Trumbull sequence is less the description of an *object* than the construction of an *environment*. The work privileges a sense of environmental grandeur: the wide-screen effect becomes an enveloping thing, such as the roiling cloudscapes that presage the appearance of the mothership in *Close Encounters*, the gorgeous and monstrous Los Angeles of *Blade Runner*, or the amorphous, infinite interiority of the starship V'ger in *Star Trek*. The Stargate sequence in *2001* features scarcely any objects; it emphasizes instead a continuum of spatiotemporal transmutations.

Trumbull's effects are grounded in a phenomenologically powerful spatial probing, and emphasize the spectatorial relationship to the effect/environment. To some degree all special effects are so inscribed: the effect is designed to be seen, and frequently the narrative pauses to permit the audience to appreciate (or groove on) the technologies on display (what, in a somewhat different context, Laura Mulvey once referred to as "erotic contemplation"). However, Trumbull's sequences are different. Where John Dykstra's work in *Star Wars* or *Firefox* (1982) is all hyperkinesis and participatory action, Trumbull's work is especially contemplative.

Further, and regardless of the director involved, the extended effects sequences typical of Trumbull's films frequently include an explicit, pronounced spectatorial position within the diegesis: the cutaways to an astronaut's frozen features, Spielberg's typically slack-jawed observers, the crew of the Enterprise, or the disembodied eye that holds the infernal city reflected in its gaze. Dykstra's work on *Star Wars* is not so inscribed: the passage of the first, impossibly enormous spaceship is witnessed by the audience, but there is no spectator *within* the diegesis (the same holds for the climactic explosion of the Death Star). Trumbull stages an extended encounter with the sublime by including the presence of the diegetic spectator, rehearsing (and hyperbolizing) the filmic spectator's own response.

Through the prevalence of such temporally distended special-effects sequences, science fiction clearly participates in the presentational mode of cinematic discourse. While audiences may use a diegetic human figure as a guide through the immensities of alien space, these characters do not serve to deflect the spectator's own experience of the action. The passage into the kinetic lights and amorphous shapes of the Stargate sequence in *2001* is directed *right at* the viewer. The close-ups of David Bowman, the astronaut, do not reintegrate us into a fictional (representational) space, neither do they situate Bowman as a psychologized subject to focus audience identification. The cutaways to human observers in Trumbull's sequences re-establish scale and re-emphasize the Otherness of the sublime environment. They do *not* mediate the experience through the psychology of characters who are, uniformly, stunned into a profound passivity. The fictive and the theatrical spaces are collapsed, as the diegetic and cinematic spectators are, in a metaphorical sense, explicitly united (Michelson has argued that *2001* is predicated upon just such a phenomenological confusion between astronaut and spectator). The presence of diegetic spectators, then, here actually enhances the presentational aspect of the cinema, while also evoking the sublime.

America (and Beyond the Infinite)

In the nineteenth century, America revealed its obsession with the relation between nature and human power and human destiny in prose, paint, and politics. A rhetoric of progress mingled with the sense of a people chosen by God and history, privileged to engage with and tame a New World that still seemed to bear the fresh touch of its Creator. The vast reaches of the American West seemed to test the will of the nation's new citizens and the emerging technologies of industrial capitalism were extraordinarily suited to the colonization and economic exploitation of these territories. Alan Trachtenberg has written that "the American railroad seemed to create new spaces, new regions of comprehension and economic value, and finally to incorporate a prehistoric geological terrain into historical time'. (This powerful spatiotemporal collapse echoes Buck-Morss's contention that spatial movement analogized historical progress.)

In an oft-quoted section of *Nature* (1836), Emerson – who also could be somewhat delirious about train travel – narrates a state of mind characteristic of the transcendental sublime:

> Standing on the bare ground, – my head bathed by the blithe air and uplifted into infinite space – all mean egotism vanishes. I become a transparent eyeball; I am nothing; I see all; the currents of the Universal Being circulate through me; I am part and parcel of God ... In the wilderness, I find something more dear and connate than in streets or villages. In the tranquil landscape, and especially in the distant line of the horizon, man beholds somewhat as beautiful as his own nature.

Emerson's debt to Kant is evident in his version of the sublime as exaltation, and in his description of the ego's dissolution, which is ultimately recuperated in the beauty of human nature. His "transparent eyeball" anticipates those infra-diegetic, but impossibly positioned, spectators that populate Trumbull's effects sequences, and provides a strikingly direct gloss on Trumbull's evident transcendentalist bias.

The landscape took on a centrality in American painting during this period, which became "immersed in nature." On the union of sublime aesthetics and transcendental philosophy, one critic has written, "the sublime experience was transformed into a new mode of landscape expression; the traditional sublime setting was augmented by the transcendental sublime sensibility, a sensibility that found its roots in man's internal perception of time and space." This mix of the sublime and the transcendental found its clearest expression in the genre of Luminist painting, which emphasized impersonal expression, horizontality, minute tonal gradations, intimate scale, immobility, and silence. And, of course, the Luminist work is defined by its representation of light: a cool, hard, palpable light (not diffuse), spread across a glassy surface. "The linear edges of reality are pulled taut, strained almost to the point of breaking."

Luminism was not the only means of evoking the sublimity of the American landscape. The monumental paintings by such nineteenth-century figures as John Singleton Copley, Thomas Cole, Church, Albert Bierstadt, and others constructed a visual rhetoric of the sublime far removed from the solitude and silence of the Luminists, although there were numerous shared concerns. "The landscape painter must astonish his audience by the immediacy of his effects," Andrew Wilton writes. While much of this immediacy was achieved through the hyperbolized detail of the rendering, the scale of the works also served to overwhelm the sensibility of the spectator. These representations of exotic landscapes in the American West or South America were too large and too detailed to be "taken in" with a single glance; the spectator's gaze had to be put in motion to assimilate the work. Furthermore, this especially exhibitionistic mode of representation was often exhibited like a fairground attraction. In its creation of a dynamic, kinetic spectatorial gaze, as well as in its mode of exhibition, the monumental landscape painting takes a place alongside such contemporaneous "phantasmagoria of progress," in the words of Buck-Morss, as the diorama and magic-lantern show.

The paintings of Church are particularly appropriate to consider alongside Trumbull's effects. The astonishing, bold color experiments (special effects) that Church unleashed in depicting his twilight skies and volcanic eruptions were the result of new technologies in cadmium-based pigment production. These effects were put in the service of atmospheric and astronomical phenomena: not just the sky, but also the sun and moon, a meteor, and the aurora borealis. One critic has pointed to the promise of revelation that underlies the dramatic scenography and monumental scale of Church's later paintings. Another writes of *Twilight in the Wilderness* (1860) that "The painting defies simple categorization as a 'luminist' work of art, but there can be no doubt that the subject of the picture is, literally, American light, symbolic of the new world Apocalypse. It is a compelling work of art which combines two aspects of the sublime, the traditional interest in nature as object and the transcendental concern for nature as experience, through color, space, and silence." The dual contexts of Luminism and "great pictures" provide a further context for understanding the Stargate sequence. The passage through the Stargate is a voyage "beyond the infinite": a movement beyond anthropocentric experience and understanding. Through slitscan technology, Trumbull created a set of images that were little more than organized patterns of light – the very stuff of cinema. Light, with its implications of revelation and blinding power, is also the very stuff of the sublime:

> Light is ... the alchemistic medium by which the landscape artist turns matter into spirit ... In American art especially, light has often been used in conjunction with water to assist spiritual transformation, either

dissolving form, as in some of Church's large South American pieces, or rendering it crystalline, as in the works of [Fitz Hugh] Lane. In the former, light is more closely attached to what we generally call atmosphere, and has a diffusive, vaporous quality. In the latter, light itself partakes of the hard shiny substance of glass. In all instances, the spirituality of light signals the newly Christianized sublime. In the large paintings by Church and Bierstadt light moves, consumes, agitates, and drowns. Its ecstasy approaches transcendence, but its activity is an impediment to consummating a complete unity with Godhead.

In *2001*, light's transformative power illustrates, embodies, and enacts the supercession of the human (and the human's rebirth as a super-human; a Star Child). The *sturm und drang* of the Stargate sequence is clearly different from the Luminism of Lane, but I would argue that the sequence involves both topoi of light, moving from the diffusion and mutability of the first section to the color-tinted, crystalline silence of the landscapes at the end. Light "moves, consumes, agitates, and drowns," but there is nevertheless a stillness that subtends the sequence's last minutes. Here the landscape becomes more concrete, but commensurably more barren, and the sky and sea blend as the horizon disappears. The penetrating camera movements persist, but are now overwhelmed by the quietude of these enormous and empty worlds. Luminism produces a sense of distance from the aestheticized landscape, unlike the sense of the immersion; nevertheless, a similarity abides in their suspended temporalities.

"While Church's handling of composition and paint only peripherally borders on Luminism," John Wilmerding writes on Church, in terms applicable to the Stargate sequence, "the sense of vast stillness verg[es] on an imminent crescendo of light and sound." The "imminent crescendo" directs us to the function of sound here and in other sequences. While most are accompanied by tumultuously loud sound effects or scoring, language is, in every instance, *absent*. Again, there is a conflation of two tropes found in the American landscape sublime: the evocation of Apocalypse ("sublimity overwhelms with a deafening roar") and the quietude of Luminism ("the spectator is brought into a wordless dialogue with nature").

TECHNO ENCOUNTERS

Mark Seltzer has astutely proposed that "Nothing typifies the American sense of identity more than the love of nature (nature's nation), except perhaps the love of technology (made in America)." To the American paradigm that opposed nature's might and human will, American painters, poets, essayists, and novelists added the newly unleashed forces of technology to produce what Leo Marx has labeled "the rhetoric of the technological sublime." The anxiety surrounding the new prominence of technology has received much attention since the Industrial Revolution, and its representation has hardly been limited to science fiction.

In nineteenth-century America, technological anxiety was transformed by a sense of destiny. "Above all, the rhetoric conveys that sense of unlimited possibility which seizes the American imagination at this remarkable juncture." This rhetoric of unlimited possibility does not, however, mask some residual anxieties, as a surfeit of landscapes featuring decimated woodlands and smoke-obscured vistas demonstrates: "The new significance of nature and the development of landscape painting coincided paradoxically [!] with the relentless destruction of the wilderness in the early nineteenth century." As Rosalind Williams notes in her study of subterranean environments in the nineteenth century. "Technological blight promotes technological fantasy." The presence of the sublime in science fiction – a deeply American genre – implies that our fantasies of superiority emerge from our ambivalence regarding *technological* power, rather than nature's might (as Kant originally had it). The might of technology, supposedly our own creation, is mastered through a powerful display that reveals anxiety but recontains it within the field of spectatorial power.

What Buck-Morss refers to as the "phantasmagoria of progress" (panoramas, world's fairs, and the like) are visual displays that concretized metaphors of progress to provide some means of contending with the complexity of what Walter Benjamin called a "new nature." By this, she contends, Benjamin meant:

> not just industrial technology but the entire world of matter (including human beings) as it has been transformed by that technology. There have been, then, two epochs of nature. The first evolved slowly over millions of years; the second, our own, began with the Industrial Revolution, *and changes its face daily*. This new nature, its powers still unknown, can appear ominous and terrifying to the first generations confronting it, given "the very primitive form of the ideas of these generations" who have yet to learn to master, not this nature itself, but humanity's relationship to it.

The sublime is thus figured in these spectacles as an idealist response to significant and continuing alterations in lived experience. Hence the sustained reappearance of the sublime in popular, technologically based entertainments. Then and now, the language of consumption and the display of spectacle grounds the spectator/visitor, and hides the awful truth: that an environment *we made* has moved beyond our ability to control and cognize it. Therefore the experience of technology is both alien and enveloping in Trumbull's effects sequences. The simultaneous fascination with, and fear of technology's beauty, majesty, and power reveals a necessary ambivalence, and through this ambivalence, the sublime becomes a crucial tool of cognitive mapping.

Technology has come to comprise an environment, a second nature "with its own attendant pleasures and hazards." Nature is displaced by technology in *2001, Close Encounters*, and *Silent Running*, and this displacement is complete in *Star Trek* and *Blade Runner*. Buck-Morss notes that the new space of the

Crystal Palace, a space permitted by new technologies of glass and steel architecture, "blended together old nature and new nature – palms as well as pumps and pistons." Technology permits a containment of nature in the Crystal Palace and in the crystalline domes of *Silent Running* (the garden in the machine, perhaps). But the appearance of nature has become little more than nostalgia for a pastoral ideal. If the rhetoric of the technological sublime in nineteenth-century letters was characterized by the appearance of "the machine in the garden," then, as we leave the twentieth century, we would have to note that the machine is the garden.

A clue to the significance of this shift can be found in Thomas Weiskel's emphasis on the distance between our experiential realm and those of the eighteenth and nineteenth centuries:

> To please us, the sublime must now be abridged, reduced, and parodie the grotesque, somehow hedged with irony to assure us we are not imaginative adolescents. The infinite spaces are no longer astonishing; still less do they terrify. They pique our curiosity, but we have lost the obsession, so fundamental to the Romantic sublime, with natural infinitude. We live once again in a finite natural world whose limits are beginning to press against us and may well crush our children.

In the absence of *nature's* grandeur, technology constitutes a new ground for human definition and for our obsession with infinite power and possibility.

Recent theorists of the postmodern have emphasized the moment's techno-cultural underpinnings and the rise of invisible networks and decentered fields of power that characterize electronic and nuclear technologies. The aesthetics of John Pfahl's series of photographs (from the early 1980s) of power plants in their "natural" settings are troublingly, shockingly ambivalent: nuclear (and other) technology becomes truly aweful – somehow simultaneously coexisting with nature, dominated by nature, and dominating overall. The startling rise of mediating electronic technologies has precipitated a crisis of visibility and control. If cultural power now seems to have passed beyond the scales of human activity and perception, then culture has responded by producing a set of visualizations – or allegorizations – of the new "spaces" of technological activity. Most science fiction remains unflaggingly conservative in its language and iconography, but it still remains the genre most committed to narrating the ambiguities that mark the technologyical contours of contemporary culture.

The ambivalent relation between technological and human definition is evident in the mothership sequence in *Close Encounters*. First, one must note the sky in the film's night scenes – abundant stars allude to the infinite reaches of space: as we know, "theorists of the sublime attached much importance to the associational significance of the sky, and usually placed the night sky full of stars at the head of their list of its sublimities." For landscape painters, clouds also afford the opportunity to depict "the storm cloud, with its obvious propensities for sublimity," and *Close Encounters* provides strikingly exaggerated clouds; substantial yet strangely liquid, and far more animated than the dumbfounded characters themselves.

The star-filled skies presage the appearance of the mothership. The ship's design was inspired, according to Spielberg, by the sight of an oil refinery – the sublime is thus constituted around an anxious technological object (recalling Pfahl's contemporaneous reactor shots). Additionally it might be noted how nature, in the form of Devil's Tower, dwarfs the humans who nestle against it until the mothership, in its turn, dwarfs nature. The complex relationship between nature and technology is also manifested in the first appearance of the mothership, which emerges from behind the mountain; that is, *from the earth*, instead of from the improbably starry sky. The scale of the ship further indicates the subjugation of nature by the power of technology – Spielberg wanted it to be so big it would blot out the stars. Finally, while the ship is defined by brilliant and beautiful light, it is also distinguished by the black shadows that swallow the observers: for all its beauty, the mothership is a dark, visually negative force. Burke noted the same dialectic between light and its absence in Milton's descriptions of God: "Dark with excessive light thy skirts appear."

ARTIFICIAL INFINITIES

Artificial infinities abound in science fiction: generation ships, outer space, cyberspace, boundless cities, cosmic time, galactic empires, 2001's mysterious monolith, the endless underground cities of the Krell in *Forbidden Planet*. Rosalind Williams has written about the craze for artificial environments that punctuated the fancies of the nineteenth century, noting that these industrial fantasies have continued unabated into the present era "in the form of retreats into personal or collective environments of consumption – the artificial paradises of the shopping mall or the media room, for example. This is a journey further inward, a retreat from technology into technology."

Trumbull's accomplishment is the articulation of the tension between anxiety and identification, as we strain to assimilate the imagined infinities of technological power. Such tension is exemplified in the opening sequences of *Silent Running*, as a lush, natural forest is slowly revealed to exist within the hyper-technologized spaces of a vast spacecraft – nature is now enclosed and redefined by the experience of the technological, as "man's traces" become increasingly more evident until they finally overwhelm. The ending is even more complex: the drones are left to care forever for the forests as they drift through deep space. The spaceship explodes in a, well, *sublime* pyrotechnical display (a new sun). The drones tend to the forest in a series of interior shots. Then the drifting, domed biosphere is seen in its entirety, slowly receding in the visual field. Culture (the ship) is superseded by nature (the pure light of the explosion); then the natural (forest) is contained by the technological (dome), which in its turn is contained by the cosmological (space).

The archetype of the artificial environment is, of course, the industrial city, revisited and hyperbolized in *Blade Runner*. The oil refinery motif of *Close Encounters* has become more pronounced as the entire city is now explicitly figured as an anxious technological object. There is no more nature, only its simulacra in the form of synthetic animals and humans and no escape from the encompassing technological landscape. Williams argues that "in the late twentieth century, our technologies less and less resemble tools – discrete objects that can be considered separately from their surroundings – and more and more resemble systems that are intertwined with global systems, sometimes on a global scale." In *Blade Runner*, as the hovercar glides above and through the city, we indeed "take a proud flight" and attain a position of conceptual mastery over the complex and superbly synchronized urban scene. The film provides two fields of vision – the physical reality beyond the windshield and a graphic display of what must be an electronic traffic corridor along which the car is gliding. Each view explains the other as urban space, and maps the other to produce an intertwined global system.

The phantasmagoria of progress involves a sustained immersion within an artificial environment *that suggests technology's own ability to incorporate what it has generally excluded*. If the disappearance of nature is seen as a consequence of a burgeoning technosphere, then utopian technologies will incorporate Arcadia (Crystal Palace, Futurama, *Silent Running*). If technology is seen as a dehumanizing force that leads to an impoverishment of spirit, then utopian technologies will permit a new emergence of spirituality and cosmic connectedness (Enterprise, virtual reality). It even might be argued that cinema is the very paradigm of an artificial, technological environment that has incorporated utopian fantasies of nature, kinetic power, spiritual truth, and human connection.

17

NEO-EXPRESSIONISM AND BRITISH CINEMATOGRAPHY: THE WORK OF ROBERT KRASKER AND JACK CARDIFF

Duncan Petrie

The persistence of critical auteurism has hindered adequate appreciation of creative collaboration in the cinema. While the cinematographer's contribution to the creative process in film is gaining gradual recognition, this has some way to go and is still not fully understood. Cinematography is the meeting point of science and art, technology and aesthetics, for the practitioner must not only understand the technical properties of light, film stocks and lenses but also the creative possibilities of chiaroscuro, colour, composition and movement. Such elements lie at the heart of film's ability to convey the ideas, moods and emotions which give the spectator both intellectual and sensuous pleasure. In this respect, British cinema between 1945 and 1950 has been regarded by many as a period of unprecedented achievement. The names of filmmakers that spring immediately to mind are David Lean, Carol Reed, Michael Powell and Emeric Pressburger, but what distinguishes their work is the quality of collective endeavour, their integration of screenwriting, directing, acting, cinematography, design and music into the final product.

At the core of this is the relationship of cinematographer and director: of Robert Krasker, using black-and-white photography, and David Lean or Carol Reed, and Jack Cardiff, using Technicolor photography, and Michael Powell. Lean's *Brief Encounter* (1945), Reed's *Odd Man Out* (1947) and *The Third Man* (1949) are all matched in this respect by Powell's *A Matter of Life and Death* (1946), *Black Narcissus* (1947) and *The Red Shoes* (1948). Not only does the critical reputation of these films owe much to their cinematography. The nature of their visual construction is a key to understanding the aesthetics of British cinema at this time. In rethinking British film, Charles Barr traces a shift from critical discourses of realism and quality, dominant from the 1940s to the 1970s, to a championing of alternative traditions rooted in popular genre and fantasy.[1] These contrasting paradigms create contrasting visions of film history. The former stresses restraint, social responsibility and community, which are epitomised by the documentary movement, by wartime consensus dramas such as *In Which We Serve* and *Millions like us*, by Ealing comedy and by the new kitchen sink realism of the early 1960s. The latter celebrate excess, desire and individuality whose touchstones are Gainsborough melodrama, Hammer horror, and Powell & Pressburger.

Barr cautions against the use of such a crude binary opposition between "outmoded" realist and "progressive" non-realist traditions. He suggests instead that a significant shift occurred at the end of the war from a concern with the public sphere, serviced by documentaries and wartime propaganda, to a fascination with the private sphere, the world of subjectivity and states of mind, with its corresponding stress on vision and fantasy. In this respect, he sees fundamental similarities between two films regarded as representing the two opposing traditions, *A Matter of Life and Death* and *Brief Encounter*. Both films share a concern with internal rather than external experience, and with aesthetic modes of subjectivity and reflexivity. They also herald the brief flourishing of a neo-expressionist sensibility, and in cinematographic terms, an expressive art of light and shade.

I

Krasker's work with Lean and Reed is part of this bold new style of high contrast, low key black and white cinematography.[2] As well as Krasker there were other skilled exponents, young technicians such as Guy Green, Erwin Hillier and Douglas Slocombe as well as older émigrés like Mutz Greenbaum, Gunther Krampf and Otto Heller. Their approach to lighting had similarities with developments in the USA, notably in the work of Gregg Toland, Stanley Cortez and James Wong Howe, and also in the emergence of *film noir*. Just as *noir* had been characterised by suspicion, mistrust and paranoia, so the British cinema shared its concern with complex states of mind. The emergence of this style was facilitated by key technological developments. By the end of the 1930s the Kodak Company had introduced new black and white stocks in America.[3] They were considerably more light sensitive then their predecessors, allowing a higher quality image that could incorporate a wide range of tones from bright highlights to strong blacks and also produce a greater depth of field. These new stocks began to be used more frequently in Britain in the mid-1940s, providing new aesthetic possibilities. The prestige productions discussed here also tended to have budgets allowing lighting levels that produced a sharper image with greater focal depth than black and white films made during the war.

Traditionally, *Brief Encounter* has been regarded as a model of restrained realism, and while *Odd Man Out* and *The Third Man* were more overtly stylised, they also correspond to the format of verisimilitude at the heart of the "classical realist text". All three films achieve almost seamless integration between studio and location sequences, regardless of where the sequences were shot. The town of Milford in *Brief Encounter* was represented by the railway platforms of Carnforth in Lancashire but also by the streets of Beaconsfield near Denham Studios. The Belfast of *Odd Man Out* is a combination of studio sets, of the city itself and of sequences filmed in Islington and Shoreditch, chosen for their similarity to the terraced streets of Belfast. *The Third Man* elevates significance of place to new heights. Rather than merely providing a backdrop, the narrow cobbled streets and piled rubble of post-war Vienna serve to constrain the action, conveying claustrophobia, corruption and danger in nearly every scene.

Krasker's approach to lighting on location was to simulate and enhance existing sources. Yet the use of such techniques demonstrates that realism was never allowed to get in the way of the creation of mood and visual effect. In addition to the careful use of light and shade, cinematographers were prepared to enhance dramatic effects by forms of artificial manipulation both in the studio and on location. Water and paint were frequently used on the set, particularly in night sequences and Alan Hume recalls a shoot with Krasker where he had prop men throwing buckets of water into the road to darken it down for a night effect. As it dried off it would glisten and shine.[4] A similar technique was used to great effect with *The Third Man*, with the cobblestones constantly being hosed down between takes. But the wet look was primarily for visual effect rather than being realistically motivated by bad weather, as it was in *Odd Man Out*.

Although made in the winter of 1944, *Brief Encounter* avoids direct connection with the war by being set in the late 1930s. Laura Jesson falls in love with Alec Harvey but their unconsummated affair lasts only a few weeks. Barr remarks that Laura's world "is structured not as documentary surface but as a projection of psychic states".[5] Here Krasker's subtle manipulation of lighting and camera angle plays a major part in the external rendering of Laura's subjectivity. The film begins in the station buffet in the third person, focussing on Laura and Alec's final moments. Yet on her train home, we are privy to Laura's thoughts signifying a shift in narrative perspective. Three times interior monologue begins on the soundtrack only for Laura's reverie to be interrupted by external stimuli. The third monologue introduces the Rachmaninov piano signifying her interiority, and the background to her face slowly fades to black, isolating her from her surroundings and drawing the spectator into her consciousness.

Later as she sits at home with her husband, she plays Rachmaninov and the music begins again. The image of the Jessons fades out and we are back in the station buffet just prior to the lovers' first meeting. The rest of the film takes the form of her silent confession to her husband, but her narrative is not only an unheard confession of transgressive desire. It is recounted through a haze of guilt influencing all of the retrospective images we see. Krasker's photography comes into its own here in a series of telling shots: Laura, distraught and running down a dark rainswept street, a high overhead suggesting vulnerability and loneliness, a composed image of solitude as she sits alone under a war memorial, a series of tilted shots as she rushes across the station platform intending to thrown herself under a passing train.

His touch is just as crucial in *Odd Man Out* but this time the play of subjectivity is more complex. The film narrates the last hours of Johnny MacQueen, an IRA commander wounded in a bungled robbery, and takes place between four in the afternoon and midnight. In this winter scenario the films opens in weak sunlight but darkness soon falls, followed by rain and snow, which has turned to blizzard by the end of the film, covering the city streets in a thick white blanket. The darkness provided Krasker with ample opportunity for brooding chiaroscuro effects. Narrative perspective is more externalised than *Brief Encounter* creating different ways of exploring the relationships between characters and environments, which drew much critical praise. Lightman, for example, enthused over the way urban locations were used photographically:

> (Krasker) took full advantage of the converging lines formed by rows of reflections shed by street lights onto damp pavement, of the web-like shadow patterns cast by catwalks and fire-escapes. Unlike many cinematographers, he did not commit the artistic error of over-lighting his night scenes. Rather, he spotted in highlights at specific areas, allowing the remainder of the composition to go appropriately dark.[6]

The streets are highlighted by simple sources of direct illumination, forming dramatic patterns of darkness edged with light. Depth of field is created by wide-angle lenses and by face-on framing of narrow streets and alleyways through which Johnny's gang attempt to evade capture. The compositions serve to hem the men in, trapping them in an urban maze from which the only escape is a police bullet. There is a constant use of low-angled shots and low ceilings pressing down upon the fugitives, confining and oppressive. In sharp contrast the decaying Victorian house inhabited by the grotesque trio of Lukey, Shell and Tober has rooms so cavernous, it renders the occupants almost insignificant, and the snow that falls through the broken skylight in the stairwell enhances the sense of its dereliction.

The film starts in objective, representational mode: images of Belfast shot from the air, a cut to a city clock tower and streets teeming with life. The first intrusion of MacQueen's subjectivity comes on the way to the robbery, as disorienting images of tramlines are intercut with large close-ups of the hero's face as he wipes away the blurred image of passing buildings bending over him. After he is wounded, he hides in a dark shelter on waste ground and hallucinates it as a prison cell. A strong diagonal shaft of light illuminates a warder entering the cell and picking something from the ground. The image then fades into a shot of girl with a single roller-skate, holding a ball. Later hallucinations occur in a pub, where MacQueen sees faces of characters encountered earlier in the bubbles of his spilt beer, and also at Lukey's studio where the paintings begin to fly around the room and he hallucinates the figure of Father Tom preaching to him. Here the use of extreme low angled shots and tilted framing convey the hero's increasingly tenuous grasp on a world slipping away from him.

In *The Third Man* Krasker developed his neo-expressionist style even further. As noted, one of the most striking aspects of the film is the important role played by war-scarred Vienna. The picture can be seen as a part of a group of "rubble" films shot against the backdrop of urban devastation in the aftermath of the war. This sub-genre includes Rossellini's *German Year Zero*, Staudte's *The Murderers are Amongst Us*, Zinneman's *The Search*, and the Ealing comedy *Passport to Pimlico*. Krasker's filming of Vienna conveys the reality of the streets, the squares and the partially demolished buildings. It also captures an oppressive environment. As Moss points out, "enclosure rather than quaintness . . . the elaborate statuary, marble staircases, brooding stone facades, only create a burdensome and foetid atmosphere, the sense of a city smothering in its own past".[7]

As in *Odd Man Out*, Krasker makes use of simple direct lighting techniques to augment existing street lighting, resulting in a combination of strong highlights and deep looming shadows. This creates a world of disorientation and distrust that frustrates Holly Marten's quest to find Harry Lime. The visual play of concealment and revelation is perhaps most effective in the scene where Holly discovers his friend is still alive. As his attempts to woo Lime's acquaintance, Anna, become increasingly hopeless, the camera detaches itself from their conversation to track straight through the flowers on the windowsill and reveal a shadowy figure in the street below. We cut to a low angle of the street cobbles, then a shot of a pair of shoes. Anna's cat approaches and begins to rub against the shoe of the stranger. On leaving Anna's apartment, Holly becomes aware of the stranger's presence and starts shouting at a shadowy doorway. Provoked by the rumpus, an apartment light is switched on and Harry's face is revealed for the first time, a brief moment of illumination as the camera moves in on him. A tram passes before Holly can cross the street and Harry escapes, leaving only the sound of running footsteps and the image of fleeting shadows. Thereafter shadows are used to great effect at other points in the film. We see the menacing shadow of the moon-faced Hans, the child who leads the mob suspecting Harry of some part in the murder of the child's father, and later the disorienting and elongated shadow we assume to Lime, until it turns out to be a balloon seller.

The framing also stresses the oppressiveness of architecture and place. The most notable element of visual style is the use of Dutch tilts used throughout to enhance unease and uncertainty, to create a sense of place where nothing seems to make sense and danger lurks around very corner. The technique had been used sparingly in *Brief Encounter* and *Odd Man Out*, but here it pervades Holly's, and the viewer's, experience of Vienna. The first tilt occurs in Harry's apartment when the porter tells Holly of his friend's "accident". Thereafter they recur in an almost arbitrary way; when Holly first discusses Harry with Anna, when he escapes from Popescu's thugs up a spiral staircase, then out of a window and across rubble-strewn wasteland; when Harry escapes from Holly outside Anna's apartment, when he appears at the bar where the trap has been set for him, and when, finally, he flees through the sewers.

Along with Anton Karas's famous zither score, the tilted shots remain the stylistic highlight of the film. The combinations of lighting and skewed camera angles have led, inevitably, to the label of *film noir*, and in many ways this is legitimate. The Anglo-American co-production and the presence of Orson Welles and Joseph Cotton echo earlier thrillers such as *The Stranger*, *The Lady from Shanghai* and *Shadow of a Doubt*. More important, Krasker's style creates the same atmosphere of mistrust and suspicion that pervades many *films noir*. The construction of narrative around an investigation with a perplexed investigator, although here with less cynicism than the hard-boiled private eye, is also a hallmark of *film noir*. The dark urban setting, the descent (both literal and figurative) into a criminal underworld, and the psychological complexity of the hero are also key points of convergence.

Yet perhaps the most impressive link of all is the careful construction of style on location, both in the dark narrow streets and the labyrinthine sewers. The style not only mirrors Holly's growing confusion as he attempts to resolve the mystery of Harry's "death". It also conveys something of the political background to the drama. As Carpenter notes, the films emerged out of a moment when Europe was entering a new stage of international conflict, as a geopolitical zone of contestation between the new superpowers, the United States and the Soviet Union.[8] The politics of the emerging cold war, then, are central to a wider understanding of the film, and compound the comparisons with American *film noir*, which many commentators have seen as an expression of the new climate of fear in the West.

II

The development of colour cinematography in Britain also embraced an expressionistic sensibility in the post-war period. Most of the early British Technicolor productions, for example, share an imperialist interest in the exotic: from Korda's films of Empire, *The Drum* and *The Four Feathers*, to Wilcox's biopic of Queen Victoria, *Sixty Glorious Years* and the Orientalism of *The Mikado* and *The Thief of Bagdad*. These films are consequently dominated by dazzling images of oriental splendour, British military pomp and exotic foreign landscapes. But the power of such effects owed much to a combination of production and costume design and the pre-existing spectacle of geographical terrain. The creativity of cinematographers was constrained by the dictates of Technicolor who insisted on high key, low contrast lighting to guarantee the technically "correct" levels of colour exposure. Technicolor stock was also very slow and required high levels of carbon arc lighting to achieve a "correct" exposure. In interiors this also had a tendency to flatten areas of colour. But nevertheless the company had a virtual monopoly on colour processing at the time they wielded a great deal of power and influence over how their system, was used in practice. This aesthetic conservatism was to be challenged by a handful of younger cinematographers in the post-war period interested in appropriating certain black and white lighting techniques to produce a more dramatic combination of light and shade in colour rather than simply relying on the colours themselves to produce depth, separation and, crucially, mood. At the forefront of this revolution was Jack Cardiff.

In his autobiography Michael Powell describes his first Technicolor feature, *The life and Death of Colonel Blimp*, as essentially "a black and white film coloured".[9] That is to say the production had not been planned for colour but rather colour was simply a pre-given which was allowed to happen. *A Matter of Life and Death* was to be a very different prospect in that this time an overtly experimental approach to colour was central to the basic concept of the film. It tells the story of Peter Carter (David Niven) a British airman who is forced to bail out of his burning aircraft over a fog-bound English Channel without a parachute. His miraculous escape starts the alarm bells ringing in heaven and a messenger (Marius Goring) is despatched to persuade him to take his place in the other world. Audacious visuals immediately set up a bold contrast between a Technicolor earth and a black and white heaven. To facilitate a smooth transition from one dimension to the other rather than a sharp and potentially jarring cut, Cardiff suggested using a monochrome image derived from the three strip Technicolor process. As Lightman remarked, this produced "a soft velvet quality devoid of the flatness that might have been expected" given that the monochrome sequences were lit for colour.[10] The dissolve process is particularly effective in the sequence when the messenger, an aristocrat executed in the French Civil War, is first despatched. A close-up on a rose in his buttonhole is slowly flooded with vibrant colour and the camera tracks back to show him against a backdrop of equally vivid rhododendrons. The effect is enhanced with his jokey self-reflexive line "One is starved for Technicolor, up there".

In addition to the visual pyrotechnics the film is als concerned with exploring subjectivity and vision. The opening titles state that "this is a story of two worlds. The one we know and another which exists only in the mind of a young airman whose life and imagination have been violently shaped by war". This suggests that the visions of heaven are Carter's fantasy. Yet within the structure of the film they have a solidity which renders them as something more than psychic projection. Ellis argues persuasively that the film is actually embraces two realities rooted in conflicting discourses: narrative fiction and documentary realism, signified by earth and heaven respectively. The Technicolor realm embraces the disruptive forces of sexuality, passion and individual desire while the latter is concerned with social order and rational administration.[11] The discourse of realism was of course championed by critics who used it to construct a particular "dominant" aesthetic tradition in 1940s British cinema. This is a tradition which is profoundly challenged by *A Matter of Life and Death*. Narratively the power of individual desire wins the day. But the film embodies a profound meditation on the construction of cinematic vision. The most powerful examples of this include the arrival of the conductor noted above and the use of subjective point of view gaze when Peter is being rushed to the operating room – culminating in the frequently – noted image of an eyelid closing from the inside. Carter and June's friend Dr Reeves (Roger Livesay) also has a camera obscura set up in his house from which he surveys unseen the life of the village around him. The voyeuristic potential of the device is foregrounded, anticipating Powell's later, darker study of voyeurism in *Peeping Tom* (1960). The images were photographed by Cardiff and then combined with the main images by way of a standard matte shot. Reeves justifies his peeping both in the interests of science – "A village doctor has to know everything – you'd be surprised how many of diagnoses I've formed up here . . ." and art: "you see (the village) all at one and clearly, as in a poet's eye".

A Matter of Life and Death is also marked by a subtle approach to lighting with effective use of coloured light and filters in certain sequences, and the kind of bold chiaroscuro normally associated only with black and white cinemato-graphy. Cardiff took these techniques a step further in *Black Narcissus*. Adapted from the novel by Rumer Godden the film recounts the doomed attempt by a group of nuns to establish a convent in the Himalayas. In the exotic remote location the nuns are gradually unsettled by the eruption of repressed desires, driving one of them, Sister Ruth (Kathleen Byron), to madness and a tragic death. The film was shot entirely in the studio and on the back lot at Pinewood, the Himalayan backdrops being a mixture of glass paintings and photographic plates. While this works more as classical illusionism rather than self-reflexive artifice, the use of the studio allowed the filmmakers total control over the atmosphere, mood and texture.

For the daytime lighting of the palace of Mopu and its environs Cardiff adopted a crisp, clear light which is as important a part of the prevailing atmosphere as the constant breeze. Much of the visual effect is generated by the contrast between the nuns in oatmeal habits and the exotic colour of the locals, the Young General (Sabu), Kanchi (Jean Simmons) and even Dean (David Jarrat) who wears an array of brightly coloured shirts set off by expanses of bare flesh. Cardiff enhances these elements of design with bold chiaroscuro and coloured lighting. The sequence when Clodagh, the sister superior, confronts Ruth who has discarded her habit for a deep red dress and make-up owes its power to a combination of light and shade, the blue backing simulating external moonlight and the big close-ups of Ruth's dark eyes and red lips. Colour is intrinsic to the design but the lighting and cinematography are equally important in the creation of subjective mood and atmosphere.

By now colour stock was faster, allowing greater latitude in the image, but the only suitable lighting remained the relatively large carbon arcs. It is therefore a testament to Cardiff's skill that he produced such subtle modelling without recourse to the smaller incandescent lights by now commonplace in black and white cinematography. His inventive use of colour light is just as impressive, and he describes his approach in the following way:

> In order to enhance the dreamlike strangeness and sensuous beauty of the nuns' environment I exaggerated my effects, sometimes using more blue than usual in the shadows; in the dawn sequence I used soft greens in the shadows, not only because this coolness is always evident at dawn, but because the juxtaposition of green and red is uncomfortable and suggestive of tragedy – like Van Gogh's billiard room at Arles.[12]

The dawn sequence building up to the climax of the film as Clodagh is stalked by Ruth is a *tour de force* of cinematic power, where the audience is forced to share Ruth's POV as stalker. As she emerges into the dawn light, her pale face and black rimmed eyes are an image of palpable evil. Attempting to push Clodagh over the precipice, she falls to her own death. Cardiff enhanced the ethereal quality of the sequence by using a diffusing filter on the last few shots, against the advice of Technicolor who argued that it would degrade the image. Powell stood by his cameraman and the effect remains. Cardiff's bold experimentation won him international plaudits and the Oscar for best colour cinematography.

The final collaboration between Cardiff, Powell and Pressburger was *The Red Shoes*. A young ballerina, Vicky Page (Moira Shearer), joins a famous company run by impresario Boris Lermontov (Anton Walbrook) and is given the leading role in a new ballet, *The Red Shoes*, scored by a young composer Julian Craster (Marius Goring). In the ballet a young girl tries on a pair of magical red shoes. They dance away with her all day and all night. Exhausted she tries to return home but the shoes won't stop and they dance her to her death. The tragedy is mirrored in life when Vicky becomes embroiled in a conflict between her passion for ballet and her love for Julian. When the tensions are finally too much, her shoes appear to run away with her, carrying her to her death under a train.

The centrepiece of the film is the seventeen-minute ballet of the red shoes. The construction of the ballet involved Cardiff working closely with Powell, the designer Hein Heckroth and the composer Brian Easdale on a range of optical effects including variable camera speeds, transparent colour screens and a travelling matte process developed by George Gunn at Technicolor which was used to superimpose the figure of a dancer against a constantly changing backdrop of cellophane sheets and chemical effects produced in water. The ballet also required the use of two massive 300-amp water-cooled arc lamps developed by the Mole-Richardson company, the only lights capable of providing enough power to simulate a theatre spot in the Technicolor process. The ballet is also the focus of the film's interest in the realms of subjectivity. The first flashes occur when Vicky dances Swan Lake at the small Mercury theatre. We see through her eyes as she pirouettes, a series of whip pans across the audience ending on a brief shot of Lermontov in the audience and a big close-up of the ambitious young ballerina in her stage make-up. It is this performance which leads directly to her being offered a place on tour with Lermontov's company. The new ballet of the red shoes not only brings Vicky and Julian together, he assures her that his music will unlock her imagination allowing her to see and experience emotions far beyond the material limitations of the stage, so it also provides a vehicle for the projection of inner turmoil and fears.

The sequence begins with an objective rendering of a stage ballet. The first brief subjective image is when the girl imagines herself dancing in the red shoes she gazes at in the shoemaker's window. After the shoes have danced away with her all night long and prevented from returning home (aided by the grasping hands of the shoemaker's huge demonic shadow), Vicky begins to hallucinate on-stage. The image of the shoemaker turns first into a vision of Lermontov, then Craster, signifying the conflicting pressures imposed on her by the two men. She begins to fall into a dreamscape and dances with a newspaper figure who momentarily turns into a man before reverting back to lifeless paper. The dream turns to nightmare – dark streets populated by prostitutes and syphilitic beggars followed by a terrifying vision of faceless monsters, subconscious demons, encroaching upon her out of the darkness, surrounding her and lifting her up. She also has a vision of an empty auditorium with only Julian conducting, this transforms into a raging sea lashing the rocks, before the spell is broken when Vicky leaves the stage for a costume change before the last scene. In this way the ballet dramatises both Vicky's inner turmoil, but also anticipates the tragedy to come.

Coates has posited cinema as the techno-industrial fulfilment of the Wagnerian concept of *Gesamtkunstwerk*, or total work of art, combining narrative, spectacle, movement, music and colour.[13] The ballet sequence of *The Red Shoes* was Powell's own attempt to realise such a complete artwork. His own term was the "composed film" in which image, music and emotion are interdependent elements in an operatic construction.[14] Orr has noted that the *Gesamtkunstwerk* may be a romantic longing for wholeness but cinema has presented us with fragmentation, alienation and the uncanny image of the double – "the creation of a hallucinatory figure which lures the self impellingly towards destruction".[15] The girl in the ballet is Vicky's double, a narcissistic projection of her own desires, which will return to impinge on her conscious reality with devastating consequences. In this way *The Red Shoes* replays the "return of the repressed" theme of *Black Narcissus*, but while Clodagh survives the attempt on her life by Ruth, this time it is the heroine who falls to her death. This engagement with the dark and destructive powers of the human psyche distinguishes the expressionistic qualities of Powell and Pressburger's work. But the effective cinematic rendering of these preoccupations owes a great deal to Cardiff's lighting and camerawork.

NOTES

1. Charles Barr "Schizophrenia and Amnesia", in Barr (ed.) *All Our Yesterdays: 90 Years of British Cinema* (London: BFI, 1986) p. 15.
2. For a discussion of this new style, see Duncan Petrie *The British Cinematographer* (London: BFI, 1996) pp. 32–6.
3. These included Plus X (80 ASA) and Super XX (160 ASA). British cinematographers continued to use the slower Super X (450 ASA) for some time afterwards.
4. Alan Hume, interviewed by the author, 2 February 1995.
5. "Schizophrenia and Amnesia", p. 17
6. Herb A. Lightman "*Odd Man Out*: Suspense in Black and White" *American Cinematographer*, July 1947, p. 237.
7. Robert F. Moss, *The Films of Carol Reed* (Basingstoke; Macmillan, 1987) p. 187.
8. Lynette Carpenter "'I Never Knew the Old Vienna': Cold War Politics and *The Third Man*" in *Film Criticism* Vol 3, No 1, Autumn, 1978.
9. Michael Powell, *A Life in Movies* (London: Heinemann, 1986) p. 536.
10. Herb A. Lightman "Two Worlds in Technicolor" *American Cinematographer* July, 1947, p. 237.
11. John Ellis, "Watching Death at Work" in Ian Christie (ed.) *Powell, Pressburger and Others* (London: BFI, 1978).
12. Jack Cardiff, *Magic Hour; The Life of a Cameraman* (London: Faber & Faber, 1996) p. 88.
13. Paul Coates, *The Story of the Lost Reflection* (London: Verso, 1985) p. 15.
14. Powell, *A Life in Movies* pp. 582–3.
15. John Orr, *Cinema and Modernity* (Cambridge: Polity Press, 1993) p. 37.

18

DAYS OF HEAVEN
(TERRENCE MALICK – 1976)

Nestor Almendros

John Ford, King Vidor, and Josef von Sternberg were directors whose style was always achieved with great inspiration in lighting. Sternberg, in particular, was the visual filmmaker par excellence: everyone knows his interest in set designing, composition, and lighting. His work has always been an example to me. For Sternberg light went hand in hand with *mise-en-scène*; indeed, it was a fundamental part of *mise-en-scène*.

It is not arbitrary that I refer to Sternberg, Vidor, and Ford when I mention Terrence Malick, because Malick is also a director who puts great store by the look of his films. When Harold and Bert Schneider, the producers, asked me to do *Days of Heaven*, I asked to see *Badlands*, Malick's first film. When I saw it, I realized at once that he was the kind of director with whom I would be able to collaborate successfully. Later on I learned that Malick had very much liked my work in *The Wild Child*, which, although it is in black and white, has something in common with *Days of Heaven*, in that they are both period films. It was because of *The Wild Child* that Malick wanted to work with me.

Days of Heaven was shot in Canada, and when I got to Alberta I realized that Malick knew a lot about photography, which is oddly enough rather unusual for a film director. He has an exceptional visual sense and an equally exceptional knowledge of painting. Communication between a director and a cinematographer is sometimes ambiguous and confused, because many directors

From: Nestor Almendros, 'Days of Heaven', in Rachel Phillips Belash (trans.), *A Man with a Camera* (Farrar, Strauss and Giroux, LLC, 1984).

know nothing about the technical and visual aspects. With Terry, however, it was easy to establish a dialogue. He immediately went to the heart of each problem, and not only allowed me to do what I wanted – which was to use hardly any studio lighting in this period film – but encouraged me. It was therefore very exciting to work with him.

Days of Heaven was not a rigidly prepared film. Many interesting ideas developed as we went along. This left room for improvisation and allowed us to take advantage of circumstances. The call sheets, for example, which are Xerox copies specifying the next day's work, were usually not very detailed. The schedule was changed to suit the weather and also our frame of mind. This disoriented some of the Hollywood crew, who were not used to working in such an improvised way and complained.

Basically my job was to simplify the photography, to purify it of all the artificial effects of the recent past. Our model was the photography of the silent films (Griffith, Chaplin, etc.), which often used natural light. And in the nighttime interiors we often used just a single light. Thus, *Days of Heaven* was a homage to the creators of the silent films, whom I admire for their blessed simplicity and their lack of refinement. From the thirties on, the cinema had become much too sophisticated.

In this as in my other films, there were a number of influences from painting. In the daytime interiors we used light that came sideways through the windows as in a Vermeer. There were also references to Wyeth, Hopper, and other American artists. But as the credits indicate, we were particularly inspired by the great photo-reporters of the turn of the century (like Hine), whose books Malick had a plentiful supply of. Thanks to Bill Weber's editing, our images took on an almost musical rhythm, like a symphony, with andantes, maestosos, staccatos, tremolos, etc.

In France the light is very gentle, because it is almost always filtered through banks of clouds; this makes working with exteriors easy, since the shots are matched together with no difficulty when they are edited. On the other hand, in North America the air is more transparent and the light more violent. A figure standing against the sun appears as a silhouette. Traditionally, cinematographers solve this problem by filling up the shaded area with arc lights. Rather than compensating, Malick and I thought it would be better to expose for the shade, which would make the sky come out overexposed, burned-out, and not at all blue. Like Truffaut, Malick follows the current trend of eliminating colors. Blue sky bothers him, which is understandable when it makes landscapes look like picture postcards or vulgar travel brochures. Exposing against the sun for the shade produces a burned-out sky, white and colorless. If we had used arc lights or reflectors, the result would have been flatter and less interesting. As measured on my exposure, I set the lens stop halfway between the luminosity of the sky and that of the faces. In this way the features of the actors were delicately visible and a little underexposed, and the sky was a bit, but not totally, overexposed.

With a few exceptions, the crew (which I did not choose) was made up of old-guard, typically Hollywood professionals. They were accustomed to a glossy style of photography: faces never in the shade, deep blue sky, etc. They felt frustrated because I gave them so little work. The normal practice in Hollywood is for the gaffer and grip to prepare the lighting beforehand, so I found arc lights set up for every scene. Day after day I would have to ask them to turn off everything they had prepared for me. I realized that this annoyed them; some of them began saying openly that we didn't know what we were doing, that we weren't "professional." At first, as a token of good will, I would shoot one take with arc lights and another without, then invite them to see the rushes to discuss the results. But they wouldn't come to the showings, perhaps because they didn't want to waste their free time. Or if they came, they were not convinced. For them the sky had to be blue and the faces completely illuminated. The conflict became more acute and there were some defections. Luckily, Malick not only took my side but went even further than I did. In some scenes where I wanted to use a piece of white polyester to bounce the sunlight and reduce the contrast a little for the faces that were against the sun, he asked me to shoot without it. As the filming continued and we saw the results, we became more daring, taking away more and more lighting aids so as to leave the image bare. Some of our technical colleagues gradually were won over to our side, but others were never able to understand.

If there were conflicts on the technical side, on the artistic side I was lucky enough to have the best collaborators I could have wanted. In every film there is a small group of leaders whom the others follow. In *Days of Heaven* seven people formed this group around Malick: Jack Fisk, who designed and built the mansion among the wheatfields, and also the smaller houses where the farm workers were supposed to live; Patricia Norris, who with extraordinary care and taste designed and made the period costumes; Jacob Brackman, a personal friend of Malick, who was the assistant director; and naturally the producers, Bert and Harold Schneider. This close little unit would drive for an hour each day in a van from the motel where we were living to the wheatfields. On the way we would invariably talk about the film, so each day the trip turned into a spontaneous production meeting.

The crew in charge of the set, props, and costumes worked together to choose blended, rather subdued colors. Patricia Norris got used fabrics and old clothes to avoid the synthetic look of studio-made costumes. Fisk built a real mansion, outside and inside, not just a façade, as is customary. The interiors were period colors – brown, mahogany, dark wood. The white cloth of the curtains and sheets was washed in tea to give it the tonality of unbleached cotton, not the overbright whiteness of modern fabrics. For the fact is that it is impossible to do good, stylish photography if the set designer, the wardrobe designer, and the prop maker do not collaborate, if the objects they put in front of the camera are tasteless or discordant. What is ugly cannot be made beautiful, unless one accepts Andy Warhol's oxymoron "lovely ugliness." In our profession many people think the director of photography should concern himself only with the camera and the technical aspects. I believe that, on the contrary, he must work in perfect harmony with the people responsible for the sets, wardrobes, and props. Before my arrival in North America we had long telephone conversations about all these things; then, while we were shooting in Canada, useful adaptations and changes were made on the spot.

I had several camera operators in *Days of Heaven*, because union regulations did not allow me to operate the camera myself, which is not the case in Europe. Therefore, Terry and I would work out and rehearse the movements both of the camera and of the actors in the viewfinder; and after a series of tryouts my operators knew exactly what we wanted. Fortunately, I was working with skilled and talented people: John Bailey, who has become since then a great cinematographer; the Canadian Rod Parkhurst; Eric van Haren Norman (a Panaglide specialist); and Paul Ryan as second unit operator. These and other men would work together at the same time in several scenes: the scene of the fire, for instance. Usually I would stand near the main camera, and when ever I could, I would go around giving instructions to the other operators. Sometimes I would pick up a camera and film myself, but this was sacrilege in the eyes of the union. Some of the shots filmed by this crew on their own were excellent; strictly speaking, the praises lavished on my work when I won the Oscar should be shared among these unsung technicians. One would film the wide angle long shots, another would do close-ups with a telephoto lens, a third would follow the action camera in hand, yet another – the Panaglide expert – would run through the flames or into the crowds, and so on. All our individual efforts were unified by Terry's great talent, his technical knowledge, and his infallible taste. For Malick would never let anyone do anything that went against his own ideas. Before filming began, he laid down a series of principles. The style of the movie was outlined in such a way that each member of the crew had to follow the guidelines, the most basic of which was to remain as close to reality as possible.

For the last days of the filming I was replaced by Haskell Wexler. I worked for fifty-three days and he for nineteen. When I was asked to do *Days of Heaven*, I had already agreed to do Truffaut's next film, and the dates had been fixed. The producers and Malick had agreed to this schedule, hoping that *The Man Who Loved Women* would be postponed a little, but in fact work began on time. Of course, I could not break my agreement with Truffaut. I left Canada for France in low spirits, because I was well aware how important *Days of Heaven* was for my professional career.

A month before I was to leave, I mentally reviewed all the cinematographers I admire in America. I thought of Haskell Wexler, who was also a friend, and we asked him if he could come and finish my work. Luckily he accepted. We worked together; over lapping for a week so that he could see how the shooting was going. We also showed selections of all we had filmed up to that point, so that he could familiarize himself with the film's visual style. Haskell was wonderful, because as well as producing unbelievably beautiful images, he adjusted perfectly to the style we had established. I don't think anyone could distinguish between his footage and mine. Even I myself can hardly tell the difference in scenes with an edited mixture of shots taken by each of us. Haskell tends to use filters and diffusion gauzes (as he did in *Bound for Glory*), but since I do not, he did without them. He shot all the final scenes in the city after Richard Gere's death, as well as isolated shots in unfinished sequences; he also did the exterior sequences in the snow, because we had had a long Indian summer and no snow had fallen before my return to France.

We shot *Days of Heaven* in Canada, although the action is supposed to take place in the Texas Panhandle. In Canada we could avoid certain union limitations that are stringent in California. For instance, in Hollywood I could not have been hired. There were other reasons, too – the location the producers discovered in the south of Alberta was in an area belonging to the Hutterites, a religious sect that left Europe many years ago because of intolerance and really live in another age. As a community they cultivate wide expanses of land, where they grow a different kind of wheat, longer than today's strains. They make their own austere utensils and furniture. They have neither radio nor television. They eat natural food, which makes their faces different from ours. Some of these people took part in the film as extras. That whole area belongs to another epoch, and an hour's travel took us daily from the twentieth to the nineteenth century. There is no doubt that the atmosphere peculiar to this place heightened the authenticity of the images in *Days of Heaven*. And there were also the tall, wine-red silos and the old steam-driven farm machines belonging to private collectors who let us use them, as well as the extraordinary virgin landscapes of Banff.

I used the Panaflex camera for the first time. This is now the most popular camera in America, but at that time it had not yet reached Europe. This light, noiseless instrument was a belated but perhaps superior American response to similar European cameras. The present trend is to make equipment smaller and lighter, and therefore more mobile; it is very versatile, because it takes magazines of different footage and can be used for studio or hand-held work. When we were shooting *Days of Heaven*, the Panaflex's only drawback was its not very luminous viewfinder, but this has been upgraded in the latest models. It is a sophisticated camera, almost a gadget. By using it along with the wide-aperture, super-pana-speed lenses, one can shoot in the most adverse conditions, which would have been considered impossible until a few years ago. This film could not have been made with a different type of camera.

Hollywood technicians suffered from a certain inertia. Since they did everything first, they found it hard to keep up with the new procedures which had appeared, mainly in Europe, since World War II. I have already mentioned the lightweight cameras that reached America only years later. But there are other examples. In Hollywood dolly shots have always been done on sheets of plywood. The technique of putting the camera on tracks is still not completely accepted. For simple movements I prefer the Italian Elemack, which is versatile and quite light. These Hollywood technicians insisted on using the heavier dolly, which is too big to fit anywhere. When I tried to convince them, they paid no attention to my reasoning, simply telling me they had always done it this way and it had never been a problem. I half believe that they purposely choose the harder way so as to protect themselves indirectly. That is, if the job is simplified, laymen may more easily penetrate what has always been a closed world. Some still defend themselves by this hostile reaction to any novelty, particularly any new device that simplifies their work, although recently I have noticed the attitude is changing.

Another example: they still refuse to discard the gear heads. Nowadays there are fluid or hydraulic heads (Satchler, Ronford, etc.) which produce pan shots just as smoothly and steadily. The new heads can be handled without a great deal of experience. Anyone with a good sense of rhythm can get perfect pan shots and follow moving figures without losing them from the frame. However, not everybody can handle these gear heads, a thing that must please them. I myself like cameras with a simple head and a handle to operate them with. The operator becomes all of a piece with the camera, which makes it almost human. The mechanical perfection of the gear head cannot be compared with the almost human feel of a handmade pan shot.

The relatively recent innovation of noiseless, large-screen editing tables at which one can sit down and work in comfort has also been greeted with suspicion. Our editor in *Days of Heaven*, Bill Weber, who belongs to the new wave, worked at an editing table. But most of the old guard went on using their small-screened, vertical Moviolas, even though these are noisy and must be worked at standing up, and a side table is still needed for splicing.

Something similar has happened with the Reflex focusers in the new cameras' viewfinders. Brands like Arriflex and Cameflex were introduced in Europe during and immediately after World War II to eliminate the parallax effect produced by external viewfinders. Through a system of mirrors and prisms the operator can even check the focus. But in the States these were not available until much later on. A Reflex system was added to the old Mitchell camera, and this arrangement was not improved for a long time. Then Panavision made a series of truly extraordinary Reflex cameras, which proves that when the Americans set their minds to solving a technological problem, they produce something that can top all that has appeared before.

Days of Heaven was the first film to use the Panaglide prototype. This is the Panavision version of the Steadicam process. The operator wears a plastic-metallic harness from which an arm sticks out with various hinges and springs, and on the end of this hangs the camera, almost as if it were defying the laws of gravity like a spaceship. The operator moves the camera by hand, but the weight is mostly on his body. The suspension system lets the camera move freely, climb stairs, even run; the operator's movements are not transmitted to the camera, which literally glides through the air. The camera also has a small built-in video viewfinder so the operator does not have to put his eye to a conventional viewfinder but can see the scene he is filming on a small monitor. There is also a remote-control motorized system for focusing. The assistant cameraman has a small wireless transmitter with knobs with which he can focus the lens without touching it. The Panaglide is so sensitive that it would move if the assistant touched the lens. And this, in fact, is one of its shortcomings. Its very sensitivity makes it swing in the wind, so that shooting may be impossible.

At first Terry was so taken with the new device that he wanted to shoot the whole film with the Panaglide. We soon realized that although it was very useful, sometimes indispensable, it was not to be used exclusively. In fact, to a certain extent we paid for the initiation. It was like the early days of zoom lenses, when filmmakers made their audiences seasick by using their new toy too much. The Panaglide left us free to move in all directions, so the scenes turned into a merry-go-round. The whole crew, sound technicians, scriptgirl, director, and I, were all constantly scurrying behind the operator so as to keep out of the frame. The rushes were brilliantly executed, but with too much virtuosity; the camera was like another protagonist intruding in the scene. We soon found out that often nothing competes with a rock-steady tripod shot or the slow, invisible, regular movement of a classic dolly on wheels.

Nevertheless, some shots and sequences in *Days of Heaven* would not have been possible without the Panaglide. And these are some of the scenes that attracted the attention of both public and critics. For example, Bill (Richard Gere), in the river, convinces Abby (Brooke Adams) to accept the marriage proposal of the boss (Sam Shepard). It would have been impossible to put tracks under the water to do a dolly shot, and besides, the actors were improvising and were wandering aimlessly with the water up to their knees. The camera never lost them for a minute. In the sequence where the wheatfields are on fire, the camera could get right in among the flames and follow the progress of the fire with dizzying, dramatic movements.

The fact that both actors and camera were improvising gave the editor some problems. There were times when it was impossible to cut to another shot without breaking continuity. It was also difficult to shorten a sequence. For example, one of the most successful shots had to be left out of the final cut: the camera operator was standing on the top of the crane to shoot a scene taking place on the mansion's third-floor terrace. Linda Manz leaves the terrace and comes down the staircase. The crane is lowered at the same time to follow her, and we see her intermittently through the windows. Once on the ground, the operator gets off the crane and, walking, catches up with Linda Manz. He follows her into the kitchen, where she meets Richard Gere and starts talking to him as they go to another room. The first part of the shot, where the crane is lowered outside a building so that the camera picks up different actions through the windows, was no novelty. Many years ago King Vidor had used it in *Street Scene* and Max Ophüls in *The Earrings of Madame De* ... But the second part, where the camera enters the building, was something new, impossible for the Louma, for example. (The Louma is a French device that lets the camera enter a building, as I did at the end of *Madame Rosa*, but it can only stay in one room, not twist and turn to follow someone into another area.) The Panaglide adds the feeling of a third dimension, and describes perfectly the geography of a set.

The trouble is that the camera and the harness together are fairly heavy. The operator has to turn into an Olympic athlete. If the Panaglide or Steadicam system takes over, it will demand a new generation of athlete operators and then the problem will be to find athlete artists. The three operators and I tried the apparatus and ended up breathless. Then Panavision sent us Eric van Haren Norman, their best-trained athlete, to go with the camera. Eric, who does pushups every day, is a good artist besides.

In *Days of Heaven* I began systematically to have the film pushed for night scenes. In the past, doing this with a 47 emulsion produced inadequate results, but by this time the technique had been perfected. We did tests in the Alfa-Cine laboratory in Vancouver, and they were more than satisfactory. Here they pushed the film by raising the sensitivity of the negative to 200 ASA and in some extreme cases to 400 ASA. The grain was normal and was not noticeable even in the subsequent enlargements to 70 mm. This process, plus the new super-pana-speed ultraluminous lenses, allowed me to go further with low exposures than I had ever gone before. The 55 mm lens opens at f 1.1, and makes it possible to film with literally no more light than that of a match or a pocket flashlight. In *Days of Heaven* we often shot with this 1.1 f stop, pushing the negative in the laboratory, not even using an 85 filter to catch the last daylight. I was worried about the depth of field, which was minimal when we were considering enlarging to 70 mm. But luckily I was working with Michael Gershman, a superb focus puller. He was well aware of the risks we were running. Unawed by the difficulties, he was enough of a perfectionist to insist on learning all the measurements and movements. Sometimes people got impatient, but I am grateful to him for the pains he took, because I have always been against the trend that prevailed until recently of diffusion filters. I wanted a clean, precise, crisp image. Some Hollywood technicians are excellent and extremely adaptable. They work hard and are full of ideas and solutions for every problem.

In professional filmmaking it was unheard of to take too many technical risks, because the cinematographer is responsible to the producer if a scene turns out badly. But in *Days of Heaven*, since Malick in fact wanted to experiment in this area, he let me go as far as I could. There are many night scenes in the film. The story was set in 1917, a time when the only way to get light outside in the country at night was by bonfires or lanterns. We wanted these scenes to give the impression of having really been illuminated by firelight. There are many such scenes in Westerns, usually shot by hiding a light beside the flames to supplement the natural light from the fire. I always regarded this as the wrong solution. Even a modern film like *Dersu Uzala* falls into this trap. Here the scene around the fire is ridiculous, not only because there is too much light – the artificial light overpowers the flames – but also because the light is white, in contrast with the color temperature and the atmosphere. Another solution sometimes used to film close-ups of characters around a fire is to wave some-thing in front of the lights, like a bad imitation of the natural flickering of the flames. We employed a new technique: we used real firelight to illuminate the faces. Like all discoveries it came about by accident. We had some containers of propane gas with flame-throwing jets to start the fire for the burning-wheatfield scenes. Noticing that they were easy to handle, and that the height of the flame could be controlled, I did some tests that clinched the matter. All the close-ups near flames were filmed like this, both those of the country dance with the fiddler and those of the burning fields. The propane gas produced the right coloration and movement. We shot at 200 ASA with the lens stop between f 1.4 and 2.2. In my opinion, our method achieved great authenticity.

At first some members of the crew felt confused, because the work we asked of them was unusual. If the gaffer is an electricity specialist, why did he have to handle bottles of propane gas? Why did the prop man? After all, this had to do with lighting. But soon a feeling of common purpose overcame their sense of professional etiquette.

The long shots of the fire in the wheatfields were filmed practically as they were, with no back-up lights. The fact is that, when fire is illuminated, it loses some of its visual strength. With our method the characters were sometimes silhouetted against the flames, like the negatives of prehistoric cave paintings. When super-productions have scenes with huge fires, they often make the mistake of spoiling the effect by overlighting, because the director of photo-graphy feels obliged to justify his salary and his presence by a spectacular display of his electrical paraphernalia.

We spent about two weeks filming the fire scenes. Each night we set fire to a new wheatfield. Several times we were alarmed because the fire spread too rapidly. On one occasion we were suddenly surrounded by huge flames and the air became suffocating. But our grips reacted quickly, evacuating the trucks with all the equipment – and ourselves as well – through the flames. No one wore special clothing, and we had only goggles to protect us from the smoke. It was a dangerous adventure which might have ended in a serious accident, but this was a blessed film.

In some scenes withdrawing the 85 filter made possible combinations of color temperatures that were beyond the norm but had pictorial quality. I remember a moment when Richard Gere and Linda Manz are roasting a turkey outside on an open fire. There was almost no daylight and the image took on a deep blue tone, except for the crackling fire that intermittently cast a red-hued glow on the actors.

In another scene, the oil lamps the farmhands carry to light their way and catch the locusts were props not used as decoration but as real light sources. As in *Adèle H.*, we hid tiny electric quartz bulbs inside the lamps. Under their clothes all the actors wore belt batteries, and fine electric cables hidden under their shirts led to the bulbs inside the lamps. For greater authenticity we tinted the glass of the lanterns orange, so the white light of the quartz bulbs took on the warm-toned temperature of oil lamps. Outside the frame we used soft lights with a double dose of orange gelatine, which barely filled up the shaded areas. And that was all.

Another innovation was the way we shot the cross-cutting dialogue in the outdoor scenes. Such dialogue occurs when two people are talking to each other and the camera films their faces alternately. In reality, when the sun is shining, one of these two people might be facing the light, and then the other will have the light behind him. In this situation there is no matching of luminous intensity possible in the editing, and the result is awkward. Lighting the person whose back is to the sun is only an artificial solution: the sky behind the person with the sun on his face is blue, behind the back-lit person it is white (overexposed), so the continuity is bad. Paradoxically – and in flagrant contradiction to my realist ethics – the solution we found (suggested to me by a fortunate mistake I made in *Femmes au soleil*) was to place each of the actors on the same spot with his or her back to the sun, only making sure that the eyeline was correct. Then both the faces and the background have the same luminous value, and there are no jumps when the shots are edited one after another. Obviously in this case the geography of the place, plains covered with wheat, lent itself to this solution, as the field and the crossfield were identical. Sometimes we would film one person in the morning and the other in the afternoon, so the sun had changed position and was behind both of them. Two people face to face and back-lit? Planet Earth with two suns? I don't think anyone who saw *Days of Heaven* noticed.

As a general rule, nature's most beautiful light occurs at extreme moments, the very moments when filming seems impossible, when the Kodak and Weston manuals advise against it. If a careful viewer could have counted two suns in the daytime scenes, in the evening scenes he would not have been able to find any. Perhaps this is what drew attention – unconsciously, of course – to the light in *Days of Heaven*. At Malick's insistence certain parts of the film were made at what he calls the "magic hour," that is, the time between sunset and nightfall. From the point of view of luminosity, this period lasts about twenty minutes, so that calling it a "magic hour" is an optimistic euphemism. The light really was very beautiful, but we had little time to film scenes of long duration. All day we would work to get the actors and the camera ready as soon as the sun had set we had to shoot quickly, not losing a moment. For these few minutes the light is truly magical, because no one knows where it is coming from. The sun is not to be seen, but the sky can be bright, and the blue of the atmosphere undergoes strange mutations. Malick's intuition and daring probably made these scenes the most interesting ones visually in the film. And it takes daring to convince the Hollywood old guard that the shooting day should last only twenty minutes. Even though we took advantage of this short space of time with a kind of frenzy, we often had to finish the scene the next day at the same time, because night would fall inexorably. Each day, like Joshua in the Bible, Malick wanted to stop the sun in its imperturbable course so as to go on shooting. This system of working at the magic hour was not totally unknown to me, because I had used it on other occasions for short, isolated vignettes, for instance in *La Collection-neuse* and *More*. But I had never been able to use it for long sequences as we did here. There are few films like this with so many different exteriors, so full of opportunities for a cinematographer.

In these scenes our normal procedure was also to push the development, counting on my exposure meter as if it had 200 ASA. We began with normal lenses, but as the light diminished, I would ask for lenses with wider apertures, always ending with the most luminous, the 55 mm, which opens to f 1.1. To draw out the sensivity of the film even further when all that was left in the air was a slight glow, we would take off the corrective 85 filter for daylight and gain almost one more stop. As a last resort we sometimes shot at eighteen or twelve images a second, asking the actors to move more slowly, which reconstructed the normal rhythm when the film was projected at twenty-four frames a second. This meant that instead of exposing at 1/50 of a second, we exposed at 1/16, which gave us another lens stop. When the people in the laboratory did the timing, they would have to harmonize – correct – a negative with different tonalities. The work Bob McMillan did at the MGM lab was marvelous. In the rushes certain scenes were really like a patchwork of different bits and pieces, and McMillan was able to unify everything. I am indebted to him.

The decision to shoot these scenes at the "magic hour" was not gratuitous or aestheticist; it was completely justifiable. Everyone knows that country people get up very early to do their chores (we shot at twilight to get the feeling of dawn). The scene in the river with Gere and Adams had an end-of-the-day feeling, because it took place when they were relaxing after work. At that time people worked from sunrise to sunset.

Since the film was set during the early days of electricity, I put low-watt household bulbs in the lamps to obtain a warm-toned color temperature for the night scenes inside the mansion. If I had used photofloods, which were then the usual solution, the light would have been too white, too modern. The lamps were mounted on dimmers so that we could vary their intensity in relation to the other lights – mostly soft lights – which were of course out of the frame. Dimmers were often used for black-and-white films. With the arrival of color, however, it was noticed that putting lights on a rheostat shifted the color temperature toward warm tones. But what was considered a defect of the early color films now gave me the more subdued effect of the tungsten lamps that characterized the early days of electricity. Toward the end of *Days of Heaven*, when the jealous husband (Sam Shepard) goes upstairs at night and finds his wife (Brooke Adams) in the bedroom, there are period lamps in the room. These justified the lighting outside the frame, which came from the same direction as the light of the lamps, reinforcing it. In the images of the mansion seen from outside, at night as well as during the "magic hour," the light coming from the windows was the electric light of ordinary household bulbs.

Apart from these scenes, we used hardly any artificial illumination in the film. For the few interior day scenes we followed Vermeer's example and used the light coming in through the windows. I had experimented with this technique earlier, particularly in Rohmer's *The Marquise of O.* But Malick went even further. Since Rohmer does not like any great contrasts in lighting, I had had to add some extra light to make the backgrounds visible, too, and fill up the shadowy parts of the faces. For his part, Malick did not want anything added. Therefore, the background remained in shadow and only the characters stood out. This method produced some positive results, apart from the most obvious, which is that we retained the beauty of this natural light. The actors work better because they are not fatigued by the excessive light and suffocating heat of artificial lights. No time or money is lost in complicated electrical installations. On the negative side is the fact that the lens stop must often be wide open, which produces minimal depth of field. Malick is one director who is very familiar with photographic techniques. Someone else might not have taken this lack of depth into consideration, but Malick organized the scene so that the actors were all on the same focal plane.

Like everything else in *Days of Heaven*, the special effects we used were extremely simple. Malick's basic principle was that they should be achieved in the camera, not by altering the original negative with opticals in the laboratory. Audiences have learned a lot, and recognize these things at once, because when the film is manipulated in the laboratory, the grain and coloration change. My European experience had taught me something my American assistants at first considered sacrilegious: fades at the beginning or end of a scene were often done directly with the camera. They did not have to be created in the laboratory. Just closing the lens stop slowly to f 16 (if the exposure for the shot was f 2.8, for example) was enough, followed by the Panaflex's variable shutter control, until everything became completely dark.

In the sequence of the plague of locusts we used a technique which some experts on the crew considered both heterodox and "unprofessional," though later on they had to bow to the evidence. For the inserts and close-ups we used thousands of live locusts, captured for us by the Canadian Department of Agriculture. But in the extreme long shots of the plague-infested fields we used seeds and peanut shells scattered from above by helicopters outside the frame. This had been done in other films: *The Good Earth*, for instance, in 1937. Here our innovation was to use a camera (an old model Arriflex) that could shoot running the film backward; then we asked the actor and extras to walk backward, and we also had the tractors driven in reverse. So when the printed film was projected, the characters and tractors were going forward and the locusts (seeds) were not falling but seemed to be flying up the wheatfields. Because it was first-generation negative, the grain was very fine and matched the rest.

We used day for night for some scenes. Since the days of black and white, night scenes have been produced by shooting during the day and underexposing the negative (I discuss this in the chapter on *The Wild Child*). The procedure still works for color films, but now a polarizing filter is used which darkens the sky somewhat, though not enough. In my opinion, this method produces unsatisfactory results. In *Days of Heaven* we solved the problem by trying to avoid the sky. We would raise the camera and shoot downward, or we would choose places from which the horizon was out of sight, like the foot of a hill. To heighten the nocturnal effect we underexposed and also eliminated the orange-colored 85 corrective filter that we used for daylight, so the images took on a bluish, lunar quality. This is yet another advantage of working in color.

Though Malick is very much an American, his culture is universal, and he is familiar with European philosophy, literature, painting, and music. So he spans two continents, and consequently it was not hard for me to adjust to shooting *Days of Heaven* in the New World.

When the Hollywood Academy awarded me the Oscar for my work on *Days of Heaven*, my career entered a new phase.

19

MICHAEL CHAPMAN
(INTERVIEW WITH MICHAEL CHAPMAN)

Dennis Schaefer and Larry Salvato

"You see, I wish I could have some more profound things to tell you. I wish there were some great thing dredged up from my psyche that I could say was the key to all these things, but there isn't. It's a mechanical medium and you've got to do the mechanics and let the mechanics give the aesthetic pleasure."

Perhaps the one of the most gifted cinematographers who now works only infrequently is Michael Chapman. He has shot just over a dozen films but has explored a great variety of styles and viewpoints. In a certain sense, he feels he's done it all; he now has no desire to take up the camera just for the sake of doing a film. So he does a film every twelve or eighteen months and then only when he feels he will be artistically and emotionally challenged by the project.

Once described as "a disciple of Gordon Willis," Chapman does not shoot like Willis or even have a comparable style. But he was Willis's operator for over four years, working on films including *Klute*, *The Godfather* and *Bad Company*. The most important thing he learned from Willis was not "how to" information but the philosophy that film is a mechanical medium of cameras, lenses and film stocks and the mechanics are the road to whatever aesthetics there are in movies. He also found that if you take your work seriously and concentrate your efforts, it will show up, sometimes even unconsciously, in the quality of your work.

From: Dennis Schaefer and Larry Salvato, 'Michael Chapman' (interview with Michael Chapman), in Dennis Schaefer and Larry Salvato (eds) *Masters of Light: Conversations with Contemporary Cinematographers* (University of California, 1984).

On over half of his films he has worked with only three directors; these good relationships have formed the basis for a high level of visual collaboration. His three films apiece for Martin Scorsese and Phil Kaufman are indicative of his ability to view things with a fresh perspective: his off-center framing and garish use of bright colors to emphasize the pop-art, comic-book texture of *The Wanderers* is one example; his innovative use of variable-speed cinematography in the boxing sequences of *Racing Bull* is another. While *Racing Bull* challenged him with an opportunity to shoot in black-and-white, *Dead Men Don't Wear Plaid* required that he match, scene for scene, vintage black-and-white Holly-wood films, a situation that called for a preciseness and a finesse that he had not achieved before.

The excitement of a new idea and the taxing of his creative energy to the fullest extent is what Chapman is looking for, a process that he describes as rejuvenating. It's not surprising, then, that he has taken on directing with *All the Right Moves*. Perhaps it's the ultimate filmmaking challenge.

[...]

On Taxi Driver, *what kind of preproduction discussions did you have with Marty Scorsese? What was the visual style that you were kind of going for?*

Well, we looked at a lot of movies beforehand. Lots and lots of movies; I can't even remember them all. That's the wonderful thing about Marty; he sees all movies and we looked at things that didn't have a hope of having anything to do with *Taxi Driver*. Things that were in no way relevant and then things that were obviously relevant like New York movies, *film noir*, *Sweet Smell of Success* and things like that. Strangely we looked at a lot of black-and-white. But we looked at all sorts of movies and that was wonderful because it just made us sort of at ease with each other and confident that when we were talking about something we were talking about the same thing. And as far as a specific visual style, I don't know that we ever decided anything. Fortunately Marty and I and Bobby DeNiro were all New Yorkers, or had lived in New York. I felt a lot about New York and, I think, knew a lot about New York, and Marty and Bobby certainly did; a lot of the people who were responsible for making it be what it was had some passionate concern about New York. And I do think that *Taxi Driver* is enormously a New York movie and that we got the way New York looks. It isn't a terribly realistic movie, so maybe we didn't get the way New York looked, but we got some emotional equivalent, some vision of New York now, and I can't think of any other films that capture it quite that way. It sounds quite arrogant and I don't want it to be. Well no, by God we did, I can't think of any New York movies that get it that way. And I think that's what we went for more than a specific visual style, though Marty certainly has a visual style that all of his movies have. It's not my movie, by any means, it's Marty's. More than a visual style, it's the New Yorkness of it. I would come back to what Gordy Willis talked about: a point of view, some vision of New

York that we did turn out to hold in common, some of it spoken and a lot of it unconscious. A lot of the unpleasantness of *Taxi Driver* is about a kind of paranoia that you can get in New York and that you have in New York if you live below a certain income level. And I think that, by whatever lucky accident or whatever you want to say, we shared some need about New York that we wanted to express.

Was the movie shot as fragmented as it seemed to be on the screen, or was that mostly in the editing?

Yes, I think it was, although it's in the script too. It's a great piece of movie writing. And an enormous amount of what you think of as that fragmentation, that sort of nervousness that begins to be one thing and then it is something else, is in the script. And Marty for once had an excellent script to deal with and he sure as hell dealt with it. I'm trying to remember; I wish I could think if Marty said some specific set of things about how he wanted it to look. You know, you say those things before a movie starts. You always say it's going to do this and it's going to do that, but after a while any given movie has a life of its own. It dictates to you and its style comes out of what happens, and if that style begins to come out, no matter what happens, then the only thing you can do is to let yourself go and let the movie go with it. If that unconscious material seems to be working coherently in some way, the best thing you can do is just let yourself go and just trust that impulse that is not quite expressable, and concentrate on the mechanics that will let that impulse be brought out. And I think that's what we did on *Taxi Driver*. That's what you do on a good movie that works, at least from my point of view. For what I do, I know that I work best if I concentrate on the mechanics of how. I mean, if the angle of the light, the way the camera moves, seem to be determined in some way I can't quite express, the best that I can do is concentrate on the ways to let those things happen.

There seemed to be a real difference between day scenes and night scenes; and the day scenes are like almost sort of normal for a city like New York. But at night, I mean, it was ominous; evil was lurking around that next corner. What kind of consideration went into getting that kind of effect?

I think that's quite true, but I think that the hardest photography in the world to do is day exteriors. I find it the hardest because you have so much less control. I'm only now beginning to think I have some clue of how to deal with it; how to impose myself on daylight rather than let daylight force itself on me. I mean, you never can. If you have a totally dark room and you have a night scene, it doesn't do anything, you do it all. You put the lights, you put the people, you do that. But if you have a day exterior, there's just plain less you can do. And the ordinary reality of the situation forces itself on you far more than you do on it. With all the elaborate camera moves and arc lights and scrims and things in the world, my God, there is just that ordinary daylight there. You can't get away from it. And I think it is the very hardest stuff in the world to do. In something like *Comes a Horseman* you have wonderful clouds and stuff like that, but that is something very different. I'm talking about the kinds of scenes where people are on the street and talking and there's all that light that's just there. And it determines you more than you determine it. It's the very hardest stuff in the world for me and I think for most people whether they even know it. I don't think there was a conscious attempt to make the nighttime scary; that just goes with the territory. That's the screenplay. It doesn't take any great insight to say that that's what you're going to do because that's what the movie's about. But I think a lot of it is simply the enormous recalcitrance of daytime. It's simply unavoidable. If it isn't I wish somebody would tell me because I struggle and struggle. I once did a western which was, as westerns are, filmed entirely outdoors. That was where I had to face that daylight, day after day.

How do you deal with that?

Well, it's mostly a matter of angles. It's a matter of using the angles. It's not just a matter of using back light, sometimes it's a matter not of using back light, but of letting it be a very elaborate pattern of flat light. A lot of it is in the locations, of trying to use the locations where some large contrast of light and shadow is there for you to play with, so that people can move from light to shadow and so that the screen is split up between heavy light and shadows. It gives you the equivalent of moving people say as in *Invasion of the Body Snatchers* where you can move a person into a light where it's shining like that, and then you move them into darkness and then into the light. It's a way of making the daylight give you some of that contrast, where you at least can, by playing with the actors and playing with the angles from which you attack it, achieve some contrast. It's hard.

What about that whole scene in, what was it, Columbus Circle? Having the political rally . . . ?

Yeah, Columbus Circle. A lot of the time we used people to create blockages and we kept inside the crowd. We took dolly shots with Bobby coming forward and reaching for his gun and then dolly shots of the candidate. We kept inside the crowd and kept it almost claustrophobic and jammed, so that kind of myriad of faces and the shuffling and the blocking and opening and blocking did some of that for us. And that has some of the tension that I hope some of the nighttime stuff had. And there's another big daylight scene where he's going to perhaps try and kill the candidate. It's a rally where he talks to a Secret Service man about some secret signal that the Secret Service has and then he makes up a goofy telephone number in New Jersey, and we tried to do some of that there, and also we did it from strange angles there. We shot them almost on top and we just did whatever we could. We tried to do it those ways but it was not as successful from my point of view, not from the movie and not from Marty and Bobby's point of view but from my own. That one just doesn't work as well as some of the others, because it's so bloody hard. You have to be able to force yourself and your will onto it the way you can on a set or you can at night. I mean, night is essentially a set.

You had all kinds of dolly shots in Taxi Driver.

Marty loves dollies, Marty loves to move the camera around and around and around, all the time. And I had been working in the movies in New York for years and knew the crews and things there. And by accident the town was very slow when we started *Taxi Driver*. And I got together, because of that fortuitous circumstance, a very, very good crew. Really wonderful. And Marty is a real charmer when he wants to be, like anybody who has real charisma. He really can seduce a crew if he wants to. And after a while they loved him. They made jokes about him. And so they really went out of their way to make all these elaborate moves, well and fast. So Marty just dollied and dollied and dollied and the guys did it. You know, there was the famous overhead shot and everything at the end after the killing takes place. We finally said, "Well, the only thing you can do is cut a hole in the floor of the next apartment upstairs," and so they cut. It was an old abandoned building and I drew a line where I wanted the opening and we just cut the ceiling out. Crews, if they're good, are a lot smarter than some people think they are, and they respond to something unusual if it is amusing. They're very sophisticated about movies. A good crew can be extraordinarily sophisticated about movies without having any theoretical background for it. They just are from doing it. And they got challenged and turned on by Marty.

And so the dollies just went on and on and I think by and large they worked. A lot of what you see is edited, and many of the moves were excessive and turned out to be excessive in the editing. But it certainly is a movie full of looks here and there and looks everywhere, like a walker in the city, you just keep wandering and looking. And I think appropriately.

With the student filmmaker in mind, what type of dolly equipment do you use?

Oh, nothing special, one of the early pipe track systems of dolly, and a lot of the time I seem to remember we used a western dolly with big tires. I made them get special big golf-cart tires that are quite large but are very soft so that you can dolly over small obstacles and things without even knowing it. Then we would put a sputnik on top of the western dolly and chain the sputnik down, and the sputnik has a great advantage in that the seat will swivel 360° around the central axis so that the cameraman, if he's good, can put his feet on any of the four little wheels of the dolly and swivel himself around and can follow action anywhere like that. In fact, all that stuff in Columbus Circle where the candidate is walking forward was done exactly that way. We just built a little lip off the sidewalk onto the street and you never noticed that the track is bumpy as hell. The western dolly with soft tires absorbs so much and the operator, Freddy Schuller, was so good that you get away with it. While it's very good to be fussy about bumps in a track and things like that, if you have one of these systems of 20-foot lengths of pipe that are joined end-to-end, you know, and you have the little flange wheels that roll on them, you get a bump say at every 20 feet if they're not joined right. So it goes very smooth and then bump, very smooth and then bump ... Well, that bump is very noticeable. But sometimes if you have a western dolly with soft tires and you dolly down the street and there's a constant sort of slight movement and wobble in the dolly, you don't notice that at all. Especially if there are people, as there were for instance in that scene, surging back and forth in Columbus Circle, you can get away with murder, and you will never notice it. And sometimes trying to make a dolly too smooth to begin with just is an enormous problem. Sometimes it's better to do something like a thing with a soft-tire western dolly and some kind of pedestal that you can sit on or even sit hand-held on the dolly, rather than try and make it enormously smooth where you defeat yourself. Because you get it smooth and then each little thing shows up. But if you do allow a certain roughness, and especially if it's a scene where there is movement and there are things swimming in and out of the frame, it's better just to trust that the eye will absorb the bumps and not notice it. Now a lot of that you have to either be the operator yourself or trust your operator to know when you can get away with it and when you can't. It's very much a judgment call. When I did *The Last Detail*, which was the first feature I did and operated myself, we did a lot of it in Toronto in the snow in winter and we had one of those soft-tired western dollies with a sputnik on it. And we dollied over ice and off the sidewalk and all kinds of stuff. You see it, but you don't care. It was there and the interest of the scene gets you past it and you can go a lot faster and do a lot more. There's no sense pretending that getting a lot of work done in a day is not important; it is.

[...]

Raging Bull *was the first film you've shot in black-and-white and one of the few films shot in black-and-white in the last ten years. What kind of problems did that present?*

It presented a problem in that I didn't know anything about it. I'd never shot anything in black-and-white. It made me feel young again, if being young is being inexperienced and terrified. On the simplest level, it's very hard to find a lab that will develop and print black-and-white. And if they do it, they don't do it well and there are terrible static problems and they just tend to screw it up. The technology doesn't seem to exist anymore, for some reason. The only people who could do it here, with any pretense of familiarity, was Technicolor because they do black-and-white for Disney. All the cells, in the various stages of animation, are done in black-and-white for money reasons. So they have a black-and-white film bath and they do black-and-white every day. Now Gordy had done *Manhattan* in black-and-white and he had terrible trouble; he had ruined negative and endless static problems. They had done it in New York and had a small lab do the developing and then Technicolor in New York did the printing. But the lab that did the developing just drove him crazy. People just do not know how to do it anymore.

He's very meticulous so he must have gone berserk.

Yes, he did go crazy. And I was going to use the same people because they had got their act together and he had beaten them into submission. But then, for various reasons, we came back here and we did all the fight sequences here. That took nine or ten weeks so there was no use sending it to New York. I sent it to Technicolor here and I stayed with Technicolor afterwards.

Black-and-white is just more complicated. You have to do the same number of things and there are fewer ways to do it. It's difficult and, as such, was interesting. I'd like to do more black-and-white. You know the reasons that it's more difficult: things don't separate by color, you have to separate them by light essentially. You can do it by backlight, or by having dark objects against a light background or by having light objects against a dark background. There are simply fewer ways to make things separate from each other. That's the essential reason. And except for the fight sequences, everything in *Raging Bull* is shot on real locations, which means low ceilings and no place to put the backlights that they used to have in the old days of the studio system. And we didn't have any of that because we were shooting in apartments and houses in the Bronx.

Do you think black-and-white is totally outmoded for use in features?

No, I don't see why. It's more abstract and thus, in some ways, more interesting to me.

How and who did Marty Scorsese have to convince on the black-and-white issue?

I don't know. He just called me up and asked me if I wanted to shoot it in black-and-white. I think perhaps Bobby DeNiro wanted to do it in black-and-white also. I think it was a very wise decision. I think that if you are above a certain age, you tend to think that real movies are black-and-white anyway. I certainly do. I mean the movies that formed me and that are deepest in my unconscious are black-and-white, by and large. And certainly you think of fight movies in black-and-white. *City for Conquest, Gentleman Jim* and all the classic fight movies I can think of, even *Champion*, which I don't like much, are all in black-and-white. So it seemed a reasonable thing to do. Anyone's memories of Jake LaMotta are black-and-white memories.

What are your favorite fight films?

I like *City for Conquest* and *Body and Soul*. But Bobby DeNiro is a better fighter than any of those guys. He looks and moves like a fighter. He has the punches and convincingness of a fighter, much more so. With Cagney or Garfield, you always have a sense that they are actors portraying a fighter. But Bobby is really a fighter. He spent a year not doing anything, just working out every day, obsessively. Finally he got to be a pretty good middleweight, I understand. He really can rock professionals with a punch. And he just looked and moved like LaMotta.

On Raging Bull *you did some different things as far as intensity, direction of light and stylization because it wasn't in color?*

Yes. We spent more time on the fights than the whole rest of the movie. In terms of screen time though, it doesn't play more than ten or fifteen minutes. So those scenes are very, very elaborate.

Choreographed?

Very, very choreographed. Just as *The Last Waltz* was. We had the camera inside the ring dollying around them. We were almost always shooting inside the ropes. We have huge crane moves that go through the ropes and come up and come down. It's done as if it were a dance. But, at the same time, they are really fighting and they're inside a regulation-size ring with a dolly, camera, grips and everybody pushing around. It's very elaborate stuff. And often it's very abstract. Things go from twenty-four frames per second to forty-eight frames per second and back to twenty-four frames per second in the same shot. Things like that. Most of the fight stuff is twenty-four frames per second. Everything else is at widely varying speeds; a man in the corner of the ring may be ninety-six frames per second. When people put water on him in the corner between rounds, it runs down his face at ninety-six frames per second and then you come out of that and slowly go to twenty-four frames per second when the fight begins again. You do this by changing rheostats and opening diaphragms and closing them down.

You're talking about doing it all with one camera?

Yes, and if you do it right, you don't get any change in density. We did things where Bobby would knock a man down and he would go to a neutral corner and that would be at forty-eight frames per second. When the other guy got up off the mat, Bobby would be standing there just like a raging bull, at forty-eight frames per second. Then as they began fighting again, it would switch back to twenty-four frames per second. We did all kinds of stuff like that. We had very elaborate light cues. Because if the camera does a 360-degree pan of the ring, and you always want to have back light and no front light, then you've got to dim the lights all the way around in sync with how they go. It's very complicated and it takes forever.

But there never have been any fight sequences even remotely like this. Some of them go into enormous abstraction, like when he's being badly beaten, the lights all dim, people are just silhouettes and there's smoke. There's also a great difference between his life in the ring and his life outside the ring. So they're shot in very different styles. What started out as a simple little black-and-white movie that wasn't going to cost much – it's just like *The Last Waltz* – it started out as one thing and ended up as something else.

You seem to be trying to move further into abstraction in your work. A bit of it shows up in The Wanderers *and now the stylization and abstraction in* Raging Bull.

Yes, that is true of the scenes in the ring, but the rest of *Raging Bull* is straightforward. It's as simple as we could make it. You shoot a wide master; if the character goes here, you pan here, if the character goes there, you pan there. If somebody looks at something, we pan over to what he looks at and pan back. We did the simplest kind of stuff on purpose.

But you personally are beginning to work more on a certain level of abstraction.

I guess so. But the other kind of shooting is also interesting too, which is *really* simple, like Renoir. You know in *Rules of the Game*, where they all arrive for the houseparty in the rain. And the butlers go out to them with the umbrellas. And the camera just follows the butler out and follows him back in again with the guests. And then he goes out to get more people. The camera does the same thing: back and forth with the people. It just couldn't be simpler; it would be impossible to be simpler. It's just a wide shot with a 25-millimeter lens and it pans back and forth. It's just one shot and it does everything. It has an enormous economy and it tells you everything you need to know about the people, the cars, the rain, the butlers and the house. That sort of ultra, ultra-simple shooting also is interesting. In a way, from where we have been, that also is something like an abstraction. It's so simple that it's back to 1926 and Buster Keaton. That to me, is really interesting if it could be thought out and pursued with real intelligence. It's just that you don't find many people, you know, who see far enough into films to know about that. Marty is one of them. Marty and I worked that stuff out and it could not be simpler. A lot of big scenes are done in just one master. There's no coverage; it's ultra-simple.

You've quoted Godard something to the effect that the choice of angle is a very complicated thing. Could you elaborate on that?

True, it's very complicated. I remember Godard saying that. I'm sure he once thought he understood them when he was the hot-shot moviemaker. He said he no longer understood angles anymore. They seemed much more mysterious to him than they had ten years before. And they certainly do to me too. They seem enormously mysterious.

In what sense?

Angles tell us emotional things in ways that are mysterious. And emotional things that I'm often unaware of. I think a particular angle is going to do one thing and it does something quite different often. I no longer have any sure sense that I have a grasp of it. Angles seem the most mysterious thing about movies to me, I think. I'm talking on a visual level. Occasionally you will hit an angle that is absolutely inevitable; it's just the right angle. But that only happens sometimes. A lot of times, what angles give you emotionally is puzzling and mysterious. I don't have any sense that I understand them.

Do you think there are a lot of subconscious things that go into the selection of an angle?

Yes. I realized that the first time I was a director of photography. If you were doing it as well as you could and working as hard as you could, there was a lot more unconscious material that went into what you did than you had any idea of. I thought it would be much more in the open than it is. I found that I was drawing on unconscious sources amazingly more than I would have had any idea I was. Anybody who was going to be honest about it would say the same thing. Unless they are just hacks. If they really are trying, and trying to do something for the first time, then you are using unconscious material surprisingly intensely. And I think one of the ways that that unconscious material reveals itself is in angles: in what it says about the relations of characters or the relations of characters to place. Or what it says about dominance and submission. It's genuinely mysterious. And I don't like mystery. You should never count on anything being mysterious or new or wonderful. Or that in the joy of doing something, you're going to create something new. I think the more planning, the more meticulous, the more anal-retentive you are, the better off you are. But there's no sense pretending that that mystery isn't there. I don't think you should ever count on it or ever even think about it until afterwards. This is all pretty abstract, I realize.

Are there other people who think the same way you do?

I have no idea.

Do you ever discuss this with anyone? With Scorsese?

Everything's unconscious to Marty; everything's mysterious to Marty. No, I've never talked about it to other cameramen much. I once had the opportunity to get together Gordy, Almendros, Nykvist, Ondricek and myself in one room because we were all in New York for some reason. And if I could have just worked it out, I could have got us all together just to talk. I was halfway to setting it up and I stopped myself because it was not going to be that interesting. I don't think that cameramen have a lot to say to each other, in a funny way. I mean, Gordy and I were the only two I knew who did talk to each other. But then I was his operator and we spent night after night on location with nothing else to do but drink and talk. So we talked. Other than that, I've never had a successful conversation about cameras, about cinematography with a cameraman. Nestor Almendros is a wonderful, sophisticated and cultivated man to talk to. And he's marvelous to talk to about literature or politics but we've never much talked about the mechanics or aesthetics of cinematography. But I know I'm right when I say that – I know I'm right for me, maybe not for anybody else. But I can't believe I'm not right about the unconscious things for someone who really is trying in some way to let some kind of energy loose. *Do you have any designs on directing?*

Yes, I'd like to. I don't mean that I've done everything that can be done in cinematography. I just mean that, for me, I don't have the energy for it that I used to. And it's no longer as terrifying as it once was, even black-and-white. And therefore it's harder to deal with. I should do something else. Maybe I should be a grip. I'd like to run a bookstore. Something. But I'm not sure that I shouldn't leave it alone for a while.

I expect all cinematographers to say they want to direct.

Some cameramen don't. Nestor Almendros doesn't want to. Gordy's already done it. Lazslo and Vilmos, I'm sure, want to direct. It's inevitable in a way. Any good cameraman who gets passed from hand to hand, through a lot of different directors, ends up doing a certain amount of ersatz directing. And that's what cinematography is, a lot of it. I suppose you want to see your name or really have the chance to do it yourself.

Touch of Evil (1958) © Artificial Eye. Source: BFI Films: Stills, Posters and Designs.

Tokyo Story (1948) © Artificial Eye. Source: BFI Films: Stills, Posters and Designs.

Pierrot le Fou (1964) © Canal Image International. Source: BFI Films: Stills, Posters and Designs.

Landscape in the Mist (1988) © Theo Angelopoulos.

Il Deserto Rosso (1964). Source: BFI Films: Stills, Posters and Designs.

Days of Heaven (1978) © Universal International Pictures. Source: BFI Films: Stills, Posters and Designs.

Odd Man Out (1947) © Carlton. Source: BFI Films: Stills, Posters and Designs.

Ulysses's Gaze (1995) © Theo Angelopoulos.

SECTION 2
INTERNATIONAL CINEMA

INTRODUCTION

Olga Taxidou

The selection of chapters that follows, while mirroring many of the concerns of the previous section, does not simply function as the 'practice' to the 'theory' that came before it. Indeed such a distinction blatantly ignores one of the greatest anxieties of the film makers of the post-war period. To separate theory from practice amounts to divorcing form from content (plot from narrative, image from language etc.), all issues directly confronted in the work shown in this section. All the directors mentioned here and the film-texts themselves propose and embody a theory of cinema as much as they tell a story.

What becomes clear in any attempt to summarise and draw parallels, or to talk of 'schools' of cinematic production is the diversity and complexity not only of the work itself but also of the approaches taken in writing about it. This is markedly different from the pre-war period in the study of cinema. This may be due to the fact that cinematic studies as both academic discipline and aesthetic theory have established their own epistemology; one that is distinct from other plastic and discursive arts. While this is apparent the parallels/relationships between cinema and theatre, cinema and painting and, of course, cinema and literature remain formidable analytical categories (but not paradigms), used in most of the studies in this section.

Once again, cinema transpires as the quintessential modern art form, the epitome of modernity, as Eisenstein would have it. All the experiments of both 'high', literary modernism and the avant-garde with its combative stance are taken on board and furthered by the film makers during this period. The relationships between form and content, between low and high culture, between orality and writing, between the real and representation, between aesthetics and the culture industry – to name a few – are confronted as almost 'stock', inevitable, as both themes and modes of production in the analyses that follow. There are some significant shifts, however, in the study of film since the period of the so-called historical avant-garde. These are influenced mostly by reception theory, and in particular feminist readings of reception and more recent developments in post-colonial studies. Several of the accounts that follow take up these approaches, sometimes in tandem, pointing out the structural link between the study of gender and the study of otherness.

In her essay on the cinema of Godard Susan Sontag quotes the director saying, 'we novelists and film-makers are condemned to an analysis of the world, of the real; painters and musicians aren't'. This relationship to the real and its mediation is an aspect of film making that almost all the chapters here touch on. In the case of Godard, as Sontag mentions, this meta-filmic quality makes his work consciously theoretical, and makes Godard himself a 'destroyer of cinema' very much in the modernist tradition. Schoenberg and Brecht are, of course, in the background. For Godard, this analysis follows, the real rivals are not music and theatre but language itself. Language, almost in a structuralist tradition, is used as 'both model and rival'. Godard's further innovation, Sontag claims, lies in combining the energies of this high-level experimentation with an equally highly commercialised art form like film.

When the mediation of the real also involves the re-writing of history then a whole new field of theoretical exploration opens up; one that deals with the poetic and the political in the same gesture. Ismail Xavier subtitles his essay on the Brazilian film *Black God, White Devil* directed by Rocha, 'The Representation of History'. In a classical materialist analysis Xavier presents through his reading of *Black God, White Devil*, the main concerns of the Cinema Novo movement in Brazil of the mid-1960s. At once aware of its narrative devices but also quite keen to tell a story the film borrows strategies from the *cordel* popular literary tradition. In doing so it touches on one of the main concerns of the Cinema Novo project: the relationship between film and the oral tradition (which is also another way or articulating the tension between tradition and modernity). Xavier's reading suggests that the film resolves this tension not by schematically siding with one against the other, but by favouring heterogeneity and maintaining a critical stance of film and orality at once. In this way the film combines both historical and metaphysical themes, using a language of representation at once traditional and avant-garde.

Rey Chow claims that Zhang Yimou's films follow a very different path in their treatment of the past and of tradition. Chow's essay, conspicuously entitled *The Force of Surfaces* puts forward the argument that Zhang's China is an imagined one, constructed by modernity in the guise of anthropology, ethnography and the power of the cinematic image itself. Where Rocha critically uses the *cordel* tradition Zhang adapts the strategies of the so-called *butterfly* novels, creating a 'melodramatised and dreamed homeland'. This constructed ethnography of China Chow claims is mainly mediated through a fetishized femininity. Her analysis also touches on the 'ambiguous dilemmas of cross-cultural interpretative politics'. Chow's essay points to the complexities involved in combining postcolonial approaches with feminist reception theories. The work of Zhang Yimou occupies a very important position in the recent New Wave of Chinese cinema. However, it has almost always been read uncritically. Chow's essay looks more closely at the politics and the aesthetics of Zhang's work and hopefully sets an agenda for a more subtle and informed debate.

Ousmane Sembene's *Xala*, set in Senegal after independence tackles similar issues. Laura Mulvey's reading, however, states that Sembene's approach rather than fetishizing and constructing a tradition is critical of both mechanisms. In a postcolonial reading that is also informed by psychoanalysis Mulvey states that the psycho-sexual is juxtaposed to the socio-economic in a story that is also about modernity and tradition. Mulvey's reading brings together Marx and Fanon; two theoretical traditions formative for the work of Sembene and African cinema in general. Rather than being geographically specific, Mulvey states that these debates have made a valuable contribution to the overall history and aesthetics of contemporary cinema.

Another film which problematises the representation of history is Tengiz Abuladze's *Repentance*. Made for Georgian television during the period 1982–84, just before *perestroika* (although the film has been read as representative of that spirit) Abuladze's extravagant tale tries to recuperate the secret years of Stalinism. As Denise Youngblood stresses, the reception of the film was highly controversial. Not so much because of its subject matter. By then everyone agreed that this period in Soviet history was a legitimate area of investigation. What was shocking for most critics was the complex and highly experimental manner it chose to tell its tale. Abuladze utilises most of the techniques of the European avant-garde of the thirties to cinematically cover the same period. Its surrealism is constantly framed and meticulously structured. Youngblood's essay leads us through the complex narrative of this strange and seductive film.

Many of the striking images in *Repentance* draw their inspiration from a combination of the surrealist and the Georgian Byzantine tradition in painting and iconography. Indeed the relationships between painting and cinema and their respective claims to discursive hegemony is probably one of the oldest debates on the power and the autonomy of cinematic art (with the relationship to theatre a close second). And, of course, this issue appears in many of the essays that follow. Angela Dalle Vacche's essay on Michelangelo Antonioni's *Red Desert* explores the relationships between cinema, painting and architecture in Antonioni's film. His allegiance with these art forms she believes marks the shift from neo-realist documentation to pictorial abstraction. This shift, however, Dalle Vacche states is also marked by gender. Through a reading of the role of Monica Vitti, as both actor and character, Antonioni creates a type of 'visual ventriloquism'. This Dalle Vacche states is both 'experimental and exploitative'.

The analogy with Byzantine painting appears again in Paul Schrader's essay on Bresson. Schrader states that like the images of the Alexandrine school, Bresson's work captures the transcendental in the everyday. This surface aesthetic, he claims, uses form as 'the primary method of inducing belief'; hence the transcendentalism of both art forms. Schrader compares Bresson with the Japanese director Ozu. In the work of both men the everyday is used not for the purposes of identification but more for distancing and alienation. Donald Richie's essay on Ozu also states that the camera work is static, the acting not psychological but more demonstrative and schematic. The paradigm of theatre and the Brechtian legacy in particular helps to contextualise these approaches. In the case of Ozu, the Noh and Kabuki theatres with their stylised conventions may provide yet another point of reference (as they did for Brecht).

The fascination with painting as rival and model continues in the work of Peter Greenaway. David Pascoe's reading of *The Cook, The Thief* draws parallels with seventeenth-century painting and its obsession with the *nature morte* style. This fixation with the process of decomposition becomes a comment on the 'body's containment within representation'. The body itself is juxtaposed against the book. The body/book rivalry, Pascoe claims, is transposed into the nature/culture debate, where eating and reading become competing discursive practices. The restaurant and the library in the work of Greenaway become the two crucial sites where this debate is acted out. In this reading painting and literature are not mutually exclusive, but are equally prominent in their claims on cinema. For Greenaway, in the final analysis, it might not be painting that all cinema 'constantly aspires to', but language itself. And just as in the work of Godard, any 'destruction' of cinema, any theoretical, metacinematic critique, also encompasses the critique of language itself.

The cinema which is perhaps the least aware of its own language and modes of production is the mainstream Hollywood tradition. Yet, any discussion of post-war cinema which does not recognise the power of Hollywood as both industry and aesthetic legacy would be seriously lacking. Hollywood and all it stands for features as both presence and absence in the following essays. Rainer Werner Fassbinder's work presents a fine example of how Hollywood can be appropriated by European cinema. Timothy Corrigan's essay on the *Bitter Tears of Petra von Kant* shows how Fassbinder's particular blend of Hollywood fascination and critical camp can produce an explosive result. Corrigan states that, unlike Godard who consciously creates against Hollywood, Fassbinder is almost seduced by it. 'Our films are based on our understanding of American cinema', declares the German director. This understanding of American cinema and Americana in general is something which informs a whole generation of German cinema as becomes apparent also in the work of Wim Wenders.

The two directors who work within the structures of Hollywood mentioned here are Alfred Hitchcock and Orson Welles. Both, of course, distort Hollywood and the whole cinema *Américain* tradition to use Bazin's term. Terry Comito's reading of Welles's *Touch of Evil* goes beyond the classic *noir* interpretation. As a film about dislocation and displacement, it successfully applies techniques of 'estrangement' that Welles borrows from his Mercury theatre days. Furthermore, it also blatantly distorts the seeming confident realism of the *plan-Américain*. From the famous opening shot and throughout the rest of the film, Comito claims that Welles's disorienting, dizzying, camera work isn't simply an expression of his 'baroque' stylistics but a conscious critique of Hollywood aesthetics. In other words, it is about 'a nice couple from Hollywood movies who stumble into a film by Orson Welles'.

Tania Modleski's chapter on Hitchcock's *Vertigo* points to the ambiguities and contradictions in much of the director's work. Modleski's argument combines reception theory, psychoanalysis and feminist readings of the cinematic 'gaze'. In dialogue with Laura Mulvey, she claims that *Vertigo*, like many of Hitchcock's films, isn't simply 'cut to the measure of male desire'. It is more of a 'limit text' in its treatment of the problematics of identification. Through the processes of 'masking' and 'masquerading', *Vertigo*, displays and frames the construction of both femininity and masculinity. Modleski's revisionist work on Hitchcock and feminist theory is crucial in any appreciation of the work of the director and of the function of the Hollywood machine in representing, imagining and constructing identities.

Colin MacCabe's account of the shoot of *Performance* directed by Donald Cammell and Nicholas Roeg also underlines the contradictions involved in trying to make an 'experimental' film within a studio structure. *Performance*, MacCabe states, was an almost unique phenomenon in combining the freedom 'normally only granted to a group of avant-garde enthusiasts' with the financial backing of a mega-studio. This strange and explosive cocktail was partly due to the spirit of the sixties. It also combined two genres that the studios thought would be successful: the 'pop star vehicle and the swinging London film'. It was due to these qualities, MacCabe points out, that the studios were willing to take such a huge risk in a film that seemed more influenced by Artaudian theatrical experimentation than anything derived from Hollywood. In an analysis that seamlessly combines anecdote with theory MacCabe captures the dynamism but also the ambivalence of that period.

The experimentation with audio-visual technologies of which film is a crucial part, intensifies towards the end of the century. Harcourt's essay on Atom Egoyan highlights the Canadian director's oblique take on this phenomenon. The application of these technologies to everyday life is both unnerving and dehumanising. At the same time, however, his reflexive use of these technologies gives his films a revitalised sense of cinematic space.

Angelopoulos in his use of the sequence shot is also recognised as one of the great innovators of cinematic space. Yet as Kolocotroni claims, his project is much broader. Like Godard and Antonioni he sets out to create his own cinematic world, his own language of film. Intrinsic to the sense of space, at once geographical and metaphysical, is a critical melancholy informed by historical adversity. From this analysis Angelopoulos emerges as a part of a great

European humanist tradition. One, however, that lacks the mystical resolutions of Tarkovsky. Configuring a very different type of humanism, Kieslowski re-reads Bergman's *The Silence* as a narrative of compassion rather than one of cruelty. This view of humanism is one that relies on the redemptive powers of the individual and the spiritual rather than the historical and the collective. Kieslowski's dialogue with Bergman is as much a comment on his own later work (particularly the *Three Colours* trilogy) as it is on the Swedish director.

Cold, clinical, detached, formalist; these are some of the epithets thrown at the truly innovative film makers of the this period. It is clear, however, that their film aesthetics are affective as well as cognitive. As such they demand an engaged reordering from the audience of their emotional response towards cinema itself.

20

INTRODUCTION TO *OZU*

Donald Richie

Yasujiro Ozu, the man whom his kinsmen consider the most Japanese of all filmm directors, had but one major subject, the Japanese family, and but one major theme, its dissolution. The Japanese family in dissolution figures in every one of his fifty-three feature films. In his later pictures, the whole world exists in one family, the characters are family members rather than members of a society, and the ends of the earth seem no more distant than the outside of the house.

The Japanese family, in the films of Ozu as in life, has two main extensions: the school and the office. Both are almost foster homes, traditionally far less impersonal than their analogues elsewhere. The Japanese student finds a second home in his school and keeps close contact with his classmates throughout his life; the Japanese white-collar worker finds in the office a third home, and will identify himself with his company in a way rare in the West. The Ozu character, like the Japanese himself, tends to move among the three: the house, the schoolroom, the office.

Thus Ozu's films are a kind of home drama, a genre that in the West rarely attains the standard of art and that even now is generally perceived as somehow second-rate. In Asia, however, where the family remains the social unit, the home drama has been refined far beyond the examples found, say, on American radio or television. Ozu's home drama, however, is of a special sort. He neither affirms the family as, for example, Keisuke Kinoshita does in his later films, nor condemns it, as Mikio Naruse does in many of his pictures. Rather, though Ozu

From: Donald Richie, 'Introduction to Ozu', in *Ozu: His Life and Films* (University of California, 1974).

creates a world that is the family in one or another of its varied aspects, his focus is on its dissolution. There are few happy families in Ozu's films. Though the earlier pictures sometimes show difficulties overcome, almost all the mature films show the family members moving apart. Most of Ozu's characters are noticeably content with their lives, but there are always indications that the family will shortly cease to be what it has been. The daughter gets married and leaves the father or mother alone; the parents go off to live with one of the children; a mother or father dies, etc.

The dissolution of the family is a catastrophe because in Japan – as contrasted with the United States, where leaving the family is considered proof of maturity – one's sense of self depends to an important extent upon those with whom one lives, studies, or works. An identification with family (or with clan, nation, school, or company) is necessary for a complete identification of self. Even in the West the remnants of such a need are strong enough for us to regard the plight of the Ozu character, and the predicament of the contemporary Japanese, with sympathy. The father or mother sitting alone in the now empty house is an image common enough in Ozu's films to serve as an epitome. These people are no longer themselves. We know they will somehow survive, but we also know at what cost. They are not bitter, they know this is the way of their world, but they are bereft. The reason they impel our sympathy is that they are neither victims of their own flaws, nor the prey of a badly organized society; they are the casualties of things as they are, the way that life is. And here we are, all of us, similar casualties.

Though the majority of all Ozu's films are about the dissolution of the family (as are a large number of Japanese novels and of Western novels too, for that matter) his emphasis changed during his nearly forty years of film-making. In his first important films the director emphasized the external social conditions impinging upon his characters: the strain in a family occasioned by the father's joblessness in difficult times, the children's inability to understand that their father must be subservient to his employer to keep his job, etc. It was only in later films that the director found more important the constraints on the human condition imposed from within.

This change has been held against the director: "Ozu used to have an open-minded view of society; he tried to capture the complicated aspects of its day-to-day existence ... He always had a burning fury against social injustice, but his realism began to degenerate and to decay ... I remember that when *Passing Fancy* and *A Story of Floating Weeds* were released, many of us were deeply disappointed to find that Ozu had abandoned serious social themes." Though Ozu's "pioneering achievements" in creating a realism new to the Japanese cinema are credited, and though *I Was Born, But* ... is found to be "the first work of social realism in Japanese film," the pictures after 1933 are found wanting: "Young critics who have seen only Ozu's postwar films know but one side of the director ... His craftsmanship and taste are, of course, impeccable; and his deep, mature understanding of the life that scintillates within is profound. Nonetheless, the sorry truth is that Ozu's greatest virtues those which made him what he was in his earliest days, can no longer be found."

The criticism is cogent and one may argue only with its basic assumptions: that realism must be social, and that proletarian reality is somehow more real than bourgeois reality. Ozu did not, of course, abandon realism. He did, however, abandon the idea that unhappiness is caused solely by social wrongs; he came to recognize that unhappiness is caused by our being human and consequently aspiring to a state impossible to attain. He also abandoned the naturalism of his earlier pictures. This was in part due to his changing families, as it were. The struggling middle-class or lower-class family, prey to every social current, disappears from his films. From the mid-1930s on the family was, with exceptions, of the professional class, and in the postwar years it became, again with exceptions, upper-middle-class. Ozu's sense of reality, however, did not change. One still hears the complaint that the interiors in the later Ozu pictures are too pretty, too neat. But an attempt at neatness and prettiness is, after all, one of the attributes of bourgeois life everywhere. Bourgeois life is no less real for being more pleasant than proletarian life – a fact that Ozu's critics, quite unfairly, hold against him.

If anything, Ozu's later films gain in a feeling of reality, and, more important to his art, transcend it. He is concerned not with quintessential family. He achieves the transcendental from a base in the mundane, in the bourgeois family – undisturbed by social upheavals, undismayed by financial misfortunes – where a sense of the dailiness of life is perhaps most readily to be discovered. It is precisely "day-to-day existence" that Ozu so realistically and hence so movingly captured.

The life with which Ozu is concerned in so many of his films, then, is traditional Japanese bourgeois life. It is a life singularly lacking in the more dramatic heights and depths found in society less conspicuously restrained. This does not imply, however, that such a traditional life is less affected by the universal human verities; on the contrary, birth, love, marriage, companionship, loneliness, death, all loom particularly large in a traditional society because so much else is ruled out.

A traditional life also means a life based upon an assumed continuum. As Chesterton somewhere remarks: "Tradition means giving votes to that obscurest of classes, our ancestors. It is the democracy of the dead. Tradition refuses to surrender to the arrogant oligarchy of those who merely happen to be walking around." Traditional life assumes that one is a part of something larger: a community in time encompassing the dead and the yet unborn. It assumes one is a part of all kinds of nature, including human nature.

Traditional life gives rise to an attitude that is as common in Japanese daily life as it is in the films of Ozu. Though there is a useful Japanese phrase for it, *mono no aware*, a term that will be examined later, the attitude was best described in English by W. H. Auden, when (in another context) he wrote: "There is joy in the fact that we are all in the same boat, that there are no exceptions made. On the other hand, we cannot help wishing that we had no problems – let us say, that either we were in a way unthinking like the animals or that we were disembodied angels. But this is impossible; so we laugh because we simultaneously protest and accept." Perhaps the Japanese, in accepting the conflicts of being human, would sigh rather than laugh, would celebrate this transient and unsatisfactory world rather than merely find it absurd. But the underlying, profoundly conservative attitude remains the same, and it animates all but the very young in the Ozu family.

If the family is Ozu's almost invariable subject, the situations in which we see it are surprisingly few. The majority of the films are about relations between generations. Often a parent is missing, dead or absconded, and the one remaining must rear the children. The dissolution of the family, already begun, is completed by the marriage of the only or the eldest child or the death of the remaining parent. In other films the family members move away from one another; the children attempt, sometimes with success, to reconcile themselves to their married state. Or again, the child finds the restrictions of traditional family life stifling and must, albeit against his will, defy them. There are perhaps a few more variations on the theme, but not many.

Just as Ozu's illustrations of his theme are few, so his stories, compared to the majority of those found in full-length films, are slight. A précis of an Ozu film (e.g., daughter lives with father and does not want to marry; she later discovers that his plan to marry again was but a ruse, accomplished for the sake of her future happiness) sounds like too little upon which to base a two-hour film. Any Ozu story, however, is in a way a pretext. It is not the story that Ozu wants to show so much as the way his characters react to what happens in the story, and what patterns these relations create. Ozu used progressively simpler stories with each succeeding film, and he rarely availed himself of plot. In the later films the story is little more than anecdote. Some of the reasons for this will be discussed later. For the present it suffices to observe that Ozu was perhaps primarily interested in pattern, in the design that Henry James called "the figure in the carpet."

Ozu's patterns are reflected in his stories. A character moves from security to insecurity; he moves from being with many to being alone; or, a group shifts, loses members, accommodates; or, conversely, a younger character moves into a new sphere with mixed emotions; or a person moves from his accustomed sphere and then returns with a new understanding. These patterns are stacked, as it were, one upon the other; it is the rare Ozu film that has only one pattern and one story. Through the similarities and differences of the patterns and stories with their parallels and perpendiculars, Ozu constructs his film, the sum of his thoughts on the world and the people living in it.

Ozu's pictures, then, are made of very little. One theme, several stories, a few patterns. The technique, too, as mentioned earlier, is highly restricted: invariable camera angle, no camera movement, a restricted use of cinematic punctuation. Similarly, the structure of the film (to be examined later) is nearly invariable. Given the determined limitations of the Ozu style, it is not surprising that his films should all resemble one another. Indeed, there can have been few artists whose *oeuvre* is so completely consistent. In film, Ozu is unique. Some of the noteworthy recurrences in his pictures are described below.

Many of the titles are similar (*Early Spring, Late Spring, Early Summer, Late Autumn*, etc.), and the general structure is, in the later films at any rate, invariable. The titles remind one of the novels of Henry Green, and both the titles and the general structure of the novels of Ivy Compton-Burnett. Ozu was obviously not the kind of director who said all he wanted on one subject and then turned to another. He never said all he had to say about the Japanese family. He was like a close contemporary, Giorgio Morandi, the artist who spent his life drawing, etching, and painting mainly vases, glasses, and bottles. As Ozu himself said, during the publicity campaign for his last film, *An Autumn Afternoon*, "I always tell people that I don't make anything besides *tofu* (white bean curd, a common and essential ingredient in Japanese food), and that is because I am strictly a *tofu*-dealer."

Not only did Ozu often use the same actor in the same kind of role, playing, generally, the same kind of character (Setsuko Hara and Chishu Ryu are notable examples), he also used the same story line in various films. *A Story of Floating Weeds* is the same as *Floating Weeds*, *Late Spring* is very similar to *Late Autumn*, which in turn resembles *An Autumn Afternoon*. The secondary story of *Early Summer* (children running away from home) becomes the main story of *Good Morning*, etc.

Character, too, is recurrent. The daughters in *Late Spring, Early Summer, Equinox Flower, Late Autumn*, and *An Autumn Afternoon* are, though played by different actresses, essentially the same character involved with the same problem – whether or not to get married and leave home. Minor characters, too, are often near-identical. The unfeeling sister of *The Brothers and Sisters of the Toda Family* becomes the unfeeling sister of *Tokyo Story*, and shows her insensitivity in the same way (asking for something after her parent's funeral). There is often (*Late Spring, The Flavor of Green Tea over Rice, Tokyo Story, Early Spring, Good Morning*) an old salaried man due to retire who, drunk, thinks back over his life and questions it. There is, from *The Brothers and Sisters of the Toda Family* on (including *Equinox Flower, Late Autumn, Tokyo Story, An Autumn Afternoon*) the gently ridiculed lady proprietor of a Japanese-style restaurant. Characters also tend to keep the same names. In some cases they are as invariable as the burlap backing that Ozu consistently used for the main titles of all his sound films. The father is usually named Shu something-or-other, a favorite being Shukichi, with Shuhei a close second. The traditional daughter is often named Noriko (as in *Late Spring, Early Summer, Tokyo Story, The End of Summer*), whereas the more modern friend or sister is named Mariko (*The Munekata Sisters, Late Autumn*). The younger brother is usually named Isamu (*The Brothers and Sisters of the Toda Family, Early Summer, Good Morning*), and so on. This is not primarily because the names carry special connotations (though Shukichi sounds old-fashioned and Mariko rather modern to the Japanese), but rather because Ozu was arbitrarily consistent with what he had already created.

The activities of Ozu's characters are also consistent. They almost all admire the civilized nature that they view in their gardens or in Kyoto or Nikko, they all are acutely aware of the weather and mention it more often than any other characters in films, and they all like to talk. They also like bars and coffee-houses. The former, in film after film, are named Wakamatsu or Luna, the later Bow and Aoi and Bar Accacia. Here Ozu characters sometimes get drunk, though they are more likely to do so in nameless small Japanese restaurants and drinking stalls. More usually they sit and enjoy the slightly foreign flavor so gratifying to city Japanese. (There are many foreign references in Ozu's pictures, mostly from the movies: characters speak of Gary Cooper in *Late Spring*, of Jean Marais in *The Flavor of Green Tea over Rice*, of Audrey Hepburn in *Early Summer*. In the background of *That Night's Wife* is a large poster for *Broadway Scandals*; Marlene Dietrich has a poster in *What Did the Lady Forget?*, as does Joan Crawford in *The Only Son* and Shirley Temple in *A Hen in the Wind*.) They also eat, more often than most film characters, and seem to favor Japanese food, though they handle knives and forks as easily as chopsticks, just as they are equally at home on chairs and tatami matting. This ease, however, is one they share with other Japanese film characters and with most Japanese them-selves. Western critics who believe that Ozu is commenting on Western influence in his country are mistaken; he is simply reflecting Japanese life as it now is.

The father or brother in an Ozu film is typically shown sitting in his office (we almost never see him doing any actual work), and the mother or sister doing the housework (hanging out towels to dry is a favorite occupation, but there are others; *The Brothers and Sisters of the Toda Family* and *Early Summer* have identical scenes in which the women fix the *futon* bedding) or serving tea to guests who are always appearing in the Ozu household. The children often study English (*What Did the Lady Forget?*, *There Was a Father*, *Tokyo Story*, *Good Morning*), and the daughter of the house can type in English (*Late Spring*, *Early Summer*).

The family (and its extension in the office) likes games (go in *A Story of Floating Weeds* and *Floating Weeds*, mah-jongg in *A Hen in the Wind* and *Early Spring*), riddles (*I Was Born, But ...* , *Passing Fancy*), puzzles, and jokes. Another pastime to which the Ozu family is addicted is toenail cutting, an activity worth mentioning because it occurs possibly more often in Ozu's pictures (*Late Spring*, *Early Summer*, *Late Autumn*) than in Japanese life.

Outdoor activities are also few, including only hiking or bicycling (*Late Spring*, *Early Spring*, *Late Autumn*), fishing (*A Story of Floating Weeds*, *There Was a Father*, *Floating Weeds*), and golfing (*What Did the Lady Forget?*, *An Autumn Afternoon*). The outdoor activity, though no sport, most often depicted is train-riding. To be sure, movies have from their inception featured trains, and Lumière, Gance Kinoshita, Hitchcock, and Kurosawa have all been fascinated by them. Ozu, however, probably holds the record. Almost all his films include scenes with trains, and in many of them the final sequence is either in or near a train. *A Story of Floating Weeds*, *There Was a Father*, *Equinox Flower*, *Floating Weeds*, and others all end in trains; *Tokyo Story*, *Early Spring*, and others all have trains in their final scenes. One reason for all the trains is simply Ozu's liking for them. Another is that for the Japanese, if no longer for us, the train remains a vehicle of mystery and change. The mournful sound of a train in the distance, the idea of all those people being carried away to begin life anew elsewhere, the longing or nostalgia for travel – all these are still emotionally potent for the Japanese.

In some Ozu films the nostalgia for a once visited place is stated directly. In *The Munekata Sisters* there is a scene in which the two sisters sit on the steps of Yakushiji. The elder is very subdued. Later she returns with the man she loves, and we learn that they had met there before when their love was new. Her feelings during the scene with her sister are thus explained without our seeing the event that prompted them. Sometimes an occurrence in one film is mentioned in another, even though all the characters are different. In *Late Autumn* the mother is reminded while traveling of a pond of carp at Shuzenji; these are the same carp that appear in *The Flavor of Green Tea over Rice*, a film made eight years before. The same line of dialogue expressing a sense of life passing will recur in a number of films. One such recurring line is "*Owarika?*" (Is this the end?), an utterance typical of Ozu in its simplicity, clarity, and use of familiar vernacular. It is used by the father in *Tokyo Story* when he learns his wife is dying; it was used, we are told, by the father as he lay dying in *The End of Summer*, and it is also used by the father when he learns that the girls will have to close the Bar Accacia coffeehouse in *The Munekata Sisters*.

Ozu's most potent device for nostalgia, however, is the photograph. Even though family pictures, class pictures, company pictures, remain in Japan something of the institution they once were in the West, there is a surprising amount of formal portrait-taking going on in Ozu's films. There is the group picture, of students and teacher, for example, in front of the Kamakura Buddha in *There Was a Father*; there is the wedding portrait, as in *Late Autumn*; there is the family portrait, as in *The Brothers and Sisters of the Toda Family*, *Early Summer*, *The Record of a Tenement Gentleman*. Except in the first example cited above, we do not see the finished picture. No one drags out the portrait of his dead mother and gazes fondly at it. Rather, we see the family gathered (invariably for the last time), smiling bravely into an uncertain future. Nostalgia lies not in later reflections, but in the very effort to preserve the image itself. Although Ozu's characters occasionally lament that they have no photos of a missing loved one, the actual use of photos is restricted to prospective brides and grooms. Death, in the films of Ozu as in life, is simple absence.

All these similarities (and there are many more) among the films of Ozu came about partly because he saw each film as either a continuation of the preceding picture or a reaction to it. The notes written by Kogo Noda, the well-known scenarist and collaborator in more than half (twenty-seven) of Ozu's films, in the joint diary the two men kept at Tateshina are indicative: "Feb. I, 1962. As preparation for our work [on *An Autumn Afternoon*] we read some of our old scenarios. Feb. 3. We talk [about the new film]; ... it will be in the genre of *Equinox Flower* and *Late Autumn*. We consider some story about a [widowed] man and his child, and a woman trying to find a bride for him ... June 10. For reference we reread *Late Autumn* ... June 11. For reference we reread *Equinox Flower*." Such a method of construction (more common for the later pictures than the earlier ones) inevitably meant strong similarities from picture to picture, particularly since Ozu and Noda apparently defined genres in terms of their own earlier work.

Similarities, then, are many, and differences few in the extraordinarily limited world of the Ozu film. It is a small world, closed, governed by rules apparently inflexible, controlled by laws that are only to be deduced. Yet, unlike Naruse's narrow family-centered world, Ozu's does not provoke claustrophobia, nor do its apparently inflexible governing rules give rise to the romantic idea of destiny seen in the apparently wider world of Mizoguchi. What keeps Ozu's films from these extremes are Ozu's characters, the kind of people they are and the way they react to their life. The simple and real humanity of these characters, their individuality within their similarity, makes it difficult and ultimately misleading to categorize as I have been doing for these past several pages. Although Ozu's stories certainly are few, the pictures do not seem repetitious; though a précis of the anecdote is thin, the film never is; though the roles are similar, the characters are not.

Human nature in all its diversity and variation – this is what the Ozu film is essentially about. It must be added, however, that as a traditional and conservative Asian, Ozu did not believe in any such essence as the term "human nature" may suggest to us. Each of his characters is unique and individual, based on known types though they all may be; one never finds "representative types" in his films. Just as there is no such thing as Nature, only individual trees, rocks, streams, etc., so there is no such thing as Human Nature, only individual men and women. This is something that Asians know better than Occidentals, or at least act as if they do, and this knowledge is responsible, in part, for the individuality of the Ozu character; his entity is never sacrificed to a presumed essence. By so restricting our view and confining our interest, Ozu allows us to comprehend the greatest single aesthetic paradox: less always means more. To put it another way, the several invariably indicates the many; restriction results in amplification; endless variety is found within the single entity.

Ozu never said this, and for all I know never thought it. He did not question his interest in character or his ability to create it. Yet that interest never failed. When he sat down to write a script, his store of themes firmly in the back of his mind, he rarely asked what the story was to be about. He asked, rather, what kind of people were to be in his film.

21

FEMININITY BY DESIGN: *VERTIGO*

Tania Modleski

In criticism of *Vertigo* (1958), as in that of *Rear Window*, one repeatedly encounters the assertion that "the spectator constructed by the film is clearly male." My analyses of Hitchcock have in part been meant to demonstrate that this male spectator is as much "deconstructed" as constructed by the films, which reveal a fascination with femininity that throws masculine identity into question and crisis. This fascination opens a space for the female spectator of the films, providing for a more complicated relation to the texts than has generally been allowed in contemporary film criticism. As I hope to have made clear by now, the questions relating to spectatorship and identification, despite the difficult theoretical language in which they are often couched, have often been posed too simply. Take, for example, Mulvey's contention that *Vertigo*, like all narrative films, is "cut to the measure of male desire" because it is from the male point of view: "In *Vertigo*, subjective camera predominates. Apart from one flashback from Judy's point of view, the narrative is woven around what Scottie sees or fails to see." What Mulvey dismisses as an aberration, an exceptional instance that proves the rule (of Hollywood cinema as male cinema), has been seen by at least one critic – quite rightly, I think – as a privileged moment, the flashback producing "a spectator position painfully split between Scotty and Judy for the rest of the film." Thus identification is, in the words of Robin Wood, "severely disturbed, made problematic." My analysis will suggest, however, that identification is "severely disturbed" long

From: Tania Modleski, 'Femininity by Design: *Vertigo*', in *The Woman Who Know Too Much: Hitchcock and Feminist Film Theory* (Routledge, 1998).

before this moment and that the film may indeed be taken as a kind of "limit text" in its treatment of the problematics of identification first introduced in the film *Rebecca*.

Vertigo begins with the credits shot over an extreme closeup of a woman's face; spiral shaped figures emerge from her eye and form themselves into the names of the credits, and then the camera moves directly into the eye as the spirals continue to shape themselves into words. At the end of the sequence the camera returns to the eye and the final credit emerges from it: "Directed by Alfred Hitchcock." Immediately we are placed into a state of anxiety: a man is being chased across some roof tops in San Francisco by two men, one in police uniform and the other – the Jimmy Stewart character, Scottie Ferguson – in plain clothes. In a leap from one building to another, Scottie loses his footing and winds up hanging precariously from the edge. The man in uniform abandons his pursuit to help Scottie but slips and falls; the sequence ends with Scottie clinging for his life to the gutter of the roof.

After the fade, Scottie is shown in the apartment of Midge (Barbara Bel Geddes), a woman to whom he was once briefly engaged. One of the more benign of Hitchcock's many bespectacled female characters, Midge is a "motherly" type, as the film continually emphasizes, too prosaic for Scottie's romantic imagination. Scottie explains that he has quit the police force because he is suffering from vertigo as a result of his recent traumatic experience. He says he has received a message from an old schoolmate of theirs, Gavin Elster (Tom Helmore), who, when Scottie visits him, says that he wants Scottie to follow his wife in order to find out why she has been behaving peculiarly. Scottie at first resists the idea of doing detective work, but soon finds himself lured into it by the mystery of Elster's beautiful wife, Madeleine (Kim Novak), with whom he rapidly becomes obsessed. In his investigation of the woman, he follows her around San Francisco and learns that she appears to be "possessed" by an ancestor from the past, Carlotta Valdez, whose portrait hangs in the art gallery in the Palace of the Legion of Honor. In order to find out more about this mysterious figure, Scottie asks Midge to take him to Pop Liebl (Konstantine Shayne), a bookstore owner conversant with San Francisco lore. According to Pop Liebl, Carlotta Valdez was the beautiful mistress of a wealthy and influential man, who at length wearied of her and "threw her away," keeping their child. "A man could do that in those days," says Pop Liebl reflectively. "They had the power, and the freedom." The woman pined away for her lost child, becoming first "the sad Carlotta," and then at length "the mad Carlotta," stopping strangers in the street to ask, "Have you seen my child?" and eventually committing suicide.

One day, in an apparent suicide attempt, Madeleine jumps into the bay, and Scottie rescues her, brings her to his home, and puts her into his bed. Soon after, they go "wandering" together, and Scottie learns of Madeleine's hallucinations of death, her vision of walking down a long corridor that ends with the sight of an open grave. He becomes desperate to solve the mystery, and when she visits him one night to tell of a recurring dream she has had of a Spanish mission where she believes she lived as a child, he joyfully tells her that her dream has a basis in reality. The next day he takes her to the mission in order to convince her that she has been to the place before. She, however, becomes distraught and runs into the tower. He tries to follow her up the stairs, but his vertigo prevents him from reaching her before she falls.

After an inquest, which reaches a verdict of suicide, Scottie is placed in an asylum where Midge attempts to get him to respond by playing Mozart records, but Scottie is inconsolable. Later we see him walking the streets, becoming upset when he sees Madeleine's car, which has been sold, and mistaking various women for Madeleine. Then he spots a woman who looks uncannily like Madeleine and follows her to her hotel. At first the woman is annoyed at being importuned by a stranger, but then she relents and allows him to come inside her room, where she shows him her identity cards to persuade him that she really is Judy Barton from Salina, Kansas, rather than the woman he seems to be mistaking her for. When he leaves, the camera for the first time deserts Scottie and stays with the woman. A flashback and a letter Judy writes and then tears up tell the whole story: Scottie was part of Gavin Elster's plan to murder his wife, Madeleine. Elster had made up Judy, his mistress, to look like his wife, in order to get Scottie to witness Madeleine's "suicide." Knowing that Scottie's vertigo would prevent him from reaching the top of the mission tower Elster had waited that day for Judy to ascend the stairs and then had flung his own wife from the roof.

Out of love for Scottie Judy decides not to run away, but to stay and try to make him love her for herself. He, however, becomes obsessed with recreating Madeleine, and he dresses Judy in the same clothes and shoes Madeleine had worn and even has her hair dyed and restyled. One night at her hotel room while they are preparing to go out for dinner, Judy puts on the necklace worn by Carlotta in the portrait and Scottie suddenly understands everything. He forces Judy to go back with him to the mission and to climb the stairs while he relates the events of Madeleine's death. Cured at last of his vertigo, he makes it to the top and the panic-stricken Judy tries to convince him that they can still go on together. As they begin to embrace, a dark shape suddenly looms up at the top of the stairs and Judy screams at this apparition – which turns out to be a nun – and falls from the tower. The last shot of the film shows Scottie emerge from the arched door of the tower onto the roof as he looks blankly downward, arms slightly extended.

If in *Rear Window*, the hero continually expresses a masculine contempt for the feminine world of fashion (while the film itself exhibits and elicits a near obsessional interest in what Grace Kelly is wearing), this is hardly the case with *Vertigo*'s hero, Scottie. In attempting to re-create Judy as Madeleine, Scottie displays the most minute knowledge of women's clothing, to the point where the saleswoman twice remarks on how well the gentleman knows what he wants. To reinvoke the metaphor central to my analysis of *Rear Window*, the female character, Madeleine/Judy, is like a living doll whom the hero strips and changes and makes over according to his ideal image.

Indeed, it might be said that the film's preoccupation with female clothing borders on the perverse. Midge's job as a designer in the female "underwear business" has gone largely unremarked in criticism of *Vertigo*, perhaps because it is felt to be unworthy of the film's great theme of love and death, a theme which places it in the tradition of Tristan and Isolde. (In fact, critics tend to slight all those parodic elements of the film which work against the seriousness of the "love theme," and in this they reveal themselves to be like Scottie, who rejects Midge's demystificatory act of painting her own face into the Carlotta portrait as "not funny.") In the early scene in Midge's apartment she is shown sketching a brassiere that is prominently suspended in the air from wires. Scottie is attempting to balance a cane in his palm, and as it falls he utters an exclamation of pain and then speaks his first line in the film: "It's this darned corset – it binds." Midge replies, "No three-way stretch? How very unchic." From the outset, then, with his failure to perform his proper role in relation to the Symbolic order and the law, Scottie is placed in the same position of enforced passivity as L. B. Jeffries, a position that the film explicitly links to femininity and associates with unfreedom: "Midge," Scottie asks a moment later, "do you suppose many men wear corsets?" He is elated because tomorrow is "the big day" when "the corset comes off" and he will be a "free man."

Shortly thereafter he spots the brassiere, walks up to it and points to it with his cane. "What's this doohickey?" he asks, and Midge answers, "It's a brassiere; you know about such things, you're a big boy now." And she proceeds to describe it as the latest thing in "revolutionary uplift," explaining that it was designed by an aircraft engineer down the peninsula, who built it on the "principle of the cantilever bridge." Now, given the prominence in the film's mise-en-scène of high places – the Golden Gate Bridge, for example – and given the association of these places with Scottie's vertigo, it seems clear that the film is humorously linking his condition to femininity, a relation that later sequences will treat with deadly seriousness. (An association between femaleness and fear of heights may also be found in *North by Northwest* [1959]. Roger O. Thornhill [Cary Grant] claims that Eve [Eva Marie Saint] uses sex "like some people use a flyswatter," and throughout the film we see him performing a human fly act, hanging over precipices, scaling walls, and clinging, as it were, to nothing as he attempts to gain possession of the woman, who is mistress to the villain.)

It is as if at this early moment in *Vertigo*, the film is humorously suggesting that femininity in our culture is largely a male construct, a male "design," and that this femininity is in fact a matter of external trappings, of roles and masquerade, without essence. This is an idea that the film will subsequently evoke with horror. For if woman, who is posited as she whom man must know and possess in order to guarantee his truth and his identity, does not exist, then in some important sense he does not exist either, but rather is faced with the possibility of his own nothingness – the nothingness, for example, that is at the heart of Roger O. Thornhill's identity ("What does the 'O' stand for?" Eve asks, and he answers, "Nothing"). In this respect, it is possible to see the film's great theme of romantic love as something of a ruse, a red herring – and Hitchcock, of course, was master of the red herring. Hélène Cixous writes, "the spirit of male/female relationships ... isn't normally revealed, because what is normally revealed is actually a decoy ... all those words about love, etc. All that is always just a cover for hatred nourished by the fear of death: woman, for man, is death." Certainly these words have a strong resonance in relation to *Vertigo*, since the source of the man's fascination with the woman is her own fascination with death, with the gaping abyss, which she hallucinates as her open grave and which is imaged continually in the film in its many arch-shaped forms of church, museum, cemeteries, mission.

But for this moment at least, the film is lighthearted; and the "hatred nourished by fear" will be suppressed until later in the film. Until that point the film will only be concerned to arouse in us as spectators a curiosity and desire for the woman as idealized object of romantic love. When Scottie goes to see Gavin Elster, a shipbuilding magnate from the east, Elster articulates a longing for the past which will eventually be Scottie's own, and he speaks of the old San Francisco as a place where men had "freedom" and "power," terms that Pop Liebl will later echo. As in *Marnie*, with which *Vertigo* in some ways invites comparison, the film first presents the woman as object in a dialogue between men, creating the triangle on which desire so frequently depends. Then, as in *Marnie*, the camera itself takes over the enunciation: in Ernie's Restaurant it first shows Scottie sitting at a bar and then detaches itself from his searching gaze to conduct its own search for the woman through the restaurant. Finally, it comes to rest in a long shot of a woman seated with Elster at a table, with her back to the camera. Romantic music emerges slowly on the soundtrack, and the camera moves slightly forward. It cuts back to Scottie looking and then to a point of view shot of Madeleine, who gets up from her chair and walks into a closeup shot of her profile. Only much later will we be able to see her entire face and only at that time will we get to hear her speak; for much of the first part of the film she will be the mute, only half-seen object of man's romantic quest: the eternal feminine.

When Scottie starts to follow Madeleine in her car, she leads him in a downward spiral – a typical trajectory of Hitchcock heroines – to a back alley, gets out of her car and disappears into a building. Scottie follows her through a dark back room, with the camera insistently wedding our subjectivity to his through point of view shots. Then the door is slowly opened in a very striking point of view shot, the romantic strains of the love theme again come on the soundtrack, and a long shot reveals Madeleine standing with her back to the camera amidst an array of flowers and bathed in soft light. The mise-en-scène at once conveys the woman's ideality and links her to death, the flowers adding a distinctly funereal touch. Madeleine turns around and comes toward the camera, and with the cut we expect the reverse shot to show that, as is usual in classical cinema, the man is in visual possession of the woman. Quite startlingly, however, it turns out that the door has a mirror attached to it, so this shot shows both Scottie, as he looks at Madeleine, *and* Madeleine's mirror image. Donald Spoto says of this shot, "by implication he (and we) may be seen as her reflection." Spoto, however, does not pause to note the extraordinary significance of this observation, which suggests that identification is "disturbed, made problematic" *at the very outset* of Scottie's investigation – just as we saw his identity as a man thrown into doubt with his very first words. The shot is in many ways prophetic: despite all his attempts to gain control over Madeleine, Scottie will find himself repeatedly thrown back into an identification, a mirroring relationship, with her and her desires, will be unable to master the woman the way Gavin Elster and Carlotta's paramour are able to do.

It is as if he were continually confronted with the fact that woman's uncanny otherness has some relation to himself, that he resembles her in ways intolerable to contemplate – intolerable because this resemblance throws into question his own fullness of being.

[...]

The uncanniness of woman for man is also rendered in a lengthy, dreamlike sequence in the middle of the film after Madeleine has been at Scottie's house. He is following her in his car, and she leads him on an especially circuitous route, while the camera, continually cutting back to his face, emphasizes his increasing perplexity. To his great surprise and puzzlement, they wind up back at his house, where she has come to deliver a note. Scottie's pursuit of the mysterious other, then, inevitably takes him to his own home, just as Freud has shown that the uncanny, the *unheimlich*, is precisely the "homelike," the familiar which has been made strange through repression.

As for Madeleine, she herself becomes the very figure of identification, which here is realized in its most extreme and threatening form in the idea of possession. Hitchcock draws once again on the du Maurier plot, the Gothic plot he disparaged in his discussion with Truffaut, to tell Madeleine's story, a story of a woman who appears to be so obsessed with a female ancestor that she actually *becomes* that other woman from the past and finds herself compelled to live out the latter's tragic fate. It is ironic that the woman whose initials are M.E. (like those of Marnie Edgar) is a person with no identity, not only because Madeleine's persona has been made up by Elster in imitation of his wife, whom he murders, but also because Madeleine continually merges into the personality of Carlotta Valdez, who has committed suicide and who, we are led to believe, attempts to repeat the act through Madeleine (so much is death, and woman's association with death, overdetermined in this film). Madeleine represents the lost child whom "the mad Carlotta" had sought everywhere to no avail. A powerless and pitiful figure when she was alive, Carlotta becomes on her death a figure of terror and omnipotence. In contradistinction to the Lacanian scenario, according to which the dead *father* is endowed with an omnipotence that "real" fathers lack, Hitchcock presents us (not for the first or the last time), with the imago of a mother who assumes unlimited power in death. Dispossessed in life, discarded by her lover, who also takes their child, the dead woman wields this new power in acts of psychic possession, thereby avenging her losses on patriarchy.

Scottie becomes progressively absorbed in Madeleine's situation, and we as spectators are made to share in his absorption, as the camera continually works to draw us into a closer and closer identification with the woman and her story. When Scottie enters the museum where Madeleine sits before the portrait in a hypnotic trance, the camera shows a closeup of the bouquet placed beside Madeleine, then tilts up and tracks forward into a closeup of the bouquet in the portrait. A similar movement begins with a shot of the spiral-shaped knot of hair at the back of her head, and then the camera tracks into a closeup of Carlotta's hair. These constant forward tracking shots do more than simply trace Scottie's observations; in their closeness and intensity they actually participate in his desire, which, paradoxically, is a desire to merge with a woman who in some sense doesn't exist – a desire, then, that points to self-annihilation. As a result of this threat posed by the figure of woman before the portrait, Scottie is driven to break the spell she exerts by competing with Carlotta for possession of Madeleine.

[...]

When Madeleine jumps into the bay Scottie rescues her and brings her home, later indicating that by saving her he now has a claim over her: "You know, the Chinese say that once you've saved a person's life, you're responsible for it forever." At one point he kisses her feverishly, insisting, "I've got you now"; during another embrace he urgently declares, "No one possesses you" – no one, the implication is, but himself. The more Scottie finds himself absorbed by this fascinating woman, the more he resorts to a rather brutal interrogation of her in his search for the "key" to her mystery.

At the heart of *Vertigo* lies the lure and the threat of madness. As Scottie desperately searches for the key to Madeleine's strange behavior, she says, "If I'm mad, that would explain everything." He looks horrified and then pursues her when she runs from him in order to grasp her ever more tightly. It is crucial for Scottie that he convince Madeleine of her sanity so that he can be assured of his own, and thus it is imperative that he make her *recognize* him, force her to turn her inward gaze away from the "mother" and to acknowledge his presence and his supremacy. "Where are you now?" he keeps asking, and she answers, not very convincingly, "Here with you." It might be said that Scottie's project is to reverse the state of affairs at the beginning of their relationship, and from being a reflection of the woman, to use Spoto's observation, he needs to make of her a reflection of himself.

[...]

Scottie's "cure" for Madeleine involves bringing her to the scene of her dream in order to convince her of the "reality" of the place and to force her to remember a previous visit there. Scottie counters his truth – which is the law of representation and verisimilitude – to hers, which appears to masculine "reason" as mad and supernatural. Throughout the film Scottie will be concerned with staging these re-presentations in order to gain mastery over them: at the end, for example, he forces Judy to return to the tower and reenact the occurrences of the day Madeleine supposedly died.

[...]

The woman will die. The very effort to cure her, which is an effort to get her to mirror man and his desire, to see (his) reason, destroys woman's otherness.

Scottie's failure to cure Madeleine deals a mortal blow to his masculine identity, as the dream that he has shortly after Madeleine's presumed death indicates. The dream begins with a closeup of Scottie's face, over which flashing lights of various colors are superimposed. A cartoon image of Madeleine's bouquet is seen disintegrating and then the camera tracks into an extreme closeup of the necklace in Carlotta's portrait and we see Carlotta come "alive" standing between Elster and Scottie. Scottie's "beheaded" face (castration has been "in the air" since the credit shots) is superimposed over a "vertigo" shot of vertical lines on a purple background, and he walks forward toward an open grave into which the camera descends. Finally, there is a cartoon-like image of Scottie's silhouette falling first toward the red tiles of the mission roof and then into a blinding white light, an image of nothingness, of infinitude. What is most extraordinary about this dream is that Scottie actually *lives out Madeleine's hallucination*, that very hallucination of which he had tried so desperately to cure her, and he *dies Madeleine's death*. His attempts at a cure having failed, he himself is plunged into the "feminine" world of psychic disintegration, madness, and death. Even the form of the dream, which is offputting to many viewers because it is so "phoney," suggests the failure of the "real" that we have seen to be the stake of Scottie's confrontation with Woman.

Looking for the source of this renewed identification with the woman implied by the dream, we find a clue in Freud's important paper, "Mourning and Melancholia." According to Freud, melancholia, the state of inconsolability for the loss of a loved person, differs from mourning in part because the former involves "an extraordinary diminution in [the sufferer's] self-regard, an impoverishment of his ego on a grand scale. In mourning," says Freud, "it is the world which has become poor and empty; in melancholia it is the ego itself." Freud attributes this diminution in self-regard to the fact that the melancholiac internalizes the loved object, who had been the source of some disappointment to the subject and who henceforth becomes the object of severe reproaches which, as a result of internalization, appear to be self-reproaches (it might be said that the judge at the inquest who speaks so harshly of Scottie's "weakness" utters the reproaches that later get internalized). In effect, says Freud, "an *identification* of the ego with the abandoned object" is established. "Thus," he continues, rather poetically, "the shadow of the object fell upon the ego, and the latter could henceforth be judged by a special agency, as though it were an object, the forsaken object". This identification with the lost object that Freud takes to be characteristic of melancholia involves a regression to an earlier narcissistic phase, that same phase evoked in the film in the mirror image of Madeleine at the florist shop. "This substitution of identification for object-love ... represents ... a *regression* from one type of object-choice to original narcissism. [Identification] is a preliminary stage of object-choice, ... the first way – one that is expressed in an ambivalent fashion". The shadow of the object having fallen upon him, Scottie not only identifies with Madeleine in his dream, but becomes caught up in the very madness he had feared in her. In his quest for his lost Madeleine, he becomes like "the mad Carlotta," who had accosted strangers in the street as she desperately sought the child that had been taken from her: after the dream we see Scottie wandering around the city and repeatedly mistaking other women for Madeleine, approaching them only to be bitterly disappointed at his error. Importantly, the film at this point emphatically *discredits* his vision – and by extension, *our* vision – on several occasions. On each of these occasions it sets us up for one of the point of view shots Hitchcock has employed throughout the first part of the film to draw us into Scottie's subjectivity, and then it reveals the sight to have been deceptive. In a way, we experience through Scottie the split that Freud says is characteristic of melancholia: on the one hand we identify with him, as before, but the repeated disqualification of his vision makes us wary; we become more judgmental than we had previously been. Further, Scottie's faulty vision provides additional proof that he now occupies a *feminine* position, in that Hitchcock frequently impairs the vision of his female protagonists in one way or another.

Finally, Judy appears walking down the street with some other women. A brunette dressed in a cheap, green, tight-fitting dress and wearing gaudy makeup, she is not, as Truffaut observes (without, however, recalling the early scene in Midge's apartment), wearing a brassiere. Though we have not yet been apprized of the situation, Judy is the "original" woman, who will soon be remade (for the second time) into the fully fetishized and idealized, "constructed" object of male desire and male "design." The camera lingers on her profile as she bids her friends goodbye, and the romantic music once again is heard on the soundtrack. But it doesn't altogether work. Not only are we wary of this "apparition" because of all the previous faulty point of view shots, but she looks "wrong," a disappointing counterfeit of the beautiful Madeleine. That woman seems to become at this point in the film a debased version of her former self is not surprising. The melancholiac's disappointment in the love object results, says Freud, in hatred coming to the force: "the hate comes into operation on [the] substitutive object, abusing it, debasing it, making it suffer and deriving sadistic satisfaction from its suffering". Before this sadism receives complete release, however, Scottie tries to restore the lost object by making Judy over into Madeleine – forcing her to wear the same clothes, shoes and makeup and to change her hair color and style.

But by this time we have been let in on the secret and we know that Judy was a tool of Gavin Elster's nefarious plot to murder his wife. This knowledge makes us much more sympathetic toward the woman, who finds herself continually negated and manipulated by men, and it contributes as well to our increasing tendency to condemn Scottie for having become, in Hitchcock's word, "a maniac." As if to emphasize a shift in interest and point of view, Hitchcock includes a scene in Judy's hotel room, which at the beginning shows her in profile, the camera tracking forward in a shot which resembles the subjective shots of Madeleine that predominated in the first part of the film. By the end of the scene, however, Hitchcock has changed camera positions and placed the camera in front of her while Scottie remains to one side, so that we are made to see a part of her that he in his obsession cannot see. As a result of the expanded sympathetic consciousness Hitchcock arouses in the spectator, we feel the full irony and poignancy of her situation – as when Scottie is begging Judy to let herself be made over and urges, "It can't matter to you." Judy acquiesces, in great anguish, out of love for Scottie.

When the process of makeover is complete, Madeleine emerges, ghostlike, into the room where Scottie awaits her; she walks slowly toward him, and the two embrace in a famous shot in which the camera circles around the couple who, in turn, are placed on an (unseen) revolving pedestal. The romantic music swells and the background. Judy's hotel room, metamorphoses almost imperceptibly into the livery stable of San Juan Bautista. Ironically, the place where Scottie had attempted to cure Madeleine's hallucination by restoring her to the real now returns to signal the triumph of *Scottie's* hallucination over the real.

But "real" women, it seems, are not so easily vanquished, and Judy gives herself away by putting on the necklace worn by Carlotta in the portrait. At this moment Scottie's sadism reaches its peak for it becomes clear to him that he never was in possession of the woman, that she has always eluded his grasp. He forces her to return to the scene of the crime, his words as he drags her up to the tower making clear what has been at stake for him all along:

> You played the wife very well, Judy. He made you over didn't he? *He* made you over just like *I* made you over. Only better. Not only the clothes and the hair, but the looks and the manner and the words. And those beautiful phony trances. And you jumped into the Bay! I bet you're a wonderful swimmer, aren't you … aren't you … *aren't you*! And then what did he do? Did he *train* you? Did he *rehearse* you? Did he tell you exactly what to *do* and what to *say*? You were a very apt pupil, weren't you? You were a very apt pupil! But why did you pick on me? Why *me*? I was the set-up, wasn't I? I was the made-to-order-witness. This is where it

happened. And then, you were his girl. What happened to you? Did he ditch you? Oh Judy, with all of his wife's money, and all that freedom and all that power … and he ditched you.

Scottie's pain results not only – not even primarily – from discovering that Madeleine was a fraud, but from realizing that she had been made up by another man, who "rehearsed" and "trained" her in the same way that Scottie had rehearsed and trained Judy. Just when Scottie had thought himself to be most in control of the woman, to have achieved the "freedom" and "power" that he has been longing for and that the film associates with masculinity, he discovers that he is caught up in repetition, like Judy/Madeleine/Carlotta, repetition which, as Freud has shown, is linked to unfreedom, to masochism, and to death. Scottie must now confront the fact that, like a woman, he was manipulated and used by Gavin Elster, that his plot too had been scripted for him: "You were the victim," writes Judy in the letter she tears up – just as Judy and Carlotta and the real Madeleine Elster are all ultimately victims in the plots of men.

"Some portion of what we men call 'the enigma of woman' may perhaps be derived from [the] expression of bisexuality in women's lives," Freud wrote. This bisexuality is attributable both to the fact that the little girl undergoes a "phallic phase" – an active phase, in contrast to the passivity typically associated with femininity – and that her first love object is the mother, just as is the male's. In order to achieve what Freud called "normal femininity," the female must turn away from her mother and shift her object of desire to the father – a trajectory we have seen is traced in the film *Rebecca*. In that film, however, Freud was forced to recognize how frequently desire for the mother persists throughout the woman's life, affecting her heterosexual relationships as well as her relationships with other women. Woman is thus often caught up in a "double desire," and feminist film theory has tried to draw out the implications of this double desire for a theory of female spectatorship. Speaking of *Rebecca*, for example, Teresa de Lauretis argues that there are "two positionalities of desire that define the female's Oedipal situation." In contrast to those feminists who claim that the situation of woman at the cinema is an either/or situation (either she is a masochist, or she is a transvestite), de Lauretis believes that female indentification is double.

[…]

De Lauretis contrasts *Vertigo* unfavorably to *Rebecca* because for all their similarities, in *Vertigo* it is through the male protagonist that we experience events. As I observed at the outset, however, the situation is considerably more complicated. There is first of all the "painful split" in identification between Judy and Scottie opened up by Judy's flashback and sustained throughout the last part of the film. But even before this point, we have seen how one of the major attractions of Scottie to Madeleine is his identification with her, an identification that the film works to elicit in the audience as well: we are identifying with Scottie identifying with Madeleine (who is identifying with Carlotta Valdez). Woman thus becomes the ultimate point of identification for *all* of the film's spectators. Not only is "a double desire" on the part of a female viewer not precluded by this set-up, but it is possible to see the film as soliciting a masculine bisexual identification because of the way the male character oscillates between a passive mode and an active mode, between a hypnotic and masochistic fascination with the woman's desire and a sadistic attempt to gain control over her, to possess her. (Hence the aptness of the famous "vertigo shot," the track-out/zoom-forward that so viscerally conveys Scottie's feeling of ambivalence whenever he confronts the depths.) Of course, sadism wins the day, and the woman dies.

[...]

The mother/daughter relationship central to the enigma of bisexuality is presented over and over again in Hitchcock films as the main problem. No doubt this is partly because it signifies that woman never wholly belongs to the patriarchy. But perhaps too it is troublesome because it provides a model of "overidentification" in which the boundaries between self and other become blurred, and desire for and identification with the other are not clearly separable processes. This "boundary confusion" can be intimidating to the male who, unlike the female, appears to achieve his identity through establishing a firm boundary between himself and woman. But *Vertigo* shows just how precarious the boundary can be. As Freud noted in *Mourning and Melancholia*, it is always possible to "regress" to narcissistic identification with the object. And this is so because identification is *"a preliminary stage of object choice."* Far from being opposed to object love as Freud at times argued, narcissistic identification is in fact *constitutive* of it, and thus, he here implies, the boundaries between self and (m)other tend to be more fluid for the male than is sometimes supposed.

22

INTRODUCTION TO
ORSON WELLES, DIRECTOR

Terry Comito

Orson Welles has always been difficult to place along the mise-en-scène/ montage axis, just because he so clearly employs, with dazzling virtuosity, the resources of both. And while it has generally been felt that *Touch of Evil* somehow places itself in the context of *film noir* (as well as of Welles's own earlier films), the nature of its relation to its predecessors has never been worked out with much care. To call it the "epitaph" of *film noir*, as Paul Schrader does, is suggestive but scarcely a definition. I am not sure we will arrive at a definition either, nor even that a rigorous definition is possible in such matters. But by setting *Touch of Evil*'s opening sequence against some of these earlier sequences, to which it can be seen as at least in part a response, we ought to be able to isolate some of Welles's defining differences.

To begin with: we know what is going on. We are waiting for a car to explode. The very first frame of the film thrusts into the camera a bomb's timing device, the instrument of a mechanical inexorability; and the blond victim's last words are a complaint about "this ticking noise." But the camera does not, as it does in *Scarface* or *White Heat*, move about in order to concentrate and guide our attention. Rather, it seems teasingly to withhold from us what we want to see, what we know – from what we've been permitted to see and also from other movies we've seen – must be coming. Welles's camera seems less concerned with monitoring the events on the screen than in disorienting the spectator. The use of a twenty-two foot crane means that vision is constantly in motion, up and

From: Terry Comito, 'Introduction to *Orson Welles, Director*', in Terry Comito (ed.) *Touch of Evil* (Rutgers University Press, 1985).

down as well as laterally; and the use of a wide angle lens gives it an exaggerated depth of space in which to play. And play is precisely what it seems to do, with no mimetic function – neither the point of view of a character nor the logic of events – to rationalize the camera's apparently independent life. Its long, graceful swooping, now speeding up in relation to the movement of the car, now slowing down, constantly changes both the angle and the distance from which we follow, or attempt to follow, the bomb's fatal progress. We lose sight of the car as it swings around behind a building; it reappears only to be half lost in a milling crowd; the camera tracks back slowly enough to let the car approach and then suddenly speeds up, leaving it far behind; Susan and Vargas pass in front of it and we turn to follow them, obviously the film's "stars," though the car, not quite forgotten, keeps crossing their tracks, as if (though we know better) it were only an accidental intrusion on the margins of the frame. We "lose track" not because our gaze is fragmented, as it is by Wilder or Aldrich, but because it is distracted, provided with too much information to pick and sort into stable hierarchies of attention.

We are not confused, as we are by the opening of *Kiss Me Deadly*. We are disoriented, dizzy. It is important that we insist upon this distinction. Near the end of the opening sequence, Susan and Vargas have crossed the border into America, and Susan realizes that "this is the first time we've been together in my country." But the camera is not allowed the easy access to their intimacy we might expect. However Susan may feel about her homecoming – this is a theme to which we will have to return – we see the lovers only through, and as a part of, a network of incommensurable movements – whirling, without stable center. This may seem a somewhat rhetorical way of speaking. French critics, especially, are fond of intoning "vertiginous" or "delirious" by way of evading any need really to explain Welles's "baroque" stylistics. But in fact I am trying to describe as literally as possible what goes on in these few frames. As Linnekar's car drives off from the customs booth in foreground, moving out of the left of the frame, we see: two MPS at the right of the frame striding purposefully toward the camera and eventually passing off in the right foreground; two civilian pedestrians passing from left to right in front of the MPS; and, in the far background, emerging from an arcade just as the MPS turn from the street to come forward, Vargas and Susan, walking from right to left. Meanwhile the camera, too, is in motion, but not along any of these paths. It moves toward Vargas and Susan, not directly, but diagonally, heading back and to the left as if hoping to intercept them. As it does so, Susan and Vargas continue to walk from right to left; in back of them a pedestrian moves from left to right and a black car moves from right to left, overtaking and passing them. Still more disconcertingly, a stream of pedestrians passes in front of them in the foreground of the frame, blurred forms, half silhouetted, moving into the camera along a diagonal – off toward the right foreground – directly opposed to the camera's course. When Susan pauses long enough to speak her line about homecoming, the camera has got ahead of them; and the lovers, though now in medium range, are nearly out of the frame on the right. There is in all this no lack of distinctness. Each of the simultaneous movements I have been cataloguing is perfectly lucid, the interplay precisely choreographed. But it is a dance in which we lose our bearings. Our heads spin. With everything apparently in motion, there is no fixed point of reference by which to chart or rationalize any single trajectory. Welles's world is not a chaos but, as Welles himself repeatedly tells us, a whirling labyrinth – one without a center, however, without a key that will unlock its mystery.

The uncentered labyrinth is of course a familiar iconographic or thematic motif in many of Welles's films: the hall of mirrors in *Citizen Kane* and in *The Lady from Shanghai*: the fruitless search for Rosebud (it vanishes in smoke before our eyes, and leaves in place, in the film's last shot, the No Trespassing sign at Xanadu); the search for Arkadin by which the secret of the past, the truth of origins, is not pieced together but expunged. But I have been implying that the labyrinths that express most fundamentally Welles's sense of the world and his artistic intentions are not those he represents but those he creates. *Touch of Evil* invites us into a world that seems to resemble the one with which we are all familiar – but cut loose from its moorings, from the frames of reference by which we habitually seek to stabilize our situation in it. It has a share, I suppose, of the *angst* we associate with *film noir*, but without the glum claustrophobia: our anxiety is born not of powerlessness or confinement but of too much freedom. And there is, too, in Welles's films generally and in *Touch of Evil* in particular, something of the desperate exhilaration we find in the best of the crime thrillers. But it is an exhilaration associated less with theme and character, which may seem sombre enough, than with Welles himself, the prestidigitator on heights more dizzying than Tony Camonte ever dreamed of.

CROSSING THE BORDER: SPACE AND MEANING

In Whit Masterson's *Badge of Evil*, the assassin's bomb is an intrusion into the comfortable precincts of the wealthy victim's San Diego beach house. The task assigned the protagonist of this routine thriller is to restore the equilibrium upset by an outsider's violence. It is a matter of keeping the peace. In transferring the story's action to the Mexican border, Welles suggests a more subversive vision. Los Robles is the sinister foreign place we discover on the margins of our own world, just over the border from the comfortingly familiar. As the film's critics have not failed to notice, Welles's most fundamental theme, from the opening sequence on, is the crossing of boundaries; or rather, the impossibility of sustaining an effective boundary between a world we recognize as normal and a realm of violence at once uncanny and, as in a dream, disquietingly familiar. To our discomfort, Welles engineers our complicity in violent fantasies, sexual and racial, of the most devious sort, at the same time he appeases the liberal in us with safe homilies on the evils of prejudice. But the crucial border, in spite of the swarthy rapists with whom Welles teases us, is not the one between Mexico and the United States. It is just Janet Leigh's error to suppose that it is a simple matter to go home again, that she will be safe in the reassuring banality of an American motel, that the half-heard whispers behind its surprisingly flimsy walls have nothing to do with her. The most precarious boundary is one overseen by no friendly customs man. It is the boundary between the apparent solidity of our rational daylight world and the dark labyrinth in which, if we yield to its solicitations, we will lose our way. Welles's "Mexico" is a place of the soul, a nightmare from which a lost Hollywood sweater girl begs, mostly in vain, to be awakened.

Which is simply to reiterate what has already been implied in the first section of this introduction. Mexico is not a geographical place Welles represents so much as it is a visual space he creates – a reorganization of the data of perception in order to betray the spectator, as Susan is betrayed, into a new and disturbing way of experiencing the world. I know of few films whose expressive content is so indistinguishable from its visual style, so wholly illegible in the dialogue alone. A good many episodes in the script, in fact – the acid throwing scene (nothing comes of it) or, more especially, the hysterical scene in which Uncle Joe chases Risto and loses his hair piece – seem no more than pretexts for the kind of vertigo we have already defined as a characteristic effect of Welles's cinematic technique. In choosing to tell a story about crossing boundaries, he has been able to thematize, to take as his subject matter, just that characteristic visual experience. What *Touch of Evil* is most immediately "about" – certainly more than it is about race relations or police corruption – is the confrontation with the labyrinth or vortex that opens before us once we transgress the boundaries of a world in which we are pleased to suppose ourselves to be at home. Or to put it differently: it is about a nice couple from Hollywood movies who stumble into a film by Orson Welles. We need to consider in more detail the dimensions of that deviousness, and then look at the effect it has on our misplaced star and starlet.

The French critic André Bazin has indicated why the eye-level medium shot (what is called in France the *plan-Américain*) gives classical Hollywood cinema the appearance of a kind of spontaneous and unselfconscious "realism." However fanciful or fraudulent the director's subject matter may be, his camera appeals to "the natural point of balance of [the spectator's] mental judgment." It is just this natural balance that Welles is continually, with every means at his disposal (the angle of the camera, its distance, its movement) seeking to subvert; and with it our sense that we can take for granted the stability of the "real." The *plan-Américain* almost never appears. Quinlan looms up in extreme low angle or is dwarfed in empty space or in networks of light, shadow, and architectural detritus. He seems not so much to enter a frame or occupy a fixed position as to shape the space around him in accord with his own megalomania or despair. The optics of Welles's wide angle lens means not only that deep space is present to us in a hallucinatory sharpness of detail but also that figures move toward us out of that space, or disappear into it, with a preternatural swiftness, imposing themselves upon us or slipping away before we have had a chance to get our bearings. A favorite framing device is the torso swollen so large that it no longer fits within our field of vision but nevertheless looms over and dominates what we *can* see. (Susan's first trip across the border is framed in this way by Pancho's leather-jacketed form; Quinlan's dazed emergence from Tanya's, near the end of his rope, is framed by Menzies" brooding profile.) These are only a few of the effects that contribute to our sense of the radical, dreamlike subjectivity of space in *Touch of Evil*. Space is no longer a neutral and measurable vacancy between stable objects. It seems almost palpable, plastic, even viscous – shaping and being given shape by, in ways wholly unpredictable, the action that transpires within it. Welles's space is in this respect less baroque than manneristic. One thinks of the tempestuous plaza of Tintoretto's *St. Mark*. Even Sartre's over-heated characterization of the delirious triumph of perspectivism in Tintoretto is not wholly inappropriate to our sense of the peculiar centerless mobility of Welles's world:

> ... reality slipped away, and the relationship of the finite to the infinite was reversed. Once an immense plenitude had supported the torments and fragility of the body. Now fragility was the only plenitude ... Infinity was emptiness and darkness ... the Absolute was absence.

Doubtless we should be cautious about claims so portentous. Nevertheless, it may not be wholly absurd to say that the world of *Touch of Evil* is without that "absolute" (in something like Sartre's sense) whose cinematic expression would be the confident realism of the *plan-Américain*. Just because its explosions and contractions are not measured against anything fixed, the space of Welles's film is radically contingent as well as subjective. The habitual use of deep space, and the violent motion Welles sets plunging through it, means that any place a character may for a moment inhabit is only the edge of a depth that opens dizzily behind him. "Foreground and background no longer serve as static frames for a comfortable middle distance ... Instead, all three are points in a single [constantly shifting] system, through which, just beyond the circle closed around a given moment's awareness, the assassin pursues his prey, and through whose sinuous passages the investigator must seek out an unknown evil." And since "foreground" and "background" are not only optical terms but measures as well of significance or importance, our bafflement is not merely visual. Welles's world is not one where it is ever simple to relegate anything to "the background." Just beyond your field of vision, but ready at any moment to make itself felt, is something that undermines the certainties you suppose you possess – that undercuts your "position." When Vargas talks on the phone to Susan at the motel (shots 261–271), Welles crosscuts with shots of Janet Leigh reclining in her nightie, hair unbound, dreamy eyed, looking like the pinup girl we know her to be. It is an image whose deliberate parodic banality signifies the limits of Vargas's imagination and understanding. But his spatial situation at the drug store makes abundantly obvious to us the fragility of this day dream and the complacency of his delusion. Behind him, visible to us out the window, Menzies arrives with Uncle Joe Grandi, the owner of the motel where Vargas thinks Susan will be safe and the source of her coming torments. (Grandi himself, in turn, keeps wondering "What am I doing here?": placement is never self-explanatory in Welles's world.) In the foreground, a blind woman, the proprietor of the shop, squints just past the camera. In part, she is merely an ironic commentary on Vargas's own blindness; but the odd hieratic stolidity of her skewed gaze also suggests she is the bearer of some knowledge we are unlikely ever to share.

It is because these spatial depths so brutally unmask the contingency of our situations that they are felt in *Touch of Evil* to be so menacing. Welles uses the arcades of Venice (California) to calibrate the depths from which violence emerges or into which victims are lured. Space is constricted, narrowed down into corridors in which the eye can no longer range at will but is led inexorably toward infinity. The form of these arcades is echoed or alluded to again and again in *Touch of Evil*: in the vortex of buildings pulling away behind Vargas and Schwartz as they drive through narrow streets; in the bar down whose length Vargas assaults the Grandi gang; in the corridor of the jail where the camera tracks with Vargas to discover Susan, drugged and violated, in her cell. The depths of perspective become, in fact, something like a conventional signifier of the onset of violence. Crossing the border alone, Susan is engulfed in space: Pancho, leather-jacketed, leering, in the foreground; the street and arcades receding behind her. Vargas steps out of the brightly lit hotel lobby and all at once is swallowed up in distance, a tiny figure pursued through arcades and empty squares by a hoodlum with a bottle of acid. As Grandi's gang plots its blackmail scheme, we can barely make out Vargas and Susan, in the extreme distance, in front of their hotel, ignorant of the menace that rushes toward them through the empty foreground. Even in the confines of Marcia Linnekar's apartment, Welles punctuates the jumpy disequilibrium of the interrogation with a series of small eruptions from the background. When Menzies produces the dynamite Quinlan has planted, Grandi springs forward, exclaiming inconsequentially ("Dynamite?"): the momentary spatial dislocation gives visual form to Vargas's suspicion, his sense that something is awry. As all these instances suggest, the fundamental violence in Welles's world is the assault not on our bodies but on our certainties.

Nor is it just Welles's manipulation of deep focus that assaults us in this way. His editing creates its own sort of spatial labyrinth. The function of "classical" editing is logical and analytic. It breaks an event down into its essential components, so that, undistracted by irrelevancies, we can attend to fundamental relationships. This is how the Russian director Lev Kuleshov describes the "American" way of dealing with (for example) a suicide:

> when it was necessary to show ... a person suffering they showed only his face. If he opened the drawer of a desk and took a pistol from it, they showed the desk drawer and the hand taking the pistol. When it came to pressing the trigger, they filmed the finger pressing on the trigger, because

other objects and the surroundings in which the actor worked were irrelevant at the particular instant. This method of filming only that moment of movement essential to a given sequence and omitting the rest was labeled by us the "American method," and it was thus placed in the foundations of the new cinematography which we were beginning to form.

Welles's editing, on the other hand, tends always to explode the event – shatter it into bright shards like the fun house mirrors in *The Lady from Shanghai*. The explosion of Linnekar's car coincides with an eruption in the style of the film itself. With the kind of self-referentiality that is prevalent in *Touch of Evil* – as if bemused with its own outrageousness – Welles uses the moment to mark a transition from the sinuous continuities of the opening shot to a jagged montage sequence. Instead of the graceful movement of the crane, we get a tilted, hand-held camera; instead of a labyrinthine density of space, we get a sense of disconnected fragments – flame, wreckage, shouting men, looming headlights, abrupt closeups – that we find difficult to assemble into a single spatial field. In one case as much as the other, we lose our grip on such centering concepts as "essential" or "irrelevant." Rather than being spectators of a world in whose important features the director patiently instructs us, we are drawn into the vortex of the event itself, an event whose peculiar violence is precisely the shattering of the world's familiar outlines.

This disintegration is most extreme in the sequence of Grandi's murder. Welles fragments the event into some seventy-eight different shots (412–490), many of them, as the hysteria mounts, of only an instant's duration. And the blinking light – during much of the sequence, the only illumination comes from a neon sign outside the window – introduces a further source of discontinuity, almost as if a second layer of montage, a light montage, had been superimposed on the primary one. The principle of Welles's cutting is always a constant shifting of spatial relations, not only in the alternation of high and low angle shots, long shots and closeups, but also (and especially) in the unpredictable realignments of figures within the shot. For example, when Susan is first apprehended by the Grandi gang, Welles alternates between shots where we see Grandi on the left of the frame and Susan reflected in a mirror on the right and shots where we see Susan (in the flesh) on the left and Grandi on the right. Even in the relatively rare scenes of quiet dialogue where Welles approximates the traditional shot/reverse shot alternation, he usually introduces some such variation to throw the rhythm off balance. In the murder sequence, these relatively minor disturbances become an absolute frenzy. The climax alternates shots of Susan as she wakes up, seen from above and upside down, with shots of Grandi's grotesquely contorted head, seen from below and also upside down, as he dangles over her bedpost. What is shocking is not so much the violence of the deed (by now, certainly, we are used to mutilations far more spectacular) as the violence of our own dislocation. In traditional montage, each shot represents a distinct act of attention. A cut from one character to another, or from a mid shot to a closeup, indicates that something of particular importance demands our scrutiny. But Welles gives us no fixed point of vantage from which to attend to events, no place to stand in the midst of the dizzying whirl of images. The succession of shots seems not to focus or concentrate our attention so much as to disperse or defeat it. We are helplessly caught up in an uproar that is – like the cacaphony that greets the hysterical Susan as she stumbles out onto her fire escape – more than we can ever hope to take in.

As this analogy suggests, the sound track is equally unhelpful. Welles's habit of dubbing in the sound after the shooting of a film is complete no doubt grew out of economic considerations. It's cheaper than using live sound. But the practice allows Welles to shape and control the audio dimension of his films with the same disregard for ordinary modes of perception as he exercises in the case of the visuals. The sound is not dead, precisely, but it has lost its spontaneous life and become raw material for Welles's own devious projects. So it is not surprising that what we hear in *Touch of Evil*, or don't *quite* hear, has the same perplexing density as what we see. Welles as an actor – notoriously – grunts, hisses, or drawls out his lines rather than speaking them. All the characters habitually speak at cross purposes, or all at once. Welles's fondness for improvisation is evident in the stream of muttered asides and nonsensical byplay that forms a sort like the counterpoint to what we would like to suppose are the dialogue's serious concerns – Quinlan's complaint about sweet rolls, for example, or the whole distracting business with Grandi's wig. It is as if the aural and dramatic surface, like the visual, were continually fracturing, splitting into incommensurable pieces.

Furthermore, much of the time the aural pieces and the visual ones don't fit one another. A remarkable percentage of the film's dialogue is conducted off camera. Sometimes it is simply a matter of looking at one character while listening to another, or of being situated in one place while straining to hear what is going on somewhere else. In the interrogation sequence, we hear bits of the third degree Quinlan is conducting off camera only in the interstices of an apparently trivial conversation in the bathroom. Elsewhere, the trick of overlapping dialogue Welles had been developing since his Mercury Theater is carried a step farther – given a cinematic equivalent – by letting lines from one shot spill over into the next one. This may serve to link shots together, but in a subtly disorienting – labyrinthine – way. We don't see a speaker finish his line; instead, we hear it in a new shot where it distracts us from what we do see. The two dimensions of our experience of the film, seeing and hearing, are out of phase, never *quite* cohering. This effect may seem a minor one, but, even where we are not fully aware of it, it conditions in a pervasive way our experience of the film's texture.

Its most flamboyant development comes in the last sequence. Not accidentally, one supposes, *Touch of Evil* ends with a bravura display of montage that parallels the display of Welles's mastery of mise-en-scène with which the film opens. Space is fragmented and reassembled to present us with a landscape wholly of the mind. The transitions between closeup and long shot are abrupt and managed in such a way that we cannot rationalize them in terms of the point of view of any of the characters. The transitions, that is, have no mimetic explanation. They occur according to the logic of dreams rather than the logic of realistic narrative. As a consequence, we cannot visualize the shifting spatial relations between the characters, nor map out in our imaginations the terrain through which they prowl and scramble. Bridges, derricks, scaffoldings, and echoing distances are elements in the expressionistic architecture of the frames of the film, rather than a representation of any conceivable place outside. The tape recorder in which Vargas captures the disjointed tale of Quinlan's life – in the end Quinlan slumps listening to it as if that life were no longer his own – becomes an emblem of the similarly denaturing and objectifying work of Welles's own soundtrack. There are three distinct kinds of sound in the sequence: "live" voices, recorded voices, and voices that are live but heard from a great distance, often doubled by echoes. A given sequence, or even line of dialogue, will characteristically pass through at least two of these registers and often all three. In this kind of sound montage, words become as fragmented as the images, literally disembodied, sundered from their presumed origin. It is as if the centerless labyrinth, which has been implicit all along just below the still marginally realistic surface of the film's story, now manifested itself, both visually and aurally, in its pure form; and manifested itself as the terrain in which Quinlan's life has in fact been played out.

People seeing *Touch of Evil* for the first time invariably notice that Janet Leigh and (perhaps to a lesser extent) Charlton Heston seem out of place in such a terrain. They don't fit. It is not only that the characters are uncomfortable on so treacherous a border, which is after all explicit enough in the script. It is as if the actors themselves shared the characters" anxieties and their determination to assert the reality, in spite of what they take to be an accidental or temporary transgression, of the border between Welles's nightmarish labyrinth and the world in which they believe themselves at home. The deliberate antinomies of the script – the good cop and the bad cop, the young bride and the aging whore – emphasize rather than smooth over the disparities between the actors, disparities in their bearing, their styles of physical presence. If what Leigh and Heston offer, a kind of well-scrubbed clarity of demeanor, speech, and bearing, is not precisely realistic, it is at least familiar: normal in the sense that Hollywood versions of reality have become normal, corresponding to our habitual expectations. In contrast, Welles and Dietrich, not to mention the outrageous Akim Tamiroff and Dennis Weaver, seem bizarre, exaggerated, close to parody or self-parody. Even visually, Heston and Leigh seem to inhabit a world that reminds us of the "rationality" of their Hollywood past. In the scene at the hotel where Susan is menaced by the Gandi gang, we see Pancho and Uncle Joe in progressively more portentous low angles, distorted in mirrors or by the lens through which we regard them, lit from below and thrown into garish shadow. Only Susan is seen in eye level shots, her white sweater, like her angry eyes, ablaze with light. "You've been seeing too many gangster movies," seems like an indictment not only of Uncle Joe's extravagant manner but also of the overheated visual atmosphere of the sequence itself. (A similar contrast appears in *Citizen Kane*, where "The March of Time" purports to return us to "reality" after the gothic excesses – we might suppose we are in for a James Whale thriller – of the film's mysterious opening.) Later, when Susan and Vargas are reunited in the lobby of their hotel, their space is shallow and evenly lit (a nondescript wall in the background, a phone booth to one side); they are seen in a medium two shot, the *plan-Américain* of our waking lives. Even the slight staginess of the scene, its banality, is reassuring in its intimation that we have returned to a mode of seeing with which we are familiar.

But just outside the hotel are those depths where Risto waits for Vargas with his bottle of acid – just as the confusions of an unwonted perspective entangle Susan the moment she makes her way alone across the border. As Vargas and Susan are increasingly drawn into the foreign place, it becomes increasingly difficult for them to maintain the boundaries of their normalcy. The clean well-lighted places where they seek security turn out to be singularly porous, riddled with gaps and subject to alien incursions. The windows of Susan's hotel room have no shades: she is transfixed in the flashlight beam that penetrates them. The "safe" American motel turns out to be a cube perched on the edge of nothingness. Inside, a low angle shot exaggerates the geometrical bareness of the looming bed, the low ceiling, the stark walls. It is a parody motel, a parody of the flimsiness of the shelters by which Yankee reasonableness seeks to shut out the void. Raucous music pours in through an implacable loudspeaker. The crazed Night Man bobs in and and out windows and doors. (In shot 240, Susan stands caught between these two ruptures in the security she hoped to find, the window with the gurgling Night Man on the left, the blaring speaker on the right.) Later there are yet more threatening intrusions: whispers from the next room of drugs and sexual violation. "What's that got to to with me?" Susan asks, though she's beginning to find out. The shots are lit in such a way that she seems to be interrogating her own shadow on the wall, her own sinister double beginning to emerge from behind inadequate barriers. The violence of the Grandi gang is dramatized less as a physical assault than as an invasion of Susan's space, its gradual but inevitable disintegration. Through windows and doors she anxiously observes a swarmlike gathering of hotrods. A window shade opens on Pancho's leering face. The final terror is the terror of a door opening, silently and without resistance. The repetition of this shot – each time the hoodlums are a bit further into the room – has an effect like slow motion, distending and prolonging the moment of violation.

The fixity whose disintegration is most traumatizing for the lovers is their intimacy with one another. The explosion that interrupts their kiss exiles them from the emotional center by which their world of chocolate sodas and straightforward expectations had been guaranteed. At first, it is only a series of irritations and misunderstandings that divide the lovers. But soon it is physical distance as well. Instead of embracing Susan, Vargas must address her fantasy image on the telephone. We know how unreliable such mediations can be, particularly when the switchboard is presided over by a leather-jacketed nemesis. The labyrinth in which Susan and Vargas lose their way, and eventually Quinlan as well, is a place whose winding corridors and unexpected gaps permit one to see or to be seen but not to communicate. The jumpy byplay of Susan and the Night Man, popping in and out of doors and windows in a fruitless attempt at dialogue, is a comic version of her later ordeal after the murder of Grandi. Half naked on the fire escape, she can see her husband but her cries are lost in the cacaphony of street sounds as he disappears in the crowd and traffic of the narrow road. His blindness, oblivious beneath a "Jesus Saves" sign, is complemented by the jeering voyeuristic awareness of the crowd, pointing and laughing at the spectacle just outside the range of Vargas's perception. "I want to watch" (shot 378) might be the slogan of the alien world through which Susan finds herself wandering. The final sequence of the movie engulfs Quinlan in a similar, though more complex, network of voyeurism, violated intimacy, and unreliable mediation. He supposes he is communing with himself, or with himself through Menzies; but in speaking to Menzies he is in fact opening himself to Vargas's scrutiny. He is speaking not to a person from whom he can expect an intimate response but to a "walking microphone" that steals from him his own language, objectifies it, sets it over against him. His words become a trap whose only outlet is the rubbish heap on which, as he dies, he listens to their mechanical iteration.

The difference between the dream of intimacy and the voyeuristic labyrinth in which the characters stray is marked by two contrasting gazes. As Tanya, Marlene Dietrich is almost invariably filmed in close-up, staring moodily into camera. What she is looking for is the human being beneath the "mess" Quinlan has become, beneath the accretions of candy bars, booze, and despair. The gaze of the voyeur, however, the gaze of Uncle Joe licking his lips in the hotel, or of Pancho looming over Susan in a fish-eye lens, or of the sullen moll who wants to watch: such a gaze is one that denies the humanity of its victim, that turns the person on whom it is directed into an object. The shadow that crosses Susan's face in the course of her ordeal – several times and then, definitively, darkening her terrified eyes – signalizes this obliteration of the self. The last and most frightening dislocation suffered by those who lose their way in Welles's labyrinths is just this loss, this displacement from one's own vital center.

23

BRESSON

Paul Schrader

The films of Robert Bresson exemplify the transcendental style in the West, but, unlike Ozu's, are estranged from their culture and are financially unsuccessful. In a medium which has been primarily intuitive, individualized and humanistic, Bresson's work is anachronistically nonintuitive, impersonal, and iconographic.

The transcendental style in Bresson's films has not been unchronicled. Amédée Ayfre, André Bazin, and Susan Sontag have all written perceptive analyses of Bresson's "Jansenist direction," "phenomenology of salvation and grace," and his "spiritual style." The qualities of transcendental style have also been chronicled by Bresson himself. Bresson is a rarity among film-makers: he apparently knows exactly what he does and why he does it. The many statements Bresson has made in interviews and discussions, properly arranged, would constitute an accurate analysis of his films (a statement which can be made of no other film-maker to my knowledge), and any study of Bresson must take into account his astute self-criticism.

Bresson's output has been meager: nine films in twenty-seven years. Bresson's career, like Ozu's, has been one of refinement, but, unlike Ozu, he served no lengthy apprenticeship. His first film, *Les Affaires Publiques* (1934), has apparently been "lost," but his second, *Les Anges du Péché* (1943), displayed what one critic called a "vision almost mature." After *Les Dames du Bois de Boulogne* (1944), a film which found Bresson somewhat at odds with his

From: Paul Schrader, 'Bresson', *Transcendental Style in Film: Ozu, Bresson, Dreyer* (Da Capo Press, 1972).

material, Bresson entered into a cycle of films which present the transcendental style at its purest. The four films of the prison cycle deal with the questions of freedom and imprisonment, or, in theological terms, of free will and predestination. "All of Bresson's films have a common theme: the meaning of confinement and liberty," Susan Sontag writes. "The imagery of the religious vocation and of crime are used jointly. Both lead to 'the cell.'" All of Bresson's prison cycle films concern spiritual release: in *Diary of a Country Priest* (*Le Journal d'un Curé de Compagne*, 1950) this release occurs within the confines of a religious order, in *A Man Escaped* (*Un Condamné à Mort S'est Echappé*, 1956) it concurs with escape from prison, in *Pickpocket* (*Pickpocket*, 1959) it concurs with imprisonment, in *The Trial of Joan of Arc* (*Le Procés de Jeanne D'Arc*, 1961), it occurs both within the confines of religious belief and a physical prison. Bresson's latest three films – *Au Hasard, Balthazar* (1966), *Mouchette* (1966), and *Une Femme Douce* (1969) – have explored and expanded some of his traditional themes, but do not as yet seem (it may be too early to tell) to have achieved the resolution of the prison cycle.

Bresson's prison cycle provides an excellent opportunity to study the transcendental style in depth for several reasons: one, because the prison metaphor is endemic to certain theological questions; two, because Bresson's statements clear up much of the ambiguity in which critics are often forced to operate; and three, because there are few cultural elements intermingled with transcendental style in his films. In Ozu's films the transcendental style had to be extricated from the culture; in Bresson's films this has already happened to a large degree: Bresson is alienated from his contemporary culture.

Like Ozu, Bresson is a formalist: "A film is not a spectacle, it is in the first place a style." Bresson has a rigid, predictable style which varies little from film to film, subject to subject. The content has little effect on his form. Bresson applies the same ascetic style to such "appropriate" subjects as the suffering priest in *Diary of a Country Priest* as he does to such "inappropriate" subjects as the ballroom sequences in *Les Dames du Bois de Boulogne* and the love-making sequence in *Une femme Douce*. In discussing how accidents on the set can affect a director's style, Raymond Durgnat remarked, "It's no exaggeration to say that such stylists as Dreyer and Bresson would imperturbably maintain their characteristic styles if the entire cast suddenly turned up in pimples and wooden legs."

Spiritual sentiments have often led to formalism. The liturgy, mass, hymns, hagiolatry, prayers, and incantations are all formalistic methods designed to express the Transcendent. Form, as was stated earlier, has the unique ability to express the Transcendent repeatedly for large and varied numbers of people. Bresson's statement on his art is also applicable to religious forms and rituals: "The subject of a film is only a pretext. Form much more than content touches a viewer and elevates him."

Susan Sontag has gone so far as to say that Bresson's form "is what he wants to say," a statement which is somewhat ambiguous because when a work of art is successful the content is indiscernible from the form. It would be more helpful to say that in Bresson's films (and in transcendental style) the form is the *operative* element – it "does the work." The subject matter becomes the vehicle (the "pretext") through which the form operates. The subject matter is not negligible; Bresson has chosen his subjects very carefully, as the term "prison cycle" indicates. But in transcendental style the form *must* be the operative element, and for a very simple reason: form is the universal element whereas the subject matter is necessarily parochial, having been determined by the particular culture from which it springs. And if a work of art is to be truly transcendent (above *any* culture), it must rely on its universal elements. Appropriately, Bresson has set his priorities straight: "I am more occupied with the special language of the cinema than with the subject of my films."

Both Ozu and Bresson are formalists in the traditional religious manner; they use forms as the primary method of inducing belief. This makes the viewer an active participant in the creative process – he must react contextually to the form. Religious formalism demands a precise knowledge of audience psychology; the film-maker must know, shot for shot, how the spectator will react. "I attach enormous importance to form. Enormous. And I believe that the form leads to the rhythm. Now the rhythms are all powerful. Access to the audience is before everything else a matter of rhythm."

THE TRANSCENDENTAL STYLE: THE EVERYDAY

The everyday in films has precedents in religious art; it is what one Byzantine scholar calls "surface-aesthetics." A fanatical attention to minute detail is evident in Chinese porcelain, Islam carpets, and Byzantine architecture (*belopoeika* and *thaumatopoike*). In the third-century Alexandrian School the study of Scripture became a matter of minute detail; the Alexandrine exegetes believed that mystic meanings could only be reached through concentration on each detail of the text.

In film, "surface-aesthetics" is the everyday, and is practiced by Bresson: "There is a nice quote from Leonardo da Vinci which goes something like this: 'I think about the surface of the work. Above all think about the surface.'" Cinematic attention to the surface creates a documentary or quasi-documentary approach. Concerning *A Man Escaped*, Bresson told a reporter: "I really wish that it would almost be a documentary. I have kept a tone bordering upon the documentary in order to conserve this aspect of truth all the time." A screen title to *A Man Escaped* reads: "This story actually happened. I set it down without embellishments." Similarly a title at the beginning of *The Trial of Joan of Arc* reads, "These are the authentic texts." Like the Alexandrine exegetes Bresson believes, "The supernatural in film is only the real rendered more precise. Real things seen close up."

By taking all fact as reality, each fact with neither significance or connotation, Bresson creates a surface of reality. The "surface" is achieved, writes Ayfre, through "a very precise choice of details, objects and accessories; through gestures charged with an extremely solid reality." Bresson's "reality" is a celebration of the trivial: small sounds, a door creaking, a bird chirping, a wheel turning, static views, ordinary scenery, blank faces. He uses every *obvious* documentary method: actual locations – Fort Monluc in *A Man Escaped* and the Gare de Lyon in *Pickpocket* – nonactors, and "live" sound. Yet there is no desire to capture the documentary "truth" of an event (the *cinéma-vérité*), only the surface. Bresson documents the surfaces of reality.

Bresson's everyday stylization consists of elimination rather than addition or assimilation. Bresson ruthlessly strips action of its significance; he regards a scene in terms of its fewest possibilities. A seeming trivial anecdote may illustrate this: while shooting a scene in *Diary of a Country Priest* Bresson instructed an assistant to have a man without a hat walk through the background of the scene. When, a short time later, the assistant told Bresson that the bareheaded man was ready, Bresson corrected him saying that he didn't want a bareheaded man, but a man without a hat. Bresson defines reality by what Aristotle called "privation," by the qualities that an objects lacks yet has potential for. Water, for example, is defined as potential steam. In Bresson's films the bareheaded man is potentially a man with a hat, and the everyday is potentially stasis. A reality defined by privation is as desolate and without significance as one defined by nihilism, but it is also predicated upon a change. To use a scriptural metaphor, a privated universe groaneth and travaileth for its potential.

Bresson admits that the everyday is a sham: "I want to and, indeed, do make myself as much of a realist as possible, using only the raw material taken from real life. But I end up with a final realism that is not simply 'realism.'" The realistic surface is just that – a surface – and the raw material taken from real life is the raw material of the Transcendent.

Bresson's use of the everyday is not derived from a concern for "real life," but from an opposition to the contrived, dramatic events which pass for real life in movies. These emotional constructs – plot, acting, camerawork, editing, music – are "screens." "There are too many things that interpose themselves. There are screens." Screens prevent the viewer from seeing through the surface reality to the supernatural; they suppose that the external reality is self-sufficient.

This is why Bresson's work seems so perverse to the uninitiated viewer: Bresson despises what the moviegoer likes best. His films are "cold" and "dull"; they lack the vicarious excitement usually associated with the movies. Bresson, Sontag writes, "is pledged to ward off the easy pleasures of physical beauty and artifice for a pleasure which is more permanent, more edifying, more sincere" – and the average moviegoer is unlikely to relinquish these "easy pleasures" easily. What are the "screens" and "easy pleasures" and how does Bresson ward them off?

Plot

Like Ozu, Bresson has an antipathy toward plot: "I try more and more in my films to suppress what people call plot. Plot is a novelist's trick." The plot "screen" establishes a simple, facile relationship between the viewer and event: when a spectator empathizes with an action (the hero is in danger), he can later feel smug in its resolution (the hero is saved). The viewer feels that he himself has a direct contact with the workings of life, and that it is in some manner under his control. The viewer may not know how the plot will turn out (whether the hero will be saved or not), but he knows that whatever happens the plot resolution will be a direct reaction to his feelings.

In Bresson's films the viewer's feelings have no effect on the outcome. *A Man Escaped* would seem of all Bresson's films the most plot-oriented; it is about a prison break. But the title dispenses with any possibility of suspense – *Un Condamné à Mort S'est Echappé* (a man condemned to death has escaped). In *The Trial of Joan of Arc* the viewer, of course, knows the ending, but in case of any doubt the English guard repeatedly reiterates the fact: "She will die." "She must burn." The events are predestined, beyond the viewer's control and beyond – seemingly – Bresson's.

By using plot to evoke audience empathy, a dramatist limits the ways in which he can manipulate his audience. Even if he toys with the plot, confusing the viewer's emotions, he nonetheless restricts the result to the emotional level. "As far as I can I eliminate anything which may distract from the interior drama. For me, the cinema is an exploration within. Within the mind, the camera can do anything." The internal drama is in the mind, Bresson seems to say, and emotional involvement with an external plot "distracts" from it. (There is emotional involvement with Bresson's films, but it is the emotional involvement which follows recognition of form.)

Bresson's films, of course, are not entirely devoid of "plot"; each has a succession of events which have a rise and fall, a tension and relaxation, however slight. By the term "drama," however, Bresson does not mean simply the manipulation of events, but the appeal to the emotions through the manipulation of events. This sort of drama is something imposed on films; it is not endemic to the cinematic form: "Dramatic stories should be thrown out. They have nothing whatsoever to do with cinema. It seems to me that when one tries to do something dramatic with film, one is like a man who tries to hammer with a saw. Film would have been marvelous if there hadn't been dramatic art to get in the way."

Acting

Bresson's most vehement denunciations are reserved for acting: "It is for theater, a bastard art." The acting process is one of simplification; the actor modifies his personal, unfathomable complexities into relatively simple, demonstrable characteristics. "An actor, even (and above all) a talented actor gives us too simple an image of a human being, and therefore a false image." "We are complex. And what the actor projects is not complex."

An actor is primarily concerned with the character of the man he portrays. Bresson is concerned with how he can use that actor to convey a reality which is

302

not limited to any one character. The actor's most convenient approach to a character is psychology, and Bresson despises psychology: "I do not like psychology and I try to avoid it." Psychological acting humanizes the spiritual, "good" psychological acting even more so than "poor" psychological acting. Bresson, Bazin pointed out, is "concerned not with the psychology but with the physiology of existence."

Psychological acting is the easiest and most appealing of all the screens, and therefore Bresson must work the hardest to avoid it. If not properly restrained an actor will exert a creative force in a film – and in a Bresson film, Bresson is the only one who does the creating. "You cannot be inside an actor. It is he who creates, it is not you."

In order to reduce acting to physiology, Bresson carefully instructs his actors in nonexpressiveness. He forces the actor to sublimate his personality, to act in an automatic manner: "It is not so much a question of doing "nothing" as some people have said. It is rather a question of performing without being aware of oneself, of not controlling oneself. Experience has proved to me that when I was the most "automatic" in my work, I was the most moving."

Bresson's treatment of actors is remarkably similar to Ozu's, and for the same reasons. Both strove to eliminate any expression from the actor's performance. Neither would give the actor "hints" or explain the emotions that the actor should convey, but would give only precise, physical instructions: at what angle to hold the head, when and how far to turn the wrist, and so forth. Both used repeated rehearsals to "wear down" any ingrained or intractable self-expression, gradually transforming fresh movement into rote action, expressive intonation into bland monotone. Bresson's instructions to Roland Monod, the pastor in *A Man Escaped*, explain both the method and rationale behind this theory of acting: "Forget about tone and meaning. Don't think about what you're saying; just speak the words automatically. When someone talks, he isn't thinking about the words he uses, or even about what he wants to say. Only concerned with what he is saying, he just lets the words come out, simply and directly. When you are reading, your eye just strings together black words on white paper, set out quite neutrally on the page. It's only *after* you have read the words that you begin to dress up the simple sense of the phrases with intonation and meaning – that you interpret them. The film actor should content himself with *saying* his lines. He should not allow himself to show that he already understands them. Play nothing, explain nothing. A text should be spoken as Dinu Lipatti plays Bach. His wonderful technique simply releases the notes; understanding and emotion come later."

Camerawork

A tracking shot is a moral judgment, Jean-Luc Godard once remarked, and so, for that matter, is any camera shot. Any possible shot – high angle, close-up, pan – conveys a certain attitude toward a character, a "screen" which simplifies and interprets the character. Camera angles and pictorial composition, like music, are extremely insidious screens; they can undermine a scene without the viewer's being aware of it. A slow zoom-out or a vertical composition can substantially alter the meaning of the action within a scene.

Bresson strips the camera of its editorial powers by limiting it to one angle, one basic composition. "I change camera angles rarely. A person is not the same person if he is seen from an angle which varies greatly from the others." Like Ozu, Bresson shoots his scenes from one unvarying height; unlike Ozu, who prefers the seated *tatami* position, Bresson places the camera at the chest level of a standing person. As in Ozu's films, the composition is primarily frontal with at least one character facing the camera, seeming caught between the audience and his environment. Again and again, the static, well-composed environment acts as a frame for the action: a character enters the frame, performs an action, and exits.

Bresson's static camerawork nullifies the camera's editorial prerogatives. When each action is handled in essentially the same nonexpressive manner, the viewer no longer looks to the angle and composition for "clues" to the action. Like all of Bresson's everyday techniques, his camerawork postpones emotional involvement; at this stage the viewer "accepts" Bresson's static compositions, yet is unable to understand their full purpose.

Similarly, Bresson avoids the self-serving "beautiful" image. "Painting taught me to make not beautiful images but necessary ones." The beautiful image, whether attractive like *Elvira Madigan*, or gross like *Fellini Satryicon*, draws attention to itself and away from the inner drama. The beautiful image can be a screen between the spectator and the event – the pictorial images of *Adalen 31* tell the viewer more about Widenberg's idea of revolution than all his rhetoric. Bresson, on the other hand, "flattens" his images: "If you take a steam iron to your image, flattening it out, suppressing all expression by mimetism and gestures, and you put that image next to an image of the same kind, all of a sudden that image may have a violent effect on another one and both take on another appearance." André Bazin pointed out that the pictorial sumptuousness of Bernanos' *Diary of a Country Priest* – the rabbit hunts, the misty air – is most vividly conveyed in Renoir's films. Bresson, in his adaption of Bernanos' novel, rejected the obvious interpretation, emphasizing instead the cold factuality of the priest's environment.

[...]

THE TRANSCENDENTAL STYLE: DISPARITY

One of the dangers of the everyday is that it may become a screen in itself, a style rather than a stylization, an end rather than a means. The everyday eliminates the obvious emotional constructs but tacitly posits a rational one: that the world is predictable, ordered, cold. Disparity undermines the rational construct.

Disparity injects a "human density" into the unfeeling everyday, an unnatural density which grows and grows until, at the moment of decisive action, it reveals itself to be a spiritual density. In the initial steps of disparity Ozu and Bresson use different techniques to suggest a suspicious and emotional quality in the cold environment. Because Ozu's everyday stylization is more "polite" in the traditional Zen manner than Bresson's, Ozu can use what Sato called a "break in the geometrical balance" to create disparity. Ozu also makes more use of character ambivalence than Bresson does (possibly because of Ozu's background in light comedy), but both employ irony. Bresson, unlike Ozu, uses "doubling," an overemphasis of the everyday, to create disparity. Both, however, create disparity by giving their characters a sense of something deeper than themselves and their environment, a sense which culminates in the decisive action. All the techniques of disparity cast suspicion on everyday reality and suggest a need, although not a place, for emotion.

Bresson overemphasizes the everyday through what Miss Sontag calls "doubling." Through the use of repeated action and pleonastic dialogue Bresson "doubles" (or even "triples") the action, making a single event happen several times in different ways. For example: in *Pickpocket* Michel makes a daily entry into his diary. Bresson first shows the entry being written into the diary, then he has Michel read the entry over the soundtrack, "I sat in the lobby of one of the great banks of Paris." Then Bresson shows Michel actually going into one of the great banks of Paris and sitting in the lobby. The viewer has experienced the same event in three ways: through the printed word, the spoken word, and the visual action.

Bresson's favorite "doubling" technique is interior narration. In *Diary of a Country Priest, A Man Escaped*, and *Pickpocket* the main character narrates the on-screen action in a deadpan narration which is often only an audio replay of what the viewer has already witnessed. In *Diary of a Country Priest* the priest calls anxiously on the Vicar of Torcy. The housekeeper answers, obviously informing the priest that the vicar is not at home. The door closes and the priest leans dejectedly against it. When we hear the priest's voice, "I was so disappointed, I had to lean against the door." In *A Man Escaped* the order is reversed: first Fontaine narrates, "I slept so soundly the guard had to awaken me." Then the guard walks into his cell and says, "Get up."

Interior narration is customarily used to broaden the viewer's knowledge or feelings about an event. In Ophuls' *Letter from an Unknown Woman* and Lean's *Brief Encounter*, for example, the heroines recount their romantic experiences through narration. In each case the reflective and sensitive female voice is used as a counterpart to the harsh "male" world of action. The contrast between "female" and "male," sound and sight, narration and action expands the viewer's attitude toward the situation. Bresson, however, uses interior narration for the opposite reason: his narration does not give the viewer any new information or feelings, but only reiterates what he already knows. The viewer is conditioned to expect "new" information from narration; instead, he gets only a cold reinforcement of the everyday.

When the same thing starts happening two or three times concurrently the viewer knows he is beyond simple day-to-day realism and into the peculiar realism of Robert Bresson. The doubling does not double the viewer's knowledge or emotional reaction, it only doubles his perception of the event. Consequently, there is a schizoid reaction; one, there is the sense of meticulous detail which is a part of the everyday, and two, because the detail is doubled there is an emotional queasiness, a growing suspicion of the seemingly "realistic" rationale behind the everyday. If it is "realism," why is the action doubled, and if it isn't realism, why this obsession with details?

[...]

Techniques like doubling cast suspicion on the everyday, and the next step of disparity goes farther: it tries to evoke a "sense" of something Wholly Other within the cold environment, a sense which gradually alienates the main character from his solid position within the everyday.

24

GODARD

Susan Sontag

"It may be true that one has to choose between ethics and aesthetics, but it is no less true that whichever one chooses, one will always find the other at the end of the road. For the very definition of the human condition should be in the mise-en-scène itself."

Godard's work has been more passionately debated in recent than that of any other contemporary film-maker. Though he has a good claim to being ranked as the greatest director, from Bresson, working actively in the cinema today, it's still common for intelligent people to be irritated and frustrated by his films, even to find them unbearable. Godard's films haven't yet been elevated to the status of classics or masterpieces – as have the best of Eisenstein, Griffith, Gance, Dreyer, Lang, Pabst, Renoir, Vigo, Welles, etc.; or, to take some nearer examples, *L'Avventura* and *Jules and Jim*. That is, his films aren't yet embalmed, immortal, unequivocally (and merely) "beautiful." They retain their youthful power to offend, to appear "ugly," irresponsible, frivolous, pretentious, empty. Film-makers and audiences are still learning from Godard's films, still quarreling with them.

Meanwhile Godard (partly by turning out a new film every few months) manages to keep nimbly ahead of the inexorable thrust of cultural canonization; extending old problems and abandoning or complicating old solutions – offending veteran admirers in numbers almost equal to the new ones he acquires. His thirteenth feature, *Deux ou Trois Choses que je sais d'elle*

From: Susan Sontag, 'Godard', in *Styles of Radical Will* (Bodley Head, 1970).

(1966), is perhaps the most austere and difficult of all his films. His fourteenth feature, *La Chinoise* (1967), opened in Paris last summer and took the first Special Jury Prize at the Venice Film Festival in September; but Godard didn't come from Paris to accept it (his first major film festival award) because he had just begun shooting his next film, *Weekend*, which was playing in Paris by January of this year.

[...]

Practically no other director, with the exception of Bresson, can match Godard's record of making *only* films that are unmistakably and uncompromisingly their author's. (Contrast Godard on this score with two of his most gifted contemporaries: Resnais, who, after making the sublime *Muriel*, was able to descend to *La Guerre est Finie*, and Truffaut, who could follow *Jules and Jim* with *La Peau Douce* – for each director, only his fourth feature.) That Godard is indisputably the most influential director of his generation surely owes much to his having demonstrated himself incapable of adulterating his own sensibility, while still remaining manifestly unpredictable. One goes to a new film by Bresson fairly confident of being treated to another masterpiece. One goes to the latest Godard prepared to see something both achieved and chaotic, "work in progress" which resists easy admiration. The qualities that make Godard, unlike Bresson, a culture hero (as well as, like Bresson, one of the major artists of the age) are precisely his prodigal energies, his evident risk-taking, the quirky individualism of his mastery of a corporate, drastically commercialized art.

But Godard is not merely an intelligent iconoclast. He is a deliberate "destroyer" of cinema – hardly the first cinema has known, but certainly the most persistent and prolific and timely. His approach to established rules of film technique like the unobtrusive cut, consistency of point of view, and clear story line is comparable to Schoenberg's repudiation of the tonal language prevailing in music around 1910 when he entered his atonal period or to the challenge of the Cubists to such hallowed rules of painting as realistic figuration and three-dimensional pictorial space.

The great culture heroes of our time have shared two qualities: they have all been ascetics in some exemplary way, and also great destroyers. But this common profile has permitted two different, yet equally compelling attitudes toward "culture" itself. Some – like Duchamp, Wittgenstein, and Cage – bracket their art and thought with a disdainful attitude toward high culture and the past, or at least maintain an ironic posture of ignorance or incomprehension. Others – like Joyce, Picasso, Stravinsky, and Godard – exhibit a hypertrophy of appetite for culture (though often more avid for cultural debris than for museum-consecrated achievements); they proceed by voraciously scavenging in culture, proclaiming that nothing is alien to their art.

From cultural appetite on this scale comes the creation of work that is on the order of a subjective compendium: casually encyclopedic, anthologizing, formally and thematically eclectic, and marked by a rapid turnover of styles and forms. Thus, one of the most striking features of Godard's work is its daring efforts at hybridization. Godard's insouciant mixtures of tonalities, themes, and narrative methods suggest something like the union of Brecht and Robbe-Grillet, Gene Kelly and Francis Ponge, Gertrude Stein and David Riesman, Orwell and Robert Rauschenberg, Boulez and Raymond Chandler, Hegel and rock 'n' roll. Techniques from literature, theatre, painting, and television mingle freely in his work, alongside witty, impertinent allusions to movie history itself. The elements often seem contradictory – when (in the recent films) what Richard Roud calls "a fragmentation/collage method of narration" drawn from advanced painting and poetry is combined with the bare, hard-staring, neo-realist aesthetic of television (cf. the interviews, filmed in frontal close-up and medium shot, in *A Married Woman, Masculine Feminine*, and *Deux ou Trois Choses);* or when Godard uses highly stylized visual compositions (such as the recurrent blues and reds in *A Woman Is a Woman, Contempt, Pierrot le Fou, La Chinoise,* and *Weekend*) at the same time that he seems eager to promote the look of improvisation and to conduct an unremitting search for the "natural" manifestations of personality before the truth-exacting eye of the camera. But, however jaring these mergers are in principle, the results Godard gets from them turn out to be something harmonious, plastically and ethically engaging, and emotionally tonic.

The consciously reflective – more precisely, reflexive – aspect of Godard's films is the key to their energies. His work constitutes a formidable meditation on the *possibilities* of cinema, which is to restate what I have already argued, that he enters the history of film as its first consciously destructive figure. Put otherwise, one might note that Godard is probably the first major director to enter the cinema on the level of commercial production with an explicitly critical intention. "I'm still as much of a critic as I ever was during the time of *Cahiers du Cinéma,*" he has declared. (Godard wrote regularly for that magazine between 1956 and 1959, and still occasionally contributes to it.) "The only difference is that instead of writing criticism, I now film it." Elsewhere, he describes *Le Petit Soldat* as an "auto-critique," and that word, too, applies to all of Godard's films.

But the extent to which Godard's films speak in the first person, and contain elaborate and often humorous reflections on the cinema as a means, is not a private whim but one elaboration of a well-established tendency of the arts to become more self-conscious, more self-referring. Like every important body of work in the canon of modern culture, Godard's films are simply what they are and also events that push their audience to reconsider the meaning and scope of the art form of which they are instances; they're not only works of art, but meta-artistic activities aimed at reorganizing the audience's entire sensibility. Far from deploring the tendency, I believe that the most promising future of films as an art lies in this direction. But the manner in which films continue into the end of the twentieth century as a serious art, becoming more self-regarding and critical, still permits a great deal of variation. Godard's method is far removed from the solemn, exquisitely conscious, self-annihilating structures of Bergman's great film *Persona*. Godard's procedures are much more light-hearted, playful, often witty, sometimes flippant, sometimes just silly. Like any gifted polemicist (which Bergman is not), Godard has the courage to simplify himself. This simplistic quality in much of Godard's work is as much a kind of generosity toward his audience as an aggression against them; and, partly, just the overflow of an inexhaustibly vivacious sensibility.

The attitude that Godard brings to the film medium is often called, disparagingly, "literary." What's usually meant by this charge, as when Satie was accused of composing literary music or Magritte of making literary painting, is a preoccupation with ideas, with conceptualization, at the expense of the sensual integrity and emotional force of the work – more generally, the habit (a kind of bad taste, it's supposed) of violating the essential unity of a given art form by introducing alien elements into it. That Godard has boldly addressed the task of representing or embodying abstract ideas as no other film-maker has done before him is undeniable. Several films even include guest intellectual appearances: a fictional character falls in with a real philosopher (the heroine of *My Life to Live* interrogates Brice Parain in a café about language and sincerity; in *La Chinoise*, the Maoist girl disputes with Francis Jeanson on a train about the ethics of terrorism); a critic and film-maker delivers a speculative soliloquy (Roger Leenhardt on intelligence, ardent and compromising, in *A Married Woman*); a grand old man of film history has a chance to reinvent his own somewhat tarnished personal image (Fritz Lang as himself, a chorus figure meditating on German poetry, Homer, movie-making, and moral integrity, in *Contempt*). On their own, many of Godard's characters muse aphoristically to themselves or engage their friends on such topics as the difference between the Right and the Left, the nature of cinema, the mystery of language, and the spiritual void underlying the satisfactions of the consumer society. Moreover, Godard's films are not only idea-ridden, but many of his characters are ostentatiously literate. Indeed, from the numerous references to books, mentions of writers' names, and quotations and longer excerpts from literary texts scattered throughout his films Godard gives the impression of being engaged in an unending agon with the very fact of literature – which he attempts to settle partially by incorporating literature and literary identities into his films. And, apart from his original use of it as a cinematic object, Godard is concerned with literature both as a model for film and as the revival and alternative to film. In interviews and in his own critical writings, the relation between cinema and literature is a recurrent theme. One of the differences Godard stresses is that literature exists "as art from the very start" but cinema doesn't. But he also notes a potent similarity between the two arts: that "we novelists and film-makers are condemned to an analysis of the world, of the real; painters and musicians aren't."

By treating cinema as above all an exercise in intelligence, Godard rules out any neat distinction between "literary" and "visual" (or cinematic) intelligence. If film is, in Godard's laconic definition, the "analysis" of something "with images and sounds," there can be no impropriety in making literature a subject for cinematic analysis. Alien to movies as this kind of material may seem, at least in such profusion, Godard would no doubt argue that books and other vehicles of cultural consciousness are part of the world; therefore they belong in films. Indeed, by putting on the same plane the fact that people read and think and go seriously to the movies and the fact that they cry and run and make love, Godard has disclosed a new vein of lyricism and pathos for cinema: in book-ishness, in genuine cultural passion, in intellectual callowness, in the misery of someone strangling in his own thoughts. (An instance of Godard's original way with a more familiar subject, the poetry of loutish illiteracy, is the twelve-minute sequence in *Les Carabiniers* in which the soldiers unpack their picture-postcard-trophies.) His point is that no material is inherently unassimilable. But what's required is that literature indeed undergo its transformation into material, just like anything else. All that can be given are literary extracts, shards of literature. In order to be absorbed by cinema, literature must be dismantled or broken into wayward units; then Godard can appropriate a portion of the intellectual "content" of any book (fiction or non-fiction), borrow from the public domain of culture any contrasting tone of voice (noble or vulgar), invoke in an instant any diagnosis of contemporary malaise that is thematically relevant to his narrative, no matter how inconsistent it may be with the psychological scope or mental competence of the characters as already established.

Thus, so far as Godard's films are "literary" in some sense, it seems clear that his alliance with literature is based on quite different interests from those which linked earlier experimental film-makers to the advanced writing of their time. If Godard envies literature, it is not so much for the formal innovations carried out in the twentieth century as for the heavy burden of explicit ideation accom-modated within prose literary forms. Whatever notions Godard may have gotten from reading Faulkner or Beckett or Mayakovsky for formal inventions in cinema, his introduction of a pronounced literary taste (his own?) into his films serves mainly as a means for assuming a more public voice or elaborating more general statements. While the main tradition of avant-garde film-making has been a "poetic" cinema (films, like those made by the Surrealists in the 1920's and 1930's, inspired by the emancipation of modern poetry from storylike narrative and sequential discourse to the direct presentation and sensuous, polyvalent association of ideas and images), Godard has elaborated a largely anti-poetic cinema, one of whose chief literary models is the prose essay. Godard has even said: "I consider myself an essay writer. I write essays in the form of novels, or novels in the form of essays."

Notice that Godard has here made the novel interchangeable with film – apt in a way, since it is the tradition of the novel that weighs most heavily upon cinema, and the example of what the novel has recently become that spurs Godard. "I've found an idea for a novel," mumbles the hero of *Pierrot le Fou* at one point, in partial self-mockery assuming the quavering voice of Michel Simon. "Not to write the life of a man, but only life, life itself. What there is between people, space ... sound and colors ... There must be a way of achieving that; Joyce tried, but one must, must be able ... to do better." Surely, Godard is here speaking for himself as film-maker, and he appears confident that film can accomplish what literature cannot, literature's incapacity being partly due to the less favorable *critical* situation into which each important literary work is deposited. I have spoken of Godard's work as consciously destructive of old cinematic conventions. But this task of demolition is executed with the élan of someone working in an art form experienced as young, on the threshhold of its greatest development rather than at its end. Godard views the destruction of old rules as a constructive effort – in contrast to the received view of the current destiny of literature. As he has written, "literary critics often praise works like *Ulysses* or *Endgame* because they exhaust a certain genre, they close the doors on it. But in the cinema we always praising works which *open* doors."

[...]

Instead of a narration unified by the coherence of events (a "plot") and a consistent tone (comic, serious, oneiric, affectless, or whatever), the narrative of Godard's films is regularly broken or segmented by the incoherence of events and by abrupt shifts in tone and level of discourse. Events appear to the spectator partly as converging toward a story, partly as a succession of independent tableaux.

The most obvious way Godard segments the forward-moving sequence of narration into tableaux is by explicitly theatricalizing some of his material, once more laying to rest the lively prejudice that there is an essential incompatibility between the means of theatre and those of film. The conventions of the Hollywood musical," with songs and stage performances interrupting the story, supply one precedent for Godard – inspiring the general conception of *A Woman Is a Woman*, the dance trio in the café in *Band of Outsiders*, the song sequences and Vietnam protest skit performed outdoors in *Pierrot le Fou*, the singing telephone call in *Weekend*. His other model is, of course, the non-realistic and didactic theatre expounded by Brecht. An aspect of Godard Brechtianizing is his distinctive style of constructing political microentertainments: in *La Chinoise*, the home political theatre-piece acting out the American aggression in Vietnam; or the Feiffer dialogue of the two ham radio operators that opens *Deux ou Trois Choses*. But the more profound influence of Brecht resides in those formal devices Godard uses to counteract ordinary plot development and complicate the emotional involvement of the audience. One device is the direct-to-camera declarations by the characters in many films, notably *Deux ou Trois Choses*, *Made in U.S.A.*, and *La Chinoise*. ("One should speak as if one were quoting the truth," says Marina Vlady at the beginning of *Deux ou Trois Choses*, quoting Brecht. "The actors must quote.") Another frequently used technique derived from Brecht is the dissection of the film narrative into short sequences: in *My Life to Live*, in addition, Godard puts on the screen prefatory synopses to each scene which describe the action to follow. The action of *Les Carabiniers* is broken into short brutal sections introduced by long titles, most of which represent cards sent home by Ulysses and Michelangelo; the titles are handwritten, which makes them a little harder to read and brings home to the movie audience the fact that it is being asked to read. Another, simpler device is the relatively arbitrary subdivision of action into numbered sequences, as when the credits of *Masculine Feminine* announce a film consisting of "fifteen precise actions" (*quinze faits précis*). A minimal device is the ironic, pseudo-quantitative statement of something, as in *A Married Woman*, with the brief monologue of Charlotte's little son explaining how to do an unspecified something in exactly ten steps: or in *Pierrot le Fou*, when Ferdinand's voice announces at the beginning of a scene: "Chapter Eight. We cross France." Another example: the very title of one film, *Deux ou Trois Choses* – the lady about whom surely more than two or three things are known being the city of Paris. And, in support of these tropes of the rhetoric of disorientation, Godard practices many specifically sensorial techniques that serve to fragment the cinematic narrative. In fact, most of the familiar elements of Godard's visual and aural stylistics – rapid cutting, the use of unmatched shots, flash shots, the alternation of sunny takes with gray ones, the counterpoint of prefabricated images (signs, paintings, billboards, picture postcards, posters), the discontinuous music – function in this way.

Apart from the general strategy of "theatre," perhaps Godard's most striking application of the dissociative principle is his treatment of ideas. Certainly ideas are not developed in Godard's films systematically, as they might be in a book. They aren't meant to be. In contrast to their role in Brechtian theatre, ideas are chiefly formal elements in Godard's films, units of sensory and emotional stimulation. They function at least as much to dissociate and fragment as they do to indicate or illuminate the "meaning" of the action. Often the ideas, rendered in blocks of words, lie at a tangent to the action. Nana's reflections on sincerity and language in *My Life to Live*, Bruno's observations about truth and action in *Le Petit Soldat*, the articulate self-consciousness of Charlotte in *A Married Woman* and of Juliette in *Deux ou Trois Choses*, Lemmy Caution's startling aptitude for cultivated literary allusions in *Alphaville* are not functions of the realistic psychology of these characters. (Perhaps the only one of Godard's intellectually reflective protagonists who still seems "in character" when ruminating is Ferdinand in *Pierrot le Fou*.) Although Godard proposes film discourse as constantly open to ideas, ideas are only one element in a narrative form which posits an intentionally ambiguous, open, playful relation of *all* the parts to the total scheme.

Godard's fondness for interpolating literary "texts" in the action, is one of the main variants on the presence of ideas in his films. Among the many instances: the Mayakovsky poem recited by the girl about to be executed by a firing squad in *Les Carabiniers*; the excerpt from the Poe story read aloud in the next-to-last episode in *My Life to Live*; the lines from Dante, Hölderlin, and Brecht that Lang quotes in *Contempt*; the oration from Saint-Just by a character dressed as Saint-Just in *Weekend*; the passage from Elie Faure's *History of Art* read aloud by Ferdinand to his young daughter in *Pierrot le Fou*; the lines from *Romeo and Juliet* in French translation dictated by the English teacher in *Band of Outsiders*; the scene from Racine's *Bérénice* rehearsed by Charlotte and her lover in *A Married Woman*; the quote from Fritz Lang read aloud by Camille in *Contempt*; the passages from Mao declaimed by the FLN agent in *Le Petit Soldat*; the antiphonal recitations from the little red book in *La Chinoise*. Usually someone makes an announcement before beginning to declaim, or can be seen taking up a book and reading from it. Sometimes, though, these obvious signals for the advent of a text are lacking – as with the excerpts from *Bouvard and Pecuchet* spoken by two customers in a café in *Deux ou Trois Choses*, or the long extract from *Death on the Installment Plan* delivered by the maid ("Madame Celine") in *A Married Woman*. (Although usually literary, the text may be a film: like the excerpt from Dreyer's *Jeanne d'Arc* that Nana watches in *My Life to Live*, or a minute of film shot by Godard in Sweden, reputed to be a parody of Bergman's *The Silence*, that Paul and the two girls see in *Masculine Feminine*.) These texts introduce psychologically dissonant elements into the action; they supply rhythmical variety (temporarily slowing down the action); they interrupt the action and offer ambiguous comment on it; and they also vary and extend the point of view represented in the film. The spectator is almost bound to be misled if he regards these texts simply, either as opinions of characters in the film or as samples of some unified point of view advocated by the film which presumably is dear to the director. More likely, just the opposite is or comes to be the case. Aided by "ideas" and "texts," Godard's film narratives tend to consume the points of view presented in them. Even the political ideas expressed in Godard's work – part Marxist and part anarchist in one canonical style of the postwar French intelligentsia – are subject to this rule.

Like the ideas, which function partly as divisive elements, the fragments of cultural lore embedded in Godard's films serve in part as a form of mystification and a means for refracting emotional energy. (In *Le Petit Soldat*, for instance, when Bruno says of Veronica the first time he sees her that she reminds him of a Giraudoux heroine, and later wonders whether her eyes are Renoir gray or Velásquez gray, the main impact of these references is their unverifiability by the audience.) Inevitably, Godard broaches the menace of the bastardization of culture, a theme most broadly stated in *Contempt* in the figure of the American producer with his booklet of proverbs. And, laden as his films are with furnishings of high culture, it's perhaps inevitable that Godard should also invoke the project of laying down the burden of culture – as Ferdinand does in *Pierrot le Fou* when he abandons his life in Paris for the romantic journey southward carrying only a book of old comics. In *Weekend*, Godard posits against the petty barbarism of the car-owning urban bourgeoisie the possibly cleansing violence of a rebarbarized youth, imagined as a hippy-style liberation army roaming the countryside whose principal delights seem to be contemplation, pillage, jazz, and cannibalism. The theme of cultural dis-burdenment is treated most fully and ironically in *La Chinoise*. One sequence shows the young cultural revolutionaries purging their shelves of all their books but the little red one. Another brief sequence shows just a blackboard at first, filled with the neatly listed names of several dozen stars of Western culture from Plato to Shakespeare to Sartre; these are then erased one by one, thoughtfully, with Brecht the last to go. The five pro-Chinese students who live together want to have only one point of view, that of Chairman Mao; but Godard shows, without insulting anyone's intelligence, how chimerical and inadequate to reality (and yet how appealing) this hope actually is. For all his native radicalism of temperament, Godard himself still appears a partisan of that other cultural revolution, ours, which enjoins the artist-thinker to main-tain a multiplicity of points of view on any material.

All the devices Godard employs to keep shifting the point of view within a film can be looked at another way – as adjuncts to a positive strategy, that of overlaying a number of narrative voices, for effectively bridging the difference between first-person and third-person narration. Thus *Alphaville* opens with three samples of first-person discourse: first, a prefatory statement spoken off-camera by Godard, then a declaration by the computer-ruler Alpha 60, and only then the usual soliloquizing voice, that of the secret-agent hero, shown grimly driving his big car into the city of the future. Instead of, or in addition to, using "titles" between scenes as narrative signals (for example: *My Life to Live*, *A Married Woman*), Godard seems now more to favor installing a narrative voice in the film. This voice may belong to the main character: Bruno's musings in *Le Petit Soldat*, Charlotte's free associating subtext in *A Married Woman*, Paul's commentary in *Masculine Feminine*. It may be the director's, as in *Band of Outsiders* and "Le Grand Escroc," the sketch from *Les Plus Belles Escroqueries du Monde* (1963). What's most interesting is when there are two voices, as in *Deux ou Trois Choses*, throughout which both Godard (whispering) and the heroine comment on the action. *Band of Out-siders* introduces the notion of a narrative intelligence which can "open a parenthesis" in the action and directly address the audience, explaining what Franz, Odile, and Arthur are really feeling at that moment; the narrator can intervene or comment ironically on the action or on the very fact of seeing a movie. (Fifteen minutes into the film, Godard off-camera says, "For the latecomers, what's happened so far is ...") Thereby two different but con-current times are established in the film – the time of the action shown, and the time of the narrator's reflection on what's shown – in a way which allows free passage back and forth between the first-person narration and the third-person presentation of the action.

Although the narrating voice already has a major role in some of his earliest work (for instance, the virtuoso comic monologue of the last of the pre-*Breathless* shorts, *Une Histoire d'Eau*), Godard continues to extend and complicate the task of oral narration, arriving at such recent refinements as the beginning of *Deux ou Trois Choses*, when from off-camera he introduces his leading actress, Marina Vlady, by name and then describes her as the character she will play. Such procedures tend, of course, to reinforce the self-reflexive and self-referring aspect of Godard's films, for the ultimate narrative presence is simply the fact of cinema itself; from which it follows that, for the sake of truth, the cinematic medium must be made to manifest itself before the spectator. Godard's methods for doing this range from the frequent ploy of having an actor make rapid playful asides to the camera (i.e., to the audience) in mid-action, to the use of a bad take – Anna Karina fumbles a line, asks if it's all right, then repeats the line – in *A Woman Is a Woman. Les Carabiniers* only gets underway after we hear first some coughing and shuffling and an instruction by someone, perhaps the composer or a sound technician, on the set. In *La Chinoise*, Godard makes the point about its being a movie by, among other devices, flashing the clapper board on the screen from time to time, and by briefly cutting to Raoul Coutard, the cameraman on this as on most of Godard's films, seated behind his apparatus. But then one immediately imagines some underling holding another clapper while that scene was shot, and someone else who had to be there behind another camera to photograph Coutard. It's impossible ever to penetrate behind the final veil and experience cinema unmediated by cinema.

I have argued that one consequence of Godard's disregard for the aesthetic rule of having a fixed point of view is that he dissolves the distinction between first-person and third-person narration. But perhaps it would be more accurate to say that Godard proposes a new conception of point of view, thereby staking out the possibility of making films in the first person. By this, I don't mean simply that his films are subjective or personal; so is the work of many other directors, particularly the cinematic avant-garde and underground. I mean something stricter, which may indicate the originality of his achievement: namely, the way in which Godard, especially in his recent films, has built up a narrative presence, that of the film-maker, who is the central *structural* element in the cinematic narrative. This first-person film-maker isn't an actual character within the film. That is, he is not to be seen on the screen (except in the episode in *Far from Vietnam*, which shows only Godard at a camera talking, intercut with snippets from *La Chinoise*), though he is heard from time to time and one is increasingly aware of his presence just off-camera. But this off-screen persona is not a lucid, authorial intelligence, like the detached observer-figure of many novels cast in the first person. The ultimate first person in Godard's movies, his particular version of the film-maker, is the person responsible for the film who stands outside it as a mind beset by more complex, fluctuating concerns than any single film can represent or incarnate. The most profound drama of a Godard film arises from the clash between this restless, wider consciousness of the director and the determinate, limited argument of the particular film he's engaged in making. Therefore each film is, simultaneously, a creative activity and a destructive one. The director virtually uses up his models, his sources, his ideas, his latest moral and artistic enthusiasms – and the shape of the film consists of various means for letting the audience know that's what is happening. This dialectic has reached its furthest development so far in *Deux ou Trois Choses*, which is more radically a first-person film than any Godard has made.

The advantage of the first-person mode for cinema is presumably that it vastly augments the liberty of the film-maker while at the same time providing incentives for greater formal rigor – the same goals espoused by all the serious post-novelists of this century. Thus Gide has Edouard, the author-protagonist of *The Counterfeiters*, condemn all previous novels because their contours are "defined," so that, however perfect, what they contain is "captive and lifeless." He wanted to write a novel that would "run freely" because he'd chosen "not to foresee its windings." But the liberation of the novel turned out to consist in writing a novel about writing a novel: presenting "literature" within literature. In a different context, Brecht discovered "theatre" within theatre. Godard has discovered "cinema" within cinema. However loose or spontaneous-looking or personally self-expressive his films may appear, what must be appreciated is that Godard subscribes to a severely alienated conception of his art: a cinema that eats cinema. Each film is an ambiguous event that must be simultaneously promulgated and destroyed. Godard's most explicit statement of this theme is the painful monologue of self-interrogation which was his contribution to *Far from Vietnam*. Perhaps his wittiest statement of this theme is a scene in *Les Carabiniers* (similar to the end of an early Mack Sennett two-reeler, *Mabel's Dramatic Career*) in which Michelangelo takes time off from the war to visit a movie theatre, apparently for the first time, since he reacts as audiences did sixty years ago when movies first began to be shown. He follows the movements of the actors on the screen with his whole body, ducks under the sea when a train appears, and at last, driven wild by the sight of a girl taking a bath in the film within a film, bolts from his seat and rushes up to the stage. After first standing on tiptoe to try to look into the tub, then feeling tentatively for the girl along the surface of the screen, he finally tries to grab her – ripping away part of the screen within the screen, and revealing the girl and the bathroom to be a projection on a filthy wall. Cinema, as Godard says in *Le Grand Escroc*, "is the most beautiful fraud in the world."

25

ANTONIONI'S *RED DESERT*

Angela Dalle Vacche

Shot during the fall of 1963 in the industrial harbor of Ravenna, Michelangelo Antonioni's first film in color, *Red Desert*, has been repeatedly compared to abstract painting. In 1942 the director drew an equivalence between color and painting: "In the cinema, black and white is to color what drawing is to painting." With another statement made in 1964, Antonioni linked color to the future: "In our contemporary daily life, color has acquired a meaning and a function it did not have before. I am sure that black and white will be stuff for the museum." Although the director's statements associate color with painting and the future, the purpose of this chapter is to expand our thematic understanding of the meaning of color in *Red Desert*, by paying attention to the representation of history, to art-historical allusions, to the dialectic of word and image, and to the sexual politics that characterize Antonioni's direction of his leading actress, Monica Vitti.

As the film's title suggests, red rules over an empty space, but the desert is born again through the most intense of all colors. It is unclear whether the desert of *Red Desert* is the vacuum left behind by an ecological catastrophe or a brand-new space of unexplored possibilities. In either case, Antonioni seems to be fascinated with the imaginative potential of emptiness. This openness toward an uncertain future suggests that Antonioni's project in *Red Desert* is to explore an uncharted territory of creativity. The director, however, shares this penchant for the new with his female protagonist.

From: Angela Dalle Vacche, 'Antonioni's *Red Desert*', in *Cinema and Painting: How Art is Used in Film* (The Athlone Press/University of Texas Press, 1996).

In reentering normal life after a stay in the hospital, Giuliana (Monica Vitti) casts a look on the world that ranges from suffering and troubled to inquisitive and exploratory. Giuliana's existential crisis not only echoes the director's willingness to experiment with color but also resonates with radical changes in the landscape around her.

If *Red Desert* is indeed a film about historical transformation and psychological change, it is not surprising that Antonioni uses color to alter the nature of cinematic language, namely to paint the world anew according to an abstract sensibility. Yet, despite his bold statements about color as abstract painting and color as the language of the future, Antonioni is aware that he is first and foremost a filmmaker who relies on direction of actors, framing, and camerawork to tell a story. The director's self-consciousness that painting with color in film implies a statement about his artistic persona transpires from a remark published by *Positif* in 1985: "I am not a painter, but a filmmaker who paints." Because throughout his career Antonioni has never denied his interest in painting, while always reminding his listeners of his identity as a filmmaker, a certain aura of transgression hovers over the images of *Red Desert*. The transgression, however, is double: one from a cinema of architecture to a cinema of painting, and the other from neorealist documentation to pictorial abstraction.

By devoting the first sequence of *Red Desert* to a strike, Antonioni immediately echoes Vittorio de Sica's *Umberto D* (1951), a neorealist film that begins with a public protest by retired government employees to signal how the civic ideals of the Resistance movement have been betrayed. With this kind of opening Antonioni also alludes to the social turmoil that characterized the early sixties in the wake of the so-called economic boom of the previous decade. Factories and refineries have replaced churches and trees, while new financial ventures and cutting-edge technologies have upset traditional relations, not only between workers and management but also between human beings and their environment.

The production history of *Red Desert* – a film shot in real locations that were, however, literally painted over to accommodate the director's experimentation with color, and a film in which professional performers (Monica Vitti, Richard Harris) worked with a newcomer to the set (Carlo Chionetti, a Milanese lawyer in the role of Ugo – spells out the director's oscillation between a neorealist background and the ambitions of contemporary abstract art. In regard to natural settings and to an art that uses walls (and, in the case of *Red Desert*, swamps, fields, docks, riverbanks, shacks) to liberate textures and surfaces in a painter's canvas, the director declared to *L'Express* in 1960, "They stimulate me more. It is the same as it might be with a painter to whom someone said, 'Here is a wall which is to be covered with frescoes, so many yards long and so many yards high.' These are the kinds of limitations which aid rather than fetter the imagination." To pursue further Antonioni's links to neorealism, his observations here seem to refer back to Leonardo da Vinci, who felt that artists could find creativity by staring at a crumbling wall and letting the mind wander:

> When you look at a wall spotted with stains, or with a mixture of stones, if you have to devise some scene you may discover a resemblance to various landscapes ... or, again, you may see battles and figures in action, or strange faces and costumes, or an endless variety of objects, which you could reduce to complete and well-drawn forms. These appear on such walls promiscuously, like the sound of bells in whose jangle you may find any name or word you choose to imagine.

During a strange winter party, inside a shack with little heat and wooden walls painted in an aggressive red – Corrado (Richard Harris) tells Giuliana that her question "What should I look at?" echoes his dilemma "How should I live?" This analogy between looking and living suggests that for Antonioni painting in *Red Desert* is no decorative citation; rather, it is the other side of lived experience, for the landscape itself in true neorealist fashion, furnishes the materials of art.

Antonioni's parallel between looking and living sets up a corollary equivalence between subjectivity and context, perception and placement, which points to André Bazin's insight that the neorealist documentary image can shift its orientation from the outside to the inside and become a private hallucination. In an essay entitled "Reflections 1964," Antonioni explains,

> It's something that all directors have in common, I think: this habit of keeping one eye open inside and another outside. At a certain point, these two visions begin to resemble each other, and like two images coming into focus, they overlap. It is from this agreement between eye and brain, eye and instinct, eye and consciousness, that the desire to speak or to show comes.

Thus, in *Red Desert*, the dialectic of an inward-bound eye and an outward-bound one parallels the mirroring between internal psychological development and external, historical transformation.

Finally, that natural settings are the other side of art, and vice versa, is confirmed by the following statement from Antonioni, published in 1958 by *Bianco e Nero*: "I cannot understand how they manage to shoot from little designs and plans they have drawn on paper ahead of time. I feel that the composition is a plastic, figurative element which ought to be seen in its exact dimensions."

Here Antonioni rejects drawings on paper and seems to describe him self standing outdoors and arranging actors and objects, colors and shots, in relation to real buildings. Indirectly the filmmaker's words set up an opposition between creating indoors and directing outdoors. While it is well known that Hitchcock planned all his films shot by shot on little scraps of paper, it is also true that the painter as well as the architect works indoors. Yet by virtue of its final execution in public outdoor spaces, architecture has historically addressed the social sphere more forcefully than traditional painting, for the latter is an art form that usually travels from the walls of the studio to the safe enclosure of the museum.

From whose standpoint is Antonioni, therefore, speaking? When the director offers these statements, does he define himself as a filmmaker, or as a painter, or as an architect? I feel that Antonioni purposefully speaks in an ambiguous manner that interlaces architecture with painting, thus inadvertently evoking a comparable overlap at the heart of the International Style, an experience marked by Le Corbusier (who worked both as a painter and as an architect) and by Ludwig Mies van der Rohe (who, as an architect, was especially sensitive to modern abstract painting).

Nevertheless, as I readjust this key feature of the International Style to *Red Desert*, I propose that Antonioni's statement – I feel that the composition is a plastic, figurative element which ought to be seen in its exact dimensions" – has an especially powerful, active ring, in which making, arranging, directing, and moving around prevail over seeing, responding, reacting. This is why I would argue that here Antonioni talks more like a filmmaker and an architect than like a painter, as if he had unconsciously aligned architecture with his power to control performers and spaces as a male director, whereas painting comes to fall under the rubric of femininity, or at least to that artistic side of himself he is exploring in innovative ways through color and his direction of Monica Vitti.

Antonioni's most incisive self-description and most famous statement about the roots of his inspiration sounds closer to architecture than to painting: "When I shoot a film, that is all I am doing. I arrange things and people the way they ought to be." It is as if Antonioni were trying to mask his transgression from a cinema of architecture to one of painting by allowing the male characters in *Red Desert* – as well as the critics of the film – to frame Giuliana, the director's female alter-ego, in the role of a neurotic who primarily reacts to circumstances instead of reorganizing the world or ruthlessly carrying out an action.

Despite his attachment to real locations and natural landscapes, Antonioni's painting in *Red Desert* is more abstract than figurative, more avant-garde than traditional. Precisely because this was a project born under the auspices of artistic creativity rather than of documentary accuracy, the director finds in the female protagonist's malaise an expedient set of eyes through which to unleash freely (but also conveniently to justify) his most daring images and delirious metamorphoses.

Much more than all the other characters, Giuliana senses the prodigious and unsettling quality of historical change – a situation she recasts in the solipsistic effort to recuperate from a suicide attempt after a car accident. Early on in the film, Antonioni establishes a clear contrast between Giuliana's uneasiness with the industrial world and her husband Ugo's unquestioning faith in scientific and rational values. Ugo's identification with the factory, however, accounts for his one-dimensional personality, whereas Giuliana's crisis heightens her desire for change – an orientation that a brief affair with Corrado, one of Ugo's colleagues, hardly fulfills. In the narrative universe of *Red Desert*, therefore, oppositional elements such as old and new, technology and the past, a masculine penchant for science and a woman's attachment to memories, are not stable categories; rather they often exchange positions in an eerie circularity. For instance, Giuliana's child, Valerio, paints with vivid colors while his art hangs on the wall of his mother's bedroom. Just like Valerio, Antonioni wants to paint a picture of the future, even though he cannot forget that his origin lies in a woman's womb.

During her wanderings across the industrial wasteland of Ravenna, on one hand Giuliana aspires to a new sense of self as a woman, while on the other she regrets the permanent loss of a former way of being. Giuliana's oscillation between old and new resurfaces in a statement made by the director in 1961: "While we are eager to get rid of old scientific notions, we wallow in the close analysis, the dissection of . . . outdated feelings. Unable to find new attitudes, we fail to bridge the gap between moral man and scientific man." Were we to rethink Antonioni's opposition of scientific man and moral man in the light of the tensions that upset Giuliana and Ugo's marriage, we can guess that the contrast is not so much between science and morality as it is between the traditional association of masculinity with technology and the future and of femininity with nature and the past.

Inasmuch as *Red Desert* is "an account of individuation," the story of a woman searching for her own individuality at a time when gendered power relations are changing, the film also tells us about Antonioni's struggle as a filmmaker who wants to become a painter engaged in the depiction of vanishing objects with unstable contours and of industrial products glowing with the harshness of alien creatures. More specifically, in order to paint with colors, Antonioni relies on Giuliana, whose illness has exasperated her perceptual abilities to such an extent that moments of unexpected clarity alternate with instances of blurred vision.

In his astute commentary on *Red Desert*, Pier Paolo Pasolini has summarized Antonioni's subterfuge of using a woman to paint in film as a "soggettiva libera indiretta," or "free indirect subjective," approach. Antonioni's strategy of giving prominence to a feminine vision or a special kind of hypersensitivity is well known all across his films, from *Le Amiche* (1955) to *La Notte* (1961). Yet in the case of *Red Desert*, stepping into a woman's shoes, so to speak, is a measure of his will to change and experiment, while it also conveys a certain uneasiness with painting, an art form he has cultivated with the same intensity he has always shown toward architecture.

Although Antonioni sees through Vitti's eyes, and he does not really speak through her body, he establishes a visual ventriloquism with her. In a way my comparison of Antonioni to a ventriloquist makes more precise the sexual politics underpinning Pasolini's insight that a "free indirect subjective" approach is at work in *Red Desert*. Although *ventriloquism* means to speak through someone else's belly – or better, to make it seem that a silent dummy is speaking, when it is really the person who holds the dummy who does all the talking from behind – Antonioni does not quite endow Vitti with the power of winning words but only lets her have visions so pictorial and so abstract that they push outward the boundaries of what until now we have considered acceptable for the visual track of a European art film.

Thus, the metaphor of ventriloquism specializes Pasolini's insight to the extent that through Vitti, Antonioni gains representational freedom, even though the images he assigns to his actress are subjective in an unsettling way, if not visceral, to return to the corporeal etymology of ventriloquism.

In short, ventriloquism is only another way of saying "free indirect subjective" approach, by throwing together the belly with the word, the body with the mind; it is this odd combination of elements that discloses how Antonioni, in *Red Desert*, strikes a very precarious balance, for his allegiances are deeply split between the past and the future, a masculine and a feminine position, innovation and tradition.

Ventriloquism implies a transfer of authorship from director to actress, an operation that emerges between the lines in this remark by Antonioni: "Of all my films *Red Desert* is the least autobiographical. In this film I kept looking at the world outside. I tell the story as if the plot were unfolding right in front of my eyes." By combining a denial of autobiographical elements with a self-portrait of visual apprehension, Antonioni offers us a contradictory model of detachment and involvement, removal and observation.

As a directorial stand-in – who sees in ways that Antonioni does not extend to other characters" points of view but reserves only for himself as the filmmaker – Giuliana might more appropriately be called, instead of a neurotic, a convalescent. Indeed there is a long tradition in European culture (Baudelaire, D'Annunzio) that equates convalescence with creativity and artistic expression with pathology. William Arrowsmith reminds us that the neurotic patient is a born artist: "In Jung's judgement, the courageous neurotic is the patient who copes creatively with his own life, who comes to terms with himself by confronting the reality of his own nature and his responsibility for his illness or health. The neurotic in this sense is of course only the classical hero in disguise." Giorgio De Chirico, a painter beloved by Antonioni, understood that convalescence, even in the form of a lingering sickness, is "the ground of a new consciousness"

> Let me recount how I had a revelation of a picture that I will show this year it at the Salon d'Automne, entitled "Enigma of a Summer Afternoon." One clear autumnal afternoon I was sitting on a bench in the middle of the Piazza Santa Croce in Florence. It was of course not the first time I had seen this square. I had just come out of a long and painful intestinal illness, and I was in a nearly morbid state of sensitivity. The whole world, down to the marble of the buildings and the fountains,

seemed to me to be convalescent. In the middle of the square rises a statue of Dante draped in a long cloak, holding his works, clasped against his body, his laurel-crowned head bent thoughtfully earthward. The statue is in white marble, but time has given it a gray cast, very agreeable to the eye. The autumn sun, warm and unloving, lit the statue and the church facade. Then I had the strange impression that I was looking at all these things for the first time, and the composition of my picture came to the mind's eye.

In short, the scenario of convalescence at the heart of *Red Desert* not only fits the theme of artistic creativity for the director and of attainment of a new sense of self for the female protagonist, but it also intertwines with the need to clear the ground, to start with a tabula rasa, to produce a temporary void, which is typical of traumatic historical change and melodrama.

By melodrama I mean, in Peter Brooks's footsteps, a mode intended to acknowledge that something sacred or original or ideal has been forever lost. Melodrama, therefore, cherishes impossible values to compensate for this trauma, while it is capable of meditating on public experience only in personal terms. In other words, *Red Desert* is an existential melodrama that suggests an evaluation of how far Italian society has come since the end of World War II in its pursuit of modernity and technology.

To someone familiar with Antonioni's rejection of facile plot lines, with one coup de théâtre leading into the next, or to someone aware of the director's tendency to undo narrative development into *temps morts*, waiting and duration, the label "melodrama" may seem wholly inappropriate for *Red Desert*. Furthermore, the allusion to the legacy of postwar neorealist cinema at the beginning of the film may also discourage the association of *Red Desert* with a melodramatic mode. Yet neorealist cinema, just like melodrama, is characterized by a certain muteness, since for its construction of character it relies more on gesture and mimicry, on landscape and architecture, than it does on dialogue and introspection.

The painful clash of old and new that Antonioni analyzes in *Red Desert* using Ravenna's periphery as an allegory for Italian society, finds an appropriate channel of expression in the director's use of color. As a nonverbal element of the mise-en-scène invested with a poignancy that well fits the radicalized polarities of an old order dying and a new system about to be born, color in *Red Desert* makes up the "text of muteness" that Peter Brooks finds to be typical of melodrama, a mode concerned with those "extreme moral and emotional conditions" that, I would add, always characterize historical change.

To sum up, besides making a case for *Red Desert* as a melodrama concerned with historical change and psychological transformation, the purpose of this chapter is twofold: to explain that Antonioni's allegiance to both painting and architecture in his cinema is predicated on the battle of the sexes; and to argue that Antonioni's visual ventriloquism through Monica Vitti in *Red Desert* is both experimental and exploitative, for while he uses his actress's eyes to work innovatively with color in film, her power resides more in the muteness of the images she shares with the director than in the dialogue. Put another way, from an artistic point of view the word is less daring than the image, yet Giuliana's impact on the world is limited by the alignment of the dialogue with a masculine perspective.

Although other critics before me have argued how Antonioni's cinema is torn between a fear of the future and a dissatisfaction with the past, my discussion strives to show how in *Red Desert* Antonioni on one hand needs a woman's vision to experiment with painting and abstraction, while on the other, by linking color to muteness and femininity, he pushes his female protagonist away from technology and verbal assertion into a primitive and speechless realm. It is precisely because the director's project is so contradictory and multilayered that *Red Desert* is not only a melodrama but also a film tinged with a baroque sensibility.

Giuliana's and Ugo's antithetical personalities, besides reiterating the struggle between art and technology, can also be said to repeat the well-known opposition between modernism, with its penchant for ordered rationalism, and the baroque, with its rejection of closure and fixity. By honoring a certain madness of vision, and by celebrating the dazzling, disorienting, ecstatic surplus of images, and by expressing intense emotion through coloristic impressions, the baroque in *Red Desert* underpins all the pieces of the puzzle: Giuliana's illness, Antonioni's striving for creativity, and the stereotypical association of femininity with excess.

By decrying the loss of pure values, melodrama is a modern form that idealizes the past or an ahistorical realm of unattainable ideals, such as the defeat of evil and death by innocence and love, whereas the baroque, although invented to promote the status quo and seduce with a plethora of discontinuous and curvilinear effects, has an open-ended quality that points toward the future. One may wonder, however, how these two modes can coexist in the same film. As we learn from Brooks, melodrama originates from the ashes of the French Revolution. By contrast, the baroque is a program of restoration to prevent a revolution rather than a post-revolutionary response to a traumatic experience. It is because melodrama and the baroque offer an oppositional but complementary orientation to the historical process that Antonioni can interlace the battle of the sexes in *Red Desert* with the tension between old and new, by situating color right in the middle, ranging from melodramatic muteness to baroque sinuosity, so that color is the element that marks the strange circularity of futurism and primitivism.

THE CHALLENGE OF HISTORICAL CHANGE

In *Red Desert* Antonioni stages the clash of old and new, especially through the interplay of history and geography and through his use of objects and decors. One could argue that Antonioni has found the iconography of this staging in the paintings of Giorgio De Chirico. One sequence in particular looks like a whole canvas by De Chirico: The deserted, gray street where Giuliana plans to open a store winds up into a claustrophobic rather than empowering vanishing point. Meanwhile an abandoned sheet of newspaper is blown along the pavement, bearing witness to the banality of time. Nearby a self-absorbed old vendor stands next to a cart covered with whitish fruits that loom like someone's mementos.

In De Chirico's paintings, the train of technology is allowed to run only on the borders of piazze punctuated by monuments and arcades, which transform a very theatrical space into a site of archeological investigation. In *Red Desert*, as the credits roll on the screen, a thick fog envelops the industrial skyline of Ravenna, where high-rises recall the elongated shape of medieval towers. Likewise, the workers on strike wear transparent raincoats, which make them resemble Hieronymus Bosch's frantic but also fragile figures in an allegory about damnation. Thus images of contemporary social turmoil slip back into ancient icons of mankind's plight between heaven and hell, the skies above and the abysses of the earth. In a sense Ravenna's modern look is only one side of an environment slipping back into the past, much in the same manner that Giuliana dreams of herself sinking into quicksand during a restless night. In a similar fashion, De Chirico's iconography oscillates between the tall, dark chimneys of factories and the equestrian statues of innumerable ancient Italian towns.

Such a precarious placement between old and new also characterizes the parallel Antonioni establishes between Italy and Patagonia, a virgin land at the end of the globe where Corrado wants to start a cutting-edge industrial enterprise. As he stands in front of a blue, green, and yellow map whose color scheme meaningfully repeats the juxtaposition of natural and artificial waste in Giuliana's neighborhood, Corrado coolly explains to the workers what their work in Patagonia will entail. Antonioni's camera slowly surveys these nameless men's weathered faces, which silently remind us of the scorching sun in southern Italy, of painful immigration stories, and of neorealist cinema's reliance on physiognomy. Finally, the workers" questions about details of daily life in the new land reveal that even the most radical geographical displacement can hardly lighten their baggage of memories, attitudes, and habits concerning women, leisure time, and family.

Antonioni's ambivalent stance between technological rebirth and nostalgia for a natural past plays itself out in geographical terms through one more episode – a fairy tale Giuliana tells her son, Valerio, one morning when the child says he cannot move his legs. Valerio's paralysis can be read as a psychosomatic response to an excess of technology. Just like the child who is not in control of his legs and freezes into a sort of inorganic immobility, the adults are so out of touch with their emotions that during the party in the red shack they engage in futile gossip until the arrival of an ominous ship releases a chain of repressed emotions ranging from fear to loneliness, from desperation to rejection.

The setting of Giuliana's fairy tale is a deserted island, off the coast of Sardinia in the Mediterranean, the same sea that witnessed De Chirico's childhood in Greece and nourished his eerily sunlit museological settings. In this enchanted place, a girl happily swims, plays with the birds, and explores the huge anthropomorphic rocks of the beach. In contrast to the foggy opening sequence in Ravenna, on the fantasy island the horizon is open, the air is filled with light, each shade of color breathes along with the reverberations of the sea. Even if it stems from Giuliana's imagination, this virgin landscape is far less hallucinatory than the documentary images of Ravenna's industrial area that Antonioni offers us at the beginning of the film.

In comparison with the red desert of postwar Italy, the pink beach appears to be the perfect site for a recovery of humanity according to natural laws. The innocence of the girl suggests a perfect unity between body and landscape, even though the huge rocks, with curvilinear, gigantic contours, stand like arcane presences. Their prodigious size implies that the price for this organic fusion might be, after all, a certain loss of humanity, or at least a regression into the darkest times, when only gods and giants and not human beings ruled. Furthermore, Antonioni's island, as beautiful as it may be, is somewhat conventional. The pink sand and the blue-green sea recall the perfect pictures advertising a hidden paradise for a vacation in a travel brochure. Since the island cannot quite belong to the mediocre present, but only to a mythical past, it can only deceive humans, soothing them with a certain longing for a primitive origin that was never entirely their own.

A song without words performed by a female voice floats over the industrial landscape of the credit sequence and the beautiful beach of Giuliana's fairy tale. In the island scenes the voice grows out of the rocks; it is full of desire, as if it belonged to an ancient soul forever imprisoned in the stone but still striving to reach out. In the credit sequence, the voice is so melodious that it seems full of corporeal abandon. This half-human, half-divine voice follows a mixture of industrial noises, whose calculated dissonance is reminiscent of Futurist concerts where traditional instruments are replaced or accompanied by the sounds of technology. Needless to say, Antonioni's combination of melodic singing and the jazzlike, discontinuous music of Giovanni Fusco points not only to the melodramatic nature of *Red Desert* but also to its baroque integration of emptiness and fullness, of jagged outlines and round volumes. And the baroque sensibility is involved with the effort of transition, with the painful breaking through of new forms out of old molds.

By setting references to De Chirico's art next to Futurist music, Antonioni reminds us that these two branches of the Italian avant-garde at the beginning of the twentieth century became a foil, one for the other, in that they explored the painful but also exhilarating impact of technology in a society that lagged behind other European countries in its progress toward modernity.

After all, De Chirico's puppetlike intruders in his airless piazze are nothing but the other side of F. T. Marinetti's mechanical man, whose direct descendant we encounter in the toy robot moving up and down Valerio's room and interrupting Giuliana's natural sleep. Through allusions to the Futurists and De Chirico, Antonioni sets up a middle ground of art and industry, nature and technology, which allows him to associate the objects and the decors of *Red Desert* with the great tradition of industrial design in Italy – a practice which, just like this director's cinema, combines an ancient aesthetic sensibility with a daring penchant for innovation.

According to Andrea Branzi in *Learning from Milan*, industrial design is a tradition especially intertwined with the contradictions of delayed industrialization in Italy. In Fortunato Depero's and Giacomo Balla's workshops of applied art, "it was more a question of applying the Futurist code to reality than genuine design activities. In short, the idea of producing on an industrial scale was totally absent."

How do we explain, then, the flourishing of design during the postwar economic boom that surrounds the making of *Red Desert*? As the historian Fernand Braudel would say, Milanese stylists have capitalized on "the advantage of delay." It is appropriate, therefore, for Antonioni to mix a high-tech look with antique pieces of furniture in Giuliana's apartment, since *Red Desert* is a film about the impact of technology upon a society not quite accustomed to it. Likewise, natural plants sit on the old-fashioned table of a worker's apartment. This domestic space, in turn, is situated in a building whose street entrance spells out high-tech, rationalist values. This mixing of old and new characterizes Giuliana's taste in clothes as well. As she speaks to Corrado in her newly painted store, she wears a formless, handmade country shawl on top of a svelte urban outfit.

While Valerio's bedroom is cluttered with mechanical toys and the den where the child plays with his father resembles a scientific lab for experiments in physics and chemistry, Giuliana and Ugo's bedroom includes a rococo chest and some upholstered mahogany chairs. Thus the aseptic, nearly chilling atmosphere of the upper-floor landing where Giuliana seeks refuge during a sleepless night – with metallic, tubular railings and long, rectangular windows – blends in with a few collector's items that spell out the economic power of a social class used to purchases from antique dealers. In contrast to Giuliana and Ugo's taste for a few precious, old pieces set amid rather barren, pristine white walls, within an infrastructure of opaque glass doors, the apartment of the worker whom Corrado would like to recruit for Patagonia is a darker but also much warmer space.

The building where the worker lives with his family is so modern that its blue, green, and yellow walls in the internal courtyard preceding the silvery and Plexiglas lobby seem to defy our expectations for solid volumes, with an orchestration of flat panels veering toward a traditional Japanese architectural taste. This modern beginning, however, is quickly superseded as soon as Giuliana and Corrado stand in front of a thick wooden door, from behind which the worker's wife emerges wearing a traditional black dress underneath a bright red apron, which she embarrassedly takes off. The comfortable but outmoded furniture of the worker's apartment well fits the wife's opposition to the possibility that her husband will leave his family to pursue profit and a career in Patagonia.

On one hand, the wife's apron signals the worker's dependence on the factory, where red, yellow, and dark blue, as primary colors, announce the birth of a new epoch. On the other hand, the worker and the woman who show up at the red shack during the party wear black and brown, the muted colors of the dying landscape. Even if Max, one of Ugo's colleagues, crassly questions his employee on sexual technique, the episode's conclusion – with the working-class couple walking in the winter fog with nowhere to go on a Sunday afternoon – suggests that a sense of desolation and emotional disorientation pervades everybody's life, regardless of level of income.

THE BATTLE OF THE SEXES

That heavy industrialization has had a deeply psychological impact on sexual roles, well beyond superficial class adjustments, becomes especially clear as soon as we compare two episodes of *Red Desert* that raise once again the question of how much interior design mirrors a changing sense of self.

In Giuliana's newly painted store, where she hopes to start a career as an independent businesswoman, the ceiling is green and the walls are light blue. Through color she has inverted the predictable scheme of sky and earth, of mind and body, and thus, thanks to her willingness to experiment, she has distanced herself from that stereotypical association of the ground with the womb, of femininity with nature, which always seems to place her in opposition to the world of science, factories, and cerebral coolness.

Giuliana's unconventional placement of colors, however, is not enough to dispel the aura of helplessness that surrounds her. She wavers in deciding on the type of merchandise she should sell, and neither does she seem capable of using the telephone to organize her business. By contrast, at the beginning of *Red Desert*, to help his colleague Corrado, Ugo relies heavily on a series of quick phone calls to gather the names of workers to be sent to Patagonia.

Giuliana is so afraid of crossing the line between old and new, of transgressing, that Antonioni repeatedly shows characters standing behind grids, which either enclose them in their obsessions or isolate them from each other. One element of the mise-en-scène especially captures Giuliana's endless wavering between liberation and resignation. A mysterious vessel that the girl in the fantasy island sees from afar promises adventure, whereas the cargo ship that stops by the red shack, flying a yellow flag to signal an epidemic on board, stands out as the symbol of a society plagued by unknown diseases.

Giuliana's constant touching of objects and fabrics, her testing of the solidity of the ground on which she walks, and her lingering footsteps on the newspaper that lands between her and the enigmatic street vendor suggest a tactile, regressive orientation, an instinctive probing for what is visceral, arcane, and below. Significantly, for Pier Paolo Pasolini, *Red Desert* was an excellent example of the "cinema of poetry," because Antonioni's stylistic liberty with the medium signaled that underneath the film there was another irrational film, one "that springs from cinema's deepest, and most essential, poetic sub-stratum."

This drive toward hidden, unconscious forces, however, is not antithetical to her interest in a group of huge radio towers, which like magic antennas stretch across the sky, listening to the voice of the stars. These towers signify escape, perhaps through voyages into the unknown reaches of outer space, but however futuristic they may seem, they look like skeletons of prehistoric monsters.

In contrast to Ugo and Corrado, Giuliana truly inhabits a no-man's land, an in-between region where the garbage of civilization mingles with the earth and propels its cycles forward; at the same time, the landscape exercises a strange pull on her, to the point of inhibiting her progress. In the red shack, she cannot take her eyes off the movement of the waves in the sea, as if their constant reconfiguring were symptomatic of her flexibility and openness toward the future but also of her inability to hold on to a well-defined identity.

This is perhaps why Antonioni insists on framing Giuliana in compositions that are highly self-conscious about the dialectic of figure and ground. Such an approach harks back to the tradition of Renaissance painting in which the body is a unit of measure of the architectural surroundings, and in Arrowsmith's words, it also conveys "her fear of separation – of being cut away from a landscape, from the past, from the 'ground' of her own being."

Unlike Giuliana, who is caught between the sky and the ground, Corrado has once and for all abandoned his work in geology, and in the aftermath of his father's death, he is much keener on building tall silos in Patagonia. This drastic change in career calls attention to Corrado's desire to pass on a masculine legacy under the auspices of science between himself and Valerio. It also marks the triumphs of the superego and of paternal authority at the expense of more libidinal energies, which the frequent outpourings of smoke from the factory's boilers barely manage to discharge. Despite all his vertical yearnings, Corrado can engage only in a directionless survey of the Italian territory, as he keeps changing city, from Trieste to Bologna, from Milan to Ravenna.

Although Ugo, as a male, lives much more in the public sphere than his wife, he is hardly aware of the historical transformations – big and small – occurring around him. When Giuliana has her car accident, he ignores the event and chooses not to return from London to Ravenna. Unlike his wife, who declares to Corrado that were she obliged to leave, she would take everything and every-body with her, Ugo is inclined to dismiss the past with indifference. He despises Giuliana because she keeps wearing the same old pair of shoes, while he allows an old hut on the riverbank to go to ruin, with little regard for a vivid picture of wild zebras on one of the walls.

In contrast to that form of mural art, which is reminiscent of the prehistoric cave graffiti discovered at Lascaux, Ugo is far removed from the deep, primitive, emotional core of his being. This is certainly not the case with Giuliana, who is the only one to experience the aphrodisiac effect of the quail eggs eaten during the party in the red shack. Ugo's metaphors about Giuliana's difficult recovery after the accident all depend on his technological training, as if his wife were a machine incapable of functioning despite several attempts at repair. Regardless of all his futuristic ideas, Ugo clings to old-fashioned views about the role of women in society and finds distasteful his wife's intention of starting her own business.

It is also true, however, that Ugo has an exploratory, creative side, even if his curiosity is strictly limited to science. With the help of a yellow toy, Ugo introduces Valerio to the gyroscope, a mechanism that allows ships to keep their balance during storms. Were we to compare the effects of heavy industrialization to a sea storm, we would conclude that to resist the waves, holding onto a reflective stance, is Antonioni's intellectual ambition. This is why at the end of *Red Desert*, when Giuliana is dressed very much as she was at the beginning of the film, as if hardly anything had really changed, she delivers a statement of acceptance from the standpoint of Antonioni's alliance with Ugo in the name of technology. In answering Valerio's question about the danger a poisonous yellow flame represents for birds, she simply concludes that natural life has to adjust to technological conditions. Somehow her words stressing compromise are at odds with the radical nature of her vision, one that suggests no mediation, but traumatic change.

Precisely because the director seals his story as a true ventriloquist by speaking through the body of his main actress, *Red Desert* is punctuated by many confrontations between the sexes. When Ugo tries to soothe Giuliana during a nocturnal crisis, they are both wearing white pajamas. While their similar outfits contribute to a desexualization of the couple, as spectators we cannot help wondering whether this visual echo between male and female at the level of clothing is nothing but Antonioni's projection of a utopian time of togetherness beyond sexual difference. Still, Ugo looks helpless in front of Giuliana's desperation, and his words make him sound more like a reassuring father than a companion on an equal footing.

Despite its obvious transgressive nature, even Giuliana's affair with Corrado ends with a disappointing return to the status quo, namely a lack of productive communication between men and women, one so extreme that Giuliana's attempt to talk with a Turkish sailor who cannot understand her is paradoxically more satisfying. To this foreign listener she can fully express her evaluation of how far she has come in the struggle to change her life. This is not to say that at least for a while she does not view Corrado as a catalyst for transformation. In fact, when the two embrace in his hotel room, Vitti's acting reaches a peak of protean effort, an extreme of discontinuities at the level of posture and gesture, to the point that her erratic, curvilinear, ever-shifting silhouette reminds us of the contortions performed by the divas of silent melodramas. In a sense, Vitti is Antonioni's diva, for *Red Desert* is a historical melodrama about the female condition, which captures a woman's ambition and ends with her containment.

Finally, this aura of ambiguity hovering over Giuliana's progress is echoed on the fantasy island, where the young girl, cut away as she is from the world of adults and the company of people her own age, seems to enjoy an unparalleled degree of freedom. Her life truly unfolds outside the demands of sexual awakening. This interpretation stems from the girl's decision to remove the top of her bathing suit, thus staging a self-image of androgyny. When the mysterious vessel appears, an icon of civilization disturbing a perfectly un-contaminated landscape, it overlays the theme of impurity onto a female sexuality still in search of self-expression. Thus, after the failure of Giuliana's affair with Corrado and the limitations of her marriage with Ugo, Antonioni's film ends by asking the viewer to contemplate only one possible strong couple: that of mother and child.

26

TRANSFORMATIONS IN FASSBINDER'S
BITTER TEARS OF PETRA VON KANT

Timothy Corrigan

That Rainer Werner Fassbinder is at once the most prolific of the New German directors and the most controversial of the group has a significantly causal relationship: the very rate at which Fassbinder makes films, along with the rapid changes of subject and style, alone is enough to alienate and confound viewers who, at a more leisurely pace, might accustom themselves to perspectives and materials which are deceptively difficult to grasp.

[...]

Fassbinder's films, in short, provoke, and this provocation may be far more important to cinema's rapport with its audience today than at any other time.

The nature of this provocation is, however, the elusive question, again bringing to the forefront the problem of audience and the relationship that Fassbinder's films have with that audience. Most importantly this relationship can not be tied to an ideal conception of the spectator, nor to a similarly static notion of Fassbinder's films. For, unlike Godard, Fassbinder does not aim to return to a utopian zero ground in order to create a new cinematic viewer as he creates a new cinematic syntax. Rather, like many of his German colleagues, Fassbinder has a decided sense of the historicity of his audience, German and otherwise, and he develops the formal and thematic features of his film in accordance with that knowledge. From Fassbinder's position, the point is not to convince viewers of the sophistication and depth of his own mind and politics but to motivate the

From: Timothy Corrigan, 'Transformations in Fassbinder's *Bitter Tears of Petra von Kant*', in *New German Film: The Displaced Image* (Indiana University Press, 1994).

viewer's own emotions and thought along a syntactical path that is accessible to emotional comprehension. Filmic revolution is, for him, an insidious affair.

Obviously the much documented love affair that Fassbinder has had with the films of the German-bred Sirk and other American directors derives in large part from this notion of filmmaking and its demand to communicate with an audience that, in most Western countries, has been weaned on Hollywood tropes. As he says in a 1971 interview, "American cinema is the only one I can take really seriously, because it's the only one that has really reached an audience. German cinema used to do so, before 1933 . . . But American cinema has generally had the happiest relationship with its audience . . . Our films have been based on our *understanding* of the American cinema." In other words, as Fassbinder remarks in his celebrated article on Sirk, "the main thing to be learned from American films was the need to meet their entertainment factor halfway. The idea is to make films as beautiful as America's, but which at the same time shift the content to other areas."

Fassbinder came gradually to this awareness that good politics are incidental without effective avenues of communication, his strategies moving through intellectual phases associated with Straub, the "anti-theater," and the French New Wave. Yet ultimately, with the assistance of his extraordinary cameraman Michael Ballhaus, he allied himself with the American cinema so that they could use its highly developed and proficient syntax to subvert its ideologically unsuspecting perspective. Through his manipulation and intellectual transformation of the Hollywood idiom – from the early seventies to his latest commercial successes, such as *The Marriage of Maria Braun*, *Veronika Voss*, and *Berlin Alexanderplatz*, Fassbinder's efforts have been, as he claims, "to learn how to show viewers the things they don't want to see in such a way that they *will* watch because it's excitingly made."

No Fassbinder film demonstrates these strategies and the problematic response that they have generated better than *The Bitter Tears of Petra von Kant*, a film which appears late in Fassbinder's Hollywood phase and which makes use of what becomes one of the defining marks of his films during this period: Sirkian melodrama transformed into critical kitsch or camp, use of popular entertainment formulas but with critical, self-conscious distance. Midway through the film, Fassbinder underlines this not at all facile use of basic emotional formulas when the relatively uncultured Karin says to Petra: "Oh yes, I love the cinema. Seeing pictures about love and suffering. Lovely." The phrase sparkles with a multifaceted irony, most particularly since this is exactly the kind of film *The Bitter Tears of Petra von Kant* is. Yet Fassbinder's film of course becomes more than this: his is also a film about the way individuals relate cinematically amidst those central experiences of love and suffering, and so the film doubles back on itself. Whereas Karin can respond enthusiastically to that fundamental pleasure of the filmic text, Fassbinder's film is an extremely disconcerting attempt to move the viewer to a point where he or she can not only respond on that level but can also examine the murky middle ground where cinema and social life confuse the clarity of each other's communications. "I don't believe that melodramatic feelings are laughable," Fassbinder has remarked; from his semi-Brechtian perspective on those melodramatic formulas comes his critical camp, his mixture of surface art and real emotions.

This confusion of the cinematic and the social that Fassbinder puts in play in this film accounts to a large degree for the outcries it has drawn from nearly every sexual group with enough political sensitivity to react to the volatile issues that Fassbinder raises. Fassbinder's films are not mimetic; nor are they examples of social realism or utopian politics. They are, rather, relational mergers of different surfaces which do their work along the circuit that makes social reality itself a product of the psychoanalytic identifications that cinema initiates. Missing this relationship, a viewer finds inaccurate distortions where Fassbinder would say there are only distortions. Or put another way: if Fassbinder regularly uses transparently bourgeois figures, it is because these are the figures and images that bourgeois and nonbourgeois audiences alike have been trained to understand and enjoy. To alter ideas structured on these images, moreover, a filmmaker does little good in refusing the mechanisms of his audience's understanding but instead must manipulate those mechanisms toward a new understanding. Hence, as Judith Mayne observes, the crucial import of Fassbinder's use of Hollywood melodrama is that it "invites a consideration of the social significance of popular culture and the extent to which the entertainment factor can function in a critical way."

Like Wenders then, Fassbinder situates his films in an American tradition and employs a high degree of critical reflexivity to mark his distance from that tradition. Yet, whereas *Kings of the Road* uses a realistic surface to tell the tale of two men and their wandering encounter with their own identities, *Petra von Kant* is a film of claustrophobic pessimism in which a lesbian couple substitutes for the standard heterosexual drama. Both films confront the threadbare cliché of the happy or normal family of American films. Yet, conversely, the two films appear as nearly inversions of each other not only in their contrasting use of sexes and space but, most notably, in the relations that the films establish between themselves and a pro-filmic reality: while *Kings of the Road* seeks to introduce new filmic relations by short-circuiting the closed circle that describes the perspective of classical cinema, *Petra von Kant* turns inward to trace the exploitative grip that cinematic posturing has on life. That *Petra von Kant* is so radically insular does not of course mean that it is any less engaged with a social and political audience than *King of the Road*: the exaggerated isolation of this drama is – as with all Fassbinder films and as much as with any film in this study – a function of a complex horizon of historical expectations which have their center in the Hollywood subject but which also include a number of social formulations of a specifically German kind. Of these, there is most particularly the crisis of a social self in Germany as it developed out of the mass spectacle of the Third Reich, through the economic miracle of Adenauer's laissez-faire fifties, to its present condition where it remains haunted and divided by those past constitutions of self. Seen in this context, *Petra von Kant* consequently becomes, in the very irony of its negations and omissions, as much a social and historical statement as any other Fassbinder film: a *Lola* without an explicit description of the street politics, a *Maria Braun* without the larger history of her economic progress to the insulated and fragile home of the final scenes. While both *Kings of the Road* and *Petra von Kant* serve, in short, as historical critiques of film's tyrannical power over perception and descriptions of the problem of identity in modern Germany, *Petra von Kant* argues this point not so much in the discursive or essayistic fashion of *Kings of the Road* but through an exaggerated style and decor which delineate the internal mechanics of the problem while not textually opening it (as Wenders often attempts to do). In this way, Fassbinder's pessimism becomes a pessimism of base content only, his negations traces of historical positives: for, in presenting that negative content, Fassbinder's stylized irony works ultimately to deflect and reflect its emotional pessimism and social isolation to a level which allows an understanding of those emotions and a clear view of those missing historical landscapes.

In *The Bitter Tears of Petra von Kant*, this work begins with the content itself, where those common cinematic motifs of love and suffering are displaced from a heterosexual couple to a lesbian one. Beginning with this switch in a Hollywood formula, the story then proceeds in a quite unremarkable way. Petra von Kant, a successful designer of women's fashions, lives with her servant-lover Marlene. Once married, Petra has rejected that way of life and men in general, because of the exploitation and oppression that marriage and capitalistic sexual relations engender. In the second of the six sections of the film, Petra meets Karin, with whom she falls passionately in love, only to be abandoned by her at the end of the fourth section when Karin returns to her husband. The final sections describe Petra's complete breakdown and her last attempt to reconcile with the hitherto ignored Marlene. At this point, Marlene leaves.

In terms of audience expectations, the story itself is formulaic, with the important exception that the players of the melodrama are lesbian, a minority group generally ignored by films. In addition to this ripple in the standard Hollywood situation, moreover, the film entwines within the love story several long and self-dramatizing conversations that abstract and underline the important role that political economy plays in the usually foregrounded loves and desires of the characters. Early in the film, for example, Sidonie visits Petra to console her about the collapse of her marriage. In a dialogue that could serve as a subtext for the entire film, Petra explains how the relationship deteriorated, beginning by dispelling Sidonie's conventional expectation that the husband asked for the divorce or that adultery was involved. When Sidonie reproaches her for lacking humility and failing to use feminine wile, Petra snaps back: "I had no time for conjuring tricks. It only makes you unfree ... It's all very well for you and Lester. Maybe this lack of freedom is just what you need ... Frank and I wanted a higher love ... We wanted to be free, awake, know what's going on at all times ... We wanted to be happy together ... You understand: *together*." This romantic ideal of clarity and understanding begins, however, to turn to disgust when male dominance asserts itself through its principal vehicle, economics. "Men and their vanity," Petra complains; "He wanted to molly-coddle me and see I lacked nothing ... He wanted to be the breadwinner ... That way lies oppression, that's clear." In a patriarchal society, she says, there are two sets of rules, and her own financial success made these painfully apparent: "at first, it was: all you earn, my girl, will be put on one side; later on we can use it to buy a house, a sportscar ... At first, it was funny seeing his ridiculous pride being pricked, especially when I thought for sure he realized how absurdly he behaved ... And later when I tried to tell him that it made no difference who was on top or not, it was too late."

Economic resentment becomes sexual resentment, her husband's failure to control her financially resulting in a desperate attempt to dominate her physically. Sexual and economic exploitation merge, and while glossing over the economic dimension, Petra reacts bitterly against the sexual exploitation and abuse:

> The last six months were excruciating. He obviously saw it was all over, felt it at least, but wouldn't accept it ... He tried to keep the wife, if not wholly, then in bed. I let him possess me, I bore it ... That man was filth to me. He stank, stank like a man. What had once its charms now turned my stomach, brought tears to my eyes ... The way he bestraddled me, he served me like a bull would a cow. Not the slightest respect, no feeling for a woman's pleasure. The pain, Sidonie, you can't imagine ...

The honesty of this description and the reality of the suffering behind it should not be doubted. Yet, at the same time, Fassbinder sets in motion around this verbal discourse a complex series of visual and narrative qualifiers, which clearly reestablish its significance. Much in the fashion of the majority of his films, *Petra von Kant* offers a rather fundamental premise about love, need, and exploitation in a capitalistic society, and so exposes itself to the often facile criticism that the film itself is facile. Yet, the film then goes on to achieve its particular density by ironically layering that base theme again and again, in this way becoming an analysis and critical exposition of the surface predicament itself. Petra's long denunciation of men and description of the pain they have caused her is accordingly tangled through the course of the film in a larger visual and psychological drama which, in recontextualizing Petra and her dialogue, shows her (and all the other women in the film for that matter) exploiting and degrading women in the same manner that a male-dominated society and its cinema does.

Most explicitly, the film exposes the bombastic and indefatigable theatrics of Petra's personal and professional relationships. Elsaesser has rightly recognized these histrionics as a recurring element in Fassbinder's films, and notes that what results from Fassbinder's perspective on them is a "sometimes terrifying and often grotesque distance between the subjective *mise-en-scène* of the characters and the objective *mise-en-scène* of the camera."

[...]

The camera's first encounter with Petra begins on this note. After the credit sequence, during which the camera holds on the base of the darkened steps which lead down into the room, it tracks slowly across the wall-sized reproduction of mythically scaled nudes to the shadowy figure of the sleeping Petra. Light suddenly floods the body, and Petra awakes and quickly telephones her mother, saying, "Mother, I had no time yesterday ... No, I've been up for ages." She then turns, looks directly into the close-up angle, smiles, and insists, "It's true!" While this lie is ostensibly for the mother, the camera work and direction are clearly for the audience, turning to grotesque mockery the played reality that the audience observes, severing the theatrics of Petra from a perspective on them, yet concomitantly assuring the spectator's complicity in the act. The audience and Petra, in brief, have the advantage of their privileged positions.

The theatrics gain momentum from this point on. Petra's first act after she leaves the bed is to don one of her many wigs and elaborate dressing robes. Her second phone call (to the department store Karstadt) is another hypocritical ruse; during her long monologue with Sidonie, the camera focuses on the preciously tiresome process of making up her face as if for a performance. These painstakingly exaggerated warm-ups then culminate in the third section of the film when Petra and Karin confront each other in outlandish Wagnerian costumes and perform a dance-like ritual of seduction and melodramatic intimacy. It is here that Karin expresses her love of the cinema, and it is here that theatrics and cinema blend most effectively in stylized movements of emotion and manipulation, more like Brechtian "gests" than naturalistic gestures. In the final moments of this sequence, Petra tells Karin, "I can see you now parading in public ... I'll make a first class model of you, Karin ... You're beautiful, Karin." And as she convinces Karin to move in with her because "it's cheaper," the statement coincides neatly with the climax of their mutual seduction through sex, theatrics, and economics. The scene as spectacle thus becomes, in Judith Mayne's words, a quintessential "guise through which the commodity form permeates social relationships," a theatrics of sexual reification.

The most salient sign of this reifying conjunction of theater, economics, and sex is Petra's profession itself. As a fashion designer, she markets appearances, self-images made through clothing; the success of that marketing is appropriately the product of sexual appeal and financial interest. In short, she sells sexual images and does it with a great deal of success. Visually the film is punctuated from beginning to end by the tools of this trade – Marlene working with fabric, the mannequins, and so forth – so that as Petra and Karin work in the foreground at their sexual relationship, the business of desire superimposes on the business of design in the background. Both occupations must purvey a more or less fantastic image to a client; both subsist on the repeated and persistent cycle of production-consumption, the underpinning of a capitalist culture. To emphasize this last point, eating and drinking (the elemental and natural art of production and consumption) take place only on the bed, which is also the place where Petra makes her business calls, makes love, and gives work orders to Marlene.

While this business of theatrics has an obvious and neat correlation with the business of cinema, two other central motifs have a perhaps less obvious but equally significant connection with the film mechanism itself: nostalgia and dreams. Of these two, nostalgia interrupts the action regularly, and it thus contributes most strikingly to the confusion of temporal spheres in the film. Shortly after telephoning her mother, for instance, Petra plays the fifties recording of "Smoke Gets in Your Eyes" by the Platters, while she dances in a circle with Marlene. The reverie it inspires is repeated at the end of the film's second section when she plays the Walker Brothers" "In My Room" for Karin, and then comments: "... records from my past. They either make me very sad ... or very happy." That these two instances (along with the Platters' song which ends the film) are American tunes from the postwar years is clearly not insignificant. But, more importantly, they and the parade of period costumes that the various characters wear signal an entrapment in memories which muddle and blur any sort of historical perspective which might lead to self-knowledge. After Petra's comment about her inconsistent emotional reaction to old records, she drifts into a memory of her former husband, and, with her new lover standing before her, she ironically remarks on the inescapable cruelty that emotions perpetrate and which she will soon become the victim of: "That was romance ... Pierre was killed in a car. He loved driving. He thought he was immortal, but wasn't ... Yet everything is predestined in life, I'm convinced ... People are terrible, Karin. They can bear anything ... anything. People are hard and brutal. They don't need anyone ... That's the lesson." For Petra, however, these very words suggest it is a lesson unlearned again and again through the alternating periods of her life.

This tragicomic inability to distinguish time and experiences and thus to escape the bitter circle of love and suffering appears most dramatically in the second and third parts of the film. Stylistically and structurally the two parts parallel each other along anchoring points such as the elegant poses of Petra and Sidonie later reenacted by Petra and Karin. Likewise, there are the long monologues which form the core of each episode, in the first Petra telling of the collapse of her marriage, in the second Karin recounting her childhood and adolescence. Petra, moreover, delivers a small speech on humility in each of these sections, the second mirroring and reversing the first according to a pattern which describes the course of the entire film: first, she rebukes Sidonie's belief that humility is the key to a successful relationship; later she mildly urges that same humility on Karin. "You have to learn humility," she explains. "Everyone has his own theory of the world ... I believe you have to be humble to bear better what you comprehend. I'm humble before my work – and the money I earn ... In the face of things stronger than myself." These reversals outline the part-ludicrous, part-tragic pattern of the whole film through which Petra changes her stance to suit her desires: her nostalgic desire for what might have been (those "wonderful chances for that man and me" of her first marriage) forces her to switch her roles and her realities rapidly, and thus to become trapped again and again in the oppressor/victim cycle of sexual desires. This is most evident in Petra's chaotic movement through her sexual oppression by males, her dominating of Karin in part 3, Karin's exploitation of her in part 4, and finally Petra's offering of a new start to Marlene at the conclusion of the film, an offer which actually means a return to the state of the relationship at the beginning of the film. Stuck in a reality which is fundamentally nostalgic and hence utopian, Petra must act out her desire repeatedly in the bombastic terms of a grand soap opera, the artificial pomp of the gestures thus masking the flat redundance of the meaning. When Petra and Karin first meet, both comment that "nothing much can change in Germany." Similarly, while Petra views her history and future only from the perspective of her libidinal longings, her temporal reality stalls in nostalgia, the immobile voyage of cinema itself.

These longings and moments of nostalgia naturally manifest themselves as kinds of waking dreams in *Petra von Kant*, thus adding another layer to those central motifs of theatrics, nostalgia, and a film economics whose business is to manufacture dreams. Petra's first statement in the film is "Marlene, have some consideration ... I've had such awful dreams," which ironically signals her awakening into a world she will people with equally awful dreams. Later, after Karin arrives for her date with Petra, Petra begins her inquiry into Karin's past by saying, "tell me about yourself ... what you dream of." Petra then sets out to fulfill those dreams of Karin, "to make something of [her] life" by transforming her into a "first-class model," the dream-image of both their desires. Finally, Petra's profession itself is a fairly transparent case of an occupation that sells dreams through appearances, and its obtrusive economic base begins to suggest more strongly the crucial connection between Petra, the designer, and Fassbinder, the filmmaker, whose business is likewise the purveying of dreams through appearances and images.

The connection exists, in fact, at the film's center: just as the theatrical costumes that pervade the film as manifestations of the individual's dreams seem anarchically nostalgic (recalling without much order a mélange of different historical periods), the cinema itself relies on a manipulation of time apart from the actual present and makes its meaning through the reworking of filmic types and characters that originate in different historical eras. Indeed, establishing this correlation between Petra's temporal and imagistic disorder and filmmaking is, on the one hand, Fassbinder's usual attempt at self-criticism, seen in many of his films from *Beware of a Holy Whore* to *Germany in Autumn*. Yet, on the other hand and more importantly, this correlation allows Fassbinder the distance needed to investigate and criticize at once the dynamics of a personality such as Petra's and the dynamics of a traditional cinema whose internal and external workings are the mirror reflection of that personality. In *Petra von Kant* the story of the loneliness and need that drive an individual to manipulate a personal history by means of artificial images becomes a descriptive figure and demonstration of a psychoanalytic and cinematic apparatus, which exploits desire with images, and especially images of women.

[...]

That these desires, exploitations, and delusions are so explicitly bound here to that cinematic figure of the circle and the specular giants associated with the filmic screen is the specific center of the film's argument about a perceptual figuration, a particular figuration of the body traditionally fostered and supported by a Hollywood ideology. Besides the many obvious connections in *Petra von Kant* between Hollywood representation and the drama of the characters themselves, Fassbinder's use and critique of this aesthetic, in other words, has focused most importantly on the motif of the human figure as object of desire, a motif which since its historical inception has been film's central subject and the cultural base of its representation. Theoretically, Metz, Baudry, and others have persuasively discussed this cinematic figure in terms of a psychoanalytic model in which scopic desire inscribes itself onto the body as text. And as a material and communication model, this figure as trope has been the dominant presence in film from the time of Méliès's erotic conjuring of dancing girls and polar giants to Pasolini's studies in film as sado-eroticism, the body consistently being the mystery to be resolved and the source of audience fascination. In the middle of this tradition and exemplary of it, moreover, is *Citizen Kane*, a film in every sense about the jigsaw-puzzle pursuit of a figure and lost body across a space whose notoriety is its flamboyant physical depth and different representations of that lost body. More so than in any other medium, as Fassbinder's film makes clear, on the cinema screen the body has been, in Foucault's words, "the inscribed surface of events (traced by language and dissolved by ideas), the locus of a dissociated Self (adopting the illusion of a substantial unity), and a volume in perpetual disintegration."

Petra von Kant engages the representational base of this pervasively established cinematic figure on several levels. As I have indicated, the story itself depicts Petra's sexual desire as fundamentally a producer of two-dimensional postures which are the mirror-image of her inflated ego; underlining this point, the camera presents and examines the depth of the film's single space *not* in order to generate an erotic surface (across which scopic desire can play off the ambiguity of depth) but to delineate the separate planes of action which when demystified indicate precisely the emotional mechanics of imagistic desire. What the film describes in this manner is a predicament (that of Petra and of classical cinema) in which scopic desire fluctuates between the utter absence of an object and its exaggerated presence, between the body as an unmarked surface and the body as resplendent giant. The economy of finances of this predicament are, moreover, a crucial element in the dialectic since, in both cinema and social life, the power to seduce a perspective is often a function of the quantitative value attached to the image, a value frequently indexed by size, texture, and material investment. In *Petra von Kant*, in short, Petra's exploitation of her lovers parallels the exploitation of the spectator by the cinematic image, and Fassbinder's technical deconstruction in this film becomes a bi-level project in which the financial erotics of social life share a space with the desiring machine which is the film industry.

27

BLACK GOD, WHITE DEVIL:
THE REPRESENTATION OF HISTORY

Ismail Xavier

Accusations of "formalism" are often addressed to films in which the work of narration, rather than being effaced, is made present and visible. Such films foreground their own narrative operations; the discursive operations of the text come to the surface and, as a result, the usual immersion in a fictive universe is rendered difficult or impossible. While conventional films allow the spectator to witness the unfolding of an imaginary world that gradually takes on the density of the "real," *Black God, White Devil* offers no such satisfaction. An adequate analysis of the film, therefore, must go beyond the represented fiction (the diegesis) if it is to account for the wealth of significations. The film cannot be reduced to the subjective whims of an auteur, nor to simplistic labels such as the "baroque," presumably expressing some hypothetical Brazilian "essence." This reading focuses, therefore, on the complex play of relations between the fictional world posited by the film and the work of narration that constitutes that world. The film's densely metaphorical style virtually pleads for allegorical interpretation even while its internal organization frustrates and defies the interpreter searching for a unifying "key" or implicit "vision of the world." And this resistance to intepretation is by no means incidental; it structures the film and constitutes its meaning.

The "fable" of *Black God, White Devil* is organized around a peasant couple. Manuel and Rosa. The film speaks of their social condition, their hopes and representations, and their links to two forms of contestation: messianic cults

From: Ismail Xavier, '*Black God, White Devil*: The Representation of History', in R. John and R. Stam (eds), *Brazilian Cinema* (Columbia University Press, 1995).

and what Hobsbawm calls "social banditry" (*cangaço*). We can identify, and the narrator clearly distinguishes, three stages in their evolution. In the first stage, the cowherd Manuel lives with his wife Rosa and his mother on a backwoods plantation. He takes care of the local landowner's cattle in exchange for a small portion of the herd. Rosa, meanwhile, cultivates the crops necessary to their survival. The first "break" in this stage occurs when Manuel, cheated out of his due allotment of cattle, kills the landowner (Colonel Morais) whose henchmen pursue him and murder his mother. Hounded by the powerful and seeing his mother's death as a sign from heaven, Manuel joins the followers of Sebastião, the miracle-working saint (*beato*), the black God. In the second stage Manuel, ignoring Rosa's objections, places his destiny in Sebastião's hands. To prove his devotion, he performs the necessary purification rites. Sebastião's cult, meanwhile, begins to preoccupy both the local landowners and the Catholic Church. Together, they call on Antônio das Mortes – "killer of *cangaceiros*" – to repress the movement. The break in this stage occurs when Antônio das Mortes agrees to exterminate the *beatos*. At the same moment that Antônio massacres the beatos, Rosa slays Sebastião, ending his domination of Manuel. In the final stage, blind singer Julião leads Manuel and Rosa, the lone survivors of the massacre, to Corisco, survivor of another massacre, that of the *cangaceiro* Lampião and his band. Manuel transfers his faith to Corisco, whom he sees as another divine emissary. He and Corisco discuss the role of violence in the struggle to master destiny. A poetic "challenge" (*desafio*) revolves around the relative grandeur of Sebastião versus Lampião, an argument that comes to absorb all the protagonists: Manuel, Rosa, Corisco, and Dadá, his mate. The final break occurs when Antônio das Mortes fulfills his promised mission of eliminating Corisco. With both the black God (Sebastião) and the white Devil (Corisco) slain, the *sertão* opens up to the headlong flight of Manuel and Rosa.

The three phases outlined here do not occupy equal intervals in the temporal development of the narrative. The first is relatively short, suggesting a kind of prologue. Already in this phase, however, the film develops its central procedure: the synthetic representation of social existence. This procedure distinguishes *Black God, White Devil* from films like *Vidas Secas* whose scenic conventions derive from the Neo-Realist tradition. The "prologue" of *Black God, White Devil* already "condenses" ordinary activities and situations, making them emblematic of a mode of existence. This process occurs, for example, in the scenes beginning with Manuel's return to his farm when he tries to communicate the shock caused by his first encounter with Sebastião and that ends with his traversal of the small-town corral to meet Colonel Morais. At the same time, this scene, by its precise way of preparing the spectator to grasp the dramatic significance of the dialogue with Colonel Morais, fully demonstrates a style of narration announced in the prologue and reasserted throughout the film.

The film's credits – superimposed over shots of the arid *sertão* – announce the narrative style. The crescendo of Villa-Lobos's "Song of the *Sertão*" coincides with images (two close shots of the decomposing skull of an ox) emblematic of the drought afflicting the region. Contrasting in scale with the preceding long shots, these images are still reverberating in our mind when we first see Manuel. These brief shots, then, concentrate a dramatic charge of information concerning the drought and the precarious conditions of *sertão* life. The drama erupts, and dissolves, rapidly. The synthetic style and the information-laden shock-image condensing a broad range of significations already anticipate the film's constant modulation of contrasts and energetic leaps.

This modulation becomes clearer in the sequence of dialogue with Colonel Morais. Rather than evoke tension through a conventional play of shot-reaction shot, Rocha exploits composition within the frame and the slow movement of the actors. The tension is primarily created by the dilatation of the scene over time, especially in the long hiatus preceding the conflict's resolution. Manuel's violence responds to the colonel's violence; it discharges the accumulated tension, finding resonance in the montage as long takes give way to a rapid succession of short duration jump-cut shots. The narration "short-hands" the struggle between Manuel and the colonel, the chase by a cavalcade of *jagunços*, and the exchange of gunshots leading to the death of Manuel's mother. At the same time, coincident with this discontinous visual montage, silence gives way to a saturated soundtrack that superimposes the sounds generated by the action with the music of Villa-Lobos. This aural saturation is proleptically "triggered" by the stomping hooves of the cavalcade, heard even before the colonel's death. This rush of sounds and events then give way to the prolonged shot in which Manuel, after closing the eyes of his murdered mother, slowly rises while looking back at the house. Complete silence, broken only by the singer's hushed lament, translates the pensive immobility of the character. Within this sequence, then, dilated time, relative immobility, and silence "frame" a more contracted time of multiple actions and crucial decisions in a contrastive scheme typical of the entire film. Rosa's mounting exasperation with Manuel's idolization of Sebastião, for example, transforms itself into a scream that "cues" Antônio's exuberant entrance into the film.

The sequence in which Manuel performs penance by carrying a boulder up an interminable slope brings dilation to the exasperation point. At the altar, Sebastião quietly tells Manuel to bring his wife and child to the sacrifice. The film opposes the interior of the chapel, space of ceremonial silence and equilibrium, to the exterior, space of hysteria and agitation, evoked by the permanently gyrating hand-held camera and the strident cries, amplified by the blowing wind, of the *beatos*, in the same dialectic of rarefaction-excess that commands the narrative as a whole. In the chapel, the ritual evolves in a silence marked by fixed glances and stylized gestures. The itinerary of the camera's glance, meanwhile, gradually transforms the central instrument of the rite (the dagger) into the center of the gravity of the composition. The hieratic disposition is broken only with Rosa's slaying of Sebastião and the fall of icons and candles from the altar, the clatter of which "signals" the eruption of gunfire and cries originating from the scene of the massacre. Extremely brief shots render the agitation and fall of the devout under the relentless fire of an Antônio das Mortes multiplied in a montage effect that recalls Eisenstein's *October* and even "quotes" images from the Odessa steppes sequence of *Potemkin*. The massacre completed, the film reverts to slow camera movements over the victims, as shots of a pensive Antônio install a new phase of reflection.

This dialectic of scarcity and saturation marks the temporality of *Black God, White Devil* as a whole. On a semantic level, this narrative organization might be seen as metaphorizing the psychology of the characters, here taken as typical representatives of the peasant class. The exasperating passivity, the verbal awkwardness, the atmosphere of hesitant rumination, alternating with sudden explosions of violence, characteristic of peasant life, thus find resonances within the narrative style. This metaphor could be extended to the environmental conditions of the *sertão* with its rude challenges to human survival, where drought alternates with deluge. More important than these plausible homologies between character and milieu, however, is the conception of temporality, historical in one of its dimensions, inherent in this modulation. The narrative, in its very texture, molds time so as to privilege disequilibrium and transformation. What seems immobility is in fact accumulation of energy, moments of apparent stasis that mask and express hidden forces. The slow passages are not neutral moments of pure extension; they engender the strong moments and the qualitative leaps. The internal movement of the narrative, in its swift changes and irreverent lack of measure, asserts the discontinuous but necessary presence of human and social transformation.

Functionally, this modulation opens "breaches" for the diverse interventions of the narrative voices, creating space for explicit commentary on the imaginary world represented in the film, and making possible the autonomous development of sound and image tracks. What guides the movement of the images, apart from the unifying "stage" of Monte Santo, is the contrasting articulation of Sebastião's messianic discourse versus Rosa's disbelief. We accompany the play of questions and answers on the soundtrack; it matters little that a sentence spoken during one scene is completed in a different scene. The same criteria operate in the *cangaceiro* episodes. The film emphasizes the rhetorical elaboration of Corisco's argument; the changes of tonality are always subordinated to the discourse rather than to the action.

Black God, White Devil is dotted with ritual stagings of its own central ideological debate. The succession of phases weaves an overall movement of reflexion, and everything in the film – the *mise-en-scène*, the montage, the singer-narrator, the dialogue, the discursive use of image and sound – foregrounds this movement. Although the film speaks of historical struggles, it never reproduces those events through naturalistic spectacle. The film is not preoccupied with the reconstitution of appearances, or with showing events as they actually transpired. Unlike spectacular, expensive, dominant cinema, it does not seek "legitimacy" in the illusory transfer of the "real" life of another epoch to the imaginary universe of the screen. In its refusal of the dominant industrial esthetic, *Black God, White Devil* affirms the basic principles of "the esthetic of hunger." The film attunes its style to its own conditions of production and thus marks its esthetic and ideological oppositon to the colonizing discourse of the film industry. Its very texture expresses the underdevelopment that conditions the film, transforming its own technical precariousness into a source of signification. And within this multiple operation, it adds a crucial element: it uses as the mediating figure of the discourse, the central narrative instance of the film, a poet from the oral tradition, a personage belonging to the same universe that constitutes the film's object of reflection.

This mediation, if not the only source of the film's cavalier attitude toward historical data, at least partially explains the fact that the film speaks of Corisco, Lampião, Antônio Conselheiro, and Padre Cícero without seeking any rigorous fidelity to the official history of dates and documents. The "figural" method of the film transforms history into a referential matrix covered with layers of imaginary constructions. The mediation operates as a kind of permeable membrane that allows passage only to selected fragments and transfigured characters. This precipitate of the popular imagination takes the form of exemplary tales whose purpose is not fidelity to fact but rather the transmission of a moral. The historical process is represented as a parable that retains only what the narrator sees as essential, in a style reminiscent, in its criteria of selection and its narrative poetics, of *cordel* literature. In the film, this tradition is embodied by the singer-narrator, although it would be simplistic to see the narration as merely the expression of his values. Popular poetry is but one of the multiple mediations that inform *Black God, White Devil*, for the film exploits all the parameters of the medium. The material of its representation (industrialized sound and image) is not homogenous to the material of oral literature and its conditions of production are not those of the *cordel* tradition. To state the obvious, *Black God, White Devil* is a film, with all that this fact implies. The mediation of *cordel* literature, resulting from an impulse of identification with popular art, interacts with the other processes involved in the film's construction, and this interaction generates the displacements that render the discourse ambiguous. The story of Manuel and Rosa "transfigures" the accumulated experiences of the peasant community. These experiences, schematized and encapsulated within an individual linear trajectory, are mediated by a narrative instance that constantly shifts its position. In this sense, the film constitutes a decentered and problematic reflection on history itself, in which the memory of peasant revolts is both revealed and questioned from diverse points of view.

The singer's narration, the work of the camera, and the musical commentaries of *Black God, White Devil* are not always in accord. In the sequence of Manuel's first encounter with Sebastião, for example, the image of the sky coincides with the singer's first chord on the guitar. While the camera pans vertically to frame Sebastião, the singer begins his song. He presents the characters and anticipates the special character of the encounter. The initial camera movement seems to define a unity of perspectives: sound and image define the saint as blessed by God. As Manuel approaches on horseback, however, the voice of the singer is stilled and the visual composition interprets the encounter in a way that anticipates the subsequent unmasking of Sebastião. Manuel excitedly circles Sebastião and his followers, staring at the saint. The play of shot/counter shot, however, underlines Sebastião's indifference to Manuel. The subjective camera shows that the saint does not look at Manuel, who becomes present to him only when Manuel places himself directly before the saint's impassive eyes. This treatment helps characterize Manuel by discrediting in advance his account of the incident in the following scene. At the same time, the image does not support the singer's description of Sebastião ("goodness in his eyes, Jesus Christ in his heart"). There is a total divorce between the actor and the camera, and the distance that characterizes the play of glances only becomes more pronounced as the film progresses. In these encounters, Sebastião remains an enigma as the camera identifies more and more with the perspective of Rosa, the focus of skepticism. Sebastião, for his part, stimulates this skepticism by his vain air of aristocratic indifference and by a certain sadistic touch in his ministering of the ceremonies. His behavior culminates in an inglorious, almost cowardly, death, the ordinary humanness of which contrasts with his former haughtiness and definitely unmasks him in our eyes. Only minutes before Rosa's attack, after all, had not this same man resolutely murdered a child?

This process of demystification, however, hardly exhausts the film's account of the social phenomenon of messianism. Manuel's "surrender" to Sebastião is constructed so as to celebrate a religious force capable of uniting the peasant masses. The camera anticipates Manuel and Rosa climbing the mountain up to Sebastião's domain, thus providing a rare moment of apotheosis. Processions of banners and symbols outlined against the sky and agitated by the wind find an echo in the symphonic music of Villa-Lobos. The solemn grandiosity of the scene comes, interestingly, not from the *cordel*-singer's voice but rather from the music of a non-regional "universal" composer. Even here, however, the figure of Sebastião is treated with great subtlety, since the camera emphasizes the pomp and circumstance surrounding him, ignoring his "good eyes" in order to emphasize the collective force of religious ecstacy. The following sequence points up the hysterically repressive side of this same religion by showing ritual humiliations and flagellations. The violent confrontation between the *beatos* and the larger society is rendered in a kind of strident shorthand, and the critique of messianism implicit in this passage is subsequently confirmed by the extended sequences on Monte Santo, locus of retreat and contemplative longing. Metaphorically exploring the topography of the mountain, the narration crystalizes the idea of proximity to heaven and imminent ascension, of retreat to a kind of antechamber to Paradise (the island that constitutes Sebastião's fundamental promise). In this privileged space, detached from the earth and its sordid involvements, the possibility of direct intervention in the world ceases to be a goal. Messianic rebellion takes the peasants out of the process of production and distances them from the official church. It frees them from the domination of landlord and boss, but in their place proposes only the passivity of prayer and the initiatory rituals that will define them as elect in the moment of cataclysm.

After the massacre, Manuel continues to be faithful to Sebastião. The saint's demystification takes place within the work of narration, without the knowledge of the characters. With the appearance of Corisco, however, the *mise-en-scène* changes significantly. An element from within the diegesis now becomes the focus of critical reflection. As master of ceremonies, Corisco's reflection is directly addressed both to us as spectators and to Manuel within the fiction. From this point on, the extended passages of rarefied action involve the characters' discussion of their own experience, a discussion in which Corisco collaborates. A new kind of dialogue appears with the insertion of the singer himself, or of his double, within the scene. At the same time, image and sound, by repeating similar elements within apparently opposite conditions, suggest that Sebastião and Corisco are merely two sides of the same metaphysic; in the symmetry of their inversions lies a deeper unity.

The same voice (Othon Bastos) delivers the words of both Sebastião and Corisco. And the same Villa-Lobos music consecrates Sebastião's triumph on Monte Santo and Manuel's initiation – by castrating the *fazendeiro* – into *cangaço* violence. The same metaphor marks the horizon of their practice: "The *sertão* will become sea, and the sea *sertão*." Both speak in the name of Good and Evil. The unity that underlies their contradictions is expressed in symmetrical presentations; Corisco too is announced as a kind of advent ("as fate would have it") in versification similar to that of the beginning of the film.

At the same time, there are significant inversions; the vertical pan from sky to earth associated with Sebastião becomes a creeping horizontal pan over the *sertão* with Corisco. This inversion opposes Corisco's rootedness in the "lower" world of "that devil Lampião" to the "elevated" world of the saint. The *beatos* straight-lined progression toward Monte Santo, furthermore, is replaced by the back and forth movements of Corisco's violent rituals. In long shot, he promises vengeance, as his circular movements underline the clearly limited space of his action on the close-cropped sertão. The perspectival view of his stage, staked out by his immobile henchmen, project on his figure the shadow of a closing and an absence of horizons that will only be reaffirmed and rendered explicit as the film progresses.

In its theatricality, the *cangaceiro* phase of the film takes on the tone of a ritual of the living dead, of survivors without hope or prospect. While Manuel lives the experience as an optimistic present, Corisco stages the events in a very different spirit, as the accomplice of the very forces that condemn him. More than once it is he who defines this condition of living death. In the metaphor of the two heads (one killing, the other thinking) he sees himself as a repetition of Virgulino, as the vestige of an historically condemned practice that he carries to its foredoomed conclusion. Corisco himself represents the limitations of social banditry on his backlands stage. His most daring strokes seem like ritual expositions of a doctrinaire solution, without practical consequence but relived symbolically as a hymn of praise to violence as a form of justice. This violence involves no program beyond "turning things upside down," and its loyalties and vengeance are based only on circumstance and personal connection. They become legitimate only when enlisted in the service of "Good" and "Evil." Corisco sees himself as the agent of Good and the figure of the just avenger (he is Saint Jorge, the people's saint, versus the dragon of wealth) and as the agent of Evil in the figure of the condemned man, who, when confronted with the greater indignity of death by starvation, chooses violence. He takes on his destructive task in the name of justice, knowing that it involves, by the ironic economics of destiny, his own condemnation. His discourse is caught in self-defeating circularity; it creates a short circuit of means and ends, and alternation of revolt and accommodation with the enemy. The exuberant rhetoric with which Corisco demystifies Sebastião (Manuel's myth) implies the demystification of Virgulino (his own myth).

In its simultaneous praise and demystification of both Sebastião and Corisco, the narration discredits messianism and *cangaço* as practices likely to generate a more just human order. The underside of the metaphysic of Good and Evil is exposed in the equivocal expression of its rebellion. The film clearly favors the willed defeat and exemplary revolt of the White Devil to the radical alienation of the Black God, whence the similarity between Corisco's discourse and that of Antônio das Mortes, figure of infallible efficacity. Like Corisco, Antonio defends his own violence as a kind of euthanasia – the people must not die of hunger. He defines himself, furthermore, as the condemned agent of destiny within the same logic of "kill and be killed" proposed by Corisco. But while Corisco exposes his contradictions in a frenetic back-and-forth movement, Antônio is enigmatic and laconic, mysterious in his physical presence and contradictory in his words. His hesitation in accepting the task proposed by the priest and the colonel implies that he understands the conversation on some other level ("it is dangerous to meddle with the things of God"). When he accepts with the words "Sebastião is finished," his tone of voice, suggesting both power and resignation, impresses solemnity on the moment. And in the conversation with blind Julião he posits once and for all the larger meaning of his acts, a meaning that his conscience intuits but that he never really explains.

Our task now is to reflect on this "larger order" affirmed by the symbolic recapitulation of the peasant revolts and their religious ideology, along with its narrative elaboration. By foreseeing the outcome of the encounter between Manuel and Sebastião, the singer suggests the idea of Destiny. The *beato* enters Manuel's life without Manuel having done anything to provoke the encounter. At the same time, Manuel's revolt is perfectly explicable in more earthly terms – the material conditions of his life, the social relations of his work, his visionary tendencies, Rosa's despair. To explain Manuel's violence, one need only assume a minimal notion of right and wrong and an elementary aspiration to justice.

Angered by an obvious fraud and frustrated in a very precise hope (the possession of land), Manuel fails to understand the structural nature of his oppression, and therefore invokes metaphysical entities to explain his adversity and justify his revolt. Sebastião's presence in this moment of revolt encourages Manuel to adopt the saint's interpretive system. Manuel attributes the tragedy to a divine plan that requires his devotion to the saint, an option that placates his guilty conscience and protects him from police pursuit.

The singer's authority remains ambiguous, not only because he says nothing about the destiny supposedly manifest in these events, but also because image and sound reveal situations that hardly require supernatural stratagems to explain them. The providential presence of Sebastião remains the focus of this ambiguity; he offers Manuel, at precisely the right moment, the option for which his consciousness is prepared. It is the narrator, admittedly, who brings Sebastião to Manuel, but Manuel must also play his part for destiny to be fulfilled. It this coincidence, this complexity, which triggers movement and concretizes the first moment of rupture in the film.

In the second major rupture, the intervention of Antônio, also a stranger to the devout world of Monte Santo, coincides with Rosa's act of violence. Her act too is explicable in terms of her own situation. She does not kill the saint to serve some transcendent design, but rather in her own name. Antônio's intervention, already ambiguous in itself, becomes doubly ambiguous by this precise coincidence with Rosa's violence. In the two moments of rupture, external forces and human actions converge to create a turnabout that projects the characters into a new phase of life. Transformation arises from this correspondence, which marks a double determination: the narrative creates a situation in which the characters, unconscious of the stratagems mounted against them, and moved by both personal and extra-personal motives, act at the right time, participating actively in a process controlled by these same stratagems. Everything moves toward a goal that remains unthinkable for Manuel and Rosa but that is palpably clear to the spectator.

In reality, events do not evolve according to Manuel's expectations. The narration works, in fact, to discredit his interpretation, suggesting instead the existence of a pre-ordained end. After the Monte Santo massacre, the projection of the singer (blind Julião) into the fiction, visibly conducting Manuel and Rosa, makes palpable the presence of the agents of the grand plan behind the whole arrangement. In his first dialogue with Julião at the crossroads, Antônio explains that he allowed Manuel and Rosa to survive so they could "tell their story." He thus reinforces the notion that he collaborates with the larger order that controls individual destinies. He makes the protagonists the spokesmen of his own legend, bastions of the oral tradition that organizes the film. He hints, then, at the very level at which the narration is engendered, for it is in the nature of the narratives to organize themselves within a certain teleology. *Black God, White Devil* "confesses" this condition and comments on it, even as it fulfills it.

The *cangaceiro* phase inaugurates a new system. Corisco arrives via the voice of the singer, and the couple comes to Corisco via blind Julião. Manuel, after the encounter, has his reasons for carrying out the predetermined; he joins the *cangaço* in order to avenge Sebastião. Prepared for violence, he sets out on a new trajectory of equivocations, in which his actions follow one design (that of a dimly glimpsed teleology) while his consciousness imagines another (based on the very metaphysic being discredited). Without knowing it, Manuel completes a circle; he descends from his messianic flight only to return to the down to earth practicality of Rosa. At this point, however, a subtle dislocation distances Manuel and Rosa from the central events of the fable. Although they remain present to the end of the film, their survival is determined by Antônio ("I didn't kill once, and I won't kill again"). In the final sequence, the most relevant fact within the larger order is the duel between Corisco and Antônio; the song makes no reference to Manuel and Rosa. For the couple, survival marks a new opening and the reassertion of immediate natural bonds. Their conscious future consists in liberation from both Sebastião and Corisco in favor of the life-oriented immediacy of Rosa.

If Manuel initially shows capacity for revolt, the Manuel of the end shows only minimal initiative. Corisco gains strength, paradoxically only in so far as he participates in the ritual representation of his own inevitable defeat. Antônio das Mortes, despite his infallibility, relinquishes all personal ambition, seeing himself as merely the doomed agent of a predestined scheme. None of the characters in the film consciously make their own history and the film advances no project for taking control of destiny. The narration moves in the opposite direction, from initial ambiguity toward explicit definition of a teleology. Initially, this teleology is merely suggested by the singer and by the *mise-en-scène*, while the characters retain some initiative. With the dialogue between blind Julião and Antônio, however, this teleological scheme, implicit in Corisco's style of representation, becomes explicit. Antônio, by his infallible action, consummates the scheme; his revelatory word evokes the final term of the overall movement: "the great war, without the blindness of God and the Devil." His own behavior, furthermore, favors this progression from implicit to explicit teleology. His slaying of the *beatos* is explicable, on one level, by his earthly code of money, but his enigmatic attitude hints at more transcendent considerations. His duel with Corisco is not commercially motivated – killing *cangaceiros* is simply his destiny. The film refers only to his commitment to the future whose teleology leads to a great war whose preparation is the only motive proposed for Antônio's action. The overall development of the film, and Antônio's specific course, suggests that progress is not determined by human beings. In this sense, the film moves toward a determinism whose focus is outside of the characters whose consciousness is completely alienated, at worst, and capable, at best, only of vague intuitions of a more comprehensive order. And it is precisely Antônio who most clearly professes this radical agnosticism.

There are, then, two major criss-crossing movements in the film: the questioning of a dualistic metaphysic in the name of the liberation of human beings as the subjects of history is superimposed on the gradual affirmation of a "larger order" that commands human destiny. This coexistence does not develop along parallel paths, but rather through a fundamental interdependence: the very person who furthers liberation and humanistic values is also the fated agent of a dim larger order. Antônio, incarnating this short circuit of alienation-lucidity, constitutes the nucleus of both movements, in which History advances along the correct path thanks to ambiguous and equivocal figures. Antônio's repressive violence is not an unfortunate incident but a basic necessity, not a *despite* but a *through* by which History-Destiny weaves itself. Messianism and *cangaço* are moments through which human consciousness moves toward lucid acknowledgment of human beings themselves as the source, the means, and the end of transforming praxis. This ascension to consciousness does not take place, however, within the perspective of the protagonists. There is a hiatus between their experience and the final term, the revolutionary *telos* around which the narrative organizes its lesson. Manuel need not complete this trajectory because he does not liberate himself alone; he is not the center of his own trajectory. The horizon of History is not delineated by Manuel or even by Rosa; the "larger order" requires that the certainty of the end be affirmed through incompletion.

The dominant voice in the fable of *Black God, White Devil* is that of the narrator. He composes the story as a propedeutic recapitulation of a historical process (peasant revolts) that the narrator understands as propedeutic, as incorporating the movement toward the "great war," an essential subterranean movement that the recapitulation, by its symbols, tries to make clear and palpable. This "making palpable" is realized by the transfiguration of the Marxist idea of "historical necessity" into the idea of "Destiny" – a version of "necessity" familiar to popular oral traditions and to *cordel* literature. The carrying out of the revolutionary telos is a certainty, but its mechanisms remain ambiguous. The crucial point is that, under the form of Destiny, the film paradoxically affirms the apparently opposite principle of human self-determination.

This paradox is clearly inscribed in the final sequence. Antônio arrives at the duel, observing Corisco without being seen. He easily aims his rifle, but before shooting, he hesitates. It is only with the beginning of the singer's ballad that Antônio resumes his arbitrarily frozen gesture. His raising of the rifle is synchronized with the words "surrender, Corisco!" in the song. From this point on, the montage schematizes the diegetic action in such a way as to make it illustrative – by its rhythm and tonality, and by its chivalric style – of the song. Cordel literature dominates the representation. The singer draws the moral of his own story: "this world is ill-divided – it belongs to Man, and not to God or the Devil." He affirms a conception of change that places history in the hands of human beings themselves, thus confirming Antônio's allusions to the "Great War" and completing the demystification of the metaphysical based on both

Black God and White Devil. The hope of transformation, or rather its certainty, is reasserted by the refrain: "the *sertào* will become sea, and the sea *sertào*." Manuel and Rosa's headlong *corrida* toward the sea – the first straight-lined vector within a trajectory marked by a constant circling of glances, movements, and even thoughts – reinforces the projection toward a dimly glimpsed future. The narrative discourse, however, does not end with their *corrida*. It offers one last reversal by celebrating revolutionary certainty in such a way as to challenge the secular humanism implicit in the singer's final words. By an imagistic leap, the narration visually realizes the metaphor of transformation used by Sebastiào and Corisco: the surf invades the screen; the *sertào* becomes the sea. The ritual sounds and voices of the Villa-Lobos music elaborates the transformation. The waves break again and again, connoting omnipresence, domination. The image strengthens and renders actual the telos that guides the entire film, lending to Manuel's *corrida* on the level of immediate appearance nothing more than a blind flight across the *sertào* – a note of hope.

The discontinuity between this narrative leap and Manuel's trajectory situates the certainty of transformation on the level of the Universal ("Man") and reaffirms the hiatus between his lived experience and his meaning as a figure within the frame of the stratagems of destiny. His trajectory constitutes an oblique, transfigured representation of the certainty, just as Antônio's "repression," finally, both liberates and represents this same certainty. Everything in *Black God, White Devil* denies the possibility of thinking in terms of lost trails, irrecoverable detours, or insurmountable gaps. The redemptive power of its teleology is radical. The story evolves as the fulfillment of Destiny, at the same time that it grants humanity the condition of subject. Everything in the story only reaffirms this problematic condition, as it is expressed in the contradictory movement of the film.

The winds of History are ubiquitous. Its modulations are palpable in moments of violence, and there is no doubt about its final direction. But who or what impels it? *Black God, White Devil* gives no univocal response to this question, and it would be obtuse to require one, for what is fundamental in the film is the very heterogeneity of its representations. The interaction of voices renders ambiguous the principle of its revolutionary lesson, thus creating an unresolved tension, deriving from the criss-crossing movements in which "Man" and "Destiny" struggle for primacy. There is no definitive answer concerning the knowledge that sustains this certainty because the mediations in the film mark the debate with different systems of interpretation of the human experience within history.

Crystallizing an esthetic and ideological project that affirms popular forms of representation (as a focus of cultural resistance, and a *logos* where national identity is engendered) and striving for social transformation, on the basis of a dialectical vision of history, the film neither idealizes nor downgrades popular culture. Rather than dismiss popular forms in the name of ideological correctness, Rocha uses them even as he questions the traditional character of their representation. Cinema Novo confronted this task – of reelaborating popular traditions as the spring board for a transformation-oriented critique of social reality – in diverse ways. *Black God, White Devil* is a key film because it incorporates within its very structure the contradictions of this project. It avoids any romantic endorsement of the "popular" as the source of all wisdom, even as it discredits the enthnocentric reductionism that sees in popular culture nothing more than meaningless superstition and backward irrationality, superceded by bourgeois progress and rationalism. Adopting the didactic formula, *Black God, White Devil* decenters the focus of its lesson and, contrary to the "edifying" and dogmatic discourse of the "models for action" school, challenges us with an aggressive fistful of interrogations. Rather than offer, in a single diapason, an insipidly schematic lesson about class struggle, it encourages reflection on the peasantry and its forms of consciousness, and more important, on the very movement of History itself.

28

THE SHOOT

Colin MacCabe

There can be few more legendary shoots than that of *Performance*. Even today there are still people in the film business in London who will tell you that the film was a disorganised mess because everybody involved was out of their heads on acid. Others speak of the live sex scenes which caused crew members to depart and labs to refuse to develop the material. Proof of this steamy material is to be found in the further legend that the out-takes from *Performance* won first prize at the Amsterdam Wet Dream festival in the autum of 1968. According to rumour, Keith Richards would prowl outside the set as Pallenberg's onscreen affair with Jagger came closer and closer to reality. Other stories recount how Robert Fraser was banned from the set for unspeakable behaviour; Jimmy Fox came apart at the seams as the film progressed and fled both set and industry when the film wrapped in order to rescue a soul torn apart by the demons that the film had invoked. Warner executives were so disturbed by the rushes of the bath scene that they closed down the production. And the one that most impressed me as a student viewer of the film: the shot which follows Chas' bullet into Turner's head before exiting through Borges' shattered image into Powis Square starts with a miniature camera travelling up Pallenberg's vagina.

Jagger has probably the best take on the fog of gossip that surrounds *Performance*: 'those stories are so good I couldn't possibly deny them.' In fact the reality is both more banal and more extraordinary. Banal because many of the more extreme stories like Fox's rumoured real-life crime and the use of

From: Colin MacCabe, 'The Shoot', in *Performance* (BFI, 1998).

Pallenberg's vagina for the hole in Turner's head are simply untrue. Banal because all film sets are the setting for scenes of sex and drugs even if they involve no more than straight affairs and excess alcohol. Extraordinary because it is difficult to think of any studio film since the coming of sound where the production was more out of the control of the studio that paid for it. Extra-ordinary because Cammell and Roeg used this freedom to improvise with both actors and camera in a manner that can find few Anglo-Saxon parallels outside the very early history of the cinema as Porter and then Griffith developed the language of narrative cinema.

To understand the conditions that allowed Cammell and Roeg, Jagger and Pallenberg, Fox and Shannon to work through the dynamics of the film untroubled by the pompous ministrations of studio execs, it is important to recognise the commercial status of the film. The first and most significant fact is that from a financial point of view this film mixed two hot mini-genres, the pop star vehicle and the 'swinging London' film. Cinema's appetite for the stars of popular music goes back to Sinatra and beyond but the coming of the 45 single and the pop charts signalled the birth of a new teen market.

It has taken the studios a long time to work out the premises of the action film and the various other Hollywood genres which have kept teenagers of the 80s and the 90s amused; in the meantime Hollywood found the easiest access to the youth market was to provide vehicles for their music idols. Thus was the endless tedium of the Elvis Presley movie born. In Britain, Cliff Richard and Tommy Steele were rolled out to much the same effect and *Spice World* proves that one can never pronounce the final death of even the most terminally suffering genre.

But genre is simply a theoretical shorthand for audience's expectation of what they are going to see. The pop music vehicle's promise to its audience is nothing more than a view of their pop idol more intimate than that offered by the stage performance or the magazine photo – it is the most minimal of genres, and this provides the basic financial justification for the investment by Warner Bros. and for their nonchalance about what was being produced. The solid commercial asset at the centre of the film was Mick Jagger, the lead singer of the world's second most successful pop group – and provided he was on camera and in focus that asset was secure.

But the ambitions of Warner Bros. were in fact set higher than what must have been their worst case bottom line calculations. The new Seven Arts management who had bought the company from the ageing Jack Warner were busy proving their credentials as a home for creative talent. They also wanted to make a film which would capture the new youth culture and its capital, London. The American studios had proved spectacularly bad at this exercise; *Duffy* had been one of many painful exercises now consigned to the dustbin of history. But there had been a series of films which had got closer: Dick Lester's film with the Beatles, *A Hard Day's Night*, Roman Polanski's *Repulsion* and, above all, Michelangelo Antonioni's *Blowup*. All had shown a foreigner's view of the capital. Now through the agency of an American who lived in London, a Hollywood studio was on the real inside track. A film about swinging London by a swinging Londoner.

It is these contexts which explain what is finally the most extraordinary fact about this extraordinary movie. A Hollywood studio committed a serious budget to a film in which almost all the principals, both cast and crew, were absolute beginners. More than that, Warner Bros. allowed them to shoot entirely on location with no representative of the studio to ensure that they would produce an acceptable movie. This trust was partly the result of the personal relationship between Ken Hyman who, along with his father owned Seven Arts, the parent company of Warner Bros., and Sandy Lieberson but it was also undoubtedly a sign of the times. *Performance* was shot in the summer and autumn of 1968 following a spring when the youth culture which had been building since the early 60s looked set for a brief instant to change all the known rules. It cannot have been difficult to argue that Cammell and Roeg were using new methods for new times.

Finally, and probably most significantly, *Performance* was produced extremely efficiently. In the end financial control and aesthetic control come down to the same thing in nine cases out of ten. Corporate wisdom would dictate that if the cash flow was under control then so was the film. However, corporate wisdom had reckoned without the decision to use as a line producer David Cammell, Donald's younger brother. While Sandy Lieberson quietened the suits, David Cammell was to ensure that the film stayed on budget and to schedule. So concerned was Donald Cammell to avoid all appearances of nepotism that it was Lieberson and Roeg who approached his brother to ask whether he would 'run' the film with the credit of associate producer. In one way it was an inspired choice, David Cammell at that time owned a commercials company with Hugh Hudson and Robert Brownjohn. Commercials were by the mid-60s the industrial cutting edge of the film business. A commercials producer would not baulk at the vast array of lenses or even the changes of gauge that the directors were contemplating for *Performance*. And Lieberson was particularly taken by the thought of running the film out of the company's offices in Chelsea. But, at the same time, it is difficult to believe that Cammell and Roeg were not influenced by other considerations. Donald's brother would be less likely to mind the improvisations and changes of schedule that the directors must have known would take place in the second half of the film. And if he did mind, he was much less likely to go running to Warner Bros. than a seasoned professional with no loyalty to the director. And David Cammell, whatever his experience in advertising, was anything but a seasoned professional. Thus, to the team of debutantes and novices was added a line producer who had never produced a feature film. By a series of events in which both luck and judgment played a part, the cast and crew of *Performance*, as they started shooting in the week of 29 July 1968, were enjoying a degree of freedom normally only granted to a group of avant-garde enthusiasts working with a mechanically operated 16mm camera and 400 feet of black and white stock. By an even greater stroke of good fortune their inexperience meant that most of them did not realise how lucky they were. Wasn't this how all films were made? And if it wasn't, then wasn't it how all films would be made in the future?

Performance was not by any means the first film to eschew studios for locations, nor to use non-professionals; both of these choices classed it firmly within the European traditions of Italian neo-realism and the French New Wave; improvisation too was part of these European traditions as well as playing a much larger part in Hollywood history than is often allowed. It was the combination of all these features with studio financing and a genuinely stellar cast which makes *Performance* such a unique production.

David Cammell's first task was to find the locations that the directors were demanding. The insistence on location shooting, apart from the bonus of removing oneself from the surveillance of the executives, was that it allowed the camera access to a reality that studios could only simulate but never recreate. Cammell had been friends in Paris with Raoul Coutard, Jean-Luc Godard's cameraman, and it is impossible to know how much Cammell had learned from him but both Roeg and Cammell seemed to follow a Godardian aesthetic insisting that the initial reality with which the camera is confronted is as authentic as possible. This authenticity is not however an end in itself but the raw material from which the film is then fashioned. If that raw material is produced from a studio in which actors and technicians take their accustomed and easy physical and social places then the material has not enough interest to warrant further work. It is the interaction of people and place on location which allows a spark of life to pass on to celluloid.

The locations were almost all found by David Cammell, who had himself argued strongly to make the film an all-location shoot. As they searched London for a cavernous house to be Turner's domain, he remembered an illegal gambling club in Lowndes Square where he had been thoroughly fleeced in the early 60s. This not only provided the setting for much of the second half of the film (the basement scenes were shot in Hyde Park Gate) but it was here that the sets for Chas' flat were built. Other significant locations were the Royal Garden Hotel in Kensington, which provided Harry Flowers' bedroom, and the top floor of a Chinese restaurant in Wardour Street which housed the gangster's office.

All film productions are beset by difficulties. *Performance* certainly had its share: some familiar, some unique. In the familiar category was the threat delivered to David Cammell and Sandy Lieberson three weeks into production by their next door neighbour in Lowndes Square. After informing the startled producer that he should be aware that there were 'more titled people living in Lowndes Square than in any other Square except Eaton Square', the lady went on to complain about the noise and disturbance that the film crew were causing. When it became clear that she meant business and that the film's landlord had broken the terms of his lease in allowing the house to be used for filming, both

David Cammell and Sandy Lieberson were forced to spend some anxious days at the High Court before a solution was found.

But if it is usual on location shooting to find that some locals are less than appreciative of the arrival of a film crew and equipment in their midst, it is less frequent to have the financiers suspend the shoot or a lab threaten to destroy the negative.

Every day executives would turn up to Warner Bros. screening rooms to watch with Sandy Lieberson the previous days rushes. The story goes that they rarely saw anything, mainly because their lunches had been so good that they were soon fast asleep, particularly as the inexperienced editor insisted on screening all the takes rather than a selection as is usual. The film was shot in sequence, so it wasn't until halfway through the movie that the normally somnolent executives were confronted with Turner sharing his bath with Pherber and Lucy. Sleep was banished as the well-fuelled execs realised that they were watching a film that was going to break every notion of what might or might not be acceptable on a Hollywood screen. The plethora of naked bodies and the simple acceptance of an easygoing polymorphous perversion were not only genuinely shocking but clearly unreleaseable.

The script was not being followed, the directors clearly didn't know what they were doing, there was only one solution: abandon the film. And that was the news that an irate Ken Hyman delivered to Sandy Lieberson, the friend that he felt had betrayed him. The shoot was indeed suspended over a weekend. Lieberson finally persuaded Warner Bros. to finish the movie, but from now on the studio was to regard the film with the gravest of suspicions as a mistake that they never should have made. It would be wrong to underestimate the extent to which the executives were genuinely shocked by a film that presented sex and violence without any of the veils or the glosses that Hollywood demanded. At the same time it is worth recalling that this was a film which had been given the green light in the spring of 1968, at the high point of the wave of the 60s, and that the bath scene had been shot in September by which time reaction had triumphed in both Paris and Chicago. *Performance* was thus born at the moment of the death of the 60s; it is what makes the film so wonderful for us now, it was what made it so difficult for its makers then.

If the first half of the film follows the approved script closely, the second half abandons almost all but the setting and the characters. When this decision was made and to whom it was communicated is almost impossible to determine. It is certain that Warner Bros. didn't know, but neither it seems did James Fox who would turn up with his memorised script under his arm day after day when it should have been clear to him that the new pages with which the directors arrived had little to do with the script and everything to do with the improvised drama being played out on the set.

It is this improvisation, and its 'edginess' (to use Jagger's term again) which is the real basis for the rumours that surrounded the *Performance* shoot from the beginning of September as they began to film the second half. When one has discounted the more extreme claims of 'Spanish Tony' Sanchez about the drug intake at Lowndes Square and when one is sceptical of those who claim that Cammell was having affairs with all four principal actors, it is still the case that a fair amount of drugs were consumed and that the sex scenes with Jagger, Pallenberg and Breton were the most explicit ever recorded for a Hollywood picture.

But it is not the sex and drugs which were the real scandal on the set of *Performance*; it was the fact that the performance of the actors ceased to be the representation of a text and became instead the acting out of their fundamental relationships. Fox, himself, has the clearest perception of this as he recollects the filming of nearly thirty years ago. He remembers sitting in the green room while Pallenberg and Jagger played sexually with each other in an attempt, certainly encouraged by Cammell, to break down any distinction between representation and reality. More importantly he recalls Pallenberg's dislike of him as too 'straight' and sees this as crucial to the power of the scenes between them. Pallenberg disclaims such emotions in favour of an account which makes a joke of her continuous promises to spike Fox's drinks with acid. However, the power of her laugh in the film as Chas pathetically clings to his normality makes nonsense of her disclaimer. And, indeed, Pallenberg was the best placed of the actors to understand exactly what was happening; for it was Pallenberg's own excursions into the avant-garde which were, according to Cammell, the initial inspiration for much of this aspect of the film.

The 60s were, in general, the decade in which representation came under attack. Happenings and situations, the breaking down of the divide between actor and audience; this was the currency of the era. Like much else of that period, the intellectual impetuses often stretched back to the Parisian avant-garde of the 20s. In this case the crucial figure is Antonin Artaud whose thought is consciously echoed in *Performance*'s single most famous line, when Turner tells Chas: 'The only performance that makes it, that really makes it, that makes it all the way is the one that achieves madness.'

Artaud's dissatisfaction with the theatre of his day found expression in the elaboration of the theory and theses of the Theatre of Cruelty. These writings imagined a drama in which the artificialities of text and speech had been left behind in favour of a drama of gesture and screams. It is doubtful whether Artaud was ever really proposing an actual strategy for the stage because any one performance which accomplished his aims would also have inaugurated an entirely new cycle of civilisation in which the whole relation between body and spirit would have been transformed. But many of his insights into the relation of theatre to primitive ritual were central to experiments such as those carried out by the Living Theatre in the 60s. Those experiments had enchanted Anita Pallenberg and it is clear that it was through her that these ideas had influenced Cammell.

Artaud was also an indirect influence on both directors. For his work is part of the context of Cocteau's *Blood of a Poet* (1931) which was a key reference point for both Roeg and Cammell. Despite Artaud's considerable career as a screen actor which included Marat in Gance's *Napoleon* (1927) and a part in Dreyer's *Jeanne d'Arc*, he only saw one of his own projects reach the screen, *The Seashell and the Clergyman*, and he disowned this film at its premiere in 1928. However, when Cocteau's film was unveiled four years later, Artaud was to claim that it had stolen its hallucinatory images and elliptical cutting from his own project. Ignoring the charge of direct plagiarism, there is no doubt that Cocteau's 'realistic documentary of unreal events' is in both method and matter close both to Artaud and to *Performance*.

Artaud was to despair finally of the cinema's potential because the cinematic apparatus seemed to split audience from representation so thoroughly that it was impossible for the events on the screen to touch the audience in the fundamental fashion that he demanded. But Artaud had reckoned without the technological advances of the cinema and without the genius of someone like Roeg who was able to take those advances and place them at a service of an aesthetic devoted to understanding a reality which cannot be reduced to a simple question of representation. Roeg's use of lenses, camera position, filters and even of different stock (at some points the film lapses into black and white) and gauges (the threesome in Powis Square was shot in 16mm) means that the viewer is never simply observing the events of the film for the viewer's vision is part of the action. The climax of this engagement comes at the end of the film where Chas and Turner become one. It is at this point that interpretation cannot avoid relying on drives and identifications that come from the spectator's side of the screen. Vision has so clearly been divorced from knowledge that it is only our own beliefs that guarantee our understanding. The film's inability to interpret what we see for us is foregrounded in the opening sequence of the film in which the black Rolls Royce and Chas' and Dana's lovemaking are intercut in such a way as to leave it completely unclear as to the direct relationship between them. The very first impression is that Chas and Dana are actually inside the Rolls. When it becomes obvious that they are not, the interior of the Rolls becomes a mysterious space hiding one knows not what infamy and perversion. Such visual riddles are the standard fare of Hollywood films and it is the business of such films to produce a narrative which resolves the riddles and leaves the viewer in the clear. *Performance* refuses such solutions and as the Rolls (now white not black) drives away at the end of the film our vision can no more warrant our knowledge of what it contains than it could at the beginning. If we know the car's contents it is because of the journey we have taken with the film, the performance that we have been obliged and delighted to undertake.

The first historic surge of realism is always an emphasis on what is being represented; the delight in the power of representation; the moment of a Balzac or a Rossellini and the laying out of society as spectacle. The even more potent mimesis is when the representation itself is understood as essential to the reality it depicts: the moment of Joyce or Godard when turn of the century Dublin or 60s Paris includes *Ulysses* or *A Bout de souffle* as part of their very definition. Now we are no longer spectators but participants. Cammell's and Roeg's movie reproduces London in 1968; it makes us part of that metropolis, a reality that it promises for us each time it unwinds.

And one aspect of that reality is sex presented in ways that are unprecedented in mainstream cinema. Cammell wanted to get the viewer under the sheets in an intimacy which the camera had never before attempted. Roeg realised that the only way to achieve the effect was to abandon the 35mm camera and to use a wind-up 16mm Bolex. And so as Jagger, Pallenberg and Breton busied themselves in the huge double bed, they were accompanied by Cammell on one side and Roeg plus Bolex on the other. Roeg claims to this day that he can still see Donald's face lifting the sheets and asking 'How was it for you?'

The rushes from that day went off to the studio as usual although not before the clapper loader had warned David Cammell that he expected trouble. Sure enough David Cammell received a call from Humphry's, the film's lab, very early in the morning saying that the previous day's film contravened the obscenity laws and that the lab were going to destroy it forthwith. After a hastily arranged meeting and much negotiation, Sandy Lieberson and David Cammell managed to retrieve the negative but they were then obliged to sit and watch as the chief executive of the lab destroyed the print with a hammer and chisel.

And so legends are born. It is true that Keith Richards patrolled the streets outside Lowndes Square ferrying Anita to and from a shoot that he despised. It is true that Robert Fraser who had let his flat to Anita Pallenberg for the duration of the production then refused to move out and that each night Richards and Fraser would pour scorn on the efforts of the film-makers. It is true that Fraser was finally banned from the set although nobody can remember the specific offence. And so on and so forth. None of this would be of the slightest interest were it not for the fact that the method of film-making caught and refracted every tension and nuance that played across the cast. It is the method that is crucial to understand and it was a method that required genuine discipline. The furore at Humphry's was not allowed to disrupt film or schedule and processing was simply transferred to Technicolor. *Performance* came in on or about both schedule and budget. The shoot that was famous for its indulgence and excess had in fact been conducted with extraordinary rigour and dedication.

29

THE CARAPACE THAT FAILED: OUSMANE SEMBENE'S *XALA*

Laura Mulvey

> *The film language of* Xala *can be constructed on the model of an African poetic form called 'sem-enna-worq' which literally means 'wax and gold'. The term refers to the 'lost wax' process in which a goldsmith creates a wax form, casts a clay mold around it, then drains out the wax and pours in pure molten gold to form the valued object. Applied to poetics, the concept acknowledges two levels of interpretation, distinct in theory and representation. Such poetic form-aims to attain maximum ideas with minimum words. 'Wax' refers to the most obvious and superficial meaning, whereas the 'gold' embedded in the art work offers the 'true' meaning, which may be inaccessible unless one understands the nuances of folk culture.*

This quotation illustrates the intense interest that recent African cinema holds for any film theory concerned with the 'hieroglyphic' tradition, and potential, of cinema. The catch-all phrase 'hieroglyph' is useful in that it evokes three processes: a code of composition, the encapsulation, that is, of an idea in an image at a stage just prior to writing; a mode of address that asks an audience to apply their ability to decipher the poetics of the 'screen script'; and, finally, the work of criticism as a means of articulating the poetics that an audience recognises but leaves implicit. My critical perspective cannot include the 'nuances of folk culture' or, indeed, other important aspects of African culture and history but attempts to present *Xala*'s significance for film theory beyond its immediate cultural context. While as a critic I would like to fulfil the third deciphering function, that of 'articulation', my critical process does not aspire to go beyond making explicit the first two hieroglyphic processes, that is the 'screen script' and its mode of address to an audience. African cinema should no longer be

From: Laura Mulvey, 'The Carapace that Failed: Ousmane Sembene's *Xala*', in *Fetishism and Curiosity* (BFI, 1996).

seen as a 'developing' cinema. It has already made an original and significant contribution to contemporary cinema and its cumulative history and aesthetics.

The germinal ground in which the African cinema developed in the post-colonial period was the francophone sub-Sahara, above all Senegal and Mali, and first of all with Ousmane Sembene. Geographically, this area has its own cultural traditions dating back to the old Mande empire founded by Sundiata in the 11th century, and revived in resistance to French colonialism as the Dyula Revolution led by Samoury Toure in the late 19th century. It was not until independence in 1960, when the French were abandoning most of their African colonies in the hope of holding on to Algeria, that the conditions for an African cinema came into being. Sembene's work, first as a writer, then as a film-maker, crosses the 1960 divide and is also divided by it. During the 50s, he had made his name as an African writer, writing, of course, in French. His first novel, *Le Docker noir* (1956), was written while he was working in the docks and as a union organiser in Marseille. *Les Bouts de bois de Dieu* was published in 1960 (after a number of others) based on his experiences during the famous 1947–8 strike on the Bamako–Dakar railway. Then, in 1961, immediately after Senegal achieved independence, he went to the Soviet Union to study at the Moscow Film School and his first short film, *Borom Sarret*, was shown at the Tours film festival in 1963. *La Noire de ...* , released in 1966, was the first full-length feature from the sub-Sahara.

Sembene's novels were written during the period in which African poets, novelists, Marxist theorists and intellectuals in Paris were grouped around the journal *Présence Africaine*. Sembene was critical of the *négritude* movement with which they were identified. He considered the concept to be irrelevant to the popular resistance that grew into the independence movement, and he identified himself with, and was part of, the anti-colonial struggle in Senegal rather than intellectual circles in Paris. While he wrote novels in French during the colonial period, the cinema offered Sembene a means of contact with popular traditions and his films are directed towards the cultural needs of the ordinary people, who had no access either to the French language or to traditions of written culture:

> Often the worker or the peasant don't have time to pause on the details of their daily lives; they live them and do not have time to tie them down. The film-maker, though, can link one detail to another to put a story together. There is no longer a traditional storyteller in our days and I think the cinema can replace him.

This last observation is characteristic of Sembene's commitment to promoting and transforming traditional culture, to using the technological developments of Western society in the interests of African culture. Sembene was more interested in finding a dialectical relationship between the two cultures than in an uncritical nostalgia for pre-colonial pure Africanness. This position is underlined by his background as a worker and his Marxism.

The cinema can speak across the divisions created by oral tradition and written language and is, therefore, a perfect mechanism for a cultural dialectic. It can perpetuate an oral cultural tradition as the spoken language plays a major role in cinema; and it can bring oral traditions into the modernity of the post-colonial. Sembene himself was the son of a fisherman and self-educated into French literacy. His own Wolof language, like the Mandinke, had no written equivalent. In the social structure of the Mande tradition, the task of maintaining and creating oral culture devolved onto a specific social grouping, the *griots*, dependent on the nobility in pre-colonial times. They functioned as the repository of historical memory, traditionally that of the kings and their families, and as creators, among other things, of poetry and music. African culture has had to negotiate a contemporary *modus vivendi* between writing in French, its own traditional oral forms and the facts of post-colonial cultural life. While the figure of the *griot* may evoke the oral culture of the pre-colonial past, he (and, sometimes, she) spoke primarily to an elite. The cinema economically and politically had to address a mass audience in post-colonial Africa.

In *Xala* the question of language is at the political centre of the drama. The economic division between the indigenous entrepreneurial elite and the impoverished people is reflected in a division between French and Wolof. The elite use French exclusively to communicate among themselves and as their official language. They speak Wolof only across class and gender lines and their reat it as inferior and archaic. In the novel *Xala*, which Sembene wrote up from his script while searching for funds for the film, the young people on the Left have developed a written equivalent for Wolof and are publishing a journal in their native language for the first time. In the film, Sembene sets up a parallel between two figures who are quite marginal to the story but significant for its politics. One is a young student selling the new journal; the other is a peasant, robbed of his village's savings which he had brought to town to buy seed. Both get caught in the police round-up of beggars that forms the film's central tableau, and become integrated into the beggar community. Any moves by the people towards cultural and economic advance and self-sufficiency are dashed in the polarisation between the entrepreneurial elite and the underclass it creates.

Although the cinema has often been evoked as a continuation of the *griot* tradition, there are important points of difference besides those of class. The oral tradition of the *griot* was based on verbal language as such. The cinema sets up a dialectic between what is said and what is shown. One can undercut, or play off, the other. In *Xala*, Sembene uses the language of cinema to create a poetics of politics. He gives visibility to the forms, as opposed to the content, of social contradiction and then, through the forms, illuminates the content. He forges links between underlying structures, or formations, and the symptoms they produce on the surface, stamped, as it were, onto everyday existence, across all classes. This is an aesthetic that depends on making visible those aspects of economic and political structure that are either invisible or repressed in articulated language. It is a cinema of what cannot be said. Underlying structures mark the lives of the ruling elite as well as the people, and as the story unfolds signs and symptoms signal an insistent return of the repressed. The repression is both political, of the people by the ruling elite, and psychoanalytic, of the ruling elite by their relation to Frenchness, its consequent phobias and fetishisms. The two spheres become increasingly interlinked throughout the film. While Sembene's analysis of signs is always historical and, in the last resort, materialist, he also acknowledges the place of sexuality and the structure of the psyche in the symptomology of neo-colonialism. There are shades of Frantz Fanon's *Black Skin, White Masks*.

Xala is set in Senegal after independence when the presence of the colonial power is concealed behind a façade of self-government. The story's premise is that independence politics had become inextricably compromised with colonial financial structures. The opening, pre-credit, sequence of *Xala* shows a crowd celebrating as a group of African businessmen expel the French from the Chamber of Commerce and take control of their own economy. The people in the crowd are depicted in such a way as to evoke 'Africanness', with bare breasts, dancing and drums. These connotative images never appear again in the film; (thereafter the characters' clothes and appearance are appropriate for the Islamic sub-Sahara). The businessmen are dressed in loose shirts and trousers made out of 'African'-type materials. They appear at the top of the steps, ejecting a few objects that evoke the colonising culture (including a bust of Marie-Antoinette). The camera is placed at the bottom of the steps. As the men turn to go into the building, the camera dips slightly to change its angle and the steps suddenly resemble a stage on which a performance has just taken place. When the camera joins the men back in the Chamber, they are dressed in the dark European business suits that they will wear for the rest of the film. While the crowds still celebrate, a posse of police arrive and, under the command of one of the recently expelled Frenchmen, push the people back from the central space in front of the Chambre de Commerce, literally enacting the process of domination and repression. The other two Frenchmen then enter the Chambre and place an attaché case in front of each African businessman. Each case is full of money. The two men step backwards with the silent subservience they maintain, as 'advisers', for the rest of the film. The sequence closes as El Hadji Abdou Kader Beye invites his colleagues to the party celebrating his marriage to a third wife. All the speeches are in French.

I have chosen the word 'carapace' to evoke the central poetic and political themes in *Xala* in order to convey an image of vulnerable flesh covered by a protecting shell. The carapace doubles as a mask behind which the ruling elite camouflages itself, adopting the clothes, language and behaviour of its former colonial masters. The carapace also evokes the social structure of neo-colonialism. The entrepreneurial bourgeoisie live the life of an upper crust, floating and parasitical on the lives of the people. In *Xala* the carapace conceals not simply vulnerable flesh, but flesh that is wounded by class exploitation.

Whereas a scab indicates that a wound has developed its own organic means of protection, the carapace of neo-colonialism denies and disavows the wound and prevents healing. The elite encase themselves in expensive Western cars, while the beggars' bodies are crippled by deformed or missing limbs. Concealed corruption at the top of the social hierarchy manifests itself on the wounded bodies of the dispossessed. During the film, the gap between the two groups, the beggars and the elite, narrows until the final scene which brings them together. The central character is El Hadji, a member of the entrepreneurial elite, who finds he is impotent when he marries his third wife. A tension then runs through the film between the vulnerability of his body, his failed erection, on one side and, on the other, his outward carapace made up of European props. In the end, his sexual vulnerability has brought him to realise that the carapace has failed and he exposes his own body, naked and covered in spit, to the beggars' ritual of humiliation and salvation.

During a climactic scene just before the end of the film, El Hadji is being hounded out of the Chamber of Commerce by his equally corrupt colleagues. His most vindictive antagonist seizes his attaché case, and opens it to find it empty except for the magic object with which El Hadji had attempted to ward off the curse of impotence, the *xala*, that has afflicted him. His enemy holds it up for public ridicule. El Hadji seizes it and waves it defiantly in the faces of the others, shouting: 'This is the true fetish, not the fetishism of technology.' At this moment, Sembene brings into the open the theoretical theme of his film, that is the different discourses of fetishism. Up until that point, these different discourses had been woven into the story implicitly, creating the complex semiotic system that makes special demands on the spectator's reading powers. Suddenly the three strands are condensed together in one object. The object acts simultaneously as a signifier of religious belief that predates Islam and colonialism, as a signifier, in the context of the story, of El Hadji's sexual impotence, and it is enclosed, concealed, in the attaché case, a key signifier of financial corruption and the commodity fetishism that corruption breeds.

Sembene weaves a series of reflections on fetishism across the film. As something in which are invested a meaning and a value beyond or beside its actual meaning and value, a fetish demands the willing surrender of knowledge to belief. The fetishist overrates his object, and ignoring the commonsense value attributed to it by society, secretly attaches mysterious powers to it. But, however intensely invested, this secret belief is vulnerable, acknowledging, even more secretly, what it simultaneously disavows. For an individual, the fetish object may be invested with private magical or sexual significance, but distortions of value and attributions of inappropriate meaning may also be shared by social groups in a kind of collective fantasy. The fetish thus acts, either individually or collectively, as a sign, signalling the intervention of fantasy into the normal course of the reality principle. And the intervention of fantasy signals a point of anxiety which cannot face the possibility of knowledge, and in the process of avoiding it, erects a belief in an object that, in turn, denies knowledge of its actual value. While supporting the suspension of disbelief, the fetish also materialises the unspeakable, the disavowed, the repressed.

The cinema, too, appropriates objects, turns then into images and wraps them in connotations and resonances that are either collectively understood, or acquire specific significance within the context of a particular story. Sembene makes use of the language of cinema, its hieroglyphic or pictographic possibilities, and creates a text which is about the meaning of objects and objects as symptoms. His use of cinematic rhetoric is the key to *Xala*. The form of the film engages the spectators' ability to read the signs that emanate from colonialism and its neo-colonialist offspring. And, because the film shows an African ruling elite accepting and appropriating the fetishisms of European capitalism, it allows a double reading. As a comedy of fetishistic manners *Xala* uses signs, objects and the rhetoric of cinema to allow its audience direct engagement with, and access to solving, the enigmas represented on the screen. But *Xala* also sets off a kind of chain reaction of theoretical reflections on fetishism, linking together otherwise diverse ideas, and highlighting the age-old function of fetishism as a conduit for the to and fro of cultural and economic exchange between Europe and Africa.

[...]

I

After the credits the film proper opens with El Hadji collecting his two other wives to go to the party. The elder, Adja Awa Astou, is traditional and religious. In the interview cited earlier Sembene says 'He got his first wife before becoming a somebody.' The second, Oumi N'Doye, is Westernised and mercenary. Sembene says 'Along with his economic and social development, he takes a second who corresponds, so to speak, to a second historical phase.' Awa's daughter Rama, who stands up to her father throughout the film, synthesises progressive elements in both African and Western cultures. She has posters of Amilcar Cabral and Charlie Chaplin in her room; she dresses in African style and rides a motor scooter; she is a student at the university and will only speak Wolof. N'gone, El Hadji's new wife, is dressed for a Western white wedding and her face is covered with a bridal veil. Sembene says: 'The third, his daughter's age but without her mind, is only there for his self-esteem.' Then, on the wedding night, ElHadji finds he is impotent. During the rest of the film he tries to work out who could have cursed him and visits two *marabouts* to find a cure. His financial affairs unravel, unable to sustain the cost of three households and the lavish wedding, until he is finally expelled from the Chamber of Commerce.

The central enigma in *Xala* cannot be deciphered until the very last scene, when the beggars, who at the beginning of the film are marginal to the story but gradually come to occupy its centre, invade El Hadji's house. Then the different clues that have been signalled by Sembene throughout the film fall into place and complete the picture. El Hadji does not function as a knowing narrator and the only character with whom the spectator is given any identification, personally and ideologically, is Rama, who plays only a small, though important, part in the film. El Hadji is a didactic hero. He is made into an example, rather as Brecht makes an example out of Mother Courage. He only engages sympathy through the disaster he has brought on himself, and, like a tragic hero of the cathartic theatre, he is stripped literally to nakedness. On a more significant level, he cannot command the narration because he is unable to understand his own history and the audience are thus deprived of the safety and security of a hero who will guide them through events, and provide them with an appropriate moral perspective. And the spectator realises, at the end, that the film itself has held the clues to the enigma of El Hadji's *xala*, and these linked images and figurations can, retrospectively, be deciphered. Sembene's use of cinema demands a spectator who is actively engaged with reading and interpreting the sounds and images unrolling on the screen.

There are certain parallels between *Xala*'s narrational strategy and that of *Citizen Kane*. Both films also tell the story of a man's relationship to money, fetishised objects and sexuality. Both films are constructed around a central enigma. In *Citizen Kane*, the audience's investigation of the enigma is conducted by a surrogate, the journalist, Thompson. However, he is unable to see or interpret the clues contained in the visual discourse of the film. The pieces finally fall into place when the camera allows the audience a privileged look at the little sled as it is thrown on the flames. Thompson cannot see how these signifiers link together like the rings of a chain and mark the movement of associated ideas, objects and images that map out the process of displacement. The camera, or rather the rhetoric of the cinema, assumes the position of master narrator, and directly addresses the audience.

As in *Xala*, the audience of *Citizen Kane* then has to think back over the whole course of the film to translate the 'sensitive areas' retrospectively, and solve the enigma by deciphering the sliding of the signifiers. Just as the glass snowstorm allows a 'reference back' to the log cabin, so the name on the sled at the end of the film returns the missing signified to the enigma, seeming to halt and restore order to the slippage of the signifiers. But the signified 'Rosebud' then sets off on another journey, as a signifier for the lost mother and a memorial to that loss. As Jacques Lacan points out in his essay 'Agency of the Letter in the Unconscious', a signifier's ability to suggest multiple signifieds creates the leap of association that allows the unconscious mind to displace one idea onto another. Where the conscious mind has set up an impenetrable wall of censorship, the unconscious disguises its ideas through displacement, but not so completely that the link between the original idea and the disguised idea will be lost. Psychoanalysis tries to trace the process backwards, following the links and deciphering the clues in reverse, restoring the links between the signifiers lodged, but indecipherable, in the conscious mind and the unconscious idea they represent. Describing the language of dreams, Freud used the image of a rebus and compared dream interpretation to the decipherment of the clues in a pictogram.

In *Xala* the visual coding of ideas is even more marked and further emphasised by the absence of a surrogate narrator. This mode of cinematic address is perfectly suited to the film's subject matter: fetishism. El Hadji and his colleagues have lost touch with their own history and society through adopting Frenchness as a sign of superior class position. There is an unbridgeable gap between the elite's own origins, their present masquerade of Westernised commodity culture and the condition of the people. The gap is demonstrated by the elite's use of French rather than Wolof, and safeguarded by a fetishisation of European objects. These things, for instance El Hadji's Mercedes, are the literal materials of the carapace, his defence against political and economic reality, and the outward manifestations of a corruption that sucks the life blood of the people. When the Mercedes is repossessed, Modu, the chauffeur, carries a wooden stool as he guides his employer along the street. The stool is like a shrunken or wizened version of the proud object of display. It is a trace of, or a memorial to, the Mercedes and its meaning for El Hadji. Because Modu has been so closely identified with the car and its welfare, his presence links the two objects ironically together. Sembene consistently links people with things, things substitute for people or for each other, things acquire associations and resonances that weave like threads of meaning through the film. At the same time, he raises the issue of substitution and exchange in a social and economic sphere. The *marabout* who cures El Hadji's *xala*, Sereen Mada, restores it when the cheque that El Hadji gave him in payment is bounced by the bank.

As the members of the Chamber of Commerce arrive at El Hadji's wedding party, the camera is positioned so that, as each man walks past, his attaché case is framed in close-up. On the outside, the attaché case is emblematic of the power of the international business community, but inside, as only the audience can know, is the secret evidence of corruption and collaboration with the old colonial masters. While seeming to be signs of power and authority, the attaché cases represent the real impotence of the entrepreneurial elite in relation to neo-colonialism. Once the film has established these associations, the image of the attaché case evokes them whenever it appears. So that when El Hadji walks dejectedly away, carrying his attaché case, from N'gone's house after his failed wedding night, he seems to be bowed down with a double impotence. And, in his final confrontation with his colleagues, his case is empty apart from the fetish given him by the phoney *marabout*. The failed fetish is found in the place formerly occupied by the colonialists' banknotes.

Although the particular discourse of sexuality, on which Freud's theory of fetishism depends, cannot be imposed carelessly on another culture, Sembene's juxtaposition of the psycho-sexual with the socio-economic is explicit. He uses the sexual as the point of fissure, or weakness, in the system of economic fetishism. El Hadji's impotence is a symptom of something else, a sign of the eruption of the unconscious onto the body itself. In Freud, the fetish enables the psyche to live with castration anxiety; it contributes to the ego's mechanisms of defence; it conceals the truth that the conscious mind represses. When the fetish fails to function effectively, the symptoms it holds in check start to surface. In *Xala*, the fragile carapace collapses under pressure from class politics and economics but these pressures are expressed through, and latch onto, sexuality and work on the body's vulnerability to the psyche. For Sembene, class politics determine over and above sexuality. Sexuality plays its part in the drama as the site of the symptom, the first sign of a return of the repressed. In his representation of repression, Sembene makes full use of the *double entendre* that can condense its political and psychoanalytic connotations.

The morning after the wedding El Hadji's secretary opens his shop. Modu delivers El Hadji in the Mercedes. El Hadji asks his secretary to telephone the President of the Chamber of Commerce who comes over to see him at once. Interspersed and separate from these events, the beggars are slowly collecting and taking up their usual positions outside in the street. As the local women empty their slops into the drain outside the shop, the secretary runs out with her disinfectant spray to ward off infection. As El Hadji's car appears, so do the beggars and their music; as the President's car appears, so do the cripples. In the back office, El Hadji tells the President about the *xala*. The President reacts with horror saying 'Who? Who could have done this to you?' At that moment the beggars' music drifts into the room. El Hadji gets up from his chair without answering and goes through to the front office and closes the window. He asks the President to call the police and remove this 'human refuse', adding that 'it's bad for tourism'. The police arrive, and under the direction of their French commander, load the beggars and cripples into a lorry and drive them out of town. They are left miles away, in the middle of nowhere, and start their slow, painful, trek back into town.

When watching this scene, the spectator cannot but be conscious of a figuration of 'repression'. The President orders that the beggars be removed from sight and from consciousness. And their return then figures a 'return of the repressed'. To the mutilated limbs of the cripples is now added a baton wound on the head of the boy who guides the blind man and whom Modu employs to clean the car. The repression is both physical and social, and the bodies of the beggars are symptoms of social and economic injustice. But this scene also contains a clue to the enigma, to the source of the *xala*, to its source in El Hadji's social and historical position. This other, psychic, dimension is not revealed until the final scene in the film. El Hadji's fall is complete: Oumi has left him, N'gone's Badyen (her father's sister) has repudiated the marriage, his cheque to the *marabout* had bounced so the *xala* has returned, his bank has refused to extend his loans, and his colleagues have voted unanimously to expel him from the Chamber of Commerce for embezzling 30 tons of rice destined for the country people. As Modu takes him to Awa's house, he tells El Hadji that the blind man can cure the *xala*. The scene builds up to the final revelation as the beggars invade the house under the blind man's leadership. While some of the beggars loot the kitchen, the blind man sits in judgment. He says to El Hadji:

'Do you recognise me? . . . Our story goes back a long way.' He tells how El Hadji had taken his clan's land. 'What I have become is your fault. You appropriated our inheritance. You falsified our names and we were expropriated. I was thrown in prison. I am of the Beye family. Now I will get my revenge. I arranged your *xala*. If you want to be a man you will undress nude in front of everyone. We will spit on you.'

It was this first act of expropriation that had set El Hadji on the road towards entrepreneurial success and had taken him from the country to the town, away from loyalty to family and towards individualism, from traditional modes of inheritance towards falsified written legal documents, away from the continuity of his own history and into a charade of Frenchness. His failure to recognise the beggar indicates that he had covered his tracks by 'forgetting'. But when the President asked who had cursed him, his response was to shut out the sound of the beggar's song. This gesture signified both an acknowledgment of the truth and the need, quickly, to re-enact its repression.

During the final scene with the beggars, the tailor's dummy with N'gone's wedding veil, returned contemptuously to El Hadji by the Badyen, stands clearly visible in the corner. The presence of these objects sets off a chain of associations that run back through the film as the links between them begin to emerge. N'gone acts as a pivot between the two fetishistic systems: the economic and the sexual. She is woman as commodity, woman as fetish and woman as consumer of commodities. This sphere of capitalist consumption has been traditionally the province of women; Luce Irigaray, in her essay 'Women on the Market', traces the development from the anthropological exchange of women to the emergence of women as both consumers and consumed in modern, urban society. N'gone's marriage to El Hadji was based on exchange. At the wedding his gifts are displayed including, most prominently, a car key. The car, which stands decked out with ribbons outside the gate of the villa on the back of a truck, is El Hadji's present to her in exchange for her virginity. As he leaves the villa after his unconsummated wedding night, he stops by the car and touches it mournfully, so that it seems to substitute for N'gone's unattainable sexuality. The car's fetishistic quality, its elevation out of ordinary use, the ribbons, are displaced onto her figure. She is first seen concealed behind her wedding veil, packaged like a valuable commodity, and she speaks only once throughout the film. To emphasise this 'thingness' and 'to-be-looked-at-ness', Sembene places her next to a large, nude but tasteful, photograph of her as the Badyen prepares her for her wedding night. As she is undressed and her wedding veil placed on the tailor's dummy, the camera pans up from her naked back to her body in the photograph. In a later scene the same camera movement reiterates this juxtaposition.

N'gone's fetishised erotic appearance contrasts with Oumi's immediate, vital, demanding and corporeal sexuality. N'gone is image and commodity and, half concealed behind the wedding veil, she evokes the double nature of commodity fetishism. The commodity, to circulate and realise the capital invested in it, must seduce its consumer and, in its very seductiveness, its 'packagedness', disguise the secret of its origins. That is, the inherent unglamorousness of the production process should be invisible and, most of all, class relations, the extraction of surplus value, must be concealed by seductive surface. N'gone's image as fetish evokes the processes of veiling, disguise and substitution necessary to commodity fetishism and it is perhaps significant that when El Hadji, temporarily cured of his *xala* by Sereen Mada, goes triumphantly to his new bride she has her period and is 'not available'. Her perfect surface is tarnished by menstrual blood. Although the depiction of N'gone suggests links with the appearance and circulation of the commodity under capitalism, the story is taking place in a non-industrialised and 'underdeveloped' country. The money El Hadji needed to acquire her as commodity, in the specific economic conditions of neo-colonialism, came from financial corruption and exploitative entrepreneurial capitalism. He paid for the wedding and N'gone's gifts by embezzling and illegally selling the quota of rice intended for the country people. The secret corruption is displaced onto the little car that N'gone will receive in exchange for her virginity; the car's fetishistic qualities are displaced onto N'gone for whom a photograph and a tailor's dummy become substitutes and metaphors.

Marx evolved his theory of commodity fetishism in the process of developing his theory of value. The problem Marx perceived to be at stake in the theory of value is connected to the question of visibility and invisibility of labour power and of value. Here the question of materiality and abstraction returns, in the context of a capitalist system of thought that Marx can show to be deeply imbricated with fetishism, its phobic other. W. J. Mitchell says: 'Marx's turning the rhetoric of iconoclasm on its principal users was a brilliant tactical manoeuvre; given nineteenth-century Europe's obsession with primitive, oriental, "fetishistic" cultures that were the prime object of imperialist expansion, one can hardly imagine a more effective rhetorical move.'

Marx identified commodity fetishism as emerging out of the gap between a belief in the commodity as its own autochthonous source of value and knowledge of its true source in human labour. This gap is finally papered over and disguised under capitalism, as the labour market necessary for mass industrial production can only function by transforming individual labour power into abstract and generalised wage labour. The commodity's glamour, verging into sex appeal, seals these complicated processes into a fixation on seeing, believing and not understanding.

[...]

The circulation of European commodities, in a society of the kind depicted in *Xala*, caricatures and exaggerates the commodity fetishism inherent in capitalism. Rather than representing an enigma that may be deciphered, politically and theoretically, to reveal its place in the historical and economic order of things, the commodity's ties with history have been effectively severed. The chain of displacements that construct the concept of value is attenuated to the point that all connection with the source of value is irredeemably lost in the movement from capitalism to colonialism. Floating freely outside First World economy, the gulf between luxury objects monopolised by a Third World elite and the labour power of the working class in the producing country seems vast. Belief in the commodity's supposedly self-generated value does not demand the process of disavowal it depends on at home so that it can live out its myth as an object of cult. In *Xala*, Sembene uses the neo-colonial economy to show the capitalist commodity 'superfetishised'. Modu, for instance, only puts imported bottled water into the Mercedes. These things take on pure 'sign value' (as Baudrillard would put it). However, the objects enable another process of disavowal. Sembene suggests that these fetishised objects seal the repression of history and of class and colonial politics under the rhetoric of nationhood. His use of the concept of fetishism is not an exact theoretical working through of the Marxist or Freudian concepts of fetishism, however; his use is *Marxist* and *Freudian*. The interest of the film lies in its inextricable intermeshing of the two.

In its final images, *Xala*'s class and psychoanalytic themes are suddenly polarised into a new pattern. Sembene invokes horror of the body and its materiality through the desperate and degraded condition of the beggars and cripples. As El Hadji is denounced by the blind man, their wounds and their missing limbs demonstrate the political fact that financial corruption and profit are manifested on the bodies of the poor. The Western objects that the entrepreneurial elite fetishise inflict not impotence but castration on those they impoverish. The wounded body, the source of horror in the Freudian concept of castration anxiety, returns in the wounded bodies of the beggars and the hunger of the peasants. These bodies break through the barriers maintained by the French language and symbolised, for instance, by El Hadji's cult of Evian water. The otherness of Africa which horrified Europeans is perpetuated in colonialism's real horror of the ordinary people, and grotesquely more so, in the irresponsible greed of the new ruling class.

For Freud, the site of castration anxiety is the mother's body. For Julia Kristeva, the mother's body is the site of abjection. The child's relation to its mother was a time of boundarilessness and a time when the body and its fluids were not a source of disgust. For Kristeva, the ego defines itself by a demarcation of its limits through mastering its waste and separating itself from those of the mother. It establishes itself as an individual, in its oneness. This concept of individualism is, it has been extensively argued, a crucial basis for the ideology of entrepreneurial capitalism. And, as has also been extensively argued, the residue of disgust, bodily waste, is the matter of ritual. In the last moments of *Xala*, the beggars take their revenge on El Hadji in a role reversal of power and humiliation. As El Hadji stands naked in front of his wife and daughter, the beggars crowd around and spit on him. This is the price that the blind man exacts for lifting the *xala*. And as the scene seems to continue beyond endurance, the film ends with a freeze-frame.

30

THE BOOK DEPOSITORY

David Pascoe

Michael is a gentle soul who dines out most evenings at the Hollandais restaurant and spends his nights in a book depository, 'a large – very large – dusty hall of books with high vaulted ceilings', a place whose shapes and colours evoke the plenty and the culture of the Dutch Golden Age:

> The colour is brown – various browns from almost cream to almost black. Overall the colour is predominantly a Rembrandt golden brown with touches of orange – a warm inviting space despite its huge size. Deep chiaroscuro – dramatic dark spaces and bright highlights on pale brown polished wood. There are stacks and stacks of books – ranged on tall bookcases whose upper shelves can only be reached by ten-foot-high wooden banistered ladders on wheels.

In his spare time Michael is cataloguing French history: 'Louis XV', 'Versailles' and 'The French Revolution' are among the headings that he has inscribed on his bookcases to organize the contents of the depository. Georgina, the lover whom he has brought back to his residence for the first time, asks him, nonplussed, 'What good are all these books to you? You can't eat them. How can they make you happy?' And she continues, 'If you had to make a choice between me and your books, which would you choose?' Michael avoids a direct answer and, before plumping for Georgina's thighs, responds, 'Print and flesh are both equally attractive'.

From: David Pascoe, 'The Book Depository', in *Peter Greenaway: Museums and Moving Images* (London, Reaktion Books, 1997).

The choice between print and flesh, the book and the body, is one which many of Greenaway's projects over the last decade have set out in explicit detail. He observed in 1996: 'It may be that there are two simulations in life that can be, sooner or later, guaranteed to excite and please – sex and text, flesh and literature. Perhaps it is a commendable ambition to try to bring both these two simulations together, so close together in fact that they can be considered, at least for a time – perhaps for the length of a film – as inseparable'. And certainly, his films have sought to present the kinds of actions that might be undertaken under the influence of a book and, further, the harm books might do to lives.

[...]

CONSPICUOUS CONSUMPTION

The choice that Greenaway tries to articulate, then, is always between flesh and print; but if the wrong choice is made, for whatever reason, then the body may need to become a text, or words may have to be eaten. In such cases, Greenaway ensures that the metaphor – making a book of the body, seeing the body as a book – becomes a grisly and shocking reality. Hence, in the closing section of *The Cook, the Thief, his Wife and her Lover*, Georgina, the wife of Spica, the Thief, will find the corpse of her Lover, Michael, in the darkened book depository. Some hours earlier, Spica has force-fed Michael the pages of the *History of the French Revolution* by Pascal Astruc-Latelle. At first glance, the image of a mouth stuffed with bloodied pages might seem to be an allusion to one of Dürer's most bizarre and explicit woodcuts, where St John devours the book that will secure his faith: 'Take it and eat; it will be bitter to your stomach, but sweet as honey in your mouth' (*Revelations* 10:8). But the leaves have been rammed down Michael's throat with the handle of a wooden spoon, in revenge for having goosed Spica's wife, becoming a bizarre act of *gavage*, which might bring about an enlarged *foie* but not an augmented *foi*. It is an act of pathological cruelty, its scenic arrangement modelled, unsurprisingly, on Rembrandt's *Anatomy Lesson of Dr Joan Deyman*, painted in 1656, which also appears in *Prospero's Books*. In it, the position of the corpse, shown lying directly facing the spectator, amounts to a bold foreshortening, akin to Mantegna; but this has been done to avoid having to offer any visual account of the removal of the stomach and intestine – what Ezra Pound might call 'the brown meat of Rembrandt' – and in their place is only an undifferentiated red mass. This, translated to Michael, becomes a stain on his chest, which can only mean life is about to become *nature morte*.

The combination of this image with Rembrandt's brings together, finally and terribly, the twin poles of the film: nature and culture, body and mind, restaurant and library. Michael is the first to admit that the book depository's kitchen and toilet facilities are a bit 'primitive', and no doubt that is why he eats out so regularly; but from the vantage point of this 'dusty hall of books', a kind of ivory tower, the lack of facilities is balanced by 'an extraordinary view'.

Yet a diet of culture is insufficient; one cannot live on books, and Michael dies when he is fed with them. Deny consumption and defecation and you deny two of the three most basic rhythms of life; the third, of course, is well known to the lovers, Michael and Georgina.

On the other hand, Spica the Thief has no sense of culture other than that prefaced by enterprise. Because his is a world dominated by false accounting, Spica thinks Michael could only be a bookkeeper; someone capable of appreciating a joke about cooking the books. So he picks up Richard's volume and suggests it be 'grilled with some mashed peas'. In several interviews, Greenaway has drawn attention to the political impetus behind the film. He told Gavin Smith that Spica represents 'a man who knows the price of everything and the value of nothing' and that the film conveys 'my anger and passion about the current British political situation'. He was even more explicit when he stated:

> *The Cook, the Thief, his Wife and her Lover* is a passionate angry dissertation for me on the rich vulgarian Philistine anti-intellectual stance of the present cultural situation in Great Britain ... There's a lull in the film where Spica says to the lover who is reading, 'Does this book make money?' That line really sums up this theme. In England now there seems to be only one currency, as indeed one might say about the whole capitalist world.

Spica is operating a protection racket, squeezing money out of businesses in the area; but the restaurant that he patronizes is no ordinary establishment. It is 'Le Hollandais'. Its back wall is covered with a reproduction of the *Banquet of the Officers of the Haarlem Militia Company of St George, 1616* by Frans Hals, 'the first monumental landmark of the great age of Dutch painting ... [which] exults in the healthy optimism and strength that helped build the new republic'. This pictorial quotation fulfils several roles. For one thing, in its depiction of these amateur archers of Haarlem it represents the burgeoning bourgeoisie as a class, and Albert, for all his money and pretensions to 'class', cannot escape his bourgeois bloodlines and habits. For another thing, Hals himself represents both Spica and what Spica might have been, had he been successful in his attempts to purchase class. Moreover, the feasting Haarlem *corps de garde* give an impression of secure masculine power which is not without parallel in Spica's world; one representation of conspicuous consumption gazes on the other, just as the diners at one table in a restaurant might cast knowing glances at those on the next.

Yet the central painterly fascination in Greenaway's film is not with Hals's work, but lies instead more generally with representations of inanimate objects, bereft of narrative context, representations that nevertheless combine the illusion of vitality and the reality of inertia; representations that came to be known in the Dutch Republic as *stil-leven*. In 1988, giving an account of *Drowning by Numbers*, a film which features 'Dutch morality metaphors' – reminders of transience in the form of the bursting bubbles on the pink soap, or a ground beetle soon to die stranded on its back – Greenaway discussed how the genre broke its strict bounds altogether and came to depict corpses:

> the Dutch were adroit at painting dead meat – plucked or unplucked, butchered or merely just slaughtered. Some painters of the art were such slow practitioners that their subjects deteriorated before their eyes – flowers faded, fruit decayed, vegetables decomposed, meat rotted – prophetic activity when the painting was commissioned to be a moral reminder of time passing – an ironic still-life would self-reflexively include the mould and the fungus.

Hence, in *The Cook, the Thief*, two vans loaded with produce arrive in the opening moments, courtesy of Albert Spica: 'racks of red and white meat and tiers of blue and white fish; pigs' heads, trotters, bulls' tongues, offal, kidneys, tripe; squid, clams, herring, flatfish, lobsters, prawns. The rich, colourful boldly lit raw food is examined with both enthusiasm and nausea'. In these stunning ensembles 'reminiscent of Dutch seventeenth-century painting' there is an attempt, particular, to alert us to Rembrandt's *Slaughtered Ox*; and, with regard to the fish, to the work of the master of the piscine still-life, Abraham van Beyeren. Such a style of painting placed high demands on the physical integrity of its subject-matter; ripeness was all, but inevitably decay would follow *ad nauseam*. And so, by the midpoint of Greenaway's film, the two vans are filled with flies and the once-solid contents have deliquesced. When the doors are opened, 'the inside of the [fish] van is a gruesome mess of rot and decay – liquid rot, maggots and flies – including the deeply rotted bodies of two large dogs'. Consequently, *nature morte* must somehow arrest the stages of putrefaction by freezing life into stasis; but refrigeration by means of paint was an expensive process, possibly costing more than the products to be preserved. Hence, it was the art itself rather than the subject-matter that was advertising its opulence, its luxury, its conspicuous consumption of time and money.

In particular, the spectacular work of Jan Davidsz. de Heem, in which the depicted objects arouse a marvel second only to that evoked by his rendering of them, provides a point of departure for many of the more ornate table displays created for the benefit of Spica's party. De Heem, who was born in Utrecht, moved to Antwerp in 1636 because 'there one could have rare fruit of all kinds, large plums, peaches, cherries, oranges, lemons, grapes and others in fine condition and state of ripeness to draw from life'. The distinction of his *pronkstilleven* lies in the lavish brightness of the colours and the extraordinary attention to detail, both in the fruits and the swathes of opulent fabric that so often frame his canvases. Take his *Still Life with a Parrot*, a triumph of illusionism in its rendering of textures and light effects, used to present a rich conglomeration of objects in an encyclopaedic fashion. It features objects representing the elements: the birds of the air, in the form of the macaw; the oysters and shells; the fruits of the earth; and the metal vessels that required heat for their fabrication. Yet, as recent critics have suggested, it is difficult to read such images of *pronk* without recalling that the banquet piece was often also a warning against decadence and ostentation. No doubt the gold – and silver-ware, the blue jewellery box and the shells all suggest the vanities of collecting and spending money on costly, worldly goods; but other elements caution the beholder against over-indulgence. Because of their presumed qualities as an aphrodisiac, oysters were traditionally reported to lead to sexual excess; while, for instance, melon consumed in large amounts was sometimes thought to produce insanity. By contrast, other objects in the picture imply spiritual strength (the unbroken column) and salvation through Christ (the bread, wine and grapes all have Eucharistic associations); but the Last Supper was never like this.

So many of Greenaway's shots frame Dutch still-life paintings and include minor subgenres. At one point, the lovers copulate in the plucking room, a sequence that may allude to the moral narrative of a canvas such as Gerrit Dou's *A Poulterer's Shop*. As Erika Langmuir explains: 'Seventeenth-century texts indicate that in Dutch and German *Vogel* (bird) was often synonymous with the phallus, *vogelen* (to bird) was a euphemism for sexual intercourse, and *vogelaar* (birdcatcher) could refer to a procurer or lover'. Hence, Michael and Georgina make love in the midst of 'some fifty or more dead birds ... lined up on the cold slabs – chickens, turkeys, geese, ducks'; and when they are inter-rupted by a bashful kitchen hand who removes a large bird, Michael, in the best traditions of British music hall, observes, 'Someone's having goose for dinner'. And of course, the most horrifying example of *nature morte* and of the body's containment within the space of representation involves the presentation of the dead Michael, cooked in aspic, and as brown as Rembrandt's beef. By pre-senting this signature dish, the French chef of the restaurant 'Le Hollandais' has become a Dutch artist in his ability to bring the real into representation. It is a movement that determines the style of the film; but, as so often, the emphatic artifice of Greenaway's image tends to have the effect of curbing our identifica-tion with it.

Beginning with a shot of several dogs, including a Dalmatian whose decay was filmed in *Z&OO*, the camera climbs up through the scaffolding of a stage set before pausing at a curtained portal flanked by two waiters. This is the point of no return. They turn and then conduct us through the curtains where the camera pauses high above a car park adjacent to the restaurant's back entrance, which itself seems to be way below the level of the street down a long gradient. At this point two vans and a car arrive and screech to a halt, and a group of men haul out a victim, strip him, force him to eat dog excrement and then urinate over him. The whole narrative is made literally groundless by this establishing shot, its *mise-en-scène* proven physically ungraspable at the very outset. With images of scavenging dogs and back entrances, Greenaway reminds us that everything above the backside, the zone of the scatological, is a fiction; and, of course, he saves his own film from the charge of cerebrality by treating it as a body he enters from the rear end.

After the assault on the hapless Roy, Sacha Vierny's camera pans laterally past the food vans along a blue ramp, where a road sign with the name 'La Concourse' is partially obscured, revealing only 'course' (part of a meal); it also shows the neon sign 'Luna', perhaps a reminder of the tics that characterize criminal madmen, as well as an allusion to *La Luna*, Bertolucci's 1977 film about mother – son incest, the metaphorical consumption of one's own kind, a kind of familial cannibalism. Continuing on its ineluctable way, the camera pans left to right again through the kitchen, a space much too voluminous for a restaurant kitchen. The camera pauses during the panning to pick up more signs (the SPICA and BOARST names), the many work surfaces for cutting and preparing food, the varied staff and many more partly obscured or hidden places: a ladder walk-up; a draped room for poultry and game, another for bread and bakery products along the back wall. It quickly becomes clear that the fourth wall, which might be expected to be behind the camera, does not exist, so the panning does not stop or go around; it merely continues, left to right, resolutely two-dimensional.

The action takes place over the course of eight days, and at the beginning of each day there is usually a period of entry into the restaurant where, after considering the *à la carte* menu, the camera pans along tables composed of still-lifes and the Hals in the background. Occasionally it comes across a wedding party and various couples, but the camera 'swallows' them up in its passage to the Spica table – the bodies arranged like Leonardo's *Last Supper*, or the parody of it in Bunuel's *Viridiana* – which is always shown with some detail of the Hals painting visible. In consequence, the self-important figures in the canvas seem to share the same space as the actors, in part because of the manner in which the colours of the painting match those of the room. Moreover, in transforming these painted figures at the Haarlem table – figures who look straight out from Hals's painting – into the watchers of its beholders, the cinema audience, Greenaway uses the canvas to position both viewer and viewed within a common space. The scene is still depicted in wide angle and showing more ceiling than floor, but here space is deceptive. We don't know the true dimensions of the Hals painting; we rarely stop for any vantage point far enough away from the Spica table to convey true distance (one rare exception is when Georgina stops at Michael's table to look at his books and we see both Albert and Richard looking at her, and the room seems enormous); and, finally, we never discover the true dimensions of the back wall until the last scene when that wall is the point of entry for Albert.

Whenever the camera pans in the opposite direction, moving from right to left to leave the restaurant, it often accentuates the event in the narrative by pulling back and up and even travelling slightly faster than the characters, so that there is both a tension of speed and an emotional distance from the characters. It is clear that such travelling movements are carefully considered by Greenaway, as is suggested by his discussion of the murderer in Prud'hon's *Divine Justice Pursuing Crime*, 'running out left, the sinister direction, against the grain of a positive left to right reading'. As Alan Woods has noticed, Spica, as aggressor – attacking Patricia, harassing Michael, hectoring Richard, torturing the porter Pup – is often on the right of the screen, facing left. The disposition of processions and recessions is not simplistic but it is simplified by the set: in the book depository the lovers are given the bad news of Pup by Richard entering from right to left, and this is followed by Georgina's visit to his hospital, where she enters from left to right, a kind of ministering angel. The characters traverse from right to left in order to perpetrate acts of violence (Spica, on several occasions, dragging Georgina), to have sex (Michael and Georgina; Fitch and Patricia) and finally to escape the clutches of Spica.

The lovers escape from under Albert's very nose, as Georgie says, in the van full of now putrefying meat. Naked like Adam and Eve, they are confronted by the decay of the flesh and expelled from the paradise of the restaurant. The allusion here is to the convention of the flight from Eden, in particular that depicted in Rembrandt. Later, after being hosed down by a black attendant named Eden, they take refuge in the book depository and wander nude through its dusty corridors. The colour of this place of exile is brown, the shade of a leather binding or an oak shelf, or of the lovers' flesh even; and light reflected from water plays against the ceiling. But the book depository is yet one more paradise from which they will be ejected for their naivety in thinking that physical love can be pure; in believing that they can return to the state of innocence.

The whole structure of the film is based on artificially coloured areas such as the depository; and the colours' function is not simply decorative but a structural element. The film commences in the 'dark blue' of the car park, a glacial and hostile place redolent of putrefaction and depravity, where the weak are literally pissed on and the dogs scavenge. From here, the film moves to the kitchens, whose predominant colour is green – 'hooker's dark green, leaf-green, emerald, faded turquoise and eau-de-Nil – like the colours of a dark wet jungle'. This is a serene work space where creativity expresses itself naturally. Jets of gas shoot from the hobs like sacramental flames, and the kitchen is echoic and resonant: 'the acoustics are like those of a cathedral', and so Pup will sing *Psalm 51* like a choirboy, an incarnation of innocence. Yet this quasi-mystical place also suggests a factory, not simply by dint of the honest graft that goes on here but also because of the enormous fans and ducts whose design 'may suggest the aircraft industry of the 1940s'. The dining room is carpeted in several tones of red and on the wall is the large reproduction of Hals's painting. The toilets, which are reached through a narrow corridor, are in fact immaculate, sanitized and white, bathed in what might at first glance seem to be an absence of colour until one recalls Newton's *Opticks*. White light is promiscuous, a fusion of all the colours of the spectrum; and so they become a place where the lovers come together for the first time, until they are interrupted by the braying of Albert. Aware of the way context inevitably colours our view, Greenaway makes the hue of a costume change from red, say, to white as its wearer passes from dining room to bathroom. And in the bathroom where cleanliness and dirt coincide we have the greatest contrast – the red sash of Albert, the thief, turns white against his still black suit.

However, such colour-coding is not merely pictorial. Greenaway's film develops the theme of consumption as a means of incorporating the real, a notion that is ironically addressed by the cook when he wonders whether Georgina wishes him to cook her dead lover so that she can eat him and absorb him into herself. The idea is seen more seriously in the attempt to create in the restaurant an ambitious system of visual signification, based on the peristaltic movements of the body's digestive tract. Greenaway, as we have seen, creates his film out of long travelling shots which take us through the different parts of the set. First of all, the kitchen displays the raw materials, rendered aesthetically pleasing, perhaps, by the conventions of still-life; next, the dining room, whose walls are as red as a mouth, announces itself as the place of ingestion, of consumption; and finally, the toilet, the site of waste, of excretion, of private functions. The kitchen communicates with the dining room by a swing door which opens and closes like a mouth; and with the toilets by means of a narrow corridor, the connecting tube between the two orifices, top and bottom. And as Albert wryly observes', ... the pleasures are related. Because the naughty bits and dirty bits are so close together, it just goes to show you how sex and eating are related'. This is close to Freud, who in 1905 attempted to explain the origin of excremental theories of birth; and why so many believed that 'people get babies by eating some particular thing (as they do in fairy tales) and babies are born through the bowel like a discharge of faeces'.

Greenaway notes: 'All the metaphors of the film are about putting things into the mouth'; and this includes putting words into others' mouths, as the self-conscious allusions to language merely reinforce the obliquities of the film. At the beginning we see letters taken out of vehicles – among them an A and an O, alpha and omega, beginning and end. Soon after, these letters are arranged to read ASPIC & BOARST, then unscrambled once again to become the sign SPICA & BORST. Later, Michael is forced to eat his books. His manner of dying makes Georgina's demand at gunpoint that her husband eat her lover's cooked penis – the veritable phallic signifier – all the more appropriate, as this materialization of his earlier threat that he will kill Michael and eat him means that Spica is being forced to eat his words; to consume himself, conspicuously.

31

THE FORCE OF SURFACES: DEFIANCE IN ZHANG YIMOU'S FILMS

Rey Chow

This reading centers on three films by Zhang Yimou – *Red Sorghum* (*Hong gaoliang*; Xian Film Studio, 1988), *Judou* (co-directed with Yang Fengliang; Star Entertainment, 1990), and *Raise the Red Lantern* (*Da hong denglong gao gao gua*; China Film Co-Production Corporation, 1991).

ELEMENTS OF A NEW ETHNOGRAPHY

The three films in question constitute a distinctive type. Their characteristics have become the "trademarks" of Zhang's style. The "background" in these films is uniform: it is an oppressively feudal China. The historical details are blurred, even though we know from the original novellas from which the films are adapted that the events take place in the precommunist period. The oppressiveness of feudal China is usually personified by an unreasonable, domineering older male figure, such as Jiuer's leper husband in *Red Sorghum*; Judou's husband, Yang Jinshan, the owner of the dye mill; and Chen Zuoqian, the landlord who owns several wives in *Raise the Red Lantern*. Because they are powerful within their class, these old men have the license to be abusive: they purchase wives, use them for both perverse sexual pleasure and reproduction, and sometimes murder them when they become disobedient or inconvenient. In terms of representing the maltreatment of women, the blurriness of historical background in Zhang's films is matched by an obliviousness to class differences. The mental or psychical suffering of Songlian, the new concubine

From: Rey Chow, 'The Force of Surfaces: Defiance in Zhang Yimou's Films', in *Primitive Passions: visuality, sexuality, ethnography and Contemporary Chinese Cinema* (Columbia University Press, 1995).

in *Raise the Red Lantern*, is as intense as that of Judou, even though Songlian has attended university and Judou is an illiterate peasant. For Zhang, woman is very much a typical sexual body that is bound by social chains and that needs to be liberated.

These tales of gothic and often morbid oppression are marked by their contrast with the sensuous screen design of the films. Zhang's film language deploys exquisite colors in the depiction of "backwardness." The color red in *Red Sorghum*, the bright solid colors of the dyed cloths in *judou*, the striking, symmetrical screen organizations of architectural details, and the refined-looking furniture, utensils, food, and costumes in *Raise the Red Lantern* are all part and parcel of the recognizable cinematographic expertise of Zhang and his collaborators such as the talented cinematographer Gu Changwei.

In many respects, these three films can be described as constituting a new kind of ethnography. The first element of this new ethnography is that it presents the results of its "research" in the form not of books or museum exhibits but of cinema. Zhang's films have become a spectacular and accessible form of imaginative writing about a "China" that is supposedly past but whose ideological power still lingers. While many of the ethnic customs and practices in Zhang's films are invented, the import of such details lies not in their authenticity but in their mode of signification. Such import makes up the second major element of the newness of Zhang's ethnography: the use of things, characters, and narratives not for themselves but for their collective, hallucinatory signification of "ethnicity."

[...]

The difference between the ethnic detail as such and its self-conscious articulation is not the kind of difference that separates the time of the ethno-grapher's "fieldwork" and the time of her writing. Rather – and here we come to the third major element of the newness of Zhang's ethnography – because the ethnographer here is himself a "native" of the culture he is transcribing, the difference made conscious by the second order articulation becomes in effect a culture's belated fascination with its own datedness, its own alterity. Although Zhang may think that he is making films about China, what he is doing is representing a timeless China of the past, which is given to us in an imagined because retrospective mode. This "China," which is signified mythically, is the China constructed by modernity – the modernity of anthropology, ethnogra-phy, and feminism. It is also a "China" exaggerated and caricatured, in which the past is *melodramatized* in the form of excessive and absurd rituals and customs.

In his mythical construct, what Zhang accomplishes is not the reflection of a China "that was really like that" but rather a new kind of organization that is typical of modernist collecting. The chaotic, overabundant elements of the past are now (re)arranged in a special kind of order. In this way Zhang's films enact cinema's capacity, described by Paul Virilio, for gratifying the wish of those away from home for a dreamy "homeland" at the same time that it turns everyone who watches into a kind of migrant:

Mandarin Ducks and Butterflies, Oedipus, and the Tactics of Visuality

Zhang astutely places the center of interest on femininity in his construction of this "new aboriginality." Femininity in his films is the place where the contradictory nature of culture-writing – as a retrospective capturing of the past's violence and chaos, and as a progressive, forward-looking investment in the possibilities of rewriting and enlightenment – becomes clearest. Women are here the prototype of "the primitive" in all the ambiguities of that word – they are the bearers of the *barbaric* nature of a patriarchal system that has outlived its time and place; their abuse is a sign of China's *backwardness*; through them we come to understand the *fundamental* horrors about a culture. At the same time, women's sufferings reveal a larger human *nature* that has been unjustly chained and that seeks to be liberated; they are a kind of wronged, maligned, exploited *noble savage* whose innocence must be redeemed.

Insofar as they melodramatize womanly events in what often turn out to be trivial, hackneyed narratives, Zhang's films are, in terms of ethnic lineage, inheritors of the popular Mandarin Duck and Butterfly fictional modes that run throughout Chinese literature and film in the twentieth century. I have argued elsewhere that the predominant feature of Butterfly fiction is that women's problems serve as the hinges of many narratives. If we translate the Butterfly novelists' narrative strategies into cinematic terms, we may say that it is women who are the objects of cinematic close-ups and slow motions, and that it is women who provide the suturing points at which the narratives "hang together." Unlike Butterfly novelists who had to focus on women with the abstract means of verbal language, however, Zhang has in the film medium an obvious means of visual display. Whereas Butterfly novelists must devise strange plots in which women characters' loved ones mysteriously disappear so that they are left alone for dramatization, Zhang has at his disposal a much more palpable means of externalizing and thus reifying women's oppression. If the subject matter of these films is the kind long decried by canonically minded critics as feminine and thus insignificant, Zhang makes us realize anew the fascination of such trivial matter. His films do not change the mundane nature of the stories but enlarge the possibilities of our enjoyment of precisely those unspeakable, at times pornographic fantasies that are, shall we say, a culture's "shame."

Furthermore, whereas in the traditional Butterfly novels, the enjoyment of such fantasies still had to be "covered up" by moralistic prefaces and didactic justifications, in Zhang such a "cover-up" is not necessary because film, at the same time that it provides him with a palpable means of expressing womanly contents, also provides him with an alibi: he is merely showing such (pornographic) contents in order to give a "realistic" picture of China. The didactic excuse, which the Butterfly novelists had to insert explicitly into their narratives, is already there, in the silence and ambiguity of the filmic image.

Indeed, there is every indication that whatever Zhang does, he does in order to emphasize not the thematic concerns or even characterization but the filmic or visual nature of his films. This is where the prominence of womanly content – that conscious invention of an ethnic primitivism – must be seen as part and parcel of the cross-cultural significance, the emergent ethnographicity, of his practice. This practice is, above all, a conscious and tactical mobilization of every kind of event toward visual display, a display that is most effectively achieved through women. Hence, even though Zhang's interest is not inherently in women's problems themselves, he relies for his culture-writing on a focalization, a "zoom-in" on the women characters.

To this end – that of skillfully displaying women as bearers of his filmic ethnography – Zhang makes full use of the modernist conceptual method that many have called, after Freud, *Oedipalization*. Examples: In *Red Sorghum*, Jiuer's husband was mysteriously murdered before "my grandpa" shows up to claim her. In *Raise the Red Lantern*, there is the suggestion that the eldest son of Songlian's husband, the young man called Feipu, might be romantically attracted to her but there would be no hope for such a romance since his father is alive and well. The woman's body/sexuality becomes, in both films, the place where Oedipal rivalries – rivalries between men – are visually, visibly staged.

In *Judou*, Oedipal rivalries literally take the form of incest: Judou lives her life between her husband and his nephew Tianqing. Apart from the background of a dye mill, Zhang introduces a significant number of changes in the Judou story in order to enhance the Oedipalist focus on femininity. First, the title of the story is changed from the name of a mythic male figure in Liu Heng's novella – Fuxi is the mythic emperor who invented the *bagua* (octogram) and the weaving of nets – to that of a poor and insignificant woman, a female subaltern, in modern times. Second, Zhang rewrites Liu Heng's plot in such a way as to connect the dramatization of femininity with patricide. Whereas in Liu Heng's novella, the old man Yang Jinshan dies a quiet natural death with a smile on his face and Tianqing, Judou's lover, commits suicide in a vat, in Zhang's film these two men, both of whom are fathers to the youngster Tianbai, are killed by him (accidentally in Jinshan's case and deliberately in Tianqing's). Third, instead of living to a great old age as she does in the novella, Judou burns down her house in what seems to be a revolutionary but suicidal ending. The implications of Oedipalization are the twin deaths of the father and the mother. If fathers are often murdered, mothers, if not murdered, commit suicide or go mad.

Together, the repeated associations of patricide typical of Oedipalization – the physical impotence, symbolic castration, and ultimate death of fathers – constitute a reading of China's modernity and "ethnicity" that is a *self-subalternization*: we are made to feel that, being fatherless, China is deprived of power; China is a subaltern in the world of modern nations. At the same time, this self-subalternization is unmistakably accompanied by the fetishization of women – fetishization that can, I think, be more accurately described as a *self-exoticization* through the tactics of visuality.

Such tactics of visuality are apparent once we examine other alterations Zhang made in the literature he borrowed. For instance, the background of a dye mill in *Judou* was not present in the original story by Liu Heng but added in the film so that the audience can see the drama on the screen as primarily a drama of colors. In *Raise the Red Lantern*, the eye-catching family ritual of lighting lanterns in the courtyard of the favored concubine is not present in Su Tong's novella "Qi qie cheng qun" [Wives and concubines], from which the film was adapted. Moreover, in Su Tong's story there is a well in which concubines were thrown previous to Songlian's arrival. The well, located in a neglected part of the garden, is a symbol both of femininity and of the inevitable death that awaits women in the Chen family. In Zhang's film, the well disappears. Instead we find an architecturally spectacular rooftop where various members of the household make their presence and where stylized singing, conversations, and conflicts take place. The space of murder is changed to a small house locked up on one side of the roof. Unlike the well in Su Tong's novella, this house, in which concubines who commit adultery are hanged, is much more prominently visible on the screen.

Examples like these indicate that what Zhang performs here is not really a liberation of sexuality – neither a vibrant male sexuality nor a repressed female sexuality – in the narrow sense but, first and foremost, a production of filmic signs. To return to Barthes, Zhang is building one semiotic system on another, in such a manner as always to bracket the denotative meaning of the "raw" first level of signification.

The Art of Seduction

While Barthes uses the word *myth* to describe the bracketing of this first level, Jean Baudrillard, in a more dramatic manner, calls it death, a death he associates with seduction: "To seduce," writes Baudrillard, is "to die as reality and reconstitute oneself as illusion."

Borrowing from the etymology of the word *seduction*, which refers to the act of leading astray or leading away, Baudrillard defines seduction as the turning of a sign away from meaning, from its own truth. Following Baudrillard, we may say that what we see in Zhang's films is a "transubstantiation of sex into signs that is the secret of all seduction." What is displayed is not so much woman or even feudal China per se as the act of displaying, of making visible. What Zhang "fetishizes" is primarily cinematography itself. If we speak of a narcissism here, it is a repeated playing with "the self" that is the visuality intrinsic to film. *This* play is *the* sexuality of Zhang's works.

Barthes writes that "myth is not defined by the object of its message, but by the way in which it utters this message." Baudrillard writes that "seduction . . . never belongs to the order of nature, but that of artifice – never to the order of energy, but that of signs and rituals." Accordingly, the seduction of Zhang's films – the appeal of his visual ethnography – is that they keep crossing boundaries and shifting into new spheres of circulation. The wish to "liberate" Chinese women, which seems to be the "content," shifts into the liberation of "China," which shifts into the liberation of the "image" of China on film, which shifts into the liberation of "China" on film in the international culture market, and so on.

With the shifting of attention from "message" or "nature" to the form of utterance and to artifice, meaning – that culturally loaded thing – is displaced onto the level of surface exchange. Such a displacement has the effect of emptying "meaning" from its conventional space – the core, the depth, or the inside waiting to be seen and articulated – and reconstructing it in a new locus – the locus of the surface, which not only shines but *glosses*; which looks, stares, and speaks.

In the light of this seductive locus of the surface, which constitutes the space of a new culture-writing, Zhang's modesty about his own work becomes very interesting. Speaking in regard to *Red Sorghum*, for instance, Zhang has said that he has not really thought too clearly about how to shoot the film (or films in general) and that he likes discussing with friends in "theory circles" because they can help him figure out many problems. Speaking guilelessly thus, Zhang is like the seducer described by Baudrillard – the seducer who does not consciously know that he is seducing even though he is fully engaged in the game of seduction. Zhang's films, it follows, are the seducer's snares – the enigmatic traps he sets up in order to engage his viewers in an infinite play and displacement of meanings and surface – and, most important, to catch these viewers in their longings and desires, making them reveal passions they nonetheless do not fully understand.

THE SEARCH FOR CONCRETENESS

Oppressive feudal practices, ethnic details, myth making, magnificent cinematography, female sexuality – these elements I have summarized as the recognizable trademarks of Zhang's films are also those that have most interested his critics, whether or not they are sympathetic with his projects. What I find most revealing about readings of Zhang's films is that regardless of their evaluation, they all tend to revolve around assumptions about depths and surfaces. I will begin with the readings that are critical of his works, readings that fall into three main types.

First, we hear that Zhang's films lack depth, a lack that critics often consider as the *reason* why his films are beautiful. For instance, in a short review of *Red Sorghum*, David Edelstein writes that "Zhang's superb eye masks his lack of interest in his subjects' psychology." Edelstein concludes that the film is a "robust crowd-pleaser from mainland China" and that "the depth of its dumbness must have been a secondary consideration, a small price to pay for sweep and novelty and unimpeachable politics." H. C. Li writes that *Red Sorghum* is "a film intended to please the eye and excite the senses, and a film endowed with superficial brilliance but not deep content." Wu Ruozeng says that one should not talk about *Red Sorghum* in terms of "profundities" (*shenke*) but should simply understand the strong feeling (*ganjue*) it puts forth for a return to human nature.

Second, Zhang's "lack of depth" is inserted in what become debates about the politics of cross-cultural representations. The beauty of Zhang's films is, for some critics, a sign of Zhang's attempt to pander to the tastes of foreigners. Yang Zhao, for instance, writes that the visual design of *Judou* is specially made to cater to those who are familiar with the established rules of American film culture, which is characterized by a kind of "tourist's psychology" (*guanguang xintai*). Dai Qing, who charges the crew of *Raise the Red Lantern* for taking "outrageous liberty with such details as decor, dialogue, and diction," writes that "this kind of film is really shot for the casual pleasures of foreigners." For Paul Clark, who is speaking about 1980s mainland Chinese films in general, the international awards won by films such as Zhang's suggest that "the strong visual qualities of these films could reach across borders," even though "for the comparatively tiny Chinese audience who followed these films ... the new movies were distinctively Chinese." There is in these remarks a feeling that the use of appealing visual qualities exoticizes China and that it is such exoticization, rather than the genuine complexities of Chinese society, that accounts for the success of such films in the West. Even though Zhang and his contemporaries are "orientals," then, they are explicitly or implicitly regarded as producing a kind of orientalism.

Third, this lack of depth, this orientalism, is linked to yet another crime – that of exploiting women. Zhang's films are unmistakably filled with sexually violent elements, such as the kidnapping of Jiuer by "my Grandpa" in *Red Sorghum*, Jiuer's eventual submission to him, the voyeuristic treatment of Judou, and the commodification of women in *Raise the Red Lantern*, in which wives and concubines are portrayed as jealous enemies preying upon one another in order to win the favor of the despotic husband who dominates them all. It is said that by fetishizing the female subaltern, or the female-as-subaltern, Zhang is simply reinforcing the patriarchal interests for which women are merely sex objects. Hence feminist critics such as Esther Yau and Peter Hitchcock write of Zhang's films: women such as Jiuer are "being engaged in excessive sexist exchanges motivated by male desire"; Zhang and Chen Kaige "remain remarkably mute about how reactionary technologies of gender may inform their own discourse"; Zhang's "close-ups of [Jiuer's] face and soft focus are entirely traditional in their aesthetic effects"; and so forth.

I would like to clarify at this point that I am fully in agreement with the feminist intent of critics such as Yau and Hitchcock. Insofar as he adopts a traditional, mainstream understanding of male-female relations, it is clear that Zhang's films do not depart at all from the politics of the polarization of male gaze versus female body that was problematized by Laura Mulvey's influential essay "Visual Pleasure and Narrative Cinema." On the contrary, Zhang's films provide a demonstration, from the perspective of a non-Western culture, of

Mulvey's incisive observation of what in many ways is still the predominant heterosexual problematic. It seems to me, however, that rather than simply reinscribing Zhang within this problematic (and condemning him for it), we need to go further and ask what we would be disabling and prohibiting from surfacing once we adopt, as we must from time to time, the moral overtones of this admittedly justified feminist position. The reason why we need to go further is that, in criticizing Zhang's "traditional" or "patriarchal" treatment of women, feminist criticism may unwittingly put itself at the service of a kind of conservatism that values depths over surfaces, and nativism over universalism, in a manner that is, ultimately, antifeminist. How so?

Jia chou bu ke wai yang

To explain what I think is the central problem here – the universal prejudice against exhibitionism and self-display – let me return to one of the most reactionary responses to Zhang, such as that coming from the mainland Chinese authorities. Apart from the explicit sexual contents of Zhang's films, it is believed that the Chinese authorities are displeased by Zhang because his films transgress the "Chinese" taboo, *jia chou bu ke wai yang*. The English equivalent to this Chinese expression would be something like "Don't air your dirty laundry in public." But the Chinese phrase is much more precise in that it points to the exact area that is being tabooed – not the "dirty laundry" itself but *wai yang*, the act of showing, brandishing, exhibiting (to the outside). The point, in other words, is not that there should not be such dirty laundry around – *that* is taken for granted, as a matter of course about *jia*, the family. The point is rather that such shame and dirt should not be flaunted.

In the language of visuality, what the Chinese authorities" disapproval signals is a disciplinary surveillance from above, but it is not exactly a surveillance over the "content" of backwardness in Zhang's films as is often assumed (many mainland films of the past few decades also use such content to point their morals). Rather, the surveillance is over the act of exhibiting and displaying. The reactionary response of the Chinese authorities in fact contains much more intelligence than most of their critics are willing to grant them, for in their disapproval lies the correct intuition that Zhang's films are not simply about backwardness but about a different kind of signification. Hence even though all the settings of Zhang's three films date back to the 1920s, 1930s, and 1940s – the period before the People's Republic of China was established – the authorities remained firm for a long time in their prohibitive resolve. Zhang's casual remarks about his filmmaking are revealing in this regard, for they point precisely to this deliberate flaunting, this defiant display of difference that disturbs the authorities:

> In *Red Sorghum* I did not deliberately try to combat or contradict the traditional way of making film . . . [However] that was indeed the purpose when we made *One and Eight [Yi ge he ba ge]* and *Yellow Earth*, and

especially when we made *One and Eight*. At that time I was filled with anger whenever I set up the camera. All of us were basically fed up with the unchanging, inflexible way of Chinese filmmaking, so we were ready to fight it at all costs in our first film. I would set down the camera and take a look, and [say to myself,] Oh, god, the composition is still the same as the old stuff! No! Turn the lens around – just turn it around, raise it, just for the sake of raising it. Actually *if you ask me whether there was any concept in this kind of incomplete composition, the answer is no; but the point was simply and deliberately to be different.*

What the Chinese authorities sense is perhaps exactly this kind of *gestural* force that, according to Zhang, has nothing "beneath" it. In its "emptiness," Zhang's filmmaking challenges the deep-rooted attitude of approval, ingrained in the understanding of representation across cultures, toward depth, profundity, and interiority. This attitude, which associates depth, profundity, and interiority with "virtue," is also the preference for a *somethingness* in representation.

Shi *versus* xu: *The Ethnic Paradigms of Evaluation*

It is well known to the practitioners and scholars of Chinese literature and culture that this attitude toward deep meanings is part of a pervasive bifurcated moralism of *shi* (fullness or concreteness) versus *xu* (emptiness), which are often used as criteria for judging virtues of aesthetic representation. Ultimately, such criteria must also be seen as major ways of *producing value in a culture*. For the purposes of our discussion, a table schematically contrasting the associations commonly attached to *shi* and *xu* may be drawn up as follows:

SHI	XU
full	empty
concrete	abstract
deep	shallow
earnest	superficial
authentic	fake
real worth	cosmetics
content	form
history	fiction
male	female

The notion of *shi* is linked to an approved concreteness of content in any representation, a concreteness that by extension would also be described with metaphors such as *shendu* (depth) and *neihan* (inner meaning). On the other hand, with the exception of philosophical discussions (typically, of Daoism) in which *xu* is attributed with the significance of the nonsaid, and with the exception of moralist advice of modesty and open-mindedness, the notion of *xu* is almost always invoked pejoratively in the language of cultural evaluation, as a way to express contempt for the kinds of associations listed in the right-hand column of our table. We think of expressions such as *xuruo* (weak, debilitated), *xuwei* (pretentious), *xufu* (superficial, slick), *xurong* (vanity), *xuhuan* (illusory), *xuwang* (fabricated), *xujia* (fake, artificial), *xu you qi biao* (superficial; literally, "possessed only with the surface"), *xuqing jiayi* (hypocritical display of affection), and *xu zhang sheng shi* (much ado about nothing; literally, "making empty noises and gestures").

When Zhang's critics criticize him for a lack of depth and an empty display, they are hence simply reinvoking the criteria of the reactionary *xu/shi* structure. As we will see in the following, precisely because this structure has to do not only with evaluation but with the production of value itself, it becomes even more crisis-laden once it is confronted with the politics of cross-cultural interpretation.

The Eyes of the Foreign Devil

In postcoloniality, this traditional or ethnic polarization of the criteria for aesthetic merit is complicated by the presence of that entity called the *foreign devil*. What may be added to our table now are "China" and "native" in the left-hand column and "the West" and "foreigner" in the right.

Among the Chinese, as among many non-Western peoples, there is a *postcolonial way of expressing contempt for one's fellow "natives"*: *zuo gei waiguoren kan* – such-and-such is done "for the eyes of the foreigner," with "foreigner" usually meaning those from the advanced industrial West. (See remarks from critics such as Dai Qing, cited earlier.) One thinks of expressions of contempt such as *chongyang* (worshiping the foreign) and *meiwai* (fawning on the foreign), which allude to the obsequious ways in which "natives" identify with the foreign devil rather than with their own culture and countrymen. These expressions, however, also reveal a highly ambivalent attitude toward the foreign, for the contempt they proclaim is, in fact, not possible without a keen observation or imagination of the foreigner's gaze and what may be done to attract or please that gaze. In other words, these expressions of contempt already contain *in themselves* the acts of looking at foreigner – of natives looking at or imagining the foreigner looking, of natives looking at or imagining fellow natives being looked at by foreigners, and so forth. And yet, while clearly recognizing in the foreigner a power to authenticate and endow value themselves, those who harbor such contempt are frequently quick to repudiate such acts of looking *in others*. Their contempt for fellow natives' looking is thus, we may say, ultimately an attempt to censor or prohibit this exchange between native and foreigner, even though, in their very mode of proclamation, they have already attested to the inevitability of this exchange.

Very often, and I think this is the case with the reception to Zhang's filmmaking, the expression of contempt is really the expression of an envy or jealousy at the success enjoyed by those who *have* captured the gaze of the foreigner. These ambivalent sentiments, which are laden with the injustices of history and politics, and which are transindividual, nonetheless manifest themselves prominently in the behavior of many individual "natives," in academia as much as in other circles, who look upon their fellow "natives" with suspicion, belittlement, and scorn, even while the same people who accuse others of pandering to the foreign devil remain themselves subserviently respectful to the foreign. Whenever the phrase *zuo gei waiguoren kan* (or its equivalent) is invoked, therefore, it is always the symptom of a self-contradictory sentiment, the meaning of which is "They have made it! They are actually being seen by the foreign devil!" – followed by a moralistic type of dismissal and selfassurance: "But of course they did it only by improper, shallow means." The fantasy that lies at the heart of such contempt is that we must prove "from within" that we are worthy of that foreign gaze and that if we do it properly, the foreign devil will look closely and deeply "inside" us for our authentic value.

Zhang, Too, Is Concrete, Not Empty

Although no books are written on how these postcolonial sentiments translate into aesthetic criteria, it is possible to see in the attempts to evaluate an artist like Zhang the inscriptions of the dilemmas of cross-cultural interpretative politics. If the more reserved of these evaluations tend to focus on the "superficial" quality of Zhang's films, the laudatory evaluations, too, are symptomatic of the bifurcated structure of moralaesthetic criteria. These laudatory evaluations, which come by and large from male critics, would show how *meaningful* Zhang's films are.

For instance, H. C. Li writes that *Red Sorghum* is "a Dionysian ode to life . . . a tribute to the heroic spirit of the Chinese people." Yan Xianglin praises *Red Sorghum* for its portrayal of a nonidealized humanity, which "returns aesthetic truth to values of simplicity and authenticity" [*dui yishu zhendi de fanpuguizhen*]; while Wu Ruozeng, who rules out using "profundities" as a criterion for *Red Sorghum* praises the film for returning us to the forces of human nature. Others draw on authors such as Bakhtin and Racine to compare the carnivalesque atmosphere and intensity of Zhang's films. Perhaps the most articulate of this type of reading is Yuejin Wang's, who sees *Red Sorghum* as a return of the collective repressed and an evocation of the cultural unconscious. Basing his interpretation of feminine sexuality entirely on Jiuer's looks, which he describes as "autonomous ecstasy," Wang upholds the film as containing a theory about a strong femininity as well as a marginalized but transgressive masculinity. These critics' interpretations are close to Zhang's own. Among Zhang's favorite descriptions of *Red Sorghum* are *reqing* (passion) and *huoli* (energy). When speaking about Mo Yan's *Red Sorghum Family*, on which his film was based, Zhang repeatedly refers to the "sensuous motion of life," the "enthusiastic human pursuit of life," and the "eulogy of life" signified by the narrative.

In their laudatory mode, the masculinist reviewers disprove the more negative conclusions of Zhang's critics but not their premise, which they in fact share. This is the premise that the value of a work of art consists in the concreteness, the "somethingness," of its content. What these enthusiastic reviewers uphold here is the "somethingness" of what we might call primitivism. In a way that reminds one of the eulogies of "nature," "life," and "sexuality" that characterize male modernist writers such as D. H. Lawrence and Henry Miller, we find in the positive readings of Zhang an overwhelming consensus about "energy" and "human nature" *in spite of* the apparent superficiality of his films. Instead of accusing Zhang of a lack of depth in the mode of being *xu*, then, these reviewers affirm, by their identification of the "energy" in Zhang that his films are *shi* – that is, sanguine, earthy, instinctual, close to the people. Together they produce a reading based on male homosocial bonding, a reading that says, Zhang, too, is concrete, not empty.

Feminist criticism, when confronted with the basic masculinism of this kind of "pro-life" clamor, has little choice other than pointing out the untenability of Zhang's "energy." Once it does this, however, it is putting itself at the service of the *xu/shi* interpretative machinery. Against the kinds of *shi* qualities affirmed by male critics, feminists must charge that Zhang's films are false representations of women's sexuality, that they fictionalize women's sufferings, and so on. In other words, feminists must *demystify* Zhang's films by saying that they are inauthentic representations of women. In the words of Yau, for instance, *Red Sorghum* is an example of China's "filmic fantasies" whose "defenses" are to be undone by "history." Another way of putting this would be to say that Zhang has left out the truth (*shi*) that is female subjectivity in favor of the lie (*xu*) that is the (fetishized) female image. In a manner perhaps unintended by most feminist critics, this type of feminist criticism would then, by implication, be helping to consolidate the kind of conservatism that would distrust all filmic representation on account of its superficiality, or that would repudiate all Westernized ethnic representation on account of its eagerness to cater to "foreign" consumption.

Whether positive or negative, therefore, evaluations of Zhang's films tend to leave the central problem of the moral-aesthetic polarization of *shi* and *xu* intact, allowing the values espoused therein to return under multiple guises. Despite their otherwise different or opposed politics, these readings have one thing in common – the assumption that there is a hidden truth, a core of meaning that is other than or interior to what we see on the glossy surfaces of Zhang's films

[...]

My primary objection to these interpretations is not that they do not tell the truth about Zhang's films – they do, and with great sensitivity and sophistication – but rather that, in concentrating on the search for concrete meanings, they seem to miss the predominant fact that filmic images operate as images, as surfaces whose significance lies in their manner of undoing depth itself. In order to deal with the problem of reading that Zhang's films cause, it is hence not enough simply to provide alternative analyses and hermeneutical exegeses of the "deep meanings" of the films.

This is the place where a kind of reading different from those legitimated by the "repressive hypothesis" must intervene and where a reference to someone such as Baudrillard is necessary. As is characteristic of all of his writings, Baudrillard's target in his book *Seduction* is Western culture's ingrained beliefs in production, depth, and the metaphysics of interiority. He argues that even ground-breaking, subversive modern theories such as Marxism, psychoanalysis, and feminism are complicitous with such beliefs when they systematically *avoid* seduction in favor of interpretation. While I do not find Baudrillard's deliberately scandalous rhetoric unproblematic – this rhetoric is itself an example of seduction, aimed at turning the reader away from even the most intimately held "truths" – I think that in a context in which the "deep" and "concrete" tendencies of interpretation are adamant, such as the present one, Baudrillard's theoretical excessiveness can be useful. Baudrillard's mistake lies in his assumption that "deep" interpretative tendencies are diseases of "the West" only. His orientalist romanticism about non-Western peoples blinds him to the fact that what he is criticizing is also a firmly cultivated legacy of the non-West, in this case China.

APPROACHES TO ILLUSION: ZHANG AND CHEN KAIGE

Inherent in Zhang's tactics of visuality is an astute, almost militaristic understanding of the way *time* works in cinema and, even more so, in mass culture. In order to be successful, film must communicate as if it is automatic and unmediated, in such a way as to make people feel that they can follow without having to make an effort. In their crudity and simplicity, Zhang's films contain this shrewd grasp of the essential illusion of transparency that film audiences are after. The following lucid remarks reveal his mastery of what makes film not only a formally specific medium but also a mass event:

> [In film adaptation] even very good literature . . . has to become filmlike. The first thing I can do is to reduce the complexity of the events, and make the story simple and popular [*tongsu*]. Film is a "one-time deal." The form of its watching is compulsory: there is no time for turning back, and there is no time for thinking; you must follow the screen. When it is a matter of concise, charming words, you can keep reflecting; even when you have arrived at the last chapter [of a book] you can turn back to the front. Film [however] is a one-time deal, and very few ordinary people watch the same film two or three times. Everywhere else in the cinema it is dark and silent; only the screen has light and sound. Watching can only follow screen time. You can't let people pass without having understood what is going on.

In other words, the irreversible time (or speed) of watching imposes itself on the filmmaker as a strict discipline. For Zhang, filmmaking is about learning and submitting to the *dominance* of this "one-time deal."

Zhang's pragmatic and disciplined (pragmatism-cum-discipline) approach is one of the major differences between him and his contemporary Chen Kaige. Whereas Zhang makes maximal use of the limited but predominant mode of time on the screen to construct the kinds of images that would be accessible to a large number of people, in Chen's films there is, as my foregoing discussions indicate, a fundamental distrust of the positivity of screen images. Hence the images in Chen's films are much less accessible and much more "allegorical" in the sense of not saying everything. This approach to the image is part of Chen's way of bringing a traditional Daoist understanding of (visual) presence – as only the partial truth if not altogether a distraction – to bear upon his use of a medium that, ironically, is predominantly defined by visuality. Juxtaposed with Zhang, Chen can be described to have put into play the *philosophical* meaning of *xu*, as a steady *emptying* of presence. In Chen's films, blanks signify and silences speak: this is why they invite *interpretation*. Moreover, interpretation must supplement the predominant imagistic and narrative presences in the films with nonimagistic and nonnarrative significations such as (as I demonstrated in the previous two chapters) music and nature.

As a result, however, Chen's films demand from their audiences a kind of attentiveness that automatically excludes a large number of people. Juxtaposed with Zhang's, Chen's approach presents itself as a more traditional scholarly belief in truth as that which is inward and invisible, and which can be apprehended but not positivistically seen. Zhang, by contrast, does not rely on the audiences' philosophical perceptiveness, patience, or fondness for contemplation to get his films across; instead he operates at an obvious and crude level that guarantees him an audience. Instead of an idealist and idealistic notion of truth as that which resides inside his own mind, inside the nuances of his films, or inside his characters' or the audience's subjectivities, Zhang, like popular novelists and mass culture-producers, relies on attention-seizing strategies that seduce audiences away from whoever they happen to be and whatever they happen to be doing. If "plot" has become weak in both Chen and Zhang, it is for entirely different reasons. In Chen the weakening of the plot has to do with the distrust of storytelling as a means of arriving at the truth; it is the distrust of a convention because it is too conventional, because it has already been used by too many people and has thus become uninteresting. In Zhang the weakening of the plot is really a heightening of effects. Zhang's films do rely on storytelling, but it is storytelling purged of its more cumbersome complexities. The story is now used for the most direct purpose of generating and sustaining interest. If storytelling is mobilized in the most conventional way, it is simply because convention is where the crowds are.

If Chen's way of critiquing culture is deconstructionist, in the sense of a careful, meditative, vigilant disassembling of culture's components *from within*

397

its structures, Zhang's critique comes from a more popularized Marxist and Maoist idealism, in the sense of a belief in the force of the masses and in the changeability and adaptability of cultural production. Zhang, who bought his first camera by selling his own blood, often speaks of a close identification not only with China but in particular with China's peasants, and of art as a liberation from oppression. In other words, Zhang's social critique follows Chinese communism's way of discrediting tradition *from below* rather than from within culture's core of coherence. If Chen has inherited the traditional Chinese literati's way of doing "culture" through philosophy and poetry, Zhang's lineage is that of the popular dramatist, novelist, and street performer whose modes of enunciation are inseparable from the masses. For Chen, even a simple act like that of pissing becomes, as I indicated in the previous chapter, an occasion for philosophical reflection (on the animalistic truth about human culture). For Zhang, piss is, as it is in *Red Sorghum*, what unexpectedly makes wine taste better, what enhances the quality of a collective form of production.

These differences also mark their respective treatments of women. While Zhang uses women for the obvious, conventional, pornographic purposes of representation – as fetishized body parts complete with the melodrama of mental suffering – in Chen women occupy a much less clear-cut, because *much more idealized*, space. Cuiqiao's brave determination to change her life leads her to her death in *Yellow Earth*; women do not appear in *The Big Parade* except in idyllic scenes that are brought about by feverish daydreams; Laidi in *King of the Children* appears in the role of a coarse, fat sister and mother; the women in *Life on a String* are either mysteriously motherly or frustrated and suicidal. The hardly visible or hardly material place women occupy in Chen's works is the symptom of an idealism that regards truth as that which is hidden, which is *other* than the here and now. Chen's critique of traditional Chinese culture stems from a belief in the invisible inward depths that have been veiled and distorted by culture's untrustworthy surfaces. Zhang's critique stems, instead, from the material force of such surfaces – from their vulgar womanly focus, their seductive accessibility, their irreversible time, their illusion of transparency.

32

MONUMENTS OF TIME:
THE WORKS OF THEO ANGELOPOULOS

Vassiliki Kolocotroni

We who set out on this pilgrimage
we looked at the broken statues
forgot ourselves and said that life was not lost
        so easily
that death has unexplored ways
and its own justice
that when we die standing
like brothers in stone
united with hardness and weakness,
the old dead left the circle and were
        risen
and are smiling in a strange calm.
George Seferis, '21', *Mythistorema*[1]

In the opening sequence of *Eternity and a Day* (1998), Theo Angelopoulos's latest film, a group of young boys rush down to the beach on an early morning escapade; repeating a favourite ritual, they run into the sea for another look at the submerged city, which one of their grandfathers remembers having once glimpsed. The older boy leads the younger ones onto the site and exclaims: 'Here it is!' The boys descend together. When they come back up, breathless, the older one asks quietly, as if respecting the strange calm of the site, 'Did you see her? Did you see the head of the smiling woman?' 'I saw columns, broken statues, pieces of marble', replies the youngest. 'That is the ancient city', announces the eldest boy, who continues: 'Grandfather says that it sleeps beneath the sea for centuries. It only surfaces once in a while, but for a moment only, and then everything stops; time stops'. To the youngest boy's question, 'what is time?', the elder replies, with a definition freely adapted from Herakleitus: 'Grandfather says that time is a child playing marbles by the seaside'. The boys dive once more while the sun slowly breaks through the clouds. This is an appropriate opening sequence, setting the tone for a meditation on time, memory, nostalgia, loss; it also frames one of Angelopoulos's signature motifs: the broken statues, pieces of marble, which the children rediscover with every plunge into the depths. Though broken and submerged, the statues are reconstructed through the children's gaze, shown here to belong in the constant past of legend. At the same time, their absence from the frame suggests their impossibility, as if they must necessarily elude the gaze of the adult spectator. In this coexistence of the absent and the present, the invisible and the invoked, lies a poignant double gesture: the magical aura of the broken statues is both reinforced and defused, offering itself at once as 'hardness' and 'weakness'.

This mini-oxymoron is a characteristic trope. A synecdoche made visible, the broken statue represents both what was once whole, becoming in that sense a vehicle for nostalgic allusion, while also putting the imaginary in its place, grounding it in the reality of the fragment. Engaging the spectator in a similar process, (though this time through the conflation of the child-like and adult gaze) a lingering *plan-séquence* in *Landscape in the Mist* (1988) follows the transportation by helicopter of a giant stone hand, a fragment of some monumental statue, across the harbour of Thessaloniki. The aura of the marvellous exists here too, but this time what is evoked and simultaneously undermined is the magnificence of a once potent symbolic image; when intact, the hand would have pointed in a masterful, reassuringly paternalistic way, but in Angelopoulos's *mise-en-scène* it hangs from the sky with the index finger missing.[2] Appearing as it does, half-way through two young children's journey in search of their father, the broken hand both crystallises and sets in motion a set of contradictory effects. By its sheer size and the drama of its prolonged drift over the city, it confirms and monumentalises their quest; by its brokenness, it makes concrete the fact of the Father's limited, transient, even truncated, glory. And there is a further significance: for the first time in a film which, true to its title, is almost uniformly shot in wintry and misty landscapes, this sequence is shot at dawn, with a warm and soothing light gradually filling the frame. The light is beautiful and benign, but it is unclear whether it emanates from the hand or from its slow disappearance, and the dawning realisation that the era of the Father has passed.[3] Either way, it is a temporary effect, an interruption. The children proceed with their journey regardless, to arrive at an end, which is another point of departure; the film closes at the imagined frontier of Greece and Germany, a realm of impossibility but beyond which the father may still be waiting.

The broken statue is firmly lodged in Angelopoulos's own cinematic imagination, though, one could also say that it was first erected in the minds of a whole generation to which he feels he belongs. In *Ulysses's Gaze* (1995), he stages another farewell to a monumental father, this time as the emblem of a revolution. 'A', the Greek-American director in search of three lost film-reels, products of the pioneering 'gaze' of two early-twentieth-century Greek filmmakers, follows an Odyssean trajectory through the ravaged Balkan landscape and reaches the Romanian port of Constanza. There he boards a Russian ship which carries the pieces of many gigantic statues of Lenin, precariously held together with ropes and propped up by rusting supports. The temporarily reconstructed structures are on their way from Odessa to Germany, to be sold on to collectors. As the ship sails through the Black Sea and out onto the Danube, a long-take records the reaction of by-standers following the ship's progress from the shore. Some make the sign of the cross, as if in front of a religious icon, or, perhaps a miracle. As the ship approaches the borders with former Yugoslavia, the broken head dominates the screen while the camera pans a full revolution. To the guards' question if there is anyone on board, a voice from the ship replies 'Nobody', recalling the episode of Ulysses's outwitting of the Cyclops. This elegiac sequence performs a sort of simultaneous burial and restoration of the broken statue, albeit only for a moment, or for as long as the sequence lasts; it also serves as a final farewell: bound for Germany, Lenin, or the revolution returns to its origins.

A statue fixes an image and an era; it is a representation, but also, a relic of history and, in that sense, a petrification of processes, relationships and ideas which can never be static. Statues, then, may fall but will contain in their fractured state echoes of what was once visualised in them. The fragment of an original gaze is what the film's 'A' seeks to encounter, in an attempt to realign the seemingly divergent perspectives of the past and present.[4] This realignment is presented as a necessity in *Ulysses's Gaze*, all the more urgent because of the risks involved in the extinction of past visions.

The search for a lost gaze belies a further anxiety: that when the ghosts of the past have been laid to rest, when the fathers' 'historical errors' and absences have been analysed, rationalised and forgiven, in other words, when the backward look at history may yield no further insights, then there might be little left but empty reconstructions.[5] This is an anxiety which Angelopoulos dramatised and dissected in *O Megalexandros* (1980), the most iconoclastic of his films, which examines the process by which an emancipatory vision transforms itself into totalitarian practice. A charismatic bandit abducts a group of English aristocrats on a visit to Poseidon's temple at Sounion (an adaptation of an actual incident from 1870), and takes them to a mountain village where, with the co-operation of Italian anarchists, he is attempting to establish an agrarian commune. The film proceeds to follow the gradual mutation of leader into despot, as 'Megalexandros' isolates himself, becomes unable to communicate and convey his vision, imprisons himself in silence and is finally destroyed by his subjects. In the final, ritualistic scene, he is literally consumed whole by the communards, and in his place is left a shattered shard of marble, his own head; a broken statue.[6]

'Megalexandros' is a composite figure: in Greek, his name alone invokes an amalgam of heroic, imperial, mythical and folk nuances, and he is in that sense bolted together, a construct, or even a parody. His relationship with his daughter suggests an ambiguous and incestuous genealogy (she is a product of his marriage to his mother/wife), which further reinforces a sense of claustrophobia and inexorable self-destruction. 'Alexander' is both the vehicle and the victim of a false consciousness, which attempts to freeze history into myth. Angelopoulos stages here a critique of an abstraction, of the phantom of ideology and power, which echoes Karl Marx's famous analysis in *The Eighteenth Brumaire*:

> Men make their own history, but not of their own free will; not under circumstances they themselves have chosen but under the given and inherited circumstances with which they are directly confronted. The tradition of the dead generations weighs like a nightmare on the minds of the living. And, just when they appear to be engaged in the revolutionary transformation of themselves and their material surroundings, in the creation of something which does not yet exist, precisely in such epochs of revolutionary crisis they timidly conjure up the spirits of the past to help them; they borrow their names, slogans and costumes so as to stage the new-world historical scene in this venerable disguise and borrowed language.[6]

O Megalexandros then presents an historical imagination in crisis; revolution as phantom and isolated, incommunicable vision. At the same time, the film engages in a critique of the power of cinematic representation, in itself a potentially mystifying, or mythopoeic medium. The absence of a subjective perspective and the interaction of rigid *tableaux* with long *plans-séquences* force a detachment upon the gaze of the spectator. The film's silence is partly a reflection of the main character's inability to communicate and his increasingly internalised vision, but it is also simultaneously an intensification of and a critical commentary on the power of the image.[7]

Angelopoulos's critique in *O Megalexandros* is all the more poignant when considered alongside the work that preceded it; as a coda to the epic trilogy composed of *Days of '36* (1972), *The Travelling Players* (1975) and *The Hunters* (1977), it adds a cautionary note to the work of historical analysis. *Days of '36* and *The Hunters* frame that analytical project by exposing the brute force but also the fragility of a political victory founded on repression, silencing and civil strife. The pre- and post-war dictatorships which provide the films' backdrop are haunted by the possibility that their crimes may yet be avenged. The paranoia suggested by the murderous reaction of the Metaxas regime to the threat of political scandal in *Days of '36*, is amplified and taken to its extreme horrific conclusion in *The Hunters*, in which the body of a dead partisan is discovered in the woods by a group of hunters. As fresh blood begins to flow from the stone cold body, the group, all members of the ruling elite, the side that won the civil war, act out their fears and fantasies. Having dreamt of their own execution by partisans, they awaken to the decision to rebury the corpse and with it the reminder of their collective guilt.

If *Days of '36* prepares the ground and sets the tone for the crimes which will haunt *The Hunters*, *The Travelling Players* pushes them on stage. The film follows a group of itinerant actors in a period of fourteen years (1939–52) as they wander through Greece's cities and villages, staging a nineteenth-century pastoral melodrama. In true Brechtian-epic style, history constantly interrupts the reconstruction of the folk idyll and involves the actors in political action.[8] On that much bloodier 'stage', they assume their roles and live and die accordingly, while it gradually transpires that the travelling players are also enacting the revenge tragedy of *Agamemnon*, Aeschylus's retelling of the fall of the House of Atreus. However, this performance does not signal a ritualistic acceptance of mythical fate; nor does it allow the meting out of justice where it is due. The film ends with the actors lined up, as if taking a curtain-call, in front of a deserted provincial train station, in a direct echo of the film's opening. In that frame, the heroic dead take their places next to the traitors and collaborators, the opportunist survivors, those whose spirit has been broken and those whose mind has surrendered to dreams of what could have been. Yet this is no reconciliation, but rather a reminder that, even the most resounding of 'victories' may not be a conclusion. The collective psychodrama of *The Hunters* imagines one way in which such decisive outcomes may be re-interrupted, but the suggestion is already there, economically and hauntingly, in *The Travelling Players*.

Formally and thematically, the film sustains a rigorous dialectic between history and myth, realism and allegory, collective action and individual fate; dazzlingly choreographed *plans-séquences*, in which two separate moments in time are simultaneously set in motion, coexist with static *tableaux* and monologues spoken directly to the camera. Most impressively of all, Angelopoulos avoids melodrama, psychological lure and didacticism, yet creates sequence after sequence of great emotional potency. One of the most memorable of these occurs towards the conclusion of the film. The year is 1950 and the players sit waiting around a seaside taverna table. It is a crisp and clear winter day. A military jeep arrives, its brakes screeching and delivers an excited group of American marines and their girlfriends. Among them, dressed in white, is Chrysothemis, the sister and counterpart to idealistic Electra, who runs to the assembled group holding a bouquet of flowers in one hand and in the other, an American sergeant whom she has just married. The party begins. The couples dance to music coming from the taverna, while the players watch. The music pauses and the old woman in the group stands up, visibly moved, nods to the accordeonist and requests 'a song for the bride'. One of the marines' girlfriends translates the phrase into English and the woman begins. The sound of her voice and the lyrics of this traditional wedding song transform the atmosphere of the scene, as if a shift in time has occurred. Meanwhile, the marines retrieve their own instruments from the next table and attempt to accompany the old woman and the accordeonist. Chrysothemis is instructing her American husband in the complexities of the ceremonial dance; suddenly a trombone breaks in and draws the other instruments into a jazz rhythm. The old woman, confused, stops singing and sits down, but the newlyweds quickly pick up the steps and dance wildly to the loud cheers of the Americans' girlfriends. Returning to the table, the sergeant raises his glass and shouts excitedly, 'A toast!', but before he can say another word, a young man, Chrysothemis's son, suddenly gets up, lifts the end of the tablecloth and pulls it away violently. Glasses, plates, paper flags and flowers tossed into the air. The young man walks away towards the sea, dragging the white fabric behind him like an unfurled flag. The 'marriage' of differing traditions, emotions and temporalities forces the issue; the progeny of coloniser and colonised. The young man's gesture is the last of a series of interruptions in the sequence, and carries a sense of justice in it, though only as a reminder. Ultimately, the flag he is left with is the wrong colour.

The valedictory tone struck here provides evidence for those critics who seek to argue that Angelopoulos's work represents the last authoritative act of a political and artistic modernism which has been force to come to terms with the demise of its heroic vision.[9] The director's gaze has increasingly turned, so it is claimed, to a form of inner scrutiny, the contemplation of the predicament of the individual in an increasingly divided and divisive world.[10] Furthermore, the exploration of the theme of borders and national boundaries, of an enforced homelessness and globalisation – with its attendant new mix of cultures and languages in films such as *The Suspended Step of the Stork* (1991), as well as *Ulysses's Gaze* – has been read as a shift of focus from his earlier concern with the processes of history as experienced by and engraved on national and collective consciousness. In Fredric Jameson's view, Angelopoulos's films since *O Megalexandros* 'drift decisively away from Greece itself towards some transnational situation which they cannot properly fix or identify'; similarly, he finds that 'a sadness and a frustration of the frontier seem to have more affinities with the "existential" melancholy of an Antonioni'.[11] For Jameson, these are themes bound to a 'formally regressive structure', they are too 'easily deflected into metaphysics, and made to serve as "symbols" of some more generalised human condition'.[12] Such a critique echoes Pier Paolo Pasolini's earlier definition of artistic practice in the 'neocapitalist' era, which 'ascribes to poets a late humanistic function: the myth and the technical consciousness of form'.[13]

It is true that Angelopoulos considers himself and his outlook to be a humanist one: 'in dealing with borders, boundaries, the mixing of languages and cultures today, the refugees who are homeless and not wanted, I am trying to seek a new humanism, a new way'.[14] Yet, in a different context, and seeking to distance himself from the metaphysical and mystical vision of Andrei Tarkovsky, Angelopoulos has stressed the *critical* tenor of his own, and as he argues, peculiarly Greek, blend of humanism: 'There is no mystery in the Greek character, as there is in the Slav. Crudely put, that is the difference ... [I]n us, there is a Cartesian element ... [an emphasis on] doubt, the dignity of thought'.[15] This is a significant emphasis for another reason: Angelopoulos is a committed secularist and, in consequence, immune to the appeal of any kind of apocalyptic angst or existential melancholy, such as Jameson might have detected in Antonioni. Yet there is a symbiosis between the two directors,[16] glimpsed perhaps in the open letter Roland Barthes wrote to Antonioni in 1980:

> Unlike the priest, the artist admires and is amazed; his gaze may be critical, but not accusatory ... Unlike the thinker, the artist does not evolve; he scans, like a sensitive instrument, the successive New that his own history brings before him: your work is not a fixed reflection, but a watery silk screen[17]

Similarly, Angelopoulos's work does not evolve, nor does it attempt to fix history on the screen; instead, he records its fluency. His journey is not a progress but a wandering, and its most characteristic moment the return, as either homecoming or retribution. Formally, too, scenes, images, and names from earlier works recur in every new one, evoking the past but also absorbing elements from this momentary immersion in the present. Depths charged with layers of past meanings generate constantly dynamic, but never truly novel, reflections on the surface of Angelopoulos's films. As the children in *Eternity and a Day* come to know, time only stands still for the statues.

The tone of the film's watery opening – bitter-sweet delight in the return to childhood through memory, to 'the time when it was still time', as Samuel Beckett put it in a rejected line from the little play 'Gloaming'[18] – gives way to the setting of the scene of a sombre and anxious present. A man in his early sixties is lying in an armchair, with eyes closed, as if daydreaming. The grey and wintry morning has an air of steely melancholy about it, as it transpires that 'Alexander', terminally ill, is preparing to go into hospital. In the course of that day, he is to say his last farewells: to the Pontic immigrant woman who has looked after him for the three years since his wife's death; to his daughter; to the old family home on the beach which is to be demolished; and, finally to his mother. Throughout, in voice-off, and in occasional returns to the dream site of the once-elegant seaside villa, a belatedly yearned-for happiness appears in the form of 'Anna', the dead wife, whose letters to Alexander are read and re-read. Regret at what was left unsaid, guilt for what was left unlived are conveyed by the juxtaposition of the wife's voice and his own fractured monologue-apology, and the emotional struggle seems both futile and oppressively self-contained.

As is usual in an Angelopoulos film, the release from the hauntings of memory and the self appears in the form of a child, in this case, a young Albanian boy, a type immediately recognisable to a contemporary Greek audience, who is saved by 'Alexander' from the clutches of a sinister mafia dealing in child labour. For a day, the boy becomes companion and guide, another trigger for the memory device, although this time, for an elegiac exploration of the political and the poetic. In a familiar motif, the protagonist is an artist of sorts, in this case a writer, whose unfinished project (his 'scattered words') consists in completing another poet's sketch: Dionysios Solomos's *The Free Besieged*, the early nineteenth-century poet's account of a famous episode from the Greek revolution, in which the inhabitants of the town of Missolonghi under siege by the Turkish army attempt a mass exodus, choosing death over bondage. Although appearing in a period cameo, the poet is used here not so much as an historical figure, but as a referent for the elemental relationship between language and freedom[19]; the Albanian boy is then witness to and cipher for the filmmaker's conviction that with each generation the fundamental bond between poetry and liberation is reconstructed, a fact as inevitable as the succession of ever-new forms of bondage. For the older man, the conclusion is more ambivalent: his reconciliation with lost time and love is effected, though through the reawakening of the desire for more time, for one more day.

Eternity and a Day was awarded the Palme d'Or at Cannes, conferring a belated accolade on a consistently celebrated career.[20] This elegiac exploration of a personal and emotional temporality is probably the most autobiographical of the director's films to date, yet it also aims to convey a sense of collective or generational introspection. The retrospective gaze at a life lived in pursuit of ideals or ideas, political and creative visions, suggests both melancholy and celebration; it is in this latter sense an affirmative vision, and in the context of this latest film, it is also offered as a patrimony, a personal and collective bequest.

NOTES

1. My translation. George Seferis's celebrated poetic sequence, *Mythistorema* [Mythical Story] (1933–34), has been a consistent source of inspiration for Theo Angelopoulos.
2. As Angelopoulos jokingly claims, 'Andrei [Tarkovsky] would have kept the pointing finger, but there you have our difference in one' (from an unpublished interview conducted by the author, Athens, December 1998). Another visual echo may be found in the opening sequence of Federico Fellini's *La Dolce Vita* (1960), where a statue of Christ is carried over Rome in a helicopter; in Fellini's film, the aura of the image mutates in the final scene on the beach at dawn, with the apparition to the revellers of a giant rotting fish.
3. Angelopoulos's epigrammatic summary of the film is that it concerns 'the silence of God'; it is the last film in his 'trilogy of silence', and is preceded by *The Beekeeper* (1986), or 'the silence of love', and *Voyage to Cythera* (1983), or 'the silence of history' (interview conducted by the author, Athens, December 1998). See also, *Theo Angelopoulos: A Retrospective 27 May–21 June 1998* (ed. by Elly Petrides et. al., Athens: The Greek Film Centre and London: Riverside Studios, 1998): pp. 28–33.
4. As the director put it to Michel Ciment, 'It is the theme of my film, that of the lost gaze, which is imprisoned … and must be freed. The gaze of the beginning of the century must meet that of the end of the century.' ('Entretien avec Théo Angelopoulos', *Positif*, 415, September 1995): p. 27. My translation.

5. 'I posed the following question to myself: "Do I still see clearly?", a question that all directors must ask of themselves' ('Entretien avec Théo Angelopoulos', *Positif* 415, September 1995): p. 21. My translation.

6. From *Marxist Literary Theory: A Reader* (ed. Terry Eagleton and Drew Milne, Oxford: Blackwell, 1996): p. 36.

7. As Akira Kurosawa remarked, 'It is the weight of this silence and the intensity of the immobile stare of Angelopoulos's camera which makes O *Megalexandros* so powerful that the viewer cannot break away from the screen. This kind of filmmaking, so personal and unique in its particularity, tends to return to the roots of the cinema'. Cited in *Theo Angelopoulos: A Retrospective 27 May–21 June 1998* (ed. by Elly Petrides et. al., Athens: The Greek Film Centre and London: Riverside Studios, 1998): p. 22.

8. As Walter Benjamin put it, 'Epic theatre does not reproduce conditions; rather, it discloses, it uncovers them. This uncovering of the conditions is effected by interrupting the dramatic processes; but such interruption does not act as a stimulant; it has an organizing function. It brings the action to a standstill in mid-course and thereby compels the spectator to take up a position towards the action, and the actor to take up a position towards his part' (*Understanding Brecht*, trans. Anna Bostock. London and New York: Verso, 1977): p. 100.

9. See David Bordwell, 'Modernism, Minimalism, Melancholy: Angelopoulos and Visual Style', in Andrew Horton ed., *The Last Modernist: The Films of Theo Angelopoulos* (Trowbridge: Flicks Books, 1997): pp. 11–26.

10. See Andrew Horton, *The Films of Theo Angelopoulos: A Cinema of Contemplation* (Princeton, N. J.: Princeton Univ Press, 1997).

11. Fredric Jameson, 'Theo Angelopoulos: The Past as History, the Future as Form', in Andrew Horton ed., *The Last Modernist: The Films of Theo Angelopoulos* (Trowbridge: Flicks Books, 1997: pp. 78–95): p. 92, 91.

12. Jameson 'Theo Angelopoulos: The Past as History, the Future as Form': p. 92.

13. Pier Paolo Pasolini, 'The "Cinema of Poetry"', *Heretical Empiricism* (Ed. Louise K. Barnett, trans. Ben Lawton and Louise K. Barnett, Bloomington and Indianapolis: Indiana Univ Press, 1988): p. 185.

14. Andrew Horton, 'National Culture and Individual Vision: An Interview with Theodoros Angelopoulos'. *Cinéaste*, XIX: 2–3 (1992): p. 30.

15. Interview conducted by the author, Athens, December 1998.

16. Since 1983, Angelopoulos has worked on his screenplays with Antonioni's long-time collaborator, Tonino Guerra. As a film student in Paris in the 1960s, Angelopoulos remembers the daily visits to the Cinemathèque for a 'dose' of Antonioni, who, in those early years was a favourite, along with Mizoguchi, Murnau, Dreyer, Welles and Minnelli. For an account of the director's formal influences, see Michel Ciment, 'Entretien avec Théodore Angelopoulos', *Positif* 174, October 1975.

17. 'Cher Antonioni ... ', in *Œuvres complètes. Tome III 1974–1980* (ed. Éric Marty. Paris: Seuil, 1995): p. 1208. My translation.

18. Cited in James Knowlson, *Damned to Fame: The Life of Samuel Beckett* (London: Bloomsbury, 1997): p. 432.

19. Solomos's work was inspired by the Greek uprising against the Ottoman empire. His *Hymn to Freedom* is set to music as the national anthem.

20. For a list of awards, see the brief filmography that precedes this bibliography.

BIBLIOGRAPHY

Angelopoulos, Thodoros. '*Le Voyage des Comédiens*'. *L'Avant-Scène du Cinéma*, 164 (December 1975): pp. 3–45.

Angelopoulos, Théo. 'Le plan de mes neuf ans'. *Cahiers du cinéma* 443/444 (May 1991): p. 6.

Angelopoulos, Theo. 'A few shots rescued from oblivion', in *Projections 4 1/2: Film-Makers on Film-Making* (In association with *Positif*), ed. John Boorman and Walter Donohue (London and Boston: Faber and Faber, 1995): p. 14.

Angelopoulos, Thodoros. *10 3/4: Σενάρια. Πρώτος Τόμος* Αθήνα: Αιγόκερως, 1997.

Angelopoulos, Thodoros. *Το βλέμμα του Οδυσσεά: Σενάριο.* Αθήνα: Εκδόσεις Καστανιώτη, 1995.

Angelopoulos, Thodoros. *Μιά αιωνιότητα και μιά μέρα: Σενάριο.* Αθήνα: Εκδόσεις Καστανιώτη, 1998.

Antonioni, Michelangelo. 'Two Statements', in *Film makers on Film making: Statements on Their Art by Thirty Directors.* Ed. Harry M. Geduld (Bloomington and London: Indiana Univ Press, 1967): pp. 195–223.

Barthes, Roland. 'Cher Antonioni . . . ', in *Œuvres complètes. Tome III 1974–1980,* ed. Éric Marty (Paris: Seuil, 1995): pp. 1208–12.

Ciment, Michel. 'Entretien avec Théodore Angelopoulos'. *Positif* 174 (October 1975): pp. 2–9.

Ciment, Michel. 'Entretien avec Théo Angelopoulos sur *L'Apiculteur'*. *Positif* 315 (May 1987): pp. 4–6.

Ciment, Michel. 'Entretien avec Théo Angelopoulos sur *Paysage dans le brouillard'*. *Positif* 333 (November 1988): pp. 6–10.

Ciment, Michel. 'Alexandre, ou la mélancolie: Entretien avec Théo Angelopoulos'. *Positif* 363 (May 1991): pp. 16–22.

Ciment, Michel. 'Entretien avec Théo Angelopoulos'. *Positif* 415 (September 1995): pp. 21–27.

Demopoulos, Michel and Frida Liappa. 'Entretien avec Théodore Angelopoulos sur *O Thiassos'*. *Positif* 174 (October 1975): pp. 10–14.

Eagleton, Terry and Drew Milne eds. *Marxist Literary Theory: A Reader.* Oxford: Blackwell, 1996.

Estève, Michel ed. *Théo Angelopoulos.* Paris: Lettres Modernes Minard, 1998.

Heinich, Nathalie. 'Notes sur la trilogie de Théo Angelopoulos (*Jours de 36, Le Voyage des Comédiens, Les Chasseurs*)'. *Cahiers du Cinéma*, 283 (December 1977): pp. 10–14.

Hill, John and Pamela Church Gibson eds. *The Oxford Guide to Film Studies.* Oxford and New York: Oxford Univ. Press, 1998.

Horton, Andrew. 'Theodor Angelopoulos and the New Greek Cinema'. *Film Criticism*, VI: 1 (Fall 1981): pp. 10–20.

Horton, Andrew. 'National Culture and Individual Vision: An Interview with Theodoros Angelopoulos'. *Cinéaste*, XIX: 2–3 (1992): pp. 28–31.

Horton, Andrew ed. *The Last Modernist: The Films of Theo Angelopoulos.* Trowbridge: Flicks Books, 1997.

Horton, Andrew. *The Films of Theo Angelopoulos: A Cinema of Contemplation.* Princeton, New Jersey: Princeton Univ. Press, 1997.

Katsounaki, Maria ed. *Θόδωρος Αγγελόπουλος: Αφιέρωμα. Η Καθημερινή* (Κυριακή 18 Οκτωβρίου 1998): pp. 3–32.

Markaris, Petros. *Το Ημερολόιο "Μιάς Αιωνιότητας".* Αθήνα: Εκδόσεις Γαβριηλίδης, 1998.

McArthur, Colin. 'The Travelling Players: Marxist History as Pleasure'. *Dialectic!: Left Film Journalism* (London: Key Texts, 1992): pp. 135–37.

Mitchell, Tony. 'Angelopoulos's Alexander'. *Sight and Sound* 49: 2 (Spring 1980): p. 85.

Mitchell, Tony. 'Animating Dead Space and Dead Time: *O Megalexandros'*. *Sight and Sound*, 50: 1 (Winter 1980–81): pp. 29–33.

Orr, John. *Cinema and Modernity.* Cambridge: Polity Press, 1993.

Pasolini, Pier Paolo. *Heretical Empiricism.* Ed. Louise K. Barnett. Trans. Ben Lawton and Louise K. Barnett. Bloomington and Indianapolis: Indiana University Press, 1988.

Petrides, Elly et al. ed. *Theo Angelopoulos: A Retrospective 27 May – 21 June 1998.* Athens: The Greek Film Centre; London: Riverside Studios, 1998.

Romney, Jonathan. 'Make It Yellow: Interview with Theo Angelopoulos on *Eternity and a Day*'. *Sight and Sound* 5 (May 1999): 9–11.

Soldatos, Yannis. *Ιστορία του Ελληνικού Κινηματογράφου* (1967–1990) Η΄ Έκδοση Αναθεωρημένη. Αθήνα: Αιγόκερως, 1999.

Themelis, Konstantinos A. *Θόδωρος Αγγελόπουλος: Το Παρελθόν ως Ιστορία, το Μέλλον ως Φόρμα*. Αθήνα: Ύψιλον, 1998.

Wilson, David. '*The Travelling Players*'. *Sight and Sound*, 45: 1 (Winter 1975–76): 58–9.

Wilson, David. 'Out of a Dead Land: *The Beekeeper*'. *Sight and Sound*, 57: 1 (Winter 1987–88): 64–5.

FILMOGRAPHY

1965   *Forminx Story* unfinished

1968   *The Broadcast* (short)

1970   *Reconstruction*, full-length feature: Best Foreign Film at the Hyères Film Festival (1971); Georges Sadoul Award (1971)

1972   *Days of '36*, full-length feature: FIPRESCI Award, Berlin (1973)

1974–75   *The Travelling Players*, full-length feature: FIPRESCI Award, Cannes (1975); Interfilm Award Berlin 'Forum' (1975); Best Film of the Year, British Film Institute (1976); Italian Film Critics Association; Best Film in the world for the decade 1970–1980; FIPRESCI: One of the Top Films in the History of Cinema; Grand Prix of the Arts, Japan; Best Film of the Year, Japan; Golden Age Award, Brussels (1976)

1977   *The Hunters*, full-length feature: Golden Hugo Award for Best Film, Chicago (1978)

1980   *O Megalexandros*, full-length feature: Golden Lion and FIPRESCI Awards, Venice (1980)

1981   *One Village, One Villager*, documentary

1983   *Athens, Return to the Acropolis*, television documentary

1983   *Voyage to Cythera*, full-length feature: Best Screenplay and FIPRESCI Awards, Cannes (1984); Critics Award, Rio Film Festival

1986   *The Beekeeper*, full-length feature

1988   *Landscape in the Mist*, full-length feature: European Film of the Year Award (1989); Silver Lion Award for Best Director, Venice (1988); Golden Hugo Award for Best Director, Silver Plaque for Best Cinematography, Chicago Film Festival

1991   *The Suspended Step of the Stork*, full-length feature

1995   *Ulysses's Gaze*, full-length feature: Special Jury and FIPRESCI Awards, Cannes (1995); Critics' Felix for Best Film of the Year (1995)

1998   *Eternity and a Day*, full-length feature: Palme d'Or, Cannes (1998)

33

IMAGINARY IMAGES: AN EXAMINATION OF ATOM EGOYAN'S FILMS

Peter Harcourt

There is a sequence in *Exotica*, the latest film by 35-year-old Canadian film-maker Atom Egoyan, that makes me think of Andrew Wyeth. There is a long shot of an extended grassy field. In the distance, a number of people appear on the horizon, walking in unison. They are looking for something. As in Wyeth's "Christina's World," there is a surreal combination of beauty and dread. Are they on a ramble, these people, looking at flora and fauna? Or are they looking for something else? Not until well into the film, as we continually return to this particular sequence, will we receive an answer to these questions.

Like other Egoyan films, *Exotica* (1994) interweaves three narrative elements. Images are established, characters are introduced; but their relationship to one another is unclear. This is Egoyan's form of cinematic suspense. Like other Egoyan films, *Exotica* focuses on the problems of looking – on the desire to specify the need to see.

During the first scene, at an airport, we watch Thomas, an eccentric character, shuffling through customs. We can also see a customs officer peering at him through a pane of one-way glass. He is exhorting his assistant to also look. He must learn to detect the officer explains, that something hidden which they have to find. "Look at him!" he exclaims. "Carefully What do you see?"

This exhortation also applies to us. When we are watching a film by Atom Egoyan, there is always something hidden that we have to find. In *Exotica* there are the scenes involving Thomas, who runs an "exotic" pet shop and who goes

From: Peter Harcourt, 'Imaginary Images: An Examination of Atom Egoyan's Films', in *Film Quarterly*, vol. 48, No. 3. Spring 1995, pp. 2–13.

to the ballet in the evenings; there are the search scenes already referred to; and there are scenes involving Francis, a tax inspector, who frequents a strip club called Exotica. These scenes crisscross one another in the contrapunctual motion that characterizes Egoyan's work, sometimes gesting parallels, sometimes differences.

[...]

Although it hasn't seen itself in this way, Canadian cinema has often reflected the insecurities of a colonial world. It has also registered inclinations toward a postcolonial escape.

In the early days, *À tout prendre* (1963), *Nobody Waved Goodbye* (1964), *Le chat dans le sac* (1964), and *Paperback Hero* (1973) all constructed cultures of entrapment, as *Termini Station* (1989) and *Léolo* (1992) do today. Furthermore, *Entre la mer et l'eau douce* (1967), *Goin' Down the Road* (1970), *l'Acadie, l'Acadie* (1971), and, more recently, *Highway 61* (1991) are all films of displacement and migration. The classic Canadian dilemma as formulated by Northrop Frye a good many years ago concerns less the existential question, Who am I? than the cultural one, Where is here? Canadian ontology has always been bound up with a dialectics of space, and one of the dominant narrative modes both in literature and film involves the quest.

As if to underline this colonial dependence, many commentators have remarked on the absence of real men in Canadian films, on the absence of father figures or even of elder brothers. During the 1960s and early 1970s, there are no fathers at all in Quebecois films; and when an actual father appears in an Anglophone film like *Nobody Waved Goodbye*, his authority is so flaccid that the filiation is refused.

While the faces and the colors of Canada are changing, metonymically in our films the situation remains the same. In *Sitting in Limbo* (1986), a quasifictional study of a group of young English-speaking blacks in Montreal, there is a distinct absence of responsible males. Similarly, in *Welcome to Canada* (1989), *Perfectly Normal* (1990), *Masala* (1991), and *Léolo*, there are few admirable authority figures.

Most consistently contestational, however, about the inadequacy of fathers is the work of Atom Egoyan. As a deliberately self-constructed Canadian of Egyptian birth and Armenian descent, Egoyan devises films that register the personal uncertainties of people who are striving to find a place of rest within a culture not their own. His six theatrical features, together with a number of shorts and television dramas, reflect and analyze the cultural uncertainties of the Canadian situation.

[...]

In *Next of Kin* (1984), his first feature, Egoyan both acknowledges the twin cinematic inheritance established 30 years ago by *Nobody Waved Goodbye* and *Le chat dans le sac* and refuses to accept their cultural implications. Like the protagonist in *Nobody Waved Goodbye*, Egoyan's character is called Peter. He too lives in a suburban split-level home in which there is no privacy. And here too, the parents are always quarreling about their son's future. Peter (Patrick Tierney) wants none of it. He doesn't want to do anything. He wants to pretend. He wants to be someone else.

The film opens with shots of an airport, the site both of flight and of change – a scene, incidentally, that will not be diegetically placed until later in the film. After a shot of Peter in bed, pulling the duvet over his head to block out his parents' quarrelling, we see him sitting by a swimming pool. He introduces himself. "My name is Peter," he says. "I'm 23 years old and I've lived at home all my life, watching my parents dislike one another." The film then constructs what Peter is planning to do to escape from his suburban cultural trap.

Recognizing that identity is less a matter of essence than of cultural positioning, less an inheritance than a potential politics, Egoyan's Peter refuses his West Coast Angloceltic filiations in order to ally himself with an Armenian family in Toronto. It is through this deliberate repositioning that Peter is able, so to speak, to come into his own. As he says later in the film:

> I've figured out a long time ago that being alone was easier if you became two people. One part of you would always be the same, like an audience; and the other part would take on different roles, like an actor.

Only by accepting some form of cultural schizophrenia – indeed, a chiasmatic sense of self – can Peter begin to negotiate his way out of the stifling inheritance of the Angloceltic middle classes. By exchanging his wimpy, WASP father for a passionate, if bigoted, Armenian father, he is able to devise a new feeling of identity.

[...]

Next of Kin establishes what will be, for Egoyan some recurring themes and stylistic strategies. First of all, there is the family. For Egoyan, the family provides a microcosm of the social world. However, its values must always be contested. This leads to the second theme that pervades Egoyan's world: the characters' need to reconstruct their identity, to try on different roles until they find one that might fit. This entails an abrogation of inheritance and an appropriation of the ideas of difference, of alterity, of something other – out less an *external* other than the other which although inside us, has been denied.

It is through Peter's fictional transformation of himself into Bedros, the family's long-lost Armenian son, and through his intimate conversations with Azab (Arsinée Khanjian, the film-maker's wife), his new-found "sister," that Peter can begin fully to be himself If at the beginning of the film we see him *pretending* to play the Spanish guitar, at the end we see Bedros *actually* playing it. Meanwhile, Azah is arranging her new photographs in her family album.

This acceptance of the immanent other often entails some kind of exile – the third recurring theme in Egoyan's films. Where Peter chooses his exile, Azah has hers thrust upon her. She is thrown out of her home for dressing "like a whore," as her father says. So Azah, too, must renegotiate her inherited identity. As a woman, she wants some of the freedoms established by Angloceltic culture in North America, while Peter wants some of the commitments of his adopted Armenian household.

If there are three basic themes in Egoyan's work involving family, identity, and the necessity of exile, there are also three stylistic strategies. These strategies relate to acting, dialogue, and narrative structure.

Egoyan instructs his actors to deliver their lines in a flat, deadpan way. This style of acting, however, is also appropriate to the characters' uncertain sense of self, to their efforts to relinquish received identities and to renegotiate new ones, as cinematic spectators must negotiate new ones with them.

Allied to this strategy is Egoyan's Pinteresque dialogue. His characters speak in a series of non sequiturs – in staccato, absurdist statements that enact a dimension of alienation but which also serve to abstract the *personae* from any simple notion of psychological realism, from a merely reflective mimesis.

Thirdly, both the flatness of the acting and the deployment of absurdist dialogue facilitate Egoyan's desire to achieve a contrapuntal structure for his films. Skilled in music and theater, he thinks out his films' structures in deliberately musical ways, like three-part inventions as we know them from Bach. Furthermore, the absurdist repetition of situations and scraps of dialogue bestows upon his narratives a serial dimension. We sense the presence of a rational intelligence ordering these experiences and directing our attention to relationships among them. Indeed, we might be profoundly moved by them – especially by the thrill of their intricate orchestration – but the "meaning" is seldom clear.

Finally, if through his treatment of actors, his dialogue, and his contrapuntal structures Egoyan's cinema is a cinema of surfaces, these surfaces are generally troubled in his films by photographic or televisual technologies of reproduction. *Next of Kin*, *The Adjuster*, *Calendar*, and *Exotica* all utilize photographs; *Next of Kin*, *Family Viewing*, *Speaking Parts*, and *Calendar* all utilize television. Video is everywhere – recording experience, mediating experience, "survelling" experience, reducing reality to replica.

Egoyan's cinema is an art of images within a culture supersaturated with the overproduction of images.

[...]

This intense concern with images is distinctly Canadian. Growing up saturated with images of the United States, we have a special problem in distinguishing between what is imaginary and what is real. This was the situation of Rick Dillon in *Paperback Hero*, and it certainly provides the central theme of David Cronenberg's *Videodrome* (1982). In fact, *Videodrome* is perhaps the *Urtext* for a whole generation of Toronto film-makers. Containing in the figure of Brian O'Blivion a parodic representation of Marshall McLuhan, *Videodrome* charts the central character's growing inability to distinguish between his real life and his video imaginings. "Television is reality: reality is less than television," as O'Blivion declaims. "Your reality is already half video hallucination ..."

From this film springs not only *Family Viewing* and *Speaking Parts*, but also Patricia Rozema's *I've Heard the Mermaids Singing* (1987) and David Wellington's *I Love a Man in Uniform* (1993). It is a specifically Canadian dilemma to sort out the differences between images imagined for us by ourselves and images imagined for us by other people – let alone making a distinction between all these imaginary images and what we might still want to call, on occasion, the "real world."

In Egoyan's *Family Viewing* (1987), his second feature film, video images are everywhere. The film takes as its central theme the desire to make connections – away from false images toward true images away from pornography toward affection, away from the father toward the mother, and away from the Angloceltic world toward an Armenian world, a large part of which has been lost. Indeed, the central character in this film is called Van – a name that implies links, that requires completion.

Van (Aidan Tierney) lives in a sterile condominium with his father, Stan (David Hemblen), and his father's lover, Sandra (Gabrielle Rose), who appears to be Van's lover as well. Stan likes to video tape all his lovemaking with Sandra although he requires the stimulus of an additional female voice on the telephone to get him started. This voice belongs to Aline (Arsinée Khanjian) who makes her living by offering telephone sex. She is also a friend of Van.

When Van discovers the sexual tapes of Stan and Sandra, he also discovers that his father has been recording over previous tapes of Stan's original family when the mother and *her* mother were still part of the home and Van was just a child. A section of this childhood tape is returned to again and again in the film, in a kind of Edenic garden, like a prelapsarian dream.

This scene is extraordinarily choreographed. We see Stan at the left of the screen, watching his family in the garden through a window, separated both by glass and by language. Young Van is there, a Mickey Mouse doll clutched to his chest, with his mother and grandmother, talking in Armenian. Stan gives instruction to his son through the window by miming gestures that he wants him to imitate. This moment suggests both continuity between the generations and patriarchal control. Finally, in the fullest version of this scene, the mother brings Van inside to Stan, for whom Van sings "Ba, Ba, Blacksheep" in English. In its recurrence, intensified by ascending string octaves supplied by composer Mychael Danna, this scene haunts the film like a discarded memory of familial affection.

The story of *Family Viewing* centers around Van's repeated attempts to find a proper home for Armen, the grandmother, whom Stan had dumped in a home when his wife ran away. He moves her first to Aline's, then into an unused wing of a hotel in which he is now working, where he finally disguises her as a bag lady, just to keep her away from Stan's clutches.

The penultimate scene intercuts images of Van watching Armen being carted off in an ambulance to some unknown destination with shots of Stan racing up the hotel stairs as if to find Armen, but actually to encounter the memory of his wife, appropriately (if alogically) appearing on a television screen.

The film ends with Aline and Van visiting Armen in a women's hostel. Television cameras are in place as part of a surveillance system, but also, for spectators, to trigger a visual echo of the video memories that we have previously seen. Miraculously, (because again alogically), the mother is also there.

But where are they, really, this reconstructed family? Where will they go? And what will they do? What is the meaning, finally, of the concluding moments in this film? Although Egoyan's work resists simple paraphrase, a few things might be said.

First of all, there is Van's quest, his need to make connections. On this level, the film has a "happy ending." He is there in the frame with his mother and *her* mother and with the young woman, Aline, who is also Armenian and might well become his wife. He has made connections both with the feminine and with his past. He seems to have rediscovered his ancient, ethnic soul, to have encountered his "other," the other that he has always felt was within him.

At the same time, on a social level, what has been accomplished? These characters have all endured a series of displacements in their journey toward this family reunion. They end up, moreover, within the confines of a site more restrictive than any other within the imaginative world constructed by this film.

If the film ends with a mystery, it is a deliberate mystery. Although there are no narrative resolutions for this or for any other Egoyan film, by recapitulating all the visual motifs in these final moments, including the prelapsarian dream, the director can bring his film, formally, to an end.

Speaking Parts (1989) further refines the polyphonic structure of the narrative and continues Egoyan's investigation of images, but now the ubiquity of television images is associated with morbidity and death. The first image we see is of Clara (Gabrielle Rose) walking through a graveyard on her way to a video mausoleum. On each gravestone is a photograph; the mausoleum contains a haunting collection of looped video records of lost loved ones. Throughout the film, we repeatedly see Clara in this mausoleum, reviewing the ghostly footage of her brother – ghostly because he died in the attempt to donate one of his lungs to her and because the footage is eerily without sound.

The opening sequence is intercut with one of Lisa (Arsinée Khanjian) watching a video that is equally eerie because, except for Mychael Danna's music, this moment is also without diegetic sound. The subject of the scene is a piano recital, but that is of little interest to Lisa: the camera of her imagination tracks in past the foreground of the image to isolate a young man sitting in the audience, someone whom we will later know as Lance (Michael McManus) – the obscure object of Lisa's desire.

Egoyan again advances three stories simultaneously, while suggesting links among them – a procedure assisted by the continuity of the music. Lisa is drawn by images of Lance; Clara by images of her dead brother; Lance by the desire to move beyond the image into speech – to achieve a speaking part. Through its visual organization, however, *Speaking Parts* might seem to endorse the voodoo belief that televisual reproductions of the self can behave as the extractor of human souls, that reproductions can rob the self of essence. Certainly, in *Speaking Parts*, the televisual representations consistently lead to a death-desiring nostalgia for something that is either not really there (the indifferent Lance) or no longer there (Clara's dead brother).

Throughout the film, all events are mediated through these televisual representations. The telephone sex in *Family Viewing* becomes television sex in *Speaking Parts*. Everything from orgies to weddings requires a video record. During the wedding sequence, the busy producer is also there – but only on a television monitor. If Lance and Clara employ teleconferencing technology to simulate sex with each other, the producer uses it to maintain the distanced authority of his masculine control.

The penultimate sequence, staged as a television talk show, not only brings together the three narrative units in a kind of cinematic stretto but also collapses the real into the imaginary. As the characters in Egoyan's film momentarily trade places with the characters in the film being made by the producer, we cannot distinguish reality from representation.

The film ends in silhouette, with Lance collapsed on the floor of Lisa's room – initially reaching out for her only to be rebuffed. Lisa then reaches out for him. Finally, ever so tentatively, they kiss.

Has Lance been so burned out by his involvement with the televisual imaginary that he is prepared to return to the real? Lisa's face now looks softer, her hair less severely drawn back, her attitude perhaps chastened. After all the media interventions, are both now prepared to accept each other as one another's other, as one another's "real"?

With *The Adjuster* (1991), Egoyan expanded both his palette and his budget. His previous films had been made for virtually no money at all. In Canadian dollars, *Next of Kin* cost $37,000; *Family Viewing* $160,000; *Speaking Parts* (the first to be shot on 35mm) $800,000; but *The Adjuster* was budgeted at $1,500,000 – still a modest sum, even by Canadian standards.

The film opens on a close-up of a hand moving within the darkness. The hand belongs to Noah Render (Elias Koteas), the "adjuster" in this film. He floats through life, dealing with the aftermath of fires, shooting arrows into the darkness at the billboards that mark the extremities of the estate on which he resides.

Noah lives with Hera (Arsinée Khanjian), *apparently* his wife. Reinforced by the silence of her sister, Seta (Rose Sarkisyan), who is constantly "in touch with" Hera's son Simon (Armen Kokorian), Hera seeks to be a center. While Seta and Simon are always holding each other, Hera is often in bed, troubled by unrecallable dreams. Actual, physical touch dominates the film, within and across both gender and generation. The less the characters have a settled sense of their own identities, the more they seem "out-of-touch" both with themselves and with one another.

This extended family inhabits a model home built for an urban subdevelopment that has never taken place. Although the billboards display names like "Sherwood Forest Estate," there is scarcely a tree in sight. If this terrain comments on the speculative insanities of late capitalism, it also creates an atmosphere that is increasingly surreal.

Like the motel which provides the other principal site in this film, the pop-art patterns of its balconies color-coordinated with the parked cars below, the model home suggests impermanence. "Something had to change," says one of Noah's clients later in the film, as she observes the spark that sets her house on fire. "So I watched while it did."

In *The Adjuster*, although fire is a source of trauma for many of the characters, it is also an agent of purgation. Fire eliminates the past futility of their lives. It also projects them into the "ark" of this motel that Noah has arranged for them. Noah is their savior. All his clients love him. As the chambermaid exclaims one evening, "They think you're an angel."

Noah's angelic role, however, is largely impersonation. He has no imagination. He endlessly repeats to all his clients the same professional clichés. "You may not feel it, but you're in a state of shock." In order to value anything, he has to quantify it. He takes photographs. He makes lists. He has to put a price on everything. Questioning a client who had everything destroyed by his fire, even his academic diploma, Noah enquires, "What did it cost to frame?"

Although there is no intimacy at all between him and Hera in the film, he beds all his clients, whether male or female, while discussing their claims. Hera, on the other hand, who as a film censor also makes lists, surreptitiously records all the pornographic films she views for her sister, who stays at home all day looking after Simon. Furthermore, both Seta and Simon are locked within the mute Armenian space of their incomprehension of the English language. In the course of the film, "Bubba" is the only word that Simon acknowledges.

The characters in *The Adjuster* are not what they seem. If they are all acting out parts only partially of their own devising, the potential madness of the imaginary life is centered in the character who is actually named Bubba (Maury Chaykin) and in his companion, Mimi (Gabrielle Rose). Uselessly rich and terminally bored, they try on different roles in the effort to flagellate themselves into a meaningful existence. Like Peter in *Next of Kin*, they pretend. They play games. The games they play, however, lead not to the liberation of self-realization but to a maniacal desire for self-immolation.

All the characters in *The Adjuster* are drained of initiative through living less within the real than through mediations of the real. While Noah is reluctant to awaken Hera from her sleep when he is in the bedroom with her, he does so on his cellular phone when he is driving away in his car. Although the speechless Seta is unaffected by the pornographic violence of the pirated videotapes, she screams in terror when a flasher appears at her window.

If the film opens with an extreme close-up of Noah's hand, it ends with a shot of his hand held up within the darkness against the flames, as if trying to touch the reality of watching his own house burn down. The final scene is the culmination of the need for touch in this film and of the sense of fire as a necessary purgation. It is complicated, however, by a sudden cut back in time.

Hera and Seta are there, looking distressed. Hera is carrying a baby in her arms, someone too small to be the Simon we have seen. Noah approaches them, as if he had never seen them before, touching Hera tentatively on the shoulder. "Is this your house? I'm an adjuster." Meanwhile, the Arabic sounds of a *duduk* within the plaintive "emotional minimalism" of Mychael Danna's music reinforce the traumatized silence of this Armenian family to suggest the "otherness" which, in *The Adjuster*, has been denied. As Noah holds out his hand to the fire, moving toward the final image, we are left once again with an uncertain sense of the meaning of this film.

Did Noah acquire his family through adjusting their claim? Is he, in fact, married to Hera? Where did Simon come from? While watching the film, we might have imagined that he was also Noah's son. Where lies the reality in what we have just witnessed? Have we just *imagined* what we have seen in this film?

Egoyan has suggested that the most powerful moments in cinema are analogous to dreams, as if wanting his own work to enter directly into consciousness, bypassing intellectual controls. With its absurd objets trouvés, its barren landscapes, and isolated model home – itself both replica and parody of what a true home might be – with the recurring presence of irrational and bizarre moments. *The Adjuster*, more than any other Egoyan film, achieves a surreal force.

Calendar came about by chance; through a prize won at the Moscow Film Festival, Egoyan was given $100,000 to visit Armenia and shoot whatever he wished. The resulting film, shot on 8mm video and 16mm film, is simple in the extreme. Indeed, for spectators who resist the intricate irrationalities of Egoyan's cinema, it is their favorite film. Certainly it is his most accessible.

As money was tight, Egoyan cast himself as the photographer on assignment with his wife (Arsinée Khanjian) and an Armenian driver (Ashot Adamian) to shoot 12 ancient Armenian churches for a photographic calendar. The churches lend to this film not only an enormous beauty but also a spiritual dimension. More deliberately than other Egoyan films, *Calendar* (1993) is about the passing of time and its irretrievable changes. Yet here there is the sense that something will survive the impermanence of relationships and the uncertainty of individual identities.

Because the photographer speaks no Armenian and the driver no English, his wife serves as translator. The photographer is more comfortable with his technology than he is with either his partner or his driver. He likes to point but refuses to touch. When asked to go for a walk with the two of them, the photographer declines. He wants to remain apart. What he really wants, as he explains later in what appears to be a letter to his wife, is to go on standing there, "watching while the two of you leave me and disappear into a landscape that I am about to photograph."

In *Calendar*, we witness the gradual transfer of the wife's affection from her past relationship with the photographer to a future relationship with the driver. At the same time, by choosing the driver, she is also choosing to return to her Armenian roots – an option not available to the photographer, who has been too thoroughly assimilated into North American culture. Furthermore, as we gradually realize, the faded color of the video footage is appropriate for the photographer's fading memory of the Armenian events.

If *Calendar* is concerned with time, it is also concerned with space. Early in the film, referring to the differences between himself and his wife, the increasingly alienated photographer says, "We're both from here; yet being here has made me feel as if I'm from somewhere else."

At the end, when the photographer has returned to Toronto, we can hear his wife on the answering machine – as always with Egoyan, a mediated communication – wanting to explain what has happened to them. She wants to describe the moment when he lost her, when the car was surrounded by sheep and the driver first reached out for her. "He grasped my hand," she explains, "while you grasped your camera. Did you know? Were you there? Are you there?"

As he moves toward greater acceptance, anxious at the same time not to alienate his present-day admirers, Egoyan is finding ways to flesh out more engagingly the characters in his films. Although the Pinteresque non sequiturs still abound and a deadpan detachment continues to inform the acting, there is now a richer sense of psychology. In *Exotica*, the characters elicit our compassion. The film still displays, however, a triadic, polyphonic structure. There are three recurring sites and three different men, each of whom relates to the three women in the film.

First of all, there is the exotic pet shop, inherited by Thomas (Don McKellar) from his mother. We have already seen him smuggling exotic eggs for his shop past the customs officers at the airport at the beginning of the film. Because of this illegal activity, his shop is visited by Francis (Bruce Greenwood), an auditor for the federal tax department. (In the evenings, Thomas also attends an opera house, in which we hear – but do not see – Prokofiev's *Romeo and Juliet*. This opera house, however, more European than North American in design and therefore just as "exotic" as the pet shop, is as much a pick-up joint for homosexuals as it is a site for cultural consumption.)

The second major site is that extended grassy field – the "Wyeth" sequence with which I began this essay. In a way structurally similar to the prelapsarian dream in *Family Viewing*, this scene is returned to repeatedly – finally, as a postlapsarian nightmare.

Thirdly, there is Exotica, the strip club presided over by Zoe (Arsinée Khanjian), which she inherited from *her* mother. The club specializes in table dancing, where the men may look but never touch. Eric (Elias Koteas) serves as Master of Ceremonies. From the past, he is also emotionally involved with Christina (Mia Kirshner), the major female character in this film.

Before the opening airport scene, the sequence behind the credits consists of a slow track right along the tropical decor of this club, its exotic nature further emphasized by the eastern strains of Mychael Danna's music, with a *shehnai*, a kind of Indian oboe, sounding unsettlingly unfamiliar to our Western ears.

This exotic club becomes the site of the feminine in this film. It is the center to which all the men are drawn, a place of dreams and desire – even of fertility, since Zoe's pregnancy is very much in evidence. Indeed, if the clients of the club are not allowed to touch the dancers, most visitors to Zoe's womb-like central office are invited to touch her belly – an invitation that is generally accepted with embarrassment.

In *Exotica*, although all of the characters have their grief, it is Francis's story that most securely grips the viewer. It is his pain that spills over to affect the others and to establish the empathetic center of the film.

Francis leads a double life. An auditor by day, he frequents Exotica by night. At the club, he too has developed a special relationship with Christina, largely because she reminds him of the daughter he has lost. Playing upon her youthful appearance, Christina wears a schoolgirl's uniform and displays a sense of great distress during her public performances on stage.

"What gives a schoolgirl her special innocence, gentlemen?" Eric intones into his microphone as Christina dances. "Is it the way that they smell? The sweet perfume of their hair . . . ?" Indeed, as if to *protect* this innocence, Francis mutters private words of concern to Christina when she dances at his table, baring parts of her vulnerable body less for his sensual pleasure than to allay his physical fears. He keeps explaining that he wants to protect her, to save her from harm.

His fears relate to his lost daughter – the object of the search in that extended grassy field. They also relate to Tracey (Sarah Polley), his young niece, who babysits for him as, when she was younger, we eventually learn that "Chrissy" also had done. Yet now, since his daughter is no longer alive, Tracey plays as much a fantasy role in Francis's life at home as Christina does at the club. If the serial structure of the film still involves the repetition of scraps of dialogue and particular events, it also entails an interlinking of these young women, as (at least in Francis's mind) their roles all tend to merge. And if Francis's pain is privileged, it is because he is the most connected with the others. Furthermore, his obsession with the youthful Christina is less pornographic than compassionate; it is an attempt obsessively to recreate moments from his past as if to bring them to a different conclusion – a desire that can never be fulfilled.

Francis pays money to young women to enact his fantasies for him, to create for him an imaginary world; this activity is analogous to the activity that we all indulge in when, as spectators, we go to the movies. In *Exotica*, Egoyan has not relinquished his critique of our obsessive consumption of images.

During the film's final moments, we see a younger Christina, scarcely recognizable – with her braids and braces – as Mia Kirshner, entering the family home. The scene is full of anguish. The assumed security of a family is now felt as a threat.

Why do those Ionic pillars on that four-square home convey such a strong sense of dread? Is it through their implicit assertion of suburban rationality – a rationality inadequate for all the problems in the film? What is Christina's relationship to the later Tracey or, more distressingly, might her destiny one day be the same as Lisa's – the slaughtered child who was finally found, actually by Eric and Christina, in her schoolgirl's uniform in the middle of that extended grassy field?

For Egoyan, has the linear quest of classic Canadian cinema become a circle? Will the characters go on enacting their compulsions over and over again, devising similar imaginary images, only to encounter the very destiny they have been striving to avoid?

The enduring theme, the evolving theme in all of Egoyan's work is the need for personal transformation. Whether assuming a fictitious identity to escape an unwanted inheritance or descending into fantasy in the effort to combat feelings of pain or failure, Egoyan's characters never feel sufficient being what they are. They simulate. They impersonate. In this sense, they are all in retreat, not just from culture – as in the early films – but from nature. Nature seems "natural" only in the old world – in Armenia with its enduring presence of sheep and churches and of people belonging to the earth out of which they have grown.

In North America, within a technologized, urbanized, and increasingly migrant culture, a wondrous stretch of meadow can serve to conceal terrors too horrible to imagine. Nature has become unnatural, as has human nature. It is the fear of the depths of human nature, finally, that either silences Egoyan's characters or drives them into madness – that makes them exiles from themselves.

Within the context of Canadian cinema, Egoyan's earlier films seemed a positive repositioning in relation to our Angloceltic inheritance, a desire to escape the postcolonial uncertainties of the Canadian world. Yet even these films were not revolutionary. They all ended by endorsing the ideology of the family.

As his work has progressed, however, if the concept of alterity remains precise and alluring, the concept of self has become uncertain and obscure. It is as if Egoyan's characters, in their imaginings, have irretrievably abandoned their "originary" home.

34

BERGMAN'S SILENCE

Krzystof Kieślowski
(Translated by Paul Coates)

Bergman's silence is as piercing as the absences of Fellini, Bunuel and Tarkovsky, as the beautiful but unalluring films of Kurosawa, or the ungainly ones of Wajda. It has to be said clearly that we who are younger by a generation or two have not succeeded in stepping into their shoes.

If the truth be told, when I think of contemporary cinema increasingly often the image of a graveyard appears before me. Graves – and bent over them a few elderly men, uncertain and careful in their movements, with a motorway nearby, chock-full of cars that are technically perfect but as alike as peas in a pod.

I reflect on what it was that set Bergman's *The Silence* apart from other films of its time, thirty years ago, and why so many people in so many countries wanted to see it. It was its tone.

That is something that is very hard to put into words but can be clearly felt and is patent during the screening and long afterwards. It was the first Bergman film to be so uncompromisingly personal and uniform in its style, its mode of narration. It had taken seventeen years of work (he began in 1945 with *Crisis*, and *The Silence* comes from 1962) for him to grasp that a film's power comes from the unrelenting honesty of its maker, his courage in refusing to retreat by as much as one step. Not from its philosophical construction (*The Seventh Seal*, which I do not like), its original and beautiful record of dreams and overpowering nightmares (as in *Wild Strawberries*), its social elucidation of dramatic events (as in *Summer with Monika*, which I like a lot) – but from its delineation of feelings we all experience and understand, as we tremble incessantly between

Reproduced with the permission of Maria Kieślowski.

love and hate, between fear of death and a longing for rest, between envy and generosity, between a keen sense of humiliation and the joy of revenge.

The Silence takes place in the oppressive stickiness of a baking day and a hot night, which has room for eroticism and lust but none for love, in which the absence of pity, sympathy or even a drop of understanding is a thoroughly natural condition. Throughout this dark, bleak, fearsomely sad film – outside its action and utterances – there pulses a tiny groundless flame of hope.

I know where the bright trace comes from in this dark film. From Bergman's profound belief in humanity, even where circumstances or feelings compel the protagonists to be cruel and ruthless. To aver that the hope is associated with little Johann (Jorgen Lindstrom) – with the presence of the child – would be too facile. It would be an oversimplification to find it in the letter Ester (Ingrid Thulin) writes to the boy before they leave her or believe that it is given in the words of the foreign language Ester understood, translated, and now passes on to Johann.

It would be even more inappropriate to discern it in the figure of the old maitre d'hotel (Hakan Johnberg), who helps the sick Ester, brings her vodka and food, wipes the sweat from her face and plays with Johann. No, the hope in this film – invisible but ever-present – is hidden much deeper. It is in Ester's delicate, actually fleeting gesture as she watches Anna (Gunnel Lindblom) sleeping naked, with little Johann snuggled up to her, and suspends her hand in mid-air, then withdraws it, fearing to stroke her sister: fearing a gesture that would indicate feeling. It is surely that. Is it love? Yes. It is in the violent reaction of Anna, who, after humiliating Ester by letting her see her in the arms of a casual lover, laughs, happy to have caused her sister pain, and then suddenly, unexpectedly, the laughter turns into tears as despairing as the laughter had been hateful. Why does Anna laugh? Because she hates her sister. Why does she cry? Because she loves her. Love: the love one cannot show if one has plunged so deeply into the display of hostility, into reciprocal humiliation; the love one cannot admit to, even to oneself: this is the hidden, invisible, yet continual small flicker of hope in *The Silence*. How Ester and Anna must have loved one another in their childhood before they discovered that their father gave them great love but each felt it to be unjust. When did they understand this? Did a word, a gesture or perhaps just a look from their father engender jealousy, then ecstatic hatred? Somewhere, somebody made a mistake. But who? The father? One of the sisters? The mother, who goes unmentioned throughout the film? If one ponders these questions in earnest, with the knowledge one now has of *Fanny and Alexander* (the mother quickly forgets the father's death and marries the severe pastor) – it seems as if it must have been the mother. It is possible that where the future is concerned the mistake that will sow uncomprehended complexes and pain in Johann is the moment when he sees his mother shamelessly kissing the waiter (Briger Malmsten).

We never learn why the sisters set off on their trip, nor where to. We do not learn why they have stopped in a small foreign town where no-one speaks

German, English, French or Swedish, and the people in the streets exchange not a word. We do not learn what country this is or with whom it is at war. We do not learn whether Ester dies in this town or returns home. We do not learn what was in Ester's letter to Johann. I do not think Bergman knows either. The pleasure of watching this film does not lie in the solving of riddles, for there is no solution. It lies in the search for a solution.

Bergman's silence is no riddle. The question remains whether he ran out of strength or patience, but the answer is of scant importance. Bergman's silence is a fact. When I look at the photographs of him from a year or two back my heart bleeds. He looks at the camera, his left hand resting on the arm of Bille August in a way that is friendly but not overdone. He is wearing a shirt buttoned up to the neck and a windcheater like the one he always wore: a simple suit-length jacket with no lapels and a high collar. He smiles somewhat queasily. His dark eyes looking at the camera, their eyelids drooping at their outer edges, are slightly misted, absent. This man is one of the few film directors – perhaps the only one in the world – to have said as much about human nature as Dostoevsky or Camus. He built *The Silence* very simply.

Everything superfluous has been removed from the film. Either it was not in the script or he threw out unnecessary scenes, dialogues and situations during the editing. The film has no passages or shots to define the action's location (establishing shots). The protagonists are in a train, then all at once they're in a hotel; we do not see them descend from the train, go through the town or look for a taxi. If Anna walks down a street it is not to get from one place to another but to allow us to grasp the growth of her desire. So she walks quickly (to the right), passing the silent walkers, hastens across the street, still affected by the brutal erotic scene she has just witnessed in the cabaret. Then she halts abruptly, stands still for a moment. She doubles back. This time she goes more slowly (and leftwards), swinging her hips ever so slightly. She returns to the cafe where the waiter had earlier eyed her legs for a moment while pretending to drop a coin. She halts between the tables. She waits for a moment in a wide shot until the waiter appears, glances at him, then exits the frame. The waiter follows her with his eyes then goes up to a colleague; we understand that he has asked him to take over from him. Cut. Watched by Ester, Anna enters the hotel room. She takes off her knickers and places them in the basin to wash them, which she does almost out of frame. This is not prudery on Bergman's part: we see just as much as we need to in order to judge that she removes her knickers out of distaste for what must have remained there from her relations with the waiter.

Bergman needed four shots to recount the scene on the street – five for the scene of the washing of the knickers. In *Images* he writes that he was short of money when it came to shooting the scenes in the cafe and the cabaret, and immediately comments – correctly – that a lack of money is not always a drawback for a film. Both scenes are clear and dramatic in their spareness. The film's editing is harsh, clear-cut, shot and countershot. On several occasions Bergman uses parallel montage, which helps greatly in maintaining tension. As far as I recall he edits within the frame twice: once at the beginning in the train (the first shot of the film) and it isn't such a great move; and then in the fine scene of the sisters' conversation at dusk by the hotel window. This is the scene in which Anna lies to provoke Ester's jealous outburst. The grey faces of Ingrid Thulin and Gunnel Lindblom in big close-ups, picked out by Nykvist's camera shifting focus at the most perfectly chosen moments. I do not want to analyse the entire film in this way, I simply want to demonstrate through a few examples how simple and precise was the method Bergman used when filming *The Silence*.

I'd like to dwell on one shot for a moment. It lasts a few seconds, maybe seven, maybe four. I have already mentioned that a war is underway or ending in the country where the heroines are staying. There are only a few signs of the war, but it is obvious. The wonderfully lit shot of Johann beside the train window as we see on his face the shadows of tanks moving on freight wagons on the neighbouring track. The cries of the newspaper vendors (we do not understand what they are shouting) clearly relating to the course of the war. And finally the shot I have in mind. A close-up of a water carafe and a glass beside it. The carafe and the glass start to shake. Small ripples begin to appear on the water. One can hear the unpleasant heavy sound of large machines and a moment later Anna (or is it Ester?) looks through the window and sees a column of tanks rolling down the street. Excellent editing short-cut, perceptive use of a metaphorical image to evoke a totally real fact.

I remember how, during the screening of Kaufman's *The Unbearable Lightness of Being*, when the glasses shaking in the cupboard told of the Russian tanks' arrival in Prague in 1968, I had the feeling that I knew that idea from somewhere. Now, watching *The Silence* after many years, I know where it came from – from Bergman. There is nothing wrong with copying: the thing is to imitate the best, and Kaufman found a good solution to the task before him. As did Bergman: the shot of Johann's face with the tanks also has a source, the Lumières' *Arrival of a Train at a Station*, one of the world's first films. It would be good if someone marked the centenary of cinema with a monograph on these "wandering notions'.

In many of his films Bergman touched on death, and his dead even visited the living (*Fanny and Alexander*). It is ever-present in *The Silence* too: "when father was still alive ..."; "father, before he died ..."; "just before his death, father ..." – all said by Ester, herself severely ill and, in the penultimate scene, dying.

Death is a theme of the cinema because it is a theme of life. Two weeks ago a newspaper report: *Fellini in hospital*. Today I look at the photograph of Bergman embracing Bille August in a way that is friendly but not overdone. At his direct look at the camera, slightly misted and absent. What do you see beyond the camera, Mr Bergman? On the cover of the French edition of *Images* (Paris, 1992) is the well-know – photograph of the man in the black cloak and close-fitting black skull-cap. He extends his hand to the left, drawing out the cloak, and the image is three-quarters black.

35

REPENTANCE: STALINIST TERROR AND THE REALISM OF SURREALISM

Denise Youngblood

For 150 years, art served as a substitute for political power in the Russian empire and its successor state, the USSR. For most of the 53 years between the Cultural Revolution of 1928–32 and Mikhail Gorbachev's accession as first secretary of the communist party of the Soviet Union in 1985, art in the USSR had been "tongue-tied by authority." Therefore, it is not at all surprising that for most Soviet intellectuals the *glasnost* era was symbolized not by politicians, speeches, and congresses – but by a novel and a film: Anatolii Rybakov's *Children of the Arbat* (Deti Arbata) and Tengiz Abuladze's *Repentance* (Monanieba [Georgian]/Pokaianie [Russian]).

That these two works are historical, focusing on the terrible 1930s, is also no surprise, given the centrality of the reexamination of history as a foundation for *perestroika*. Yet neither *Children of the Arbat* nor *Repentance* is a product of *glasnost*. Rybakov wrote his epic novel in the 1960s and 1970s "for the drawer"; Abuladze wrote and produced *Repentance* from 1982 to 1984 for Georgian television, under the protection of a powerful patron, Eduard Shevarnadze. Otherwise, these two iconographical works seem to have little in common. *Children of the Arbat* is firmly situated in the tradition of Russian realism (with some vestigial remains of socialist realism). In its scope and structure (especially its blend of fictional and historical characters), the novel pays conscious homage to Lev Tolstoi (especially to *War and Peace*), and it was

From: Denise Youngblood, '*Repentance*: Stalinist Terror and the Realism of Surrealism', in Robert Rosenstone (ed.), *Revisioning History: Film and the Construction of a New Past* (Princeton University Press, 1995).

warmly embraced by Russian readers as "theirs." *Repentance* is an altogether different matter – a Georgian slap in the face of the hallowed Russian realist tradition, sanctified in the Soviet period by the official aesthetic of socialist realism. Only tenuously "historical," extravagantly surrealistic, irritatingly mannered, and difficult to grasp, the film was a sensation.

Inside the USSR, *Repentance* provoked paradoxical reactions. The film received officialdom's highest accolade, the prestigious Lenin Prize, in 1988, but audience responses ranged from tears and passionate admiration to non-committal shrugs to outright hostility. *Repentance* has been lauded as a "strange but great picture" – and excoriated as a "political porno film" that sensationalizes and trivializes its material. Outside the USSR, the movie received lavish praise from critics, garnered film festival prizes (including several at Cannes and Chicago in 1987) and was extensively distributed, a rarity for a Soviet film. As befits a work of its richness and complexity, *Repentance* is a film open to varied readings, yet unexpectedly (given its stature in the history of Gorbachev's cultural revolution) it has rarely been analyzed in depth. Most often considered as political or moral exegesis, the film has also been studied as a specifically Georgian work, the final installment in Abuladze's trilogy of Georgian "nationalist" films. But despite its obvious engagement with burning questions of the *Soviet* (as opposed to Georgian) past, no one has explored it as a serious work of Soviet history. Though R. W. Davies reports that at least one Soviet professor was moved enough by *Repentance* to declare that "he was going to make big changes in his lectures on the 1930s," most Soviet critics have explicitly rejected it as a historical film, finding its self-conscious surrealism fundamentally antihistorical. As Igor Aleinikov put it:

> Unfortunately, the film is not even an adaptation of Solzhenitsyn. It is not a TV serial with a full list of the victims and the killers of Stalin's regime . . . The time for solving the aesthetic issues of the material of the 1930s is not yet here. The urgency is to call a spade a spade first; otherwise the historical issues will not be clear for the majority of the audience.

Film as a medium is poorly suited to the transmission of factual information if it is to remain true to its own aesthetic imperatives. Yet this kind of pedantic criticism – making factual accuracy (or inaccuracy) the chief criterion for judging the merits of a historical film – has been around a long time. In the 1920s the Soviet poet Vladimir Maiakovskii, ardent defender of facticity in historical films, led the charge against movies as diverse as the costume drama *The Poet and the Tsar* (about Pushkin) and Eisenstein's revolutionary masterpiece *October*. A few comparatively recent historical movies, like Daniel Vigne's *The Return of Martin Guerre*, have more or less succeeded in passing the litmus test for "accuracy," but *Repentance* is not one of them. There can be no argument about *Repentance* on this score: it is not "factual," and indeed Abuladze seems to go out of his way to avoid any such accusation. The NKVD, of course, did not make their nightly rounds decked out in full suits of armor. Soviet artists' wives in the 1930s likely did not wear red satin gowns and ermine headbands. Police interrogations did not take place in sunny, abandoned gardens with inquisitors dressed in tails playing grand pianos.

Yet *Repentance* is most definitely "real." It succeeds, moreover, as a true representation of the epoch it depicts *because* of its surrealism, not despite it. No period in Soviet history (and perhaps in all of history) was more surrealistic than the Great Terror, a time when black was white and day was night. The transcripts of the show trials demonstrate this, contemporary newspaper accounts demonstrate this, survivors' memoirs demonstrate this – and so does *Repentance*, as vividly and profoundly as any other source. Abuladze utilizes the tools of a master filmmaker, but he thinks like a historian in this picture. Through the construction of his cinematic "metanarrative," he has brought the *mentalité* of the 1930s to life. As one sympathetic and perceptive Russian critic put it, "The historical parallels are not obvious but grasped inwardly."

For these reasons alone, *Repentance* should be considered a landmark historical film, but it is far more than an imaginative re-creation of the Stalinist Terror and an exploration of the mentality of terror. It is also a film about history, the persistence of memory, and the relationship between the past and the present. That this was early recognized is demonstrated by the way *Repentance* was introduced to the audience at a preview for Moscow's literati. A critic quoted none other than Lev Tolstoi (an artist quite remote from Abuladze in style), but as philosopher of history rather than as legendary realist writer: "We say, why remember? Why remember the past? It's no longer with us, so why recall it? What do you mean, why remember? If I were gravely and dangerously ill and recovered or got over it, I would always recall life with joy. I wouldn't remember it only when I got sick or became more ill and so wanted to fool myself." Abuladze, who was present at the screening, laconically responded to this unusual tribute by saying: "After hearing Tolstoi's words, what can one say? Let's watch the film."

So let's "watch" the film by deconstructing it. In so doing, we will see revealed not only Abuladze's understanding of Stalinism but also a sophisticated engagement with the problems of historical interpretation. Abuladze's approach to the story is "structuralist": the chronology (or sequence of events) is critical, and he eschews seamless transitions for discrete episodes that function like chapters. The narrative heart of *Repentance* is the protracted flashback that occupies more than half the film's two and one-half hours' running time. Flashbacks are standard devices in historical films, but Abuladze's use of the flashback is as unconventional as everything else he does in this picture. *Repentance*'s flashback is complicated, as we shall see, by the existence of not one but *two* framing narratives, a fact that is not obvious until the very end of the picture and that has a serious impact on interpretation.

The film's surrealism is carefully constructed and transmitted in six main ways: plot details (beginning with the appearance and reappearance of the corpse); symbols (unnaturally large figs hanging like microphones in the conservatory); costumes and mise-en-scène (Guliko's appearance in court in a black sequined dress with white fur boa); eclectic music (ranging from the "Moonlight" Sonata to "Sunny"); mordant humor (Varlam's corpse cavalierly tossed into the paddy wagon); and purely cinematic techniques (exaggerated camera angles, unexpected shot perspectives, and unusually long takes). The overall effect is to keep the audience constantly unbalanced, so that we will see, feel, and think in new ways about familiar material.

That *Repentance* will be completely out of the ordinary is evident from the opening shot, a close-up of a woman's hands making a marzipan flower. The scene that follows confirms this initial impression and beautifully illustrates how Abuladze establishes the atmosphere and succeeds in keeping the viewer perpetually off guard. The marzipan flower is destined for an elaborately decorated cake, which the baker hands out the window to a woman, who (despite her modern clothing) is picked up by a horsedrawn carriage. The baker has a visitor, who is eating cake and chatting with her when he suddenly reads in the newspaper that a "great man" has died. Listening to his emotional expostulations with evident lack of interest, the baker simply remarks how lucky he was to have known "such a man." A close-up of the obituary notice is followed by a cut to the funeral of the late, great Varlam Aravidze.

Abuladze sustains this oddly unsettling mood at the funeral. The camera pans the flowers on the casket and then, very, very slowly, the faces of the mourners. Expressions of grief are highly stylized. A diminutive bearded man dressed in worker's garb appears; he is applauded and identified only as "our benefactor." He reads a bizarre poem intended as the funeral oration. The guests join hands and sing "Samshoblo," a Georgian Menshevik anthem. The transition to the next sequence, the funeral procession, is another abrupt cut, to the face of Guliko Aravidze (wife of Varlam's only child, Abel), then to flowers, then to the coffin being carried down a staircase – further examples of the constant and unsettling changes of perspective.

The pacing is so slow and the "action" so meaningless that by this point, the viewer is impatient for something to happen. Abuladze obliges. That night Guliko, investigating her howling dog, discovers Varlam's corpse propped against a tree in the garden. He is reburied in an eerie nighttime procession. The next morning, he has reappeared, again leaning against a tree. The police arrive in a comic opera scene to "arrest" Varlam for their investigation (very characteristic of Abuladze's use of black humor, not only to mock but also to relieve tension). When Varlam reappears, he is sitting on a bench, the chain used to lock the cemetery gate wrapped around his neck. The police and the two Aravidze men, Varlam's son, Abel, and his grandson, Tornike, stake out the cemetery. Tornike shoots and captures the miscreant, who appears to be the baker we saw in the opening scene.

Her name is Keti Barateli. Dressed in a white suit with elaborate white hat (the woman in the white hat?), Keti arrives at court for her trial, flanked by armored guardsmen. The head judge, who looks bored, plays with a rubik's cube. Keti, asked to enter her plea on the charge of malicious mischief (for disturbing the corpse) makes a startling announcement: "I confirm the fact but do not admit guilt ... For as long as I am alive, Varlam will not rest. The sentence is final." She proceeds to tell her story: "You must all want to know why I'm pursuing the deceased ... I have no choice." And like a good historian, she poses the central question and establishes the context for the transition into the past: "And so, who was Varlam Aravidze? I was eight years old when he became mayor of this city ..."

Now we see Varlam Aravidze clearly for the first time, standing on a balcony watching his inaugural parade, decked out in generic dictator's garb: a fascist-style uniform and a Hitlerian moustache. Early suspicions are confirmed: in appearance and mannerisms, he bears a stunning resemblance to Lavrentii Beria, native son of Georgia, who was party chief in the Transcaucasus during the Great Terror and who at the end of 1938 became head of the NKVD as a reward for his "outstanding" service. This is not to say, however, that Abuladze intends to establish a direct parallel between Varlam and Beria. Such a parallel would be far too limiting; Abuladze is no reductionist who finds simple relationships between cause and effect.

We begin to understand how carefully crafted the protracted introduction to the story is – that the fantastic details are not so fantastic after all. Varlam was lauded at his funeral as a "modest man" who "had an outstanding gift for turning a foe into a friend and vice versa ... a gift of the chosen." This was Stalin's persona; this was Stalin's "gift." There is no death for Varlam Aravidze. He is the "undead" – the embalmed corpse "sentenced" to remain on public display – like Stalin.

And the trial of Keti Barateli? It is a show trial, with the same aura of unreality that characterized the actual events of the 1930s. Her statement "I confirm the fact but do not admit guilt," echoes the bizarre confessions of those accused at the show trials, for example, Bukharin's: "I refute the accusation of having plotted against the life of Vladimir Ilich [Lenin], but ... [I] endeavored to murder his cause." Indeed, the very title of the film provides another connection between the events of *Repentance* and the show trials, where the words *repent, repentant*, and their synonyms made frequent appearance in confessions.

The flashback is constructed in two parts, with the fulcrum a long scene that begins with Varlam's arrival at the Barateli apartment and ends with Sandro Barateli's arrest. The first part consists of four scenes of approximately equal length and weight, and the historical content of each is powerful, whether manifested directly or indirectly. At every juncture, Abuladze takes on the icons of Stalinism.

The opening sequence, showing Varlam's inauguration as mayor, is a farcical one strongly reminiscent of Fellini. The day is lovely, warm and sunny. Varlam waves and smiles benignly as people give speeches in his honor; a secretary sits on the balcony busily transcribing these words (which we cannot hear) for posterity. But a water main has broken, and the action at the main, as the workers struggle unsuccessfully to stem the flood of water, becomes the unintended focal point of the "celebration." Everyone, including Varlam, is soaked – and yet they stoically continue the revelries. No matter the reality, as the ubiquitous slogan of Soviet power had it, "communism will conquer"; adhering to the form is more important than the substance.

The eight-year-old Keti Barateli is standing on her balcony, blowing bubbles and watching the unexpectedly comical festivities, when her father, Sandro, sternly orders her in. As Sandro closes the balcony window, we see in Varlam's gaze a subtle but sinister change of expression. These two men, who will become bitter antagonists in the struggle between art and authority that follows, appear to make eye contact (though they are never shown in the same shot). The lighthearted mood evaporates like Keti's bubbles, never to return.

The next scene, which takes place in a church being used as a vibration testing laboratory, establishes the conflict between religion and science, between culture and political power, which is central to the flashback (and paradigmatic to Soviet history). As the Baratelis (Sandro, Keti, and the madonnalike Nino) wander wonderingly through the church, we hear, quite incongruously, a doomsday speech by Einstein on the radio followed by a program of cheerful 1930s' song-and-dance music.

Sandro is handsome but otherworldly and obviously an intellectual (Edisher Giorgobiani is the kind of actor who could never have been cast as a protagonist in a socialist realist film). This man turns out, quite fittingly, to be an artist, a dangerous occupation in Stalin's time, with profound political reverberations. Sandro takes his moral and social responsibilities as artist quite seriously; his cause is saving the church and its frescoes from the depredations of the vibration experiments. In the company of two elderly "bluebloods" with biblical names (Mose and Miriam), Sandro has an audience with Varlam (in a lush, almost tropical garden) to discuss the disposition of the laboratory. That this plot line is similar to that of *Out of the Way!* (Khabarda, 1931), an antireligious comedy by Mikhail Chiaureli, the Georgian who became Stalin's favored director, is surely no accident.

Varlam's first reaction to Sandro's pleas on behalf of the church serves as a tocsin: "So you're opposed to science and progress" (watchwords of Stalinism) – but Sandro is not deterred. He refuses to be silenced. He speaks persuasively about the preservation of culture as spiritual nourishment for the people, whereupon Varlam nods sympathetically, saying of the church, "It's our history, our pride" (the first of several admiring references he makes to the past).

Yet Varlam is willing to go only so far in respecting the artifacts of the past, pointing out that financial considerations make this odd arrangement a necessity. When Mose persists, claiming that "the city will be blown up," Varlam suddenly and dramatically destroys the order permitting the laboratory to be situated in the church, and begins to talk about history again, in the form of genealogy.

He insists that he and Sandro share an illustrious ancestor (one Tarasi Taraskoneli), then smilingly reminds Sandro of the incident on election day with these chilling and prophetic words: "I notice everything. So beware of me. Some blow bubbles while others track down enemies of the people."

Varlam becomes unaccountably agitated, talking about the "sluts" and "criminals" populating the nation, ending his tirade screeching in Russian: "*Is this normal*?!" (one of only three times the Russian language is used in the film). The camera sweeps upward, and we notice for the first time that the scene is not located outdoors (in a free and open area) after all. They are sitting instead in a closed space, in a conservatory guarded by medieval knights walking on the glass ceiling.

The ominous implications of this sequence are borne out in the next, which takes place in the office of Mikhail Korisheli, Sandro's longtime friend, apparently the party secretary and certainly a "true believer" – one of those fervent communists who perished by the tens of thousands during the Terror. Mose and Miriam have been arrested, and Korisheli telephones Varlam. Relieved to hear that "Varlam looked into the case and released them," Korisheli, with some amusement, wags his finger at Sandro and twits him as a "strange fellow." Sandro's somber face and the room shrouded in darkness belie the optimism of Korisheli's words and mood.

These four episodes set up the turning point in the flashback. Their slowly building sense of doom then explodes in a scene remarkable for its skillful combination of realism and surrealism. The doorbell of the Barateli apartment rings, and Keti skips to answer it. She flings open the door to Varlam, his son Abel, and his dim-witted flunkeys Doksopulo and Riktafelov, as Sandro, his wife, Nino, and their guest Elena Korisheli (Mikhail's wife) exchange concerned glances (arrests occurred at night, almost without exception). Varlam is wearing a Cossack cape over his uniform; Doksopulo and Riktafelov are in tails. They are singing bel canto and present Nino with flowers and Keti with a caged bird.

Varlam's mood is jovial. He apologizes for the inadvertent arrest of the "old couple"; the trio sings again; and Varlam turns to admire Sandro's paintings, which line the walls of the apartment covering almost every available space. Varlam looks searchingly at the paintings, and his admiration is obviously sincere as he tells Sandro, "This is the kind of art we need – serious, thoughtful, and deep," and "Artists like you must be with us now." Varlam also, however, labels the work "intimate boudoir art" and "an escape from reality" (words that were a death sentence for Soviet artists in the 1930s and beyond). And when Sandro protests against the role that Varlam wants to assign him as an enlightener of the people, Varlam is plainly annoyed, but he remarks (in Russian for the second time), "Modesty is a fine quality in a man" (another allusion to Stalin's well-known "modesty").

The impromptu musicale continues, and even the skeptical Sandro is able to laugh, applaud, and enjoy himself. The trio is in fact quite brilliant; this is no "amateur hour" presentation. Varlam reveals himself to be not the ignorant thug we have supposed but someone far more disturbing: a highly cultured, perceptive, and complex man who looks on his minions with a great deal of disdain. As he prepares to leave, Varlam smilingly accedes to his listeners' request for one last song. He does not, however, sing. Rather, he recites (and quite movingly) a poem that, were the author not William Shakespeare, one would say had been written to commemorate the evils of Stalinism. Certainly we are to understand the sonnet as the quintessence of Abuladze's interpretation of Stalinism, for every word rings true to the story that is unfolding:

> Tired with all these for restful death I cry,
> As, to behold desert a beggar born,
> And needy nothing trimm'd in jollity,
> And purest faith unhappily forsworn,
> And gilded honour shamefully misplaced,
> And maiden virtue rudely strumpeted,
> And right perfection wrongfully disgraced,
> And strength by limping sway disabled,
> And art made tongue-tied by authority,
> And folly, doctor-like, controlling skill,
> And simple truth miscall'd simplicity,
> And captive good attending captain ill,

Varlam leaves the final two lines of the sonnet unspoken, but we know from the expression on Sandro's face that he could supply them:

> Tired with all these, from these I would be gone,
> Save that, to die, I leave my love alone.

Shepherding his son and followers together, Varlam bids his reluctant hosts goodbye. ("Routine is routine," he says cheerfully a Russian for the third and final time, referring perhaps to the prosaic workings of the Terror.) Laughing, the four visitors – "needy nothing trimm'd in jollity" – jump out the window, and we hear the sound of horses galloping away. As Sandro is rather inexplicably pronouncing Varlam a "buffoon" (he has revealed himself as anything but in this scene), the doorbell rings once again, foreshadowing doom. Varlam has come to return the crucifix Abel pilfered. (The two children spent the evening talking about Jesus and heaven.) Varlam kisses Nino's hand and says with heartfelt emotion, "Count me on the list of your many admirers, dear Nino." Cut to Sandro, playing Debussy's elegiac "Les pas sur la neige" on the piano, a piece used in another Soviet film featuring a similarly Christ-like figure, Larissa Shepitko's *The Ascent* (Voskhozdenie, 1977). Sandro, "captive good at tending captain ill," knows he is dead from this moment on.

As Sandro plays, Nino dreams the nightmare that is about to befall them. She and Sandro are running through sewers, through city streets, through a field on the hills high above Tbilisi with Varlam and his knights in hot pursuit. They are buried alive in the newly ploughed field as Varlam sings and laughs. As she awakens, she urges Sandro to run away, but Sandro, resigned, tells her there is no point, that they would be "tracked to the ends of the earth." The doorbell rings for the third and final time. The knights (one of whom, as we see behind his iron mask, is Doksopulo) have arrived, muttering the incantation "Peace unto this house." The nightmare is real; peace will be no more. The interlopers take Sandro away and strip the apartment of his paintings, while Doksopulo bangs discordantly on the piano that Sandro had been playing so beautifully moments before. "Right perfection" has been "wrongfully disgraced."

This long transitional scene in the apartment – the longest sequence in the film – encapsulates, as does the sonnet, the major themes of the film: the struggle of humanity against abstract idealism, of essence against appearance, of art against authority. And yet there is no "simple truth" to be found. As though acknowledging this, the tone and pacing alters considerably, to a gritty realism and quick shifts of location.

Following Sandro's arrest, there is a cut to Korisheli's office, as the outraged Korisheli, still unaware and unafraid, demands to know the reasons for Sandro's arrest. Varlam calmly reads from a letter denouncing Sandro, a document replete with the stock phrases of the denunciation ritual, painfully familiar to anyone who knows the rhetoric of Stalinism: "This pompous artist is a hooligan ... an individualist ... an anarchist ... His art is a menace to our society." Korisheli, the true believer, angrily informs Varlam that "those who write this are enemies of the nation," to which Varlam, the true democrat, sorrowfully responds that by arresting his "close relative" (Sandro), he has fulfilled the will of the people, adding that "in this matter I must support the majority." Korisheli is at last unmasked as an intellectual and an elitist (like most Old Bolsheviks) when he retorts: "An intelligent person is worth one thousand idiots." Varlam, unmoved, replies in a classic example of Stalinist transference: "He's our foe, and we're his victims." Enraged, Korisheli slaps Varlam and breaks his pince-nez glasses, thereby sealing his own fate (as we can see recorded in the slight twitch on Varlam's face).

This dramatic scene is followed by a cut to the prison – a long line of women and children waiting to learn, from a never-seen bureaucrat, the fates of their men. Nino and Keti are told that Sandro has been "exiled without the right to correspond," the standard euphemism during the Terror for the death penalty, though Nino does not yet know this. Nino runs to party headquarters; Korisheli has also been arrested. In anguish and frustration, she smashes one of Varlam's posters; Varlam is, of course, there watching her. (He, like Stalin, is every-where.) She falls to her knees, begging him to save Sandro, but with a look of subtle satisfaction, he moves on. It is obvious that this desirable woman ("maiden virtue rudely strumpeted") would have done anything for him; by rejecting her, his power over her is complete.

The final episode in this series of relentlessly realistic scenes takes place at the railway station. A little boy has informed Nino and Keti, who are sitting listlessly in their darkened, denuded apartment, that a shipment of logs from a labor camp has just arrived and that sometimes the exiles carve their names on them (yet another historically accurate detail). Nino and Keti rush to the yard, slogging through the mud, running from one log to another in the company of a few other women and children. They, of course, find nothing (since Sandro has not been exiled), but there is a lingering medium shot of a woman crying, stroking, kissing, and talking to her log, a shot held so long that its emotional intensity is absolutely unbearable. Nino and Keti disconsolately walk away.

At last, Abuladze returns to the surrealism that has characterized most of the film, and the viewer realizes that this style has another advantage. Yes, surrealism is formally suited to the expression of the Terror, but it also serves as a shield against the intense pain of these events. So we experience a real sense of relief when the location shifts to a sunny neglected garden, with a man and woman in evening wear playing the Mendelssohn Wedding March on a white piano. It is Sandro's interrogation. As Sandro appears in a torn, bloodied shirt, the woman becomes a living statue – of Blind Justice. The cheerful inquisitor informs Sandro that he has been arrested because Mikhail Korisheli, head of a secret organization, has implicated him. We know that such a sequence of events cannot possibly be true, since Korisheli was arrested after Sandro (not that the truth ever mattered at this stage of the proceedings). Sandro defiantly (though naively) replies that "if men like him are being arrested, you might as well arrest the entire country." The interrogator regards Sandro with an indulgent smile and offers to produce Korisheli.

A gray-faced, obviously disoriented Korisheli staggers in. He mechanically confesses his crimes to the shocked Sandro: he plotted with his 2,700 conspirators "to dig a tunnel from Bombay to London" and "to poison corn to annihilate the population." He takes Sandro aside and feverishly explains his plan – and why, true believer to the end of his life, he had informed on Sandro: "We must accuse as many people as possible – and call them enemies of the people ... We'll expose the malefactors who are deliberately misleading the government ... We must sign everything and reduce it all to complete absurdity ... We'll sign a thousand stupid statements." As Sandro watches and listens in horror, Korisheli's lips tremble, and his haggard face crumples. The wretched man ("purest faith unhappily forsworn") is overcome by tears, impotent rage at his plight, and hysteria. Once again, as so often in this film, we see the line between unreality and reality blurring and disappearing in a way totally suited to the material. Was anyone arrested for attempting to die a tunnel from Bombay to London? Perhaps not, but as all available evidence indicates, it is too close to the truth for disbelief. Korisheli's naming of names is definitely the truth – many party faithful, "gilded honour shamefully misplaced," implicated others for this very reason.

Varlam, in the meantime, is giving speeches on his balcony, his previous persona of thoughtful, reasoned kindliness abandoned in favor of crazed bombast. His language is now purest Stalin-speak:

> We must be vigilant and prepared to unmask enemies ... Four out of every three persons are enemies! ... Numerically, one foe is greater than one friend ... Our motherland is in danger! ... It's difficult to catch a black cat in a dark room, especially if there's no cat there. We are faced by a most difficult task, but nothing can deter us. If we want to, we'll catch the black cat in the dark room, *even if there's no cat there.*

Cross-cut to Nino, who meets with Elena Korisheli, like her husband Mikhail still a true believer despite all the evidence at hand. Elena feels that Sandro's and Mikhail's arrests were a mistake, but even if the errors were never uncovered, the sacrifice the women were making would be worth it, since "we're serving a great cause." Her face shining with fanaticism, she begins singing the Schiller "Ode to Joy" from the Beethoven Ninth Symphony. The jubilant, exalted music continues as we see Sandro confessing, and being condemned and finally crucified.

At the moment of his death, the church (the symbolic foundation of this tragic conflict) is dynamited, the triumph of political authority over culture. The past has been obliterated, reduced to rubble. Nino, awakened by the blast, pulls Keti close to her and tells her that Sandro is dead. Nino goes to Elena's, but it is too late. Elena has been arrested as well, and Nino's despair is complete as she sits weeping on the steps outside the abandoned Korisheli apartment. In the meantime, we are treated to a little, quite necessary black comic relief in which Varlam finds that the Terror, "doctorlike," has assumed a life of its own. Thus, he is forced to accept the folly of Doksopulo's "truckful of enemies': everyone named Darbaiseli has been rounded up and arrested, an ironic reference to the arrest quotas of the Terror.

And then, at long last, it is Nino's turn. Keti is torn from her, screaming and crying, as we see Nino's hands vainly stretching through the bars of the horse-drawn van (a turn-of-the-century Black Maria). "That was the end of Nino Barateli," says the middle-aged Keti, back in the courtroom, and that is the end of the flashback.

The flashback personalizes history, as flashbacks often do, and that is an important contribution, especially in this case. The catastrophe that took place in the USSR under Stalin can all too easily become a mind- and soul-numbing matter of numbers. In Tofik Shakhverdiev's 1989 documentary *Is Stalin with Us?* (Stalin's nami?), one contemporary Stalinist notes in all seriousness that while he does not believe 20 million people died at the hands of the state, if it were true, that would represent "only" 10 percent of the population.

But *Repentance* is not just about the Aravidzes and the Baratelis, hence the stylized "everyman" shape of the parable and Abuladze's refusal to use real names. Every detail of this tale, fantastic or mundane, was repeated countless times from 1936 to 1938 as eight to ten million people were arrested, most of them, like Sandro and Nino Barateli, never to be seen again. Abuladze's description is a complete one, despite its deceptive simplicity: he has shown us the support the regime enjoyed, the extent of the collusion and collaboration that fueled the engine of terror, the creeping paranoia and ruthless illogic of the witch hunt, and the way "class conflict" was manufactured, with the "people" on one side, and artists and intellectuals on the other. Perhaps most importantly, in the person of Varlam Aravidze, Abuladze and Avtandil Makharadze have given us a chilling and thoroughly believable portrait of the inscrutable mask of twentieth-century terrorism.

With so many witnesses dead, it is mainly those hopelessly implicated (whether through action or through inaction) who are left to remember. How can the past survive under such circumstances? *Repentance* has been presented as Keti's story, but we must keep in mind that it is only infrequently told from Keti's point of view. There is much we see that Keti did not, and that it is highly unlikely her parents would have told her. How does she know the story she told? Through research? Through imagination? Through collective memory? Is her story therefore suspect?

These are questions that cannot be answered by reference to the flashback alone, and we must return to the film to see the way the framing story plays itself out. In the second part of the framing story, it rapidly becomes apparent that Varlam's grandson Tornike is a key figure, not the peripheral character he seemed at first. He is the Keti of the next generation of the tragedy. Tornike has appeared since the beginning of the movie as a voyeur, or witness; in the opening scenes as the corpse is discovered and rediscovered, we see him constantly in the background, quietly observant. During the police stakeout, he is the only one alert and aware. (His father and the police chief have gone to dinner, and the other policemen are crouched behind a tombstone, drinking and joking.) At the trial, there are frequent cuts to his ever vigilant countenance, none more important than that at the end of the flashback.

As the courtroom erupts in exclamations of disbelief and shouts of "She's insane!" Tornike looks shell-shocked. He immediately sinks into a reverie in which he imagines his grandfather blindly staggering about in a towerlike enclosure, mortally afraid of the light (the light of the truth that has just been revealed). After the trial recesses, Tornike accusingly asks his father Abel: "Did you know all that?" It is a rhetorical question, since Tornike, like the viewer, is now aware that there is much that Abel knows. Keti and Abel are, after all, acquainted (on that fateful evening in the Barateli flat, Abel even kissed her and promised to return soon), but Abel has taken some pains to conceal this fact. Abel's response to his son's question is a troublingly evasive justification, but one oft-heard in "real" life: "Those were complicated times ... It's difficult to explain now ... The situation was different then." As Tornike persists, Abel becomes defensive, arguing that Varlam "never personally killed anyone" and asking, "What are the lives of one or two people when the well-being of millions is at stake?" Desperate, Abel pleads with his son: "What am I guilty of?" and receives the answer he does not want to hear: "You justify Grandpa and follow in his footsteps."

At home, Tornike dreams his second dream: he sees his mother, Guliko, dancing provocatively and mockingly around Varlam's corpse (another sign of disrespect for the past and for the story that Keti has told). In a nearby room, the Aravidze clique, now clearly depicted as a kind of mafia, plots to rig the outcome of the case. Abel knows that Keti is not insane and is reluctant to manipulate the trial, but the hard-bitten Guliko prevails. They will coerce a court psychiatrist, who is one of "theirs," to declare Keti unfit to stand trial. As Abel listens to the court pronouncing Keti insane on the basis of the fabricated "new evidence," his own sanity is in doubt. That night, he goes down to the cellar of his palatial home, where he has a long conversation about good and evil with a figure, shrouded in darkness, who is eating a raw fish. It turns out to be Varlam – openly contemptuous of Abel's doubts. As the camera pans around the gloomy cellar, we see a stunning sight. Sandro Barateli is more than a memory: Varlam may have ended Sandro's life, but he preserved Sandro's art, which is now stacked against the walls, decaying in the damp cellar, seen only by the Aravidzes.

Is this strange scene no more than Abel's nightmare? It would seem so, but at the final session of the court the next day, Guliko, in disgust, removes a fish skeleton from Abel's limp hand. He says, to no one in particular, "My life's over." Keti's final statement, before being committed to an asylum, is determined and defiant: "Aravidze is not dead. He's alive and continues to corrupt society."

Tornike believes this, too. After visiting Keti in prison, a surrealistic scene in which he begs her forgiveness, he returns home to confront his father for the last time. Abel, as musically gifted as his father (and Sandro), is pensively playing the "Moonlight" Sonata (well known to Soviet audiences as Lenin's favorite). Tornike shatters the mournful mood, screaming at Abel in horror: "How can you go on lying forever? ... You'd swear the innocent were guilty; the sane, insane." He runs to his room. With guests arriving to celebrate Keti's conviction, "Sunny" blaring loudly on the stereo, and Guliko pounding at the door, Tornike shoots himself with the gun his grandfather gave him, the same rifle he had used to shoot Keti.

Abel can no longer avoid his fate. Weeping piteously over his son's coffin, he cries out "Why were you born, you fiend, Abel Aravidze?" (*not* Varlam Aravidze). He feverishly digs up his father and throws the corpse over the cliff to the ravens.

The meaning of this is all very clear: classic tragedy (if overwrought by Western standards). Then Abuladze pulls his most inexplicable and maddening stunt. The film is not over, as it should be. We return to the bakery, and see – the woman who may be Keti, not in prison or the asylum but as she was at the beginning of the movie, in the company of the man in the uniform, surrounded by her fanciful cakes, reading Varlam's death notice in the newspaper. An elderly woman carrying a suitcase taps at the window: "Does this road lead to the church?" Keti looks at her sadly: "This is Varlam Street. It will not take you to a church." The old woman responds, "Then what's the use of it? What good is a road if it doesn't lead you to a church?" As the camera backs away, Keti watches her walking slowly down the narrow alley. And *this* is the end of the film.

What are we to believe? Was it all a dream?

Keti functions in this film as Abuladze's surrogate; she is *Repentance*'s historian. Her account of events has been reconstructed, but no more (or less) so than any historian's account of any historical situation. She is driven throughout by the historian's fundamental imperative: not only to remember the story but to *tell* it, in such a way as to ensure that it will not be forgotten. Varlam, too, respects history: he exploits it for political purposes (when he manufactures the putative blood tie between Sandro and himself as descendants of the same ancient hero) and fears it (hence his dynamiting of the church). Varlan manipulates the past for his own ends and destroys the past when it suits him, but by so doing he implicitly pays tribute to the past by acknowledging history's power over the present.

Abel, on the other hand, is history's true enemy, counterhistorian to Keti's historian. Abel is simply silent, the ultimate subversive act. His silence is worse than a lie, and it is for this that he must repent, not for any blood debt the Aravidzes owe the Baratelis. Tornike kills himself because of what Abel has *not* done, not for what Varlam did. Abel knows this, hence his heart-wrenching cry "Why were you born, you fiend, Abel Aravidze?" and his decision, finally, to resurrect the past by unearthing Varlam's corpse.

So how should we construe the ambiguous ending? It seems to me that the key lies in the identity of the elderly woman who makes her way to Keti's window. As is true of so much in *Repentance*, she is not what she appears to be. She is not just "any" old woman but Veriko Andzhaparidze, one of the most beloved actresses of Georgian cinema in her final role. Andzhaparidze's career, which began in 1923, spanned the entirety of Georgian cinema; she *is* Georgian film history – personified. "Then what's the use of it?" she asks Keti when she is told that there is no church on Varlam Street. She walks off without expecting an answer, because the answer is obvious.

What's the good of a street without a church? Of a people without their culture? Of a nation without its past? Of art "tongue-tied by authority'? Keti will tell her story, Abel will unearth Varlam, the Soviet people will remember – and Tengiz Abuladze will make movies, openly and honestly.

As William Faulkner said (and as *Repentance* forcefully demonstrates): "The past is never dead. It's not even past."

INDEX